D0225686

Wilhelm Raabe

Wilhelm Raabe

THE FICTION OF THE
ALTERNATIVE COMMUNITY

JEFFREY L. SAMMONS

PRINCETON UNIVERSITY
PRESS

Copyright © 1987 by Princeton University Press
Published by Princeton University Press, 41 William Street,
Princeton, New Jersey 08540
In the United Kingdom: Princeton University Press,
Guildford, Surrey

All Rights Reserved
Library of Congress Cataloging in Publication Data will be
found on the last printed page of this book

ISBN 0-691-06709-0

Publication of this book has been aided by
the Whitney Darrow Fund of Princeton University Press

This book has been composed in Linotron Janson

Clothbound editions of Princeton University Press books
are printed on acid-free paper, and binding materials are
chosen for strength and durability.
Paperbacks, although satisfactory for personal collections,
are not usually suitable for library rebinding

Printed in the United States of America by
Princeton University Press
Princeton, New Jersey

CONTENTS

CONTENTS

ACKNOWLEDGMENTS

ACKNOWLEDGMENT is due to the American Council of Learned Societies for a travel grant that enabled me to work in Wolfenbüttel and Braunschweig, and to the administrators of the Duke August Library in Wolfenbüttel, who arranged comfortable and agreeable quarters in that lovely town and otherwise showed me every hospitality. I am grateful to Dr. Manfred Garzmann and his associates in the Municipal Archive and Library of Braunschweig, who granted me permission to use unpublished materials in the Raabe Archive and assisted me in every way, and to Professor Josef Daum, currently president of the Raabe Society and head librarian of the Technical University of Braunschweig, for allowing me access to materials in his institution. A special debt in friendship is owed to Professor Hartmut Steinecke of the University of Paderborn, who sacrificed his valuable time to guide me through Raabe's Weser River landscape. Permission to republish in revised form previously published or forthcoming sections of this book was graciously granted by Dr. Mark Gelber of the Ben-Gurion University of the Negev, Israel, editor of the forthcoming Festschrift for Sol Liptzin, for Chapter 7; by Dr. Hans-Jürgen Schrader, co-editor of the *Jahrbuch der Raabe-Gesellschaft*, for Chapter 13; by Professor Bengt Algot Sørensen, editor of *Orbis Litterarum*, for Chapter 18; and by Dr. Hans-Werner Peter, co-editor and publisher of *Wilhelm Raabe: Studien zu seinem Leben und Werk* (Braunschweig: pp-Verlag, 1981), for Chapter 19. I must particularly express my lively and cordial gratitude to my colleague Professor Leo A. Lensing of Wesleyan University for his expert, observant, and thoughtful criticisms generously provided at considerable expense of his time and effort. Finally, I am deeply obliged to my wife Christa for meticulous proofreading and such copyediting as was possible in the face of my obstinate infatuation with the sound of my own voice.

New Haven, Connecticut
Fall 1985

The Works of Wilhelm Raabe
in Chronological Order of Publication with the
English Titles Used in This Book

Berlin and Wolfenbüttel

Die Chronik der Sperlingsgasse (novel; 1856) *The Chronicle of Sparrow Alley*

Der Weg zum Lachen (story; 1857) *The Way to Laughter*

Ein Frühling (novel; 1857) *One Springtime*

Der Student von Wittenberg (story; 1857) *The Student of Wittenberg*

Weihnachtsgeister (story; 1858) *Christmas Spirits*

Lorenz Scheibenhart (story; 1858) *Lorenz Scheibenhart*

Einer aus der Menge (story; 1858) *One of the Crowd*

Die alte Universität (story; 1858-59) *The Old University*

Der Junker von Denow (novella; 1858-59) *The Squire of Denow*

Die Kinder von Finkenrode (novel; 1859) *The Children of Finkenrode*

Wer kann es wenden? (novella; 1859-60) *Who Can Change It?*

Aus dem Lebensbuch des Schulmeisterleins Michel Haas (story; 1860) *Michel Haas*

Ein Geheimnis (story; 1860) *A Secret*

Der heilige Born (novel; 1861) *The Holy Spring*

Die schwarze Galeere (novella; 1861) *The Black Galley*

Nach dem großen Kriege (novel; 1861) *After the Great War*

Auf dunkelm Grunde (story; 1861) *On Dark Ground*

Unseres Herrgotts Kanzlei (novella; 1862) *Our Lord God's Chancellory*

Das letzte Recht (novella; 1862) *The Ultimate Justice*

Die Leute aus dem Walde (novel; 1862-63) *The People from the Forest*

Stuttgart

Eine Grabrede aus dem Jahre 1609 (story; 1863) *A Funeral Eulogy of 1609*

Holunderblüte (story; 1863) *Lilac Blossom*

Die Hämelschen Kinder (story; 1863) *The Pied Piper of Hamelin*

Der Hungerpastor (novel; 1863-64) *The Hunger Pastor*

Keltische Knochen (story; 1864-65) *Celtic Bones*

Drei Federn (novel; 1865) *Three Pens*

Else von der Tanne (novella; 1865) *Elsa of the Fir*

Die Gänse von Bützow (novella; 1866) *The Geese of Bützow*

Sankt Thomas (novella; 1866) *St. Thomas*

Gedelöcke (story; 1866) *Gedelöcke*

Im Siegeskranze (novella; 1866) *In the Victory Wreath*
Abu Telfan (novel; 1867) *Abu Telfan*
Theklas Erbschaft (story; 1868) *Thekla's Inheritance*
Der Schüdderump (novel; 1869-70) *The Rumbledump*
Der Marsch nach Hause (novel; 1870) *The Homeward March*
Des Reiches Krone (novella; 1870) *The Crown of the Empire*

BRAUNSCHWEIG

Der Dräumling (novella; 1872) *The Dräumling Swamp*
Christoph Pechlin (novel; 1873) *Christoph Pechlin*
Deutscher Mondschein (story; 1873) *German Moonshine*
Meister Autor (novel; 1873, imprint 1874) *Master Author*
Zum wilden Mann (novella; 1874) *At the Sign of the Wild Man*
Eulenpfingsten (novella; 1874-75) *Owls' Pentecost*
Frau Salome (novella; 1875) *Madame Salome*
Höxter und Corvey (novella; 1875) *Höxter and Corvey*
Vom alten Proteus (novel; 1875-76) *Of Old Proteus*
Horacker (novel; 1876) *Horacker*
Die Innerste (novella; 1876) *The Innerste*
Wunnigel (novel; 1877-78) *Wunnigel*
Deutscher Adel (novel; 1878-79) *German Nobility*
Auf dem Altenteil (story; 1878) *In Retirement*
Alte Nester (novel; 1879) *Old Nests*
Das Horn von Wanza (novella; 1880) *The Horn of Wanza*
Fabian und Sebastian (novel; 1881-82) *Fabian and Sebastian*
Prinzessin Fisch (novel; 1882-83) *Princess Fish*
Villa Schönow (novel; 1884) *Villa Schönow*
Ein Besuch (story; 1884) *A Visit*
Pfisters Mühle (novella; 1884) *Pfister's Mill*
Unruhige Gäste (novel; 1885) *Restless Guests*
Im alten Eisen (novel; 1887) *On the Scrap-Iron*
Das Odfeld (novel; 1888) *The Odin Field*
Der Lar (novel; 1889) *The Lar*
Stopfkuchen (novel; 1891) *Stuffcake*
Gutmanns Reisen (novel; 1892) *Gutmann's Travels*
Kloster Lugau (novella; 1894) *Cloister Lugau*
Die Akten des Vogelsangs (novel; 1896) *The Documents of the Birdsong*
Hastenbeck (novel; 1899) *Hastenbeck*
Altershausen (novel fragment; written 1899-1902, posthumously
    published 1911) *Altershausen*
Der gute Tag (story; written 1875, posthumously published 1912) *The
    Good Day*

INTRODUCTION

THE ENTERPRISE pursued in these pages is grounded in a conviction that Wilhelm Raabe (1831-1910) was the major nineteenth-century novelist in the German language between Goethe and Fontane, and a writer deserving of an honorable place in the canon of European literature. This claim may bewilder different readers in different ways, depending upon their level of knowledge. Those generally familiar with nineteenth-century European literature may never have heard of Raabe; he has been little translated[1] and has not thus far been accorded much standing in comparative literary history. Anyone who looks him up in a reference work may wonder how he comes to be placed *between* Goethe and Fontane, for Raabe was twelve years *younger* than Fontane and outlived him by the same number of years. But, as a novelist, Fontane was one of the most remarkable late bloomers in the history of literature. He published his first novel in 1878 at the age of fifty-nine; by that time, Raabe had published fifty-one novels and stories, fully three-quarters of his life's work. Raabe, as I shall try to show, was distinctly a German *Victorian* writer; the older Fontane belongs to a more recent phase in literary history. The idea that we may speak of a Victorian age in German literature was introduced two decades ago by Norbert Fuerst; he did not, however, address Raabe, who could have supplied his most persuasive example.[2]

Others may protest the claim that he was the preeminent German-language novelist of his time; what of the canonized achievements, such as Gottfried Keller's *Der grüne Heinrich* (*Green Henry*) or Adalbert Stifter's *Der Nachsommer* (*Indian Summer*)? Perhaps no single one of Raabe's novels matches these in accomplishment—though this is a concession I would not make with alacrity. But, as far as the novel is concerned, Keller and Stifter were one-book writers; their other efforts in the genre remained fragments or were otherwise failures. Raabe wrote, at a minimum, a dozen novels of significant rank. Of no other German-language novelist of the time can this be said.[3] Finally, by no means all of those to whom Raabe's name does mean something are persuaded of his stature. In large part this is owing to the peculiar and damaging history of Raabe's reputation. But I cannot be deterred by the skepticism of others, past and present. For Wilhelm Raabe is a discovery I have made for myself.

Needless to say, he was there all the time. But, although much of my training and most of my work has been in nineteenth-century

German literature, he might as well not have been as far as I was concerned. My revered mentor, Heinrich Henel, was one of those who did not hold him in very high regard, and I cannot clearly recall ever hearing his name during my studies. Over the years, the name came slowly over the horizon, one in that cloud of little-read novelists hovering on the periphery of the traditional German literary canon. I came upon him almost serendipitously, during the evolution of my shocking discovery that the widely believed dominance of the nineteenth-century German novel by the form of the *Bildungsroman* is a legend.[4] It was in my search for the elusive *Bildungsroman* and then in a determination to examine the novels which, in contrast to the claims of literary history, really did exist, that I began to read Raabe, knowing little and expecting less. Even though I did not begin with the works now judged to be his finest, it is difficult to describe my astonishment upon reading him for the first time. What I was reading resembled nothing I had ever seen before in German letters of the whole century; I was particularly struck by Raabe's narrative ingenuity and originality of tone. Someone once remarked of Joseph Conrad that, as soon as one began to read him, one knew that one was in good hands. I take this to mean that the ultimate judgment on the author's literary rank may still be reserved, but right away one recognizes competence, substance, and artistic integrity. This was my experience within a few dozen pages of Raabe. From that beginning, several years of investigation brought me to the judgment with which I began this introduction.

Those unacquainted with the peculiarities of German literary study may find all this hard to credit. Literary history, plowed and replowed as it has been, does not, as a rule, unearth neglected masterpieces by unrecognized geniuses. To put forward the kind of claim I am asserting may appear to carry the amiable eccentricity of the academic a bit too far. But German literary history suffers from the same disastrous discontinuity that has disrupted German history in general. Agonizing reappraisal has been the order of the day for a generation now, especially in regard to the traditional canon, which was formed under particularly intense ideological pressures in the Wilhelminian era. Nowhere, in my judgment, is this need more evident than in the unsatisfactory state of the study of the novel, of which the *Bildungsroman* hoax is but a symptom. If the world at large believes that the Germans in the nineteenth century were unable to write novels as other nations did, with the exception of a half-dozen rather eccentric examples, it is because the Germans arranged the canon to give that impression. Raabe's insecure position in the canon and his capture by what was in many ways an unliterary cult constitute one of the more outlandish chapters in the reception history of German literature.

I am not unmindful that the élan of discovery in a case like this may exaggerate its importance and distort judgment. But I am comforted by the clear evidence that I am by no means alone. The reconsideration of Raabe has been one of the most exciting developments in the study of German literature, especially during the last fifteen years or so. It is not without significance that some of the most worthwhile interpretive work is to be found in often unpublished British and, latterly, American dissertations. Striking about many of them—to which I owe a considerable debt—is not only their quality but their vivacity. They do not read like labored, required exercises, but reflect the fascination that reading Raabe and attempting to solve his many puzzles can afford. The much bruited malaise in the literary disciplines may in large part derive from a subliminal, naturally unarticulated feeling that every conceivable interpretive task has been done over and over, with ever more refined nuances that hardly anyone can stand or even understand anymore. However this may be, staleness is not a problem with Raabe; everything has had to be done afresh. The enthusiasm of discovery is clearly not peculiar to me, but has struck many others with equal force.

The juxtaposition of two recent examples from opposite ends of the scale of academic prestige may illustrate this unusual sea change. One is a 1981 lecture on Raabe's late novel, *The Documents of the Birdsong*, by Wilhelm Emrich, one of the most powerful intellects among contemporary German literary scholars, renowned for his profound studies of Kafka and of the symbolism of the second part of *Faust*.[5] If I am not mistaken, this positive, enthusiastic lecture was the product of quite recent experience; in any case, Emrich had never before addressed himself to Raabe in his substantial career. The other example is a touching little piece that appeared around the same time in a left-wing pedagogical journal.[6] It is the confession of a young schoolteacher, whose training in the current academic atmosphere had left him with little impetus to read literature, as opposed to literary theory, who—again, serendipitously—came across Raabe's historical novella *Höxter and Corvey* and found himself, to his surprise, reading with pleasure and absorption. That reading literature might be pleasurable is apparently something that had never before occurred to him as a student and teacher of literature. In the contentious and sometimes confrontational cultural atmosphere of Germany today, Raabe's demonstrated capacity both to excite and to beguile begins to be increasingly persuasive.

It might be mentioned in passing that Raabe, though most definitely a "bourgeois" writer, has been relatively immune from the hostile criticism of the left. On a couple of occasions he has been the object of exercises in ideological criticism familiar on the German academic left, but these seem not to have been very convincing to others; rather, leftists have endeavored in various ways to regard Raabe positively, reserving their ire for past admirers and disciples. Indeed, it seems to me that the acerbity not infrequently encountered in German cultural discourse has been largely absent from the lively modern discussion of Raabe, though there was plenty of it in the past. It would be unrealistic to suppose that his profoundly humane spirit has radiated a gentling effect over the critical community; but *something* has been radiating: admiration, respect, the excitement of aesthetic discovery—perhaps, though one trembles to suggest it, the pleasure of reading.

To be sure, none of the foregoing proves the standing I claim for Raabe. Fashions come and go, in criticism as in literature. Some years ago we experienced the flourishing of Hermann Hesse, discovered by legions of enthusiastic readers and validated by dozens of vigorous critics, but none of that, in my opinion at any rate, made of him a major writer. A skeptical cultural critic might detect motives for the Raabe renaissance as worrisome as those I imagined I saw in the Hesse boom. I do not intend to press the evaluative issue in what follows, though I shall address it from time to time. Rather I hope merely to make a contribution to the ongoing process of understanding Raabe's fiction. Much of the finest modern work on him has consisted of detailed interpretation of texts and fictional devices; it is my ambition to draw on these achievements as judiciously as I am able in order to widen the perspective to a more comprehensive, though certainly not exhaustive, account of the oeuvre as a whole.

Among the manifold difficulties that confront me in pursuing this purpose, two require particular mention. The newness of the Raabe topic, which generates high spirits in the scholarly endeavor, has another side. While certain general lineaments of consensus have been developing, the topic lacks the solid base of fundamental insight that normally accrues to the study of past literature. We are still working with basics and are perhaps not yet in a position to build the superstructure of fine nuance characteristic of the academic criticism of long reputable literary artists. Thus a certain amount of groping for the right perspective may be evident in what follows. At the same time, I want to express once and for all my obligations to my predecessors and contemporaries in this endeavor. While I am anxious to give credit where it is due, if I were to discharge every debt this study would be burdened with literally thousands of reference notes. One of the ancillary gratifications of studying Raabe is to find oneself in an international community of thoughtful minds, in limited compass a genuine republic of letters. A second, not unrelated difficulty is that a mastery of the oeuvre cannot be expected even of most specialists in German literature. Whoever writes critically about Dickens, or Tolstoy, or Proust, has a right to assume that one is familiar with the texts; if one is not, one should be. With Raabe that is not the case, so that some exposition will be unavoidable. The reader with a good knowledge of Raabe may wish to skim the entire first part of this book as well as the descriptions of the texts discussed in the second and third parts.

All quotations, unless otherwise indicated, are taken from Wilhelm Raabe, *Sämtliche Werke*, ed. Karl Hoppe et al. (Göttingen: Vandenhoeck & Ruprecht, 1960-), identified by volume and page number in parentheses; supplementary volumes are designated by E (*Ergänzungsband*). All translations are my own. Raabe's idiosyncratic style is quite difficult to render into English, and I make no claim for my versions other than a striving for literal accuracy.

PART I

In Search of Raabe

CHAPTER 1

Wolfenbüttel

◙

IN THE summer of 1906, a magazine editor solicited from the nearly seventy-five-year-old Wilhelm Raabe his autobiography. He had often received such requests and had almost always fended them off. Consistently he replied to the curious that his life and person were of no interest, that all that was worth knowing about him could be found in the encyclopedia, and that anyone wishing to know him better should read his works. To a request from Paul Heyse in 1874 for biographical information, he replied: "My biography is quickly written," and added a few dates and a list of his works.[1] In 1891 he sent to a publisher a biographical sketch in telegram style totalling 139 words and forbade him to ask for more details.[2] His touchiness on this point derived in part from what he regarded as a youthful indiscretion; in 1861 he had replied to an inquiring busybody in a more thoughtful and communicative way. There he spoke about his early life, remarked upon his character traits of indolence combined with a capacity for great energy, his shyness sometimes misinterpreted as arrogance, and the inner tensions of "my fluctuating soul": "There are a lot of contradictions in me and since my earliest youth I have occupied myself self-tormentingly with their analysis." He remarked rather offhandedly upon his literary culture, saying that he had started reading Goethe only three years before and still had not finished *Wilhelm Meister*, though he knew the first part of *Faust* by heart; that he had read less of Jean Paul than one might think; and that Schiller affected him intermittently in certain moods; to this he added that an aesthetic conversation "can drive me into the swamp." As for his way of life, he unspectacularly asserted his liking for good friends, a good cigar, and a good drink, adding a comment, more hopeful than true, on his instinctive grasp of the popular.[3] These musings, journalistically embellished, haunted Raabe in recurring versions for years; when his friend Marie Jensen wrote a parody of them in 1870, he expressed his irritation at the report and his regret at having given the interview, referring to the journalist as a "lout."[4]

Raabe was not fond of reports about him by others, either. On one such effort he quoted Samuel Johnson's remark, "No man was written down but by himself."[5] When a young admirer wrote a book about his youth, he said he would rather run across the marketplace in his undershirt than see such things published in his lifetime, and he in fact saw to it that the book did not appear until after his death.[6] In 1906, however, he relented somewhat. He actually sent several paragraphs, totalling 530 words, reporting on his birth, mother, father, education, the beginnings of his writing, his marriage, his children, and his retirement, along with a couple of retrospective reflections. Terse enough, yet it cannot be said that he left very much out. Although long "life and works" volumes have been written about him, Raabe has less of a biography than almost any other writer one can think of. He was born, grew up, began writing, travelled a bit, married, had children, lived consecutively in Wolfenbüttel, Stuttgart, and Braunschweig, and died. There are no adventures, no scandals, no great passions, no gross deviations from the pattern of life of a petty-bourgeois gentleman of his time. This mediocre existence was, to be sure, in part a consequence of limited resources, but more than that it was a deliberate strategy that reduced to a minimum all the energies expended on life in order to maximize those concentrated upon writing.

There are numerous paradoxes in Raabe's character, among them that he was a gregarious introvert. Early on he established the pattern that he was to maintain throughout his life of spending his leisure afternoon or evening hours in taverns, surrounded by an entourage of companions. Over his long life he had dozens of friends and hundreds of acquaintances. At the same time, he seems to have maintained an ultimately impenetrable reserve. Though gregarious, he was rarely talkative, and one imagines that he spent much of the time observing the behavior of others. It has been said of him, no doubt with exaggeration, that he learned the names of his reserved-table companions only when he read their obituaries.[7] Of the title figure of *Master Author*, one of Raabe's numerous ironically fictionalized self-projections, the narrator observes: "Like all of his kind, by a bashfulness very ridiculous to the worldly part of mankind, he was hindered from opening his inner self to a relatively strange person and committing himself, so naked and exposed in his thoughts, meditations, wishes, and hopes" (11: 19-20). A later character, Uhusen in *On the Scrap-Iron*, puts it more militantly: "We play our roles well and do not let the mob into our personal affairs of feeling and privacy. We know how to make faces" (16: 385). For Raabe reticence was a value in an author; he found Theodor Storm's self-promotion in his published correspondence foolish and annoying.[8] Yet he was anything but withdrawn; he seems to have liked bustle around him and he was indifferent to noise. He was completely unmusical—he told a funny story of his father's efforts to have him taught one simple piano piece[9]—and he was quite undisturbed by loud music from a summer theater near his home and cheerfully endured scales played for therapeutic purposes by an arthritic neighbor that, according to a friend, would have driven "a Kant, a Schopenhauer, a Carlyle, to raving madness" (17: 450). His correspondence shows a similar pattern. It grew to be very extensive, especially in his later years; he was a faithful correspondent and tried to answer every letter he received, even from complete strangers and an occasional crackpot. His letters, while not as undistinguished and uncommunicative as they are sometimes made out to be, are rarely very intimate; they tend toward brevity and their customarily rather laconic style contrasts markedly with the almost Baroque luxuriance of his fictional manner. The supposition that he "deliberately husbanded his energies when writing letters" to save them for his creative work is not improbable.[10]

Then there is his diary, which has united every student of him, past and present, in unanimous exasperation. He began to keep it on October 1, 1857, soon after his twenty-sixth birthday, and continued it day in and day out for fifty-three years and thirty-three days, until November 2, 1910, two weeks before his death. Its terseness and utter refusal to reveal anything much are legendary among Raabe scholars; it is not surprising that until recently no one has thought of publishing it. One can read page after page of it without encountering a complete sentence with a subject and a verb. In it Raabe keeps track of the progress of his writing—this, of course, is one of its most valuable features—and records letters received and sent, people he has met, the commonplace events of quotidian life. In 1860 he began the habit of starting each day's entry with a weather report; a meteorological historian could obtain a seamless record of the North German climate in the second half of the nineteenth century from the diary. The weather was important to Raabe because he suffered from asthma and was very vulnerable to climatic changes. The diary seems to have been rather an obsession; when he broke his collarbone in the autumn of 1909, he missed a day, but then had the entries made by someone else. He was quite self-conscious about it; for example, he noted the tenth and the thirtieth anniversaries of its beginning. As usual with him, there are sly references to his habit in his fiction. The narrator of *German Moonshine* gives as evidence of his sober nature the fact that he does not keep a diary, only appointment books (9/2: 381), and the father in

5

Gutmann's Travels advises: "Keeping a diary is sometimes silver, but not keeping a diary, in any case, is much more often gold," and things too personal should be kept out of it (18: 237). But privately he took a more serious view; he wrote to his brother-in-law that the best way to overcome the oppression of the world was to enter every misfortune into a diary, so one might see that there is a time for everything, and he advised his daughter to enter a couple of lines of what each day brings, which will provide amusement and sometimes consolation years later.[11]

It would be a mistake to measure this document against the literary genre of the diary. It is rather an ongoing memorandum of Raabe's life, which he evidently consulted from time to time. It can rarely have taken as much as five minutes out of his day. Still, it is not quite as barren as frustrated researchers sometimes suggest. Just because the diary is so very terse, one is inclined to suppose that the items recorded were of special importance to him, though the absence of discourse and commentary sometimes makes it a puzzle as to what they might mean.

That the diary is a symptom of a very strong habit of reserve seems undeniable; it is almost as if Raabe had not been intimate even with himself. In fact, it is generally true of his literary characters also that they do not directly reveal much of their inner selves; it has been observed, for example, that he rarely employs the device of inner monologue.[12] Thus Raabe, despite his volubility in his fiction, was a rather veiled personality, and he and his posterity seem to have collaborated in the erection of a public persona that is to some degree a fictive self. This public persona was that of a wise man, stable and stoic in the face of adversity, dispensing consolation and humor from the inner resources of an integrated, sovereign self. Upon closer acquaintance, this image does not stand up to scrutiny very well. The inner man was high-strung, short-tempered, beset by ambivalences and antinomies, and agonized by the labor of creation. One of his daughters recalled that his "over-refined, easily and painfully irritated nervous system reacted violently." He would get into moods that terrified his family during which "weeks, months would go by in which his dark glowing eye would not brighten, his clenched fist would not open." At such times he was happy neither at home nor with his friends; everything was "stale, flat, and unprofitable"—a phrase from *Hamlet* I, ii, often employed in the diary as a shorthand for bouts of depression.[13] It has rightly been said that every student of Raabe should read this report of his daughter three times;[14] it is not only a matter of combatting the legends that have grown up around him, but also of growing more attentive to the inner tensions, ambiguities, and ironies in his often deceptive style of fiction.

ORIGINS

Wilhelm Raabe was born on September 8, 1831, in Eschershausen, a small town in the Duchy of Braunschweig, but a few weeks later the family moved to the larger town of Holzminden, which was the real home of his earliest boyhood. The forebears of the family had been Harz Mountain miners, but more recent generations were employed in the official and learned professions. On his paternal grandmother's side he was descended from Justus Georg Schottelius, a prominent seventeenth-century philologist and literary figure. His grandfather, August Heinrich Raabe, had been postmaster in Holzminden but was also a local essayist and historian of a late eighteenth-century Enlightenment persuasion.[15] He remained a model figure for Raabe, whose short story, *The Old University*, was based on his grandfather's memoir of the defunct University of Helmstedt; to help generate the eighteenth-century atmosphere of *The Geese of Bützow* his grandfather's verses are quoted (9/2: 65, 67, 68, 70, 75); and elsewhere Raabe drew on his grandfather's studies in local history. He seems, indeed, to have meant more to Raabe than his father Gustav, a judicial official of, from all we can make out, vigorous temper and lively mind.[16] In 1842 Gustav was transferred to the town of Stadtoldendorf, a promotion for him but a misfortune for the boy, for the school of the small town was inadequate and young Raabe began what was to be a permanent alienation from schooling. In 1845 Gustav Raabe died suddenly of acute appendicitis. Raabe's interesting lack of emotional distress at this event will be mentioned later in another context. But the practical consequences were serious. His widowed mother was left with a tiny pension; she decided to move with Wilhelm, his brother Heinrich, and his sister Emilie to Wolfenbüttel, where she had relatives.

As he profoundly knew, Raabe was extremely fortunate in his mother, whose capacity for retaining good cheer and unstinting love for her son in the most trying of circumstances seems to have been inexhaustible. She was, he said, a "Sunday child";[17] upon her death he wrote to his sister: "But now she remains alive with her clear eye, her infinitely fine feeling for all life around her, with her kindness and her remarkable understanding of the world and sense of beauty."[18] In a number of his works we find mother-son relationships whose chief features are the mother's clear-headedness, calm good cheer, indifference to the common opinion of the world about, and unerring loyalty

7

to the son no matter what he does. That this pattern reflects Raabe's gratitude to his mother and his strong bond with her no one has ever doubted. Her psychological importance for him is manifest. Freud observed, in connection with Goethe: "If one has been the undisputed darling of one's mother, one retains for life that feeling of conquest, that confidence of success that not infrequently draws success after it."[19] Freud may have underestimated the inner fragility that can be masked by Goethe's notorious posture of calm and balance, but it seems altogether probable that Auguste Raabe's unconditional love armored her son's inner tensions with an invincible self-regard that served him well in the vicissitudes and bitternesses of his life, for, whatever transpired, he was least likely to blame himself for it. This may not be an altogether amiable characteristic, but without it one may doubt that he could have persisted in his career with single-minded independence against every kind of discouragement. Still, it is possible that he might have been as well off if his mother's love had not been so totally unconditional and uncritical. I would not have ventured this notion if it did not seem to me that Raabe himself implies it in his late novel, *The Documents of the Birdsong*, as I shall try to show in that connection. He did make the rather odd remark late in life: "My sainted mother could have done something more clever seventy years ago than to give me on life's path the most foolish part of her dear intellect,"[20] a thought probably reflecting his recurrent feeling that his creative vocation had been a misfortune for him.

WOLFENBÜTTEL, MAGDEBURG, BERLIN

We do not know a great deal about Raabe's boyhood. There is little reliable documentation, and his steadfast stance against autobiography effectively blocks our view. Many students of Raabe, to be sure, have found evidence in his fictional works, which often depict childhood. The boyhood of Theodor Rodburg in *Princess Fish*, for example, an isolated child withdrawn into a world of imagination and reading, has been taken as a picture of Raabe's own boyhood. But the retranslation of fiction into its antecedent reality is always a chancy business, and never more so than with Raabe, who was not a systematically mimetic realist. The elements of autobiography and personal experience, of which there are doubtless a great many in his writings, are always subordinate to the logic of his fiction. He consistently and irritably deflected all questions about the "real" model or origin of this person or that place. He wanted people to read his books, not to speculate about something behind or outside them, and he seems to have done everything he could think of to persuade people that his fictions were *fictional*, though with little success until relatively recently. We do know with assurance that he was not successful in school. His mother's chief motive for moving to Wolfenbüttel was that one of her brothers was the headmaster of the high school and another a teacher there. But, although they seem to have nurtured Raabe to the best of their ability, for one reason or another they were able to do little for him. He did well only in German and drawing; he had difficulty with other subjects, especially Latin, and he left school at seventeen without graduating.

His difficulties with school are puzzling, for he was not only, of course, intelligent and imaginative; he was actually of a rather studious nature, and he was blessed, as we can easily see later on, with a stupendous memory. It seems particularly absurd that he was unable to pass Latin, for he had, if anything, a gift for languages. In his mature years he was an altogether competent Latinist and he knew at least some Greek. Like all educated people of his time, he knew French; he acquired by himself a quite serviceable reading knowledge of English; and there is evidence that he could quote Dante in the original. He was neither the first nor the last German writer to founder in the school system; the horrors of schools are a recurrent theme in German literature. But it is difficult to make out what was so terrible about the Wolfenbüttel high school, quite apart from his presumably privileged position as the headmaster's nephew. Indeed, when his uncle celebrated his retirement, Raabe wrote very friendly words of congratulation.[21] We possess only one document from the school years, an essay notebook from the winter semester of 1847-48. The sixteen-year-old boy's exercises already exhibit signs of stylistic dexterity, imagination, and wit. On one of them his teacher wrote that it gave great hopes for future accomplishments;[22] from this unique piece of evidence it is not easy to conclude that the school was bent on discouraging and repressing him. Here, too, the fiction has been required to serve for evidence. A recurrent character type is the youth who cannot learn Latin or do well in school, an amiable good-for-nothing who becomes an active person in the world. But, as always, it is difficult to know how far we may extrapolate from the fiction to the facts. In *The Odin Field* Raabe mentions his schooldays in Holzminden "around 1840" and says it was not the fault of the school's tradition if he learned little there (17: 15). It may well be, as is customarily asserted, that his education was derailed by the static condition of the school in Stadtoldendorf. But it is difficult to understand why a boy of vigorous mind should not have been able to overcome such a disability; it does not seem to have impeded his brother, who passed his legal examinations and made a substantial if conventional career in the civil service. One can only imagine that, in his quiet, pleasant way, young Raabe simply refused to do what was required of him by others; already the firm individualist he was always to be, he seems to have been guided by a subliminal inner purpose, though he was at first far from clear about what that purpose was.

Since he was not able to graduate from school, at the age of seventeen he was apprenticed to a book dealer in Magdeburg. At this point curious parallels with the youth of Hermann Hesse begin to emerge, though without the *Sturm und Drang* that beset Hesse's adolescence. Of the four years Raabe spent in this apprenticeship, we know virtually nothing; only that he was nearly arrested for draft evasion, though eventually deferred for near-sightedness, and that he suffered a major emotional shock from the suicide, virtually in the next room, of his master's son. We also know that the apprenticeship came to nothing; it is not difficult to imagine that Raabe exhibited more interest in reading the books than in selling them. The shop contained a large number of remainders dating back to the first half of the eighteenth century, in which he read extensively;[23] he also taught himself English, in the first instance to read Thackeray's *Pendennis*. It is clear, however, that he left both his master and the town of Magdeburg on amiable terms. He always recalled the place and the whole experience with affection, and he set the town a monument in his historical novella, *Our Lord God's Chancellory* (1862), the second edition of which was published in 1889 by the very firm to which he had been apprenticed forty years before.

When the twenty-one-year-old Raabe returned home from his aborted apprenticeship empty-handed, his poor mother's worry must have been considerable; these were times in which it was certainly very unsafe for a young man wholly without means to have no orderly place in society. Surely he must have sympathized with his mother's feelings; it is not unreasonable to assume that the recurrent theme of the uncomfortable returnee in his fiction owes something to this experience. Evidently she, and perhaps other members of the family, continued to stand by him. It was thought that he should study, and he attempted a special school graduation examination, but was unable to pass it. Nevertheless, he went off to the University of Berlin; since he had not graduated from school, he could not be regularly enrolled, but it is likely that he put his four semesters as an auditor to better use than many a registered student. He attended lectures on the philosophy of history (from the Hegelian Karl Ludwig Michelet), aesthetics (from the Hegelian Heinrich Gustav Hotho), art, law, logic, literary history, Shakespeare, the *Nibelungenlied*, and Goethe; for some reason he also took a course in stenography. His attendance certificates regularly report him as having been "industrious," and he took extensive notes.[24] He seems to have lived in a quite isolated way, and could, of course, have had no knowledge that, as he realized later, "Gottfried Keller was sitting at that time in another quarter of that same rustic Berlin over his *People of Seldwyla*."[25] No doubt the two Berlin years were very educational; but once again he had to return home with no apparent progress toward a station in life. He had, however, written a book.

THE CHRONICLE OF SPARROW ALLEY

Raabe's first novel was begun, or so he was later to claim, on November 15, 1854. He and his friends came to celebrate this date as the anniversary of the "day of setting pen to paper," and he was to die on that date fifty-six years later. The book was finished in the spring or summer of 1855. The "Sparrow Alley" of the title was the Spree Alley, where he had lodged during his first year in Berlin; for his centenary in 1931 the street was officially renamed Sparrow Alley. The novel consists of the diary-like reminiscences of an elderly man, Johannes Wachholder, as he surveys from his upper-floor dwelling the life on the street below and in the building across the way. His memories concern a boyhood friend, illegitimate son of a nobleman and of a mother who drowned herself; Wachholder becomes his friend's rival for a girl and loses her to him; after the death of his friend and his beloved their daughter becomes his ward; he oversees her betrothal to a young man who is also a descendant of the wayward count.

These plot materials are not very interesting, nor are they meant to be. Raabe cared little for plot, especially of the boy-loves-girl variety; in time he came to dispose of this component of novel-writing by making it demonstratively conventional and colorless, and as he matured he seemed ambitious to reduce plot to as near nothing as was well imaginable in nineteenth-century fiction. Instead his focus is on the narration itself, on the process of remembering. An immediate present, a wider present, and layers of the past are interwoven in memory and current experience. Texts by other hands, contrasting and correcting, are interpolated into the memoir. Behind the apparently freely associating, meek, and somewhat insecure old man stands the young author, carefully organizing stresses, modulations, and contrasts. Woven into the text is a strong sense of the times, of the betrayed hopes for liberty and progress of the past, and of the torpid oppressiveness of the post-1848 present. As though in conscious parody of the famous opening sentence of Dickens's *Tale of Two Cities*, "It was the best of times, it was the worst of times . . . ," Raabe begins his first novel in an ominous tone:

> It is really an evil time! Laughter has become dear in the world, wrinkling of the brow and sighing cheap indeed. In the distance lie bloody and dark the thunderclouds of war, and sickness, hunger, and need have laid their eerie veil over the vicinity;—it is an evil time! Beyond that it is autumn, sad, melancholy autumn, and a fine, cold, pre-winter rain has been dripping on the big city for weeks;—it is an evil time! People have long faces and heavy hearts, and when two acquaintances meet, they shrug their shoulders and hurry almost without a greeting past one another;—it is an evil time! (1: 11)

The *Chronicle* has always been regarded as a remarkable achievement for a first novel. Its sureness of style and organization are impressive, and in some ways it serves as a primer to Raabe's whole oeuvre: the intricacy of the narrative perspective; the sometimes oblique but nevertheless uncompromising critique of conventional society; the search for humane hopefulness in certain kinds of personal relations in the face of a melancholy view of life and the world. It also has the weaknesses not surprising in a first novel by a bookish, essentially self-educated young man with little experience of the world. Its tone is marked by the sentimentality with which Raabe had a long struggle; it exhibits the Dickensian pathos without much of the Dickensian muscle. While Raabe may not have been much interested in his banal plot elements, the fact remains that these elements are there. The implied criticism of class and society is ingenious in some places, but schematic in others.

On the whole, however, young Raabe had reason to be satisfied with himself. He endured the customary difficulties of an unknown author in getting the book published and wound up paying for publication himself; it appeared in Berlin in 1856, receiving a number of encouraging reviews by critics of some influence. The most important was a review of a second printing in 1858 by Friedrich Hebbel, who was not only Germany's leading playwright but also a critic of considerable penetration: "An excellent overture," he wrote, "but where is the opera?" (1: 437). The *Chronicle* was not a commercial success at first; like many of Raabe's works, it had a slow start but a long life. It was twenty years before the fifth edition appeared, but by the end of his life there had been seventy editions. Still, the critical *succès d'estime* made him confident that he had found his métier, and he was sure he could do better.

Almost sonambulistically, Raabe had arrived at his true vocation: the writing of fiction; for the most of the rest of his life he did little else. I have heard students sometimes ask whether, with this obsessive concentration on the craft of fiction, he ought to be compared with Flaubert. Probably not, I think; Raabe was a relatively fluent writer, not much given to revision, especially in his mature years. While he was undoubtedly meticulous, one does not imagine him agonizing for hours or days over a single sentence or paragraph as Flaubert did. He seemed to have had no problem with inspiration; when his wife, worried about finances, asked him if he would be able to think up a new book when the current one was finished, he replied: "That is a full pot into which I need only to reach and that never gets empty" (E 4: 49). His diary gives the impression that he finished one work and began another in unending succession; only in his relatively early years did he pursue several projects simultaneously. Of course he took breaks, vacations, and so on; but the overall impression is that he wrote as though it were a job, diligently and continuously. Even his marriage and his subsequent move to Stuttgart, which occurred while he was in the middle of a novel, interrupted his pace for no more than a month. It has been estimated that he averaged a page of print a day.[26] This insistently businesslike regularity is one of several of his characteristics that remind one of Thomas Mann.

What is unusual in the context of the time is Raabe's total concentration on narrative fiction and his determination to make his living from it exclusively. In nineteenth-century Germany this was very difficult to do and almost no other major writer succeeded in achieving the earnings of some of their counterparts in other European countries. Most of the major writers of the Classical-Romantic age had employment of other kinds: Goethe was a government minister, Schiller a professor, Novalis a mining engineer, Eichendorff a Prussian official, Tieck was employed by royal courts as a reader and theater director, Hoffmann was a judge, etc. Even Heine, who is said to be the first truly professional German writer, obtained something like half of his income from other sources. Kleist was an exception, and the utter hopelessness of his material existence was certainly one of the contributing factors to his suicide. In the later nineteenth century this did not change very much. Storm, Stifter, and Keller were public officials. Fontane began as an pharmacist and then became a journalist and foreign correspondent. There were others who tried to support themselves by journalism or editing periodicals; some obtained positions in the theater; one or another found a sinecure, for example, Hoffmann von Fallersleben, the author of "Deutschland, Deutschland über alles," who became librarian of the Abbey of Corvey. In fact, upon Hoffmann's death in 1874 it was suggested that Raabe might succeed him, for Corvey is located on the Weser in the midst of his literary landscape. But he dismissed the idea without even considering it seriously;[27] doubtless an abbey was no place for him and he may also have been mindful of Lessing's disagreeable experiences as librarian in Wolfenbüttel a century earlier. He was several times offered the editorship of journals or of other publishing enterprises, but he consistently refused them; "I am thoroughly unfit to be an 'editor,' " he wrote one publisher.[28]

The specialization in narrative fiction was also unusual, especially since the novel had a rather dubious standing in the German aesthetics of the time. The most prestigious genre was the drama; most writers of the time tried their hand at it or at least hoped to, often with dispiriting results; Raabe thought about playwriting but made no serious attempt. Also highly prestigious was the epic poem, an enthusiasm that has left us with a vast corpus of totally unread literature; Raabe considered a mock epic on the Queen of Sheba but fortunately thought the better of it. He did write some poetry, however. There is a famous diary entry under the date of December 5, 1857: "*I discover that I can make verses!!!!*" Raabe wrote some seventy poems, almost all of them during this episode early in his career. In general, they are what one would expect: competent, with an occasional arresting image or passage. Many of them are derivative of older styles: folksongs, seventeenth-century mercenaries' songs, Heinesque ballads and lovesongs, the political verse of the previous generation. As one might imagine, few of them are very introspective. Raabe had a difficult time inducing anyone to publish any of them, and gradually he began to take a self-ironic view of them, putting them into the mouths of fictional characters to satirize them as pompous or tasteless.

While many of his contemporaries wrote essays, literary criticism, or other journalistic items whenever they had the opportunity, his total non-fictional prose fills no more than thirty pages. This corpus consists of a one-page review of Berthold Auerbach's *German Popular Calendar for 1859*, an essay commissioned for the hundredth birthday of a hero of the Wars of Liberation named Kleist von Nollendorf (1862), a descriptive reminiscence of the old city of Braunschweig (1865), an essay on the eighteenth-century fairy-tale adapter Musäus (1865), a brief account of his Stuttgart literary friend Edmund Hoefer

(1867), and a little speech he gave to his tavern cronies on the occasion of his fiftieth birthday (1881).[29] What is striking about all these pieces is that, with the exception of the Musäus essay, in style and content they are totally undistinguished; no one would pay the least attention to them if they were not from Raabe's hand. The last item especially is well suited to reinforce an impression of him as a petty-bourgeois provincial, but to my mind it is just one more piece of evidence of his disinclination to display his private self in public.

Raabe's most pronounced non-fictional talent was in art. In fact, there is reason to think that at one time he may have been intended for a career as an artist; his earliest efforts have clearly the appearance of academic exercises. The talent ran in the family; his brother Heinrich seems to have been a capable amateur artist, and his daughter Margarethe became a professional portrait painter. Raabe has left us four early oils, seventy watercolors, and 630 drawings. To my untutored eye the oils and watercolors do not seem very remarkable; they lack the finish of Gottfried Keller's paintings and certainly cannot compare with the work of the most talented writer-artist of the time, Adalbert Stifter. But the drawings are more compelling; to some extent they remind one of Goethe's, with their spare, swift line, their sure sense of proportion, and their skill in light and shading even in miniature compass, though it seems to me that there is a certain, perhaps significant, erect rigidity in the figures.[30] Raabe made these drawings all his life, even on his deathbed; oddly, they are often more meditative and introspective than his poems. It is evident, however, that he regarded them as nothing more than a casual pastime; most of them are on scraps of paper, discarded manuscripts, old bills, the backs of envelopes; sometimes one drawing even runs into another. In no way did his drawing talent distract him from his main occupation, the writing of fiction.

WOLFENBÜTTEL AGAIN

After the appearance of the *Chronicle*, Raabe launched upon his literary career with vigor. During the next five years he undertook no fewer than nineteen works: nine stories, five novellas, four novels, and part of a fifth. Virtually none of this early work is held in very much regard by criticism today. In retrospect, Raabe looked back on this phase of his career with dismay, repudiating all of it as immature. It may be that we have gone too far in following him in this judgment. While none of the early works reaches the excellence and potential of the *Chronicle*, some of them exhibit interesting and even impressive aspects, and perhaps Raabe studies will return to them in the future. In any case, many of them, with all their weaknesses, seem to me distinctly superior to the average of German fiction at mid-century, especially stylistically. But it is true that young Raabe found himself in what might be called a trilemma, on the three horns of which he remained painfully impaled throughout much if not all of his career. The first was fidelity to his own voice and vision, idiosyncratic and original, generating both stylistically and thematically a form of fiction very different from the literary conventions and horizon of expectations of mid-nineteenth-century Germany. The second was his strong desire to be heard, to have readers, competent ones if possible, an ambition to make his message efficacious in Germany. This was a purpose that to some considerable degree conflicted with his commitment to artistic individuality. The third horn, a particularly sharp one, was his unconventional determination to make his living exclusively by writing fiction. This exigency doubtless to some extent accounts for the appearance of over-productivity and perhaps excessive haste in the first phase, as well as the uncomfortable and ultimately unsuccessful melding of the Raabean voice and vision with the kinds of literature written by other people, for the young writer of limited experience was obliged, like many other writers, to learn about literature from the literature that was then extant.

This hybridization is especially evident in his second effort, the ambitious novel *One Springtime* (1857), which combines the Dickensian sentiment of decent young people seeking a passage through a hard, ungenerous world with melodramatic generational conflicts, wayward artistic careers, honest poverty contrasted with luxurious depravity, secret past histories and hidden family relationships. It has been said that the novel anticipates the fairy-tale pattern of the family magazine novel.[31] Critics complain regularly of "banal action" and "romantic clichés," of dissolution in sentimentality and moralism.[32] One of the most prominent critics of the time, Levin Schücking, noted without difficulty the resemblance to Dickens, but complained of harmlessness, mannerism, and over-composition (1: 480). Indeed, the novel contains five different plots.[33] This complexity of plot shows, perhaps more than any other feature, Raabe at odds with his own instincts.

Although he made revisions in some of his works in later editions, *One Springtime* is the only one he subjected to complete recasting; he began to rewrite it in 1865-66 and completed the revision in 1869-70. In fact, in 1865 he acquired and burned the remainder of the first edition, including even his brother's copy. Here there is an interesting parallel with Gottfried Keller, who attempted to eradicate the first edition of *Green Henry* (1855), burning the remainder as winter fuel and composing an entirely new version (1889-90). But the second version of *Green Henry* is, on balance if not in every detail, a clear improvement over the first. This is not the case with the second version of *One Springtime*; though it had some success with the public, the critics did not like it, nor did Raabe himself, who never seems really to have had his heart in the project.[34]

The other novels of the period are equally ambitious and bulky. *The Children of Finkenrode* (1859) is a sardonic, to some degree self-ironic novel of contemporary life, in which, however, Raabe continues to struggle with mannerism, clichés, and the clearly sensed but still unsolved problems of narrative perspective. *The People from the Forest* (1862), the longest of all of his novels, is his first effort to reproduce the *Bildungsroman* form. The book has interesting aspects and is very important for his development as a novelist, but the *Bildungsroman* form is vitiated, almost parodied, by the device of solving the protagonist's problems by having him strike it rich in the California Gold Rush. Hidden in this unpersuasive strategy is an as yet unarticulated awareness that the optimistic *Bildungsroman* pattern had become incongruous in nineteenth-century society. Raabe also wrote a number of historical works in this period, including what has been over the years one of the most widely read of his stories, *The Black Galley* (1861), and two by no means negligible works: *The Holy Spring* (1861) and *Our Lord God's Chancellory* (1862). While these are still not counted among his major achievements, in them he succeeded rather better in amalgamating his talents with a recognizable literary genre of the time. There will be something more to say of them in the chapter on the theme of history.

During these years Raabe's career certainly did not blaze brilliantly; the hopes aroused in him by the encouraging reception of the *Chronicle* had to be considerably modified. Still, his industriousness counted for something; he began to earn enough to support his modest bachelor way of life. He was able at last to cease being a burden on his mother and take a small flat of his own. In 1859 he had saved enough to undertake a journey of several weeks' duration. His original intention was to travel to Italy, but he was prevented by the outbreak of war between Austria and France; Raabe was never to visit a non-German-speaking country except for Bohemia, hardly a foreign country at that time. He played the conventional tourist; his diary during the trip is uncharacteristically detailed. Apart from his excursion to Prague, the major stops along the way were Leipzig, Dresden, Vienna, and Stuttgart. One easily sees the method in this sequence, for these were, along with Berlin, which Raabe already knew, the major publishing centers of German literature, and indeed he called on a number of prominent literary figures along the way. He may already have been thinking of abandoning little Wolfenbüttel in favor of an urban literary center, a supposition reinforced by the actual consequence of the journey a couple of years later.

On July 24, 1862, Raabe married twenty-five-year-old Berthe Leiste of a local patrician family, whom he had been courting for some time. As he was fortunate in his mother, so he was fortunate in his wife. She was an intelligent, competent woman, with, as it turned out, a pronounced talent for domestic management, a skill that was often strained to the utmost as the family navigated through lean times. She was musical and may even have contemplated a career as a singer, but she submerged any ambitions she may have had for herself in her duties as a wife and mother. Raabe's classically patriarchal household does not, of course, correspond to the pattern commended today, but this was the nineteenth century, and we should not think of Berthe Raabe as a repressed creature. She evidently possessed, like her husband, a quick, dry wit that kept them on even terms, and she was not beyond complaining about his irritating, somewhat selfish habits.[35] She brought into the marriage a dowry of 13,000 talers, but it is symptomatic of Raabe's character that he made every effort to avoid invading that little fortune, even in the hardest of times; he may well have thought that, given his precarious position in life, it was her only life insurance. Overall, the marriage must be judged to have been an uncommonly happy one; for forty-eight years Raabe and his wife remained bound by indissoluble ties of loyalty.

CHAPTER 2

Stuttgart

◻

O N H I S wedding day Raabe commenced a move to Stuttgart. He
had made the decision to do this at the end of the previous
year.¹ He did not give his reasons, but they are not hard to perceive.
Clearly he was moving to a larger, more urban environment. Stuttgart
had 62,000 inhabitants in 1862 and, like most German cities, it was
growing rapidly; by 1870 the population reached 90,000. In his tour
of literary centers, he had found Stuttgart particularly amiable and
hospitable. He hoped to associate with other writers and work in an
environment that would be advantageous to his own publishing ambitions. He promptly took up his customary pattern of life, made
numerous acquaintances, and joined a club. His first daughter, Margarethe, was born July 17, 1863. Later that year he wrote to his
mother: "For me as a writer and as a human being I could not find
any better residence in Germany."² But these hopes and expectations
were gradually eroded; in the course of time the Stuttgart experiment came to look increasingly like a failure that would have to be
abandoned.

This disappointment was certainly not owing to lack of industry.
During the approximately eight Stuttgart years Raabe undertook six
stories, five novellas, and five novels. Three of these novels were particularly important in his career: *The Hunger Pastor* (1863-64), *Abu Telfan* (1867), and *The Rumbledump* (1869-70).³ These three have become
known as the "Stuttgart Trilogy," a notion generated by Raabe when,
in the last paragraph of *The Rumbledump*, he linked them together as a
sequence: "We are at the end—and it was a long and wearisome way
from the hunger parsonage at Grunzenow on the Baltic by way of
Abu Telfan in Tumurkieland and in the shadow of the Mountains of
the Moon to this old lazaret at Krodebeck at the foot of the old Germanic magic mountain!" (8: 379). His friend Wilhelm Jensen identified
them as a trilogy in a newspaper review in 1870 (8: 399), and Raabe
several times reinforced the notion. There has been some sterile discussion as to whether the novels "really" constitute a trilogy, for they
have no overlapping characters, no continuity of place or plot. They

19

are connected, however, by an increasingly bleak view of the possibilities of the humane individual against a callous, mundane society. *The Hunger Pastor* is a *Bildungsroman* in which the process of *Bildung* is, on the whole, a series of disappointments ending in a harbor of diminished expectations; *Abu Telfan* recounts a rebellion against society that recoils back upon the rebel as though off a stone wall; *The Rumbledump*, the most deeply pessimistic of his major novels, exhibits the victory of evil, of the imperishable *canaille*, over goodness in the realm of conventional society if not of the spirit.

During the Stuttgart years he consciously strove for artistic maturation. He labored to find a form of realism; to his publisher he wrote in 1866: "There is much lying in our literature, and for my poor part I will do what I can with all my strength to expose it, although I know quite well that the comfort of my life will not benefit from it."[4] His concern was not so much for a mimetic realism of time and place, though he approached that also; the novel *Fabian and Sebastian*, written later in Braunschweig in 1880-81, nowhere mentions Stuttgart but is identifiably set in that city (15: 576). But his realism was more a matter of tone, of desentimentalization and disillusionment. This was not easy for him, for, like virtually all German-language writers of the nineteenth century, he was deeply rooted in the culture of German idealism; he never fully escaped it, but it came into productive conflict with his skeptical, often bitter perceptions of real life, society, and history. One can follow this hardening of tone in the revisions of *Elsa of the Fir* (1865), the theme of which is vulnerable to sentimentality.[5] This work also exhibits an advance in internalizing the process of perception in the protagonist's consciousness. For Raabe's search for his own voice was in large measure a search among the possibilities of narrative perspective. The multiperspective option, adumbrated in the *Chronicle*, came to fruition in the novella *Three Pens* (1865), in which three separate narrators, in two separate segments each, give their perspectives, very different by reason of age and character, on the same sequence of events. Since this novella also incorporates Raabe's new relative hardness of tone, he regarded it as a breakthrough; he said at the time that he was at last beginning to master his art, and late in life he characterized it as his "first independent work" (9/1: 492, 493).

But all this artistic progress, which the modern observer can recognize as genuine, merely impaled him more painfully on the horns of his trilemma. The more he found his way to his skeptical, experimental, narratively complex mode, the less successful he became. Even *The Hunger Pastor*, in the long run his most famous novel, had a modest start; *Abu Telfan* and *The Rumbledump* failed with the public. The critics were cool and began to honor his experiments in narrative perspective with complaints about mannerism and subjectivity. The meager response naturally brought with it a meager income; he seemed to be working harder and harder for less and less return. A pattern of bitterness toward a public for whose approbation he was deeply ambitious began to assert itself. The deterioration of his spirits during the 1860s can be followed, at a distance but unmistakably, in his diary. On October 1, 1864, he records a "homeless mood"; on January 3, 1865, there appears the first thought of leaving Stuttgart; he feels "dull, defeated." A year later, on January 9, 1866, he records "the doubts and irritations of society." By August 14, 1868, he is "tired of life"; his favorite *Hamlet* quote, "stale, flat, and unprofitable," appears on December 9 and recurs at intervals thereafter. He seems to have suffered from anxiety attacks and sleepless nights. As he had begun to study Greek, he entered on December 9, 1868, "*ademonia kai lutta*," anguish and rage, and "*mania*," and again on January 27, 1869, this time in German letters, "in the evening suddenly mania." On a draft of *Elsa of the Fir*, dated May 3, 1864, he wrote: "Scriptum in miseria" (9/1: 459).

His distress had several causes, along with his anxiety about his career. Though at root a sturdy man, he was plagued by irksome ailments that he bore with anything but patience. He was asthmatic and therefore susceptible to bronchial attacks, which he blamed on the Stuttgart climate. He developed an ear disease, apparently Ménière's syndrome, that required an operation. When the doctors told him that it was only the seventh case of this condition in their experience, he wrote to his mother in the distinctly unstoic spirit with which he endured his own sufferings: "Isn't that disgusting? I could have played all the lotteries of the world without winning the least thing, and *this* must happen to me among the millions and billions!!!!!!"[6] His wife's health, also, was threatened by stillbirths in 1864 and 1865. One perhaps minor but recurrent annoyance was that his wife seems to have had difficulty getting along with the local servant girls; the diary shows a constant hiring and firing of them. However, these problems may have had a little to do with Berthe's personality, for they continued in Braunschweig; diary entries in April 1871 show that one servant ran away and the police had to be involved. The manner of the entries suggests that the monotonous recurrence of these scenes began to strike Raabe as wryly comic. More seriously, he had misjudged the value for him of Stuttgart literary life, which was lively but mediocre. Almost none of his literary friends has any identity at all today except as they appear on the margins of his biography.[7] The finest writer in the neighborhood, Eduard Mörike, Raabe did not attempt to meet. Many years later he explained that Mörike "led such a hypochondria-cally withdrawn life that probably only his oldest *Swabian* friends were in intimate contact with him."[8] It is true that Mörike was intro-verted and withdrawn, but he was not a hermit, and one imagines that Raabe could have made his acquaintance had he tried; one of his close Stuttgart friends, Friedrich Notter, was also an intimate of Mö-rike. The busy life of largely commercialized potboiling was doubtless more a threat than an impulse to Raabe's own literary aspirations. In time he resigned from his club and reduced his contacts with the mi-nor writers around him.

The most important cause, however, of his increasing discomfort in Stuttgart was political. He had come to be a vigorous nationalist, strongly committed to the unification of the German nation, of neces-sity under Prussian leadership, since that appeared to be the only realistic option. These convictions conflicted with the particularist sentiment and democratic suspicions of Prussia widespread in Swabia and in the German southwest generally. With the Prussian victory over Austria in 1866 and the manifest ascent of Bismarck, this conflict deepened; Raabe's letters of the time express increasing impatience at local Swabian particularism. At one point he believed he had been denounced to the security service of the Kingdom of Württemberg as a "very dangerous individual."[9] Berthe, easily identifiable by her northern dialect, seems to have been subjected to considerable rude-ness. Raabe noted in his diary on August 1, 1866, that someone had insulted her as a "Prussian-head" (*Preußenkopp*), and in later years he recalled that she had been thrown out of stores as a "Prussian pig" (*Schweinepreußin*).[10] At the same time, however, as his political convic-tions were alienating him from his Stuttgart environment, they brought him the most enduring friendship of his life.

THE JENSENS

One day in 1866, so the story goes, Raabe was bodily thrown out of a political meeting for having too vigorously opposed particularist po-sitions. Thrown out with him was another man, like Raabe a tall, handsome northerner and like Raabe a writer. He held the same mil-itant nationalist convictions; in fact, the Kingdom of Württemberg had briefly incarcerated him as a subversive in one of the most notorious of German prisons, the Hohenasperg. His name was Wilhelm Jensen (1837–1911). Within a few weeks the Raabes and the Jensens were bound together in an affectionate relationship that was to last through the remaining forty-four years of Raabe's life. Since they lived apart for most of those years, their friendship was carried on mainly by mail, so that their letters constitute the largest segment of Raabe's correspondence.

Today Wilhelm Jensen is remembered for only two reasons: as Raabe's friend, and as the author, late in life, of a novella, *Gradiva* (1903), which was taken by Freud as the object of his first extended analysis of a literary text (1907).[11] In his time, however, Jensen was a successful and prominent writer, more successful and prominent than Raabe. Though Freud, with his deep literary culture, did not over-estimate *Gradiva* as a work of art, his attention to it nevertheless says something about Jensen's continued visibility in the first decade of this century; Freud and Jensen (who was delighted by the attention, if baffled by the analysis) got into a courteous correspondence with one another.[12] Jensen's professional career was quite the opposite of Raabe's, taking a more conventional shape. He published not only fiction but also poetry and dramas. He wrote literary criticism and essays on contemporary and historical topics. He edited newspapers and journals, and lived a public literary life from one end of Germany to the other. Altogether he must have written considerably more than twice as much as Raabe in a career of about the same length.

Although in some respects, intellectually, politically and in certain aspects of his character, he resembled Raabe, he was a quite different kind of writer: more direct, more "objective," that is, naive in his narrative stance, more explicit in his ideological biases, and certainly more in tune with the taste of the reading public. Now the vicissitudes of taste have reversed the judgment. Virtually no one reads Jensen today, hardly even literary historians of the period. His works gather dust on library shelves or are scattered in the heaps of unread anti-quarian books that litter the world. Nor is it easy to imagine that this will change, for, though not without imagination, fluency, and a cer-tain technical competence, he was a heavy-handed, one-dimensional writer, lacking in irony, often pretentious, regularly melodramatic, sometimes priggishly salacious, and frequently quite gory. (*Gradiva*, as a matter of fact, does not give a complete notion of these qualities, for it is one of his more graceful works.) While reading his *Chiemgau-novellen* (*Chiemgau Novellas*, 1895), which purport to illustrate Ger-manic mores beginning with the sixth century, I was reminded of nothing so much as the *Prince Valiant* comic strips I used to read as a boy. Furthermore, his comments and occasionally quite critical book reviews on Raabe's works do not suggest a very penetrating insight into his friend's writing; indeed their friendship was more personal than literary, so that their correspondence exhibits relatively little literary depth or interest.

In fact, it was Jensen's wife Marie who showed more sensitivity to Raabe's art. Born in Würzburg on August 31, 1845, she was eleven years younger than Raabe, but she always celebrated her name day, September 8, as her birthday, which, being also Raabe's birthday, annually gave occasion for mutual felicitations. Half Jewish in origin, Catholic by upbringing, and raised for a time in Vienna, she was more vivacious than the relatively reserved North Germans and also, judging from photographs, pretty and stylish. She was musical and artistic; in 1880 she painted quite a good portrait of Raabe.[13] Her gaily exuberant letters to him—sometimes in verse—were more than friendly, and her comments on his works close to worshipful. Needless to say, some observers, doubtless vexed by the absence of escapades in Raabe's life, have wondered if there might not have been an erotic undercurrent in this relationship. Might not Raabe have been drawn to this bright, cheerful woman with her unfeigned admiration for his every creation, in contrast to his not unintelligent but staid, domestic, perhaps fairly unliterary wife? But, quite apart from the fact that such a thing would have been completely out of character for Raabe, and apart also from the clear evidence in the correspondence that Marie and her husband were at least as affectionately and intimately bonded as Raabe and his wife, Raabe gave no sign of more than a friendly attachment to Marie and at times—we shall see an example in a moment—seemed to feel that she was crowding him a little.[14]

Long and cordial as the Raabe-Jensen friendship was, it was not without some mild but persistent subliminal strains. They had essentially two sources. In the first place, it could not wholly be ignored that Jensen achieved the success and prosperity that long remained out of Raabe's reach. Jensen was much more a man of the world. After living for a time in Stuttgart, in south central Germany, he moved to the extreme north, to Flensburg in 1868 and Kiel in 1872, then to the extreme south, to Freiburg in 1876, and to Munich and Chiem Lake in 1888; at each stage his surroundings seem to have become more luxurious. In contrast to the almost immobile Raabes, the Jensens vacationed in Switzerland, Austria, the Shetland Islands, Holland, Belgium, and Italy. With prosperity came social prestige; one of the Jensen daughters was morganatically married to Prince Ernst, son of the Duke of Saxe-Meiningen.[15] Raabe could not help but feel this difference, not because he envied Jensen, but because he was embittered at his own fate. A curious symptom of his feelings is the ingenuity with which he avoided visiting his best friends, though the most imploring invitations were a leitmotif for years of their letters to him. He visited them once, alone, in Flensburg in 1870, then, with his family, exactly ten years later, in Freiburg in 1880. Again ten years later, in 1890, a visit was talked of, but fell victim to one of the many excuses Raabe had employed over the years to decline visits or postpone them indefinitely. In October 1904 they met again, for the last time, in a public place in Magdeburg. Fairly early on Raabe made it clear that the financial difference was the hindrance: "Until people buy my books, I must, as regards seeing one another again, depend on *your* mobility."[16] Raabe cannot have been encouraged by the enthusiastic accounts the Jensens intermittently sent of their surroundings and their travels. At some point Marie seems to have sensed this, for she began to find occasion to insist that her family was not that well off and also had financial troubles.[17]

This difficulty was not unconnected with another, more delicate one. Despite Jensen's success, Raabe knew in his heart that he was the finer writer; Marie knew it also, and Jensen, though not much given to self-disparagement, probably did, too. Marie rather undiplomatically brought the matter to a head near the beginning of their relationship, in 1869; she urged Raabe "to tell me in confidence, candidly and completely honestly, what *you* think of Wilhelm's productions. Nothing will be taken ill but a lack of honesty."[18] Raabe did not have to be urged to sincerity; that was his nature, and he must have been seriously embarrassed by this request. One may imagine that he spent the next week and a half trying to compose a reply to it at once truthful and evasive. Why, he answered, should one so successful ask others how they like his things? Raabe, for his part, likes them very well, but he is not sure *Jensen* will like them five years hence. He writes well, but he doesn't make his *own* figures dance; he brings his pleasure in things to paper, but not the things themselves. Between the lines Raabe gives an impression that he senses Jensen's combination of energy and shallowness, and his comments are buried in friendly jokes and comic drawings.[19] Marie thanked him and agreed that Jensen never had written with his heart's blood; Jensen took the critique with as much good humor as he could muster, and a little later concluded a letter with the words: "Above all keep me in your affection and to this end don't read my works too often."[20] Some years afterwards Marie commented on Raabe's *Horacker*: "Dear Wilhelm, I wish Wilhelm would write as thoughtfully as you!"[21]

Acknowledging Jensen's works must have been one of Raabe's most stressful writing tasks. On *Minatka: Ein Roman aus dem dreißigjährigen Krieg* (*Minatka: A Novel of the Thirty Years War*, 1871), he observed: "The book is often *very beautiful*; but often you have made too many concessions to your notorious rage; —Count Marek has a certain similarity to Sir Leicester Dudley [i.e., Dedlock] in *Bleak House*"; and concerning *Karin von Schweden* (*Karin of Sweden*, 1878) he commented that he knew King Christian [II] of Denmark had been a bad man, but he had never supposed him that bad.[22] One must have read *Minatka* and *Karin of Sweden* in order to perceive the diplomatic irony of these remarks and the restraint they must have cost to formulate. Jensen's melodramatic, ideologically aggressive, black-and-white characterization is very evident in both of them. For one thing, he was militantly anti-Catholic and was constantly refighting the Reformation. In 1883, one of his dramas, *Der Kampf für's Reich* (*The Struggle for the Empire*), in which the Archbishop of Cologne appears as a drunken political manipulator, so incensed the Catholic population of Freiburg that a mob besieged his house.[23] Raabe, too, was a Protestant partisan, insofar as Protestantism for him, as for most German liberals of his time, stood in the succession of Reformation, Enlightenment, and liberty; but he deplored the sectarian strife that had plagued Germany for more than three centuries and in his mature works he always treated it even-handedly. Similarly in politics; Raabe yielded to no one in his nationalist sentiment, but he did not employ it for chauvinistic militance against other nations in his fiction as Jensen did, fighting the Danes even in a historical novella like *Karin of Sweden*. Marie, too, recognized this difference; at the time of the Franco-Prussian War she wrote that her husband was celebrating every victory, while she was too depressed by the misery and bloodshed to participate;[24] she may have been aware that in such matters her sensibilities were closer to Raabe's than to her husband's. In the far-fetched comparison of the truly awful *Minatka* with Dickens one senses Raabe's struggle to devise something positive to say. In fact, his repressed competitiveness broke through his politeness in an odd way; he developed the habit of praising Jensen's *poetry and dramas*, advising him to abandon fiction: "What business does he have," he wrote to Marie, "on our worn and exhausted field of epic prose?"[25]—that is, on Raabe's own field, worn and exhausted as it might be.

In late years the relationship may have grown less important to the Raabes and Jensen, if not to Marie; the letters are less frequently written, in some years only on birthdays and Christmas, and become preoccupied with domestic events. In 1896 Jensen "forgot" Raabe's birthday, which is a little odd, since it was the same as his wife's.[26]

By the end of the century they were very old friends, no less, but also no more.

But in 1868, Jensen's decision to leave Stuttgart in order to edit a Flensburg newspaper in the Prussian interest[27] was a painful loss to Raabe and intensified his unwillingness to continue living there. It is a curious fact, however, that his increasing unhappiness in Stuttgart, documented beyond any doubt, dissipated in his memory after he had left the city behind. He did not forget the political aggravations, but otherwise he looked back on the episode with good humor and maintained affectionate contact with some of his friends there for many years. His departure took place amid expressions of mutual regret. He wrote a poem, now something quite rare for him, entitled "Parting from Stuttgart" (20: 409-10), while his wife wrote rather sourly to the Jensens that everyone was extremely sorry to see him go after having ignored him for eight years and that the publisher who had refused *The Rumbledump* now gave him a banquet and offered to build him a house if he could be induced to stay.[28] But by then the die was cast.

CHAPTER 3

Braunschweig

◙

IN JULY 1870 Raabe moved from Stuttgart to Braunschweig. He chose an inconvenient moment, for he and his family found themselves riding trains and shipping goods in the midst of the mobilization for the Franco-Prussian War. But after a certain amount of chaos he settled down in Braunschweig, and there he remained settled for forty years. At first glance this seems in no way puzzling. Literary disappointments, political abrasions, and the departure of his new friends had exhausted any desire to continue in Stuttgart. In Braunschweig he was moving to the capital of his homeland, a city he knew well, with friends and relatives in the neighborhood, close to his old home of Wolfenbüttel and not far from the Weser River landscape where he had been born and that inspired much of his fiction. Berthe, who was even more out of place in Stuttgart than her husband, may well have encouraged the move to a more familiar environment. Raabe was, as usual, close-mouthed about his reasons, saying only to his brother-in-law that the main one was to give his children a North German, meaning, of course, Protestant education.[1]

Nevertheless, Raabe experts have always felt that this move required an explanation, as though its motives were not altogether obvious.[2] Braunschweig was not exactly a backwater, but it was not exactly a metropolis, either. With 60,000 inhabitants it was two-thirds the size of Stuttgart at the time, and it was growing less rapidly than many German cities, having only doubled its population by the end of Raabe's life. It was somewhat to the side of the main transportation arteries in Germany, and the cultural life of the late eighteenth century, with the brilliant Lessing at its center, was scarcely a memory. In his time Raabe was the only writer of national importance living there, and for a good many years Braunschweig seems to have been only dimly aware of his presence. His love for the city was hardly fanatical. When Jensen in 1877 gave some thought to moving there, Raabe replied that it was nice enough, but only for someone who would not care if he fell out of the world completely for a number of years.[3] Looking back in the last year of his life, he realized that he had isolated himself with the move and associated his loneliness and friendlessness (exaggerated in retrospect) with the image of the sunken garden in *Master Author*.[4] Within the city he was restless, moving four times, until in the spring of 1901 he found the apartment on the Leonhardstrasse that today serves as a Raabe museum.

What apparently keeps Raabe's admirers restless is a potential charge of provinciality that would diminish his stature. Braunschweig *was*, after all, a provincial capital, and Raabe did not get very far out of it very often. It is true that he did not much like big cities. The narrator of *The Documents of the Birdsong* probably expresses the author's feelings when he says that he shudders every time he hears of another German city exceeding a hundred thousand inhabitants (19: 218). In that novel as well as in *Master Author* more than twenty years earlier we see traditional town neighborhoods being destroyed by urban development. Although thirteen of his works take place wholly or partly in Berlin, typically the perspective, as in the archetypal *Chronicle*, is a relatively narrow, individualized space.[5] Of all of his works, only *On the Scrap-Iron* (1887) and *The Lar* (1889) come close to the representations of modern urban life familiar from other nineteenth-century realists, though there are ineffectual probes in minor stories such as *One of the Crowd* (1858), *Thekla's Inheritance* (1868), and the posthumously published *The Good Day*, written in 1875. Raabe was early aware of his predilection and defended himself, for example, in *The People from the Forest*, where one character remarks that the purview of the world-traveler Faber need not be wider than that of the meditative police clerk Fiebiger in his garret (5: 71), and in *The Dräumling Swamp*, where Rector Fischarth argues that anyone is blind who does not believe that the Muses as soon sing in Abdera as in Athens (10: 143). When Raabe's first interviewer asked him if he did not find little Wolfenbüttel constricting, he is said to have replied:

> I have never missed the busier life of a big city in my home town, because I have no need of so-called "stimuli." The world and life seem to me, seen even from Wolfenbüttel, so rich that I often secretly regret the brevity of life on earth because one cannot say all one has to say. Too many images, too many situations, too many characters always buzz in my head. (E 4: 34)

Finally, there is a passage in *Cloister Lugau* (1894) where the narrator slightly ironizes the protagonist's willed provinciality, then takes the irony back:

> The whole wide world with all its wonders could not offer him what this middle-sized provincial town and great German university fully supplied: satisfaction of his antiquarianism and his sense

of world citizenship, his personal vanity and his philosophical striving for complete detachment from the things of temporality, in brief, his stupidity and cleverness, his foolishness and wisdom. Even more briefly: nowhere in the world, neither in Copenhagen nor in Berlin, neither in London nor in Rome and Paris, could he, as his own personal fool, tower so far above the others as here. So he said, at any rate, but we know better. . . . (19: 15)

These, it seems to me, are permissible views for an author to hold; it is tyrannical to assume that every writer must have the same urbane and cosmopolitan perspective on the world. But in Germany the matter is complicated by the ideological history of regional literature. This is a peculiarly German problem. Who, in our culture, worries that Thomas Hardy or William Faulkner were regional writers? But in Germany, regional writing, called *Heimatdichtung*, though clearly a chapter in the search for realism—one of its pioneers was the Jewish author Berthold Auerbach—became linked to nationalist, anti-modern cultural politics and is widely perceived to have flowed into the fascist "blood-and-soil" literature of noxious memory. Raabe was uncomfortable with the label of *Heimatdichter*. In 1903, when his active writing career was over, he growled that he did not want to be known as a "Lower Saxon tribal writer," but as a truly German one (E 4: 179)— an assertion that does not, of course, cut the link of regional literature with nationalism. Therefore it seems to me that some defense of Raabe against the charge of provinciality might be ventured in this place.

First of all, there seems to be a notion among scholars that a person who is not intimate with major writers or intellectuals does not know anyone. In Raabe's case there may be a vague perception that his entourage consisted primarily of minor local officials, schoolteachers, parsons, and other small-scale provincials. This is by no means true, and I want to try to dispel this perception by quickly mentioning a few names. Among his Wolfenbüttel friends was the extremely wealthy German-American Theodor Steinweg, or Steinway, his father's partner in the famous piano-manufacturing enterprise. Also in Raabe's circle there were Gustav Spiess, later president of the state church consistory; Wilhelm Spiess, who became a Braunschweig government minister; Karl Justus von Schmidt-Phiseldeck, subsequently head of the state archives; Adolf Glaser, for thirty years chief editor in the influential publishing house of Westermann; and Karl Schrader, later a leading railroad director, a pioneer in progressive education, and a left-liberal member of the Reichstag. One of Raabe's closest friends in Stuttgart, Friedrich Notter, also became a Reichstag deputy. Another Stuttgart intimate was the eccentric Albert Dulk, play-wright, revolutionary socialist, and Near Eastern traveler. He became famous for swimming across Lake Constance in 1865 and notorious as a Social Democratic Reichstag deputy who was imprisoned in 1879 for press law violations and blasphemy; in 1882 he founded the first German liberal religious congregation. The Victorian Raabe does not seem to have been at all troubled by the unusual circumstance that Dulk, on principles brought home from the Orient, lived with two wives simultaneously.[6] Among Raabe's Braunschweig intimates were Gustav Bohnsack, architect of the building in which the renowned Duke August Library in Wolfenbüttel is still housed; the classical phi-lologist Konrad Koch, who introduced the game of soccer into Ger-many; Heinrich Stegmann, a successful manufacturer of railroad sig-nal equipment; and the Latinist and occasional poet Wilhelm Brandes, who became head of the entire school system in the Duchy of Braun-schweig. These were not, of course, world-shaking figures, but neither were they insignificant or obscure. It is worth noting that such per-sonalities, successful men of affairs, rarely appear as characters in Raabe's fiction and, when they do, almost never as positive ones. One exception to this is *Villa Schönow* (1884), the protagonist of which is a prosperous, self-made roofing contractor; it is not without significance that this work is one of the least impressive of his mature novels. Late in life the inveterate bourgeois Raabe also attracted the admiration and friendship of the Grand Duchess of Oldenburg and the Prince-Regent of the Duchy of Braunschweig. His relations with them were, natu-rally, civil but in no way obsequious.

Raabe was very attentive to world affairs; in his diary one can see that he followed current events closely and there are interesting traces of them in the fictional works. In *The People from the Forest* one char-acter offers an uncanny prediction of the future power of Japan as the England of the Pacific (5: 364); when this prophecy was realized more than forty years later in the Russo-Japanese War, Raabe followed the events in his diary with special attention. In his last completed work, *Hastenbeck* (1899), there is a passage that appears to foresee the World War, "in my opinion the most terrible [of wars]" (20: 29). Mexican politics of the 1860s are woven into *Princess Fish* (1882-83, 15: 331-39), and a character in *The Documents of the Birdsong* (1896) alludes in passing to James Fisk's manipulation of the Erie Railroad, to Boss Tweed, Tammany Hall, and Sing-Sing prison (19: 230). In his diary (April 22, May 1, 1898), Raabe noted the outbreak of the Spanish-American War and the Battle of Manila. He seems to have had a particular interest in technology and communications. His diary records on July

27, 1866, the arrival of the North American end of the transatlantic cable in Newfoundland; three decades later, Velten Andres in *The Documents of the Birdsong* uses it to send a message from America (19: 318). As for the railroad, Raabe remarks in *Gutmann's Travels* that German unity could not have been achieved without it (18: 214), and his personal attitude was that the Riviera Express was a thousand times more poetic than the stagecoach; the "good old days," he said, "are a swindle" (E 4: 133).[7] On May 29, 1901, he records in his diary, he went to watch a Paris-to-Berlin auto tour as it passed through his part of the country; twenty-five years before, the clockmaker and mechanic Brüggemann in *Wunnigel* had tried, unsuccessfully, of course, to invent an automobile (13: 51-52). During a visit to his daughter in Wilhelmshaven in August 1895, a modern torpedo boat caught his eye, as he recorded in his diary. In the summer of 1908 and the spring of 1909 we find him following in his diary the flights of the *Graf Zeppelin*; his granddaughter reported that there had been a plan for the zeppelin to fly over his house and greet him, but this homage was frustrated by the weather.[8] The point is that Raabe did not, as some have assumed, resolutely turn his back on the modern world. In fact, even his contemporaries sometimes failed to understand this, as a well-known anecdote illustrates: some friends wanted to build an old-fashioned cottage for him, but he declined the offer, saying that he had always preferred modern buildings.[9] Nor was he impervious to modern ideas; it is clear from *The Lar* (1889), for example, that he accepted Darwinism, which indeed did not fit in too badly with his cast of mind.

Furthermore, although it is true that he did not get much out into the world, in a certain sense the world came to him. As his fame consolidated late in life he had a great many visitors curious about him; some were foreigners, including English and American travelers.[10] Among them, as I discovered in the diary, was a professor from Yale whom I knew personally years ago.[11] Raabe's correspondence grew to such proportions that his wife said he seemed to have become the father-confessor of the whole nation.[12] But his correspondence was by no means limited to Germany. Letters came to him from Singapore, Budapest, Guatemala, Moscow, Indiana, Rhode Island, Pennsylvania, North Dakota, Sandy Hook, Rhodesia, Mexico, Australia, and Manchuria, most though not all from German nationals living abroad. His daughter Elisabeth married a navy physician, Paul Wasserfall, from whom Raabe received postcards and letters from Nagasaki, Niagara Falls, Venice, and Liberia. With his son-in-law's travels and the new prominence of Japan on his mind, he closed one of his letters with the salutation "Banzai!"[13] It should be remembered that in the late nineteenth century some forms of communication were hardly slower than they are today, as one example in the diary impressively illustrates: on November 8, 1892, Raabe received a German-American newspaper published in Louisville, Kentucky, on October 21. Today we might be pleased if we could do that well by airmail.

During his Braunschweig years Raabe wrote four stories, nine novellas, and eighteen novels along with a fragment of a nineteenth. The shift to the novel as his true calling is evident from these figures. But it did not occur right away. His Stuttgart experiences caused him to despair for a time of success in the novel, and he concentrated at first on the novella. The most important of his several collections of shorter prose, the *Krähenfeld Stories*, so called because they were all written in the Braunschweig quarter of that name in which he originally lived, appeared in 1878 and contained six of his finest novellas: *At the Sign of the Wild Man* (1874), *Höxter and Corvey* (1875), *Owls' Pentecost* (1874–75), *Madame Salome* (1875), *The Innerste* (1876), and *Of Old Proteus* (1875). Not until he began *Old Nests* in 1877 did he again undertake a full-length novel. For the sake of symmetry, critics have matched the "Stuttgart Trilogy" with a "Braunschweig Trilogy" consisting of *Old Nests* (1879), *Stuffcake* (1891), and *The Documents of the Birdsong* (1896), although little connects them beyond the fact that all three, in contrast to the Stuttgart novels, have first-person narrators. I doubt the usefulness of linking them in this way, for, while *Old Nests* is a very characteristic but, in my view, average Raabean novel, *Stuffcake* and *The Documents of the Birdsong* are among the finest achievements of his whole career.

At this point I feel I should enter a parenthesis concerning the term "novella." As all students of German literature know, the definition of the novella has been and continues to be an inexhaustible topic of theoretical discourse. It is a discussion from which I would prefer to be excused, at least in this place. Like many nineteenth-century German writers, Raabe was much less exercised about the question than modern theorists; he tended to designate his works as "stories" (*Erzählungen*) regardless of length, when he did not give them more imaginative subtitles. In designating his works as story, novella, or novel I have with indifferent obedience followed current authorities, who, as far as I can tell, employ the minimalist definition of the novella as a fictional work of intermediate length. Nevertheless, there are generic observations on Raabe's career that can be made. On the one hand, his short stories are unquestionably the weakest segment of his oeuvre, and it is not accidental that they are concentrated in the first half of

33

his career. Some of them were the consequence of solicitation by magazine editors, and a few will strike today's reader as downright trivial. Raabe's most characteristic manner required space. The sharp silhouette, the efficient characterization, the elegantly turned plot of the short story were not among his narrative resources. But, on the other hand, the long, bulky novel was not his true vocation, either. His longest novels are all relatively early and are not counted by modern critics among his most important works. He abandoned bulk because complex plotting and large populations of characters were also not congenial to his truest purposes. This does not mean, however, that he followed the alleged movement of nineteenth-century German fiction away from the (Western) genre of the novel toward the (peculiarly German) one of the novella. Rather, with Raabe novella and novel begin to converge. He followed the contemporary tendency of the novella to get longer, but at the same time—and here he contrasts with some of his prominent contemporaries—his novels grew shorter. From around a hundred to around three hundred pages—this was, so to speak, Raabe's classical length, and virtually all the works admired today fall more or less within those limits. Here the distinction between novel and novella fades in importance.

Raabe's long years in Braunschweig were almost without incident. Three more daughters were born to him, whom he raised with devotion. But the evenness of his life was badly disrupted when, on June 24, 1892, his youngest daughter, sixteen-year-old Gertrud, died of meningitis after an illness that had not at first seemed threatening. Raabe was overwhelmed by grief, and he had great difficulty in coping with it; the stoic attitude toward life and fate that his fiction tried to inculcate did not help him in the concrete case. At the end of the year he wrote a friend that, for the first time in thirty-one years of marriage, Christmas was being celebrated without a tree, and he added that he would be just as pleased never to have to take up the pen again, but he needed the money.[14] His wife, too, was very deeply grieved, and for some time they visited Gertrud's grave every day. Gradually he regained command of himself and he resumed writing, though his pace slowed. His last work, *Hastenbeck*, appeared in 1899. He undertook one more novel, *Altershausen*, but it remained unfinished; there will be more to say about the reasons for its abandonment in a later chapter. Raabe felt that he was not meant to be a twentieth-century author; when he had laid down his pen for good, he referred to himself as "writer (ret.)."

Though visibly aging, the retired author was by no means decrepit. He continued his gregarious habits and remained, as visitors often discovered, a strong, vigorous walker. He was now a famous man who had all he could do to cope with his vast correspondence, many visitors, and the honors that increasingly came to him. But something seems to have happened to him in the summer of 1909; he began to suffer from torpor and weakness. On August 29 he broke his collarbone in a fall from bed. This injury, though painful, was not dangerous and in fact healed satisfactorily, but to him it was a bad omen that depressed his vital spirits. He hated aging and death; in the following winter he wrote: "since August of last year I have turned from a strong, healthy old man into a sickly greybeard withdrawn from all social contact."[15] He died on the fifty-sixth anniversary of first "setting pen to paper," November 15, 1910, two months past his seventy-ninth birthday. The nation mourned him, for he had at last achieved, with dogged persistence, the recognition and influence to which he had aspired; he lived to see his works, some of them, at any rate, appear in dozens of printings and tens of thousands of copies. A brief account of how this came about, and why it came about too late and at too great a cost, will require a separate chapter.

CHAPTER 4

Raabe and His Public

◘

La moralité de l'art se renferme, pour chacun,
dans le côté qui flatte ses intérêts. On n'aime pas
la littérature.

Flaubert, *Bouvard et Pécuchet*

WILHELM RAABE carried on a struggle with his public and his
publishers as long, stubborn, and bitter as that of any writer
who ever lived. The intensity of this struggle, which came to be an
obsession, was owing to the divergent horns of his trilemma: fidelity
to his own artistic originality, desire to affect the public and even be
a preceptor to the nation, and the need to earn money from his pen.
In the impossible task of reconciling these commitments he was hauled
this way and that, complaining violently all the time. Karl Heim, the
most acute analyst of Raabe's relationship to his public, remarked
justly that he thought the German people had a duty to concern themselves with him *because* he refused to accommodate himself to their
taste.[1] Indeed he thought so from the outset; in 1859, when he was
still confident about his prospects as a writer, he wrote to a publisher that the public would thank him for going his own way and for
his rejection of advice from others, which destroys freshness and
originality.[2]

This youthful letter is typical of his independent, not to say abrasive, attitude toward his publishers, of which he had altogether
twenty-two. While some of them or their editors were his personal
friends, as publishers he held none of them in any permanent regard.
Once, when he submitted a list of his works to a periodical, he refused
to list the publishers, saying that they have little to do with the development of an author and are of no interest to the public.[3] Some of
his troubles were the usual authorial experiences with unreliability,
dilatoriness, broken promises, as well as rejections, in some cases even
of solicited works. In 1875, *The Good Day*, a satire on rent-gouging,
was refused by an editor who had asked for a contribution from him;
it was accepted by another periodical but suppressed, then posthu-

36

mously printed in 1912 in a bowdlerized version, so that the true text first appeared in the modern critical edition (13: 464). Then there was the familiar tug-of-war over chiseling; it deeply offended Raabe, who, though certainly a formidable proponent of his own interests, was also strictly forthright and honest. In 1862 the publisher Westermann complained to his editor Glaser that *The People from the Forest* was not as long as he had expected and groused about the honorarium, whereupon Glaser informed Raabe that they would calculate more exactly in the future (5: 446). Thus his nose was already out of joint when, several years later, Westermann tried to reduce the honorarium for *The Rumbledump* when it was already in the press on the grounds that it was not as long as *Abu Telfan*. Raabe replied angrily that he did not sell his works by the yard, threatened to go to law, seeking legal advice from his brother-in-law, and ultimately abandoned Westermann's firm for some years.[4]

In addition, Raabe felt very strongly the author's understandable, so seldom granted wish that the publisher might print the text the author has written. He was perhaps even less amenable than most of his contemporaries to any editorial intervention, and generally he managed to hold the line, though he lost part of a hard fight over *Restless Guests* in 1885. It had been solicited by the primary family magazine of the time, *Die Gartenlaube* (*The Garden Bower*), and in retrospect it is not difficult to see that this subtle, bleak work was entirely unsuited to such a publication; the editor was subsequently to say that the "cultured" readers had praised it but that the majority had been unable to understand it and complained about it (16: 549). In order to be helpful to the majority, the editor attempted to edit vigorously; he changed foreign words and quotations, for which Raabe had a weakness, and excised an allusion to the then widely despised Heine as well as one to Laurence Sterne. Worse, he attempted to rewrite the ending to give it more closure and poetic justice. This vandalism Raabe was able to resist, though he had to get pretty rude about it; but he was unable to persuade the editor to rescind the other changes. He restored his original text in the book version (16: 548-49).

This conflict was connected with another difficulty: the propensity of publishers to serialize fiction in periodicals before bringing out the book version. Raabe combatted this practice all his life, but unsuccessfully for the most part, for here the economic exigencies were all but irresistible. Germany was still a poor country until late in the nineteenth century and books were relatively expensive; Raabe complained about prices more than once, observing in 1889 that, at seven marks fifty, *The Lar* was affordable only by those with incomes in excess of nine or ten thousand marks a year (17: 455). Throughout the entire century no major German writer earned a fortune comparable to those of Scott and Dickens in England or Balzac and Dumas in France. Raabe sensed this, though he did not fully grasp the sociological reasons for it and in 1891 blamed the German public: "If I had written the book [*Horacker*] as an Englishman for Englishmen, as a Frenchman for Frenchmen, it would have been a different matter, but Mother Germania is patient and gladly waits until thirty years after the death of one of her authors, until she gets 'such a thing' cheaply in Reclam's dime library."[5] A year later he made a similar observation in his private notes, here, however, combining his sense of neglect by his own nation with the economic awareness that, as in America in the nineteenth century, it was cheaper to publish foreign authors than native ones to whom honoraria had to be paid:

> If a Frenchman had known and described the most intrinsic French essence, an Englishman the English, as I have the German, their people would have rushed upon them with jubilation. The Germans don't want to know about anything that they themselves have. Thus I have had to carry on a hard battle throughout my whole literary life—against France, naturally—against California, against Norway, Russia, etc. etc.—against everything that is far away from the German people, thus all the more attractive, and that the book dealers can get more cheaply.[6]

Furthermore, the reading habit of many Germans was served by a network of commercial lending libraries—such an establishment is rather sorrowfully depicted in *German Nobility*—so that, while one copy of a book might have many readers, the market for books was constricted. Publishers were therefore strongly attracted to serialization in newspapers and magazines, a both popular and lucrative contrivance that had spread into Germany from France.

But, as every literary historian knows, serialization has a powerful effect on form. More or less natural breaks in the narration must be devised at relatively regular intervals, and ideally they should be devised in such a way as to whet the reader's appetite for the next installment—a strategy of which Eugène Sue, the creator of the European serial novel, was such a diabolical master. Raabe had no desire to resemble Sue, who had enough imitators already, and he chafed under these requirements as just one more external constraint on his artistic individuality; furthermore, suspense was never a high priority for him. He complained about the practice constantly. In 1867 he compared the progress of *Abu Telfan* through a periodical to that of a

tapeworm.[7] He thought *The Rumbledump* "too good" to be "prosti-
tuted" in a magazine but was forced to acquiesce (8: 400). In the case
of *Master Author* he did not acquiesce, but the book version did not
thrive (11: 455). With the *The Odin Field* he got into a fierce argument
with his publisher, who had introduced chapter divisions, probably
with an eye to newspaper serialization. Raabe often numbered chapters in his works, but in this one he did not wish to, insisting that it
was not a "feuilleton novel" (17: 413-17); this clash led to another
permanent breach with a publisher. In *The Lar* Raabe mounted a
broad satire on the journalistic and feuilletonistic culture of the time.

In these matters the publishers were obviously attempting to pursue
their economic interests, of which Raabe sometimes took an unsympathetic view. To one he wrote: "I am convinced that you are making
a much better deal than I," and to Glaser he asserted firmly: "you will
admit that I have as much right to try to turn my labor power to
account as quickly and securely as Mr. G. Westermann does his capital."[8] But it might also be said on their behalf that they were trying
to function as advocates of that public Raabe was so anxious to reach.
On the whole, they seem to have had a good deal less confidence in
him than he had in himself. Even his friend Glaser wrote to Westermann behind Raabe's back that he had become eccentric and that his
works were only curiosities.[9] Indeed, his ambition to be a popular
writer was impossible of achievement, though he seems hardly to have
realized this until a few months before his death, when he confessed
to one of his former publishers that he knew very well how much of
his failure with the public had been his own fault.[10] Quite apart from
all the other reasons one might adduce, he was just too *difficult*. Over
and over editors and reviewers made the complaint that he was too
hard to read, as well as too mannered and subjective; the constant
complaints about abstruse cultural allusions and foreign words and
phrases belong here as well.[11] One atypically perceptive reviewer, sur-
veying Raabe's work of the 1880s, remarked that his art forces the
reader to an effort of intellectual collaboration and makes the reader a
"passive poet" (17: 419). Raabe's sly, oblique, deceptive manner requires attentive reading, reflection on what has been read, re-reading.
This is not the road to popularity. Readers, as a rule, do not want to
work; they want to be entertained, comforted, and reinforced in their
sense of the rightness of things. The way to popularity—and to the
Nobel Prize—was modelled in Raabe's time by Paul Heyse's slick,
easy novellas, most of which I have found I can hardly remember a
week after reading them.

It is clear that the more Raabe found his way to his own art and style, the less the critics were able to follow him. For example, *Three Pens*, which he rightly regarded as a breakthrough, simply caused annoyance; reviewers complained of the lack of suspense and dismissed its innovative narrative strategy as a "Jean-Paulian manner," a shorthand of the time for any deviation from foursquare narration; it was thirty years before a second edition appeared, and then, in 1895, a critic *still* complained of "Jean-Paulian manner" (9/1: 493-94). It can be observed that many of the best or most understanding reviews came from the most prestigious writers: Hebbel, Gustav Karpeles, Auerbach, Fontane (with reservations), sometimes, though not always, Jensen;[12] this suggests that Raabe, contrary to his purposes, was more a writer's writer than a popular one. At the same time he allowed himself to be greatly affected by criticism. He carried a negative review of *Old Nests* from a Viennese newspaper in his wallet for eleven years as, he claimed, a "consolation."[13] Twenty-five years after *The Chronicle of Sparrow Alley*, on November 15, 1881, he recalled in his diary the first *critique* of it. He came to exaggerate the hostility of the critical response to him, even imagining that there was a conspiracy of silence among the reviewers. This was certainly not the case; a modern scholar collected 146 reviews from all parts of Germany, as well as Austria and Switzerland, some by prestigious reviewers; in them there was not a single total rejection, though, of course, they contained some criticism.[14] His late novels were well received by the critics, but by that time Raabe could not believe anyone wished him well.

He carried on his debate with the public in his only vehicle, his fiction, in tones that range from teasing, cajoling, and self-defensive to downright insulting. These remarks are not infrequently addressed to the female reader, the notorious "liebe Leserin" who was not only for Raabe an irritation. Since the eighteenth century it had been perceived that women, because of their leisure, were the major audience for literature; many observers felt that they debased literature with their requirements for sentimentality, prudery, and moralism, requirements that reacted upon the economics of literature and the preferences of publishers. In 1807 Heinrich von Kleist had written:

> If one investigates it correctly, it is ultimately the women who are to blame for the complete degeneration of our stage, and either they should not attend the play at all, or special theaters, separated from the men, must be erected for them. Their demands for propriety and morality annihilate the whole essence of

the drama, and the essence of the Greek theater could never have developed if they had not been completely shut out from it.[15]

Three-quarters of a century later, the Naturalist theoreticians, the Brothers Hart, were no less exasperated:

> Our literature, with few exceptions, has become a mere women's, indeed, perhaps girls' literature; what does not please the pampered, prudish, and silly creatures of a petty method of education is forbidden; what pleases them is set down as a guideline.[16]

Heine, like Raabe, also apostrophized the disdained female reader in the text, in his case with maliciously elaborate courtesy and pretended admiration, especially in *Das Buch Le Grand* (*The Book of Le Grand*).[17] Raabe fixed these repressive females in view early on, for example, in *The Children of Finkenrode*, where they are apostrophized as "you novel-reading delicate souls . . . citizenesses in the realm of the beautiful and sentimental" (2: 19). By the end of his career he was not feeling any more chivalrous; in *Cloister Lugau* we are told it is a good thing the "Leserin" cannot look on with us at what the protagonist is doing, for she would not understand it; not a page later it is said that readers who do not already grasp what is going on are "simply stupid, and to continue to work hopefully on their further education and enlightenment is indeed a heavy burden for the historiographer" (19: 86, 87).

But the reader as potential enemy is not exclusively female: he will be bored if not truly called to the task (1: 18); he is jumpy and inattentive (3: 378); rich readers are easily bored (5: 63); a Berlin police station will be described for those readers living in a green idyll who have no idea what it is like (13: 304). The attitude toward the reader in *The Rumbledump* is particularly hostile, resulting "in a narrator who is unusually authoritarian in his control of the reader's fictional participation."[18] In *Abu Telfan*, after devoting three pages to a defense of his literary career and his efforts to please, Raabe concludes sarcastically: "truly it is a joy to feel alive in one's skin and in one's nation" (7: 10).

He longed for a dialogue with his readers like that of his best characters with one another—allusive and sensitive to nuance—but he could not trust the reader. The communication gap is indirectly but repeatedly imaged in the fiction: Hagebucher's catastrophic effort to reach the public with a lecture in *Abu Telfan*; the wall of incomprehension between artist and public in *The Dräumling Swamp*; the charmingly normal wife who falls asleep at the narrator's reminiscences in *Pfister's Mill*; the image of the junk heap in *On the Scrap-Iron*, on which Raabe felt himself to have been thrown years before he wrote the novel.[19] At times there are gestures of resigned despair; at the beginning of *The Odin Field* the narrator sniffs: "If anyone wants to hear the story I tell here, it is fine with me. If not, I shall have to put up with that, too, and will talk of the old matters, as quite frequently before, to myself alone" (17: 7). More commonly, however, Raabe envisages a minority public of right readers, an elite self-defined by its capability and willingness to attend and comprehend. Perhaps the few will in the future become the many: "We will follow that unfortunately much smaller number of readers who for now no longer wish to dwell upon the further events in the Achtermann family; we ourselves have in this respect neither wish nor disinclination; we go where we must: after a few and, we still hope, ultimately in front of many" (*German Nobility*, 13: 262-63). The most famous passage of this kind is probably the image of the new house in *Horacker*: of a thousand people who look at it, only one will try to imagine the life that will take place in it. "For this one we are writing today and have always written. But we wish ourselves many readers" (12: 297). Doubtless these gestures, even the dismissive ones, were meant as an encouraging challenge to the reader, though one can easily imagine that many a reader would be irritated by them and wish the narrator would get on with it. More seriously, they increasingly seem to project a coterie audience, a danger against which reviewers occasionally warned, not without reason, as it turned out. For Raabe this meant defeat, because an elite audience was just what he did not want; his deepest wish was to speak for and to the German nation.

Over the years he developed a vast eloquence in bemoaning his fate. To one publisher he expressed the hope that he would not be reborn as a German writer: "I have had quite enough from the one incarnation."[20] He groaned about the triviality and density of readers. In a notebook entry in the fall of 1864 he observed: "It is really a fine time when people still believe that the final and happy union of the lover and his girl is the ultimate and highest thing with which the drama or the novel can occupy themselves."[21] *Old Nests* ends in irritation at readers' demands to know the subsequent fate of characters; Raabe may very likely be thinking of Dickens here. Spoofing the readers' inability to distinguish fiction from reality, Raabe has his narrator suggest they apply for information from one of the novel's characters (14: 268-69). His private comments were often more acerbic. When the editor Glaser reported to Raabe that the public had had enough of him and his books resembled one another too much, he entered on April 29, 1884, an uncharacteristically explicit complaint in his diary; almost two years later he brought it up again in a letter to the more successful

Heyse, to whom he was particularly inclined to confide his feelings of resentment.[22] In 1882 he wrote to Marie Jensen that his nerves had been abraded by twenty-eight years of literary campaigns, and in the following year he expressed the hope that with the daring *Princess Fish* he had thrown the charge of being boring back into the reader's teeth.[23] Once he really lost his nerve and cried out plaintively to the Jensens: "Tell me, do you know any means at all to move people to buy my books? For twenty years now I have been trying to chew my way through the pablum into the Land of Cockaigne—one could get sick to one's stomach from it!"[24]

Here we see Raabe being gored by the third horn of his trilemma. In the documents of his life there is a continuous ground bass of worry about money, of anger and despair at the poor return on his labors. In 1859, when he had realized that making coin out of the success of the *Chronicle* would not be as easy as he had hoped, he reported that he had not yet earned 500 talers from all his writings.[25] As he remembered it, he had tried to get 200 talers for *One Springtime* but was talked down to 150 (1: 478–79). Over the years he grew weary of his money troubles, often commenting on them in his letters and his diary. When the Jensens sent him a set of punch glasses for his birthday, he burst out: "Punch?!—Great God, water, water,—water is the only beverage that the noble German people have permitted people like me to drink since the year Seventy. And you ironic people send one as a birthday present a set of punch glasses!"[26] He struggled doggedly with his publishers. When in 1879 the formidable George Westermann died, he was succeeded by his son Friedrich, an admirer of Raabe, who at once took the opportunity to jack up his demand for *The Horn of Wanza* from 3,000 to 4,500 marks. Friedrich Westermann politely asked if this were a mistake, but paid it; however, for *Villa Schönow* four years later Raabe was knocked back down to the usual 3,000 (14: 491; 15: 657). From his accounts in his early days one can see that he earned a great deal more, page for page, for stories than he did for his novels, which very likely explains the concentration of short prose in the first half of his career. But in the long run he could not make the compromises of a commercial writer. As early as 1859 he had discovered that he could not, as he put it, bury the poet and writer in the *Literat*: "I thought I could, but I have learned that I can't and that I shall not earn a fortune with my pen."[27]

However, modern scholars who have looked more closely at his finances have come to regard his case a little less tragically.[28] Poverty can, of course, be very real, but it can also sometimes be imaginary. Raabe knew this very well. In *The People from the Forest* the banker

Wienand, who suffers a serious setback but is still not completely without resources, persuades himself that he is impoverished and becomes a pathological miser. The motif is repeated in *The Dräumling Swamp*: the protagonist's father dies a broken man after he must liquidate his business, although after his death his son finds a third of his fortune still intact. It is true that Raabe's income often makes a rather meager impression.[29] For his review of Auerbach's almanac he received, as he notes in his diary on December 14, 1859, twenty-two groschen; this looks more like a tip than an honorarium and may have been a factor in his decision never to write such things again. But the cost of living in nineteenth-century Germany was not high and remained fairly stable for a long time. After the first full year of his marriage he reported to his mother that he needed 1,200 talers a year and that he was entering 1864 with a substantial surplus.[30] By the end of his career he seems to have been still roughly at that level; commenting in his diary on his tax return on December 31, 1894, he notes that he had earned 3,400 marks from his literary works, the equivalent of 1,133 talers. These are certainly not princely sums; but at the same time one must observe his way of life. There is no trace of the destitution found in the lives of many other authors in the history of literature. He was always decently fed, clothed, and housed. The family normally kept a servant, without which no middle-class household could be managed at that time. While he worried about the future of his daughters, he succeeded in educating them, and, of the three surviving girls, two made proper marriages and the eldest was set up in the painting profession. Never was there any constraint of his daily habit of sitting long hours in taverns, enjoying wine and good cigars. Doubtless he owed much of this comfort to his wife's sacrifice and management abilities.

For all that he strove to wring what he believed he had earned out of his publishers, he would not accept charity. Perhaps his complaining was a little too successful, for from time to time he would receive gifts of money from admirers. When they were not anonymous he always returned them. In 1896 he became agitated when he heard that a committee had been formed to raise money for him; he replied that he had 4,000 to 5,000 marks a year, with which an author so neglected by the public had to be content.[31] He had no compunctions, however, about accepting grants from the Schiller Foundation, established to aid authors, for he regarded them as a form not of charity but of acknowledgment from the German nation. In 1864 he received a one-time grant of 300 talers, and in 1886 a pension of 1,000 marks annually for three years, renewed in 1889 and again in 1892; in 1895 the pension was awarded to him for life. From another such source, the Tiedge Foundation in Dresden, he received a prize of 3,000 marks for the twenty-eighth edition of *The Hunger Pastor*, as he notes in his diary on May 23, 1908. Indeed, his condition improved substantially at the end of his life. This was owing largely to his delayed popularity and the appearance in his latter years of new editions of works that had long lain fallow. *The Hunger Pastor* is a good example; the first three editions required thirteen years, but thirty-four editions appeared by the end of his life. For each new printing he received 1,200 marks. From his diary one can see that in the last decade of his life he was earning more in one quarter than he previously had in a year.

This delayed success did not mollify him very much, however. For one thing, he was dismayed that it consisted largely of a revival of his earliest works, the "stale junk of my youth," as he once sourly put it,[32] while his mature works, for the most part, continued to languish. For another, he did not trust his prosperity, nor could he forgive the worry he had been caused in the past. He even suffered from occasional attacks of jealousy. To Heyse he permitted himself the observation that Fritz Reuter had also received a grant from the Schiller Foundation, but in the meantime had managed to build himself a villa.[33] Since Reuter in earlier times had spent years in prison for largely imaginary political crimes, a more generous view might have been that his later prosperity was also just compensation from the nation. The fact is that Raabe probably was as financially successful as any major German-language writer in the nineteenth century. But, as Heim has acutely observed, he did not measure himself against major writers in this regard, but against ephemeral writers of quick success.[34] The example of Jensen was, after all, perpetually under his nose.

One sees in all this a deep ambiguity in Raabe's relationship to his public. In an early poem he stated that he wanted to appeal to all hearts; if the great and clever do not want to listen, he will turn to the small and simple (20: 338). But, according to his daughter Margarethe, his ambitions flew higher than that: "Between Goethe and Schiller a seat is free—Jean Paul could have taken it but didn't; now I will" (E 4: 54). He smarted under criticism while insisting on his indifference to it: "I may say with satisfaction that my striving becomes ever more earnest and all literary industrialism ever more hateful to me. To criticism, as it manifests itself at present, I am dead and glad of it."[35] At times he put his trust in the future. In 1889 he wrote of the misery of being one short step ahead of one's own generation,[36] although he must have known perfectly well that his generation believed him to be more than a step behind. He compared himself to Karl Immermann, not understood until thirty years after his death (E 4: 223). When recognition did come at last to the works he himself respected least, he was in a quandary. An example is *Our Lord God's Chancellory*, which he reckoned among the sins of his youth; nevertheless, he had to be pleased when it became a genuine book of the people (4: 518). He could be almost childishly delighted at recognition, even from persons quite foreign to him in spirit. For example, the completely unmusical Raabe was very pleased to know that Richard Wagner admired him, and he valued Cosima Wagner's good opinion of *Restless Guests* (E 4: 94, 112). (According to one source, Brahms also admired him and intended to leave him something in his will, but Raabe refused to allow it [E 4: 259].) The effect of all of this was that he was not able wholly to maintain his vaunted independence; more and more he came to express gratification at his small, intimate circle of readers in contrast to the indifference of criticism and the larger public: "*The* circle of readers that alone comes into consideration for me," he wrote to Berthold Auerbach, "I have had for long years and I will keep it, despite all the so brilliantly blown up soap bubbles now sailing through the air."[37] Raabe participated in the formation of his coterie, driven to it by his fear of isolation and ineffectuality. How important and fateful this was we shall have occasion to see.

Regarded externally, the great watershed in the history of his reputation appears to be the celebration of his seventieth birthday on September 8, 1901. Such festivals were customary in German-speaking lands; both Theodor Storm (1887) and Gottfried Keller (1889) had been given elaborate seventieth-birthday celebrations. But Raabe's was a fabulous and memorable occasion, crowded with admirers and widely reported. He received a gift of 18,000 marks, an honorary doctorate from the University of Tübingen, the honorary citizenship of his birthplace Eschershausen and of Braunschweig, 216 congratulatory telegrams and so many letters that he had to have a thank-you note printed. The event was reported even in the United States.[38] His reputation had become much more international. His works were published in England and America; he corresponded with scholars in Indiana and North Dakota; admirers sent him gifts of coffee from Guatemala and marmalade from England; as he noted in his diary on May 18, 1905, he was invited to a Schiller celebration in San Francisco. Streets were named for him in one city after another; a month before his death, he received another honorary degree, an M.D., no less, from the University of Berlin, where, we are told, the award aroused a storm of applause among the students (E 4: 274). The momentum continued after his death, when some of his works reached publication figures of tens and in some cases hundreds of thousands of copies. For example, *The Black Galley*, which became a children's book and a school text, had appeared in one of its several formats in 860,000 copies by 1941; after World War II it was made into a radio play and, in East Germany, a film; in 1979 it was reported that the Reclam edition had sold 497,100 copies since 1961.[39] In an inquiry of 1927 by a journal of the publishing industry asking people to name the dozen books that belong in the home library of an "educated German," Raabe came in fifth place in the total mentions.[40] Two years later a number of writers contributed autographed books to be auctioned off to raise money for a Raabe monument; among the contributors were Thomas Mann, Heinrich Mann, Hermann Hesse, and Arthur Schnitzler.[41]

A closer examination, however, shows that Raabe's reputation did not burgeon all at once in 1901; it had been gaining momentum for a number of years. The 1870s were probably his worst decade, and many of his bitterest comments about his relationship to the public are concentrated in those years. In the eighties a slow but perceptible improvement in the sales of his works becomes noticeable. In the early nineties Raabe began to sense that a young generation of people between twenty and thirty-five was beginning to discover him.[42] By the end of the nineties he was able to say: "See . . . the others are now going to bed—and I—I am now getting up" (E 4: 139). There were other straws in the wind. Although it has been seldom stressed in accounts of Raabe, his *sixtieth* birthday in 1891 had been celebrated with a good deal of fuss, as the diary entries show. In November 1894 his Stuttgart friends organized a celebration of the fortieth anniversary of the beginning of *Chronicle*, as a number of letters during that month show. In 1899 he was decorated with the Bavarian Order of Maximilian, as successor to the deceased Swiss poet Conrad Ferdinand Meyer; Raabe remarked characteristically that the award would have been more useful earlier.[43]

Heim has suggested that the reason for this revival had to do with a change in the literary atmosphere around 1890; Raabe represented tradition and old values for a reading public disoriented by modernism.[44] This is not improbable, and, if correct, represents simply another phase of misapprehension, so that he was right to be skeptical at the same time as he could not help being gratified. For his gratification was not full-hearted. The turn in his fortunes came, to use his original title for *Princess Fish*, "too late in the year." It could not make up for the years of bitterness, abandonment, and undeserved struggle;

his resentment had become deeply rooted in his psyche, to the point where he sometimes willfully failed to perceive evidence of success and recognition. It had, after all, always been his nature to look at things from their darkest side. This pecularity of his personality invites separate attention.

CHAPTER 5

Pessimism

◙

ONE OF Raabe's minor short stories is entitled *On Dark Ground*.
The phrase could serve as a motto for his whole oeuvre. All his
hopefulness for a conciliation of human affairs in kindness and sympathy, all his acknowledgment of the joys of life and the beauty of the
world, all his humor and comedy, are a highlighted foreground on a
dark background of tragic anxiety, a continuous threat of meaning-
lessness and futility. None of his occasional denials of pessimism, none
of the efforts of admirers to rescue him from it, for example, by the
assertion that the meaning of life was not *absent* for him, but *hidden*,[1]
can wholly alleviate the overall effect. One of the most acute of the
older generation of critics observed that an "optimism of the heart"
does not refute a "pessimism of the mind," but merely indicates that
Raabe was not gloomy; cordiality cannot change the meaning of the
world—it prevents despair, but not perception.[2] Raabe does not so
much preach pessimism as struggle in his writing both to name it and
combat it; but the pervasiveness of the struggle makes evident the hold
that pessimism retained on his spirit.

The reasons for his inclination to pessimism are by no means obvious at first sight. As human fates go, especially among writers and
artists, his life was not singularly miserable. It is clear that he looked
upon his childhood, despite its deprivations and problems, as a happy
time. No great grief impinged on him in the forty-seven years from
the early death of his father to the early death of his youngest daughter. This last event did quite overthrow him, submerging his stoicism
into the tense readiness for despair that had always characterized him:
how tragic it was, he wrote, to have his attention called in this way
to the "vanity of all things. . . . And as though it had been so very
necessary especially for me!"[3] It is perhaps not without interest that
in his second novel, thirty-five years earlier, he prefigured his unas-
suageable grief at his daughter's death in the elder Hagenheim, whose
cult of loss—he leaves his dead daughter's room unchanged for years—
suggests an innate readiness in Raabe for his inconsolable reaction.
Such a loss is undoubtedly hard, but it cannot be said that he expe-

rienced vastly more of it than other people. Of course he suffered defeats and disappointments, but so do we all.

Perhaps there is some unfathomable mystery of temperament after all. Consider the case of Raabe's older contemporary Berthold Auerbach. As a Jew he did not have an easy time in life from the beginning. His ambition to become a rabbi was frustrated because as a student he had served a short spell in jail for a harmless political escapade and the law prohibited anyone convicted of a political crime from being ordained as a clergyman. He hacked his way precariously through life as a free-lance writer, never able to convert his ultimately considerable fame or his extensive acquaintance among the prestigious and the high-born into any sort of material ease. His personal and domestic affairs, unlike Raabe's, were stressful. Yet through it all he seems to have retained a remarkably sunny disposition. In 1876 he said in a speech in Vienna: "Yes, it is a century in which the spirits are awake, and I, an atom of this century, feel today through and through, into my last indivisible particle, it is a joy to live!"⁴ One cannot imagine Raabe saying such a thing, and certainly not in 1876.

This might be taken merely as evidence that Raabe was less naive and more sensitive to the sorrows of his times than Auerbach. Clifford Bernd has stressed the extent to which Raabe's consciousness was formed by "the tangible reminders of the catastrophic events of 1848":

> the economy had been disrupted, food was scarce, prices were high, and unemployment was rampant. The destruction wrought by the revolutions had to be paid for; taxes had become oppressive, bankruptcies an everyday occurrence. Memories of the terror on the streets of Berlin—of the bloody engagements, of the wounded and dead—were still very much on everyone's mind and lips. Everywhere could be seen bedraggled and hungry people. A pall of defeat, frustration, and despair hung over the entire city, indeed over the whole of Germany. The newspapers gave daily notices of the sad exodus of hapless Germans departing for greener pastures in the United States, the southern provinces of Brazil, and even the coastal regions of Algeria. Hundreds of thousands were hurrying to flee, determined to escape the poverty brought on by political instability. Beginning with 1848, emigration from German-speaking lands soared exponentially. But the year 1854, when Raabe commenced writing *Die Chronik der Sperlingsgasse*, turned out to be the worst of all. The emigrations of that peak year surpassed every previous exodus of Germans seeking relief from pauperism.⁵

No one who reads the *Chronicle* can fail to observe the effect of this environment on the tone, which was, of course, not peculiar to Raabe in his time. One thinks of the persistent greyness of Theodor Storm's fiction, with its too-lateness, its reiterated missed connections among persons. It is not surprising that one trend of modern criticism has found the explanation for Raabe's cast of mind in social and political determinants. Lukács argued that his pessimism lay in a split between his national-liberal allegiance and the social facts of his world.[6] More recently, the pessimism of his darkest novel, *The Rumbledump*, has been relativized by associating it with the decline and degeneration of the aristocratic class.[7] There is much to be said for this perspective, especially as, carefully applied, it will increase our respect for Raabe's sensitivity to the sub-surface movements of his times. Still, one must wonder if it can fully account for the existential intensity of his pessimistic instincts.

For one thing, his characteristic outlook was firmly in place at the outset of his career, when he still had relatively little experience of life and literature. The groaning opening lines of *The Chronicle of Sparrow Alley* have already been mentioned. "Oh, we poor human beings," the narrator observes, thinking of condemned criminals on their way to be executed, "is not the whole of life such a passage to the place of execution?" (1: 29). "Seated backwards on the grey ass 'time,'" he remarks, "mankind rides to its goal" (1: 31), an observation that corresponds to one of Raabe's most often cited aphorisms, dated twenty-five years later: "The eternal illusion that life lies before one. Life always lies *behind* one."[8] *The Children of Finkenrode* begins with the narrator's desire to put a bullet in his head on his twenty-ninth birthday (2: 7), and this narrator, Bösenberg, who already shows signs of Raabe's tendency to self-parody, echoes the opening of the *Chronicle*: "Truly, it is a bad world? Love is burst, reconciliation has a hole in it, mercy has lost its handle, and the bottom has fallen out of faith" (2: 122). The permanent Baroque melancholy, the "malus hypochondriacus" (2: 468) of the title character of *Michel Haas* was so pronounced that readers complained of its bitterness (2: 606). In *The Holy Spring* there is an image of frogs gaily popping out in the cheerful springtime, not knowing it would have been better for them if they had stayed in their holes (3: 10). Often it appears that man is a victim of a systematically malign and indifferent fate, imaged at times in nature, as in the sarcastic indifference of the moon shining down on the poor human race in *Who Can Change it?* (2: 504), at times in the gods or their emissaries, as in the lending-librarian's rumination in *German Nobility*: "if there is anything that can bring the dreadfulness of our existence in this world to consciousness, it is the recognition that we have been set into the world as a *joke even to the Furies*" (13: 219). Such passages could be accumulated endlessly throughout the oeuvre. Perhaps the locus classicus is the motto to *Abu Telfan*: "If you knew what I know, spake Mohammed, you would weep much and laugh little" (7: 6).[9]

Among the several ways the *Chronicle* prefigures Raabe's life work is the employment of an old man as the central consciousness. It has been pointed out that the perspective of old age is typical of the time and is found in other writers such as Immermann, Stifter, Keller, Fontane, and Storm.[10] Doubtless this suggests something about the tenor of the times; but the device is especially pronounced in Raabe, who employs it repeatedly. There is something a little out of the ordinary in a young man who makes a very old, rather resigned man the narrator of his first literary work. Often Raabe puts the very young and the very old into an alliance against the oppressive vigor of those in the prime of life. Sometimes the young are born old. Such is the case of Theodor Rodburg in *Princess Fish*, whose old face as a child binds youth and old age together while imaging a sense of fleeting time and too-lateness (15: 222). It is significant that his shallow, odious, older brother Alexander, one of the most evil of Raabe's characters, has a "jovial, *youthful* face" (15: 252). But Raabe does not always apply the same motif in the same way. August Hahnenberg in *Three Pens* is also a young man with the spirit of an old one, a thirty-year-old misanthrope who looks much older; in him pessimism has become bitterness and an almost suicidal irony. But these characteristics are psychological consequences of an emotionally starved youth and a role played to hide disappointment; pain is shifted to aggression in a far from positive way.

Here we can see that, intellectually, pessimism for Raabe was not a philosophy but a burden imposed by reality and perception. Consequently he constantly made gestures to counter it. In 1894 he wrote:

> In regard to the word or platitude about "pessimism" in my writings, I think that I have everywhere and always represented the indestructibility of the world and of human existence on earth. That it sometimes turned out to be a matter of "making the best of a bad bargain" is something I cannot help. I consider the *Never say die!* of the English to be a brave word and I think we will stick with it to the end!"[11]

On another occasion he pointed out that the good is always victorious in his writings, though not trivial happiness; only the phlegmatic and the stupid are truly happy: "Fine nerves cannot be happy" (E 4: 247). It is true that he often represented his writing as a form of consolation for the reader. In the preface to the second edition of the *Chronicle* in 1864 he notes that the original had come out during the Crimean War and now another war was threatening; he hopes that "under *one* roof it chased away a dark hour, lightened a heavy hour" (1: 9). In the archetypically titled *On Dark Ground* the narrator asserts: "I know only that the good and beautiful becomes ever better and more beautiful, the more darkly and evilly, indeed jealously the world impinges upon it" (3: 404). While the first half of *The Holy Spring* ends with "Memento mori!," the second ends with "Memento vivere!" (3: 174, 346). Gestures of heroic resistance against inimical fate are frequent: "Forward even in chains!" cries Robert Wolf in *The People from the Forest* (5: 337). One of the aphorisms often lifted out of context by Raabe's traditional admirers is from the letter of Countess Laura Warberg in *Cloister Lugau*: "Your Excellency, the world is not so bad at all; one must only accommodate to it and know how to take it" (19: 182). The most positively balanced of all of Raabe's characters, the matured Just Everstein in *Old Nests*, finds equilibrium in a traditional organicism of a distinctly Goethean cast: "nothing else in the world draws the plagued soul into equability than quiet attention to the sprouting, blossoming, and fading of vegetable life, though it were but a weed under the hedge" (14: 143).

But mining Raabe's utterances, fictional and non-fictional, for nuggets of wisdom is an old failing that blocks insight into the full range of his mind. It should never be forgotten that his victories of goodness are achieved in a managed, fictional world. As has been pointed out in connection with *The People from the Forest*, the narrator must rhetorically instill faith.[12] The deeper message of *The People from the Forest* is not "forward in chains," but the recognition that the optimistic spirit of the *Bildungsroman* patterned on Goethe's *Wilhelm Meister* could not be sustained with integrity in the middle of the nineteenth century. Of the protagonist it is said: "His education to a human being was complete; but he felt only the more clearly the human being's helplessness" (5: 385). In *Old Nests* the well-balanced Just Everstein contrasts with the narrator, Fritz Langreuter, who remains a physical and emotional cripple and for whom the sun is an image of cruelty, laughing at man's illusions (14: 212-13); thus the Goethean organicism of Just's integration is at least partly relativized by the more modern image of a scornfully indifferent nature. Raabe sometimes himself introduced confusion into these matters. Late in life he remarked that according to literary history, his Stuttgart period was supposed to have been his "pessimistic epoch," while in fact it had been the happiest time of his life.[13] It is remarkable to what extent he misremembered or repressed his deep unhappiness in Stuttgart, about which there can be no doubt from the evidence.

The literary history viewed so skeptically by Raabe has associated his pessimism not only with Stuttgart but also with Schopenhauer. The progress of Raabe's interest in Schopenhauer can be sketched from the diary. He first read about the philosopher in the summer of 1863, that is, in Stuttgart, but did not begin to read him at first hand until towards the end of the Stuttgart period, in 1868. In 1881 he acquired a copy of *On the Fourfold Root of the Principle of Sufficient Reason* and studied it thoroughly (15: 645). On February 22, 1888, he noted the hundredth anniversary of Schopenhauer's birth. On the anniversary of his death in 1907 Raabe joked that it was a day for self-examination and contrition.[14] The philosopher turns up fleetingly in several works. In the revised version of *The People from the Forest*, published in 1889 though the revisions were begun in 1868, the amateur astronomer Ulex somewhat anachronistically pores over the then virtually unknown *World as Will and Representation* (5: 162). The protagonist of *The Odin Field* quite anachronistically cites the principle of sufficient reason (17: 163). Schopenhauer makes a cameo appearance in *Owls' Pentecost* as a grumpy pedestrian muttering in English when someone gets in his way (11: 390-91). These and several other allusions are not without an element of playfulness, and are peripheral to the question of the influence of Schopenhauer on the interior of Raabe's texts, concerning which there has been much study and speculation.

In my opinion, however, altogether too much attention has been paid to this matter.[15] Germans sometimes have a tendency to believe that writers are unable to create without the help of philosophers, as though literature were an extension of philosophy by other means. Raabe did not have a philosophical mind in any systematic or technical sense; one reason, perhaps, why some intellectuals, fixated on the primacy of philosophy, have not been able to take him seriously. He looked to philosophers as he did to writers and historical figures for models of steadfastness before an inimical, uncaring world. This is the sense of his exhortation: "Stay away from the history of philosophy. That is only a history of human ignorance about what is hidden behind earthly appearances. Spinoza, Goethe and the 'Aphorisms on Practical Wisdom' of the second *Frankforter* [i.e., Schopenhauer], in connection with the proverb, 'to make the best of a bad bargain!' now suffice me entirely for the rest of my way through the earthly vale."[16] Raabe, who did not like to be thought of as influenced by anyone, repeatedly denied Schopenhauer's influence on him. He pointed out that, in the opening sentences of the *Chronicle*, he had anticipated Schopenhauer before anyone had heard of him.[17] In 1874 he criticized Jensen for attempting to console him with Schopenhauer and for basing his view of life too much on current literature; Raabe then added the curious remark that Schopenhauer's philosophy, like the "dear God," was "novelistically very applicable and pleasant."[18] What that was supposed to mean I am far from sure, though once again it implies the distinction between fiction and life. Raabe could be very self-contradictory, a failing, no doubt, in a philosopher, but not so much in a writer or artist, for the contradictions become dynamic, generating ambiguity, irony, and polyperspectivism, preventing the apprehension of reality from becoming petrified in systematic presuppositions.

In my opinion, the key to Raabe's pessimism and the way it informed his imagination is to be found in his attitude toward death. Here there is no question of a modernist "metaphysics of death";[19] his posture was simpler, starker, and more rationalistic. While I shall try to address his views of religion later on in connection with *Restless Guests*, I will anticipate here by asserting my conviction that he was entirely devoid of religious faith; religious concepts or turns of phrase, which frequently occur, are either rhetorical commonplaces of discourse, remnants of the secularized religiosity of German idealism, or cultural elements of historical settings. For a mind so constituted, death is the ultimate negation, threatening the meaning of life and its manifold sufferings. Personally, though he did not fear death—that would not have been like him—he detested aging and dying. Although he lived a long life by the standards permitted to mortals, it apparently did not seem long to him, despite his complaints about its quality. He was constantly aware of his own aging; he brooded over his birthdays, especially his fiftieth, on which he began commenting in letters for months beforehand. He said that he felt the shadow of death when he entered his sixtieth year and did not want to be reminded of his birthday.[20] In the last years of his life hardly a letter goes by without a comment on his age; the correspondence with the Jensens grows cheerless, with loss and aging the themes. His final decay filled him with disgust; one month before his death he wrote: "How gentle and merciful it would have been if I had been called away from the healthy [year] 1909. What now? Continuous torment day and night until the last cry!"[21] In 1906 Raabe predicted that someday a doctoral dissertation would be written about the way people die in his works.[22] More valuable would be a study of the commentary on death in his works;

it would yield a bulky compendium. Here only a very few examples can be offered:

From *One Springtime*:

This wrestling against the cold, rigid monster: time! This writhing and beating of man, pinned on the needle of self-awareness, against the annihilation that inexorably approaches and from which no power in heaven or earth can deny one stroke of the bell-tones slowly following upon one another! (1: 355)

From *The Hunger Pastor*:

It is enough for us that laughter is not a monopoly and weeping not a servitude on this round, fire-filled ball flattened at both poles, on which we find ourselves without our will and from which we shall depart without our will after the space between coming and going has been made sour enough. (6: 7)

From *Fabian and Sebastian*:

Is not our whole existence mostly a sticking-our-head-in-the-sand before the unavoidable, before the trivial irritation of the next quarter hour as well as before the terrible hunter, death, who, as it were, wrapped in a cloud of dust, appears on the horizon of the desert and is behind us and over us, while we still make a joke about him or have entangled him in a net of dogma or a philosophical system? (15: 83)

From *Villa Schönow*:

Oh, God, it is true that people must die; it is in the Bible and in the books and the teachers say it and the preachers preach about it—everyone speaks of it and laughs and can go on calmly eating and drinking and think that tomorrow the seamstress is coming or that it is Tuesday, Wednesday, or Thursday.

Oh, God, and *when it suddenly really all at once—all at once—has come!* and it seems as though everything else: sun and light and green trees, people and animals and children and the houses in the streets must care about it—how terrible, how terrible! (15: 478-79)

How young, we are told in *Wunnigel*, a thousand-year-old artifact seems next to a ninety-year-old man (13: 49). The poet Lippoldes in *Pfister's Mill* recites a Christmas poem in which death is the bridegroom and nothingness the bride (16: 85).

And so on, and on. Of course, there are counter-gestures, and they are extremely varied. With the characteristic sentimentality of *The Hunger Pastor*, Hans Unwirrsch and his bride speak of love as the only palliative in the face of death; later we hear that the resources are love and work (6: 404-5, 439). In the black comedy of *Gedelöcke* the tack is entirely different: death is made clownish. Gedelöcke turns death into satire; by using his dead body for satirical and didactic purposes, he overcomes bodilessness.[23] Once in a while Raabe seems to drift toward aesthetic considerations. In *The People from the Forest* there is a wistful observation on the early extinction of individual life—but the play of colors of life has no end (5: 278-79). Raabe, however, had an instinctive mistrust of aestheticizing solutions. In Blech, the corpse photographer in *The Lar*, death has, in a sense, acquired a victory over art, motivated by material need. Blech lives from death, survives from it; death can be aestheticized if the public wants. He puts a naked skull in his shop window and gives the public the choice of prettiness or reality (17: 276). Sometimes Raabe falls into sententiousness, which, alas, was the side of him that came to appeal most to his popular audience. His disciples quoted *ad nauseam* a passage from *German Nobility*: "It is German nobility not to take death too seriously and to treat the dead with seriousness and respect" (13: 321). But even in that novel one character remarks: "the older one gets, the more one notices in what sort of retardative tragedy one has a role to play" (13: 213).

Raabe's most obvious way out would seem to have been to affirm the fleeting pleasures of life, to take up the ancient theme of *carpe diem*. Leonhard Hagebucher, in his ultimately catastrophic public address in *Abu Telfan*, pursues this solution in high style:

> My greatly honored ladies and gentlemen, there is no one on earth, of whatever station and lineage he may be, around whom these three calls do not resound continuously on his way from the cradle to the grave. Happy is he who knows and feels through all the veins and fibers of his body and soul the strength, power, and magnificence of his humanity! Happy is he who is strong enough not to become excessively proud and calm enough to be able to look at every hour into the empty eye sockets of nothingness! Happy is he above all for whom that last call is everywhere and always the first one, for whom the enormous song of praise of creation in no place and at no time is a senseless or even repulsive murmur and who can rouse himself out of every crisis and every darkness with the cry: I live, for the Whole lives above me and around me! (7: 191).

The high, even bloated rhetoric here is meant, I think, to suggest the fragility, even the desperation of Hagebucher's position, which ultimately he is unable to sustain. But there are other, less strained passages in which Raabe seems to converge somewhat with his contemporary Gottfried Keller, whose Feuerbachian denial of personal immortality—sometimes imprecisely perceived as atheism—generated in him not despair but vigorous affirmation of life in this world, to be treasured just because it is a gift that must be returned. Nevertheless, Fritz Martini was right to argue that, in the long run, Raabe was unable to hold to Keller's position, for he saw death "as an inner denial of reality. This disjointedness of his world picture, intimated again and again, is only with effort cloaked in resignation."[24]

Thus the sixteen-year-old Raabe's employment in a school essay of images of falling leaves and fading blossoms for the movement of life toward death was more than an inherited cliché.[25] It was a fundamental instinct of his being. His virtually Baroque concentration on the transitoriness of all things and the empty vanity of the temporal world, the "saeculum," as he scornfully denominated it, is so pervasive that at one time an effort was made to portray him as a mystic.[26] The mainstream of Raabe criticism has been right to resist this line of argument; his ideal was not mystical but stoic. Goethe, Schopenhauer, Seneca (especially in *The Horn of Wanza*), the Bible, all are plundered for resources of survival in an inescapably bad situation. But, as Raabe never really achieved stoical detachment in himself, so he recognized the need of mankind for illusions, for fictions, which he himself endeavored to supply even as he recognized and admitted that they were fictions. Of this we shall eventually hear more in connection with *Of Old Proteus*; for the present we will conclude with a passage from *Owls' Pentecost*:

> It is an inborn right of mankind, after every present annoyance and irritation, as quickly as possible to lie one's way into every possible and impossible blessing of the future. This succeeds, if not always, nevertheless quite frequently. Sometimes the recovered good mood lasts, but sometimes it passes by like a glance of the sun on an April day. In the latter case the world speaks in all tongues of owls' Pentecost—never-never day—postpones the enjoyment of earthly life *at latter Lammas*, ad graecas Calendas, aux calendes grecques, to the Pentecost when the goose walks on the ice; but in the end the Jewish wisdom is right for all time: Rejoice, O young man, in thy youth, while the evil days come not, when thou shalt say, I have no pleasure in them. (11: 426-27)[27]

Thus Raabe deeply disbelieved in utopias; at the same time he found them necessary. This is the need, it seems, served by fiction.

CHAPTER 6

The Case Against Raabe

◻

Fʀᴏᴍ ʜɪs time to our own, Raabe has always had critics, often cool, frequently baffled, sometimes dismissive, and occasionally hostile. During his career the general level of criticism applied to him was quite low, repetitious, and inexact. One reason for this is that the overall level of literary criticism in nineteenth-century Germany was quite low; among post-Romantic critics there are hardly any memorable figures to be compared with the great critics in the English tradition. The best minds did not write literary criticism, which, until quite recently in Germany, was regarded as an inferior genre, a form of journalism. The best minds wrote literary theory as a branch of philosophy, with its characteristic inattention to specific texts and their details. The common run of critics looked for a congenial message; if they found it or thought they did in Raabe, they praised him; if not, not. But even some of the most perceptive and sympathetic critics often expressed reservations. As early as the 1860s one observer warned, perhaps not unjustly, that Raabe was writing too much and too fast (5: 450-51). One of his most consistent supporters, Paul Heyse, wrote in a preface to *The Ultimate Justice*, which he included in a novella anthology in 1875, that Raabe still needed a great subject with typical figures for the major work he owed his public (9/1: 409-10). In modern times, when his reputation had become very firm in a segment of the public, some critics and scholars became, perhaps for that reason, unfriendly. Lukács, whose mode of literary history consisted primarily of exclusions, acknowledged Raabe's significance as a popular writer but asserted that he would never have the rank of the major German authors such as E.T.A. Hoffmann or Gottfried Keller.[1] Ernst Bloch attacked Raabe as a petty-bourgeois panderer to anti-Semitic prejudice.[2] Rudolf Majut, the author of a generally reliable compact account of the nineteenth-century novel in a major handbook of German literary study, called Raabe a pretentious, less than mediocre writer, "the worst mannerist since Jean Paul," and accused him of triviality, repetitiveness, and lack of discipline.[3] In 1950 one observer found in him "the humor of a small town reserved table at which foresters and druggists set the tone, a wash of Goethean *Bildung* highly diluted with Biedermeier water, the self-important, didactic posture of a kindergarten teacher, and a frothy mountain of sentimentality."[4]

Until quite recently Raabe was not able to gain much of a foothold in Western countries. There were some efforts at translation in his lifetime, but they seem to have succeeded only in Dutch. A bad English translation of *Abu Telfan* in 1881 was indifferently received, characterized by the *Times* as "dreamy, desultory, metaphysical and unpractical" and by the *Athenaeum* as "mere abstractions of an armchair philosopher . . . the humour is ponderous and more calculated to excite a yawn than laughter," though the *Illustrated London News* thought it "the sort of novel that might have been written by such a genius as Heinrich Heine."[5] There has been very little translation of Raabe into English and none into French since 1931.[6] Reasons for the French silence may be found in a large, detailed study published in Paris in 1939. Its author, Louis Kientz, takes a perversely negative view of Raabe as an undisciplined, disorderly person, full of the class-consciousness of bourgeois officialdom, shiftily seeking social standing as a writer. Kientz, though clearly perceptive and intelligent, invents traits and motives for which there is no evidence, is incapable of distinguishing voices in the text, and is sometimes very inaccurate. He seems mainly to deplore that Raabe was not a French realist of clearly focused rationalistic philosophy, and he is particularly bewildered by Raabe's ambiguity, irony, and refusal to take clearly defined positions: "Raabe apparaît comme un esprit incapable de prendre nettement parti, de faire un choix net, de se construire une pensée réellement à lui."[7] The book is so resolutely hostile and often downright unfair that one must suppose it was colored by the political atmosphere of the time; it indicates, however, how difficult it is to export Raabe. Kientz's book is the longest ever to have been written on Raabe in a language other than German; the experience of reading it, as I did, in succession with the longest ever to have been written in German, Fehse's Nazified biography of 1937, can threaten to break the spirit of one's admiration.

Some of the case against Raabe will simply dissolve with the application of responsible interpretation. The acknowledged pioneer of modern Raabe studies in English, Barker Fairley, remarked over thirty years ago that the excellence of Raabe among European writers was not the prevailing view: "But the prevailing view," he added succinctly and prophetically, "will have to go."[8] Some of the case can be met with reasonable argument. I tried myself, a few pages back, to defend him against the charge of provinciality. His experimental narrative eccentricities, which ran into a wall of incomprehension in his own time, are the main reason for his resuscitation in modern criticism and will require a chapter of their own. To Kientz's pervasive accusation that Raabe was a weak-minded, unreflective ideologist of the official caste it is hard to know what to say other than that the claim is non-sense; few writers of his time so persistently criticized, satirized, and undermined the complacencies and allegiances of his own class. Perhaps more difficult to refute is the complaint, which Raabe was obliged to hear in his own time, that his works resemble one another too much. To this there seem to me to be two answers. First, it is surely not unusual to find in a major writer a considerable continuity of style, manner, structure, theme, and outlook from one work to another throughout the career. If one reads large amounts of Dickens or Balzac in succession, one will certainly find elements of sameness in work after work; this is the reason, after all, that one will normally identify at a glance a page of Dickens or Balzac without difficulty. In German-language writers, too, such as Storm or Keller, one will find a tonal similarity and thematic coherence from work to work. One of today's outstanding Keller scholars has observed: "As though in a chess game, a limited number of figures and figural movements yield almost unlimited combinatory possibilities."[9]

This last remark brings us to the second point, the variety that can be found within the superintending consistency. Here Raabe's friends and enemies have conspired together to obscure his remarkable exper-imentalism; uniformly they have regarded the life work as an undif-ferentiated oeuvre, a single great confession, as Goethe once said of his career, from which the same conclusions, the same body of wis-dom, can be drawn at every point. In this regard, the traditional dis-inclination to analytic criticism has resulted in a genuine failure of perception. Only reasonably detailed interpretation can counter this misapprehension, as I shall try to show in various places, but a couple of anticipatory points can be ventured here. Careful reading will reveal that Raabe's apparently similar thematic patterns sometimes undergo subtle shifts in the course of a single work that alter what the reader might have taken to be their meaning and perspective. This is the case, for example, in *Old Nests*, in *The Documents of the Birdsong*, and, I be-lieve, implicitly in the fragment *Altershausen*. Furthermore, though some of Raabe's motifs indeed reoccur over and over in his works, they do not always mean the same thing. I will just briefly mention three examples because they belong to the commonplaces of interpretation, which, when they are handled without differentiation, can lead to the impression of monotony.

1. A frequently encountered figure is the "returnee" (*Heimkehrer*), who returns to his home society after a long absence in a strange one. This is an effective device, especially for a relatively plotless author, for it generates a conflict of values and makes ambiguous the perspective on the conventions of normal society. But Raabe's returnees do not always represent the same kinds of values. Sometimes they are wholly positive. The best example is Just Everstein in *Old Nests*, who returns from his experiences as a farmer in America as a more mature, more deeply realized self. His less persuasive antecedent is Robert Wolf in *The People from the Forest*. But sometimes the returnee's experiences have alienated him from his home society in ways that make reintegration difficult or impossible, thus highlighting the rigidity, the lack of resilience and tolerance in conventional society. The classical and most tragic example is Leonhard Hagebucher in *Abu Telfan*, who returns from captivity as a slave in Africa to find himself wholly out of phase with his home society. But alienation is not always tragic; stronger souls maintain their refusal to affirm or accommodate to the conventions they have outgrown, and live as a constant, often sarcastic reproach to the commonplace. Such figures in Raabe's works are frequently elderly women; a particularly appealing example is Lina Nebelung in *Owls' Pentecost*, who, returning from her politically motivated, twenty-year exile as a physics professor at Vassar, emerges as a redoubtable combination of independence and generosity of spirit. Another possibility is that the returnee may find that his new home, not his old one, is his true one. One such case is the Swedish soldier in *The Homeward March*, whom the fortunes of war have cast up far from home on the shores of Lake Constance. Here the homeward movement undergoes a reversal, and the old soldier discovers that his adopted home is where he belongs. Finally, the returnee can bring home values not of maturity and insight, but of evil and disruption. Examples of this are *Princess Fish* and *At the Sign of the Wild Man*.

2. The "returnee" is often a special case of the "outsider" (*Sonderling*), the alienated, unintegrated, resistant individual as erratic block in conventional society.[10] Concerning this motif there have been two serious misunderstandings. One is the reduction of the outsider to a humorously depicted eccentric, a cranky codger or appealing odd fellow with a touch of the clown (in German, *Kauz*). This cliché ought to be wholly dispensed with, for it trivializes Raabe's depth of sympathy for suffering, the desperateness of the struggle for even minimal

human survival. The other misapprehension treats him as the propagator of a dogmatic, militant individualism, as though he were, in this respect, a forerunner of Hermann Hesse. It is true that Raabe had a strong individualistic streak. He was always his own man, or tried hard to be; he did not co-operate easily with others, shunned collegiality, and more than once expressed his scorn for efforts to organize writers into professional associations. But it cannot be said often enough that his fiction is richer than his personality. In many cases his outsider incarnates positive values, but then it is not merely a matter of following one's own drummer, however odd the beat may be. Rather he (or, in some cases, she) affirms values, often acidly and impatiently, of a substance more humane and rational than the slovenly, selfish customs of conventional society. Frequently the price is high in terms of loneliness and deprivation of the common gratifications of life. An example is the isolated title figure of *Master Author*, whom the world does not understand though he understands the world perfectly well. But this is not the only type. Sometimes the outsider is neurotic, a victim of self-incurred timidity and short-sightedness; such is the case of the narrator of *Old Nests*. The outsider's individualism can be carried to dangerous extremes, to the edge of madness, to an egocentrism that expresses itself in insensitivity to others, as with the title figure of *Wunnigel*, or to a kind of spectacular irrelevance in the conduct of life that has elements of both the heroic and the pathetic, as with Velten Andres in *The Documents of the Birdsong*. Furthermore, it would be wrong to suppose that Raabe finds his ideal in isolation of the self; rather, it is one of the themes of this study that the outsiders gravitate to one another to form an alternative community.

3. Finally, there is the recurring initial constellation of the "cloverleaf" (*Kleeblatt*): three children, bound together in friendship or at least companionship in childhood, whose converging or diverging subsequent fates structure the narration. Here the variations are more obvious. The three can remain in mutually supportive alliance far into old age, as in *The People from the Forest*. Two of them can be joined together to the exclusion of the third, as in *Old Nests*. Or all three can fly apart centrifugally, as in *The Documents of the Birdsong*. In all these cases there is a need for analytic, differentiating observation in place of synthetic, comprehensive categories that would impose a reductive coherence and univalence on Raabe.

There are, however, other aspects of the case against him that are not so easily argued away. For one thing, those who hold to the dogma that an author must show and not tell will not befriend themselves with him very easily, for he was distinctly more inclined to tell than to show. We can see, for example, in the drafts of *Horacker* (12: 544) that his way of working was often to make a skeletal sketch of plot elements, then to fill it out increasingly with material on the authorial level of narration. Conversation and narration become the content. Raabe's inexorably verbose and garrulous manner is certainly not to everyone's taste; even a well-disposed reader may sometimes become irritated, though the irritation is perhaps intended, as part of the abrasive campaign against the reader, for it is true that the more the spokesmen of the public complained about his manner, the more insistently he developed it. One of the more awake critics of the time, Eduard Engel, wrote in 1881 that, while his contemporaries were mostly interchangeable with one another stylistically, one could identify Raabe from ten lines of text.[11] His style, which is inadequately researched, resembles that of no one else, before or since; in my opinion, it in no way resembles Jean Paul's, with whom Raabe has been interminably compared. If any writer comes to mind, it is Laurence Sterne; of all of Sterne's numerous German descendants, Raabe resembles him most. He was not unaware that he was a peculiar stylist; he replied to Engel's review somewhat ironically: "I know only too well where the shoe often pinches and that I often brood much too long to make a thing clear that would come out brighter, lighter, and more comprehensibly with less worry and care."[12] But to an officious chap who offered to rewrite *The Hunger Pastor* in order to raise it to the highest stylistic level by Germanicizing its foreign words, Raabe replied in comic exasperation with a whole sentence of foreign words from Oliver Goldsmith: "A book may be amusing with numerous errors, or it may be very dull without a single absurdity."[13] There is no doubt that Raabe's style requires more patience than many readers feel it is their duty to bring to bear. It also has another consequence, noted by many, including the aforementioned Eduard Engel in a review of *Hastenbeck*: that all his characters talk alike (20: 438). This is, frankly, true; at least his positive characters do. All of them speak a peculiar Raabean idiolect—digressive, allusive, wordy, ironic, and oblique—of a sort that I rather doubt has ever been spoken by anyone in real life, but that is one of the indicators of membership in the alternative community. It makes for slow reading, to be sure, but it can be highly entertaining, and even when it is not, we will tolerate it more easily if we refrain from applying mimetic canons of value to Raabe.

A more fundamental reservation might be this: the reverse of the coin of variety and experimentalism is that his oeuvre is very uneven. The unevenness is not merely a matter of chronology or genre. The impression given by some modern commentary that Raabe matured steadily to excellence is imprecise; there are works late in his career that seem weak or regressive, such as *Villa Schönow* and *Cloister Lugau*, and it is possible that *Altershausen* was turning in that direction when Raabe shut it off. There is also unevenness within works. Sometimes the garrulous author seems to run out of breath, especially in longer narratives, which appear to flag in the third quarter, becoming immobile and repetitious, thus leading to the suspicion that Raabe may have been trying to fill up a symmetrical number of chapters. Even in some of the best works, the modern reader may be put off by patches of sentimentality or sententiousness. These are the consequence, I believe, of a permanently unresolved conflict in him between a realistic but dispiriting perception of the world and a form of idealism necessary for hope but articulable only as illusion and fiction. One matter I find difficult to assess is the extent to which his works were informed and perhaps distorted by an effort to accommodate to the putative readership. In some of the early works, especially the novels, the effort to write books such as other people wrote but nevertheless in his own voice seems virtually to tear the texts apart. This became a critical problem in *The Hunger Pastor*, as I shall show in the next chapter. Like any serious writer, he eventually had to solve this problem in favor of his own voice, but he may never have got it completely off his back. Its persistence can be seen in his employment of symbol and leitmotif. His symbolism is often praised, but I am not persuaded that it is always one of his strong points, except in a few exceptional cases, mostly in the late works.[14]

One of the clearest examples of his problem with symbolism is *The Rumbledump*. The title (*Schüdderump*) is a little-known slang word for a crude cart used in past centuries to collect and dump the corpses of plague victims. There is no such object in Raabe's story, which in any case has a modern setting. It exists exclusively on the authorial level of narration, where it rumbles around at the author's behest as an emblem of the ineluctable approach of evil and death, of the hopelessness of goodness in this world, and of the vanity of all transitory, secular things. This at once unintegrated and obtrusive symbol gets on the reader's nerves because it is so clearly motivated by the author's mistrust of the reader, whom he cannot expect to follow him without being led around by the nose. Another example of the way Raabe leans on his reader is the notorious leitmotif of hunger in the *The Hunger Pastor*. Hunger is Shiva and Vishnu, destroyer and sustainer;

the book is dedicated to the sacred power of true hunger; the protagonist feels an early hunger for love; his hunger and that of his Jewish contemporary are alike but different; a schoolmaster hungers for the light of knowledge; there is material hunger, spiritual hunger, hunger displaced as ambition, hunger for innocence, loyalty, gentleness, love, fulfillment, on and on, hunger hunger hunger until the reader wants to scream. The trouble is not, as is sometimes argued, that the hunger leitmotif refers to incompatible realms: material, spiritual, psychological, moral; there is nothing wrong with that, in my view. It is rather that coherence is imposed by assertive repetitiousness and therefore does not succeed in integrating the leitmotif into the narration. There is a deep problem here of a sundered moral universe that Raabe at this time was unprepared to face, but much of the heavy-handedness of his use of symbol and leitmotif must be owing to his relationship to a public both courted and mistrusted. In his employment of leitmotif he is today sometimes thought of as a forerunner of Thomas Mann; Raabe's anticipations of Mann, long overlooked, are indeed interesting; but it must be said that in most cases his employment of leitmotif has little of Mann's elegance. (Still, it is my experience that when one has read a Mann story ten times or so, the leitmotivic machinery begins to look a little obtrusive.)

I hope the reader will agree that we can live with these faults and artistic shortcomings if they are counterbalanced, as I believe they are, with imaginative ingenuity and artistic strengths. But the case against Raabe is made weightier by a complicated and peculiarly German burden. In Germany as in no other country, reception history is a powerful determinant of literary evaluation. Since traditional bourgeois culture is perceived as having been in intimate complicity with the advent of fascism and its barbarities, any writer will be suspect to the extent that he can be seen as representative of bourgeois culture in fact or reputation. For it will in most cases be found that such reputations flowed, with greater or lesser ease, into the Nazification of German culture. With no other writer has this been more the case than with Wilhelm Raabe, and I know of no other case in which the process of freeing an author from the odium of his reception history has been beset with so many difficulties. To explain how this came about requires an unpleasant but necessary excursus.

Shortly after his death in November 1910 a group formed that called itself "The Society of the Friends of Wilhelm Raabe." That was a reasonable description, for almost all the original members came out of his entourage or were otherwise personally acquainted with him. This group developed into the second-largest literary society in Germany; only the Goethe Society was larger. It was organized in local chapters throughout the country and began in 1911 to publish a newsletter that evolved into something more like a journal. Adulation was the stock-in-trade of the Society. Raabe was virtually worshipped as a fountain of wisdom and a guide through the tribulations of life, a conserver of eternal values and a humorist who taught a reconciling, idealistic elevation above the transitory contradictions of the real world. The best mind the Society produced, Wilhelm Fehse, wrote in 1921: "If we did not see in him the highest paraclete of our people, where would our Raabe Society be?"[15] Members came to shore up their own self-regard by association with him; they identified themselves as "Raabe people," a kind of elite of sensitivity, idealism, and humor, though in retrospect they look like quite typical representatives of the educated petty-bourgeoisie. Effusions such as this, from a local chapter in 1924, were not uncharacteristic: "in beautiful hours of community we want to orient ourselves firmly on the master, to collect and elevate ourselves, indeed, to *find* ourselves in him, the inexhaustible one. . . . In short, we want *ourselves* in Raabe: our hidden essence and life, our inwardness that can never be satisfied by the external day because it is superior to the temporal world."[16]

One of the peculiarities of the Raabe Society was a strongly articulated anti-aesthetic and anti-critical attitude. The actual founder of the Society, Wilhelm Brandes, explained that, unlike the aesthetically motivated admirers of other writers, the Raabe "community" had a "quite preponderantly ethical character," and he defined the society as "a sect, a freemasonry" and as a "diaspora" of German-speaking people all over the world.[17] The practical consequences of this were, first, a kind of ransacking of Raabe's works for aphoristic wisdom without regard to their character as artistic fictions, with the result of a considerable reduction in their ironic dimension; and second, a pronounced hostility to any form of literary criticism developed outside the Society, which took an increasingly proprietary attitude toward Raabe. A corollary to this preference was a particular attachment to *The Hunger Pastor*. Perhaps no other single factor has done so much harm to Raabe's reputation as *The Hunger Pastor* and its popularity, especially as it is the one title that most people who have ever heard of him associate with him.

Probably none of this is very remarkable from the point of view of the sociology of literary societies. It is necessary to remember that the Raabe Society, with all its absurdities, nevertheless performed useful service in preserving manuscripts and materials, editing texts and publishing editions, and accumulating knowledge, not all of it trivial. Its monolithic view of Raabe was never wholly unchallenged without and even within the Society. Even within its confines one can find here and there the seeds of a more modern outlook and the early traces of later contributors to it. Under more normal historical circumstances the Raabe Society might have outgrown its parochialism and evolved together with the maturation of modern literary scholarship. But the historical circumstances were abnormal.

For the Raabe Society became completely Nazified. In 1932, after some sort of internal crisis, a sixty-six-year-old schoolteacher named Franz Hahne became president of the Society. Hahne was a Nazi and a raging anti-Semite. He regarded himself as an expert on race theory and could hardly discuss any subject without relating it to the iniquities of the Jews. For Hitler's birthday in 1939, Hahne arranged to have a Hitler Youth prepare a calligraphic manuscript of *The Crown of the Empire* as a gift, and upon Hitler's escape from the assassination attempt in the Bürgerbräukeller Hahne sent congratulations on behalf of the Society.[18] In one grotesque episode, he found it necessary to defend Raabe against a Nazi attack on him as pro-Jewish.[19] In the third issue of the Society's *Communications* in 1933, Fehse dedicated a sonnet, no less, to Hitler, and in 1939, to support Germany's aggression against Czechoslovakia, he contributed another poem denouncing the Czechs along with Woodrow Wilson.[20] Both Hahne and Fehse endeavored to present Raabe as a forerunner of Nazism, and another contributor of long standing wrote an essay on Raabe and Hitler as religious thinkers.[21] Jewish members of the society were informed by a bank of their expulsion,[22] including the literary historian Heinrich Spiero, a baptized, active Protestant and wholly assimilated German conservative, who was vice-president of the Society, president of the Berlin chapter, and Raabe's first biographer.

It is true, of course, that all corporate entities like the Society were forcibly integrated into the Nazi system, and the successors of the Society like to hint that it was coerced into conformity. But a perusal of the record does not bear this out. We find instead a steady development toward fascist attitudes long before the advent of the Nazi regime. One theme is the scorn of the Weimar Republic, expressed as early as 1922 in a piece by Fehse.[23] In the previous year, a volume sponsored by the Society carried an essay, brimming with nationalist resentment at the lost war, which contrasts Raabe to shallow Anglo-Saxon rationalism, ascribing to him a deep, instinctive, brooding soul, free of logic or thought.[24] Fehse contributed an anti-Semitic article in 1924.[25] An interpretation of Raabe according to race theory appeared in 1927, a theme continued by Hahne during the Nazi period.[26] In

1931, in a series on what Raabe might mean to modern youth, a representative of the youth movement of the time writes: "With him we fight against modern civilization, which annihilates the highest and most sacred things in man as well as in the community."[27] Thus the ground was well prepared for the Nazification of the Society, which was not a passively endured accident.

Of course, this might be regarded as a familiar story of the development of ideology in Germany, and there has been a tendency to see it in class terms.[28] Undoubtedly the Raabe community was very class-oriented.[29] Hostile remarks about the working class and the Social Democrats are not infrequently encountered in the reception materials. The founder Brandes himself asserted that only the middle class possessed the peculiar German virtue of *Gemüt*, which he defined as "the deep and inward feeling for the ethical values and the bonds of life, a feeling that, resting on premonition and insight, is composed of love and veneration."[30] Events after the war also followed a depressingly familiar pattern. The Raabe Society was more concerned with continuity than with contrition. The Braunschweig professor Ernst-August Roloff, who, under the "Führer principle," had been appointed, not elected, as president after Hahne had been incapacitated in a bombing attack, worked to pick up the pieces. His organizational achievements deserve acknowledgment, but, in the process, the Raabe Society fell into a state of near amnesia. The impossible Hahne was installed on the shelf as "honorary president," and later, in a euphemistic retrospective by Roloff's son, Hahne was praised for the resourcefulness of his leadership in difficult times.[31] There were a few oblique gestures toward reparations; one, immediately after the recovery, was an article in the newsletter by one of the old stalwarts on Raabe and Heine, a previously tabu topic.[32] But it was to be 1951 before the briefest allusion to the Nazi years appeared, and it came from a member in New York.[33] Finally, in 1956, it was acknowledged that the Nazification of the Society was a burden for Raabe's reputation in foreign countries.[34] Thus it is not surprising that the task of illuminating the Society's complicity and its history, evaded by the Society itself, was taken up in hostile quarters, in the atmosphere of neo-Marxist arraignment that began to develop in German scholarship in the late 1960s, although it is to the Society's credit that one of the earliest of the unfriendly analyses appeared in its own journal.[35]

There is little doubt that the reception history did indeed burden Raabe's reputation, making him appear as a coterie writer of harmless idylls and escapist nostalgia for provincial officials, clergymen, and schoolmasters, a writer conservative and nationalist in outlook, at one with the social caste that most vigorously committed itself to fascism. The revision of this evaluation has been an ongoing struggle. But the revision contains its own dangers, not only of excessively modernizing him, but of standing his image on its head, to make him the opposite of what he previously had been believed to be. There is, to be sure, something ludicrous about associating him, with his contempt for despotism, his hatred of war, and his sympathy with human suffering, with the Nazi atrociousness. But he *was* a nationalist; there *was* a conservative facet to his temper; he *was* a representative of his class while being deeply critical of it from within. The "friends" of the Society *were* originally his friends. He was grateful for response and was little inclined to monitor its accuracy or appropriateness. The sense of a community of a self-elected elite was fostered by Raabe himself and is thematic in his fiction, though for him superiority was less a matter of the mystical *Gemüt* than a capacity for sympathy and generosity toward other human beings in their trouble and sorrow. Thus he cannot be wholly excised from the reception history, at the same time as we recognize it as reductive and distortive.

I have never been an adherent of the currently prestigious doctrine that the literary text exists only as the sum of its reconstitutions by its readers, so that reception history obtains a priority over interpretation. Indeed, the case of Raabe seems to me to constitute a warning against the dangers of this doctrine. But in this case there is nevertheless an interactive continuity among author, text, reception history, and our present task of interpretation. We must try to separate these things from one another without isolating them, distinguish without repressing. It is with this purpose in mind that I have found it necessary to devote the first chapter of the next part to an effort, not to cut, but to loosen and perhaps untie, the Gordian knot at the center of his reputation in the world at large: the matter of *The Hunger Pastor* and Raabe's place in the catastrophic history of German-Jewish relations.

PART II

Themes

CHAPTER 7

Raabe and the Jews:
The Case of
The Hunger Pastor

◙

R EADERS of today, coming to Raabe for the first time and reading him from end to end, would not be likely to conclude that Jewish themes and characters were a major issue in his career. Such readers might be disturbed by one work, *The Hunger Pastor*, but since they would find nothing else in the oeuvre reiterating its troubling features, they might well regard it as an unfortunate aberration. But the reception history, entwined as it is with the catastrophic history of modern Germany, does not permit us to take this offhand approach. *The Hunger Pastor*, once the centerpiece of Raabe's fame, has turned into one of the main hindrances to a just appraisal of him. The problem is not a simple one, and dealing with it even summarily will require, unfortunately, a good deal of detail. That Raabe was not an anti-Semitic writer and that *The Hunger Pastor* is not an anti-Semitic novel in its intention have been so well established in literary scholarship for so long that it would seem redundant to argue the point any more. Nevertheless, legends of reception are often tenacious; for example, in Gordon Craig's widely acclaimed book *The Germans* it is said that Raabe, Gustav Freytag, and Felix Dahn "resorted in their most popular books to the technique of parallelism, placing in contrast the careers of their Christian protagonist, who was always portrayed as being honorable, idealistic and dedicated to the service of others, and his Jewish counterpart, who was self-centered, cowardly, materialistic, and unscrupulous," as though Raabe, or, for that matter, Freytag, had done nothing but write such novels their whole lives long.[1] Therefore it is not superfluous to make the case again; but in reopening it, we will find that the matter is rather more complicated than it is normally made out to be. Neither the anti-Semitic view of Raabe nor its refutation in conventional presentations has exhausted the subject of Raabe and his reputation in regard to Jews and anti-Semites.

THE CASE that Raabe cannot be regarded as an anti-Semitic writer was made long ago.[2] It can only be sketched here; there has not yet been a thorough study on modern principles of Jewish characters and their situations and of Jewish references in Raabe's works,[3] but the point is that positive as well as neutral Jewish figures appear in numerous places. The earliest example is in the second novel, *One Springtime*, in which a Jewish old-clothes dealer, Rosenstein, though portrayed with some stereotypical features, is nevertheless a positive figure amiably regarded by his fellow Gentiles, and his two kindly, well-bred daughters quite clearly belong to Raabe's ideal community of the good and the gentle. *Lilac Blossom*, written during the genesis of *The Hunger Pastor*, is the reminiscence of an elderly doctor who recalls with sorrow how, as a young student, he aroused the feelings of a girl he met in the Jewish Cemetery of Prague, but did not love her, and she dies, like her prefigurative ancestor, the dancer Mahalath, of a symbolically enlarged heart. This does not strike me as one of Raabe's most successful works; it suffers from the sentimentality that plagued his writing in its first phases, and it falls into the pattern commonly met with in nineteenth-century German fiction of regarding the Jew as exotic or "oriental," thus foreign and inaccessible. All the same, despite the stress on the filth and nastiness of the Jewish community and the stereotyping of the girl's pawnbroker father, the novella expresses sympathy and understanding for the plight of the Jews, as well as respect for Jewish dignity in the image of the grave of the great rabbi Judah Löw (which Raabe visited; his diary entry of May 18, 1859, shows a particular interest in the site). In fact, the symbol of the enlarged heart—which inspired the narrator to become an accomplished heart specialist—refers not only or even primarily to obstructed love, but to grief at the sufferings of the Jewish people, who, it has been argued, are portrayed as the suffering servants of the world.[4] It is here as well as anywhere that one can see the two reasons why Raabe could not have been an anti-Semite even had he wanted to: his strong feelings about the integrity and just rights of a people, an extension of his own pronounced nationalism,[5] and his profound gift of sympathy that vibrates through his entire oeuvre with human suffering, despair, and oppression.

Three other works must be mentioned in this connection. One is *Gedelöcke* (1866), a farcical and improbable story, which, like many of the most improbable fictions, is drawn directly from real life, a tale recounted in a book Raabe found in a flea market. The Danish freethinker Gedelöcke, owing to his friendship with Jews and his interest in learning from them, has put himself into the reputation of having

virtually converted to Judaism; while he has not actually done so, the
very idea of it drives the community and his wife into hysterics of
gossip, bigotry, and superstition. He creates a situation that makes it
impossible to bury him either in Christian or in Jewish ground, and
so he is buried and dug up and buried again and dug up and finally
deposited in the common field. Here we have an expression of Raabe's
secular and often aggressively anti-clerical outlook; the religious Jews,
who expel their cantor from the community for bringing this trouble
by associating with Gedelöcke, are no better than the religious Christians, but, on the other hand, the Christians are no better than the
Jews, and Gedelöcke's posthumous whipsawing of his fellow men with
their own prejudices certainly has the effect of making anti-Semitism
one more symptom of a mean and trivial spirit.

Of particular interest is the novella *Madame Salome* (1875), whose
title figure is in some ways the most remarkable Jewish character I
know of in nineteenth-century German fiction. Not only is she intelligent and energetic; in her competent readiness in a chaotic disaster
and as a refuge for the daughter of the half-mad sculptor Querian she
is clearly another member of the alternative community of the good,
the generous, and the sympathetic. But, even more remarkably, she
is the millionaire widow of a Jewish banker, the kind of person who
would almost never appear in a positive light in the fiction of the time.
That she can exchange urbane repartee about her Jewishness with her
Gentile friend, the Judicial Councillor Scholten, merely expresses her
and her author's sovereignty over common prejudice. Salome, Scholten, and the girl Eilike Querian are bound together by the central,
original symbol of the novella: the "ichor," the blood of the gods that
flows in their veins and sets them apart from vulgar mankind. It has
been suggested that, with this image, Raabe wished to join the Jewish
and Greek spirits as "opposing forces to the more dangerous and stifling aspects of the German mythical atmosphere."[6] The characterization of Salome not only exhibits Raabe's cross-grained opposition to
cliché and convention; I rather suspect that she may have been conceived out of a bad conscience about *The Hunger Pastor*. The novella,
incidentally, is full of reminiscences from Heine's *Harz Journey*.[7]
There is also the splendid historical novella *Höxter and Corvey* (1875),
one of Raabe's several evocations of the bloody misery of the historical
past. As is frequently the case in his historical fiction, the blood and
misery are the consequence of Catholic-Protestant conflict, but here
both factions turn on helpless and harmless Jews, and the protagonists
risk life and limb in an attempt to shield an elderly Jewish woman and
her granddaughter from murderous ruffians and howling mobs. To

these cases may be added the painter Rudolf Haeseler, the spirit of shrewd wit and realism in *The Dräumling Swamp* (1872), whose mother, the daughter of a converted Jew, was "black-haired, corpulent, and aesthetic" (10: 32); his Gentile father is the money-changer, i.e., banker.[8] It is important to observe here that Haeseler, who has the reddish hair and beard of the anti-Semitic stereotype (10: 20), is one of the alter egos of Raabe's own personality encountered in various disguises in his works. Parenthetically, it might be noted that Raabe never refers to the people of the Old Testament as Hebrews or Israelites, as an anti-Semite might have done, but always as Jews.

It is true that there are scattered, occasional, disrespectful passages. As an example one may take a quotation from *The People from the Forest*, since it has sometimes been cited by anti-Semitic admirers: "Many a black-haired, hook-nosed businessman kept his sharp Semitic eyes focused on the house in the town" (5: 177). Apart from the fact that, in this case, it is actually the Gentile servants who are systematically robbing the property, an examination of such passages would show that in almost every case they reflect the association of Jews with money and commerce, graspingness and greed, and in spirit they differ in no way from often harsher passages in Heine or Marx. Heine could easily have a written a sentence in the same novel in which party guests are referred to as "Christian bankers with Jewish veneer and Jewish bankers with feudal titles" (5: 66); along the same line is the remark in *Old Nests* that Count Everstein's property is pledged to a Shylock (14: 69). Raabe could fall into this vulgar tone in his irritation at his publishers, some of whom were Jewish; he once wrote that his vacation would depend on what the Jews were prepared to pay for *The Rumbledump*,[9] and in his diary on March 19, 1879, he grouches about the newspaper editors who had turned down *Old Nests* as "the Berlin Jewish scoundrels." He irritably referred to R. M. Meyer, who had written dismissively of him in his history of nineteenth-century German literature, as "Richard Moses Meyer" and again as "Moses Meyer."[10]

To say that these were shared commonplaces of discourse is not meant to be an excuse but simply an observation necessary to place the stereotypes in their historical context. Social, class, ethnic, and national typology is virtually universal in nineteenth-century literature, a central feature of its anthropology and, if one will, "realism"; it appears in Raabe in many forms, among which the Jewish types are neither prominent nor striking. One could write another little essay on his images of blacks, but that would lead too far afield here. Furthermore, one must be careful about voice. One must also bear in mind the sarcastic edge of his temperament, most acidly articulated in his social satire. That the Jews have it worse than all the other human types falling under his scourge no one could plausibly claim. There are several instances in which negative characters exhibit anti-Jewish attitudes.[11] In a conversation Raabe is said to have argued against stereotypes by asserting that a Jew can be anything, even a colonizer, and to the familiar prejudice that a Jew could not be truly creative he responded with silence (E 4: 131).

As far as his personal life is concerned, his acquaintances and connections included a substantial number of Jews. In his boyhood he seems to have had a Jewish friend named Seckel Falkenstein, who, we are assured, bore no resemblance to Moses Freudenstein of *The Hunger Pastor* (E 4: 14-15). In the diary we find several Jewish names among his social relations in Wolfenbüttel and Stuttgart. Paul Heyse, with whom Raabe had cordial relations, was half Jewish, as was his dear friend Marie Jensen. Wilhelm Jensen was rather militantly anti-Jewish, though he once commented that the writer Ludwig Fulda was one of the none too common "descendants of the 'old tribe' " who make one realize that anti-Semitic affects are not universally applicable.[12] Raabe's vastly expanding correspondence during his Braunschweig years contains exchanges with a number of Jewish people, from literary figures such as Gustav Karpeles and Karl Emil Franzos to a rabbi in Galicia.[13] It is reported that "at his table Lutherans, Catholics, and Israelites sat peacefully beside one another," while he observed that the Jews were "our oldest nobility . . . their ancestors climbed the stairs to the David Palace in Jerusalem in trailing garments and gold jewelry while the ancestors of our proudest German lords sat clad with skins in primitive huts in the primeval forest and slaughtered human beings at the sacrificial fire" (E 4: 263). He was curious about the Jews as he was about most things, and at the time of writing *The Hunger Pastor* he read a definitive history of the Jewish people.[14]

With the most prominent German-Jewish writer of his time, Berthold Auerbach, he maintained, by his standards, friendly relations; it has already been mentioned that his only book review is a notice of an anthology edited by Auerbach. In Stuttgart Auerbach was one of his drinking companions, according to the diary. Raabe has Eyring, the amiable eighteenth-century narrator of *The Geese of Bützow* (1866), reading the poems of the Jewish aphorist Ephraim Kuh (9/2: 69); this at least suggests an acquaintance with Auerbach's novel *Poet and Merchant* (1840), a fictionalized biography of Kuh. The diary shows that Raabe read other works of Auerbach from time to time. In the texts there are scattered references to Auerbach, for example, in *German*

Nobility (13: 211). Always grateful for recognition, Raabe wrote Auerbach a most cordial letter of thanks for his review of *The Horn of Wanza*.[15] The community of admirers that clustered around Raabe in his late years and became the core of the Raabe Society included people of Jewish origin;[16] I have already mentioned the most prominent of them, Heinrich Spiero, and shall have more to say of him shortly. There is not one shred of evidence that Raabe's associations with Jewish people differed in the slightest nuance from his habits of personal relations generally.

IN THE light of all this, *The Hunger Pastor* comes to look like an anomaly in Raabe's career, an eccentricity that we might justifiably put to one side if it were not for the reception history, which made of this episode in his grueling search for his own voice and posture his most famous work, at home and abroad. By the 1950s it had appeared in over sixty editions totalling well over a quarter of a million copies (6: 493). It is a double-plotted *Bildungsroman* paralleling the development of a model German youth, Hans Unwirrsch, to that of an exact Jewish contemporary, Moses Freudenstein. The poor shoemaker's son Hans, in his hunger for light and truth, passes through a series of discouraging and sobering social experiences, until he finds his vocation as a pastor in a bleak community of fishermen on the remote shores of the Baltic. Moses, in his hunger for power, status, and worldly goods, transforms himself into a Frenchified Catholic intellectual named Théophile Stein, ruining various women along the way, and eventually becoming a social success as well as a political agent of the oppressive German governments but, in the narrator's judgment, "civilly dead (*bürgerlich tot*) in the most terrible sense of the word" (6: 461). His political turn, as an agent of the repressive governments, is the main reason why Moses is not to be identified with Heine, despite Moses's own attempts so to identify himself. There is some reason to suppose that Raabe was thinking of Joel Jacoby, who had become a police spy and government agent in the 1840s. Raabe's amalgamation of the reprehensible Jew with repressive authority rather than with rebellious opposition, as was more common on the right then and later, is a significant indicator of his political position.

It would certainly seem that anyone familiar with mid-nineteenth-century German literature must be struck by the similarity in pattern of this novel to the great best-seller of those times, Gustav Freytag's *Soll und Haben* (*Debit and Credit*, 1855). Though obvious to the Raabe experts of the past, this connection came to be treated gingerly, and, while it seems to be accepted by now, to my knowledge a thorough comparison has never been undertaken.[17] The reason may be that, although Raabe met Freytag personally on his mini-grand tour in 1859, the two writers did not admire one another very much;[18] furthermore, a comparison may have seemed odious to Raabe admirers, for, whatever the failings of *The Hunger Pastor*, as a work of literature it is undoubtedly superior to *Debit and Credit*. But Freytag's novel, too, pairs the exactly contemporaneous careers of an innately good, if in this case somewhat priggish and occasionally slow-witted bourgeois Gentile, and a crudely ambitious, unethical, and greedy Jewish boy. In both novels the career of the Jew keeps impinging on that of the Gentile, creating nasty complications that require to be repelled and set right. In neither novel is there any pronounced sense of the Jews as a religious community; they are an ethnic foreign body in a German nation struggling for an elusive identity and cohesiveness. Both novels have very much the cast of ideological tracts in the interest of German nationalism and a liberal bourgeois ethos, although the tenets of classical liberalism are much more explicitly articulated by Freytag, whereas Raabe has a scene of a proletarian revolt that the protagonist observes sympathetically. Both novels understand the condition of the Jews to be historically and socially determined but nevertheless pass ethical judgments on them. Freytag was no more of an anti-Semite or racist than Raabe; he was a national and class partisan. But despite nuances in the texts sometimes adduced in defense of both, despite their authors' subsequent embarrassment and implicit disclaimers, the books took on lives of their own and nourished calamitous prejudices.

While this is not the place for a detailed comparison, some differences might be mentioned, apart from the considerable qualitative gap in style and thoughtfulness.[19] In the first place, Freytag was much more extensively concerned than Raabe with the Jews as a social problem. Apart from minor figures, there are six important Jewish characters in *Debit and Credit*, distributed along the ethical spectrum that is a vertical axis of the novel: three negative ones—the antagonist Veitel Itzig, the oily financier Hirsch Ehrenthal, and the *gonif* tavern keeper and fence Löbel Pinkus; and three, in a qualified way, positive ones—the ethically assimilated but physically feeble scholar Bernhard Ehrenthal, the comic and seedy but ultimately Biblically righteous Orthodox peddler Schmeie Tinkeles, and a Jewish innkeeper who represents an outpost of *German* ethics in the even more degenerate environment of the Poles.[20] In *The Hunger Pastor*, Moses Freudenstein is the only important Jewish figure. Otherwise there are Moses's father, who hoped by avarice and labor to win strength and survival for his son, only to earn his son's contempt and to die of horror when he realizes what a monster he has sired, and the Jewish housemaid of the family, who abhors Moses as a renegade (both motifs are prefigured in *Debit and Credit*). In Raabe's overall scheme of things Moses is less a Jewish type than an example of the *canaille* that he found infesting mankind everywhere; there are parallels to his brutal cynicism in other, Gentile figures, such as the obnoxious swindler and loan shark Pinnemann in *Three Pens*, the corrupt Baron von Glimmern in *Abu Telfan*, or the terrifyingly invincible Dietrich Häussler in *The Rumble-dump*. As we shall see in another context, there is a non-Jewish parallel to the exotic, mistreated, ultimately vengeful racial outcast in the Wendish piper Kiza in *The Pied Piper of Hamelin*.[21]

On the other hand, however, Moses is a much more serious and impressive antagonist than Veitel Itzig. Freytag's Jew, though he has a pronounced capacity for hard work and self-improvement, remains an unappetizing and inferior character throughout; he has no dialectical relationship to the protagonist Anton Wohlfart, who is never attracted to him, and he represents nothing in the realm of ideas. But Moses is a forceful and elegant personality, with a strong if egocentric imagination, quick in learning and in the acquisition of Epicurean taste and savoir faire, a juggler of Machiavellian and cynical ideas of some penetration. While Itzig's chief intellectual accomplishment is to learn standard German and commercial correspondence, Freudenstein becomes a scholar of Semitic languages and aspires to a professorship. Despite his conversion to Catholicism and change of name, Moses does not hide his Jewishness but employs it, for example, in his seduction of the excessively emancipated Kleophea Götz, when he stresses the heroism and stoicism of the Jewish people (6: 264-65; cf. 271). Hans, who has been his protector against anti-Semitic rough-housing in his boyhood (another motif prefigured in *Debit and Credit*), feels an unrequited friendly attachment to him and has some difficulty arriving at a true assessment of his character—an aspect of the novel rather poorly handled by Raabe. In fact it is Hans's envy of Moses's humanistic education and Latin studies that impels him to rebellion against his destiny as a shoemaker (6: 63). The figure of Moses has absorbed some of the dexterity and mental sharpness of Freytag's other parallel figure, the renegade aristocrat Fink, who despite his need for some instruction in bourgeois ethics, rather overshadows the boring Anton Wohlfart, even in the narrative voice, in attractiveness and ultimate competence. It is Moses who, in the middle of the work, denominates Hans as the "hunger pastor" (6: 254), thus contributing a faint dimension of ironic distance. The suggestion has been ventured that Moses's demonically nihilistic nature and his sarcastic vengefulness represent a fraction of Raabe's own spirit.[22] I find this hard to accept, for Raabe goes to extremes in making him a villain, but his stature and role are certainly more imposing than Itzig's, and there is no doubt that he contributes to Hans's education.[23] Finally, Raabe disposes of him differently. Itzig, while being pursued by Anton, drowns, with more melodramatic than poetic justice, in the same place where he had originally drowned his mentor, the degenerate Gentile Hippus. Raabe had originally planned to have Moses shipwrecked and washed up on the hunger pastor's shore, to die in his arms, but wisely thought the better of it and let him live on, "civilly dead," perhaps, but nevertheless surviving as an image of the endurance of human evil in the world, which continues to balk the supersession of bourgeois values.

As in the case of Freytag, critics have from time to time attempted to mitigate the effect of this portrayal, for example, by pointing to the fact that Moses is a renegade Jew, not a representative one (a tack Raabe himself took in self-defense, as we shall see), or by citing the passages about the mistreatment of Jews, now fortunately in the past, and about Moses Mendelssohn's humiliations, passages clearly showing Raabe to have been a supporter of Jewish emancipation (6: 41, 47). But the case is not wholly persuasive and readers of the past were easily able to admire the portrayal as healthily anti-Semitic.[24] Repeatedly Moses's characteristics are identified as "Semitic": his intellectual quickness, seen as sophistry and Talmudic quibbling (6: 130); his unchildlike nature, even as a boy; his tendency to materialism; his vengefulness; the cynicism with which he turns Catholic and becomes a government agent, thus in both ways an enemy of the liberal, Protestant, progressive, bourgeois German; his rootless cosmopolitanism. It is a curious fact, however, that all of this diction is on the authorial level of narration; good Hans never employs it, even when he is at last obliged to turn against Moses. In one odd passage, Hans find himself on a train with some Eastern Jews in caftans, who, we are told, do not smell very agreeably, but Hans courteously converses with them in Hebrew (6: 364).[25] This distinction might give pause to a subtle reader, aware of the complexities of Raabe's narrative technique; nevertheless, the overall effect comports too well with what Mark Gelber has defined as "literary anti-Semitism," as distinct from authorial intention: "the potential or capacity of a text to encourage or positively evaluate anti-Semitic attitudes or behaviors."[26] Undoubtedly, at the center of the portrayal lies Raabe's nationalism. Moses himself has an interesting speech in which he talks of the freedom of Jews, who are Germans only insofar as it pleases them, passengers on the ship of liberalism, cosmopolitan adherents of the idea rather than the nation (6: 130). But, as strong as the nationalistic affect was in Raabe, elsewhere in his works it does not commonly overrun his deep sympathy with the fragility and sorrowfulness of the human condition, which in fact he expresses, perhaps somewhat uneasily, in the motto to *The Hunger Pastor*, from Sophocles's *Antigone*, line 523: "I cannot share in hatred, but in love" (6: 5).[27] How, then, did the literary anti-Semitism of *The Hunger Pastor* come into being?

The answer must lie in Raabe's struggle for acknowledgment by the public. As I imagine it, Raabe read *Debit and Credit* and observed its success, then said to himself quite rightly that if that was the sort of thing the public wanted, he could do it better.[28] I have suggested that Raabe, in his earlier phases, struggled to amalgamate his own voice with the kind of literature that others wrote and the public accepted. But this is the only time, as far as I can see, that he drew direct inspiration from a specific contemporary work. The result shows that it was a compromising mistake, for, perhaps subliminally, he drew into the undertaking some of the prejudices of a public with which, in his deepest instincts, he was out of harmony. The tension continues in the ambivalence of his subsequent estimation of the novel. At times he appeared to repudiate it as immature along with almost all of his earlier writing before he began to find his way to his own voice and form in the later 1860s; at other times, his longing for recognition made him more indulgent of a work that had contributed to his fame and saw thirty-four editions by the end of his life (6: 491-93). Walking a tightrope, he fell off into a trap, but that it was a trap was far from evident for a long time.

How enduring the tension remained appeared in an episode in 1903, when Raabe received a letter from a Jewish lady, Philippine Ullmann. She must have been quite elderly, for she begins with reminiscences of Raabe's family during his earliest childhood in Stadtoldendorf. Then she goes on to express her concern about the effect of *The Hunger Pastor*, asking whether in his long life he has never met a Jew with character.[29] In this connection there emerges a set of curious parallels and coincidences. For the same thing had happened to Dickens forty years earlier: he received a letter also from a Jewish lady, Eliza Davis, observing that the portrayal of Fagin in *Oliver Twist* "has encouraged a vile prejudice against the despised Hebrew," and rather pertly suggesting that Dickens atone with a charitable donation.[30] The repetition is not without significance, for it is well known that Raabe owed much to Dickens, and in fact he re-read *David Copperfield* while working on *The Hunger Pastor*; furthermore, it has long been established that *Debit and Credit* was structurally modelled on *David Copperfield*.[31] If, as I suppose, *Madame Salome* was meant to be some kind of compensation for *The Hunger Pastor*, this would constitute yet another parallel, to Dickens's creation of the kindly, upright Jew, Mr. Riah, in *Our Mutual Friend* as an antidote to Fagin in *Oliver Twist*. That the correspondence of Mrs. Davis and Dickens is virtually contemporaneous with the publication of *The Hunger Pastor* may be mentioned as a detail.

Dickens replied to Mrs. Davis that if the Jews feel wronged, "they are far less sensible, a far less just, and a far less good-tempered people than I have always supposed them to be." He defended himself on the grounds of realistic typology.[32] But his sense of justice must have been touched all the same, for he revised *Oliver Twist* to remove some of the direct references to Fagin's Jewishness.[33] Raabe, in his response, went even more on the offensive. He thanks Philippine Ullmann for her reminiscences of his boyhood milieu, but then his reply turns testy. He says it is the Jews' fault if they count the renegade Moses as one of their own, and adds that she seems to have an accidental acquaintance with his writings, calling her attention to *Madame Salome* and *Höxter and Corvey*. He denies that he is to be counted among anti-Semites and says that Jews have always been among his best friends and most appreciative readers.[34] Here his irritable obsession with neglect by the public rises to the surface again. He quite evaded the question that had been put to him, but one wonders whether it was completely settled in his own mind. When a rabbi raised it with him in 1902, asking whether Moses was meant to be a representative figure and apparently pointing to the rise of political anti-Semitism and the agitation of the Prussian court preacher Adolf Stöcker, Raabe replied with one of the rudest letters of his life.[35] However, it is also true that he made a spirited reply to a man who solicited an anti-Semitic novella from him in 1883. Here he rejects the anti-Semitic writings and illustrations sent to him, observing that he does not think they will do the Jews much harm and adding that Israel does no harm to the real German people. He is not a partisan writer, and, if he wrote *The Hunger Pastor*, he also wrote *Madame Salome*. He ends by firmly rejecting the request.[36] Perhaps the rise of anti-Semitism induced him to avoid Jewish characterizations altogether in his late works. He had originally intended to make the wise mentor in *Princess Fish* a Jewish bookbinder named Abraham Veigel, but decided to conflate the character with a non-Jewish one (15: 598). The name of the real-life biologist Ferdinand Cohn is changed to Kühn in *Pfister's Mill*, although the microorganism named for him, Cladothrix Cohn, remains unchanged (16: 91, 90). The narcissistic aesthete Albin Brokenkorb in *On the Scrap-Iron* was originally named Levin Bodenstaub, a name that need not be Jewish but might be (16: 584).

THE BURDEN placed on Raabe's reputation by the Raabe Society has already been adumbrated. It became especially burdensome when the anti-Semitic potential of the disciples burgeoned in the Nazi period. The Society's president, Franz Hahne, in his younger days had met Raabe, who insisted that he was in no way anti-Semitic, but Hahne would not believe him. Instead, he asked himself why Raabe had never "attacked the Jews" after *The Hunger Pastor* and guessed that the reason might have been his fear of Jewish power.[37] Needless to say, the Jewish members of the Raabe community had no role to play in this phase. Most striking is the case of Heinrich Spiero, a modestly talented but productive literary historian who met Raabe during the seventieth-birthday celebration in 1901 and subsequently devoted a third of a century of service to the cause. He became vice-president of the Raabe Society and was for many years president of the Berlin chapter. Among more than forty publications on Raabe, he wrote the first general biography, composed a lexicon of Raabe's cultural allusions, and edited an elaborate Festschrift for the hundredth anniversary of his birth in 1931.[38] Spiero was completely assimilated—loyal, patriotic, and conservative, perhaps, in his own way, racist: he once wrote of "Austria's sub-Germanic Danubian peoples."[39] In his memoirs, published in 1929, he does not refer to his Jewish origins with a single word, presenting himself as an active liberal Protestant; after World War I he was a member of a committee that tried without success to devise a progressive constitution for the Protestant Church.[40] His cultic loyalty to Raabe yielded to no one's: "to grow up in succession to him is a German task."[41] No matter; he was unceremoniously forced out when the Raabe Society was Aryanized.[42] In 1937 Fehse gave him a little kick when he was down by writing dismissively of his pioneering biography.[43] As far as I can see, only one Raabe enthusiast was sufficiently offended to make a gesture: Constantin Bauer, who resigned the editorship of the *Communications*.[44]

Obviously, it has been necessary to rescue Raabe from his own reception history on this front more than any other. The task, however, is not simple. The initial post-war amnesia of his traditional admirers falls far short of meeting the need. But standing his reputation on its head will not serve the purpose, either. For the reception history is not something that just *happened* to Raabe; he himself was involved in it for particular reasons that no one in the modern phase of Raabe scholarship has yet thought worthy of attention.

WHEN RAABE replied to Philippine Ullmann that, like our Lord
God, he let his light shine upon the just and the unjust,[45] he was not
turning a phrase. For one thing, he was tolerantly curious about the
new ideas of his time, without distinguishing those that in retrospect
appear ominous and odious to us. He noted in his diary that on April
29, 1893, he attended a lecture on Jews in art and science by a prominent anti-Semitic politician and propagandist, Paul Förster. He
showed a polite interest in the race theories of Gobineau, which were
pressed on him by his friends.[46] For another, not only were there
numerous Jews in his circle of acquaintance; there were also numerous
anti-Semites. It will be remembered that the Raabe Society grew out
of that circle of acquaintance, the clubby atmosphere of his entourage
in Braunschweig. It therefore had some reasonable claim to succession
and its members to special privileges as initiates. Both Fehse and
Hahne, along with others who participated in the Nazified phase, had
been in his circle. The author of the essay on Raabe and Hitler is
found among his correspondents in 1907. One surprising character
encountered here is Adolf Bartels, the popular, hysterically anti-Semitic literary historian who devoted some two dozen publications to a
campaign to destroy Heine's reputation; this is a bit odd, since Raabe's
admiration of Heine is now well established.[47] Perhaps one might
mention here also Raabe's encouragement of Gustav Frenssen's best-
selling novel *Jörn Uhl*.[48] While this novel is a work of some substance
that may owe something to Raabe's narrative ingenuity, and especially
in its dénouement does not wholly deserve the opprobrium of blood-
and-soil literature into which it has fallen, Frenssen did evolve into a
Nazi supporter of a particularly fatuous kind, judging from his memoirs.[49] The circumstance is striking because Raabe was normally very
chary of interest in and critical approval of the work of his German
literary contemporaries.

In the writings of the closest personal friend of his old age and the
real founder of the Society, Wilhelm Brandes, I do not find much of
an anti-Semitic nature, but there is one passage that shows how the
conservative ideological attitude of that class of men in those times
had become second nature: while attempting to distinguish Raabe's
humor from the liberal succession to Jean Paul, Brandes remarks on
"the Jewish wing of Young Germany."[50] What can this possibly
mean? None of the Young Germans was Jewish. Brandes mentions
Moritz Saphir and Adolf Glassbrenner, but the shallow satirist Saphir
had nothing to do with Young Germany, and the populist Glassbrenner, who in any case was not Jewish either, was at most on the periphery of the movement. It is a defamatory transference of the Jew-

ishness of the Young Germans' model figures, Heine and Börne, and a continuation of the influential critic Wolfgang Menzel's strategy in the 1830s of denouncing Young Germany as "Young Palestine." This strikes me as unfaithful to Raabe's origins and foundations. For, apart from his demonstrably positive relationship to Heine and hints that he was also an admirer of Börne, with the sarcastic and bitter tone of the innumerable political observations in his works he seems to me to preserve more of the Young German spirit than any other mid-century writer I know.[51] It is unfortunate that we do not know what he thought of the Dreyfus Case. We can only guess; Zola was the only Naturalist writer Raabe at all admired, and in his diary on February 23, 1898, he noted without comment Zola's sentence of one year in prison. It is in such matters that the taciturnity of the diary becomes most frustrating; he also noted without comment on November 22, 1880, the debate in the Prussian parliament on the petition, signed by a quarter of a million Germans, to abrogate the civil rights of Jews. However, since his political hero Bismarck was determined to quash the petition and succeeded in doing so, one may assume that Raabe agreed with him in this policy.

If the keepers of Raabe's reputation were guilty of a breach of faith in turning him into an anti-Semite and prophet of Nazism, he was not without complicity in it insofar as he welcomed such people into his fold. But I do not think this indicates a change in him, an accommodation on his part to the Wilhelminian ideological atmosphere. His ideological commitments and social views were formed early in life and thereafter changed some in form and perspective, but not very much in substance to the end of his days. Furthermore, we do not know what Raabe, in his innermost heart, thought of any of these people. The answer must lie again in his need for an audience. He made his light to shine upon the just and the unjust, as long as the just and the unjust were his readers and adherents. He repelled out-and-out anti-Semites who made demands upon him, but otherwise he did not subject his adherents to ideological tests. This tolerance was a product of his personal priorities and helps to account for the combination of pleasant conviviality and mild aloofness in his relations with his friends. This would explain Bartels, for example, who wrote positively of Raabe during the seventieth-birthday revival of 1901. But he not only sought popularity; he also feared it, and in this he was right also. Like many major writers, he was both of his time and out of phase with it. His desire for a public created dangers that I believe he sensed but did not fully grasp. As he did not see the extent to which he had trapped himself in his imitative excursion into the commonplace with *The Hunger Pastor*, so he was in no position to see the risk of imprisoning his reputation by encouraging a band of disciples who were not content to admire and enjoy, but who enhanced their own self-regard as a chosen people by grafting their more petty vision and their parochial preoccupations onto his supple, subtle, and questioning art. It is only just and realistic to recognize that he cannot be separated or isolated from the first phases of his twentieth-century reception, that his involvement in it was rooted in his own ambivalent but intense manner of coping with the threatening isolation and homelessness of the nineteenth-century bourgeois artist.

CHAPTER 8

Politics

◙

F ROM ONE vantage point, Raabe's political views were simple and
straightforward: he was a national liberal. This means that his
chief political concern was the unification of the German nation. Since
there appeared to be no feasible means of achieving this goal with the
inclusion of the multi-national Austrian empire, he was an adherent
of the *kleindeutsch* solution: unification without Austria. Since only
Prussia was strong enough to impose unity on the German states, he
was obliged to place his hopes in Prussian policy and power, and he
vigorously opposed all expressions of local patriotism and small-state
particularism. Since all populist and democratic efforts to unify the
nation had failed, in some degree ignominiously, while Bismarck's
shrewd and often ruthless policy succeeded, Raabe was an adherent
and admirer of Bismarck almost without reservation. As the whole
national-liberal position came to be, under the pressure of these loyalties, less liberal and more nationalistic, so also did Raabe, who
shared the conviction widespread in his class and generation of the
need to put a unified Germany first in all purposes and policies—the
true meaning of the often misunderstood first line of Hoffmann von
Fallersleben's "Deutschland, Deutschland über alles."

Raabe formed these attitudes early in his life and held to them unalterably, in the main, to the end of it. In 1859 a German National
Party began to form, demanding a revision of the constitution, a central government in place of the confederation, Prussian command over
all military forces and Prussian management of all German diplomatic
representation. Raabe joined this movement and attended its meetings
in Wolfenbüttel. In May 1860 he joined the National Association and
made two speeches in Wolfenbüttel. He attended the first convention
of the National Association in Coburg in 1860 and the second in Heidelberg in 1861.[1] At the time of the war with Denmark in 1863 he
distributed propaganda fliers in Stuttgart sent to him by his brother-
in-law.[2] When one considers his temperamental disinclination to appear in public or participate in large-scale collective activities, his activism in these matters is evidence of a very strong motivation indeed.

88

In later years, when the movement became the National Liberal Party, he always voted for its candidates.

In the disposition of his own emphases, probably the most prominent was his opposition to provincial particularism. He nourished a special dislike for the Kingdom of Hanover, which he saw as an ally of foreign powers in Germany, at times England—Hanover was in personal union with the British crown from 1714 to 1837—at other times France. The Hanover of his time under the reactionary King George V opposed national unity; Hanoverian supporters of the national movement were treated as rebels. In 1860 a Hanoverian minister threatened to employ troops of foreign nations to prevent national unification, an event that Raabe never forgot and is said to have been his immediate impetus for joining the National Association.[3] In his later years he refused to set foot in Hanover.[4] While the modern observer may find Raabe's dislike of Hanover understandable, it may be less easy to take his side in regard to his impatience with Swabian particularism, which in time made him unbearably uncomfortable in Stuttgart. For in Swabia the particularists tended to be democrats, while the nationalists were allied with conservatives. It is not surprising that the Catholic West regarded with some trepidation the prospect of the hegemony of Prussia, notorious for its aggressive, court-sponsored Protestantism, with which the Rhineland had already had painful experiences; nor that the Southwest, where embryonic democratic institutions had developed, looked upon Prussian authoritarianism without enthusiasm. Raabe was not unaware of such concerns, but he tended to brush them aside as symptoms of a petty, short-sighted egotism, perversely blocking the destiny of the German nation. Thus in him as in many of his generation, such democratic components as the liberal position may originally have contained came to be to a large extent dissolved in the obsession with national unity.

In the long view, his class attitudes may be seen to exhibit the same allegiances and undergo the same liberal evolution. His mentality shows many symptoms of petty-bourgeois consciousness and, in particular, an allegiance to the petty-bourgeois sub-caste, the educated professional men and officials, who were, in a sense, outside the commercial and increasingly capitalist economy and whom he was not alone in regarding as the salt of the earth and the backbone of the nation. It is they, along with artisans and certain types of bohemian outcasts, who constitute for Raabe the "people"; the touchstone usually being a certain amount of cultural literateness. The "people" are distinguished, of course, from the oppressive nobility, and also from the members of polite society—in *On the Scrap-Iron* those who attend aesthetic lectures do not identify themselves with the "people" but with the "world," generally a pejorative term for Raabe (16: 347). But the "people" are also distinguished from the mob, the unreliable, threatening, morally and nationally homeless underclass. In a poem entitled "Royal Oath," an angry gloss on King George V's lawless breach of the Hanoverian constitution in 1855, the lines occur:

> The plebeians he could doubtless buy with gold,
> The people he cannot move with gold! (20: 358)

The root of the position is a fierce, in its initial stages, revolutionary opposition to the neo-feudal nobility. Raabe pursued this class conflict in a wide variety of forms. There is the conventional melodrama of the maiden seduced and ruined by the irresponsible aristocrat, for example in *The Chronicle of Sparrow Alley, Who Can Change it?*, and *After the Great War*; it is picked up again, with more subtlety and finesse, in *The Rumbledump*. Lieutenant Kind in *Abu Telfan*, who despite his rank sees himself as proletarian, breaks out into hysterical rage when his daughter is violated and threatens bloody revenge against a depraved nobleman (7: 327-28). In Raabe's historical fiction the nobility does not, generally speaking, play a very positive role. The Duke of Mecklenburg in *Our Lord God's Chancellory*, who spares the brutish mercenaries captured in battle against him but gives no quarter to bourgeois and peasants, is referred to as the "Ducal good-for-nothing" (4: 267), and Duke Moritz of Saxony in the same work exhibits the failing Raabe often ascribed to the feudal nobility: the inclination to make alliances with foreign powers such as France against internal German enemies (4: 471). Sometimes he takes the historical role of the nobility more from the satirical side; in *Gutmann's Travels* he alludes to the absurd "Wasungen War" of 1747-48, caused by a quarrel over precedence between two court ladies in Meiningen and Gotha (18: 244). More often he sees the nobility as a class in decline, displaced or survived by more vital classes. In *Christoph Pechlin* the narrator is pleased to see peasant dwellings around Hohenstaufen Castle, for they show that the peasants outlived those who looked down on them, while the castle is ruined and the mighty princes are scattered (10: 271). In *Old Nests*, the narrator observes how valuable it is that the land is no longer in large domains but in the hands of peasants and petty-bourgeois (14: 14); Just Everstein, from a family branch that had lost its nobility, becomes the successor to the estate not as a lord but as a modern farmer. The awareness of aristocratic decline is internalized in Juliane von Poppen in *The People from the Forest*. She is a class oddity by reason of her intelligence and ironic distance; though not without aristocratic traits herself, as shown in her treatment of her poor friend Ulex, whom she protects but also patronizes in a master-servant relationship, she sees with considerable bitterness that her clan is perishing not from hatred but from contempt. By its own conduct the aristocracy is causing itself to be laughed out of existence.

German liberals typically made a distinction between aristocracy and monarchy. While they yearned to displace the aristocracy as the dominant class in the life of the nation, they also hoped for a mutually supportive alliance with the crown, and certainly the majority of them preferred monarchy, constitutional or otherwise, to republicanism. This seems to have been, on the whole, Raabe's view also, especially after the formation of the German Reich. He regarded Kaiser Wilhelm I with genuine admiration. I have been puzzled by my inability to find any comment on the ill-fated Kaiser Friedrich III, who was looked to by many liberals with great though possibly illusory hopefulness. In his diary on April 16, 1888, Raabe noted Friedrich III's worsening condition and on June 15 entered his death, but otherwise he made no mention of him. It is curious that the events of the "Three-Kaiser-Year"—the death of Wilhelm I, the ninety-nine-day reign of the cancer-ridden Friedrich III, and the accession of Wilhelm II—which seemed of significant and perhaps ominous portent to many observers, are nowhere referred to in Raabe's correspondence with Jensen throughout 1888. Raabe was prepared to admire Wilhelm II, though he was worried by the neurotic Kaiser's policies and character,[5] and these worries might well have increased if Raabe had lived another five years.

Toward the princes and rulers of the past he was considerably less tolerant. In his diary on January 2, 1861, he noted with more accuracy than respect the death of King Friedrich Wilhelm IV "in imbecility"; perhaps he had the mentally deranged Prussian king in mind when, in the poem he wrote for his admission to his Stuttgart club, he described the mad King George III of England riding to Bedlam (20: 390-92). In *The Lar* there is a passing reference to an anecdote in which a grenadier on the battlefield of Kunersdorf growls to Frederick the Great: "for six thruppence a day this is enough for one day, Fritz" (17: 301). Such anecdotes were, of course, part of the Friderician legend, but Raabe does not seem to have been very susceptible to it. He once pronounced Frederick the Great to have been "effeminate"—by which he probably meant Frenchified—and a bad fellow, and added that the Dukes of Braunschweig were also bad fellows.[6] Raabe was anxious, as he put it, not to appear as "the boot-polisher of the hereditary dynasty" of Braunschweig.[7] As we shall see, in *The Odin Field* he drew a sympathetically nuanced portrait of Duke Ferdinand of Braunschweig. But the intelligent, cultured Ferdinand was never a ruling duke. Raabe took a different view of his reigning nephew, Duke Karl Wilhelm Ferdinand, whose egregious performance during the disastrous Prussian-Austrian invasion of revolutionary France in 1792 Goethe, with poker-faced deference, had so ruthlessly exposed in *The Campaign in France*. Raabe made reference to that debacle in *The Chronicle*, where an old veteran of the campaign reminisces about his experiences "in foreign Frenchland, where the people had grown tired of oppression and noble rule and made a clean sweep," until the "Duke of Braunschweig and the Prussians and all had to retreat through filth and rain" (1: 44). Unlike some other writers of historical fiction in his time, Raabe was not inclined to transfigure the feudal and absolutist past into a heroic age or to see its crowned heads as much more than a plague on mankind.

There can be little doubt that, in the course of time, he came to share the hostility of his class and party to the organized working class. While he did not make a major issue of it, his antipathy to the Social Democrats is plain in both public and private utterances. In his diary he noted the publication of the laws against the Social Democrats on May 20, 1878, and their passage on October 19; while he made no comment on this policy, it is quite likely that he supported it (he also noted the expiration of the laws on October 1, 1890). In 1905 he hesitantly permitted his name to be added to an appeal for clemency for the imprisoned Maxim Gorky, but he added that the imprisonment of the treasonable Social Democrats at the time of the Franco-Prussian War had been quite proper.[8] In 1909 he was pleased at a centenary celebration of the "Black Corps" of Napoleonic times, remarking: "With the state of the future and the 'people's army' of Social Democracy there is nothing doing for the time being."[9] The previous year he had received a letter from Clara Zetkin, one of the most radical of the socialist activists, that must have baffled him somewhat: Zetkin informed him that she had printed a chapter of *The Hunger Pastor* in a working women's journal, *Equality*, the purpose of which was "to cultivate and educate the female readers of the magazine artistically and purely humanly"; she wanted to give the poorest of the poor only the best, to which Raabe belongs. This communication must have put his usual civility to all admirers to a severe test, for his reply is uncommonly strained. He states that he has no desire to aid the Social Democratic state of the future but has no objection to being read in that camp, and adds a little discourteously that Zetkin's praise is as welcome as any "from the highest social positions or out of the blackest womb of the Church—it is all the same!" The main thing in his life, he continues, was to be a friend and consoler of the weary and burdened of all classes, and he disclaims any "democratic attitude of the artist."[10]

Like many people of his time, he distinguished the poor from the "mob," and in all probability he distinguished both from the Social Democratic Party, which I imagine he saw as an unpatriotic force threatening the laboriously achieved unity of the nation. Certainly he exhibits his awareness of the poor and compassion for them in many places. It may be true that there is a certain Dickensian sentimentality in some of the depictions of the poor in his early works; it is likely that the exploitative dressmaker's shop in *One Springtime* came straight out of *Nicholas Nickleby*. Sentimentality blocks the effect of the prophecy in *One Springtime* of proletarian revolution as a flood to come: the narrator prays that God may hover over the workers, and when the proletarian children desist from stealing anything in the singer Alida's luxurious room, it is taken as a sign that the flood will not come (1: 257, 266). Nevertheless, Raabe's depiction of the poor is not without a political dimension. In that same novel it is said that it is better to be a washerwoman than a reactionary aristocrat like Hagenheim (1: 376), and the grievously hard life of a washerwoman is made plain enough in the account of the protagonist's mother in *The Hunger Pastor* (6: 20-21). Poverty and ignorance, Eva Dornbluth of *The People from the Forest* notes, can kill the spirit (5: 108).[11] In *The Children of Finkenrode* a jail is defined as a place where the poor are locked up (2: 105); in a number of places in Raabe's works jails and prisons appear as gloomy loci of the repressive force of authority. Even the rather shallow Mathilde Sonntag in *Three Pens* remarks on the intimidating presence of the police, watching for "political criminals" (9/1: 327-28), while in *Abu Telfan* a policeman is described as a well-fed "messenger of the daughter of Erebus and the night," that is, Nemesis (7: 201).

The *Hunger Pastor*, for all its failings, contains some of Raabe's most explicit social criticism. Hans Unwirrsch's tutorial positions constitute a journey of the impecunious educated man through the levels of society and property: the landed gentry, the boorish capitalist industrialist, the parasitical urban nobility. In the second of these positions Hans witnesses a strike and loses his position because of his sympathy with the workers; he recognizes that he himself has been proletarianized (6: 177). Many of Raabe's most admirable characters come from the underclass, such as the streetwalker Little Red Riding Hood in *On the Scrap-Iron*, who exhibits impressive efficiency in an emergency, or the stubbornly brave sutler-woman Wackerhahn in *Hastenbeck*. Understandably, however, his most eloquent outrage is reserved for the oppression of the educated man of his own class, the teacher in a school for the poor. This passage from *The Hunger Pastor* is worth quoting at length because it reflects precisely the policy of the time of inhibiting the education of the poor in order to keep them in their place:

> In a dark dead-end, in a one-storey building that had once served as a fire station, the commune had set up the school for its poor, after it had refused as long as possible to give up any place for so superfluous a purpose. It was a damp hole; at almost every time of year the water ran from the walls; fungi and mushrooms grew in the corners and under the teacher's desk. Tables and benches were sticky-wet and covered with a light layer of mould during the vacations. Of the windows we would rather not speak; it was no wonder that the most interesting fungoid shapes formed themselves near to them. It was also no wonder that the loveliest gouty concretions formed in the hands and feet of the teacher and the most magnificent tubercles in his lungs. It was no wonder that from time to time half the school was ill with fever. If the commune had been obliged to put a marble monument on every child's grave for which it was to blame, it would have very soon arranged for another school location.
>
> Karl Silberlöffel was the teacher's signature on the receipts for the stupendous sums of money that the state paid him quarterly. Alas, the poor man bore his name ["Silverspoon"] only for the sake of irony; he had not been born with a silver spoon in his mouth. He might have given the ministry of culture much to think about if this honorable and most meritorious authority were not distracted by more important things. How can the high authorities concern themselves about the teacher Silberlöffel when the question still has not been solved: what minimum of knowledge may be permitted to the lowest levels of society without causing damage and inconvenience to the highest? For a long time the gentlemen charged with the solution of this question will regard the elementary schoolteachers as their enemies and would consider it a most preposterous and ridiculous demand if malevolent, revolutionary idealists were to require that even a high ministry might do good to its enemies and at least clothe them decently and feed them minimally. Oh, good old days, when mankind passed from the hand of one drill-sergeant into that of

another! Oh, good old days, when not only the army was subject
to the corporal's rod! (6: 30-31)

Raabe understood perfectly well that this combination of poverty and
repression was driving potentially useful and productive citizens to
emigration to America, and he repeatedly points to this circumstance
in his early works.

This may be the place for a brief digression on his view of America,
since it has been seriously misrepresented in the reception history by
resentful post-World-War-I nationalists and Nazi sympathizers, who
would have us believe that Raabe despised America as the crude land
of mammon. The evidence for this is normally restricted to the figure
of the rich, dubious businessman Charles Trotzendorff in *The Documents of the Birdsong*. But he represents only one facet of Raabe's image
of and long-standing interest in America. During the course of his life
he had numerous American connections, personal and epistolary. Like
many Germans he followed the course of the Civil War with concerned attention. In his diary on April 26, 1865, he noted with emphasis the assassination of Abraham Lincoln, and in the same year we
find him celebrating the Fourth of July with his Stuttgart friends, a
festivity doubtless connected with the gratifying conclusion of the
Civil War. For Raabe, America was in the first instance a place of
refuge from oppressive conditions in Germany. In the *Chronicle* "they"
force the schoolteacher Roder into American exile because "they" are
afraid of him (1: 122); whole families emigrate, not out of Germanic
wanderlust but out of "destitution, misery, and pressure" (1: 166). *The
People from the Forest* brings a scene of Germans who are in St. Louis
because they could not stand the "illustrious German Confederation."
In their tavern, instead of the required portraits of "potentates," there
is a picture of the revolutionary martyr Robert Blum decorated with
flowers by the innkeeper, which, as the narrator ironically notes,
"gave evidence of a very bad heart and highly depraved political
views" (5: 380-81). When Just Everstein in *Old Nests* returns from his
experiences as an American farmer, he holds his head higher, and the
narrator wonders how long the German people need a drill-sergeant
hitting them under the chin to make them stand straight (14: 100).

All the same, it would be a mistake to portray Raabe as a radical
democrat or, like some over-zealous admirers today, as a "left-intellec-
tual."[12] Often when he perceives the underclass as a mass, it appears
as a threatening, barbaric force. While the sixteenth-century Catholic-
Protestant conflict in *Our Lord God's Chancellory* is perceived as a class
war of bourgeoisie versus aristocracy, the lowest classes in the town

appear as an unreliable mob and the peasants outside are unmilitary and cowardly. A century later, the common people in *Elsa of the Fir* are dull, suspicious, superstitious, and eventually murderous in their "animalistic stultification" (9/1: 163). In modern times this seems not to have changed much; the miners in *Madame Salome* are much like the peasants in *Elsa*: hostile, threatening, allied with the underground forces of darkness and irrationality, ready to seek a scapegoat in a young girl suspected of witchcraft. In *Master Author*, cruel and selfish peasants drive a helpless, destitute old woman out of the village and abandon her in open country (11: 88-89); in *Horacker* the peasants appear stolid, balky, stubbornly conservative out of malevolence, and lacking in charity in comparison with the middle-class characters; in *Restless Guests* the mountain people are primitive, ungenerous, rather loutish. These are the perceptions, as "realistic" as they may be, of a bourgeois class consciousness.

Whoever cannot live with such things will not be able to live with much nineteenth-century fiction. More grating to the modern reader may well be Raabe's obtrusive nationalism and the insistence with which he links it to a Bismarckian allegiance. In this he seems to follow all too obediently the ideological development of his class, which sacrificed equality to an elitist individualism and downgraded social emancipation.[13] He numbered himself among "that tough generation that founded the new German Reich."[14] Indeed, his nationalism seems to have grown stronger toward the end of his life, perhaps reflecting the atmosphere portending the World War, which Raabe appears to have foreseen (E 4: 190). In 1909 we find him eulogizing the fanatically patriotic, formally regressive playwright Ernst von Wildenbruch as a "loyal *German* man."[15] He seems to have become more Bismarckian as he got older, especially after Bismarck was forced out of public life. The refusal of the Reichstag to send Bismarck greetings on his eightieth birthday embittered Raabe; he attributed it to the dominance of the Catholic Center Party, "the cold Jesuit fist at the throat of noble mother Germania."[16] He came to see the traditional enemy of liberty, the Catholic Church, in perverse alliance with the modern enemies, the socialists. The Reichstag of 1906, with its alliance of the Center Party and the Social Democrats, he characterized as a "socialist priest's whore" (E 4: 236). The victory of Prussia over Austria in 1866 was one of the most exhilarating moments of his life; on July 3, 1866, he entered into his diary with great emphasis the Prussian victory at Königgrätz and Sadowa. He began to long for war with France; to his mother he wrote in 1868, "War! War! nothing but a new and improved edition of the year sixty-six could now cheer me a little," and in his last letter from Stuttgart: "Here great enthusiasm. All partisan humbug at an end. War to the knife against the French."[17] The diary entry for July 15, 1870 reads: *"War between France and Germany!"* Now the despised Swabian particularists would be taught a lesson: "for *we we* will have the last word."[18]

Anti-French gestures, with their customary historical resentments, were a natural accompaniment to these views. In *Cloister Lugau* Napoleon is referred to as an "adventuring military hooligan" with "his stupid gangs" (19: 12). Late in life, while reading the diaries of Joseph von Eichendorff, of all people, Raabe was disturbed by what he felt to be an unpatriotic admiration for France in them, and added that Napoleon had been a blessing to cure this.[19] French allegiances frequently serve for negative characterization of Raabe's figures. We have already mentioned the malevolent, Frenchified Jew Freudenstein in *The Hunger Pastor*; military service on the French side also belongs to the reprehensible characteristics of the cavalry captain Grünhage in *The Horn of Wanza*, who ends up in association with lumpen-revolutionaries. Numerous other examples could be cited.

There is no profit in attempting to repress this very pronounced aspect of Raabe's personality, which played a large role in his reception history. Doubtless we should not forget the contribution such attitudes made to subsequent catastrophes; at the same time it is well to seek a perspective that will help us understand why he viewed the world as he did. It is of the first importance to remember that our perception of Germany in this century as a militaristically aggressive and brutal power bears no resemblance to the Germany that he perceived. His Germany was all but imaginary, weak and splintered, socially and politically a laughingstock among the nations. At the same time it was frustrating that German *culture* was the most admired in the world. When, in *The Children of Finkenrode*, a man awakening from long years of madness asks how it is with Germany, he is told it is as it was: Germany keeps school for the nations, while the suffering German people mark time in place, incapable of being one great nation (2: 196). The desire to bring the prestige of Germany as a nation-state into consonance with its prestige as the "land of poets and thinkers" was very deeply felt in the nineteenth century.

From Raabe's point of view this weakness had two particularly distressing features. There was first of all the centuries-old tendency of the Germans to engage in intermittent but constantly recurring civil war. A tavern brawl in *Christoph Pechlin*, in which no one has any idea why he is fighting, is explicitly associated with this perpetual self-laceration (10: 325-26). All of this conflict and slaughter in Raabe's view has been in the interest not of the German people but of feudal despots and foreign powers. This leads us to his second complaint: that Germany was a place where foreigners had their wars, while Germans were employed to fight for the interests of others rather than their own. In *Lorenz Scheibenhart*, whose title figure shoots his own friend in battle, it is said that wherever there is a war—in Italy, Poland, or America—one hears German curses (2: 327). The squandering of German energies and blood for foreign interests is a constantly reiterated theme in Raabe's historical fiction. We may usefully remember that he was old enough to have distinct historical memories of the tendency of German princes to finance themselves by the sale of troops to foreign powers, among whom the notorious "Hessians" in the American Revolution were but one example. Historical memories also account for his anti-French affect. Again we must remember that in the historical record he surveyed, France, not Germany, was the perpetual aggressor nation. Early in his last completed work, the historical novel *Hastenbeck*, the narrator observes wearily: "The French were, as usual, in the land" (20: 11). In *Gutmann's Travels*, set in 1860, a young man explains to the girl he is courting: "All the peoples around form themselves into fists, and our so-called German fatherland is lying there like an open hand with its fingers spread" (18: 338). As we know, this German tendency to self-pity was retained long after the complaint of powerlessness was obsolete, and sometimes combined with arrogance and aggressiveness in a most distasteful way. Raabe may well have begun to realize this, for he has young Gutmann talk himself into a rage about drawing blood with the German fist from the nations round about: "Yes, yes, blood, blood, blood, dear miss!" (ibid.). This passage has sometimes been lifted out of context by Raabe's chauvinist admirers, but in fact it is comic exaggeration on the part of an amiable but confused and politically unfocused young man.

Raabe's consciousness of recent German history was segmented by three significant dates: 1813, 1830, and 1848. For him, as for most of his generation, the anti-Napoleonic Wars of Liberation had given birth to the national spirit in its activist form. It has been pointed out that a fictional character's past in the uprising of 1813 is the "ever recurring touchstone of upright and inwardly free humanity."[20] But the German people were swindled out of their victory by the neo-feudal governments with the support of organized religion. Raabe never ceased to regard these governments with contempt. In Chapter 13 of *Abu Telfan* there is an ironic history of the principality in which it takes place, unnamed "in true Germanic modesty." "We live in the most romantic

Middle Ages; the swinishness is great, but the hereditary princely house thrives splendidly. . . . Viva Carolus, Fridericus, or something like that!"—and a couple of chapters later the narrator predicts the day when there will be no more such places, but a United States of Europe, for a republic is "a happy and truly normal condition" (7: 128, 130-33, 151). The irony becomes slapstick satire in *Owls' Pentecost*, where one of the main characters serves a principality whose name the narrator cannot remember and whose capital is "Zerotimeszeroburg" or, more simply, "0x0burg" (11: 359, 360).

But Raabe's joking, as usual, is but another way of dealing with serious matters. In a précis of recent history in *The People from the Forest* it is observed that after the Congress of Vienna the people were ordered to praise God, but God saw that it was not good (5: 84). Raabe constantly alludes to the oppression and shrewdly measured terror of the Metternichian period. In *Abu Telfan*, for example, one character is an embittered victim of the Carlsbad Decrees of 1819, and it has been suggested that Raabe was here thinking of the Low German writer Fritz Reuter, who, in consequence of the Decrees was sentenced to death for activity in a student fraternity, a sentence then commuted to a long prison term (7: 47, 417). The main thrust of the Carlsbad Decrees, as of other measures taken intermittently after them, was to throttle freedom of the press, the civil right most important to writers and intellectuals. Raabe put the issue into a historical context in *Our Lord God's Chancellory*, where Magdeburg appears as the publishing center of the Reformation and therefore of liberty and progress. On the day the citizens go out to attack their besiegers, an old printer addresses his presses, which are the real weapons; the little black marks are invincible (4: 241). All peoples and potentates listen to the printed word of the beleaguered city (4: 324).

One episode in *The Chronicle of Sparrow Alley* is particularly telling in its artistic formation: the narration of the widow Karsten, who tells of her husband's patient confidence that the Napoleonic occupation of Berlin would not endure; he raises his sons in a spirit of resistance and stoically accepts their death in the war, which is commemorated by a plaque in the church. Another writer, especially one of nationalistic commitments, might have ended the tale here. But it is not finished; in the course of time, Karsten more and more avoids looking at the plaque. When lightning strikes the church, Karsten does not lift a finger to fight the fire, and when the church burns down, destroying the plaque, Karsten is relieved: "Mother, praise God, the plaque is burned! Mother, I couldn't look at it any more!" (1: 103). Widow Karsten professes not to have understood her husband's meaning, but every reader in Raabe's time would have, and we must also: the spirit of 1813 has been betrayed, the sacrifice has been in vain, bitterness has infected loyalty to the dominant institutions.

While the Revolution of 1830 in France had relatively little impact on the well-carpentered Metternichian system, the greatest upheaval took place in Raabe's own Braunschweig, where the duke, the most detested of German princes for his rapacity and megalomania, was driven from the throne. It is obviously significant that, in *The Hunger Pastor*, Hans's rebellion against his family's assumption that he will be made a shoemaker occurs simultaneously with the Revolution of 1830. Of the reactionary past of the elder Hagenheim in *One Springtime* it is said that he fought the most terrible of fights, that against his own times (1: 347). How enduringly the atmosphere of these times remained in Raabe's consciousness is illustrated by an, in itself, trivial incident that occurred late in his life. He got into a quarrel with a friend; this is fairly remarkable, as Raabe very rarely quarreled with his friends. The friend had supported the effort of the legitimist, younger Welf line to be restored to the throne of Hanover against Prussian opposition. Raabe's dislike of Hanover has already been pointed out, but when, in a letter of reconciliation, he explained the reasons for his pugnaciousness, he put at the head of the list: "In my youth the echo of the year of the Göttingen Seven still reverberated."[21] The affair of the Göttingen Seven, when seven professors, including the Brothers Grimm, the historian Dahlmann, and the literary historian Gervinus, were dismissed for having protested the abrogation of the constitution by King Ernst August of Hanover, occurred in 1837, fifty-nine years earlier, when Raabe was six years old. Nevertheless it was still fresh in his memory in 1896.

In *The Children of Finkenrode* there is the story of Weitenweber's father, employed as a semaphore operator, who is so dismayed by the messages of the governments that he refuses to transmit them and loses his job. The image of these "devilments" of the Metternichian Confederation transmitted above and beyond the ken of the peaceful citizens below is especially ingenious (2: 177). However, Raabe also shows us cases of liberals ground into conformity under the authoritarian system. One such is the editor Wimmer in the *Chronicle*, who by 1841 has "sweated out the embarrassing political cough" and settled into philistine domesticity (1: 117-22). The theme recurs in *The People from the Forest*, where it is observed in connection with Alexander Mietze how open, frank, anti-authoritarian spirits are normally ground down and turned into what are regarded as good officials: "slow, cow-

ering to those above, autocratic, tyrannical, cantankerous to those below" (2: 36).

As for 1848, Georg Lukács complained that Raabe did not employ
the revolution as a model for the future.[22] It is true that nowhere in
his works is there an elaborated scene of the revolution, of which
Raabe himself witnessed very little, though we shall see in a later
chapter that it appears in a dream in the last, fragmentary novel *Altershausen*. The observation has been made that *The People from the Forest*, which covers that period, avoids the revolution entirely.[23] But this
silence is eloquent; it communicates a feeling of futility, even of embarrassment. Hoppe observed that the "will to life" of Raabe's whole
generation was lamed by the reactionary victory over the revolution.[24]
On Philipp Kristeller's wall in *At the Sign of the Wild Man* a print of
Dürer's *Melencolia* hangs between two 1848 street scenes (11: 166).
This and other references indicate that the painful episode was permanently in Raabe's mind. In 1863 he attended a banquet in Stuttgart
in memory of the ill-fated Frankfurt constitution of 1849,[25] and an
emphatic diary entry on February 24, 1898—"N.B. 50 years ago!"—
can only refer to the outbreak of the revolution in France. With *German Moonshine* (1873), written soon after the establishment of the new
Reich, Raabe composed a rather weird parable of the events of 1848:
an otherwise sober official is attacked by the moon in 1848 and within
a year he is filled with disgust at things and personalities he used to
revere; he becomes dissatisfied with the way he is treated and begins
to read liberal writers and poets. Even worse, he begins to write dis-
sident verse himself. The more grotesque than humorous tale welds
together the depressed post-1848 mood with an image—the moonshine—of German insubstantiality and free-floating idealism along
with the flight into the impotence of poetry.

In contemplation of this rather ignominious record, Raabe, like
many of his contemporaries, became unalterably persuaded that the
only hope for liberal institutions of a dignity corresponding to the
prestige of German culture in the world was the pursuit of national
unity under Prussian leadership. Prussia was the largest, the strongest,
the best educated, and in some ways the most advanced of the German
states, with a tradition of the Enlightenment and a historical phase of
liberal reform at the time of the Napoleonic Wars that rendered it in
the eyes of many observers of the time potentially less reactionary
than Austria.[26] After the Prussian victory over Austria of 1866,
Raabe's wife wrote to her brother, the people would be on top, Bismarck and the feudal party would have to yield, and the hegemony of
the large landowners would come to an end.[27] Raabe may not have

taken quite the same view of the matter, but he certainly was no breathless admirer of Prussia. What he thought of the Prussian "new man" we shall see later on when we look more closely at *Horacker*. In one of the verbatim political speeches cited in *Gutmann's Travels*, the liberal politician Hermann Schulze-Delitzsch asserts: "The victory of the national movement in Germany is at the same time the victory of the humanitarian cause—and that is the final goal of all history" (18: 299). Not long afterwards the young Gutmann admires his father's political enthusiasm and joyfulness; without these qualities he would not like to be subordinated to "Prussia's dry, sober sovereignty" (18: 300-1). When one delegate asserts that the convention is not giving homage to Prussia's military or even the present king [the mentally unstable Friedrich Wilhelm IV], but to the state of Frederick the Great and the liberal reformer Baron vom Stein, he gains "stormy applause" (18: 355). The late historical novel *Hastenbeck* bears a motto from Baron vom Stein: "I have only one fatherland, that is Germany" (20: 6), an assertion Stein made to defend himself against the imputation of serving only Prussian interests.

Undoubtedly there is a certain amount of wishful thinking in these attitudes and a certain amount of passive conservative drift. Nevertheless, when the founding of the nation did at last succeed, Raabe was rather less edified by the result than he had hoped to be. The new Reich was governed not by the spirit of Goethe and Schiller and humanistic philosophy, but by a frenzy of long deferred and frustrated economic development. Raabe discovered that nationalist feeling has more meaning when the project of nation-building still lies in the future, less when it has been accomplished and the nation settles into its political and social routine. In 1895 he wrote to Marie Jensen: "It was, after all, good to live at the foot of the Hasenberg [in Stuttgart] when we were still young and had the German Reich still before us!"[28] A decade earlier he had written to the equally dissatisfied Jensen: "I for my part already warned you in 1870 not to praise our nation too much. . . . On holidays we are certainly not better than other peoples and on workdays definitely not."[29] A decade before that, in 1875, he complained to Paul Heyse about the megalomania going around in the German people.[30] One of Raabe's most unappetizing figures, the sneaky social-climber Eckbert Scriewer in *Cloister Lugau*, becomes a major public figure during the Franco-Prussian War, after which he is likely to be elected to the Reichstag (19: 207). Raabe's most often quoted comment in this vein is in the preface to the second edition of *Christoph Pechlin* in 1890:

The wounds of the heroes had not yet scarred, the tears of the children, the mothers, the wives, the fiancées and sisters had not yet dried, the graves of the fallen were not yet green: but in Germany—so soon after the terrible war and difficult victory— quite strange things began to happen. As during or after a great fire a barrel of sirup bursts in the street and the mob and the urchins begin to lick, so among the German people the money bag had opened, and the talers rolled in the gutters, and only too many hands grabbed for them. It almost seemed that this would be the greatest benefit that the united fatherland could obtain from its great success in world history!

What remained to the lonely poet in his anxiety and disgust, in his unnoticed corner, than to escape into dry jesting, into quite unsentimental amusement, to pull the fool's cap over his ears and take the harlequin's sword in hand?

Moreover, it has always been the privilege of decent people in dubious times to play the fool for themselves rather than to be louts among louts in society at large. (10: 205)

The passage will serve to remind us that the often castigated withdrawal of German writers from public action need not be a matter of indifferent introversion; as likely as not, it proceeds from political disappointment and disgust.

Sometimes his habit of rather drastic expression led him into what appear to be self-contradictions but are probably more justly seen as evidence of his capacity to see things from several sides. It is interesting to observe that he expressed his nationalist sentiments more bluntly in his private utterances than in his fiction, and this at a time when many authors, including his friend Jensen, were beating the nationalist drum vigorously. For one thing, as we shall see in connection with his historical fiction, Raabe never forgot the cost of war, and there is a great deal less celebration of Prussian and German victories in his fiction than one might expect. The schoolteacher Eckerbusch in *Horacker* broods sorrowfully about his former pupils who have fallen in the 1866 war (12: 297). In *Villa Schönow* we see a young man who for years has been slowly dying from his wounds in the Franco-Prussian War. The text that deals most directly with that war, *German Nobility*, is very subdued in tone. Its perspective is not on the battlefield but on the worried home front, and the soldier is not a hero but lies wounded in a hospital, where he makes friends with a dying Frenchman next to him.

It cannot be stressed enough that Raabe did not translate his historical bitterness at French oppression and ravages in Germany or even his gratification at the victory of 1871 into hostility to the French people. He always carefully distinguished his attitudes toward institutions and collectives from his attitudes toward individuals and ordinary folk. He resisted the imputation that he hated the French and made fun of the notion of the "hereditary enemy" (12: 270); he admired Voltaire, whose outrageous farce *La Pucelle*, which had so pained Schiller that it inspired him to his tragedy celebrating Joan of Arc, was one of Raabe's favorite books. In his early short story *A Secret* he comments on the degeneration of the French nation at the end of the reign of Louis XIV, when it imagined itself the first nation of the world; but not long afterwards there is a passage on the past glories of French culture, especially Molière, "the good fighter against stupidity, hypocrisy, superstition, and vice" (3: 350, 368-69). It rains in France as it does in Germany, observes one character in *Fabian and Sebastian*, and just as the French have helped the Germans to their new Reich, so the Germans have helped the French to their new republic (15: 138-39). To Edouard de Morsier, who had written a study of Raabe in French that he privately thought rather naive, Raabe nevertheless wrote that it would be appreciated in Germany as an act of international understanding: "May good fortune keep the two races from their next conflict as long as possible."[31] On the whole, he tried, perhaps incompletely and unsuccessfully, to reconcile his nationalism with the cosmopolitanism of the Goethean age. In one of his early poems, "Songs of the Peoples," the international song swells to a chorus of freedom washing away tears and blood (20: 404-5), and elsewhere he appealed for a sense of national worth without anti-French chauvinism.[32] He prided himself that he had named each of his daughters from a different culture: Margarethe (Greek); Elisabeth (Hebrew); Klara (Latin); and Gertrud (Germanic).[33]

Although Raabe was a nationalist, there is good reason to believe that he was not an imperialist and that he regarded colonial ambitions with a skeptical eye. The futility of colonialism is exhibited in one of the bleakest of all of his works, the historical novella *St. Thomas* (1866), the setting of which is a struggle between the Spanish and the Dutch over the island of Saõ Tomé at the end of the sixteenth century. The natives are gratified by the mutual destruction of the foreigners; at the end they dance in joy on the walls of the besieged city, attack it, and kill the commander.[34] In later years Raabe rather laughed at Gustav Frenssen's notion that Romantic German softness was hindering colonial enterprises.[35] In his diary entries he followed the rebellion of the Boers in South Africa closely; he was very sympathetic to the

Boers and prided himself on having been the first to bring them into literature (in *Stuffcake*), adding that he had always been a *Realpolitiker* since Bismarck's early struggles.[36]

It is characteristic of him that, while he was hostile to Social Democracy, he was not necessarily hostile to Social Democrats, some of whom he counted among his best friends, and he pointed out that socialists wrote him from prison that his works were their only consolation (E 4: 179). Undoubtedly he had a substantial working-class readership. On his death he was attacked in a socialist magazine as a dangerous anodyne for the working class, whereupon a worker sent in a letter defending him.[37] On one occasion he is supposed to have said that he had nothing against a Social–Democratic proposal to make Braunschweig a republic, as it would save a million from the civil list.[38] He was, no doubt, far from a republican, but his chief enemy never ceased to be the neo-feudal aristocracy. In a diary entry of September 30, 1868, he noted with emphasis the victory of revolution in Spain, adding with apparent delight: "exeunt Bourbones!"

The widely held view that German literature of the nineteenth century was largely withdrawn from political and social concerns is an exaggeration, a legend based on a canon reduced with the purpose of giving just that impression. Political and social fiction abounds in nineteenth-century Germany. Even so, Raabe is remarkable for the extensiveness of the social depiction and (sometimes oblique) political commentary in his writing. A monograph much longer than this chapter would be necessary to bring out all the facets of the political dimension of his fiction from the very beginning to the very end of his career. This is not to say that political partisanship was a major motive of his writing. Instead, he seems to have shared the conventional view that the political realm was inferior to the dignity of literature. In the politically excited year of 1866 he wrote in a notebook: "For the poet preoccupation with politics is a descent, and one often finds that it is just the creative writers who look upon these patterns of the day most soberly and sensibly."[39] There are in his corpus, however, three works that can be regarded as political novels in the explicit sense, each written at or near the end of each of the three phases of his career. They are *After the Great War* of 1861; *The Dräumling Swamp*, which appeared in 1872 as the first publication of his Braunschweig period but was conceived and partly written at the end of his Stuttgart years; and *Gutmann's Travels* of 1892, the fourth-last of his published works.

After the Great War is a one-sided epistolary novel that begins in May 1816 and ends in August "of the year of the great famine 1817" (4: 130). It is therefore a reflection of the situation in Germany immediately after the Napoleonic Wars. The writer of the letters is an idealistic young schoolteacher named Wolkenjäger ("Cloudchaser"); while we do not see the letters of his correspondent Sever, we can tell from Wolkenjäger's replies that he is querulous and disillusioned, discouraged by the betrayal of liberal hopes in 1815 and unable to feel hopeful about the German future. (The device of the silent but nevertheless audible correspondent was modelled in Goethe's *Werther*.) In the face of Sever's anti-Romantic, anti-idealist realism and of the evidence of the immediate environment, Wolkenjäger strives to maintain patriotic hope, and his spirits are lifted when he falls in love. He meets an old soldier, Lieutenant Bart, and his adopted daughter, Anna, whom Bart had found abandoned on a Spanish battlefield. She turns out to be the secret offspring of a noble family von Rhoda with a long history of unpatriotic French service and other vicious depravities. The current von Rhoda is found dying, contrite about his many sins; Wolkenjäger, naturally, marries Anna and looks forward to living ever after.

As a novel, *After the Great War* is a failure in every respect. In any evaluative list of Raabe's novels, it would not be unfair to place it at the bottom. Formally it is ungainly: the letters are interrupted by a long diary entry that permits the recital of the love story and its melodramatic prehistory, while Lieutenant Bart tells stories of his military service, one of several devices to insert historical material tending to the point of the dissipation of German energies in divisive conflicts in the interest of foreigners. The humorless text is embarrassingly burdened with some of Raabe's least attractive poems. The effort to represent a Romantic spirit in Wolkenjäger's consciousness is unpersuasive and leaden, suggesting that Raabe is not to be seen in Romantic descent as much as some critics have suggested. The novel failed with the public as well; initially it sold seventy-five copies[40] and the critical reception was chilly. Hardly anyone but the most rabid nationalists has had a good word to say about it and modern commentators have almost totally ignored it.[41]

It does, however, provide a map of young Raabe's political allegiances, his liberal patriotism in the teeth of reactionary repression. Wolkenjäger cannot believe that all the power of the people is meant "to serve as ridiculed toys and frippery in the hands of a few childish priests, courtiers, women, diplomats, and imbecilic soldiers!" (4: 21).[42] All of Raabe's permanent views about the faults and misfortunes of the German past, the unpatriotic character of the aristocratic class, and the invincible potential of the German people are woven in, however clumsily. It is, moreover, not unimportant that he allows Sever's pessimistic, contrary voice to be overheard, not merely as a foil but as a partially justified attitude, nor is it unimportant that the last, shyly hopeful note of the novel is set in the famine of 1817, a grim catastrophe that impelled thousands of desperate Germans to emigrate to America. With this kind of writing Raabe certainly wished to instill hope and courage into his imagined readership. Towards the end of the *Chronicle*, the narrator calls out: "Oh you poets and writers of Germany, say and write nothing to discourage your people, as those who bear the proudest names in poesy and learning have unfortunately so often done!" (1: 166-67). But he may well have felt that this purpose could be served truthfully only by integrating the dimension of doubt and skepticism that he himself so keenly felt.

The scene of *Gutmann's Travels* is the convention of the National Association in Coburg in 1860, which Raabe had attended thirty years before. A young North German, Wilhelm Gutmann, has persuaded his initially hesitant father to travel to the convention. But in Coburg their roles are reversed: the father becomes fired with enthusiasm and rejuvenated by the patriotic spirit, while Wilhelm, though no less patriotic, seeks every pretext to escape the debates and droning speeches, of which Raabe gives a number of verbatim excerpts. For junior has met a pert young lady, Klotilde Blume, from the Franconian town of Wunsiedel, the birthplace of Jean Paul—no other text of Raabe's alludes to Jean Paul so often and so explicitly. Klotilde has been abandoned to her own devices by her politically obsessed and quarrelsome elders, and Wilhelm finds her company more gratifying than the proceedings in the convention hall. Klotilde is being courted by an old friend of the Gutmanns, an Austrian former forty-eighter named Pärnreuther. Wilhelm, of course, wins Klotilde, reconciling the disputatious families from North and South while shutting out the Austrian, who accepts the turn of events with gentlemanly goodwill. Transparently, this is an allegory of the *kleindeutsch* solution, the unification of the northern and southern German states to the exclusion of Austria, with the hope, nevertheless, that Austria will remain a friend to the German Reich.

Although Bismarck is mentioned only twice in the text, Raabe conceived *Gutmann's Travels* as his "Bismarckiad."[43] He began the book three months after Bismarck's dismissal by the young, impetuous Kaiser Wilhelm II in March 1890, an event that, as we know, worried not only followers of Bismarck and not only Germans. Raabe's homage to Bismarck is oblique and subtle, and seems quite to have escaped the critics and the public at the time. For he portrays not Bismarck, but the political conditions that, in his view, had made Bismarck necessary. Notwithstanding all of Raabe's personal sympathies with the spirit of the Coburg convention, he was obliged to face the fact that the words could not be transformed into deeds. Even the citizens of Coburg itself are complacently indifferent to what is taking place in their town. The bourgeois liberal professors and officials had not been able to solve the problem of national unity at Coburg in 1860 any more than they had at Frankfurt in 1848. What they had been unable to do, Bismarck accomplished, and if his methods were somewhat indelicate, that was just too bad. The regional self-interest, the political naivety, the indecisiveness masked by the sometimes inspirational, sometimes pompous rhetoric cited in the novel constituted, in Raabe's view, a knot that could only be undone by Bismarck's sword. Raabe once said that he owed more to Bismarck than to Goethe and Schiller (E 4: 125); no political development in his late years angered him more than what he regarded as studied ingratitude toward the man he apotheosized without embarrassment as the "Redeemer."[44]

Unfortunately, the effect of the oblique strategy is to make *Gutmann's Travels* somewhat slight as a novel, and Raabe's subsequent doubts about its value were not unjustified. Not that the literary maladroitness of *After the Great War* is chargeable against it. In 1890 Raabe was at the height of his abilities; the confident sovereign author is here at his chattiest and most digressive. Many of the details of the novel are cleverly managed, and it is certainly not without political insight. The historian Hermann Oncken wrote to Raabe in 1908 that the book gave a better picture of the political mood of the times than the historical documents (18: 477). As usual, the humorous tone is not free of darker shadows. Wilhelm's sharp-tongued mother cannot see why there should be any dissatisfaction with things as they are and remarks perceptively that the liberals are confused in their intentions; they want to found the new Reich while keeping everything intact that tore the old one into a thousand pieces, professing open cosmopolitanism and enclosed nationalism at the same time (18: 225). Her real concern is that her son's career will be endangered if he is marked as a subversive. A friend of Raabe's who had attended the convention was punished and driven out of the civil service for refusing to make a report to the authorities (18: 467-68). Wilhelm Gutmann indeed receives an ominous official communication after the convention, though we are assured by the author that he will be all right in the future. But it is just this allrightness that threatens to trivialize the book. Since the well-meant, amiable insignificance of the national movement is the theme, the overall effect is somewhat slack and ideologically affirmative. The circumstance that the father is politically engaged while the son pursues other, more personal interests, may well suggest that the political enthusiasm was old-fashioned, a crotchet of an older generation. The typically banal love story that prospectively allegorizes the founding of the Reich strikes me as an unfortunate device, for Raabe, as we know, did not much care about love stories, and consequently the whole political tone of the novel comes to seem condescending and more indifferent than he may have wanted it to be.

More successful than the first and third of these political novels is the second, *The Dräumling Swamp*, for in it Raabe confronted the political issues on the ground most appropriate to him: the national cultural tradition, the wellspring of the humane dimension of German liberalism; and he did so with wisdom and insight in a work that is not only artistically satisfying but highly entertaining. For the novel is not "humorous" like *Gutmann's Travels* but *funny*, sometimes uproariously so, and yet it lacks the arch undertone that makes the late work somewhat petty. It is set in the swampy, backwater town of Paddenau in 1859, the year of the centennial of Schiller's birth. This occasion was celebrated in cities and towns, public halls, churches, and synagogues from one end of Germany to the other, an essentially political demonstration that employed Schiller as an icon of the hope for freedom and progress against the torpid and oppressive condition of the German states. Raabe understood perfectly well the function of the occasion as a surrogate for unattainable political action. "The significant day dawned," he writes with restrained sarcasm, "and as far as the German tongue was heard, the German nation put on its clothes with the firm determination now to ventilate quite decisively the political feelings so remarkably suppressed in the summer toward the aesthetic-literary-historical side" (10: 94). *The Dräumling Swamp* narrates Paddenau's disorganized, disharmonious, and in some degree hysterical version of this famous moment in history. Every event Raabe noted in his diary during the celebration he himself witnessed in Wolfenbüttel in 1859 finds a place in the novel, and in his deflation of the event's pomposity there may be a subtext of self-irony, for on the occasion in Wolfenbüttel he had himself contributed a poem (20: 350-51) that can compare with anyone's in its grandiloquent fustian.[45]

The instigator of the Paddenau celebration is a school rector named Fischarth, a henpecked, high-strung, busily inefficient enthusiast who definitely has his heart in the right place but is rather given to an overblown, donnish rhetoric punctuated by disparate and abstruse Classical allusions. His project is invaded by a newcomer to the town, one Rudolf Haeseler, a red-haired, half-Jewish painter who specializes in swamps. Ebullient, voluble, simultaneously sardonic and idealistic, he is certainly one of the numerous disguised alter egos of the author. In this incarnation, he has a distinct touch of the anarchistic, and he swarms about, transforming the planned dignity of the occasion into a kind of Germanic hootenanny. At one point he locks the hypertense Fischarth into a room with several alcoholic beverages to calm him down and prevent him from making any more speeches. Simultaneously Haeseler is pursuing a young lady, Wulfhilde Mühlenhoff, but this love affair is livelier and less banal than its counterpart in *Gutmann's Travels*, for Wulfhilde is one of Raabe's independent, self-possessed female figures, who insists upon performing in the public ceremony against the disapproval of her conservative grump of a father and her fiancé, a Hamburg businessman with the ear-splitting name of Knackstert. The latter regards this Schiller business as hogwash, and he attempts to sabotage the celebration in alliance with the faction in town that cannot understand all this fuss over a dead writer; for, they say, "afterwards anyone could come along and be celebrated. Today Schiller, tomorrow Goethe, the day after Klopstock, and so on through the whole lending library" (10: 65). But Knackstert's machinations fail, and in the process he loses his betrothed, naturally, to Haeseler.

The basic ideological layout is plain enough: it is a conflict between the past and the future, in which the hundred-year-old Schiller is located on the side of the future, an icon of the hope of a united nation for a utopia of freedom and moral refinement. Arrayed against this hope are the forces of stasis: the peevishly short-sighted, selfish townspeople; the boorish, parochially unpatriotic businessman; officialdom loyal to the status quo, represented by Wulfhilde's father; and the clergy, for whom Schiller and all of German Classicism were dangerously unorthodox and who in this instance forbid the use of the church bells. There are some conversions, for example, of the innkeeper, who is initially an ally of Knackstert but is mollified when he learns that there is money to be made from the occasion. All of this is conventional enough, if carried off with an unusual degree of comic panache. But other features of the novel relativize the ideological pageant. The rather frantic movement of the narration is centrifugal, away from the focus of the celebration itself; for example, we do not hear the speeches, and there is some question whether anyone else can hear them, or cares to. We only catch the end of Fischarth's address, when he says that Schiller is a paraclete of the German people, who are so much in need of a helper (10: 119).

Among those who do not hear the speeches are Goethe and Schiller themselves, who have a skeptical conversation in heaven about the affair, during which Goethe remarks that he had not enjoyed his own centenary ten years before, either (10: 108). While locked up Fischarth has a vision of Goethe and Schiller, who teach a lesson about humorous relaxation, accepting the abrasions of life; they are joined by Shakespeare and then by the playwright Kotzebue, so despised by Goethe and Schiller in life but now tolerated; he in turn is reconciled with his assassin, the nationalist student Karl Sand. At the end they are all laughing together (10: 145-48). The passage seems to prefigure the phantasmagoria of the laughing Goethe and Mozart toward the end of Hermann Hesse's *Steppenwolf*.[46] Here its function is to deflate the pomposity and dissipate the gas generated by such occasions. The novel was composed during the Franco-Prussian War, and Raabe wrote to his brother that "the work is written in direct contradiction to the self-glorification of German philistinism that now often appears so disgustingly."[47] Raabe did not doubt the importance of the occasion itself; in the preface to the second edition of 1892 he wrote: "The Gutmann and Blume families would certainly not have offered one another heart and hand so readily in Coburg for the common erection of the new German Reich if Rector Fischarth, the swamp painter Haeseler, and Miss Wulfhilde in Paddenau in the Dräumling swamp had not earlier produced the Schiller festival despite everything!" (10: 7). The intended effect is a demystification of the cultural tradition to make it available to the people as a friendly possession rather than an awe-inspiring monument.

Still, the novel is in some considerable degree a satire, and there is a good deal of ambiguity about the "people," their identity and their potential. Knackstert, who thinks the whole nation has gone crazy over Schiller (10: 70), looks at first like a stuffy killjoy, but in fact the citizens of Paddenau like and admire him. The one citizen who defends progress, the railroad, youth, and the Schiller celebration is known as the "blockhead" (10: 18, 75). The artist Haeseler hardly seems to be in harmony with any segment of public opinion. On the first banner he designs for the celebration he proposes the symbol of the railroad, in contrast to Fischarth's desire for a more conventional symbol such as a Muse or a Germania (10: 53, 57). On the second version he portrays Wulfhilde as an angry Muse, with the result that the banner cannot be used (10: 130-31). He rather subverts the parade by making the piper who leads it drunk, and the procession starts out with a good deal of quarrelling (10: 104-6). Haeseler's speciality of painting swamps suggests a combination of creativity, eccentricity, and iconoclastic skepticism. The swamp is the central and most ambiguous image in the novel.[48] It represents both sluggishness and fecundity, damp philistine torpor and hope for a new life. It therefore reflects the portrayal of the people as a whole in its conflicting, often exasperating, yet in the long run hopeful substance.

Haeseler's choice of the swamp as his artistic motif is a commitment to realism, to representing things as they are, and in this regard especially he stands in for Raabe, especially at this critical stage in his career. That Raabe made this identification and saw himself in the same swamp is evident in the convoluted sentence with which the novel ends, after he has asked himself if "we stand opposite the swamp": "Oh, no, we are sitting very deeply in it and are trying, like the painter Rudolf Haeseler, only to see our way clear in the Dräumling, and consider this no mean achievement, but we will not boast and certainly will not offer from the Dräumling alleged good advice to anyone who claims to stand opposite the Dräumling" (10: 201). Perquin's observation long ago that this last passage shows "the depths of questions that were avoided but not solved" is well taken.[49] But the refusal to resolve is a strong point of *The Dräumling Swamp*, making it one of the most balanced political novels of its time. In it Raabe's nationalism appears from its best side, in its commitment to humane values, its awareness of limits, its suspicion of rodomontade and pompous ceremony, its unusual combination of a satirical vision with a tolerance for the commonplace, and—most unusual of all—its ability to laugh.

CHAPTER 9

History

◧

> Without historical knowledge the cleverest re-
> mains a stupid ass; with it, as a superior human
> being, he scientifically sticks a whole town, a
> whole community into his pocket.
>
> *Stuffcake* (18: 71)

HISTORICAL fiction constitutes just under a third of Raabe's oeuvre. The historical works, however, are unevenly distributed. All but four of them belong to the first half of his career, and they are even more heavily concentrated toward the beginning. It is not without interest that this recession of the historical genre occurred subsequently to the founding of the Reich in 1871. *Höxter and Corvey* appeared in 1875 and *The Innerste* in 1876, after which Raabe wrote fifteen successive works set in the present. Only toward the end of his career did he return to historical fiction with *The Odin Field* (1888) and his last completed novel, *Hastenbeck* (1899). The pattern of a decline in the frequency of historical fiction along with an increase in its quality is one of the most obvious features of his evolution as a writer and tells us something about his relationship to his times.

The historical fiction that began to thrive in Germany in the 1820s and remained a major mode, especially of popular literature, throughout the nineteenth century, had three closely interrelated aspects. In the first place it was a reflex of the greatly increased historical sensibility itself, which had been deepened as well as sharpened by Romantic scholarship. This was an international phenomenon in both learning and literature. The strongest initial influence on the German historical novel came from abroad, from Sir Walter Scott. Willibald Alexis (1798-1871), the early pioneer of historical fiction in Germany, published his first novel (*Walladmor*, 1824) under the pretense that it had been translated from Scott. Secondly, the employment of historical materials was one of the strategies in the pursuit of realism. Germans themselves felt that their parochial and static social conditions made the development of a modern realism more difficult than it was in more advanced societies such as France and England. They hoped to find in the historical record the substance that they felt was lacking in their immediate environment. Writers of the time were quite aware of this function. "Through the historical novel one hoped to gain a footing on real ground," wrote Berthold Auerbach in 1842.[1] Thirdly, historical fiction was a symptom and an expression of the nationalist spirit. Here, too, Scott provided a model, but in Germany the nationalist urgency was greater. It was the task of historical fiction to provide for the not yet existent nation a usable past. Alexis collectively titled his series of eight novels set in various epochs of the Prussian past *Patriotic Novels*. He wanted very much to be a loyalist, but, as was so often the case in those times, his critical patriotism brought him into conflict with the ruling powers. Among many others, however, German hope and pride came to be compounded with a resentful, chauvinistic arrogance formed in equal measure of collective self-pity and self-aggrandizement. With the approach and the final, delayed achievement of the German nation-state, fiction was increasingly employed to affirm the political development and reinforce an uncritical euphoria with retrospective glory. Among the authors who served in this role was Raabe's friend Jensen.

Against this background Raabe's own development becomes intelligible. He fully shared the historical curiosity of his age and he became a considerable amateur historian, especially of his native Lower Saxony. He rummaged around in primary sources and old newspapers, so that there is a sense in which history might be said to have been his only hobby. There is little doubt that history was of great importance in supplying substance to an inexperienced, provincial, and somewhat withdrawn young writer. The preponderance of historical fiction in his early phase is one facet of his endeavor to be successful while being himself. Its decline in his more mature period thus appears in some degree as a symptom of increased confidence in his own imagination and of a richer perception of the world in which he lived. Thus for him the genre seems to have served its purposes quite efficiently: it helped to establish him as a writer, it compensated for the limits of his personal experience, and it trained him in realism. Historical fiction also served him as a vehicle for his nationalism, but this matter will be postponed for the moment, as his development was in this regard rather more idiosyncratic.

Thus it is not surprising that some of his earlier historical tales, though certainly not unskilled, may seem to be relatively conventional and to exhibit the least of his narrative and perspectival originality. Nor is it surprising that some of these same works have been among the most enduringly popular of all of his writing. Among these has been *The Black Galley* (1861), a swashbuckling sea story of the revolt of the Netherlands from Spain at the end of the sixteenth century. It has been one of the most frequently republished of all of his works, quite commonly as a schoolbook, for it is best appreciated as children's literature. Into this category may also fall *Our Lord God's Chancellory* (1862), a dramatic novella of the siege of Magdeburg, the center of Protestant publishing, by Catholic forces in the 1550s. In 1889 Raabe found he had forgotten the book and was not sure he wanted it re-published, since, as he remarked, historical fiction had made great progress since then;[2] in a preface to this new edition he called it a "picture book" obviously written by a young man (4: 143). Despite his disclaimers, it is a good book of its kind, containing some of the most exciting action of any of his works; as recommendable reading for imaginative early adolescents it need not fear comparison with Robert Louis Stevenson.

Most of these early historical stories betray the quantity of study that went into them. Raabe's works are not as burdened with learning as those of some other nineteenth-century writers, who often legiti-mated their fictional texts with footnotes; I can recall only one foot-note, an identification of the Marquis d'Argenson in *The Odin Field* (17: 53). Still, his narrator is ironically forthright about the visible manner in which he links general history and antiquarian studies to his invented fiction, for just as he knew instinctively that fiction could not be "objectively" mimetic, so he recognized that the vaunted objec-tivity of contemporary historiography was an illusion.[3] The second chapter of *The Holy Spring* begins:

> At the town hall of the city of Holzminden there are few doc-uments, writs, and sources about the city itself and even fewer or rather none at all about Klaus. But, despite the tooth of time and the teeth of the rats and mice, we have, through immeasur-able, fabulous industry and late-night study learned much for which we will on occasion bid the thanks of the learned, for whom we have prepared the first path through the primeval for-est. We begin with the history of the town, tell where it is lo-cated, what sort of people inhabit it, and thereby reach the pre-history of our Klaus, who is a "historical figure" and well worth being brought to light out of the night of oblivion and set under the eyes and eyeglasses of the German public. (3: 21)

Despite this self-aware irony, not a few of the early stories bear sty-listic traces of the chronicle mode. In the case of *Lorenz Scheibenhart*

(1858), Raabe's editor Glaser successfully urged him to reduce the historical scene-setting somewhat (2: 572).

The early works also exhibit fairly openly Raabe's basic ideological location. Perhaps it would not be too strained to see his instinctive view of history as a German counterpart to what in England is known as "Whig history." In the case of Raabe and the majority of his post-Romantic contemporaries it is Protestant history, in the sense that it sees the Enlightenment, liberty, and modern intellectual culture in genetic succession to the Reformation. I doubt that he thought very much about this at first; it must have seemed quite obvious to him, as it always had not only to liberals but also to more radical writers such as Heine. The attitude is adumbrated in virtually every text, but appears most clearly in *Our Lord God's Chancellory*, where it is not only or even primarily the Protestant cause that is being defended in Magdeburg, but the printing press, the instrument of liberty, enlightenment, reasoned discourse, and citizen participation. Raabe was to moderate this Protestant bias in time, especially as he came to focus on the danger that religious strife had always posed to the unity of the nation. Also the nationalist spirit is implicit in many of the early works, though it varies in intensity; apart from the failed novel *After the Great War*, it appears most explicitly in *The Crown of the Empire* (1870), which takes place in Nuremberg in the first half of the fifteenth century. It is thus, with the exception of the legendary *Pied Piper of Hamelin*, the most remote in time of his historical fictions, and the breath of Romantic medievalism pervading it is not the least of its weaknesses. It concerns a young man who succeeds in recovering the Imperial crown during the Hussite Wars but returns stricken with leprosy; his beloved renounces the world to become the mother superior in his leprosarium. The rather obscure tale was a great favorite with Raabe's nationalistic admirers, but its heavy symbolism and tendency to melodramatic sentimentality are less likely to appeal to today's readers.[4] It strikes me as the most Jensenesque of Raabe's writings.

In general, however, modern criticism may have come to undervalue the early historical fiction. As immature and formulaic as some of it may be, it displays a number of Raabe's later strengths and preoccupations in embryonic form, and most of it, even when slight in conception, exhibits the precocious story-telling talent that he possessed from the beginning. One work that may have been somewhat unjustly shunted into the reject pile is *The Holy Spring* (1861).[5] It is one of those early novels upon which Raabe's own retrospective reprobation fell most severely. While reading the proofs of a new edition in 1891 he called it a "lending-library-nursery-book"[6] and in the preface to that edition he defended it lamely with the remark that everyone needs a little "childhood romanticism" in life (3: 8). Indeed it would not be difficult to run up a bill of particulars against the novel. Set in the age of the Reformation, it is an immensely complicated, melodramatic, almost chaotic book that virtually defies synopsis. The plot at one level concerns a cheerful young adventurer who loves and eventually wins the daughter of a bigoted clergyman; she, in turn, is illicitly and secretly loved by a young monk who eventually goes mad from the conflict of conscience with repressed passion. At a second level it concerns a demonic German-Italian *femme fatale* named, I regret to report, Fausta la Tedesca (even Raabe's most ardent admirers have not thought he had a vocation for this sort of thing). She is hostilely pursued by one of her justifiably horrified former lovers and manages to ensnare a lusty, well-meaning, but somewhat dissolute count, ruler of the principality in which, to his vast annoyance, a holy spring has appeared. A third level concerns a conspiracy to subvert German troops into the service of the evil French Catholic cause. Compared to *Our Lord God's Chancellory*, the novel is ungainly in structure; Raabe has a visible struggle managing the levels of time and exposition. At times the pace is frenetic; at others, especially toward the end, it drags irritatingly. The narrator jabbers throughout, giving historical instruction and telling us what to think. It is possible that Raabe even then became somewhat embarrassed at this effort and that it was not only a gesture of authorial irony when he entitled the last chapter: "The Narrator Grows Angry at Himself and Throws His Pen out of the Window" (3: 334).

However, the novel has, in my opinion, one great strength, and that is the complex of the holy spring itself. From the narrator's point of view there is nothing intrinsically holy about the phenomenon. It is simply one of those springs that bubble out of the ground in many places in Lower Saxony and Westphalia, around some of which elegant spas have been built. This one, however, acquires the reputation of a fountain of youth and comes to be a focus of all the exaltation, lunacy, and charlatanism of an age of high-pitched religious revival. Swarms of pilgrims are attracted to it and camp out in huge numbers, raising the racket that so exasperates the count, while a both pedantic and whimsical pastor draws up a futile set of rules of conduct. Prophets, evangelists, and other quacks are naturally soon on the scene; crooks, whores, and vagabonds abound. The proprietors of a competing holy spring attack the new one in a pamphlet. There is a good deal of comedy in all this, but people are growing ill and dying and losing their small store of reason in this place. In the last phase there are orgies and lethal fights with firearms. Then, upon the news of the count's death in the Battle of St. Quentin, the crowd disappears as though by magic, and the sacral aura of the spring vanishes. Much of the detail is deftly managed and in this regard the rather chaotic quality of the narration is well suited to the subject.

Furthermore, it is in connection with the holy spring that we can see some of Raabe's view of history crystallizing. It is not only that these scenes exhibit in extreme form the irrational religious strife that he saw as a major curse on German history, though this point was important to him. Later, in *Höxter and Corvey*, a work that recapitulates some of the spirit of *The Holy Spring* with much greater finesse, there is, in one of the rare quiet moments, a conversation on peace between a Jewess, a soldier turned monk, and the protagonist Lambert, who remarks that peace will come when people of different religions stop reaching for the club (11: 340-41). Not long afterward, Lambert's uncle, a militant Protestant pastor, tries to revive the conflict with the monks of Corvey again, and this starts a new riot against the Jews. But this is not the only historical insight that Raabe had already developed in the earlier novel. We begin to see that for him there was no unitary *Zeitgeist* in past ages. There is rather conflict and contradiction, a mix of regressive and progressive forces, evil and good, weakness and strength. "It was," he comments, "a believing, disbelieving, superstitious century, this sixteenth after the birth of Christ! Even in the most enlightened, clearest heads, light and darkness were intertwined in such a strange tangle that one never knew what mad, fantastic, crazy or—sublime thoughts, opinions, deeds would burst out of them in the next moment" (3: 118). It was, he goes on, a boiling, bubbling time of individual freedom, witchhunting, great art, swinishness of life, all leading to the crisis of the Thirty Years' War, in which the Middle Ages collapsed, making room for a new world to grow.

Raabe did not, in my opinion, possess anything quite so dignified as a philosophy of history, and I believe that as a historical novelist he was better off without one. Thus unencumbered, he was able to sense history as an ambiguous flux. "Raabe," Daemmrich has observed, "never states that history is unknowable, never argues against the significance of historical insight for civilized society, never counters history with a one-sided, timeless pattern of man's suffering. But he questions the false security afforded by views of historical progress, evolutionary development, and the impact of great statesmen."[7] At his most pessimistic—and he was often at his most pessimistic—he could imply an idea of eternal recurrence, and so it is not surprising that another modern critic has argued that there is no tendency to improvement in Raabe's view of history; German history especially is a continuously repeating succession of catastrophes to which the individual is exposed.[8] But that is not quite it, either. As we have just seen, he was able to extract even from the Thirty Years' War, the epic catastrophe of German history, an element of hope for the future. In *Höxter and Corvey* there is an image of the poor, plagued German people after the religious wars of the seventeenth century cropping up like sprouts after the tree had been cut down (11: 267-68). This is hardly an image of exhilarated optimism; neither is it one of hopelessness and inevitable defeat. Perhaps one might say that he saw in history potential without necessity. There is no inherent reason why human affairs should not continue to be as irrational, vicious, and discouraging as they always have been, but implied is a responsibility for the present, to take the potentialities in hand and shape them by our best lights.[9]

As with other aspects of his artistry, his development as a historical novelist was not continuous from one stage to another. An early work like *The Holy Spring* could contain elements that point to the future, while one relatively late in the sequence like *The Crown of the Empire* seems quite regressive. Nevertheless, there is a development, if in discontinuous stages. One turning point might be seen in the novella *St. Thomas* (1866).[10] Like *The Black Galley* and another once-admired novella, *The Squire of Denow* (1858/59), *St. Thomas* takes place in 1599 and is drawn from Schiller's *Geschichte des Abfalls der vereinigten Niederlande* (*History of the Revolt of the Netherlands*) or, more exactly, from its continuation by another hand. But it could not be farther removed in spirit from Schiller's *Don Carlos* and especially from Goethe's drama set in that epoch, *Egmont*, for it is one of the bleakest, bitterest, most despairing of Raabe's works. St. Thomas, the once Portuguese, today independent island of Saõ Tomé in the Gulf of Guinea, has been fortified by the Spanish, who are attacked by a Dutch fleet; a Spanish fleet sent in relief arrives too late. The Dutch overcome the Spanish defenders but are decimated by a tropical plague called "madorca" in Portuguese. This conflict frustrates a love relationship between Camilla Drago, daughter of the Spanish commander, and a Dutch sailor, Georg van der Does, whom she had met when she had been captured and held hostage in the Netherlands. Now they are on opposite sides, and Camilla rises to heroic stature in the defense of the doomed fortress. The narrator never tells us explicitly what ultimately happens to either Camilla or Georg, though it is evident that both perish in this catastrophic episode, which renders their individual fates insignificant.

However, the larger catastrophe is also insignificant in historical perspective. The siege of St. Thomas is but a sideshow in the theater of war. Both the defenders and the attackers become infected with despair at the increasingly obvious futility of the situation. Life has become pointless; among the defenders a baby cries and a mother sings a lullaby, "as though that were still necessary" (9/2: 54). The Spanish commander himself is old, tired, and uninterested in his service; he thinks of the useless, worthless condition of the war-ridden world (9/2: 10). *If* the King of Spain were to hear a rumor of the event, it *might* elicit a royal shrug of the shoulders (9/1: 56). The true victors are actually the natives, who, oppressed by both sides, view the coming doom with satisfaction and attack the burning city; at the end a black girl, wearing Spanish finery, sits on a crag singing an epic song of liberation, which Raabe endeavors to imagine in more than a page of poetic prose (9/2: 57-58). In our world the dreadful event forms but a couple of lines in a chronicle, a page or less in a history of the Netherlands (9/2: 57). An obbligato to the slaughter and brutality is provided by the preacher Leflerus, whose futile Baroque exhortations have no effect on the marauding, heat-stricken Dutch; at the end of the novella we find him, a survivor of the debacle, back in Holland, driven to the edge of almost nihilistic madness by the ghosts and flashbacks of the experience.

With this grueling text in mind we may pause for a moment to attempt to specify some of the features of Raabe's view of history and historical fiction. The pleasant Lower Saxon landscape in which he spent ninety percent of his long life was at peace for all that time. He never witnessed at first hand the horror and sufferings of war, in contrast to some of his literary contempories—Auerbach and Fontane, for instance; even of civil disturbance he experienced very little, unlike Jensen, who in 1870 found himself in the midst of the conflict between Germans and Danes and in 1883 instigated a riot in Freiburg with his anti-Catholic writings. Yet it seems that Raabe did not trust this peace. The historical ground on which he lived was drenched with the blood of the past, groaned with pain and suffering. With his sometimes underestimated attentiveness to the world around him he came to have ominous feelings about the future as well. In his last completed novel, *Hastenbeck*, he mused about those at the end of the nineteenth century "who have experienced so many wars and who have internally such great anxiety about the coming new one, the most terrible one in our opinion!" (20: 29). These feelings evidently accompanied him

through much of his life. His editor Glaser reported that, in Wolfenbüttel in the late 1850s, when the young author passed the historical
sites of witch-burning, he had fantasies of pestilence, war, and famine,
and claimed that they would come again (E 4: 40-41). On two occasions in *One Springtime*, set in the peaceful present, there are sudden
flashbacks to the violence of the sixteenth century that took place in
the now civil streets (1: 201-2, 272). When the protagonist mulls the
bloody past among Roman ruins, he is beset by pessimistic thoughts
(1: 231). Fritz Wolkenjäger of *After the Great War* has a vision, in the
midst of the peaceful forest, of the blood, flame, and destruction of
battles of the past (4: 41). Even the memory fixed in art of the horrors
of the past is oppressive and might perhaps be best wiped away: in
Höxter and Corvey the narrator remarks that it is a consolation for us
that Jacques Callot's 1,600 plates depicting the horrors of the seventeenth century, *Misères et malheurs de la guerre*, were melted down for
kitchen equipment (11: 331-32).

Thus the last thing Raabe was inclined to do, in contrast to some
other historical fictionalists, was to glorify or idealize the past. From
the outset he was sardonic about the "good old days." In the early
story *The Ultimate Justice* (1862) the narrator opens with a pointedly
anti-idyllic description of an early eighteenth-century town, a "free
Imperial city and the very unfree people in it" (9/1: 19), in the most
"romantic" corner of which the executioner and torturer dwells,
though the narrator makes it clear that the "romantic" is an imposition
of later generations. The legal machinery of the Holy Roman Empire,
we are told, allowed the executioner's father, an official, to tyrannize
the helpless and draw more powerful people into his traps. Remarks
like this were more significant than may appear to the modern reader,
for since the Romantic period there had been a good deal of nostalgia
among reactionary thinkers for the institutions of the past, and relics
of them remained intact in the political institutions of Raabe's own
time. A dozen years later, in *The Innerste*, he remarks on the savage
"good old days" of the Seven Years' War (12: 105), and the attitude is
consistent throughout his historical fiction. If he was in some ways a
conservative, he was certainly not a restorationist.

In his works there are many scenes of war, violence, and marauding. His attitude toward such things, however, was resolutely civilian.
In this he may remind us somewhat of Goethe, who, having been
obliged against his will to accompany his ducal master on the disastrous invasion of revolutionary France in 1792, ostentatiously pursued
his scientific and cultural interests in the midst of the military campaign and at one point memorably portrayed himself riding around

the battlefield with a sausage in his pistol holster.[11] Unlike some other authors of historical fiction, Raabe did not glorify war. It is true that at one point in his life he became infected with a militant spirit; to his mother he wrote in 1868 that he longed for war to settle the nationalist issue, and at the outbreak of the Franco-Prussian War he burst out: "War to the knife against the French!"[12] But this was an aberration impelled by the excitement of the times, and indeed after 1871 he became even more sober about war. In his fiction his attitude toward war and mortal conflict is consistently one of grieving and sometimes of stunned dismay at the magnitude of human atrocity. In *The Innerste* there is a quotation from the historian Archenholz aestheticizing the corpse-strewn battlefield of Liegnitz, after which the narrator comments sardonically: "We have copied the description completely, for in reading it one comes to feel so clean, light, and, as it were, friendly, that it is a true joy" (12: 149-50). Herstelle, the soldier turned monk in *Höxter and Corvey*, sits brooding at the bedside of the dying Jewish woman: "Lord, Lord, my God, when will peace come into your poor world" (11: 335), and he reflects on his own part in destruction and oppression.

By and large, Raabe avoided the great battles of history; there is no counterpart in his works to Tolstoy's description of Borodino or Hugo's panorama of Waterloo. His scenes tend to be secondary or even, as in *St. Thomas*, historically trivial episodes in larger conflicts, a device that naturally intensifies the pathos and futility of these events. The peripeteia of *The Homeward March*, when the Swedish soldier Sven Knäckabröd discovers that his true home is now in his Austrian captivity and no longer in the north, occurs at the Battle of Fehrbellin in Brandenburg in 1675, made famous in literature by Kleist's *Prince Friedrich of Homburg*, but Raabe avoids describing the battle itself. He certainly acknowledged courage, but generally it is the courage of ordinary people, sometimes devil-may-care in the case of the young, often stoic in the case of the more mature. He was not inclined to elevate heroism above its true value. The grandfather's sword from the Danish wars in *On the Scrap-Iron* is a heroic symbol, to be sure, but it is also the sword of a man defeated, in war as in life (16: 407). The great commanders, usually seen in the middle distance, are not heroized; they are more likely to be worried and distraught, or even, as in the case of the Spanish commander in *St. Thomas*, depressed.

However, this preference for peripheral skirmishes and futile engagements should not be misunderstood as a means of dehistoricizing the fiction in favor of particularized individual fates or universal verities. For in the background are always the great conflicts of European history: the Reformation, the revolt of the Netherlands, the Thirty Years' War, the Seven Years' War, the French Revolution. The Thirty Years' War was still perceived in Raabe's time as the traumatic catastrophe of German history. No German author, he remarks in *The Odin Field*, can avoid mentioning the Thirty Years' War in a historical work (17: 12). It had preoccupied him from his earliest beginnings. *The Student of Wittenberg*, originally conceived as a segment of *The Chronicle of Sparrow Alley*, takes place on the verge of the Thirty Years' War, and there Raabe gives us a picture of laughing, vivacious school-boys who are soon to plunge into "the blood and flames of the religious and civil war" (2: 248). *Lorenz Scheibenhart* (1858), a fictional memoir of the war, is subtitled *A Portrait of Life from Brutal Times*. Much of the pervasive gloom of *Elsa of the Fir* (1865) is motivated by the horrors of the war. The pastor who is the central figure has been tortured by troops and his hut has been burned down three times. Elsa's scholarly father has been displaced and declassed, and has witnessed his wife and two of his children being burned alive in his house. The story ends with the observation: "it is not to be uttered, not to be counted on the fingers, what perished through this German war, which lasted thirty years" (9/1: 198).

In one of his final four historical fictions, *Höxter and Corvey* (1875), Raabe turned to the chaotic conditions in the decades after the Thirty Years' War, the aftermath of which continued to blight the seventeenth century. Historically the conflict between Protestant Höxter and the Catholic abbey town of Corvey across the Weser River grew out of a quarrel over beer-brewing rights, but this pathetic circumstance did not interest Raabe much. Nor is he in any way concerned to take sides in the *Kulturkampf* of his own time, the struggle of the Protestant state against the Catholic Church.[13] Instead he concentrates on the continuously inflamed relations between Protestants and Catholics, with the helpless Jews wedged in as scapegoats between them. The situation is made even more chaotic and anarchic by the fact that the communities are riven also by class conflicts and resentment against authorities, who cannot keep order because they are all partisan; the common people, as has been observed, "are pawns in the game of power politics."[14]

There has already been occasion to mention *Höxter and Corvey* in connection with Raabe's depiction of Jews; here I shall add only some comments on its remarkable form. By mid-nineteenth-century standards the novella is exceptionally impressionistic. Chapter by chapter it shifts abruptly among Höxter, Corvey, and the river between them, from one group of characters to another, back and forth between interior and exterior scenes. Its very first image is one of disordered time: all the clocks of Höxter are wrong or broken down altogether (11: 261). The novella's sequence of riots and assaults barely has a plot; the narration is held together only by its central figure, the student scapegrace Lambert Tewes, who tries with varying success to retain his blithe spirit and sense of proportion in the midst of the atrocious uproar and bestiality. Some older critics have not appreciated the appropriateness of this structure. Hans Oppermann regarded its complicated composition as a weakness and denied it the status of one of Raabe's best works because it lacks clarity of form.[15] Even Fritz Martini, who recognized that the novella is antithetically constructed out of its narrated space, thought that so much associativeness made the bonds of narration too loose.[16] But it should be clear to the modern reader that the jagged structure is entirely congruent with the chaotic content,[17] which in turn is but a segment of the larger historical chaos: "Storm after storm had rolled over the precincts of Höxter since 1618. No chronicler has yet counted how often this place, the ferry and the bridge . . . had fallen victim to the sword and the torch" (11: 277). At the same time I think we should be hesitant about extrapolating from this text, as modern observers tend to do, a philosophy of eternal recurrence, of history as a repeating cycle of atrocities before which human beings are helpless. This is, of course, what it *felt* like to live in seventeenth-century Germany, as is evident from much of that century's literature. Raabe the historian not only recuperates much of that spirit but has also internalized it to a certain degree; nevertheless, the intent is more admonitory about the lessons of history than discouraging or escapist.

The other three of Raabe's final historical fictions are all associated with the Seven Years' War, which was as close to him in time as the American Civil War is to us and doubtless loomed as large in his sense of national history. It must be said first of all that his view of the Seven Years' War was rather different from the customary one of his time. For most of his contemporaries the central figure of the war was Frederick the Great. As part of the process of legitimating a national tradition culminating in the founding of the Reich under Prussian auspices, nineteenth-century German art and literature labored assiduously at the elaboration of the Friderician legend. Raabe did not focus on this aspect very much. Frederick is not entirely absent from the scene, but he is far in the background, and heroizing him was not one of Raabe's priorities. For him the war was not a historical chapter of heroic achievement but, as usual, a chronicle of misery and suffering whose larger meaning was opaque and very likely irrelevant to its victims. The protagonist of *The Odin Field* observes that it is a reissue of the Thirty Years' War, with everyone driving everyone else into war, the peasant from the plow, the workman from the workplace, the student from his book—while the foreigners laugh (17: 51). Among the main characters in *Hastenbeck* are a deserter and a disillusioned old veteran who hides him, so that the spirit of protecting the alternative community is directly subversive of the military madness. At the end of the war there is once again peace—what one calls peace—in the world (20: 191).

The war was a demonstration of one of Raabe's most persistent historical complaints: the habit of the Germans of fighting one another in the interest of potentates without national allegiance and of foreign powers invited to devastate German soil. In *Höxter and Corvey* the French have again been in the land because a German prince-bishop is allied with them (11: 262-63). In *The Innerste*, "the French were in the land" (12: 106); in *Hastenbeck*, "the French were, as usual, in the land" (20: 11). The English catch it once in a while, too; in *The Innerste* a veteran has bitter things to say of the cowardice of Viscount Sackville at the Battle of Minden, and a pompous professor from Göttingen, a Hanoverian subject, flatters himself with the illusion that he is British (12: 124, 136-37). *Hastenbeck* begins with George II, Elector of Hanover and King of Great Britain, deploring his son, the Duke of Cumberland, whose incompetence and cowardice caused the loss of the battle for which the novel is named (20: 7). At the same time Raabe is very far from a long-lived attitude of the Germans toward themselves as perpetual innocents abused and misled by sneakier and more ruthless foreigners. He will have none of that; he lays the blame at the door of the Germans themselves. In *The Odin Field* he observes: "The hail that destroyed the crops, the mice that emptied the barns and larders had been invited to it by the German people themselves, princes and subjects in one bundle," and he adds that it is not superfluous today to remind the German people of their stupidity (17: 22). He set as a motto to that novel a passage that his grandfather had written one hundred years before, to the effect that conflicts on the Orinoco had to be fought out in Germany and Canada had to be conquered on German soil (17: 6).

The Innerste, although it is set in the time of the Seven Years' War and is pervaded with historical detail and commentary, is perhaps not most effectively treated in the context of historical fiction, even though the central figure is a miller's son whose personality is altered and weakened by the experience of war. An absorbing story that has attracted a good deal of critical attention,[18] it is more profitably regarded as an experiment in the psychology of folk myth. The Innerste, which flows south of Braunschweig, is alleged to scream periodically, whereupon it requires a sacrifice of a living being. Whether this is true or not is a topic of much debate in the novella, for Raabe perceives the eighteenth century as an age of both rationality and superstition. The murderous river is identified with the wild, red-haired miller's daughter Doris Radebrecker, erotic siren and bandit princess, by far the most compelling of Raabe's demonic *femmes fatales*. Whether the story is in some extended sense an allegory of German history is a matter on which I have some suspicions but I would prefer to put them to one side for present purposes.

However, the two other late works, *The Odin Field* and *Hastenbeck*, are without doubt major exemplars of historical fiction in German literature. The *Odfeld* of the first story is a heath in the Weser hill country, quite close to Raabe's birthplace of Eschershausen; near it is the Protestant cloister of Amelungsborn, a twelfth-century structure still standing today, which in the past was used as a school. I have translated *Odfeld* as "Odin Field," which is doubtless a false etymology, as Raabe knew, but one employed in the novel for symbolic purposes. The field was the scene of a battle of the Seven Years' War on November 5, 1761: as usual, not a major battle, but one of the many bloody, rather indecisive engagements of that war. The action of the novel covers exactly twenty-four hours, from the evening of November 4. Noah Buchius, a superannuated teacher left behind in retirement in the abandoned cloister school, and his unfriendly neighbor the prefect, witness an extraordinary sight: a battle between swarms of ravens in the sky. There is great carnage among them, and the dead and wounded birds litter the ground. Buchius picks up one of the ravens and gives it shelter in his cell. In the course of the story the timid, bookish old man manages with persistence and wisdom to protect his little band of friends from the rigors of the battle and return them safely to the cloister, with the exception of one young man, his favorite pupil, who dies in the combat. The stress here, as always, is on sorrow and suffering, not on heroism or victory. The death of the bright, ebullient young rascal is perceived not as tragic but as wasteful.

The Odin Field is a dense, intense text that cannot be exhaustively treated here. There is good reason to think that Buchius, the despised, aging, maladroit, apparently useless scholar, is another of Raabe's disguised self-portraits. Against the senselessness of the chaotic historical world the depressively inclined humanist asserts meaning. He cannot do much in the face of all this chaos, but what he can do, he does: he

calls upon his knowledge and curiosity to protect himself and his companions—it is his inquiring mind that has discovered the cave in which
they find shelter during the worst of the battle. Similarly, he can do
nothing about the natural "prodigium" of the raven battle except to
register apprehensive awe, but he can gather up one wounded bird
and offer it shelter. The raven battle, one of Raabe's most curious
symbolic complexes, reinforces this autobiographical link, for Raabe's
name, of course, means "raven," and a long history in his works of
playing upon the raven image culminates in *The Odin Field*, as I have
tried to show in detail elsewhere.[19]

Instead of recapitulating this detail here, I should like to concentrate
briefly on a particular moment of the work as a historical novel. One
of Raabe's motives in *The Odin Field* was to erect a kind of monument
to the Prussian field-marshal and commander in this battle, Duke Ferdinand of Braunschweig (1721-92). Now it was never Raabe's habit to
glorify ruling houses, of Braunschweig or otherwise, and indeed he
contrasts Ferdinand, who, though a duke, never ruled, to the rest of
his house as "the most humane of his thick-headed, stiff-necked,
rough-hewn breed" (17: 181-82), and even he, when he bursts out in
anger at one of his commanders who has failed to make a critical
junction, shows "how coarse the House of Braunschweig could . . .
on occasion be" (17: 176). But it is the duke's basic mildness and generosity that Raabe wishes to celebrate, his character in some ways
mirroring that of the lowly Buchius, unassuming and unappreciated,
less heroic than bewildered, melancholy, and dutiful. So that we
should not understand the praise of Ferdinand as a parochial expression of regional pride, the narrator eulogizes him in four languages:

> Vivat Ferdinandus Dux! . . . Vive Monseigneur, le bon duc Fer-
> dinand! . . . Three cheers for prince Ferdinand, good prince Fer-
> dinand! . . . Es lebe Ferdinand der Gute, der gute Herzog Fer-
> dinand von Braunschweig und von Vechelde! (17: 181)

But even this well-meaning man is powerless to relieve the evil of
the day, as appears in a telling scene in Chapter 21. When Buchius
and his little band of refugees encounter him, the duke and the eloquently admiring Buchius briefly recognize an affinity in character
between them, or it would be recognized if the duke had any time,
but he has no time. One of Buchius's companions, the servant-girl
Wieschen, has on a previous occasion obtained a coat-button from the
duke as a token of a promise to help her; the duke recognizes the
button and tells her to bring it to Braunschweig, but it turns out later
that he has absent-mindedly put it in his own pocket. The harried

duke orders one of his captains to help Buchius's crew through the battlefield back to the cloister. The irritated, short-tempered captain passes the order on to an even more irritable corporal, who finds the task quite beneath his dignity and drives the refugees with blows of his rifle butt to the next crossroads, where he abandons them in a swamp. Thus the duke's humane goodwill is dissipated as it filters down into the inhumane reality. This is not a case of "If the Tsar (the Führer . . . Stalin) only knew!" The futility of transmitting the compassion of one of the most decent members of the dominant class is in the *system* and in the hellish circumstances that are a product of that system. It is important to read Raabe's perspective accurately here and not lose track of it in generalizations about eternal recurrence and historical pessimism. With what he shows us during the grisly twenty-four hours on the Odin Field he is indicting the political and social system of the eighteenth century, which is responsible for this hideous war and all its manifold afflictions in the lives of ordinary people, and he illustrates the indictment in a vignette of a nobleman and commander whom he regards with explicit sympathy and admiration. There is not a trace here of conservative nostalgia: the order of the past is rejected, even in its mitigating aspects. This is not all that Raabe had on his mind in *The Odin Field*, but it is an important dimension of his historical outlook.

For his final work Raabe turned to a somewhat earlier phase of the war, a battle at Hastenbeck in July of 1757. From the German point of view the battle was a defeat, and a galling one, for it was lost largely through the incompetence and cowardice of the Duke of Cumberland and it led to the humiliating convention of Kloster Zeven, at which Hanover was ceded to the French and the ruling Duke of Braunschweig, Karl I, was banned to a neutral zone, the principality of Blankenburg. (The event is touched upon and given much the same interpretation in Chapter 4 of Thackeray's *Barry Lyndon*, which Raabe had read in 1865.) This time, however, the novel does not portray the battle itself, but its aftermath, in which a number of ordinary people are entangled. If *The Odin Field*, said the author, was his "ducal Brunswickian *Iliad*," *Hastenbeck* was his "ducal Brunswickian *Odyssey*."[20] There are allusions to *The Odin Field* in it, as well as to other earlier works. The exceptionally slow-moving, verbose work had preoccupied him for a long time; he had been unable to find an objective correlative to put at its center until he received a book written by a friend about the history of the porcelain factory at Fürstenberg, located on the Weser in Raabe's home country. This enterprise, which was founded in 1747 and exists to the present day, manufacturing fine china purveyed at quite breathtaking prices, provided him with an institutional generator of Rococo delicacy and fragile art in the midst of an environment of disruption and anxiety.

As so often with Raabe, the novel *appears* to be a story of love balked and then triumphant. The initial setting is the vicarage of the kindly Pastor Holtnicker, his somewhat more severe wife, and their foundling daughter, known as "Immeken" or "Little Bee." Immeken, according to Frau Holtnicker's lights, is to marry one of her relatives, another pastor, whose name Emmanuel Störenfreden ("disrupt peace") creates an expectation of ill that the story disappoints. Immeken, however, is in love with Pold Wille, a painter of flower designs at the factory, who has been shanghaied into military service and, by the sudden vicissitudes of the war, is now a deserter in fear of his life. He is hidden and protected by another figure washed up by the fortunes of war, an old Swiss soldier named Balthasar Uttenberger, wounded in French service. When things become too dangerous for Pold, the couple is rescued by the "village witch," Wackerhahn, a most un-witch-like sutler-woman with a colorful past and what one might call "road smarts," which enable her to bring the couple through the winter landscape to the duke's court at Blankenburg—this journey is the "Odyssey" of the novel. Along the way, for propriety's sake, Wackerhahn obliges Pastor Störenfreden to marry Pold and Immeken, which he does not only in manful renunciation, recognizing that Immeken cannot love him, but also irregularly, risking and subsequently incurring the wrath of the church consistory. Ultimately, with the successful conclusion of the Seven Years' War, Pold and Immeken live happily ever after.

Anyone who has followed Raabe through his career will recognize that this banal story is not the one he really meant to tell. In fact, the several allusions to earlier works suggest that, in composing this novel, his own career was much on his mind. It has not been sufficiently noticed how systematically *Hastenbeck* mirrors and revises *The Rumbledump*, published almost thirty years earlier. The rugged sutler-woman Wackerhahn corresponds to the peddler-woman Jane Warwolf; each is, in a wholly positive sense, a kind of Mother Courage. The probably illegitimate foundling Immeken corresponds to the illegitimate orphan Antonie Häussler, while Frau Holtnicker's repressive attachment to convention in matters of marriage is reminiscent of the attitude of Frau von Lauen. But the contrasts are obvious. Whereas in *The Rumbledump* the pastor and his son, also eventually a clergyman, belong to the *canaille* bringing harm and hurt into the world, in *Hastenbeck* Pastor Holtnicker is kind and generous, while the young Pastor Störenfreden is more than generous. In *The Rumbledump* the elderly mentors are helpless to avert the tragedy of Antonie's life; in *Hastenbeck* they bring the young lovers through to safety. The gloomy image of the rumbledump itself is, so to speak, cancelled in *Hastenbeck* by "God's miracle wagon," a leitmotif from a book of early eighteenth-century piety by one Gottlieb Cober, to which recurrent reference is made. All this gives *Hastenbeck*, despite the oppressiveness of its setting, a much more optimistic tone than *The Rumbledump* and it is perhaps even meant as a repudiation of the earlier novel.

On the other hand, the plot substance has been considerably diluted. The tragic Antonie Häussler, with her clear insight into her own self and situation, is an attractive figure, and the inexorable unfolding of her fate has certain conventionally novelistic virtues. *Hastenbeck*, by contrast, is exceedingly soft at the center. This is particularly true of the lovers. Raabe had a penchant for unheroic heroes. But Pold Wille is certainly the weakest of his central figures; his very name strikes us as an ironic contradiction, for Pold is nearly devoid of will. Though an artist and, in some sort, a soldier, he is hardly more than a boy, timid and tearful, and very much in need of management by his elder mentors. Immeken, too, has nothing like the psychological stature of Antonie Häussler; she is but a sweet, pretty girl, barely distinguishable from the painted Rococo figures on china for which she has served as a model. In his last novel Raabe seems to have carried his characteristic devaluation of plot to an ultimate point. If the novel's meaning cannot be found in plot and character, perhaps it lies at another level; and so it does.

The old Swiss warrior Uttenberger has brought with him a blood-stained, bullet-scarred book he has found, the idylls of his countryman Salomon Gessner. The pastorals of Gessner are the very essence of what we mean by "Rococo" in literature; they are the literary counterpart of the decorated china of Fürstenberg. They were also the first German-language literary work of modern times to achieve a wide international reputation and were translated into all the European languages. Raabe puts great stress on the contrast between Gessner's "Daphne and Chloe story" and the grim reality described in *Hastenbeck* (20: 39-40). At the outset of the Seven Years' War, the narrator remarks, Gessner lied about the world as Arcadia and about Zurich peasants as innocent shepherds (20: 60-61). But this is only a hyperbole stressing the fictiveness of the idyllic; as long as we understand its fictive status, the idyllic can serve as a context of utopian consolation and hope, as it does for the rough, barely lettered Swiss soldier. In the chapter containing the somewhat irregular marriage of Pold and

Immeken, there are several quotations from Johann Heinrich Voss's *Luise* (20: 135-36, 139). This, too, is characterized in literary history as an idyll, but it is much closer to social reality, and, in fact, a marriage outside of the church occurs in it. Voss was also the translator of Homer into German hexameters, thus one of the path-breakers of German Classicism. Another seminal work for both Classicism and Romanticism was Laurence Sterne's *Tristram Shandy*; the narrator alludes to it in the same chapter (20: 138), even though, as he points out, it would not begin to appear for another two years. Pastor Störenfreden has been a pupil of the Protestant Abbot Johann Friedrich Wilhelm Jerusalem, identified by the narrator as "Werther's father" (20: 92), for his son's suicide in 1772 was to be one of the impulses for Goethe's *Werther*, also one of the first products of the then generally unknown German literature to achieve international fame. This event, of course, is also in the future, this time by some fifteen years. Jerusalem appears later in the novel as an advisor to the Brunswickian ducal court at Blankenburg.

The journey itself, Raabe's Brunswickian *Odyssey*, continues to touch the nascent seeds of the great age of German culture. The refugees obtain help along the way from the Countess Stolberg, whose two sons, Count Christian and Count Friedrich Leopold, were to be friends and travelling companions of the young Goethe and play a prominent role in his autobiography. The journey passes the place where the popular poet Gottfried August Bürger is growing up, as well as the vicarage that is the childhood home of the girl alleged to be the subject of Bürger's ballad on infanticide (20: 156); we are now reaching almost twenty-five years into the future. At the Blankenburg court there appears as an emissary from the court of Weimar the young Baron von Fritsch, "the future Antonio of the future Weimarian minister of state von Goethe" (20: 165), an allusion to Goethe's *Torquato Tasso*, thirty-three years in the future. The refugees are received in Blankenburg by Philippine Charlotte, Duchess of Braunschweig. She was a sister of Frederick the Great, but it is not this connection that primarily interests Raabe here; she was much more appreciative of German culture than her brother, and, as Raabe may have known, was a particular admirer of Gessner.[21] More importantly, she was the mother of Duchess Anna Amalia of Weimar, who, by attracting Wieland and Herder to that court, set in motion the sequence of events that was to make Weimar the focal point of German culture for two generations. Philippine Charlotte is concerned about her daughter and sickly son-in-law, for Anna Amalia has just given birth to a son: the future Duke Carl August, patron and intimate friend of Goethe, employer of Schiller and other figures of the great epoch. Perhaps it is not too far-fetched to observe in addition that the final scene of this configuration, Blankenburg, is also the name of the first German theoretician of the novel.[22]

In any case, the general drift of things is clear. Just over the horizon of the struggle and odyssey of these relatively unremarkable fictional figures awaits the dawn of Germany's great modern age. That this is the case lies completely beyond the awareness of any of the novel's figures; only the first harbingers, Gessner and Voss, are yet visible, though in their true importance only to the narrator, while the present consciousness of the novel's characters, fictional and historical, is marked more by dismay and anxiety than by hope. But the narrator communicates with us over their heads, linking the optimistic outcome of his foreground story with the historical outlook of imminent greatness. The utopian quality of Gessner's idylls, untruthful in their own world, nevertheless anticipates hope in the realm of the imagination. This hope joins reality not in the exploits of Frederick the Great or the outcome of the Seven Years' War, as important as these may be to the historical context, but in the Age of Goethe in its crucial importance for Germany and the world.

Hastenbeck exhibits the ultimate quintessence of Raabe's nationalism. He set as a motto to the novel a quotation from the Prussian reformer Baron vom Stein: "I have only one fatherland; that is called Germany" (20: 6). It is important not to misunderstand either the quotation itself or Raabe's use of it. Stein's meaning was that he was not an agent of parochial Prussian interests but an advocate of the nation as a whole, the "Germany" that, at the time he made this utterance, existed only in the imagination. Raabe's meaning is that, although he has written a Brunswickian *Iliad* and *Odyssey*, his concerns, too, are not regional or parochial, and that his vision of the nation was one of culture, independence, and liberty, the vision of which Stein, the political contemporary of the Age of Goethe, was for a brief, frustrating time the paladin. The vision is one of hope more than confidence. In *Hastenbeck*, as in all of Raabe's historical fiction, we see the fragility of the world of culture and civilization, of the imagination and simple decency, how the brutality and cruelty of man's customary state recurrently threaten to engulf that world and obliterate its meaning. Thus his hope was not so much a promise as an ethical imperative.

CHAPTER 10

Humor

◧

There is a sort of jesting which is very much in earnest, and includes some pretty serious disgust.
Dickens, *Martin Chuzzlewit*

Who is a humorist? He who drives the tiniest of nails into the wall or the skull of the highly esteemed public—and hangs the whole wardrobe of the times and all past times on it.
Raabe, 1873[1]

IT HAS BEEN a long-standing joke that the shortest book of the year is entitled *Four Hundred Years of German Humor*. This is, of course, a libel, but it points to a cultural difference that emerges in the terminology of literary theory; indeed, a German of traditional culture might have claimed that the Germans have *more* humor than other peoples. The *Princeton Encyclopedia of Poetry and Poetics* contains substantial articles under "Comedy," "Farce," "Satire," and "Wit," but has no entry under "Humor."[2] By contrast, a much-used German lexicon of literary terms does have such an entry, which defines "humor" quite specifically in a long sentence, part of which runs as follows:

> a mood that benignly but with distance rises smilingly above the inadequacies of human life and penetrates above and beyond the low comic and the unnatural to a healthy and natural apprehension of the world, a means of both self-criticism and self-affirmation in senseless existence, distinguished, by mild, humane forbearance and sublime composure of direct observation, from the sharp scorn of satire as well as from the figurative mode of irony and from gross comedy, and originating either from the ground of plain childish simplicity or the freedom of the spirit and the recovered psychic equilibrium after the severest shocks, always accompanied by a philosophical view of life and related through its sublimity to the tragic.[3]

133

The origin of this definition in idealist aesthetics is plain enough. The definitive codifier of this meaning of humor was doubtless Jean Paul, who wrote in Section 32 of his *Primer of Aesthetics*: "Humor as the inverted sublime annihilates not the individual but the finite through its contrast with the idea. . . . Humor thus annihilates both great and small, because before infinity everything is equal and nothing."[4] The function of humor as a means of coping with the misery of life and reality was a preoccupation of German literature and literary theory in the nineteenth century. The young Gottfried Keller saw this function as a truism: "humor often puts forth its loveliest blossoms on the dark ground of the greatest grief";[5] around the same time Friederich Theodor Vischer in his influential *Aesthetics* wrote: "Humor presumes . . . the deepest unhappiness of consciousness."[6] The same view was held by Hermann Hesse, the modern successor to the idealist tradition, who wrote of humor as "the old mediator between ideal and reality."[7]

There can be no doubt that Raabe, from the outset of his career, understood himself as a humorist in this codified German sense. His apprehension of the dark ground of life and his sense of literature as a resource of consolation were instincts that remained intact from beginning to end, though with experience they were to undergo maturation and elaborate ramification. In an early phase of his career he spoke of working on a "humorous sentimental novel."[8] The concept appears promptly in *The Chronicle of Sparrow Alley*, in this as in so many other respects a primer of his career. On the anniversary of a great pain in the narrator's life, humor appears on his threshold, calling: "Laugh, laugh, Johannes, you are old and have no more time to lose" (1: 23). April, we are told in the same novel, is the month of humor; it carries rain and sunshine, laughter and tears in one sack (1: 162). In the slight early story *The Way to Laughter* (1857), a saturnine professor, who has been told by his doctor to learn to laugh or die, exorcises his burden of sorrow through sympathy with others and acceptance of the happy family life of his lost beloved. The posture is one of stoic compassion, of kindness in immediate human relations accompanied by detachment from the mean absurdities of the social world. The police clerk Fiebiger in *The People from the Forest*, apostrophized as an "old humorist," is a man who has learned to be free in fetters and chains, with the result that he has become "a caustic despiser of all pretensions of human pride and human perfections" (5: 36, 58). In *The Dräumling Swamp* the narrator enthusiastically eulogizes the humorous spirit:

Long live free laughter that wrestles itself suddenly, unexpectedly, and irresistibly out of the confinement of the fretful day!
Long live above all the still serenity that upon more mature consideration is wrung out of all the confused, tortuous irritations of
life! . . . Praised be he who knows how to elevate the short moment of comfort out of the uncomfortable length of the day with
genuine profit! (10: 145)

There is a fine line here between stoicism and willful illusion, between employing imagination to mobilize wisdom and goodwill for
psychic survival and employing it as flight from the contradictions and
sufferings of life and society by pronouncing them insignificant *sub
specie aeternitatis*, thus serving conservative immobility to the benefit of
the privileged and comfortable. Raabe skirted this line from time to
time, but he did not really cross it, for with his extremely acute sense
of the antinomy of fiction and reality he knew where the boundary
ran. The same cannot be said so confidently of his disciples. Shortly
after his death his humor was characterized in this obfuscating fashion:

Only that this humor has extremely little in common with joking,
wit, and comedy, and is not easily found here and there, but is
poured over the works of the poet like sunshine and is the sublime
expression for the relationship between the human-earthly and
the eternal power of the light.[9]

The harmonization into "eternal values" as well as the melting of
Raabe's works into one indistinguishable mass are characteristic of the
posthumous development of his reputation. As usual, the canonized
view was reiterated monotonously. Humor in *Horacker* was defined as
equanimity before the little worries of life so that the heart is free for
the great sufferings and struggles.[10] When Adolf Suchel later admitted
the existence of the comic in Raabe, he excluded the humorous from
the discussion.[11] This is one of the aspects of Raabe's traditional reputation that has infected the modern attitude toward him. For Lukács
humor was Raabe's formal admission of his inability to solve the problem of capitalism; in other words, an evasive strategy.[12] Even his modern admirer Daemmrich sees humor as a deflective disjunction of reality and ideals that "afford[s] the reader the exquisite pleasure of
smiling at life's incongruities and laughing at human folly instead of
feeling challenged to rise in defense of needed reforms."[13] Only slowly
has the recognition come that "his humor is certainly closer to satire
than people wanted to perceive; his faces can even become distorted

into a grimace, a grotesque visage, and his portraits turn into caricature."[14]

Although Raabe often seemed quite content with the appellation of
humorist, in time he began to notice that he was being reductively
type-cast and grew uneasy about it. To a request for a humorous
contribution in 1877 he replied: "What the German calls 'humor' is
often completely the opposite of it."[15] By 1885 he had come to regard
the idea of a "humoristic Germany" as a cliché, adding that he had
experienced little of the German people as a chosen people in this
regard.[16] In *The Lar* (1889), humor comes close to being reduced to
popular entertainment; the young protagonist Kohl wants to be a serious journalist, but he is advised that he is too much of a humorist
and should stick to the feuilleton, for that is what the sixty million
Germans prefer (17: 284). Near the very end of his life Raabe remarked to his biographer Krüger: "What do people want? I am much
more a tragedian than a humorist" (E 4: 306). Certainly he adverted
often enough to the dark ground of humor. The narrator of *German
Nobility* observes that humor is opposed to heroism and related to the
insight that all of us, heroes and heroines alike, will die (13: 234-35).
Stuffcake ascribes to himself the "humor of despair" (18: 134), and in
Cloister Lugau the humor of Aunt Knowthemall turns into anger and
frantic frustration at the meanness of the world around her, leading
even to fantasies of mass murder, of the poisoning of whole towns (19:
77-78).

All the talk about humor in Raabe has paradoxically obscured the
fact that he is one of the funniest writers in German literature. As a
comic writer I would rate him above Fritz Reuter and even Keller,
and his range was greater than that of his only near competitor, Wilhelm Busch, whom Raabe found sadistic (E 4: 268-69). A definitive
study of his comedy, of which "humor" in the specific sense would be
only a facet, has yet to be undertaken. Such a study would find, I
believe, its center not in "humor" but in satire, to which his humor
constantly tends, as does his Dickensian surrealism, his black comedy,
his larking, and his grotesque farce. The mock-pompous, self-consciously hyperbolic tone of his satire may sometimes, especially in the
more mature works, remind us of Thomas Mann, who might conceivably have written this account of the quarters of the fashionable aesthete Albin Brokenkorb in *On the Scrap-Iron*:

> Where would we end if we wanted to begin to describe in detail?
> Cabinet next to cabinet, compartment over compartment in the
> most art-crafty decor through all the rooms! The museum of a

rich private gentleman from the first seal, postage-stamp, beetle, and butterfly collections to the genuine Tanagra figure! Portfolios full of copper engravings, etchings, woodcuts of the oldest and most recent masters! Portfolios full of manuscripts of famous, well-known, notorious people of all ages! Everything that had a touch of the dainty, the petite, the tiny in pastel, watercolor, wax, oil, enamel—on paper, linen, copper, wood, and china! Curiosities in lathe-work, glass-work, wire-work! The most graceful weapons, domestic and decorative articles from the wildest non-European nations! Old globes from Nuremberg and Augsburg. *Books!* Yes, books! For almost too many branches of human knowledge, the best, most copious, most abundant, most precious aids for easing the capacity of man in regard to finding himself, thinking for himself!

"Oh, God!" the female visitors used to say, when, as politely interested as possible, they endeavored to get past this exquisite library to something more interesting; and we—we say the same. (16: 358)

But to exhaust the range of Raabe's satirical tones alone in any detail would require the space of a monograph. I want here only to address briefly some examples from the spectrum of his comedy in order to release him from the pigeonhole of "humorist."

German Humor: *Horacker*

The short novel *Horacker* (1876) is probably the most refined example of the traditional concept of humor in Raabe's oeuvre. Though rather coolly received upon publication, it has grown greatly in estimation over time and is today among connoisseurs one of the best-loved of all his works. As is so often the case in his best fiction, almost nothing happens in the eight hours covered by this novel, although much seems to be happening that is not. The initial constellation of characters includes an elderly pedagogue named Eckerbusch, one of the last men to hold the now abolished post of conrector in his village school, a man whose speech is full of the tags of the classicistic humanism he has taught for so many years. His younger friend Windwebel is the drawing instructor in the school. The latter's recent bride is loving and anxious, but Eckerbusch's wife has been dubbed by her husband, with characteristically donnish humor, the "Proceleusmatica," after a Greek metrical foot of four short syllables, in recognition of her blunt, rather impatient common sense. The village community has been put into something of a tizzy by the news of the escape of a criminal, Cord Horacker, whom steadily escalating rumor has rampaging in the countryside.

This monster criminal turns out to be an undernourished, none-too-bright, nineteen-year-old boy who has been put in the workhouse for stealing a pot of lard from a woman sleeping by the road. He has escaped because a malicious fellow prisoner put a bug in his ear about the unfaithfulness of his beloved, the poor orphan girl Lotte Achterhang. The very opposite of this is true; Lotte, who has found employment in the working-class suburbs of Berlin, tramps home on foot (we may assume it is Raabe's native Weser country, some 175 miles from Berlin) in order to be with him when she hears of his new trouble. The two schoolteachers, on a walk in the country, encounter Horacker's distraught, widowed mother, and then Horacker himself; after some bumbling misadventures they induce the starving, frightened boy to come to the vicarage in the next town, where he is reunited with Lotte, who had been a ward of the pastor's wife. However, the absence of the two teachers gives rise to the rumor that they have been murdered by Horacker. Young Frau Windwebel is quite terrified by the rumor, but Frau Eckerbusch does not believe a word of it; she takes it into her head that it is a tasteless April Fool's joke of her husband, and she sets off for the next town with blood in her eye to have it out with him. She takes along not only Frau Windwebel but also, as a very unwilling passenger, a young teacher named Neubauer.

This character is the New Prussian Man as schoolmaster. Full of himself and of his sense of superiority to his elders, he is preoccupied with composing a *Sixty-sixiad*, an epic poem on the recent Prussian victory over the Danes in 1866. Raabe's little literary joke here may well escape most modern readers. He is alluding not only in general to the bad literature patriotic feeling can generate, but also to the contemporary mode of the heroic epic poem, a genre vigorously pursued in his time with many elaborate works that, one and all, have fallen into total and justified oblivion.[17] Frau Eckerbusch feels lively contempt for the busy, fussy popinjay and makes a verse upon his type:

> Rush, rush, rush;
> Tar them all with just one brush. (12: 398)[18]

What she recognizes in him more than anything else is a lack of a sense of humor: "It can be all the same to me and my old man. *We* have, thank God, the humor to enjoy many things; but I feel sorry for the poor youths who their whole lives long can't get rid of the drill-sergeant in one form or another, from the cradle through the school into their numbered cool grave" (ibid.). In the end, everything is untangled; a decent order of things, a kindly justice, and a more or less optimistic outlook for Horacker and Lotte are restored.

Here, as always, Raabe had serious things on his mind, as he emphasized when praising the book to his publisher.[19] According to his own account, the whole mood of the book proceeded from an excursus on the word *man*—"one," "they," "people," the impersonal, anonymous, conventional opinion that blocks a differentiated, sympathetic insight into human affairs.[20] The passage begins with a sequence of conventional, masked egocentric locutions:

> Who is *one*? One does not gladly see one spider devour another; —one likes to eat oysters;—one founds a business, through which one gladly competes with everyone to the utmost. One has a well-founded prospect of soon advancing in office, since one says that the man whose place one would gladly take is lying deathly ill of a nervous fever and certainly will soon bite the dust, leaving a large family behind him. . . . (12: 344)

The passage goes on to observe that individual sufferers like Horacker and Lotte are sometimes this "one," for whom "one" in general has no sympathy.

However, there are other, less aphoristic considerations in the background. *Horacker* puts me in mind of a brief but highly suggestive moment in Chapter 41 of Dickens's *Great Expectations*. Two chapters earlier, Pip has had a visit from the transported criminal Magwitch, who reveals, to Pip's consternation, that it is he who has secretly funded Pip's great expectations. Later, Pip's amiable housemate Herbert Pocket returns and is made acquainted with the startling revelation. When Magwitch has left, Herbert Pocket unconsciously takes the chair in which Magwitch has been sitting, "but the next moment started out of it, pushed it away, and took another." Here we see in tightest concentration that terror of criminality that pervades the novel, despite Magwitch's moral rehabilitation and instincts of generous gratitude. For the sake of these good qualities Dickens cannot hang him, but neither can he allow a man of criminal past, illegally returned from transportation, to go free; so Dickens splits the difference by having him die in prison before his hanging date. To my mind, *Horacker* is a gloss on this nineteenth-century bourgeois terror of criminality and exhibits a more flexible attitude toward conventional morality than Dickens was able to muster. It is true that Raabe stacks the deck by making Horacker such a harmless and pathetic figure. But in fact his harmlessness and pathos make little difference to the collective consciousness, which, out of its responses rigidified in petty-bourgeois automatism, turns him into a bogeyman. So that we should not forget that there is real crime in the world, Raabe has his characters pass on the road a memorial to a forester killed fifteen years before by a poacher (12: 395). As Martini has pointed out, even the good, helping people are beset by their fears of criminality; even the kindly Eckerbusch believes that Windwebel might have been killed by the harmless Horacker.[21] In one of the most comic scenes of the novel, Windwebel chases Horacker, catches him, and sits on him, whereupon the utterly defeated boy completely gives up, but Windwebel, not knowing what to do in this situation, gets scared; not daring to let the fearsome criminal get up, he mutters: "so he has me quite in his claws, the bandit Horacker" (12: 362).

All this critique of petty-bourgeois consciousness modifies the elegiac quality of Raabe's humor in *Horacker*, its nostalgia for an idyllic small-town atmosphere. It is undeniable that there is a conservative aspect to the novel. There is, as has been said, a mood of farewell through the whole story.[22] Another critic has characterized the work as a "farewell song to the pedagogical provinces of German neo-classical humanism."[23] Along with this humanistic culture, the values of kindness and tolerance, the virtues of humor, seem to be slipping into obsolescence. A new generation is on the horizon, represented by Neubauer: ambitious, pompous, military in bearing, both servile and tyrannical. Traditional patterns of authority, if indeed they ever existed, no longer function. When the public prosecutor dismisses as a myth Horacker's reputation as a dangerous criminal, the local peasants refuse to believe him; the peasants, the narrator remarks, "trust" the robber more than the prosecutor (12: 310). There is a great deal of antagonism between the pastor and his wife on the one hand and the peasants on the other. The peasants have discovered an ancient tradition that the pastor must appear at each family's home at New Year's with a verse greeting; out of malice they insist upon its restoration, arousing despair in the pastor and an all but murderous fury in his wife.

It must be admitted that peasants do not come off very well in Raabe's fictional world. They exhibit human beings in a primitive and elemental state, obstinate, superstitious, selfish, fixed in their mental processes, which is to say, ungentled by bourgeois humanism. Where a farmer appears as a positive figure, such as Just Everstein in *Old Nests*, it is because he has acquired a humanistic education. There is a visible stress on the class virtues of the traditional petty-bourgeoisie in

Horacker. The peasants are totally unsympathetic to Horacker and make no allowances for the extreme poverty of his background, and they regard Lotte as a vagabond who should never have been charitably treated in the first place. At every appearance their conduct is lumpish and self-righteous. But Raabe means it not self-righteously but justly when the pastor's wife asserts: "We are basically good people, whatever the village may think about it" (12: 353).

Still, Raabe is no more committed to the "good old days" here than he is elsewhere. The concept of "idyll" undergoes a continuous subversive critique in the novel. When the teachers find a picturesque place in the country, an accumulation of trash on the ground shows that others had already found it (12: 318). One scrap of paper gives the total of the casualties in the 1866 war. As always, the war is in the background not as victory but as sorrow; Eckerbusch broods over the memory of his former pupils fallen in the field. Only the impossible Neubauer (whose name, "new peasant," may suggest that he is a modern, more polished version of the traditional blockhead) strives to make something heroic out of the war. It is Neubauer who is alleged to get his notions from Goldsmith's *Vicar of Wakefield* (12: 348), misperceived in Germany since Goethe's time as a genre picture of idyllic traditional life. The pastor's wife vigorously rejects the notion that they live in anything like an idyll (ibid.). Later the narrator intervenes, not without irony, to rescue what remains of the idyllic genre:

> Almost too much ferment in the epic-tragic brew, too many errata in the idyll, and still, still, what an idyll! What a cloudless ether over the fretfulness of the world; and through a heart here and there what a cool and peaceful breeze out of a quite remarkable other world without errata, advertisements, and criticism!
> (12: 415)

Yet there are parodistic elements to this "idyll," especially of the village tale, made popular by Raabe's contemporary Auerbach.[24] The refusal to sentimentalize the peasantry belongs here. At the same time it must be said on behalf of the peasants that the conflict was initially instigated by the pastor, who found in old documents a tradition fallen into desuetude, by which the peasants owed him dues of four pennies each quarter, and he has applied to the consistory for its revival. The peasants simply retaliate on the principle that one man's traditionalism is as good as another's. To this must be added the circumstance that the obsolescence of the positive characters is too pronounced to be wholly positive. The pastor regards the eighteenth-century moralist

Gellert as a classical author (12: 305), hardly a virtue in the mind of an author struggling for contemporary acceptance of his own work. The Conrector Eckerbusch, who is said to be as extinct as a kiwi (12: 293), is rather too unworldly; he has never left his narrow horizon except for his three years at the university, and he pays no attention to current events. The drawing teacher Windwebel presents a problem of a different kind. When the teachers confront the ragged, despairing Widow Horacker, Windwebel's first reaction is to sketch her as a picturesque figure and tip her a couple of coins (12: 320-21). He does the same to the hungry, cold, and sobbing Horacker, asking him at one point to pose (12: 331). When he escapes, Windwebel chases him because he had only completed two-thirds of the drawing (12: 358). We have already seen in the preceding chapter what Raabe thought of this aestheticization of suffering.

Thus it is part of his "humor" to put limitations on his positive characters, to avoid presenting them as moral paragons. Humor is balance, sympathy, tolerance, comprehension, and a decent degree of moral relativism without losing sight of the humane priorities. No other of his works is so gracefully pervaded by this spirit as *Horacker*.

SLAPSTICK: *Celtic Bones; Christoph Pechlin*

Raabe's sense of humor had a farcical, anarchic side that has not appealed very much to his traditional admirers. Perhaps it does not add substantially to his stature, but it is important to see it in the context of "humor" as an antidote to the idealistic, implicitly escapist harmonization associated with that concept. The surreal, burlesque, sometimes just plain goofy impulse breaks out in him at various places, but is most clearly illustrated by two works in the middle of his career, the short story *Celtic Bones* (1864) and the novel *Christoph Pechlin* (1873).

Celtic Bones followed immediately upon one of his darkest and most depressing works, *Elsa of the Fir*, an indication that his profoundest pessimism required comic relief for psychic balance. The story is the consequence of a visit in 1859 to Hallstatt, southeast of Salzburg, where beginning in 1846 a Bronze Age and Early Iron Age archaeological site was excavated that has given its name to the Hallstatt Culture. At that time there was a debate as to whether the bones were Germanic or Celtic, an argument that undoubtedly had nationalistic implications but that Raabe nevertheless found ridiculous. The story is narrated by an unnamed, amused, peripheral observer, who arrives at Hallstatt, in wretched weather, along with two scholars: a funereal university "prosector," Zuckriegel, and his exact counterpart, a Berlin professor named Steinbüchse. The former supports the Celtic theory, the latter the Germanic, and they squabble comically about it though neither has seen the bones. It is Zuckriegel's plan to steal some of these bones for himself, in preparation for which he reads a *History of German Crooks* (9/1: 207); Steinbüchse has the same idea. On their excursion to the site, the narrator feels sorry for the skeletons and imagines them attacking the tourists with swords (9/1: 235). The scholars grab pieces of the skeletons and run off, the guide shrieks for help, the locals chase the scholars, who tumble down the mountain, furiously throwing skulls and bones at one another.[25]

With this fluff Raabe had several minor and less minor things on his mind. Along with the satire on scholarly striving and competition there is satire on tourism, a phenomenon that had been gaining momentum since early in the century and for which Heine in his time had also had a sharp satirical eye. Particularly annoying are fundamentalist Americans, who keep Zuckriegel awake all night in his hotel room with their loud praying. Of more importance is the background of the war in Italy between Austria and France in 1859, which had frustrated Raabe's journey to Italy; he was vexed by the ineffectual conduct of the Austrian side, upon which he makes some rude remarks in the story (9/1: 210). There is a scene of an old beggar woman whose son is a soldier, but the narrator refuses to novelize it; the boy had gone out cursing "in order to protect what others had married together" (9/1: 211), that is, dynastic interests of no importance to the people. Later in Salzburg the narrator sees a casualty list on which the old woman's son appears wounded—in the back (9/1: 240). A third concern is part of a personal self-clarification. Also visiting Hallstatt is a crazy poet with the dissonant name of Krautworst, which he has masked behind the more refined pen name of "Roderich von der Leine." (The custom of second-rate writers taking on pretentious *noms de plume* is also satirized in Gottfried Keller's novella *The Misused Love-Letters*, written in Berlin in the 1850s but not published until ten years after *Celtic Bones*.) Krautworst recites terrible poetry and must endure rude interpolations from Zuckriegel, who, to the poet's fury, compares him to "Heinrich Heine, or whatever the man's name is" (9/1: 222). The joke is that all this awful verse is from Raabe's own corpus of several years earlier. With ruthless self-parody he has cut himself away from the poetic aspirations of only a few years before.

His most elaborate experiment in the burlesque, *Christoph Pechlin: An International Love Story*, has been little liked even by his most enthusiastic admirers. Even the editor of the text in the critical edition, Hans-Jürgen Meinerts, seems to have been embarrassed by it. He notes the absence of any "deep penetration with the spirit of Raabean humor" and sees the work as caricature, "the madness of love viewed with Schopenhauerian wrath" (10: 487). Raabe himself was apparently uneasy about the work. When in 1896 someone turned it into a stage farce, Raabe refused to permit its performance, fearing that it would upset his "little community."[26] In a new edition of 1890 he added the famous preface that I cited in Chapter 8 on politics, in which he connects the work to the spirit of materialism and selfishness that pervaded Germany after the victory of 1871. Most observers have taken this to be an *ex post facto* justification; among the major modern critics, as far as I can see, only Daemmrich has taken Raabe at his word, arguing that the novel "brilliantly captures the aggressiveness of the empire builders, the hypocrisies beneath grandiose ideals, the conformity begotten by collective experiences, and the spirit of a people caught up in the rush to live a good life."[27] I am not certain that this will stand up to scrutiny of the novel, or whether it would have occurred to anyone without the nudging of the later preface. The novel's center appears to me rather to lie in a sour, even misanthropic facet of Raabe's sense of comedy. It is a tone very different from his legendary role as beneficent, comforting wise man, which is quite likely the reason his disciples have wished it away.

The noisy, abrasive, and bizarre comedy is not easy to summarize briefly; in fact the novel made sense to me only when read a second time. Pechlin, a failed theology student with literary ambitions, receives a visit from a student friend, Baron Rippgen, who has married for money—an old story hardly worth telling, the narrator puts in (10: 218). His wife, Lucie, daughter of a silk merchant, is a fat, bossy, pretentious, and conceited monster of an emasculating female. Lucie has a crony and fellow-conspirator against the male sex, Christabel Eddish, a pale, blonde Englishwoman of about thirty, who is quite pretty at first sight but is high-strung, snobbish, prudish, and ill-mannered; she has been called a "figure which exemplifies Thackeray's influence on Raabe rather exceptionally."[28] Pechlin incites the baron to the rebellion of taking a journey with him, without Lucie or her permission. But, as every commentator has noticed, the structural principle of the novel is improbable, contrived coincidence, and the principle of coincidence is that characters are constantly meeting those from whom they are attempting to flee. Thus Pechlin and Rippgen run into Lucie and Christabel on the journey. Pechlin is quite smitten with Christabel, against his better judgment, and she overcomes her initial distaste for his vulgarity in admiration of his conduct in an epic tavern brawl. Pechlin finds himself most grievously betrothed, as

Christabel undertakes to reform the cheerful anarchist into a proper bourgeois gentleman. At one point he comes to regard her as a vampire to whom he is enslaved (10: 409). Dashing in and out of the story is Sir Hugh Sliddery, a perfect ass of a travelling Englishman, who is attempting to avoid Christabel and therefore repeatedly encounters her, on which occasions she falls into hysterical fits. After much ado and general foofaraw, Pechlin is liberated by the discovery that Christabel and Sir Hugh are the parents of an illegitimate six-year-old boy whom both have abandoned. At her exposure Christabel turns into the screaming virago she is at heart; she disappears to Australia with an American clergyman—doubtless an appropriate punishment in Raabe's eyes—while Pechlin and his friends assume responsibility for the abandoned boy.

It is almost superfluous to remark that feminists may have some difficulty being amused by this tale. There is in it an unmistakable and rather atypically extreme note of misogyny; Pechlin (or Pechle, as he is nicknamed), sighs as he is preparing his marriage to Christabel: "Rippgen, I tell you, no male person knows the evil of women as it deserves to be known; but I, Christoph Pechle, am in a fair way to become unique as regards penetration into this science!" (10: 412), and the lawyer who knows the truth about Christabel breaks out into eloquent rage when he thinks of her: "Oh, you, you—you unutterable one, you—green-eyed, fish-blooded polyp, have I caught you now?! Oh you unholy, pretty, mother-of-pearl witch, shall I finally get you out of my files?!" (10: 435)

Raabe's attitude toward women is a topic that has been examined several times[29] but would bear more scrutiny because of its complexity and ambiguity. It would lead us too far afield here, but it may be remarked that there is a broad spectrum of attitudes toward women in the works, from the patriarchal and condescending through respect for forthrightness and initiative to examples of genuine emancipation. The ambiguity is detectable in Raabe's life as well, of which one example may suffice: he had his eldest daughter Margarethe trained as a professional painter, and, as a matter of fact, she was the first female pupil in the commercial art school she attended.[30] Yet in her parents' old age she was apparently obliged to nurse them; Raabe wrote that he felt sorry for her, as she would so much like to go out into the world, but there was nothing for it.[31] One gets the impression that Raabe, who by this time could easily afford a servant, apparently turned his forty-seven-year-old, professionally trained daughter into one—though this may be unfair, as the letter was written a couple of months before his death, when he was failing seriously.

His tenderness in his fiction toward unwed mothers, who seem to have filled most other nineteenth-century novelists with horror, is so remarkable that long ago it was the subject of a special study.[32] Christabel Eddish is only apparently an exception. She is abhorrent not because of her unwed motherhood, but because of her total lack of responsibility to her child and the contrast between her conduct in the past and her snobbish prudishness: she is unspeakably shocked when Pechlin refers to the navel and is determined to cure him of such vulgarities as playing the jew's harp. The target of the burlesque in the novel is not so much women as marriage. This is not the only place where Raabe, who was as happily married as any man has a right to be, took a traditional, low-comedy view of marriage, though it is doubtless the most extreme case. Whether he did so as a form of commonplace male psychic release from the restraints of marriage or in obedience to a comic literary tradition of long endurance is a question I would not know how to answer.

Another plane of comedy in *Christoph Pechlin* is the linguistic. The novel was written soon after Raabe's departure from Stuttgart and was apparently intended as a gesture of affection toward Swabia and his friends there. Therefore much of the dialogue and a number of expressions in the book, such as Pechlin's nickname "Pechle," are colored by what Raabe supposed to be Swabian dialect. I am no judge of this, for I have always found Swabian the most unfathomable of all the German dialects I have encountered, but genuine Swabians have not been impressed by the achievement,[33] just as one critic at the time denied the authenticity of the Saxon expressions put into the mouth of Baron Rippgen (10: 491-92). The lawyer speaks an alleged Frankfurt dialect, the authenticity of which I am also unable to assess. With the English language, which is called upon repeatedly in the novel, I am on a somewhat surer footing. Christabel Eddish speaks in a macaronic jumble of German and English; Lucie in a letter flatters her by quoting a number of lines from Coleridge's "Christabel," while Pechlin, when infected with his fateful passion for her, keeps muttering "yes" in English. Sir Hugh, on the other hand, speaks German fairly fluently but with a pronounced English accent, which Raabe tries to indicate orthographically. None of this, I fear, is very successful. The orthographic device has mainly the effect of slowing up the reader. Raabe's efforts at English show all too plainly that, although his reading knowledge may have been excellent, he did not possess active skills. It may be nit-picking to argue that the awkwardness of the English-language device justifies a low estimate of the novel,[34] but it is distracting to the reader, especially one with a command of English.

The language games do, however, have a function in the novel: like the recurrently improbable coincidences and the constantly hyperbolic, even hysterical quality of the discourse, they reinforce the artificiality of the narration, its pronounced literariness, and this, in turn, suggests that the low comedy of the novel is largely literary in nature and not a significant meditation on the relationship of the sexes. Thus *Christoph Pechlin* belongs among Raabe's numerous experiments in the art of fiction, and if this one did not fully succeed, it certainly obliges us to extend our concept of his sense of humor.

ELEGANCE: *The Geese of Bützow*

Just as the farcical, chaotic, anarchic dimension of Raabe's imagination has been smoothed out of the traditional image of him, so one would not normally think of applying the term "elegance" to him. Despite his resourceful dexterity, his stylistic center of gravity was the middle level, his fundamental mode the low mimetic, as the central instincts of his mind were those of matter-of-fact bourgeois reasonableness. Refinement and polish were not among his priorities; indeed, he tended to look upon these qualities with suspicion as masks for duplicity and egotism. Twice we have seen examples of his resistance to aestheticization as mendacious prettification of the grim truths of reality. Yet Raabe is not to be captured by exclusive formulas; whenever we try to delimit him, we will discover something that transcends those limits. At the opposite end of the comic spectrum from the intentionally vulgar burlesque of *Christoph Pechlin* lies the exquisite high comedy of *The Geese of Bützow* (1866). Like *Celtic Bones*, it was written contemporaneously with one of the darkest and bleakest of his works, in this case *St. Thomas*.

The story of the novella is anything but elegant; it is altogether absurd, and once again Raabe has drawn the absurdity from real life, as documented in an eighteenth-century judicial record. In Bützow, a town in Mecklenburg (the subtitle of the novella, *An Obotritian Historia*, refers with characteristic learnedness to one of the ancient tribes of the area), the authorities issued an ordinance requiring that geese be kept in stalls and no longer be allowed to run free in the town. Incensed at this assault on their traditional habits, the townspeople rose up in protest. The year was 1794, the time of the terroristic and militant phase of the French Revolution. Fear of revolutionary infection was widespread in Germany; in Bützow the authorities smelled revolution in the protest and perhaps some of the townspeople did, also. Troops were called in, arrests were made, and rebels were imprisoned, though their sentences were commuted by a more sensible higher court. This splendid example of revolution, German style, understandably struck Raabe's funny bone when he ran across it.

In managing the material, Raabe, on the one hand, personalized it, and, on the other, pressed it to the extremes of satire that it certainly invites. Central to the revolt is Mamsell Hornbostel, a thirty-five-year-old maiden who is another of his formidable females. She is courted by Magister Albus, a drab schoolmaster who, however, is sincerely committed to the constitutional ideals of the French Revolution. Mamsell Hornbostel makes use of his devotion but promises her hand, for the time being, to a more manic rabble-rouser, Dr. Wübbke; eventually she marries the commander of the troops occupying the town, for she is motivated not by ideology but by resentment against the mayor, Dr. Hane, who backed out of marriage with her. But Raabe counters this trivializing personalization with generalizing satire. The mayor is apoplectic with rage at the challenge to his authority, and he makes the immediate association, instinctive to the threatened dominant class, with radical subversion and Jacobin atrocities. He is seconded by the sanctimonious pastor, who reminds the people of their duty by reading to them from an edifying work of passive submissiveness entitled *The Spiritual Night-Cap* (9/2: 71-72). The town policeman whose task it is to enforce the ordinance is a conceited numbskull, and the burghers are utterly immobile and resistant to change. But the satirical eye also falls upon the inflated rhetoric of the protestors, as when Albus orates: "Citizens, friends, patriots! I declare the infringement of the goose freedom an invasion of the rights of man crying to high heaven . . ." (9/2: 108).

Raabe's *tour de force* in this work, his encapsulation, so to speak, of the absurd in the elegant, lies in the characterization of his narrator, the retired schoolmaster J. W. Eyring, who refers to himself in the mock-epic chapter headings as "auctor." The depiction of events in the story, it has been rightly said, is "intensified and totally engulfed by Eyring's personality. . . . His subjective view is finally what makes the tale worth telling."[35] Here Raabe's play with language works much more persuasively than in *Christoph Pechlin*. He well captures the formal, learned, witty style of an already somewhat old-fashioned late eighteenth-century man of culture. His diction is packed with literary and historical allusions and parodies, though he is up-to-date enough to allude to both Goethe and Schiller. These allusions, as has been said, "pour down upon the helpless and soon capitulating reader like a pelting rain."[36] The effect is to diffuse the events he is describing into a kind of historical relativism, a documentation of eternal recurrence. For Eyring is a man of reason, tolerance, and judicious contemplation almost to the point of paralysis. He does intervene to rescue his friend Albus from the consequences of his political activism by spiriting him off to the care of the rationalist Friedrich Nicolai in Berlin, but on the whole he remains the amused, wise, refined, and detached observer of human folly. He has no brief for officialdom and certainly none for the religious institution in alliance with it, but neither has he any confidence in the people, for whom the geese are a metaphor, or in the efficacy of political activism, behind which he detects vulgar motives. That the authorities with their anti-Jacobin hysteria are overreacting is as plain to Eyring as it is to us, but their foolishness does not make the goose revolution any more dignified. He is able to register the good sense spoken at times by the rabble-rouser Wübbke as well as the nobility amidst the nonsense in the oratory of Albus, who at one point quotes Georg Forster (9/2: 106), one of the most admirable German figures of the age of revolution, as Raabe certainly knew. But all of this is in the realm of ideas; in the cloddish world of reality, nothing can or should be done to change things that are probably as good as they can be and no worse than they are likely to get if meddled with. Eyring is a liberal-minded conservative. His mind is awake and advanced, but his civil morality is complacent and philistine. Thus the elegance, the wit, the recourse to the humanistic tradition, the posture of the objective, all-forgiving because all-comprehending observer are exposed as an absence of empathic sensibility and moral animation. It is surely no accident that the first initials of J. W. Eyring are the same as those of J. W. von Goethe. In Eyring we have Goethe without genius, but with that detached, timeless wisdom, that objective curiosity and indifference toward public and political events that so exasperated the younger generation of intellectuals in the latter part of Goethe's life.

It has long been recognized that the novella is Raabe's gloss on the fate of the French Revolution in Germany. In fact it could be numbered among his political or historical works if it were not so hugely comic.[37] But even modern commentators, who have made acute observations on the work, in my view still miss some of its subtlety by identifying Raabe too closely with the narrator Eyring. Thus, for example, Peter Michelsen sees the narrator condemned to ambiguities and ironies that are

> the expression of a resignation that was not only Raabe's: of an abandonment of the world in order to rescue oneself in the contemplativeness of the ego. This ego, which narrates about the

world of which it thinks nothing, surrounds itself with a crust, shrinks to the whimsical figure of those originals and odd fellows of the German small town such as the Rector Eyring embodies.[38]

This is not wholly mistaken, but I believe it underestimates Raabe. Daemmrich has rightly said that the "peculiar style" of the novella "serves as a distancing device."[39] Eyring's mannered elegance not only distances us from the narrated events; it also distances us from the narrator Eyring, reminding us that elegance and polish were not obvious virtues in Raabe's scheme of things.

What he actually achieves with the device is total ambivalence. Yes, it was foolish of the authorities to take a protest over geese as a prelude to an impossible revolution, and it was foolish of the townspeople to apply faddish revolutionary rhetoric to the protest. But Raabe doubtless believed, as Goethe did, that revolutions were the consequence of misgovernment, and there is plenty of misgovernment to be seen here; Raabe, *unlike* Goethe, did not believe that eighteenth-century structures of authority in Germany were generally satisfactory. Yet even this point is not unambiguous. For it must strike one that cooping up the geese was a rational and modernizing move; as so often, the rebels are the conservatives. But the improvement is enjoined without the participation of those affected; there is rationality but no persuasion; the citizen is a vassal and, in the age of revolution, is coming to resentful consciousness of his vassalage. Of course, the "revolution" in Germany was a big joke, just as the 1830 Revolution was, by and large. How ridiculous that the unworldly, servile, provincial, bumbling Germans should have a revolution—a notion laughable to both right and left. Eyring's epochal resignation and inward turning were a historically imposed response that may, as Michelsen and others have indicated, have been shared by Raabe. But he also sensed things that are beyond the purview of Eyring's complacent wisdom: the sadness of it all, as a genuinely valuable human being like Albus is frustrated and shunted to the periphery; and the humiliation of a nation that, in the age of great historical upheaval, of the founding of new orders such as the American and French republics, calls out soldiers to get geese into coops. Once again Raabe's comedy, even at its most elevated, is not harmonious. The humorist Eyring is a comic figure himself, and if the clown were not a philistine, he might have cause to weep.

CHAPTER 11

Literature

◘

THE MOST obvious fact about Raabe's relationship to literature is
his studied aloofness from contemporary literary life. This posture is not unknown among writers. One might think of Jean Paul,
who kept his distance from both the Weimar Classicists and the Romantics, or, in our own time, of J. D. Salinger or Thomas Pynchon.
But it is unusual behavior; writers commonly have a tendency to associate with one another. In the Classical-Romantic age in Germany
there were clear groups, or, as some thought, cliques. In post-Romantic Germany there was less of this, at least until the advent of the
Naturalists, but writers knew one another, formed associations, and
corresponded on literary topics; they participated in literary discourse
with criticism and theoretical essays. Raabe did none of this. He was
not a hermit and had plenty of opportunity to become acquainted with
other writers, and he did get to know quite a number, but with none
of them was his relationship intimate except for Wilhelm Jensen, and
with him, as we have seen, he generally kept the correspondence off
the literary ground. He wrote no literary commentary for publication
except for his one insignificant book review, and in his letters and
recorded conversations there is nowhere a sustained examination of
any author or work; one finds nothing but brief references and aphoristic evaluations. It is perhaps in keeping with this pattern that, unlike many of his contemporaries, he was not much interested in the
public art of the theater. He attended the theater rarely and said that
it was too much bound by the taste of the mass public to generate
true artistic works; only a book can seek the readers it needs (E 4:
144).

This consistent attitude has allowed the misapprehension that he
was a non-literary or anti-literary writer. He himself encouraged this
view. Langreuter, the narrator of *Old Nests*, when at loose ends, begins
to read literature of the 1820s; he pronounces it true and beautiful but
irrelevant to his times and troubles, and finds more consolation in
subliterature: "God's blessing on the reading fodder of the masses and
of youth" (14: 146-47). This, to be sure, contradicts Raabe's statement

on the theater, and perhaps it should be remembered that Langreuter is a narrator of rather limited spirit, but similar attitudes turn up even in Raabe's private utterances. "I have sometimes had more stimulation," he once noted, "from a piece of waste paper that accident blew into my hands than from years of study of all the classics of all the nations, as far as my knowledge of languages extends."[1] A notebook entry of 1876 implies that he was less an extensive reader than an intensive re-reader of a small stock of familiar works: "There is for me nothing more dubious than a new book that I am supposed to read" (14: 455). But these are disguises of the folksy wise man. He was an enormous and, one must think, indefatigable reader. Marie Jensen once mischievously asked his wife if she did not get afraid of him when he read all the time.[2] We will not begin to understand him if we do not grasp the point that he was literary in the extreme.

To begin with, no one can possibly miss the immense allusiveness in his fiction. Sometimes the allusions quite overwhelm the text; for example, a letter of the Judicial Councillor Scholten in *Madame Salome* contains in two-and-a-half pages no fewer than twelve literary allusions, among them to Lesage, Cervantes, Fielding, and Horace (12: 53-55). Herman Meyer, for whom Raabe was a prime example of the "poetics of quotation," estimated that there are some 5,000 literary allusions and quotations in his works, yielding an average of one every second page.[3] To some this has looked like the German philistine's addiction to familiar quotations and the tag lines of culture. But it is more accurately seen as a parody of cultural acquisition, along with the recognition that culture had become a commodity and an emblem of social prestige.[4] It is clear that he was more the master than the slave of his cultural resources. Furthermore, his early biographer Krüger made the perceptive observation that his very wide reading preserved his independence from influences (E 4: 22). It will be useful to bear this in mind, for influence-hunting has been rather a plague in Raabe studies.

His relationship to German literature of the past was eclectic but quite broad, reaching back into the Middle Ages, for he set as a motto to his early story *The Student of Wittenberg* some lines from Hartmann von Aue's Middle High German poem *Poor Henry* (2: 244). The protagonist of *The Hunger Pastor*, descendent of shoemakers, is named Hans Jakob for the two shoemaker-authors of the past, Hans Sachs and Jakob Böhme (6: 11), thus foreshadowing the lure that a life of seeking and learning will have for him. In the eighteenth century, Lessing was naturally an important figure for Raabe; he is beloved by the vivacious young Thedel von Münchhausen in *The Odin Field*, while the older and more old-fashioned Buchius knows him only as a bad fellow who attacked the excellent Gottsched.[5] That the rationalist Raabe should have praised the great Enlightenment aphorist Lichtenberg (E 4: 124) is understandable. Otherwise he seems to have regarded eighteenth-century German letters as quaint. Gellert, who, we recall, was a "classic" for the pastor in *Horacker*, had long before, in *The Children of Finkenrode*, appeared as a figure of fun; his novel *The Swedish Countess* is said to be no loss when used for tinder (2: 154). Raabe's often reiterated concern for authenticity in literature, particularly in regard to military enthusiasms, appears in *The Innerste*, where it is recalled that the poet Ewald von Kleist fell in battle, while Gleim, comfortable in his ecclesiastical officialdom, composed war poems (12: 151).

Raabe's relationship to the great German classics seems to me more tenuous than has sometimes been assumed. We have already seen in *The Dräumling Swamp* that his reverence for Schiller and Goethe could take a quite relaxed, anxiety-free form. The children in *The Documents of the Birdsong* do not read Goethe and Schiller, for they are sick of them from school; they quite plausibly prefer Dumas (19: 240), of whom something more must be said a little further along. After World War II a strenuous effort was made to argue that Raabe underwent a significant conversion to Goethe around 1880, of which the first major consequence was the novel whose title is taken from a poem of Goethe's, *Princess Fish* (1882-83).[6] I find this overargued and unpersuasive, and I expect it is motivated by a need to secure Raabe's stature by association with Goethe. This is, or used to be, a particularly German way of going about things, but I do not think we need Goethe's aid to appreciate Raabe. He tended to conform Goethe to his own categories of stoic resistance, seeing him as a survivor of the oppressions and disappointments of life. Raabe pretty much ignored the German Romantics, whose standing was not very high in his generation. The young Lina Nebelung in *Owls' Pentecost*, against the taste of her family, supports the late Romantic Hauff against the popular sentimentalist who wrote under the name of Clauren (11: 393), but the contempt for Clauren had long been conventional in the literary community. With Jean Paul, however, there is a particularly difficult problem, of which only the outlines can be sketched here.

The very first review of Raabe's very first work saw him as a distant relative of Jean Paul, though adding that "he has completely his own house and yard and does not live off his relatives" (1: 432). This association is not surprising; there are a number of allusions to Jean Paul in *The Chronicle of Sparrow Alley*, including one to *Leben des vergnügten*

Schulmeisterleins Maria Wuz (*Life of the Happy Little Schoolmaster Maria Wuz*, 1: 17), which in turn contains an allusion to Gottlieb Cober's book of piety, mentioned above (p. 130) in its role in Raabe's very last completed novel.[7] Raabe also makes an explicit connection to Jean Paul as the exemplar of idealistic humor; he compares April as the month of humor to a poem of Jean Paul (1: 162). Allusions to Jean Paul are scattered through the works, especially early ones like *The Children of Finkenrode* (2: 88, 110). In *The Hunger Pastor* a lawyer in his poverty is compared to Jean Paul's Siebenkäs (6: 353). In a self-advertisement for *Abu Telfan* he wrote of himself that literary history would "put Raabe's name next to that of Jean Paul and will add that, while he shared with the latter the rare talent, the seriousness, the humor, the many-sided knowledge, the deep view into high and low human relations, and above all the genuine, warm, love of mankind, he knew how to avoid the failings of the great poet of Wunsiedel that make comprehension of him possible only for a few" (7: 398-99). In *German Nobility* Raabe alludes to Jean Paul's typology of the imagination in the *Vorschule der Ästhetik* (*Primer of Aesthetics*, 13: 237). *Gutmann's Travels*, finally, is permeated with allusions to Jean Paul. Klotilde comes from his birthplace of Wunsiedel and is named for a figure in *Hesperus*, while her mother bears the name of the gentle Liane in *Der Titan* (*The Titan*, 18: 260, 238). Her uncle can wax enthusiastic about Jean Paul to the point of tedium while mocking the contemporary writers Klotilde prefers to read (18: 246). At this point we begin to suspect parody, perhaps self-parody, perhaps another stealthy round in Raabe's quarrel with the public.

For the association with Jean Paul turned out to be rather a liability for Raabe's reputation. Under post-Romantic German literary norms, with their fixation on "objective" narration, the subjective, chronically ironic, formally flamboyant Jean Paul figured as a horrible example of how not to do it. Raabe's intrusively authorial narration, which more than anything else put him at odds with the critics, was constantly marked down by them as a "Jean Paulian manner." A reviewer of *The Rumbledump* in 1871 complained of the "subjective formlessless recalling Jean Paul's manner" (8: 405), and this criticism was reiterated in numberless variations until the end of Raabe's career. It did him a double injustice, for it failed to recognize the particularity of his narrative art and it exaggerated Jean Paul's influence. Indeed, very near the beginning of his career, in his first autobiographical sketch, he is credibly reported to have said: "Of Jean Paul I have read less than one might think; I own of him only the two first parts of *Siebenkäs* and the *Katzenberger* [the work alleged to have influenced *Celtic Bones*]" (E 2:

68). His diary records the purchase of *Flegeljahre* (*The Awkward Age*) on August 13, 1870; this is very late to be of any substantial influence. Still, we do not want to downplay the interest: his preserved library contains nine Jean Paul titles, including the *Primer of Aesthetics*.[8]

Furthermore, it is useful to remember that Jean Paul was held in high regard by the oppositional, anti-Romantic generation of writers in the 1830s. The reason for this seems to have been an appreciation of his aloofness both from the alleged Goethean indifferentism and the reactionary proclivities of the Romantics, as well as of his populist concern for the common man. For Raabe's attachment to Jean Paul is one of several things that identifies him as a successor to the Young German generation, a connection that has not been clearly seen and that I have discussed in detail elsewhere.[9] His allegiance to Heine, long suppressed by his disciples, has already come up in the first chapter of this section. Of Ludwig Börne there are only a few traces; Raabe was, after all, five-and-a-half years old when Börne died. He is mentioned, however, in one significant context; of the girlhood of Lina Nebelung in *Owls' Pentecost* we learn that she had secretly read Börne while thinking of her beloved, whose imprisonment as a "demagogue" destroys their future together and alienates her from her surroundings (11: 394). According to his diary, in 1868 Raabe purchased a copy of *Wanderungen durch den Thierkreis* (*Wanderings through the Zodiac*, 1835) by Ludolf Wienbarg, regarded as the most radically democratic of all the Young Germans. As much as anything else, this purchase shows Raabe's attentiveness to a phase of literature that most of his contemporaries had forgotten or recalled only with scorn, for the book was certainly an antiquarian item by that time and Wienbarg himself had fallen into obscurity. But Raabe pursued associations with other writers of that epoch who were still on the public scene. On his tour of German literary cities in 1859 he developed reasonably friendly relations with the normally bearish Karl Gutzkow[10] and he read and owned a number of Gutzkow's works; in 1860 he made a rare visit to the theater to see Gutzkow's comedy, *Das Urbild des Tartüffe* (*The Model for Tartuffe*, diary, October 16), a thinly disguised attack on German censorship. Raabe doubtless did not overestimate Gutzkow, but observed fairly upon his death that "he was no poet but a great writer" and that many favorites of the day must feel quite small "against this restless, gasping man who built with everything that fell into his hands!"[11]

Raabe took note of other authors of that period. In Stuttgart he had friendly relations with the quondam radical poet and associate of Marx, Ferdinand Freiligrath (diary, April 23, 1869). To be sure,

Raabe also gave attention to Heine's bitter enemy August von Platen; Madame Salome, who quotes Heine, also quotes Platen (12: 36), and he is strongly recommended in *The Lar*, though perhaps somewhat dubiously by the corpse photographer Blech (17: 259). Just as dubiously, Eduard, the narrator of *Stuffcake*, alludes to Platen as an indication of his level of culture (18: 7). According to the diary, Raabe in December 1864 began reading *Ut mine Festungstid* (*From my Fortress Period*), Fritz Reuter's fictionalized account of his seven years as a political prisoner in the 1830s. Of particular interest is Raabe's admiration for Karl Immermann, friend of Heine and satirical novelist, for this is one of the rare cases when Raabe forcefully expressed a genuine critical opinion. Immermann is sometimes denominated as a conservative on account of his Prussian loyalties, but as a social satirist he can properly be discussed in the context of Young Germany.[12] His comic novel *Münchhausen* (1839) contains, as a foil to Münchhausen's world of bottomless mendacity and flimflam, scenes of a traditional Westphalian peasant milieu. In the course of time these segments were excised out of the novel and published separately under the title *Der Oberhof* (*The Grange*), which saw many more editions than the novel itself. Raabe perceived without difficulty that by this procedure Immermann's urbane satire had been falsified into rural idyll and regionalist nostalgia. To Paul Heyse he wrote that "the noble German people have deleted . . . Münchhausen out of *Münchhausen* in order to make it palatable,"[13] and in *Old Nests* he complained that "we have made ourselves a little entertainment piece out of a wise, bitterly serious book" (14: 53). This curt judgment, in my opinion, sheds much light on his critical principles and his own orientation as a writer.

That he avoided criticism and stayed out of the literary life does not mean that he paid no attention to what was going on. He remained quite *au courant*; a thorough examination of his knowledge and opinions of contemporary German literature would require a monograph of its own. It must be said, however, that he liked very little of what he saw; the list of writers he acknowledged positively is fairly short. He is said to have called Adalbert Stifter "a fine writer" (E 4: 191) and the lending-librarian Achtermann in *German Nobility* recommends him (13: 216). Raabe had a good word to say of Otto Ludwig[14] and he liked Hermann Kurz (E 4: 58). Raabe and Theodor Fontane were somewhat wary of one another, and they never met, but Raabe evidently respected Fontane. He was pleased to hear that Fontane read *The Horn of Wanza* and was gratified by his review, even though it was not uncritical.[15] As early as 1867, before Fontane emerged as a novelist, Raabe read his ballads (diary, December 30). In 1889 he sent

Fontane a seventieth-birthday greeting and, in his old age, he declined, on grounds of short notice and probably also out of his dislike of pompous gestures, a request to comment on the unveiling of a Fontane monument, saying that "one does not do justice to such a splendid man and high artistic contemporary with 'a few friendly lines' " on such an occasion.[16]

With Paul Heyse, who, for reasons no one today can remember, was the first German imaginative writer to win the Nobel Prize for literature, Raabe had agreeable relations, largely because Heyse was in charge of the Schiller Foundation from which Raabe received grants. Although he confided to Heyse many of his bitter feelings about his own situation, he never sought real intimacy with him and doubtless did not admire his slick, formulaic novellas, of which Raabe rightly predicted little would survive (E 4: 41).[17] Still, he seems to have liked Heyse, whose personal charm was widely acknowledged; Raabe was pleased when he heard, a few days before his death, the rumor that Heyse was to receive the Nobel Prize (E 4: 315). Similarly, Raabe was on friendly terms with Berthold Auerbach and read his works, for example, the novel that became known in English as *Court and Cottage* (*Auf der Höhe*, diary, February 1866), which the lending librarian in *German Nobility* treats dismissively as mere entertainment (13: 211). Raabe read both the major German-language novelists of America, Charles Sealsfield (diary, October 1869) and Friedrich Gerstäcker; the latter lived in Braunschweig when he was not travelling around the world and Raabe knew him personally (diary, October 30, 1870). Both writers, especially Gerstäcker, may have had some influence on the American scenes in *The People from the Forest* (see 5: 436), but if so, Raabe did not take Gerstäcker very much to heart, for Robert Wolf's acquisition of wealth in the California gold fields is precisely the kind of illusion against which Gerstäcker's novels and travel books consistently warned.

Toward other writers of the age Raabe could be downright chilly. We have already seen how, with unpersuasive excuses, he avoided Mörike in Stuttgart. In 1877 Marie Jensen tried to lure Raabe to Freiburg to celebrate their common birthday of September 8 by pointing out that it was also Mörike's,[18] but with the usual lack of success. Of Annette von Droste-Hülshoff Raabe is reported to have said: "When I look into one of her books, it is as though one opened a long locked cabinet in which old rubbish was mouldering" (E 4: 107). He found Conrad Ferdinand Meyer's *Gustav Adolf's Page* "silly and historically quite impossible" (E 4: 290). The writer of enduring reputation Raabe seems to have most disliked was Theodor Storm, which is odd, since

Storm was not the sort of man who normally aroused hostility in others. But Raabe found him irritatingly pompous and vain in his published correspondence, sitting in his own aroma, as he remarked to Jensen; and to Sträter he observed sourly that *Pole Poppenspäler* should not be discussed like *Faust* and *Hamlet*.[19] At the end of *Pfister's Mill* (16: 178, cf. 544) there is a parody of the conclusion of *Psyche*, admittedly not one of Storm's strongest novellas. The aroma one perceives here is a rather strong one of competitiveness. Indeed, although he never said so, it is my opinion that Raabe in his heart believed that *he* was the major writer of his time in the German language; he was vexed by what, in *Of Old Proteus*, he was pleased to call the "Yahoo literature" preferred by the Germans (12: 240).

For the writers more popular in his time than in ours he displayed a thinly disguised contempt. The so-called "programmatic realists" with their claims of "objective" narration did not impress him. The case of Freytag has already been taken up in Chapter 7. Raabe distanced himself as well from Friedrich Spielhagen, perhaps the most famous German novelist during the latter part of Raabe's life; he sneered when he heard that Spielhagen had described himself as a "poet-journalist,"[20] and he jabbed at Spielhagen several times in his fiction. In *Cloister Lugau* there is a rather obscure passage where a character swears "by Mylitta (here certainly not Melitta!)" (19: 25). The commentary (19: 434) identifies Mylitta as the Babylonian goddess of fertility and Melitta as a sea-nymph, but I suspect the latter is more likely an allusion to the main female character of Spielhagen's *Problematische Naturen* (*Problematic Natures*, 1861-62), Melitta von Berkow, who was so widely admired that it is said girls all over Europe were named for her. In the same novella (19: 87) he also took a swipe at Julian Schmidt, the critic who propagated Freytag, Spielhagen, and "objective" realism. The beloved magazine writer Eugenie Marlitt is read by a negative character, Mathilde the door-slammer, in *The Horn of Wanza* (14: 444).[21] Raabe asserted that he was sorry not to have met the prominent playwright Hermann Sudermann in order to tell him that he was a fraud (E 4: 127-28), a view to which some drama critics had also come after the turn of the century. For all his enthusiasm at the time of the Franco-Prussian War, he groaned at the terrible poetry it was generating and remarked that it was a good thing the poets did not have to save the fatherland.[22] For his time he was not especially prudish or moralistic in his judgments, but he did have his limits, and one writer who exceeded them was Leopold von Sacher-Masoch. In 1909 Raabe refused to oppose a ban on *Venus im Pelz* (*Venus in Furs*), saying that if, as he had heard, it touched upon sadism, then a ban on mass distribution was justified.[23]

As is the case with many though certainly not all artists and writers who live to an old age, Raabe's tastes grew less flexible with time. He is said to have hated contemporary art, especially Liebermann, though he was obliged to admit that his daughter painted in the new style (E 4: 219-20). Although he corresponded with Jakob Wassermann (diary, September 12, 20, 1898) and received a visit from Hermann Hesse in October 1909 (E 4: 298-304),[24] many of his late connections were with distinctly old-fashioned or even reactionary writers such as Lulu von Strauss und Torney, Börries von Münchhausen, and Erwin Guido Kolbenheyer (E 4: 270-72; diary, October 24, 1908). Raabe's gratified acceptance of the discipleship of Gustav Frenssen has been particularly troubling because of his later association with the Nazis.[25] Frenssen was a kind of literary idiot savant, a writer of some elemental power and shrewdness but rather seriously lacking in intelligence, and Raabe's opinion of him was not without reservations. In a colonial novel of Frenssen's, where blacks die a deserved death, Raabe firmly entered a question mark in the margin.[26] The later disciples were not so discriminating; Frenssen was awarded the first Raabe Prize in 1933.[27]

Raabe expressed to Frenssen the hope that he might do something to wean the German people from their enthusiasm for Ibsen.[28] This is but one example of a recurrent, irritable theme in Raabe's late years: a fierce dislike of Naturalism in general and of Ibsen in particular, who brought out in him some of his most chauvinistic utterances; even in his historical novel *Hastenbeck* he took the trouble to attack Scandinavian and French Naturalism (20: 29-30). Though he abhorred the works to which Ibsen owes his enduring fame, he appears to have liked *The Pretenders* (1864), Ibsen's relatively early and, as it seems to me, quite immature historical melodrama (E 4: 114). He transferred this dislike to the German Naturalists; to an inquiry as to which of them had "given the most pregnant expression to the German emotional life of the present," he replied with studied sarcasm that, judging from their success, they all seemed to have done so, and the authors "can be quite satisfied with the echo from the current day."[29] He became even more disgusted when Hauptmann turned to mysticism with *The Sunken Bell* (E 4: 239). Interestingly, the Naturalists in no way reciprocated this hostility, for they cordially admired Raabe. Arno Holz corresponded with him, and Hauptmann and Wilhelm Bölsche sent him seventy-fifth birthday greetings from Hauptmann's estate of Agnetendorf (diary, January 16, September 21, 1906). When the Naturalist theorist Heinrich Hart wrote a friendly review of *Gutmann's Travels*, Raabe was obliged to grunt that he was pleased, even though it came from *that* camp.[30] However, his late taste was not completely ossified. We are told that, to pass the time while ill with influenza, he read fifteen contemporary dramas and liked only one of them: Rostand's *Cyrano de Bergerac* (E 4: 239; of course, we do not know what the other fourteen were). And there was one very surprising exception to his disparagement of the Naturalists: he cordially admired Zola. In 1891 he said that the only French books he still read were those of Zola.[31] This enthusiasm greatly puzzled his friend Sträter (E 4: 113), and indeed it was unusual. Zola was generally disliked in Germany, an attitude that, under altered ideological auspices, remains intact in Lukács. This unexpected exception shows once again how independent Raabe could be of the conventional opinions of his times.

It also shows that his literary interests were by no means confined to Germany; indeed, they were very cosmopolitan, supported by what appears to have been a notable gift for learning languages. Despite his school troubles, he became quite competent in Latin, an occasional error notwithstanding. Latin tags are scattered throughout his works, and he was particularly attached to Horace. In *Höxter and Corvey*, odes of Horace appear in Raabe's own translation into a Baroque idiom appropriate to the times (11: passim). In 1868, judging from the diary, Raabe was teaching himself Greek, even making some entries in that language. How well he knew Greek is not clear,[32] but he cites a phrase from Homer in *The Geese of Bützow* (9/2: 75), a passage from the New Testament in *The Crown of the Empire* (9/2: 375), and a thus far unidentified phrase in *Old Nests* (14: 104); in the *The Lar* he coined a Greek neologism, "hemerographia," to denote the journalistic description of everyday events (17: 285). He evidently knew enough Italian to have Moses Freudenstein quote Tasso in the original (6: 124) and to quote Dante in the original in *The Lar* (17: 327) and in conversation with his friends (E 4: 254). Perhaps the oddest anniversary in Raabe's diary is the entry on April 13, 1900, noting that 600 years ago Dante was in Hell. Kleophea Götz in *The Hunger Pastor* scandalizes a tea-party by mentioning Boccaccio (6: 234), whose *Decameron* in Italian is found in Raabe's library.[33] He does not seem to have cared much for Russian literature. As appears in *Wunnigel*, he was resentful of Turgenev, who he thought had been contemptuous of Germany (13: 131).[34] Evidently he numbered Tolstoy among the Naturalists; he commented on him rather sourly[35] and disliked *The Kreutzer Sonata* (E 4: 114). He even worked a couple of Russian phrases into the linguistic circus of *Christoph Pechlin*, one of which is apparently faulty (10: 378, 513).

His French may have been self-taught; in any case, in his diary we find him working on it in the fall of 1858. His interest in and knowledge of French literature was quite extensive. He praised Molière in an early story, *A Secret* (3: 369) and began to read him in earnest in 1876, recommending him to Jensen in the following year.[36] In *Gutmann's Travels* he quoted in French from Lesage's *Diable boiteux* (18: 324), and in *The Dräumling Swamp*, in one of Raabe's several self-identifications with authors of the past, Haeseler lectures on La Fontaine's failure to be understood by a public that thought his fables naive and did not grasp that he was a grim and clever historian of the realm (10: 88-90). Raabe very much liked Gautier's *Mademoiselle de Maupin*,[37] and read, both soon after publication, Victor Hugo's *Les Misérables* and Ernest Renan's free-thinking *La Vie de Jésus* (diary, May 8, 1862; June 10, 1864). Balzac is mentioned in passing in *German Nobility* (13: 233); *La peau de chagrin* belonged to Raabe's early reading experiences (E 4: 20), and his diary shows him purchasing *Les illusions perdues* on February 24, 1863, and several other works along with a biography of Balzac on March 14, 1864.

Sometimes writers and intellectuals exhibit reading preferences of which literary scholars cannot wholly approve. One thinks, for example, of Karl Marx's addiction to the novels of Paul de Kock. Raabe knew him, too; the early short story *Christmas Spirits* bears a motto from him (2: 280), and the slovenly Leon von Poppen in *The People from the Forest* reads de Kock's "newest masterpiece" (5: 290); there is another passing reference in *German Nobility* (13: 233). Like almost everyone else of his generation, young Raabe read Eugène Sue "with shivering delight."[38] In the same context he names one of his most enduring allegiances: Alexandre Dumas. As I mentioned above, the young people in *The Documents of the Birdsong* prefer him to Goethe and Schiller. Raabe called him a "splendid fellow" and said to his friend Hartmann that artistically he owed most to Dumas (E 4: 20, 194); Hartmann could not see how, and neither can I. What I find most difficult to explain is his life-long attachment to *The Count of Monte Cristo*, one of the books he re-read with pleasure at the very end of his life.[39] It would have suited me better if he had preferred *The Three Musketeers*, which he also knew (E 4: 23) and which, in my opinion, is a superior book and certainly a wittier one. Along with this peculiarity and his unconventional admiration for Zola, there is one more oddity among his French favorites. In his old age there lay on his nighttable, along with the Bible and Gessner's idylls, a copy of

Voltaire's *La Pucelle*. Hartmann said that people would not believe him if he told them this, but Raabe replied: "Go right ahead; I like to read it" (E 4: 193). Voltaire's impious, salacious slapstick had in its own time so offended Schiller that he not only wrote a poem against it; he was impelled by it to write his tragedy, *The Maid of Orleans*, to restore Joan of Arc's character. Raabe's liking for the work is another sidelight on his rationalist, satirical bent and on his independence from the pieties and solemnities of the German cultural tradition.

However, the most important component of his literary patrimony was English. It was more important for him, I believe, than even the German tradition. There are seventy-three works of English literature in his preserved library.[40] But even this collection does not give an adequate idea of the range of his English interests, which reach back to the Anglo-Saxon *Widsith*, quoted in *The Documents of the Birdsong* (20: 226-27). His English was evidently self-taught; his early diary entries, which are sometimes in English, show him working on it. His command of the language was clearly limited;[41] when he says of Christoph Pechlin that "he had drawn his whole English only out of obsolete novels" (10: 407), Raabe is very likely making a joke at his own expense. To be sure, some of his English enthusiasms are common to the German tradition, beginning, of course, with Shakespeare; Raabe bought complete editions of Shakespeare in both English and German in 1863 and a new English edition in 1874,[42] and *Cloister Lugau* is pervaded with parodistic allusions to *Hamlet*. His knowledge of *The Vicar of Wakefield* has already been noted in connection with *Horacker*; in August 1873, according to the diary, he bought a biography of Goldsmith. His admiration for Sterne is rather a commonplace among German writers;[43] the intelligent Lina Nebelung in *Owls' Pentecost* prefers Sterne to contemporary German writers such as Gutzkow, Auerbach, or Spielhagen, read by her fluffy niece (11: 384). That Moses Freudenstein in *The Hunger Pastor* quotes Byron's *Manfred* (6: 272) is not remarkable; the diary records Raabe reading Byron in October 1865. Like all German historical novelists, Raabe paid close attention to Scott, whose works he purchased early in his career (diary, November 29, 1860); the Scots dialect that appears in *The Odin Field* may be derived from Scott, or possibly from Robert Burns, whom Raabe also knew (diary, May 17, 1867); to Jensen he cites "Auld Lang Syne."[44] Cooper is also not unexpected in the list; the diary reports Raabe purchasing *The Pathfinder* on February 18, 1864, and there are detailed references to Cooper in *Stuffcake* (18: 121). Poe, too, was a European enthusiasm; there is an allusion to *The Murder in the Rue Morgue* in *The Lar* (17: 294), and in 1875 Raabe's friend Caecilie Kopp, who was teaching at Vassar, sent him American periodicals with Poe items (diary, April 19, May 10). Because of the play on the meaning of his name, Raabe undoubtedly knew "The Raven" well; in 1872 we find Jensen citing it to him in German translation.[45]

But his knowledge went well beyond these expected authors and works; only a quick survey can be offered here. He knew not only of Burns, but also of John Gay, one of whose ballads he quoted in *After the Great War* (4: 68); not only Sterne but also Fielding, whose *Tom Jones* he read in November 1861 and to whom Scholten alludes in *Madame Salome* (12: 54); not only Byron but Coleridge, Shelley, and Keats, acquired in a one-volume edition (diary, April 14, 1869). He was strongly attached to his "intimate friend" Samuel Johnson;[46] according to the diary he acquired the *Life of the Poets* on February 2, 1864, and bought a copy of Boswell on January 27, 1869, probably the *Life of Samuel Johnson*, which he finished reading a year later. He even found his way into genuinely odd corners of the house of English literature. On September 24, 1866, he purchased the eighteenth-century Aristophanic comedies of Samuel Foote, and on May 24, 1867, *The Story of a Feather* by the early nineteenth-century satirist Douglas William Jerrold. Of writers closer to his own time he knew Trollope and Leigh Hunt (diary, October 6, 1865; January 27, 1869), and at an early date he purchased and read Charlotte Brontë's *Jane Eyre* (diary, October 28, 1861). One of his rare visits to the theater occurred on August 29, 1903, to see Brandon Thomas's *Charley's Aunt*.

By far the most important English writers for him were Dickens and Thackeray. This has long been recognized—in 1868 Jensen in a review had already called Raabe the German Dickens and Thackeray (6: 488), and in 1881 a reviewer of *The Horn of Wanza* said that the Germans should no longer complain they had no Dickens, for here he was (14: 492)—and a good deal has been written about these involvements, but in almost all previous study of them there has been a principal difficulty. The traditional hunt for "sources" and "influence" often unconsciously takes on the appearance of a hunt for imitations. The hostile critic of Raabe can easily extrapolate from this a view of him as a derivative, inferior writer.[47] The error has been to search for similarities in situations, characterizations, and constellations of characters. No doubt these can be found, though seldom proven. But the whole enterprise misses Raabe's originality as a *German* novelist, who imported from Dickens and especially Thackeray not material but tone, not stories but solutions to the problems of story-telling. His relationship to the two great English novelists was not imitation but inspiration.

Dickens was a very popular writer in nineteenth-century Germany—his works appeared in German translation almost as soon as they had in English—and it was apparent from the beginning that Raabe had gone to school to him.[48] There are references to Scrooge and to *The Haunted Man* in *The Chronicle of Sparrow Alley* (1: 50, 150), and the short story *Christmas Spirits* (1858) may owe something to Dickens's series of Christmas tales. An influence of Dickens on *The People from the Forest* has been seen by a number of critics,[49] and Friedrich Wolf in that novel has learned about America from *Martin Chuzzlewit* (5: 93). Pinnemann in *Three Pens* looks as though he may have been modelled on Uriah Heep in the way he gets control over his master Hahnenberg, while the ninety-year-old law case represented by Hahnenberg reminds one of *Bleak House*. *Fabian and Sebastian* has been associated with *Dombey and Son*, and it is well established that *The Hunger Pastor* was influenced by *David Copperfield*, which Raabe was reading at the time. In general, Dickens's surreal realism and, in particular, such devices as verbally inventive, ironic, or comic label names for characters may have had a liberating influence on Raabe. He paid close attention to Dickens's career and thought him a fellow struggler in the losing battle of life against death. He noted Dickens's death in his diary two days after the fact on June 11, 1870, and referred to it in *German Nobility* (13: 177). Later in that work the dying Paul Ferrari quotes, in English, "Down at last!"—the alleged last words of Dickens, "a man," the narrator says, "who with his imagination has accomplished many and great things on this earth" (13: 318).

But there are also significant differences. Dickens was clearly much less at loggerheads with his reading public than Raabe, and the heart-tugging sentimentality of Dickens is rare in Raabe, except occasionally in his early works. Oscar Wilde's quip that one would have to have a heart of stone not to laugh at the death of Little Nell is nowhere applicable to Raabe; one would need only compare the conclusion of *The Old Curiosity Shop* with that of *The Rumbledump*. Dickens, for all his social criticism and sympathy with the downtrodden, was in deep harmony with the superintending moral principles of his time; it was his office to expose the hypocritical gap between the profession of these moral principles, shared, he assumed, by all decent people, and social practice. For Raabe things in the moral world were much less clear and obvious. He was a questioner more than an affirmer of values, so that he could not be so robust a reformer of the world, of whose potential for reform he took a rather pessimistic view. A contemporary critic has held this against him, in Dickens's favor, adding that in Dickens the *villain* is isolated or an oddity, while central characters are never eccentric. Why this difference, correctly seen as it is, should be chalked up against Raabe is unclear to me unless it is believed that readers should not be troubled in their moral certainties.[50]

Raabe's early and observant biographer Krüger thought Thackeray meant more to him than Dickens (E 4: 23-24). To his friend Sträter, Raabe praised Thackeray as a genius; Sträter, mistakenly, found Raabe's apparently aesthetic evaluation of Thackeray out of character (E 4: 113). Indeed I believe that of all literary "influences" on Raabe, Thackeray was the most important. The connection has certainly been studied, but, like so many matters, it needs to be reopened and reexamined.[51] Thackeray, too, was extremely popular in Germany and had an almost continuous publication history in that country in the nineteenth century. Still, it would be difficult to name a German writer other than Raabe who showed a strong influence from him, though Fontane praised *Vanity Fair* almost above Dickens.[52] Late in life Raabe recalled that he had learned English as a bookseller's apprentice in Magdeburg in order to read the English authors, especially Thackeray. He mentions particularly *Pendennis* in that connection, interesting to him as a story of the development of a young author.[53] We see in the diary that in June 1865 he took up Thackeray again: he read Thackeray's poems and *Gehagen*, *Yellowplush*, and *Barry Lyndon*—all three, significantly, comic examples of totally unreliable narrators. Raabe kept photographs of authors in his diary, including one of Thackeray, and, as was his custom, he entered Thackeray's death on December 25, 1863. There is no explicit evidence that he read *Vanity Fair*—only *Pendennis* is in his library[54]—though it is certainly possible. That Wachholder in *The Chronicle of Sparrow Alley* is compiling a work *De vanitate hominum* might be an allusion to it (1: 15-16, 462-63); the good, kind, modest, unstylish, somewhat simple Helene Wienand in *The People from the Forest*, who is not thought much of by other girls of her wealthy class, reminds us of Amelia Sedley, as the contrasting pair Fränzchen and Kleophea Götz in *The Hunger Pastor* may remind us of Amelia and Becky Sharp, but these are not only mere conjectures; they lead away from Thackeray's main importance for Raabe. Nor is this importance to be found in parallels of their lives and personalities. The urbane, restless, boisterous, frank, sometimes charmingly gauche Thackeray lived a more widely ranging life, socially and geographically, than the reserved and relatively stationary Raabe, and the difference is reflected in the range of their fictional worlds. Furthermore, in Raabe's relatively tranquil life there is nothing, not even the sad death of his daughter, to be compared with the burden of

Thackeray's insane wife nor with his passion for another man's wife, thwarted primarily and permanently by his own gentlemanliness. Neither are the obvious similarities—the satirical bent, the sympathy with the weak and mistreated, the tendency to moderate conservatism as they grew older—near the crux of the matter.

Only quite recently has Raabe criticism clearly seen where this crux lies:

> William Makepeace Thackeray became famous in Europe after the middle of the century through his novels *Pendennis* and *Vanity Fair*, which are above all distinguished by the fact that here an author, in late succession to Romanticism, on the threshold of realism, causes his figures to act like marionettes who, despite their serious expressions, make a comic impression in their help-less dependence on his imaginary stage. The author or the au-thorial narrator is enthroned like a god in Calderon's drama above the proscenium of the *gran teatro del mundo*, and plays a varying world-comedy, as though before scenery, at the hearths of the degenerate nobility and the nouveau-riche bourgeoisie. . . .
>
> It may have been the authorial superiority or aloofness that made an impression on the young book dealer's apprentice in Magdeburg; at least neither the young nor the old author ever denied or gave up this sovereign narrative posture. This deserves to be stressed because he thereby set himself directly and con-sciously in contradiction to the fashionable tendency of his time and its demand to descend from the narrative Olympus.[55]

In other words, it is narrative technique and point of view that link Raabe to Thackeray. Thus the same objections that were made against Raabe were made against Thackeray by the pope of "objective" nar-ration, Julian Schmidt, who called up in the same way the spectre of Jean Paulian mannerism.[56] It is not necessarily the case that Thackeray generated this manner in Raabe, for it is too fundamental to his artistic instincts, but the English writer must have been an encouraging and prestigious model who showed the young author what tunes could be played on this instrument.

One can open Thackeray's novels virtually at random to find that tone so familiar to the constant reader of Raabe. I take my first ex-amples from *Pendennis*, because of the importance of that novel for his development:

—The insouciant and sovereign display of the narrator's command over his narration:

. . . we beg the reader to understand that we only commit anach-
ronisms when we choose, and when by a daring violation of those
natural laws some great ethical truth is to be advanced. . . .
(Chapter 52)

—The sudden breach of the fiction by a direct allusion to the author's
own life and experience:

Let Pen's biographer be pardoned for alluding to a time not far
distant when a somewhat similar mishap brought him a providen-
tial friend, a kind physician, and a thousand proofs of a most
touching and surprising kindness and sympathy. (Chapter 53)

—The stoic moralizing about the indifferent capriciousness of fate and
the attachment to the unheroic, moderately virtuous figure who mud-
dles his way through life, as well as the disguised and critical self-
portraiture:

If the best men do not draw the great prizes in life, we know it
has been so settled by the Ordainer of the lottery. We own, and
see daily, how the false and worthless live and prosper, while the
good are called away, and the dear and young perish untimely,—
we perceive in every man's life the maimed happiness, the frequent falling, the bootless endeavor, the struggle of Right and
Wrong, in which the strong often succumb and the swift fail: we
see flowers of good blooming in foul places, as, in the most lofty
and splendid fortunes, flaws of vice and meanness, and stains of
evil; and, knowing how mean the best of us is, let us give a hand
of charity to Arthur Pendennis, with all his faults and shortcomings, who does not claim to be a hero, but only a man and
brother. (Chapter 75, last paragraph of the novel)

Or, to turn to *Vanity Fair*:

—the self-mocking authorial conceit, the superficially courteous gesture to the mistrusted reader, the raising of false issues, misleading
information, and bogus foreshadowing:

I know that the tune I am piping is a very mild one (although
there are some terrific chapters coming presently), and must beg
the good-natured reader to remember, that we are only discours-
ing at present about a stock-broker's family in Russell Square,
who are taking walks, or luncheon, or dinner, or talking and making love as people do in common life, and without a single passionate and wonderful incident to mark the progress of their

loves. The argument stands thus—Osborne, in love with Amelia, has asked an old friend to dinner and to Vauxhall—Jos Sedley is in love with Rebecca. Will he marry her? that is the great subject now in hand. (Chapter 6; of course, Osborne does not love Amelia, though he marries her, and Jos's feeling for Becky is trivial and without result.)

—The assurance that we are not like other novelists, the allusion to the superintending leitmotif, and the awareness of the dark ground on which comedy and humor are played out:

> Sick-bed homilies and pious reflections are, to be sure, out of place in mere story-books, and we are not going (after the fashion of some novelists of the present day) to cajole the public into a sermon, when it is only a comedy that the reader pays his money to witness. But without preaching, the truth may surely be borne in mind, that the bustle, and triumph, and laughter, and gaiety which Vanity Fair exhibits in public, do not always pursue the performer into private life, and that the most dreary depression of spirits and dismal repentences sometimes overcome him. Recollection of the best ordained banquets will scarce cheer sick epicures. Reminiscences of the most becoming dresses and brilliant ball-triumphs will go very little way to console faded beauties. Perhaps statesmen, at a particular period of existence, are not much gratified at thinking over the most triumphant divisions; and the success or the pleasure of yesterday becomes of very small account when a certain (albeit uncertain) morrow is in view, about which all of us must some day or other be speculating. O brother wearers of motley! Are there not moments when one grows sick of grinning and tumbling, and the jingling of cap and bells? This, dear friends and companions, is my amiable object— to walk with you through the Fair, to examine the shops and shows there; and that we should all come home after the flare, and the noise, and the gaiety, and be perfectly miserable in private. (Chapter 19)

And so on, and on; one could multiply the examples indefinitely, but I offer these to the inexperienced reader of Raabe as indicators of what one might look for in him. One can, to be sure, collect such examples of self-conscious authorial irony from Dickens, but they are more robust, more confident about the narrative enterprise. The importance of Thackeray to Raabe has yet to be recognized in its full dimensions; it is in him, and through him to Fielding and Sterne, that Raabe's literary pedigree is to be found, not in Jean Paul or other German traditions. So it is by this roundabout route, through Raabe's passive, extensive, cosmopolitan, fragmented yet, in its main outlines, intelligible experience of literature, that we have found our way to the axial issue of contemporary Raabe criticism, which will occupy us in the next chapter.

CHAPTER 12

Narrators

◻

A genuine writer says *I!* That means: the forms
of his imagination have such reality that they
completely repel the forms of the day or subsume
themselves.— Afterwards the nation speaks of lack
of patriotism and the like.

Raabe, 1875[1]

WILHELM RAABE was the most ingenious experimenter with
narrative perspective in nineteenth-century German literature.
He was, one recent scholar has written, "constantly aware of an entire
spectrum of different narrative-structural possibilities and chooses at
random first one approach, then another. In doing so, he explores his
potentials as a writer, discovers his weaknesses, recognizes his strong
sides; as a result he establishes the firm foundation in his later highly
complex narrative structures."[2] In this regard no one in his own time
can match him. He wrote frame stories like Storm—it has been estimated that about a third of his narrations are of this type[3]—but he
did not specialize in them as Storm did, and in Raabe the relationship
of frame and story is much more subtle and varied. Of course his
contemporaries, such as Keller and Stifter, probed the possibilities of
first-person narration, but for Raabe's peers one would have to go back
to Goethe's subtly and ironically translucent narration in *Werther* or
forward to the stream-of-consciousness experiments of Schnitzler or
even to such a modern contemporary as Max Frisch. In demonstrative
third-person narration Raabe has no peers at all in his time; for com-
parisons one would have to look back to the Romantics or even to
Wieland's awareness of the stress between authorial sovereignty and
authorial limitation, between realism and illusion,[4] and forward to
Thomas Mann. Both Raabe and his critics were well aware of his
eccentricity in this regard, and almost all the public complaint of him
throughout his career is about his authorial, intrusive, subjective, in
short, "Jean-Paulian" or, in my view, Thackerayan manner. When in
1894 the influential critic Ferdinand Avenarius, in a generally positive

review of *Cloister Lugau*, complained of a confusing opening like a series of hedgerows balking the reader's access to the story and trying his patience (19: 418-19), he was reformulating objections that Raabe had been hearing for decades. For the literary establishment of his time was committed to the "objective" narration propagated by the programmatic realists, which meant nothing more profound than silencing the authorial voice as far as possible. Raabe seems to have been aware that this alleged objectivity was a delusion, since it was only technical,[5] and in retrospect we can see clearly that it was a kind of ideological hoax, presenting partial and biased perspectives as universal truth and objective reality. His traditional admirers paid almost no attention to his narrative technique, though for other reasons: they were insistent that he was a wise man rather than an artist, and the harmonious equilibrium they were determined to find in him is highly vulnerable to the irony and polyperspectivism of narrative self-consciousness.

Conversely, the recognition of his exceptional narrative variety has been the main lever that has pried him away from his "friends" and elevated his standing in modern criticism. Much of the best British and American Raabe scholarship has been focused on narrative technique, and there have been an increasing number of German contributions to this topic as well. For it is by this means that Raabe, often thought of in his own time as a stubbornly old-fashioned writer, comes to appear to us as a harbinger of the modern. Wayne Booth has said that "it was not until this century that men began to take seriously the possibility that the power of artifice to keep us at a certain distance from reality could be a virtue rather than simply an inevitable obstacle to full realism."[6] This statement may be a little misleading, in view of the eighteenth-century and Romantic roots of ironic artifice in narration, but it points up the centrality of narrative experimentation and, in its wake, narrative theory, in modernism. In this as in other matters the pioneer was Barker Fairley, who in a now classic essay stressed Raabe's polyperspectivism and observed quite rightly that he "touches, at one point or another, all the forms that fiction can take," and that, though not a theoretician, he had a "general awareness, from the start, of what is involved mentally in the process of narration."[7]

The justice of this observation can be seen if one contemplates Raabe in the light of what I take to be a representative contemporary exposition of this "modern" mode of narration, Michael Boyd's recent study of the "reflexive novel." Boyd takes as his exemplary authors Conrad, Joyce, Woolf, Faulkner, Nabokov, and Beckett. The reflexive novel, in his understanding, is parodistically attuned to the would-be mimetic, realistic novel. In it, "the self-conscious writer makes the reader equally conscious of the mind behind the fiction" and the narrator usurps the role of the hero, reducing the stature and dimensionality of the character. "Reflexive novelists often try to give their work the look of the moment in the study, the rough draft—that the reader might somehow experience the novel as an act, as something done with words by a particular person at a particular time and place."[8] One need not share Boyd's credulous deconstructionist faith and his militantly anti-mimetic stance to acknowledge that these and others of his observations can be applied to Raabe as a reflexive novelist. But when Boyd asserts: "Prior to the twentieth century, only Lawrence [sic] Sterne had insisted upon occupying the space of his fiction with the aggressiveness of a Nabokov or a Beckett,"[9] one must, as so often, deplore the American theorist's unawareness of German literary history, in which Sterne remained far more influential than he was in English literature. In particular, the historical parameters of the reflexive novel, which Boyd closely associates with the epistemological skepticism of twentieth-century thought, will have to be shifted back by more than half a century if Raabe is to be accommodated, unless we treat him as a prophetic anachronism, a view I would find irrational. In German criticism it was seen almost a generation ago that even description and dialogue in Raabe do not lead to greater realism, but to "a reflexive and at the same time subjective distancing from mere event," and "it is not the narrated occurrences that form the continuum of the narrative context, but the consciousness of the narrator."[10]

Thus Raabe has been rescued for us on essentially formalist grounds as a proto-modern. Yet, if we are honest with ourselves, there is something about this procedure that ought to make us a little uneasy. There is first of all the large question whether the modernist reevaluation of a writer often perceived in his own time as a Romantic throwback, in form, at any rate, does not imply a substantial Neo-Romantic component in modernism. More specifically, the critical concentration on narration postulates a high degree of conscious artistry, but Raabe utterly declined to play the Flaubertian role of obsessive artist. He almost entirely avoided all theoretical or aesthetic pronouncements, except for tantalizing, often obscurely aphoristic scraps in his private notebooks. He displayed a pronounced dislike of aestheticism and, except by example, did not so much combat the reigning theory of objective narration as ignore it contemptuously. He admired other writers, such as Goethe, not so much for their artistry as for the example they set in surviving the battle of life. One of his notebook entries of 1880 reads: "For real man the time is perhaps coming when he will no longer seek art, the aesthetic, in the works of authors, in order to achieve peace in the storm of life, but indications of how they found their way in the great struggle."[11]

In the contemporary critical atmosphere it has become bad form to speak of Raabe as a supplier of consolation to the reader and of *Lebenshilfe*, guidance in life. It is therefore frustrating that he explicitly claimed this to be his office from one end of his career to the other. In one of his aphoristic early poems we read: "To grasp light out of shadow, / That is the poet's vocation!" (20: 337). The apostrophe at the end of *The Hunger Pastor* became virtually proverbial: "Pass on *your* weapons, Hans Unwirrsch!" (6: 463); that is, the reader is to draw sustenance from Hans's experiences and his survival of them. Many years later, Raabe wrote in the first chapter of *The Odin Field*:

> May the consolation that we personally have drawn from the old schoolmaster, from Noah Buchius, be granted to many another. This is our most cordial wish as we arise from the folios, quartos, parchments, and bundles of documents in which we have listened from afar to the uproar, the clangor from Wotan's field, the Odin Field, in the noise of the present, the roar of the day, that tomorrow always lies behind us as though it had been a hundred thousand years ago. (17: 12)

In his embarrassed letter to Clara Zetkin of 1908 he asserted: "For me the main thing is that, through my whole literary life, I have been less an aesthetic author than a good friend, advisor, and consoler of the wretchedly burdened, of those of *all* classes in need of courage to live and to die."[12] These utterances, which could easily be multiplied, cannot be ignored, and indeed there is much evidence that he had in fact such an influence on many of his readers. For this reason there have been justified warnings from scholars of impeccable contemporary credentials against excessively formalist interpretation fixated on narrative technique.[13]

But it is not merely contemporary critical fashion that prevents us from falling back into a view of Raabe as a naive, insouciant storyteller, oblivious to the complexities of narrative perspective and subordinating artistry to message. For as soon as he was taken as such, he rebelled: "In my life work I have always cared more about the *work of art* than the effect. You call me a 'quiet and modest artist.' The noun I accept, the two attributive adjectives by no means."[14] This is not just contrariness on his part; it is merely another facet of his self-understanding, one that he rarely articulated but that is undeniably present in the texts. For him the medium and the message were compounded, and it is for us to try to understand how the message required the narrative ingenuity. We are not dealing here with a set of quirks and mannerisms, but with one of the most insistently self-conscious narrators in European literature after Sterne. One could compose a substantial and satisfactory textbook of narrative technique and point-of-view theory with no other resources than Raabe's body of fiction.

For, as we can now see, the variety in the range and intensity of his narrative devices is extraordinary, one more aspect that should deter us from homogenizing him and ignoring his experimental dimension. He shifted back and forth between first- and third-person narration; one novel, *Princess Fish*, was originally drafted in the first person but recast in the third; and in his very last work, the fragmentary *Altershausen*, he experimented for the first time with another variant: a first-person narrator tells of himself in the third person. The degree of authorial intrusiveness can differ considerably from work to work: it can be subdued but persistent; it can be concentrated at the beginning, or at chapter beginnings, or at crucial junctures, or at the conclusion; or it can be pervasively aggressive and mannered, sometimes to the point of self-parody. Traditionally, the display of authorial manipulation has been associated with humorous or, more exactly, ironic narration. It can also generate rhetorical heightening at solemn moments. When, in *Elsa of the Fir*, the narrator pauses to say, in a one-sentence paragraph: "This, however, is the story of the death of the maiden" (9/1: 180), he reminds us strongly of the famous opening of the second-last chapter of Thomas Mann's *Buddenbrooks*, describing the death of Hanno: "With typhus the course of things is as follows." Furthermore, lest we suspect that his manner is merely a matter of naivety, of not knowing the rules, it must be noted that he intermittently approached omniscient, "objective" narration in cases where his authorial presence is as subdued as one is likely to find in nineteenth-century fiction, and in one of his most mature works, *Restless Guests*, he suppressed the authorial narrator almost entirely. The suggestion made recently that he did so in order to accommodate himself to the normal family-magazine reader[15] is, in my view, to be rejected. As I shall argue in Part III, *Restless Guests* is one of his most brilliantly executed works, and the suppression of the narrator is quite appropriate to the novel's sober, thoughtful, observant tone and to its psychological realism.

This is not to say that he fully and flawlessly mastered the craft at every point. The price of experimentation is the risk of falling short

of the mark; furthermore, the annoyance of his readers at his mannerisms cannot be dismissed as total obtuseness on their part. Even the
modern, sympathetic reader will occasionally come to be irritated at
what may seem to be authorial affectation, even a relentless nerve-
wracking jabbering, as though one were locked in a room with the
Ancient Mariner. Even a modern, sympathetic critic has sighed that,
in the Stuttgart trilogy, "We cannot say that Raabe's narrators . . .
succeed in making themselves interesting at all times"; there are places
where "the intrusion is not a valid extension of the narrator's personality but rather an empty posturing."[16] One reason is probably that
Raabe's formal sense matured much more rapidly than his imaginative
mastery of content. Not unreasonably it has been argued that the
narrator of the early *One Springtime* tries to force consistency of meaning by authorial rhetoric and that the story does not show what the
narrator says it does.[17] In *The Rumbledump*, which shifts between an
exceptionally personal authorial opening and relatively omniscient narration, it is hard to get quite clear about the author's view of the
characters; he circles around them with voices of public discourse that
may need correcting. It has been said that the strategy "results in a
narrator who is unusually authoritarian in his control of the reader's
fictional participation,"[18] but whether in this case he is as persuasive
as he is authoritarian is another question. The novel falls in the Stuttgart period, which one critic has seen as a time of transition, of increasing subjectification of narrative and emphasis on the way the
story is told, and a decreasing concern with linear narrative.[19] It is
true that his instinctive polyperspectivism, when applied to relatively
conventional materials, could make his plot management overcompli-
cated and obscure. Another critic has fairly observed that in *The People
from the Forest* Raabe was "trying to be in too many characters' minds
and too many places at once."[20] While his development was not a
steady progression, over his career he undoubtedly grew stronger in
matching matter to manner, in part by dissolving plot and dissipating
suspense.

As a general principle it may be said that the effect of his authorial
technique is to stress fictionality, *poiesis* over *mimesis*. His realism is
more a realism of the narrative act than of what is narrated. To this
end he calls on a wide variety of devices, most of them, to be sure,
familiar from the history of literature. There is first of all the collapse
of the narrator into the empirical self of the author. Raabe often does
this, and we should be wary of applying to him a dogmatic point-of-
view theory or a strict insistence on the narrator's fictional second self.
The narrating self is not layered but fluid, slipping in and out of roles

from a virtually essayistically presented empirical self through various levels of fictionalized narrative selves, deflections, partial and full disguises, to fully fictionalized alter egos of the author's imagined self. A theoretical position that anything within the boundary of a fictional work must be treated as fictional will miss the point of Raabe's protean dynamic.

He begins *The Rumbledump* by telling us under what circumstances he saw a rumbledump: we know this to be a fact, and it does not become a fiction because it is recounted in the novel. He began his teasing on this point early, in the melodramatic story *On Dark Ground* (1861), where the narrator constructs a frame in which he introduces himself in his quotidian life and slides from his storytelling environment into the fictional narration, and at the end of "this touching story" he is exhausted, can't drink his tea, goes to a wine shop to read his newspaper and smoke his cigar (3: 379, 409). At the end of *The Children of Finkenrode* he inserts himself into the fictive environment under his pseudonym "Corvinus" and appears on his way to the theater to see the tragicomedy of *The Children of Finkenrode* (2: 219). Much later, in *German Nobility*, he repeats the device: in the "Epilogue" the author and his fictional characters meet (13: 321-27). In *The Holy Spring* he tells us how industrious his historical research has been (3: 21); in *Our Lord God's Chancellory* he discusses the selection process that distinguishes the work from a mere chronicle (4: 323); at the beginning of Chapter 13 of *The People from the Forest* he puzzles over how to proceed, complains that most people don't realize how hard storytelling is, and assures the reader that he should be happy he does not have to write the book (5: 148-49), a conceit that recalls Heine.[21] Later in the novel he tells us that he is a harmless, naive individual, like his characters (5: 313), and at the end the character Fiebiger recites the motto "that we have prefixed to this book" (5: 415), thus collapsing character and author. Hans and Fränzchen in *The Hunger Pastor* get married on Raabe's birthday (6: 444). At the beginning of *Abu Telfan* he mounts a self-defense of his career, then slips into the narrative role of limited omniscience (7: 9-14). To see both kinds of utterances occurring on the same fictional plane, to deny the shift from the narrator's "first" to his "second" self, would be mere theoretical obstinacy.

The examples of Raabe showing himself being a writer could be multiplied almost endlessly. In *Höxter and Corvey* he tells us that he began it on November 23, 1873, almost exactly two hundred years after the date of the story (11: 261). This almost pedantic self-consciousness can be observed in his writing habits outside the fictional context as well; from the diary we see that *Fabian and Sebastian* was begun around January 20, 1880—the name day of Saints Fabian and Sebastian (15: 575). Raabe's aunt, he tells us, would have thought the beginning of *The Lar* disorderly, but she is dead; why should he force himself for the sake of readers who prefer pleasant, light reading to his "lack of discipline" and "jumpy nature," especially as his readers, unlike his aunt, will not leave him a legacy (17: 224). In that same novel he inserted a personal reminiscence of his old Stuttgart friend Friedrich Notter (17:326) and similarly memorialized another, Johann Georg Fischer, in *Gutmann's Travels* (18: 285). The frantic arabesque of *Christoph Pechlin* opens with an uneasy defense of the author's worth:

> The man who submits himself to the heavy and fearfully responsible task of telling stories to his fellow citizens and is continually aware that he writes on the discarded shirts of just these fellow citizens, will seldom deposit on the white, innocent paper something altogether worthless, that is, something harmful to his advantage and earthly comfort or, more briefly, to his good concord with his neighbors. I, the writer of this book, keep myself constantly aware of this and so on my desk I have only with the most sensitive feeling of delicacy made the necessary new folds in the— fine linen of my dear friends in the public, male and female, after its admittedly somewhat weird journey from their body through the sack of the rag-collector. I can certify on my behalf that I have always approached my task very carefully. But today I am telling an *international* story and go to work with heightened anxiety. (10: 207)

This anxiety is justified, as the novel threatens repeatedly to escape the author's control. At one point "we tame our gasping, trembling zeal and narrate calmly and in an orderly fashion" (10: 209), but at another the usually cool narrator's nerves are shattered by a decision made by the characters (10: 418).

Raabe repeatedly reminds us of the status of the text as *poiesis*, something made. For example, he is not only familiar with the traditional inexpressibility topos, but he exhibits his awareness that it is a topos: "The epic author describes many kinds of feelings by stating that he cannot describe them; Hans's feelings on this occasion were of such a kind" (*The Hunger Pastor*, 6: 27). He was also aware that he often worked with typological characters; when the crude, self-important businessman Knackstert enters the story of *The Dräumling Swamp*, the narrator refrains from describing him, because, as he says, everyone knows what he looks like (10: 69). After having played with the possibility of conventional openings to *Gutmann's Travels*, he continues: "There is nothing new to tell people. The house, the household, and the family are already present in the imagination of every cultured reader" (18: 213). Chapter 18 of *Abu Telfan* begins with the statement that it is in form and content the middle point of the story, the peak of the pyramid upon which Hagebucher sits (7: 183-84). This is indeed, by page count, the middle of the book; Raabe calls our attention to the book as a crafted, even material object, and connects its planned, external disposition with its internal formal shape. When *Old Nests* grows rather talky and immobile toward the end, the narrator admits his repetitiousness, blandly asserting that he can't do anything about it (14: 246). Whether this is to be categorized as sovereign irony or a self-critical confession is hard to say.

Raabe knew very well that omniscience is also a fiction. Where would we be with our vocation, he asks in *On the Scrap-Iron*, if we could not pass through all doors and go uninvited where we please (16: 348)? This novel, perhaps the most realistic, even naturalistic, of his major works, not surprisingly contains a good deal of reflection on the question of realism, to which the author finds some surprising answers. He begins with half-sardonic reflections on stories that begin well and end badly, or begin badly and come to a desirable end; these are not like real life, which lacks beginnings and endings. But instead of constructing the fiction that *his* story is more like real life, he opts for the traditional conventions of a *story*; this one ends fairly well "by human standards" (16: 341), and therefore, by implication, more like literature than real life. The main thing is for the narrator to breathe freely in his own cause or that of others, and to find the right listener; he then launches into a fairy-tale tone. At the end he gives us five possible endings to choose from, of which only the first and possibly the second happen (16: 507).[22] The ironic-comic side of the choice of fiction over illusion is the pretense that the story is escaping the author's control. In *Horacker* the narrator complains that the story is getting out of hand; he has too much stuff and has to get rid of some of it, like Dutch merchants burning nutmegs to keep the price up (12: 376). At the end of the second chapter of *German Nobility* there is another complaint, this time that a narrative method has crept in that cannot please us (13: 184). Raabe's most fantastic tale, *Of Old Proteus*, opens with a rumination on how best to make it credible to the reader. One beginning, in the manner of mimetic naturalism, is tested and rejected. The narrator starts again in the romance mode of Shakespeare's *Midsummer Night's Dream*, but a voice from the public objects that no one could stand it anymore without Mendelssohn's music. Yet the narrator comes to be encouraged that it can work by hopefully imagining the right kind of reader, by the appearance of the shade of Aristophanes, and by recalling Bottom's frank rejection of illusion in the awareness of fictionality: "If you think I come hither as a lion, it were pity of my life: no, I am no such thing: I am a man as other men are; and there indeed let him name his name, and tell them plainly he is Snug the joiner" (12: 200-201).

From this and others of my examples it can easily be seen that Raabe's narrative irony comes to be closely involved with his ongoing fencing match with his reader. He alternates between wistfully projecting an ideal reader and imagining, with varying degrees of exasperation, his real readers. The most famous example of the first kind is doubtless the passage in *Horacker* with the image of the story as a new house; only one person in a thousand will ask what will happen in it—this is the reader for whom the narrator writes (12: 296-97). In Chapter 12 of *Cloister Lugau* he expresses the hope that in Chapter 6 the reader, with exact attentiveness, has begun to get a notion that the story would make some sense (19: 79). But more often he jabs irritably at the reader. In *The Good Day* he inserts a dream scene to make the "female reader" aware of "poetic intensification" (13: 340). We have seen in the chapter on Raabe's public that, whether fairly or unfairly, like many others in the literary world, he blamed the female readership for the dead weight of convention. In *Wunnigel* he tells us that he will get the young man Weyland married, though perhaps not in the way that will suit all female readers (13: 11-12). In *Hastenbeck* he projects the female reader, "her serene highness," as objecting to digressions and demanding that the narrator get on with the love story (20: 44). From early on Raabe put himself in the willfully perverse posture of balking the reader's appetite. A notebook entry of 1864 reads: "It is, to be sure, a fine age, in which people still think that the final and happy joining of the lover and his girl is the ultimate and highest thing with which the drama or the novel can occupy itself."[23] Chapter 20 of *The Rumbledump* begins with an image of the well-meaning, tepid Hennig weeping bloody tears and wringing his hands—that is the way it would be if one were to write in a way to gain the sympathy and approval of readers, but it is not the way it was (8: 194). The author informs us that he has no love story with which to conclude *Fabian and Sebastian*, no fiancé for Konstanze (15: 170-71). *The Lar* bears a motto from a private letter from a friend who wanted him to write a story where the boy and girl "get" one another; Raabe sabotages all suspense about this by writing a preface in which the boy and the girl are shown at the christening of their first child (17:

222-24). He repeats the gesture in *Gutmann's Travels*, telling us plainly that the boy will get the girl (18: 214). In *Cloister Lugau* he hints at a story that he will not tell, a scandal at a petty court, on the ground that it is too trivial (19: 9). It has been pointed out that the happy ending of *Owls' Pentecost* is "purposefully superficial because conflicts are smoothed over rather than truly resolved."[24] In that same work he rejects, less humorously and more irritably than usual, any role of the reader as a participant in the creative process: "We accede to nothing so far as the claims of the reader on the story are concerned. What we have to do, we know, and what we have to say, likewise, and this satisfies us completely" (11: 383). But obviously it did not satisfy him, or he would not have made such an ado about it.

What has been said so far about narrative irony, authorial intrusion, stressed fictionality, and ongoing confrontation of the reader, all the Thackerayan devices, applies, naturally, more obviously to Raabe's third-person narrations. It has long been noticed, however, that the boundary between third-person and first-person narration in Raabe is not sharp, and it appears even less so if we regard the intrusive narrator as a fictional figure. There is a distinction, however, which is illustrated by *Elsa of the Fir*, a text where the two modes tend to converge and which is therefore identifiable as an innovation in Raabe's oeuvre.[25] This is a third-person narration with a perspective very close to the consciousness of the central figure, Pastor Leutenbacher. The point of view, which at first might seem to be tending toward an interiorized free indirect discourse, is not strictly sustained; there is an occasional shift into the omniscient, authorial first-person plural (e.g., 9/1: 176, 177). Formally, therefore, the text is a hybrid. Nevertheless, by Raabe's standards the authorial voice is generally subordinate to the protagonist's reminiscing consciousness. More significantly, the narrative reduplicates certain reticences and inhibitions of Leutenbacher, particularly his erotic attraction to Elsa, which comes to strike the reader more and more forcibly, but which the pastor is unable to articulate explicitly and which he sublimates into idealization and worship. This technique is closely related to some of Raabe's major achievements in first-person narration.

In that department, Raabe is virtually without peer over a long stretch of German literary history. Here, as so often, the *Urtext* is *The Chronicle of Sparrow Alley*. One of the most striking features of this work—that a quite young, novice author, instead of fictionalizing his own personal experience, imagines the consciousness of a quite elderly man— already shows an intact instinct for narrative distancing in a rather daring form. As Daemmrich has observed, the memoirist

Wachholder's "attitude toward writing is precarious"; while he disclaims any novelistic ambitions, he experiments with the tenses, narrating the past in the present and the present in the past, achieving overall "a genuinely new novelistic technique."[26] The non-linear reminiscence is intended not so much for memory as an exorcism of memory: "I linger in the minute and leap over years; I paint pictures and provide no plot; I break off, without allowing the old tone to die away: I do not want to teach, but I want to forget, I—am writing no novel!" (1: 75). But the most ingenious device is the introduction of an encapsulated second narrator. This is Wachholder's friend Strobel, who criticizes the disorderly narration, its absence of firm images and rambling commentary, like the "concoction of an inexperienced literary light" (1: 140-41)—an obvious self-irony of the author. Wachholder invites Strobel to participate in the text, and he does make an effort, but falls into impressionistic association, as the same narrative spirit overcomes him. In exasperation he concludes: "the devil take the chronicle of Sparrow Alley!" (1: 150). Here young Raabe appears to be insisting that his unorthodox manner of narration is not arbitrary but necessary.

Over the course of his career Raabe experimented with several varieties of first-person narration.[27] Perhaps the most elementary of these and the one most easily available to the inexperienced writer is the epistolary novel, long familiar from literary tradition. For the first and only time, Raabe experimented with it in *After the Great War*. I do not know why he never returned to it, except to hazard the guess that the artistic failure of that novel deterred him from a second attempt. As *Elsa of the Fir* is a third-person narration on the boundary to first person, so *Celtic Bones* is a first-person narration close to third person: the narrator is unnamed and plays no part in the action, confining himself to highlighting its comic absurdity. *In the Victory Wreath* (1866) brings for the first and only time an elderly, reminiscing, *female* narrator, doubtless because Raabe had heard the story from his mother-in-law, in whose family it had occurred. But his most innovative experiment was undertaken somewhat earlier in the Stuttgart period: the short novel *Three Pens* (1865).

Here Raabe revives and elaborates the polyperspectivism of *The Chronicle of Sparrow Alley*. In his first novel, Wachholder's friend Strobel intervenes in the text and tries to write some of it himself. Variations on this technique appear here and there in subsequent works, for example, the unconsciously comic passages from Aurora Pogge's diary in *The People from the Forest*, of which the narrator observes: "We learn from this that other people view the persons of our story differently than we do ourselves" (5: 212). In *The Horn of Wanza* there is a handed-around narration of first-person reminiscences that undergo an unexpected turn. First the late old soldier Grünhage appears as a brute; then it turns out he has been laughed to death by his wife Sophie and her old friend Thekla when he postures as head of the local militia, which causes us to see him more as a victim; then previously unperceived stresses and resentments emerge between Sophie and Thekla, who turns out ultimately to have been somewhat sympathetic to old Grünhage. The absorption of all these perspectives one after another into the narration gives us something new: an unreliable third-person narrator!

In *Three Pens*, however, polyperspectivism is the structural principle. Here there are six parts by three authors, each appearing twice. This seems never to have been tried before in German literature.[28] The first part, dated 1829, is a memoir of a young curmudgeon of thirty, August Hahnenberg, whose impoverished, loveless childhood has turned him into a bitter misanthrope, aged before his time. He has loved once, but lost his beloved to Joseph Sonntag, a pleasant but sluggish, stupid, and incompetent friend. The second part, obviously written much later, is a commentary on this document by Mathilde Sonntag, wife of the offspring of that union, the young doctor August Sonntag. Mathilde is pert, confident of her own superiority, extremely conventional, and quite lacking in subtlety or insight. She regards Hahnenberg as an old monster and objects to his tone. The third part is written by August Sonntag, who after his father's bankruptcy became Hahnenberg's ward. Under his care the boy experienced a gloomy, lonely childhood as his mentor attempted to harden him, combat the traces of his father's weakness, and make him emotionally indifferent as he claims himself to be. Nevertheless, in retrospect August is not without gratitude. It soon appears that August is a much more substantial and thoughtful character than his wife's condescending view of him would lead us to believe; we later learn that he has made a significant, acknowledged biological discovery. In the fourth part Mathilde grabs the pen on the grounds that she is the better narrator; she introduces the plot line of the novel, which concerns a slimy conniver named Pinneberg who gains control over and swindles his employer Hahnenberg; he seems rather obviously descended from Dickens's Uriah Heep in *David Copperfield*. The details of this plot need not concern us here; however, it is not uninteresting that the plot line, with its rather conventional, suspenseful, and sentimental elements, is initially narrated by the most conventional and short-sighted of the narrators. August continues the story in the fifth part. Part six

is dated 1862 and is a commentary on the whole document by Hahnenberg, who must now be sixty-three. How much he has learned is
hard to say. He is still loveless and burdened by the sadness of his
life. He has striven to be strong and without sympathy, and he kept
August poor and endangered for pedagogical reasons. But he has loved
August in his own perverse way and is delighted at the boy's rebellion
against him, his emergence as an independent and competent personality.

Raabe worked very hard on this novel; it was written a good deal
more slowly and laboriously than usual. To his publisher he wrote: "I
am just beginning to master my art and have, I hope, the best years
of my life before me," and many years later he spoke of it as his "first
independent work" (9/1: 492-93). To examine it critically would lead
us too far afield here, but it is an interesting and original work not
only in its formal aspects.[29] With his polyperspectival narration Raabe
gains a dimensional depth that cannot be achieved by straightforward
realistic narration of the sort that satisfies a depressingly normal mind
like Mathilde's. We see that even so damaged a self as Hahnenberg,
an almost Balzacian villain in his constricted, malign egocentricity, can
be sympathetically understood with differentiated and patient judgment. One of the ironies of the work is that, although Hahnenberg
labored to educate empathy out of August's character, it is just that
capacity for empathy that enables him to view his tormentor with
comprehension, without hatred, even with forgiveness. Yet as impressive as this experiment in multiple narrative turned out to be, it remained an isolated one, for Raabe never employed the form again.
One reason may be that the critical reaction at the time was almost
uniformly negative, with the formal innovation once again, madden-
ingly, deplored as "Jean-Paulizing method" (9/1: 493). In any case, it
was with a different device of first-person narration that Raabe found
his most productive line of development.

This device we may, for the sake of brevity, call the "unreliable
narrator." There are few literary techniques, apart from outright obscurity, that put such demands on a reader's attention or go so far
toward making the reader a partner in the creative process. Thus there
are few so likely to lead to misunderstanding and incomprehension in
the common reader. Nothing, therefore, better illustrates Raabe's
stubbornness as a writer, his commitment to his own artistic vision,
than his pursuit of a narrative device of which hardly anyone, as far
as I can see, had the faintest comprehension in his own nineteenth-
century environment. That it must seem so obvious to us today is a

good index of the revolution that has taken place in criticism between his time and our own.

In German literature his major and, I think, only important predecessor in this regard is Goethe's *Werther*. Goethe arouses in us enormous sympathy and even identification with Werther, as the sometimes overwrought reception history of the work clearly demonstrates. Only with thoughtful and reiterated reading does the subtle and serious irony of the text begin to emerge. We are allowed to see only through Werther's eyes, yet gradually it must dawn on us that his eyesight is far from perfect. We begin to realize that Lotte is, in all probability, not the person Werther thinks she is, and then we begin to notice other moments when Werther misreads the character of others and, in some degree, also his own. This could not be apprehended for a very long time, even though it is evident that, with this work, Goethe was attempting to overcome and dissociate himself from that threatening potential in his own self that had caused his real-life entanglement with Lotte Buff and Albert Kestner. Goethe returned to the technique again, even more subtly and deceptively, in the long misunderstood sixth book of *Wilhelm Meister's Apprenticeship*, "The Confessions of a Beautiful Soul."[30] I am not, incidentally, postulating here a line of influence; I have no idea whether Raabe read Goethe in this way. The evolution of his unreliable narrator, it seems to me, was very much his own. Nevertheless, it is perhaps significant that the three works of Thackeray mentioned in Raabe's diary in 1865, *The Tremendous Adventures of Major Gahagan*, the picaresque *Barry Lyndon*, and *The Memoirs of Mr. C. J. Yellowplush, Sometime Footman in Many Genteel Families*, are all first-person narratives of this type, in which the reader sees through the narrators' comic exaggerations, self-aggrandizement, and failings of character.

The first, perhaps still rather primitive example appears quite early: Bösenberg in *The Children of Finkenrode*. His dubious character is not immediately obvious, for he is bright and amusing, but gradually we begin to sense his self-conscious use of cliché, his impatience with ordinary people, his readiness to kick a dog and become infuriated when the owner complains, and his underlying philistinism. We are driven off identification with his perspective by Weitenweber, who predicts the philistine results of Bösenberg's journey home and later savagely teases him, or by the fact that his love affair completely evaporates owing to his misreading of the young lady's behavior. A contemporary critic who has written at length on Bösenberg as an unreliable narrator has observed: "The reader eventually senses a second voice in the novel, the voice of the implied narrator, who sees Bösenberg as the affected dilettante that he is."[31] But the same critic seems to feel that Raabe is not in control of the technique, that the authorial voice and Bösenberg's tend to fall together, confusing the distinction and leading ultimately to a non-commital stance.[32] That may be fair; still, it is worth remembering that Goethe does not sharply distinguish himself from Werther but remains very close to him while at the same time putting his literally fatal failings into a subtly ironic perspective. It may be, for all I know, quite difficult to write a story in which the first-person narrator must appear to us as morally dense and reprehensible—classic examples are Ring Lardner's *Haircut* or Henry James's *The Aspern Papers*—but surely it is more difficult to remain in close moral and psychological intimacy with the narrator and still edge him into unreliability. Learning how to do this was one of Raabe's great achievements.

The intimations of this development can be traced in a number of works. One that has already been mentioned in connection with Raabe's humor is *The Geese of Bützow*, with its facetious, garrulous, philistine narrator affecting a somewhat heavy-handed tone, whose perspective, nevertheless, is not so much askew as merely limited. But a genuine breakthrough was to occur in the mid-1870s with *Master Author* (published in 1873 with the imprint 1874 but begun in 1872). This is a difficult, rather private work, and once again I will not attempt an exhaustive interpretation.[33] Its central figure, Kunemund, is an isolated, unpopular author who takes the view that he understands the world, but the world does not understand him. Clearly he incarnates Raabe's own feelings at a time when he felt himself to be at the bottom of his literary fortunes. The rambling, sometimes opaque story concerns Kunemund's effort to care for Gertrud Tofote, orphan of his forester friend. Kunemund loses her to the world of wealth, egotism, and shallow urbanity because she receives an inheritance from Kunemund's brother, an evil-spirited colonial businessman, who leaves her the legacy, out of malice toward his brother, in the expectation that it will corrupt her.

Our concern here, however, is not with these matters, but with the narrator, one Emil von Schmidt. As so often, already the name attracts our attention: the combination of one of the commonest of German surnames with the particle of nobility—presumably a very minor nobility in consequence of some public service in the family past—constitutes a kind of oxymoron that Schmidt himself finds droll (11: 11). More than that, it indicates an incongruity of the common and the elevated that marks Schmidt's character throughout. A man of independent means, he has abandoned his position as a mining engi-

neer in the civil service to become "an unoccupied amateur of inex-
pensive aesthetic pleasures" and to write "dainty novellas" (11: 16) that
no one reads; in that respect he is a comic counterpart to Kunemund.
He is a man of reasonably lively mind but rather tepid affects, whose
deprecating self-irony is a symptom of weakness rather than sovereignty and who recognizes his pleasure in being alone as "the most
sublimated egotism" (11: 135). He likes to recite Schopenhauerian
apothegms but in a wholly self-indulgent spirit. Schmidt's character
contributes considerably to the opacity of the story, which he does
not always seem intensely interested in telling. His claims of friendship with and for Kunemund sometimes seem exaggerated, and it is
not clear that Kunemund fully trusts him. Schmidt in fact belongs to
that world into which Gertrud is seduced by wealth and apparently
innate secularism. He ultimately marries a formidably self-indulgent
society lady whom he has initially perceived as a witch; the marriage
occurs together with Gertrud's bleakly conventional one in an atmosphere both cynical and banal. We will encounter this kind of character
again, even more subtly rendered, in a third-person narration, *Restless
Guests*.

The consequence is that it is hard to know what to think about what
Schmidt tells us, particularly in regard to Kunemund. Hajek has remarked justly that what Raabe means "can only be deduced when one
responds to the flickering style the author allows his chronicler with
the distrustful reserve that he obviously expects of his reader."[34] Martini has argued that Schmidt has wholly missed Kunemund's reality,
the pathos of his life of disappointments in a concrete historical reality
that includes an episode of imprisonment, instead converting these
realities into a "fairy-tale," a "Rococo idyll" sentimentalizing a lost
past.[35] That may well be true; still, we know of these things only from
Schmidt's account. In him Raabe has found the key to this kind of
narrator. He is not an ass, as Bösenberg was at bottom; Hajek points
out that he has integrity and powers of observation and warns that we
should not underestimate his intelligence.[36] He is not malign like Hahnenberg, but a vaguely well-meaning person, and he is not as complacently comfortable in his social role as he pretends, but is uncomfortable, even neurotic. He is the intellectual, aestheticist version of the
homme moyen sensuel, and as such, with all his goodwill, he points up
the profundity of Kunemund's isolation. He forces us to read through
him to the story he purports to tell and makes us worry whether we
can do it, for perhaps we are more like him than we are congruent
with Kunemund. Here is one of Raabe's most original inventions: the
basically sympathetic, intelligent narrator in whom there is neverthe-

less something lacking, some organ of perception, some ability to get out of his own skin.

He perhaps did not reach his full mastery of the technique here. Hajek has complained that Raabe sometimes collapses himself into his fictive narrator, "suddenly gives up his reserve and begins to give dictation to his chronicler."[37] I am not sure that I accept this criticism, which is similar to that made of *The Children of Finkenrode*. It may fail to perceive that the characterization of the narrator is not only an assault on the public and the undercompetent reader, but can also be a vehicle of authorial self-analysis and self-irony. Still, the characterization of Schmidt may be shifted a little too much into the pejorative for Raabe's purposes, especially toward the end of the novel. Schmidt begins to resemble the caricatured aesthete Albin Brokenkorb in *On the Scrap-Iron*. Later, in *Old Nests*, Raabe tried another variant: the subdued narrator Fritz Langreuter, crippled in body and somewhat in soul, bereft of laughter and self-confidence. He is not unreliable in *what* he narrates; he is observant and often expresses Raabe's own views, but there is something lacking in him in interpersonal sensibility; he is utterly astonished to learn, when it is many years too late, that Eva Sixtus had liked him (14: 136). Here Raabe has relieved the excessively pejorative characterization, but has replaced it with too much pathos that draws excessive attention to itself, unbalancing the delicate narrative relationship in another way. The fulfillment, as we shall see in Part III, was yet to come in the great first-person novels of his last phase: *Stuffcake* and *The Documents of the Birdsong*.

We may now return to our original question: what might the reason be for this complex, persistent experimentation with narrative technique on the part of an author who appeared to disclaim any strictly aesthetic or formalist ambitions? The question does not admit of an easy answer. Is it an unresolved dichotomy? Recently it has been said that Raabe wanted to narrate and also wanted something else "for which traditional literary typology offers no right name, something that is neither philosophy nor edifying tract nor aphorism but has something of all three of these genres and that was obviously often more important to him than carrying his plots forward."[38] Actually, I think many writers want to do something like this; Raabe thought especially hard about how it might be done credibly. What was not credible for him was the alleged objectivity of programmatic realists. As Daemmrich has rightly said: Raabe's "use of devices abandoned by other novelists and the exploration of new possibilities in the reminiscence technique prevent the hidden subjectivism in the impersonal narrator of other Realists."[39] While conventional realists seek mimetic intimacy, Raabe seeks distance, and, as Wayne Booth has said, "distance along one axis is sought for the sake of increasing the reader's involvement on some other axis."[40] The one axis, along which Raabe distances himself, is clearly that of elementary storytelling—"and then . . . and then . . . and then . . . what next?" What is the other axis along which he means to involve us? One might say that it is the ethical, and one would not be wholly wrong. But his ethical "message," as elaborate as it may have been, was not so intricate as to require this vast repertoire of narrative devices. Something more must be at stake here. I think it may have been truth and integrity. Raabe had a strong realistic *motivation*; he really wanted to tell it how it was. But how things are is complicated, elusive, subject to perspective. Furthermore, mimetic conventions, he found, could not tell how things are; they only generated illusion by masking fictionality. To tell how things *really* are required a repudiation of illusion, an acknowledgment of fictionality, and a shift of focus onto the telling. Thus by logic, instinct, and the profoundest artistic probity, not by theory, not by epistemological conundrums, not by some preternatural "modernism," he came to the narrative experimentalism that strikes us as so "modern" and obstinately held to it in the teeth of a chorus of voices insisting that he was wrong, that he should get on with the story and tell the readers what to think so that they might be reassured in their own sense of rightness.

CHAPTER 13

The Defective Family

◻

No ONE WILL deny that Wilhelm Raabe was a bourgeois writer. Years ago Fritz Martini called him "fanatically bourgeois."[1] But it is not always clear what this well-worn word really means. For the bourgeois class of western civilization is the dialectical class *par excellence*, insofar as it constantly generates its own self-criticism, even its own dissolution. To free Raabe from the putative odium of the bourgeois it is not even necessary to assert that he was not a bourgeois but only assumed a bourgeois aspect as a mask.[2] Hajek's formulation is more exact: "Raabe belongs not to the pillars of society but to its most implacable critics. But—and here lies the difficulty—he himself stands inescapably on the ground of the bourgeois form of life that he criticizes."[3]

To the characteristics of the bourgeois form of life assumed *a priori* as given belongs the reverence for the family as the core organism of society, bulwark of virtue, unalienated refuge from a fallen world. More or less classic formulations of the ideology of the family can be found in the writings of Raabe's somewhat older contemporary, Wilhelm Riehl (1823-97), who, in the very successful third volume of his *Natural History of the People as Foundation of a German Social Policy*, entitled *The Family* (1855), energetically defended the endangered patriarchial extended family and demanded its restoration. One of Riehl's more admirable characteristics is his readiness to make his ideological motivation explicit—in this case the fight against socialism. With a great display of pseudo-scientific arguments he orders women back into the house: "The real women's organization is the home."[4] The fight against the emancipation of women belongs to the defense of traditional society itself, for "only in the contrast of man and woman . . . can social inequality be shown to be an eternal law of nature in the life of mankind."[5] Thus his doctrine of the family coheres with his defense of class structure in the whole four-volume work: "Only suffrage by classes is congruent with the perception and recognition of the family."[6] The family understood in this way "is the center of gravity and fulcrum of our social-political life because it is also of our national life"; it "is a sacred thing to us not only religiously but also socially and politically. . . . To injure the family means to undermine all human culture"; and, above all: "the *spirit of authority and piety* nourished in the family shall once again permeate, consecrate, and transfigure the regimen and citizenship of the state."[7] Among the enemies of the family Riehl names the literature of the Age of Goethe (not to speak of the Frenchified Rococo or of Young Germany): "It follows with natural necessity that cosmopolitanism, disregard of the social forces, and underestimation of the family always appear together. The humanistic idea swallowed the concept of the family."[8] But Riehl is optimistic about the second half of the century; as an example for a new spirit in literature adequate to the times he mentions particularly the profoundly conservative Swiss writer Jeremias Gotthelf (recently deceased at nearly sixty).[9]

The central significance of the family in the literature and literary theory of the time can be documented in many other places. Theodor Storm, whose own family life did not entirely meet the standards of bourgeois normality, in his public persona "saw the family as the nucleus and basis of any state. . . . In the absence of a belief in any other meaningful reality transcending the individual, such as the nation-state or religion, the individual and his family were the only certainties remaining."[10] Adalbert Stifter, for whom the family was a crucial institution mediating between the demands of the present and the threatened values of the past, has his wise man Risach lecture on the family near the conclusion of *Indian Summer*:

> It is the family that our times need; it is more needed than art and science, than transportation, commerce, boom and progress, or whatever people call what seems desirable. Art, science, human progress, the state are based on the family. When marriages do not turn into happy family life, you will in vain bring forth the highest achievements in science and art, you will pass them on to a generation that deteriorates morally, for whom your gift is ultimately of no more use and that in the end will fail to bring forth such goods.[11]

Friederich Theodor Vischer, in his mid-century *Ästhetik* (*Aesthetics*), welded the bourgeois concept of the family to the novel form:

> The *bourgeois* novel . . . is the actual normal species. . . . The hearth of the family is the true midpoint of the world picture in the novel and only acquires its significance when spirits gather around it that echo the hard truth of life with the delicate chords

of an expanded spiritual world. Only in these circles is the true picture of morality, far from the extremes, truly experienced and unfolded.[12]

Such examples could doubtless be multiplied endlessly. How does Raabe fit into this picture?

Let us look first at the actual condition of the family in his works. Every attentive reader will have noticed how often his children are orphaned or grow up with only one parent. According to my count, there are sixty-three motherless figures in thirty-two texts, twenty-seven fatherless figures in nineteen texts, and fifty-three orphans in twenty-nine texts.[13] Among these the nine cases of illegitimate children form a special sub-category. It has often been complained that Raabe reduces the erotic and passionate aspect of life to a minimum. In this respect, too, he is a writer of the Victorian age, although it has been correctly observed that *Princess Fish*, as an account of puberty, was something new in the German literature of the time,[14] and it has probably been too little noticed that *Restless Guests* is, in its restrained way, an erotic novella. While Wilhelm Riehl explicitly praised the prudery of the time,[15] Raabe occasionally protested against it, for example, in *Princess Fish*, where the narrator regrets the suppression in schoolbooks of an erotic ode of Horace (15: 244). I have mentioned earlier that the hysterical horror of illegitimate birth, found everywhere in bourgeois society of the time and especially in the English novel, is largely lacking in Raabe. In most cases the blame is placed not on the mother but on the father. Thus Kienbaum in *Stuffcake* is negatively characterized by his refusal to support his illegitimate child; as a consequence the child dies and the mother ends up in prison (18: 189). Exceptions might be Christabel Eddish in *Christoph Pechlin* and Marianne Erdener in *Fabian and Sebastian*. But, in the first case, as I have argued earlier, the woman is punished not as an unwed mother but on account of her hypocritical prudishness and her heartless denial of her child. In the second case, the woman is guilty of infanticide; although certainly a sad figure, the voice of stability in the novel, that of Knövenagel, accuses her of frivolity and love of luxury, and calls her a witch (15: 141-44). In general, however, the unwed mothers are treated with indulgence and the illegitimate children with kindness, all in succession to the poor dancer Rosalie in *The Chronicle of Sparrow Alley*.

To the many cases of defective families we may add those of more or less disordered ones. Some of them are torn apart by generational conflicts that can run in either direction. In *One Springtime* there are bitter estrangements between fathers and sons in two generations. Just as bitter is the struggle of Benedictus Meyenberger with his demonic daughter Fausta la Tedesca in *The Holy Spring*. The first scene of *A Secret* brings a nasty, physical fight between the innkeeper Claude Bullot and his dissolute daughter. A recurrent motif is the rejection of the prodigal son by the father. In *After the Great War* a father expels his son because he has lamed his brother in a jealous dispute. Markus Horn in *Our Lord God's Chancellory* is banned from his father's house. At the end father and son are reconciled, but in other cases reconciliation does not occur. Andreas Kritzmann in the same novel curses his father, who has thwarted his union with his subsequently executed beloved and their child; even on his deathbed he is not prepared to forgive his parents (4: 413). The disowned Hagebucher in *Abu Telfan* is not reconciled with his father during his lifetime, though becomes more like him after his death. In this novel there are broken family relations in every direction, doubtless as symptoms of a completely hypocritical society. Even before his adventure in Africa Hagebucher had become alienated from his family; he knew he could "not be any sort of man for my dear papa" (7: 23). Nikola von Einstein is practically locked up by her family; she fears her father and is contemptuous of her mother, who is prepared to sell her daughter for thirty pieces of silver (7: 184). Klaudine is abandoned by her son; Bumsdorf does not want to know anything about his son; Viktor rebels against his father.

Schnarrwergk in *The Lar* has also been mistreated and finally expelled by his parents (17: 332-34). The son of Pastor Buschmann in *The Rumbledump* is whipped by his father and in consequence threatens revenge against his parents (8: 159). This lack of respect need not necessarily characterize a negative figure like young Buschmann. The thoroughly positive Haeseler in *The Dräumling Swamp* speaks rather dismissively of his parents and calmly ignores the reproach of impiousness (10: 32-33). In *Höxter and Corvey* the pastor refuses to take his nephew, the failed student Lambert Tewes, into his house; later, when the parsonage is besieged by rioting Catholics, the amused Lambert does not lift one finger to help his uncle and aunt, although he courageously stands by his friends and the threatened Jews. In the draft of *Madame Salome*, the Countess Marie, as the title figure was originally called, is the daughter of quarrelling parents, with the consequence "that there has probably seldom been a child who grieved so little over the death of her mother as she did over the death of hers" (12: 467). In the final text the artist Querian's treatment of his daughter Eilike is anything but healthy. On the other hand, the father Erdener in *Fabian and Sebastian* cannot overcome his bitter feelings toward his daughter, not even after her release from a twenty-year imprisonment (15: 168).

This last novel reminds us of another theme, that of contentious siblings. The prehistory of Hagenheim in *One Springtime* is a story of hostile brothers, one devoted to the strict father, the other to the weak mother. Out of the circumstance that one son is responsible for the death of the other grows the estrangement between father and son. I have already touched upon the quarrel between the Bart brothers in *After the Great War*. There is a deep opposition between the brothers in *Master Author*, each of whom regards the other as a lout and fool (11: 34). Out of rather twisted malice the evil brother leaves his wealth to the master author's ward Gertrud in the justified expectation that it will spoil her character.

Indeed it appears that whatever can go wrong in a family goes wrong in Raabe. Count von Seeburg in *The Chronicle of Sparrow Alley* abandons his son and mistreats his daughter. In *One Springtime* it is the mother Angela who abandons her daughter. The melodramatic complications of *The Ultimate Justice* grow to a large extent out of chaotic family relationships. In *The People from the Forest*, Fiebiger is the son of an alcoholic, bankrupt innkeeper, Ulex the son of a weak father and a mother who is an alcoholic chicken-thief, Helene Wienand the daughter of a banker who virtually sells her to an unwholesome aristocrat for the sake of a patent of nobility. The narrator of *Lilac Blossom* has been oppressively treated by his uncle. The Götz family in *The Hunger Pastor* is characterized by a "bellum omnium contra omnes" (6: 233); the daughter Kleophea hates her mother and regards her spoiled brother, not without reason, as a "disgusting little toad" (6: 235). The female narrator of *In the Victory Wreath* is forced to care for her insane stepsister, a wholly inappropriate task for a child. In the end she rebels "in scorn and defiance of her father, her stepbrothers, and all the rest of her relatives" and frees the prisoner (9/2: 246-47). The perpetually quarrelsome Nebelung family in *Owls' Pentecost* drives the daughter Lina to America after having thwarted her love affair on political grounds and arranging for her beloved to be jailed. Albrecht in *The Innerste* suffers severe psychic damage from his tyrannical father; he knows himself that his father "made me what I have been" (12: 182). It has been rightly observed that only the death of his parents frees Albrecht from his servitude and also exorcises the myth of the lethal river.[16] Wunnigel in the story named for him is a man who does not want any family at all; he treats his daughter accordingly. Theodor Rodburg in *Princess Fish* is another unwanted child; his father is too old and his sisters are busy elsewhere; Theodor, for his part, indifferently fails to notice the death of his father in his chair. This family is splintered by the bad temper of the father, while the moral threat to the young Theodor is generated by his own brother. Social dissatisfaction of the mother and disappointment of the father, who considers his son mediocre, overshadow Kohl's childhood in *The Lar*. Conversely, the somewhat questionable character of Helene Trotzendorff in *The Documents of the Birdsong* is attributed, at least by the other figures, to her swindler of a father and fool of a mother.

Two cases of confused family relations strike me as especially noteworthy. One, *Three Pens*, has already been briefly discussed. Here the three narrators succeeding one another so to speak write their way out of their difficult family fate. "We were," recalls the thirty-year-old Hahnenberg, "old and young, a sour, peevish, dark, dusty, worm-eaten family" (9/1: 246). His parents should have stayed single, and their children will. The stupid mother of Joseph Sonntag spoils her son, whose marriage with Karoline Spierling, from a family dominated by a tyrannical father, is a regrettable one in Hahnenberg's eyes. August Sonntag loves his father Joseph but suffers from his incompetence, and suffers still more under his eccentric guardian Hahnenberg: "probably seldom has a child hated his youth so much as I did at that time" (9/1: 300). It is a chain, for Hahnenberg himself has been made a psychic cripple by his loveless childhood (9/1: 361-62). Here we are rather far removed from Riehl's "idyll of the German home."[17] The other case, perhaps the most remarkable of all, is *The Rumbledump*. For in this novel Antonie Häussler is betrayed and sold by her own grandfather. Here Raabe seems to be engaged in outright iconoclasm. What in the iconography of bourgeois society of that time is more venerable than a grandfather? In literature the "venerable old man," in German *ehrwürdiger Greis*, had long since become a type. Dietrich Häussler displays parvenu elegance but is in no way venerable, nor does he, despite his advanced age, make a very elderly impression. When he characterizes himself as a "greybeard" (8: 234-35), it is part of his theatrical role-playing. He radiates instead an oppressive energy and vitality; he is an incarnated image of the deathlessness of the *canaille* in the world. Here at the latest the chronological reader of Raabe would be forced to suspect that his fictional world does not have much to do with the sanctity of the family.

Ought we to bring Raabe's satire on marriage into this context? In *The People from the Forest*, for example, the police clerk Fiebiger receives from his friend Faber the advice to marry in order to escape melancholy, whereupon the married police commissioner Tröster sighs: "That doesn't entirely help, either, Faber" (5: 35). In the same novel marriage destroys the light-hearted spirit of Schminkert (5: 307-10). Wife and daughter of poor Löhnefinke in *German Moonshine* fight his inclination to poesy (9/2: 401-2). Attention has already been called to the merciless satire on love and marriage in *Christoph Pechlin*. Fritz Hessenberg in *Owls' Pentecost*, who was not allowed to marry his beloved Lina, marries another after his release from political imprisonment and finds himself beset like Laocoon between his wife and his mother-in-law (11: 418). Achtermann in *German Nobility* is cruelly persecuted by his wife and daughter; he seeks relief in his work as a lending-librarian, but: "All the romanticism of the twenty thousand volumes of his library could not compensate for the desolation in his body and the emptiness in his soul" (13: 206). This no longer has a humorous sound; not humorous at all is the very bad marriage of Irene von Everstein in *Old Nests*, and one may reasonably doubt whether the bad marriage of Sophie Grünhage in *The Horn of Wanza* is to be viewed humoristically from every side. More like the farcical quality of *Christoph Pechlin* is the surreal malice and jealousy of Frau Schönow in *Villa Schönow*.

To be sure, generational conflicts, sibling strife, and tragicomic marriages have belonged since time immemorial to the basic materials of literature. An even, uneventful family life yields no novelistic art. Tolstoy began *Anna Karenina* with the observation that all happy families are alike, while each unhappy family is unhappy in its own way. The implication is that only this unhappiness yields literature. In the English novel from which Raabe drew so much inspiration, family life is often far from idyllic. One might think of Dickens's *Dombey and Son* or *Nicholas Nickleby*; Fehse compared the nasty relationship between Dietrich Häussler and his granddaughter with that between Ralph Nickleby and his niece Kate.[18] One might think also of the unpleasant relationship between Arthur Clennam and his cold mother in *Little Dorrit*. But—and this shows once again the difference between Dickens and Raabe—Mrs. Clennam is in reality *not* Arthur's mother. Dickens is, as usual, defending values that for Raabe were by no means certain; while Dickens can entertain the notion of a dangerously incompetent father in Dorrit, a cold and selfish mother goes too far, and so, as in the fairy tale, she is displaced into the figure of stepmother. Again one might sooner think of Thackeray, of the hardly edifying relations in the Crawley family in *Vanity Fair*, or, in *Pendennis*, of the well-meant but morally somewhat dubious guidance of young Pen by his uncle.

The epidemic disappearance of parents might conceivably have a technical purpose, namely of fictional population control. The socially panoramic novel with many characters in a complex web of relationships with one another was not Raabe's forte. By orphaning so many of his characters, he relieved himself of the necessity of extending their involvements laterally. But here, too, one might look at the literary environment. Again we think of Dickens with his various poor, abandoned, orphaned, pure-hearted children. The Dickensian pathos may still burden Raabe's early works, but the similarity should not be exaggerated. One modern critic has argued that "the period of idealism and idyllics in his writing, during which the innocence and naivety of children are praised uncritically," lasted until 1862.[19] But *The People from the Forest* already forces him to contradict himself: "The idyll of childhood, seen in its reality, is shown to be squalid."[20] Certainly there is a sentimental tendency in the early phase, quite likely with an eye to the public. There is no doubt that from beginning to end Raabe wants to arouse sympathy with his young people who have been abandoned or have otherwise fallen into sad circumstances. But that does not seem to me to be the basic tenor, not even at the beginning. Rather—and this is the main point of this long prolegomenon—the loss of one or both parents and of the family connection may be sad, but it is not tragic, for it is the precondition of a liberation. In other words: in the value system of Raabe's fictional world, blood relationship counts for little or nothing.

The stress here must be on the word "fictional." For to make such an assertion about the Raabe of real life would be absurd. He became a family patriarch quite in the style of Wilhelm Riehl. Even his indulgence in regard to illegitimacy does not seem to have extended to his personal life; the Raabes dismissed a maid on the first day when they discovered that she was pregnant.[21] His love for his sister, his lifelong friendship with his brother, his profound feeling especially for his youngest daughter, whose death put him into the deepest emotional crisis of his life, all testify to a pronounced sense of family.[22] His relations with his more distant relatives by blood and marriage also seem to have been free of stress to a degree that perhaps few of us experience. His strong bond with his mother is evident and well known. Only in respect to his father's early death does the temperature seem to be noticeably cooler. The relevant passage has often been quoted: "The early death of my father was my fate. If he had lived longer and educated me, I would perhaps have become a mediocre

lawyer. . . . One of us had to give way."²³ In Raabe there is no trace
of the permanent psychic load that the early death of the father left
on Gottfried Keller. The bond with his mother and, at most, a certain
distance from his father²⁴ are the only biographical parallels to the
theme of the family in the fiction; otherwise the contrast between real
life and fictive world is striking.

One conspicuous aspect of his fictional tone in these matters is the
impious indifference not seldom expressed in his works. Von
Schmidt, the narrator of *Master Author*, is pleased that his father died
early enough "in order not to be able to be a hindrance on my way
through life and in my pastimes" (11: 17). Agonista in *At the Sign of
the Wild Man* is reminded of his mother by a goat (11: 236). These two
are questionable or negative figures, but one finds similar things uttered by more positive characters. In *Old Nests*, for example, when the
father of Ewald Sixtus has a fatal accident, even under such circumstances Ewald cannot suppress his feeling of strangeness toward his
father (14: 247). Not to mention Stuffcake, whose view of his own
parents as "a not only obstinate but also weepy mama and an old man
with a downright furious fixation on whatever professional study was
nearest to hand for his master son" is extended to the father of his old
acquaintance Eduard: "your ghastly old man as well as mine"; and he
entertains a fantasy of both fathers sitting behind bars (18: 34, 47).
I shall come back to this in my discussion of *Stuffcake* in Part III, but
it should not be forgotten that the morally commonplace Eduard
has remained totally loyal to his father and his traditional patriarchal
ideology.

Beginning with *Cloister Lugau*, Raabe develops variations on the
theme of well-intentioned parents who threaten their children's happiness by regarding them as a continuation of their own will. "How
much would the Judge of the world have to expiate," we read in *Cloister Lugau*, "if He were to punish the sins and crimes of mothers committed for the welfare of their children in His world!" (19: 38). The
wife of Pastor Holtnicker in *Hastenbeck* also falls under this judgment.
In *On the Scrap-Iron*, the natural family is, so to speak, deconstructed
and replaced with an unnatural one: "the pairing of Uhusen and Mut-
ter Cruse, between whom there is no question of sexual attraction,
precludes the conjugal conclusion of the typical family-journal
novel. . . . The prospective family is an odd one . . . compounded by
the near-inclusion of the streetwalker Rotkäppchen in this motley new
family."²⁵ The natural family is by no means always healthy for the
individual. The father, who does not need to be the least bit evil, can
nevertheless, insofar as he embodies affirmative social authority in

Riehl's sense, function as a repressive superego. Jehmüller has observed concerning the first-person narrators of the so-called "Braunschweig trilogy": "As the representative of a middle-level officialdom, the father initiates the biographer into a certain mental milieu from which he can never really liberate himself."[26]

Not that Raabe polemicizes against the institution of the family; that would not have been his way. We also find intact families in his works and also cordial family relations; one may think, for example, of the friendly relationship of father and son in *Gutmann's Travels*, or, even closer and more significant, in *Pfister's Mill*. Blood relationships *can* be companionable, friendly, humane, productive. But they *need not* be; they often *are not*. If such positive results occur, let us say, in the mother-son relationship, it is a stroke of fortune, perhaps even an accident. In Raabe's fictive world a person can be more easily crippled by an intact family than by the loss of one. The bourgeois family in Riehl's sense is regarded with consistent skepticism, especially in the place where Raabe treats the theme with the greatest tact and understanding: in *The Documents of the Birdsong*. On the contrary, the orphan, robbed of an intact family, has the possibility of forming bonds with persons who are initially strangers or with family members who have been pushed to the periphery as black sheep, persons who become mentors more serviceable to his acculturation, maturation, and protection.

Whoever regards Raabe as only "fanatically bourgeois" easily runs the risk of missing the real implications of his texts. Thus Martini wrote many years ago: "in Raabe's work the sacredness of the family plays perhaps the greatest role."[27] Thus a modern ideological critic writes of the late works: "The private idyll, the bourgeois family, is all that is left, all social expectations must be dropped."[28] Dieter Kafitz asserts: "Class identification loses its significance in comparison to the family as a form of organization and as a standard of value of meaningful life. . . . The disorder of family life [in the Götz household in *The Hunger Pastor*] becomes an indicator for the inhumanity of the social order."[29] Here Raabe seems to have been confused with Schiller. Kafitz implies a development to greater skepticism in the later works, but even in regard to the early ones critics can exaggerate: "in the early work the family was still the protective refuge of intimacy, the essential educational institute for the individual developing as a whole person, a 'green place' in the prosaic conditions."[30] These seem to me to be cases of a refusal of perception, which leads to fitting Raabe to preconceived bourgeois patterns. It will be more productive to try to read him with genuinely new, unprejudiced eyes in order adequately to recognize the particular, acutely critical nature of his bourgeois mentality.

Furthermore, the fictional deconstruction of the family, its replacement with relationships that may, but need not, be familial, the formation of a supportive and sustaining community outside the natural family, bring us at last to the thematic subtitle of this book.

CHAPTER 14

The Fiction of the
Alternative
Community

◘

SINCE THE Romantic era the concept of community has been a
recurrent concern in German thought. The advent of the modern
world with its division of labor, its sometimes lonely and exposed
individualism, its dissolution of traditional, organic relationships and
of superintending institutions such as religion, has constantly aroused
anxiety, a sense of alienation in a fallen world. The anxiety generates
nostalgia for a real or, more likely, imagined past as well as imaginings
of a utopian future, and not infrequently imagined past and imagined
future are bridged in an eschatological arc over the despised real present. The pattern can have reactionary or progressive motives, sometimes both at once. The Romantics, notwithstanding the modern and
urban aspect of their consciousness, came to lean to the reactionary
side, projecting both political and religious restoration. Anxiety about
division and alienation brought a revival of Romantic notions of community in fascism, the very symbol of which—the fasces—is an image
of strength in solidarity. Kenneth Burke, in his admired analysis of
Hitler's *Mein Kampf*, rightly called attention to the great "yearning for
unity" that fascism purported to satisfy, adding, more dubiously, that
Hitler's doctrine was the "*bad* filling of a good need."[1]

But the idea of community has exhibited a constancy in German
thought that has been one of its unifying elements across ideological
boundaries. The liberal sociologist Ferdinand Tönnies made his name
in 1887 with a now classic work contrasting and comparing community formed by natural will with society formed by rational will, *Gemeinschaft und Gesellschaft*. Community, once lost, again to be re-
covered, has been an enduring theme of the radical left as well. Let
us listen for a moment to the *Communist Manifesto*:

> The bourgeoisie, where it has come to power, has destroyed all
> feudal, patriarchal, idyllic relations. It has unmercifully torn the

colorful feudal bonds that linked man to his natural superiors and left no other bond between man and man than naked interest, than insensate "cash payment." It has drowned the sacred thrill of pious devotion, chivalric enthusiasm, philistine wistfulness in the ice-cold water of egotistical calculation. It has dissolved personal dignity in exchange value and put in place of the innumerable vested and duly acquired freedoms the *single* unscrupulous freedom of trade. It has, in a word, put in place of exploitation veiled with religious and political illusions open, shameless, direct, arid exploitation. . . .

The bourgeoisie has torn the touchingly sentimental veil from the family relation and reduced it to a pure money relationship.[2]

Despite Marx's and Engels's characteristically profane, rationalistically superior tone here, despite their allegiance to progress and thus their acknowledgment of the disillusioning role of the bourgeoisie, an undertone of nostalgia for social relations that were once unified or at least believed to be so remains audible, and it has become much more audible in modern Western Marxism, for example, in Ernst Bloch's elaborated principle of utopian hope or Theodor Adorno's belief in the work of art as a vessel of unalienated resistance to the irredeemably fallen world of bourgeois, capitalist society. More recently, the obsession has re-emerged in leftist sentimentality about East Germany, where repression and what we in the West might regard as social and economic backwardness have allegedly permitted the retention of an unstressed, relatively unspoiled nineteenth-century environment and of more natural interpersonal relations (how perverse of the East German population to desire so forlornly to flee this idyll, so that it must be literally walled into it). Whether the longing for community is more strongly felt among Germans than in other nations I am in no position to guess. But in the United States the most stubbornly enduring communes—the Amish, the Mennonites, and, less barricaded against secular society, the Moravians—have been of German origin.

Wilhelm Raabe was also much concerned about community. It has long been recognized that he opposed *Gemeinschaft* to *Gesellschaft*; the latter was for him "a thoroughly negative concept, identical with philistinism, the world of illusion, or even the *canaille*."[3] He took a bleak view of worldly society—the "saeculum," as he was implacably to call it in *Restless Guests*—as an only superficially civilized wilderness of egotism, lovelessness, superstitious false consciousness, and stolid insensitivity. It is a world in some ways not very different from Balzac's, only less colorfully and melodramatically delineated, less obsessively charged with avarice and lust. While still young, Raabe seems to have thought about this vaguely in class terms, reposing a sentimental trust in the common people against the institutions and selfish ideology of the dominant classes. In the early novel *One Springtime* he celebrates the natural virtue of the underclass:

> Do you know the caritas of the alleys?—It carries no tractates in its pocket; it is not the miserable mixture of curiosity and boredom that drives it down to gloomy cellar hovels, up to windy garrets. The caritas of the alleys does not visit misery because the contrasts are piquant, because rags can be picturesque. The caritas of the alleys, the caritas *in* the people, is feeling, while the caritas *over* the people is *mostly* coquetry! (1: 190).

The rescue of Germany by the salt of the earth is implied in this novel. Of the stoic leitmotif drawn from Tacitus, *Securus adversus homines, securus adversus Deum*, one character says: "In this proverb are connected many in green Germany who believe they cannot understand one another!" (1: 403). The salvation of the community by the emancipation of the decency of ordinary people—the "German nobility" in the novella of that name—never receded beyond Raabe's horizon. But he was unable to retain his youthful faith in the virtue of the common people, who in many texts—for example, *Horacker, Elsa of the Fir, Madame Salome, Restless Guests*—appear unsympathetic, insensitive, sometimes menacing. What develops instead in his fiction is a characteristic movement of particular individuals into a protective, defensive, internally supportive subcommunity distinctive in its ethos from the "saeculum," from society at large.

In the past there has been a good deal of imprecision in apprehending the meaning and the character of this most fundamental of Raabe's strategies. He has been seen both as a nostalgic upholder of traditional structures and as a champion of "originals," odd fellows who retain an individualism threatened by soulless modern society and thus isolate themselves. It is important to see how he maneuvers between the extremes of these conventional notions. On the one hand, his general estimate of mankind was too low to allow him much faith in utopian projections, past or future. As we have seen in the case of the family, he predicated no intrinsic virtues to the given, natural structures of society. Natural communities in Raabe are not charitable; neither fraternal ones, such as the brothers in *Fabian and Sebastian*, nor traditional social ones, such as the peasant community in *Horacker*, where "the feeling of community in its blindness is pilloried and another picture of community is substituted for it."[4] His alternative communities are therefore not preformed; people choose one another, freely and rationally in recognition of mutual affinities. "The right people always find their way together," we read in *The Dräumling Swamp* (10: 185). These essentially rational personal relations transcend the normative barriers in society, as in *The Holy Spring* when the ideological enemies, pastor and priest, become friends during a disastrous fire. The priest loses his hate: "with the need for relief, mildness had entered his heart"; the pastor, for his part, frowns with clenched lips as he composes his tract against popery, but when the old priest comes to visit, his features relax, he can smile (3: 54, 57).

Many years later, in *The Odin Field*, a similar point is made: the horrors of the day partially restore the community, in that the prefect, who threw Buchius out of the cloister, at the end of the twenty-four hours of slaughter and dread begs his pardon and sincerely welcomes his return, while the prefect's wife, usually very unpleasant to Buchius, is also glad to see him (17: 211). Even when the alternative community has its origin in childhood friendship—Raabe's famous "cloverleaf"—the children tend to be heterogeneous in origin and circumstances. His positive characters do *not* seek isolation or eccentricity, or a decoupling of the responsible links among human beings, such as we see in more modern writers like Nietzsche, Rilke, or Kafka.[5] Nor do they achieve independent selfhood entirely on their own resources, or even with the aid of a single "significant other"; it takes the polyperspectivism of a group. "No one," remarks Aunt Grünhage in *The Horn of Wanza*, "has by himself alone helped another to his essence and comfort in the world" (14: 321)—just as the narrative structure of that novel provides a shifting perspective on the several facets of the events of the past. On the other hand, Raabe was too much of an individualist to submerge personality into the oversoul of an organic community. A kibbutz would not have been the place for him or his fictional characters. The members of his subcommunities share a certain ethical outlook and certain restraints on the ego, but there is space between them, respect for difference. He has no intention of recreating in the alternative community the stifling intimacy of the family.

Furthermore, the alternative community does not always work in the same way, and often its workings are far from perfect. The subcommunal relationship is fragile and labile, and can have a quite different appearance in different contexts. The individualism can become extreme and ultimately dysfunctional, as in the case of *Wunnigel* and of Velten Andres in *The Documents of the Birdsong*. It can take the shape of incompetence in life—Joseph Sonntag in *Three Pens*—or of madness—Paul Ferrari in *German Nobility*. The expelled self can fail to sustain its autonomy despite the presence of a sympathetic alternative community, as we shall see in the case of Leonhard Hagebucher in *Abu Telfan*. The young Raabe may have thought, rather sentimentally, that suffering and defeat predispose the personality to a readiness for subcommunal empathy; in *The Ultimate Justice* "it once again became true that two unhappy people much more easily find their way to one another and bind themselves much more firmly to one another than two happy people" (9/1: 32). It is true that in Raabe's fiction good fortune hardens the heart and it is the wounded and defeated souls, by and large, who are his positive figures. Yet as early as *The People from the Forest* he knew that suffering and worry can dull empathy, the sensibility for other selves, and that this is the common condition:

> Mankind has never had a very sharp eye for the internal, and we do not want to reproach mankind for that; for the winters are cold, the potatoes fail very often, and one has trouble enough with governments, wives, and children. Watch out or you will freeze! Watch out or you will starve! Watch out or you will be put under police surveillance! Watch out or your wife will threaten with her slipper! Watch out or your daughter will not get a husband!—The devil take inwardness! By heaven, poor mankind has little time to occupy itself with its most private being. (5: 57)

One might extrapolate from this that it is the office of fiction to remedy this deficiency, to form models of sympathetic insight into other selves.

One of the most important functions of the alternative community in Raabe's fiction is the mentorship of the young. It is here that the characteristic dissolution of the family becomes most important, for the child or youth, orphaned or abandoned, is taken up by elder mentors and educated by the humane principles of the alternative community. Once again, however, we have a theme with variations, not just for the sake of variety, but to open up questioning perspectives, to keep the pattern from petrifying into simplistic doctrine or "message." The theme appears in its most basic form in *The People from the Forest*. Here the police clerk Fiebiger, a lonely bachelor oppressed by the human misery with which he must deal in his daily work, adopts the young delinquent Robert Wolf. He wants to save Robert's soul, while Robert with his youth will save the aging Fiebiger from the anxieties he brings home from his police work (5: 35). The motto of the novel, which recurs as a leitmotif, is from Proverbs 27:17; in the

Revised Standard Version, which is closest to the German, it reads: "Iron sharpens iron, and one man sharpens another." But, as usual, Fiebiger is not alone in his task; he is assisted by his friends, the sharp-tongued renegade aristocrat Juliane von Poppen and the unworldly astronomer Ulex, the three of them forming the still intact cloverleaf of their own youth. Together they effect an improvement in Robert's spiritual condition and, as has been pointed out, not merely as a result of their love and concern, but also of his contact with them "as representatives of specific world-views."[6] This is the first fully developed example of the alternative community at work. Yet even here the mentors are not infallible. Fiebiger quirkily wants to raise Robert to a life of permanent bachelorhood like his own, and all three try to separate him from his true love. As Fiebiger, Juliane, and Ulex get old, they spend more and more time withdrawn into Ulex's tower, and Fiebiger turns bitter as he learns the axiom of the vanity of all things as demonstrated in his own existence (5: 407). Thus, as so often with Raabe, the idyll, if that is what it is, is an idyll of diminishment.

In *The Hunger Pastor* mentorship becomes a little more ambivalent. Hans Unwirrsch's foster parents, Aunt and Uncle Grünbaum, teach him important lessons of kindness and sympathy for the oppressed. But in their traditionalism they are also a threat to the unfolding of his individuality. When his uncle tries to force him to become a shoe-maker like his forebears, they have a serious quarrel; the moment the uncle gives in, he loses all further influence over Hans. In *Three Pens* the thematic relationship becomes still more tense; here the mentor who rescues the youth from the failed family is the misanthropic Hah-nenberg, whose surrogate parenting is anything but pleasant for the boy and probably also of limited ethical value. Of Hahnenberg it has been remarked that he is Raabe's "first educator-figure not drawn in black and white,"[7] but this judgment overlooks the evolution to increased questioning of the basic model. Later, in *Princess Fish*, the young person's stress with the absolutely well-meaning and even wise mentors becomes acute. Unable to deal with young Theodor Rod-burg's crisis of puberty, they order him out of the house, though on reflection they relent. It is perhaps a mark of Raabe's maturity that the virtually congenital loneliness of Theodor, born "too late in the year," is only assuaged but ultimately not integratively relieved by his mentors' efforts.

Just about the worst case, unsurprisingly, is found in the most pessimistic of the big novels, *The Rumbledump*. Here the alternative community fails altogether in its function of protecting Antonie Häussler, the orphaned young person put into its care. The quality of mentorship contrasts with the pattern in the thematically model case, *The People from the Forest*. While in that novel the aristocrat Juliane von Poppen forthrightly regards her own class as obsolescent and even ridiculous, here Adelaide von Saint-Trouin lives in a fantasy of the *ancien régime*, pretending to a still intact role in its long irrelevant hierarchies of privilege and respect. These are harmless, even comic quirks, tolerantly viewed in the alternative community, but at the same time they unfit her as a guide into the world of reality. Her male counterpart, the Chevalier von Glaubigern, is chivalrous and sympathetic—he makes the bravest attempt at the end of the novel to rescue Antonie from her fate—but his mental furniture is old-fashioned and he lacks the wisdom of the astronomer Ulex. He is too timid and aged; he lapses directly into senility after the failure of his attempt to rescue Antonie. The mistress of the estate, Frau von Lauen, is hospitable and generous to the illegitimate, orphaned girl, but at the same time she is on the alert to prevent her son Hennig from developing an emotional attachment to her that might lead to a mésalliance. Hennig himself likes Antonie and at the crisis even offers to marry her, but Antonie recognizes that his heart is not in it, that his sympathies are kind but commonplace, lukewarm as his name, Lauen, suggests in German. The kindness and decency of these people are not strong enough to stand against the worldly malignance of Antonie's jovial and ruthless grandfather, who attempts to sell her to a decadent nobleman. In time the clear-eyed Antonie blames her mentors for her misfortune, for having unrealistically led her to believe that she was "usable" in the world as she was (8: 304). The mentors suffer from various inadequacies of character, but more abstractly one might say that they are not sufficiently emancipated from their natural communities, in this case defined by class and the concomitant remnants of class consciousness, so that the alternative community is not fully willed and therefore does not completely take shape.

The fragility of the alternative community, its potential for failure, has sometimes been underestimated by critics. For example, Daemmrich comments on *Master Author*: "In small enclaves, people adhere to spiritual values, gentleness, and love, whereas in the technologically oriented society engineers plan to clear the land for roads, railways, and new housing."[8] But I wonder if the contrast is quite that stark, or whether the formulation shows too little distance from the dubious narrator von Schmidt. The movement of personal relations in the novel is centrifugal, away from genuine community and into diminishment, and the novel ends in an almost parodistic creation of conventional communities with the master author's ward, Gertrud, product of failed mentorship, marrying a stupid man and sinking into equally stupid domesticity, and the narrator von Schmidt coolly marrying a disturbingly fashionable lady. The withdrawn master author himself must learn a lesson about personal relations: "A person like me always thinks that he is there for his own sake, but that is not so . . . one must grow old to ferret it out" (11: 125).[9] Even some modern criticism has not entirely escaped the traditional habit of attributing to Raabe a rather rigid dualism that sets a positive but escapist utopian community against the fallen world of reality. Frau Klaudine in *Abu Telfan*, who has resigned from the social world almost entirely, expresses this view most explicitly: "We are a few against a million, we defend a little empire against a whole wild world; but we believe in victory, and more is not necessary to win it" (7: 249). Doubtless this is something Raabe would like to have believed and conveyed as a message of consolation, but how many ambiguities accrue to it in the actual working out of the fiction we shall see in the next chapter.

In contemplating the alternative community, it is important to recognize how much disruption attends its formation. In many cases it is not so much that Raabe's characters opt out of conventional communities as that they are driven out by meanness, oppression, individual and collective egotism. These disruptions have costs. It has been rightly said that at the end of *Madame Salome* an old community has been dissolved and a new one formed.[10] But accomplishing this has required, among other things, a conflagration that consumes a large part of the town and in particular incinerates a mad father from whom his daughter must be rescued. The new formation is a community of the isolated, shut out from the larger society and aware of their isolation. The childhood cloverleaf is not a model but a possibility; it functions into adulthood in *The People from the Forest*, but in other cases it does not. Of the original cloverleaf in *Madame Salome*—the protagonist Scholten, the mad sculptor Querian, and the distant mystic Schwanewede—Scholten remarks that three broken pots don't make one whole one (12: 75). Not only is Querian burned to death at the end; it turns out that Schwanewede, to whom Scholten has been writing letters, has been long dead. The childhood community in *Old Nests* breaks apart; the narrator loses track of his friends, and the community is only partially reformed at the end of the novel. The cloverleaf in *On the Scrap-Iron*— Uhusen, Brokenkorb, Erdwine—is completely unreconstructible. Erdwine has died, and the aesthetic, socially successful Brokenkorb has become too alienated from Uhusen's values. A new community is formed: the orphan children with their elderly mentors, Uhusen and the déclassée junk dealer Wendeline Cruse. In this case, however, there is a new variant: a character opts out of the *alternative* community. This is the streetwalker Little Red Riding Hood, who finds it is best for her to depend alone on her own resources and her own fate. The cloverleaf in *The Documents of the Birdsong*, as we shall see, splinters apart in emotional disruption that reflects a crisis in the very integrity of the self.

Once again Raabe is the master, not the slave, of his theme. He turns it over, upside down, and inside out, looking at it from every angle. With imagination, skepticism, and even self-criticism he explores the potential strengths and weaknesses of what is certainly an enduring central vision of an alternative pattern of human relations, a pattern of unambitious, unmanipulative empathy in shared consciousness of the vanity of all things, the pathetic brevity of life, and its ineluctable tragedy, a pattern of friendship between men and women, between elders and youth, between human beings of different religions, different classes, different geographical origins. The alternative community does have a kind of utopian aspect insofar as Raabe quite seriously regarded it as a message to the nation. In *German Nobility*, his novel of, though not about, the Franco-Prussian War, this community is expressed as a new nobility; including a German girl with an Italian name, it is characterized as "an excellent hodge-podge of German nationality—let us boldly call it, of *German nobility*" (13: 312). Hermann Böschenstein has said quite rightly that Raabe's works "gather the people who are mature for a humane founding of a state, who afterwards prove that the good material is not exhausted and will guarantee endurance and authenticity to this humane state."[11]

To this, however, must be added two things. In the first place, it is clear that Raabe came to despair of the creation of this humane state in his own time. The vision doubtless fueled his longing for the unification of the German nation, grounded, he hoped, in the finest and gentlest of bourgeois sensibilities. But he was to find afterwards that nothing had changed so profoundly, neither in the quality of community nor in the relations among human beings. As his hopes receded, his art grew stronger, probing, with increasing precision and subtlety, the depth, complexity, and boundaries of the alternative community. Secondly, and doubtlessly not unconnected with this non-realization, we must acknowledge the pronounced fictivity of the alternative community. Its fictional status is evident not only in its clear contrast with Raabe's personal way of life but even more relevantly in the stressed fictionality of his narrative technique. It is apparent in the fragility of the alternative community. "How good and how pleasant it is for brethren to dwell together in unity," remarks the narrator of *Hastenbeck*, quoting Psalm 133 and paraphrasing, as he points out, a similar remark in *The Odin Field*—"and how rarely it is the case!" (20: 34; 17: 8). It is in this light that his much criticized penchant for delineating defensive subcommunities, isolated in allegedly idyllic withdrawal from the world of reality, must be understood. The isolation and encapsulation create a protected space in which the otherwise threatened humane potentials can be imagined. In a sense, his entire oeuvre is such a space, potential rather than real, which was meant not to be enclosed in permanent withdrawal and rejection, but to alter consciousness in the jungles of the civilized world.

His failure to achieve his aspirations in this regard may have much to do with the radicality of his vision, which his admirers did not perceive and which even he himself may have failed to perceive in its full dimensions. For the alternative community implies a quite modern, Enlightenment and rationalist spirit. No traditional or conventional rootedness is binding, not in church or state, in family or regional soil. Such allegiances may persist, but they need not; they remain within the choice of the individual. The attitude actually lies on the same line as his opposition to local, particularist patriotism, while the "Germany" to which he demanded allegiance was a new creation, not an organic growth on a traditional ground but made by human will and intention. Thus his historical fiction, unlike that of many of his contemporaries, makes no effort to display a continuity from the past to the German Reich. Instead there is the hope that the dismaying and bloody eternal recurrence of history might come to an end in a new order in which the spirit of the alternative community might become more generally efficacious. It is the spirit, to borrow an image, not irrelevantly, I think, from Heinrich Böll's novel *Billiards at Half-Past Nine*, of the lambs rather than that of the buffaloes. As long as this spirit is not efficacious—and Raabe was obliged to see that its realization was not close at hand—then the non-aggressive, the non-ambitious, the empathic and gentle-spirited, the defeated rebels and the souls in tune with the pathos of living, must be shown in fiction finding and choosing one another as their community. In doing so, they also express, always implicitly and sometimes explicitly, a refusal of the inherited structures of society, to which they abjure loyalty, not by confrontation but by evasion. Thus the appearance in Raabe of flight, withdrawal from responsibility into enclaves of consolation, and humorous eccentricity; but the implied repudiations and the all but total absence of compromise with the traditional institutions of society were evidently less easily apprehended. That the values articulated in his fictional communities were perceived as expressing acceptance rather than refusal must count as one of the great blindnesses of literary reception.

PART III

Interpretations

CHAPTER 15

Irresolute Form:
Abu Telfan

◻

IN THE preceding chapters I have tried to suggest several times that Raabe's career should not be seen as a linear, progressive development from early immaturity to mastery, that in his search for forms and techniques adequate to his vision there are fits and starts, early anticipations and later regressions, and strengths and weaknesses often side by side at every stage. Nevertheless, there is a development in a rough sense, insofar as most of his peak achievements are found late in his career. The phases and junctures of this development are not always easy to define. Raabe himself was not always consistently clear about them, especially as it repeatedly happened that he would complete and offer a new work with gratification, only to have his spirits dashed once again by critical resistance and public indifference.

In the overall development of his career the Stuttgart trilogy obviously occupies an important place. The three novels are elaborate and ambitious, products of a major investment of imagination and labor. Their failure with the public one after the other was deeply discouraging. Not only did it turn him away from the novel form altogether for a number of years; it established permanently in his psyche the consciousness of failure that no amount of later success and fame could fully dislodge. Of the three novels, the middle one, *Abu Telfan*, seems to have survived best into modern times. *The Hunger Pastor*, though it exhibits a number of sometimes unacknowledged local strengths, is altogether too burdened by its injudicious handling of the Jewish theme to appeal very much to post-Holocaust readers. *The Rumbledump*, in my judgment, is burdened also, by a rhetorically reinforced pessimism that approaches melodramatic self-indulgence. *Abu Telfan*, however, continues to command respect among those well acquainted with Raabe and, I have found occasionally, among readers with a more casual knowledge. In 1980, when the influential Hamburg weekly *Die Zeit (The Times)* ran a series on the hundred "best" works of world literature, the prominent literary historian Hans Mayer, originally of Marxist provenance, chose *Abu Telfan*.[1] I, too, find much to admire in this novel. It is, even by Raabe's standards, impressively well written (except perhaps at the very end), an intensely thoughtful, in places meditative work in which he clearly invested a great deal of concentration and effort. It had a long genesis, repeatedly interrupted by other works, and, though he was not normally given to elaborate revision, he spent a full three months working on the final draft (7: 387). He had great hopes that the novel would improve his standing with the public; he propagated it vigorously and even composed advertising copy for it (7: 398-99).

In this he was, as usual, to be disappointed; the critics found the novel eccentric and it sold so poorly that three years later, in 1870, the remainder was reissued as a "second edition" with a new title page. But the first printing of 1,500 copies did not sell out for twenty years. Only in the 1890s, with the general rise of Raabe's reputation, did it post some modest gains, reaching a sixth edition in 1908 (7: 400-1). Thus its stronger standing in modern times is welcome. However, along with its strengths, the novel has problematic qualities as well. It appears to me to exhibit an irresoluteness of execution, leading to missed opportunities and an ultimate confusion in import. In these respects it shows Raabe still struggling with his vocation, and perhaps it can be employed to analyze more clearly what the terms of that struggle were.

Abu Telfan or The Return from the Mountains of the Moon is, or at first appears to be, the story of Leonhard Hagebucher, a misfit who has fallen into quite dreadful circumstances. A dropout as a theology student, he became, to the dismay of his family, something of a drifter, eventually wandering to the Near East, where he landed a public-relations job on the Suez Canal project. In this role he performed quite well, but his position was terminated and he became associated with a notorious ivory dealer. The band of traders was attacked by natives; the dealer was tortured to death and Hagebucher was enslaved by blacks in Abu Telfan in Tumurkieland, a fictitious African locale. In this captivity he remained for ten years, and he was just about at the end of his resources of endurance and courage when his freedom was purchased by a German wild-animal dealer who called himself Kornelius van der Mook. All of this is unfolded piecemeal in the course of the actual narration, which begins with Hagebucher's homeward journey, during which he is an object of police curiosity at every stage. The exposition flows into his ambivalent reception in his home town of Bumsdorf near the capital city of Nippenburg and his awkward efforts to reintegrate himself into conventional society.

We thus have here a classic case of the Raabean theme of the "re-turnee," the individual who has been propelled out of his native en-vironment and then, after experiences in alien surroundings that effect an alteration of consciousness, returns home with enhanced or at least altered perspectives. Generically we can see here the old literary theme of the criticism of Europe from an exotic perspective, with the twist, however, which turns out to be important, that the exotic ex-periences have been not enriching but horrifying and to some degree crippling. All the same, the situation affords an opportunity for acute social criticism, which is, of course, the feature of the novel that ap-peals most to a modern critic like Hans Mayer. In his first sentence the author makes it explicit that the setting is contemporary: "On a tenth of May at the beginning of the seventh decade of this, as we all know, so highly blessed, illuminated, amiable nineteenth century . . ." (7: 7)—an opening that establishes the sardonically critical tone pervading the whole novel. Bumsdorf and Nippenburg are fictitious places, but there is nothing to prevent us from associating them, as other critics have done, with Wolfenbüttel and Braunschweig.

The returned Hagebucher is at first a nine-day wonder, but when it emerges that he has not come back from the Orient with fabulous riches and swashbuckling achievements, but in as empty-handed and incompetent a condition as when he left, the townspeople promptly lose interest in him, dismiss his stories as fables, and scorn him as a parasite and good-for-nothing. As so often with Raabe, the mean-spir-ited recalcitrance of conventional society is centered most intensely in the family. Hagebucher's father, a soberly calculating tax official, lives in a house that bears over its door the verse, "Blessed be thy going out and thy coming in," adapted from Psalm 121:8, but he keeps be-hind the door a "thick club for shameless beggars, itinerant journey-men, and stray dogs" (7: 15) and before long he begins to place his long-lost son in one or another of these categories. At length a family council is held to decide what might be done to make Hagebucher, who, it must be remembered, is now nearly forty years old, into a useful member of society, during which the shrill ultimatums of his aunt make her seem more awful to him than Madame Kulla Gulla, his cruel enslaver in Abu Telfan (7: 45). His father, for whom the son's return has been even more embarrassing than his departure, "would have been the last man to speak a word on behalf of his African" (7: 42). The father loses prestige among his reserved-table tavern com-panions, and, although he fully agrees with them that his son is a lout, he is drawn into a quarrel so distressful to him that afterwards he screams at his son and slams the door of his house on him. On the larger social plane, Hagebucher eventually attempts to rehabilitate himself by offering in the capital a series of lectures on his experiences. But here the alienated perspective of the returnee breaks out in full force. His first lecture is acidly critical, drawing disagreeable parallels between the slavery of Africa and social conditions in the homeland. The police inform him firmly that no further lectures will be required, and his one effort toward recognition and respect comes to an ignominious end. Eventually he acquires an obscure position copying Coptic texts for an eccentric Professor Reihenschlager, whose chillingly normal daughter Serena he half-heartedly and unsuccessfully courts.

In these circumstances, it is inevitable in Raabe's fictional world that Hagebucher will be drawn into the alternative community. Its center is one of the best known of Raabe's loci of withdrawal from the world and society: the Cat Mill, where a wise woman, Klaudine Fehleysen, known as Our Lady of Patience, lives a hermit-like existence, offering comfort to other damaged selves. As she listens to the steady drip of water from the old millwheel, she waits in hope and trust for the return of her son Viktor, who disappeared years before in consequence of a quarrel with his father. This is an obvious parallel to Hagebucher's case, though with reversed values, for in this case the father, victim of a courtly intrigue of a Baron von Glimmern, was the decent man, while the son was egocentric and churlish. Among Klaudine's emotional dependents is Nikola von Einstein, a maid of honor at the court; she is being forced for family and social reasons into a loveless marriage with Baron von Glimmern, who wishes to use this connection to get closer to the court. The good-looking, neurotic, sarcastic, and defeated Nikola, who advises Hagebucher to give up his efforts at integration and become an organ-grinder, is one of Raabe's most attractive female figures, at least for my taste, and Hagebucher appears to be half in love with her, though he denies that he is.

Another member of the group is Wassertreter, a garrulous, hard-drinking cynic, who has been a victim of political oppression and now lives an obscure life as a road-building inspector. He represents another kind of parallel to Hagebucher, for he has had comparable experiences in the past: "See, my son, when in the year eighteen hundred and twenty-one they sent me down from the Wartburg [prison] with a gracious kick, I came home the same way you did from remotest Africa, and the Carlsbad Decrees had done their work on me just as well as the whip in Tumurkieland did on you" (7: 47). Yet another parallel figure is the tailor Täubrich, known as Täubrich Pasha, for he, too, had wandered to the Near East and during one of his adventures got hit on the head with a stone; rescued by Mormons, he wakes up at home in Germany. Täubrich has many exotic adventures to relate, but in his case it is far from certain how true they may be, for he is a man of doubtful mental health inclined to drift into dream states. Here Raabe doubles back on his fiction, setting the probably imaginary reminiscences of Täubrich in parallel to the "real" ones of Hagebucher, and implying that, real or imaginary, they are equally devoid of interest to the local public. Another figure who later accrues to the alternative community is Lieutenant Kind, retired commander of a punishment company, a harsh and angry man who is bent on a course of vengeance against Baron von Glimmern. For we learn that this Baron in the past seduced Kind's daughter and entrapped her fiancé, a sturdy, honorable conscript, into insubordination, so that he is sent to Kind's punishment company. There the young man attempts to assassinate the Baron, whereupon Kind himself is obliged to shoot down his own prospective son-in-law. Kind has been accumulating material on the Baron's corruption, in order to blow him up at the appropriate moment.

My attentive reader will have noticed that something troublesome is beginning to happen to the novel. Corrupt aristocrat ruins lower-class girl, but avenging nemesis lies in wait—my, my. "Is not the intrigue surrounding Friedrich von Glimmern," one critic asks fairly, "the substance novels are made of, and the part likely to have the greatest appeal to the reading public?"[2] Is it not, one might add, in the 1860s a little late for this sort of thing? The point where the novel takes this turn can be identified fairly exactly. When Hagebucher gives his disastrous public lecture, his rescuer van der Mook turns up in the audience. Not only is it he who brings Lieutenant Kind into the story; it soon appears that he is actually the long-lost prodigal son, Viktor Fehleysen. Secret family relationships and revealed hidden identities, of course, also belong to the stuff of the conventional novel. On top of this we get something like a detective chase. After Kind exposes Glimmern's peculations in public, the latter must flee, pursued by Kind, in turn pursued by "van der Mook," who runs them down in London with the help of the amiably efficient British police and finds them both dead, having shot one another in a duel across a table.

This sort of thing has tended to distress Raabe's critics, both traditional and modern. He himself seems to have been a little uneasy, for in one place the narrator tells us that we will not follow van der Mook's pursuit or concern ourselves with the details of the fate of Kind and Glimmern, "for we consider it neither an art nor a pleasure, and least of all our vocation, to keep the record of a criminal proceeding" (7: 350-51), but not much farther along we hear the whole story in a letter from van der Mook (7: 362-68). To sniff at such elements as "novelistic" does not seem appropriate, since such a judgment reflects the aesthetic devaluation of the novel form from which we presumably no longer suffer. Hidden in the charge is a subliminal anxiety about meretriciousness. Was Raabe merely pandering to a conventional public? No one can look into his heart in such matters; my own view is that, given the quality of his integrity generally, we do well to avoid presumptions of this kind. My inclination, rather, is to suspect a bewilderment on the author's part about the course of the novel, especially as it is generally agreed that such melodramatic elements were not Raabe's métier and he did not usually carry them off very persuasively. The most obvious effect here, especially in about the third quarter of the novel, is to distance the narrative perspective from Hagebucher's dilemma of identity, which at first appeared to be the novel's subject.

As this occurs, Hagebucher undergoes a transformation that has made thoughtful critics uneasy. His withdrawal into the alternative community, with its values of stoic resignation and patient endurance, instead of shoring up his non-conforming, critical spirit, turns him instead to an accommodation with conventional society. All readers have been struck by the portrayal of Hagebucher toward the end of the novel, with his pipe in his mouth and a stature, posture, and mien greatly resembling his father's, though he is friendlier and livelier (7: 375-76). The novel seems to trail off in "humorous" reconciliation, though in a minor key of loss and sadness, punctuated by repetition of the book's motto: "If you knew what I know, spake Mohammed, you would weep much and laugh little" (7: 6, 380, 382 [the concluding line of the work]).

It is in this context that a passage appears that may have done Raabe more harm among hostile critics than any other paragraph in his writings:

> Is that not an amazing thing in the German land, that the Cat Mill can lie and does lie everywhere and Nippenburg has its being all around and the one can never be imagined without the other? Is that not an amazing thing, that the man from Tumurkieland, the man from the Mountains of the Moon, never appears without Uncle and Aunt Schnödler? Wherever we look, German genius always and everywhere draws a third of its strength from Philistia and is crushed in the aerial regions by the old giant Thought, with whom it wrestles, if it does not betimes succeed

in touching again the ground from which it grew. There go the Sunday children of other nations, whatever their names may be: Shakespeare, Milton, Byron; Dante, Ariosto, Tasso; Rabelais, Corneille, Molière; they toil not, neither do they spin, and yet even Solomon in all his glory was not arrayed like one of these: but in the land between the Vosges and the Vistula an eternal work-day prevails, it steams continually like freshly plowed fields and every lightning-bolt that flashes up from the fruitful haze carries a smell of earth with it, with which may the gods finally, finally bless us. They all toil and spin, the lofty men who precede *us* through the ages, they all come from Nippenburg, whatever names they have: Luther, Goethe, Jean Paul, and they are by no means ashamed of their origin, gladly show a comfortable understanding for the workplace, the clerk's office, and the council chamber. . . . Long live Nippenburg and Bumsdorf, the beer stein and the coffee pot, the knit stocking and the inkwell, long live the ground on which we stand and in which we will be buried. . . . (7: 357-58)

What is this gassy, ill-written passage (the first ellipsis marks a segment that makes no sense to me at all) doing in a novel that earlier has subjected the philistine spirit, especially in the persons of Uncle and Aunt Schnödler, to ruthless exposure? Is it an ironic acknowledgment of the more privileged status of writers in other nations? Is it a convergence of the spirit of the narrative with the accommodation of Hagebucher? Is the author whistling in the dark, trying to talk courage into himself at the conclusion of what he may suspect is a failing enterprise? Or is it just a hyperbole, an overstated recognition that great literature (and not just German literature) often does have a vital connection with the earth and the common run of people, or that the notion of philistinism is elitist and subject to abuse? I find this whole passage rather a crux, and there may be others who agree with me that Raabe might better have left it unwritten. In any case, its awkwardness appears to me to be closely associated with the collapse of Leonhard Hagebucher's role as resistant outsider and with it, I believe, the collapse of the coherence of the novel.

The transformation of Hagebucher and of the narrative perspective on him has been a gradual process, so gradual that it may not emerge clearly until the novel has been read more than once. Possibly the first subtle turn occurs in Hagebucher's public lecture, in much of which he seems to speak with Raabe's own voice; indeed, toward the end, one may hear allusions to the author's own predicament and aspirations:

> You said to one another or to yourselves: here a man has come to us who lived twelve years among the underground creatures [it has been roughly that long since Raabe's literary career began], while we have been able to spin out our existence uninterruptedly in the light of the joyful ether. That fellow will know how to tell droll, strange things; let us hear his *Mémoires d'outre-tombe*, let us have the fun of watching this will-o'-the-wisp, this spook out of the grave of his own existence, dance!—My honored ladies and gentlemen, the ghost has danced, and you heard the beginning of what I would like to communicate to you. You were many wakeful people against *one* dreamer, many seers against one blind man. . . . (7: 191)

But at this point Hagebucher loses track of what he intends to say, for he has spotted van der Mook in the audience, and his lecture ends in confusion.

There is a sense in which the whole lecture is somewhat confused, its assertive idealism high-flown and woolly, as though there were an undertone of parody of Raabe's own sentiments. On the surface Hagebucher continues to exhibit positive characteristics: he reads Goethe in his effort to restore his equilibrium, sympathizes with Nikola's secret suffering, and asserts a turn to reality away from Mohammedan passivity and resignation:

> it is a joy to live in reality, as many sharp edges, evil hooks, and insidious, treacherous pitfalls as it may have. Who, by the way, gave the clever fool Mohammed the idea that everything intoxicating is forbidden!—? Who can forbid this poor, plagued, mankind the intoxicating? As long as pain, sin and death walk about in its midst, so long the intoxicating cannot be forbidden! (7: 293)

As a matter of fact, however, this turn to reality is associated with Hagebucher's unrealistic, ultimately futile courtship of Serena Reihenschlager. In this episode he cuts a rather comic figure, so that the reader may feel that the narrator is withdrawing from him. After the narrator has told us that Hagebucher has observed every aspect of love and sex during his enslavement in Africa, so that he feels that Europe has nothing new to offer him, he sets off confidently on his quest: "The experiment seemed to him easily, pliably, and smoothly manageable without excessive effort." But the very next paragraph begins:

"This cheerful attitude, however, changed in the moment he set his foot upon the street" (7: 295-96). He comes to play the role of the indecisive, sexually timid suitor, an old theme of traditional comedy.

This inconsistency in the narrative perspective appears also in the gradual change of Hagebucher's attitude toward his father, leading toward the final vignette where he has come to resemble his father physically. He comes to feel sorry for his father, who was "in the right in every respect and acted quite correctly, psychologically as well as morally" (7: 126). Some time after this we are told that, after a year at home, Hagebucher has changed in appearance, but not to his advantage. His hair is greying, his eyes have grown more shadowed, and the traces of the wild man of Africa rebel against the furnishings of civilization; he looks like a monkey dressed in a top hat and cutaway (7: 136-37). The tone of this passage strongly suggests that he is retaining his rebellious, non-conformist posture. It is only when we read the book backwards, as we so often must, that we can also see it as a phase in the process of accommodation. Hagebucher begins to be pained at the shabbiness of his surroundings, and longs for life, peace, and cleanliness (7: 272). Around this time his father dies, leaving him with a reasonable inheritance, which modest wealth in turn causes the townspeople to think more kindly of him. An implacably hostile critic like Kientz can identify this metamorphosis with Raabe's philistine values, pointing out irritably that Hagebucher refuses work, is served by his sister and mother, and lives finally an inactive life as a *rentier* off his father's investments, which he had previously condemned.[3] But Kientz, as usual, is not sensitive to the ambiguities in the narrative voice. For it is just at this point that we see Hagebucher's conformist subconscious in contrast to his conscious militance:

> "I sleep with the sword under my pillow!" cried Leonhard grimly, and when he finally did sleep, he dreamed of a warm dressing-gown, a pair of lovely, soft slippers, a long pipe, and a singing tee-urn. (7: 276)

These have been the accouterments of stodgy, complacent philistinism in German satire since Romanticism.

Associated with this metamorphosis in Hagebucher's consciousness is a considerable hostility toward Lieutenant Kind and his plans for revenge against Baron von Glimmern. Hagebucher objects to Kind's project first of all on stoic grounds, on the uselessness of activity in this vain world:

Who on earth has anything but his just deserts! So let everyone have his just deserts! Who is so stupid as to arouse himself except under the whip of buffalo hide; who is such a fool, after so many thousands of years of experience, still to want to play the knight errant and straighten out the heads, hearts, and stomachs of mankind! (7: 275)

Can this be Raabe's true voice? No, but it is an aspect of the unresolved dilemma of the novel, as we shall see shortly. More specifically, Hagebucher is concerned that Kind's vengeance will thrust Nikola deeper into her misery. In this he is right; when Glimmern is exposed in a spectacular scandal and driven from the scene, Nikola, instead of being relieved by her emancipation from an unloved, corrupt husband and a false position in society, falls into total despair and hopelessness, in which state she can only be nursed by Klaudine and eventually by Hagebucher, her protector. (In my judgment, Raabe mishandled this feature of the novel, but it, too, is evidence of his irresolution.) But even though Hagebucher may be right in his understanding of Nikola and her situation, Kind is deeply offended by Hagebucher's attitude. When, after the scandal has broken, Hagebucher is rude to the high-strung, ecstatic Kind, the lieutenant accuses him of having become *like the others*:

> Have you got as far as the others and cry havoc because a man has taken justice into his own hands like a man! The dog is always mad who runs up the silk stockings and under the velvet dress-trains. I wish you luck, Herr Hagebucher! Have you already learned so much since your return? (7: 326)

This is a serious charge, even if we are meant to regard Kind's proletarian belligerence as overwrought—and I frankly do not know whether we are meant to do so or not.

Part of the difficulty in Raabe's perspective on his protagonist, I believe, lies in his disinclination to create heroic figures. Hagebucher has undergone extreme suffering: ten years of humiliation and physical torment in slavery; a return home that, instead of providing him with comfort and restoration, results in rejection and isolation; failure in his efforts to establish himself in the community. These are make-or-break experiences calling upon exceptional resources of courage and spiritual energy. Hagebucher is not a man with such resources and never has been. Here lies, the reader may feel, the main missed opportunity of the conception; for Hagebucher does not seem to be sufficiently affected in mind and character, apart from his tendency to discouragement, by his experiences in slavery to support his role as the novel's protagonist. Despite his flashes of intelligence, imagination, and independence, he is basically a mediocre man, and Raabe could apparently find no course other than to lead him to a mediocre consummation. It is in such matters that we can see his long maturation as a writer. For by *The Odin Field* he had discovered how a man of modest intelligence and timid character might develop heroic qualities in an extreme situation, and in *The Documents of the Birdsong* he shows that an existential choice in favor of the conventional can appear dignified and thoughtful. Here, however, it seems to me, Raabe comes to be at a loss, because he is unable to organize conflicting values in a coherent relationship to one another.

This is the case also with the most difficult problem of interpretation and evaluation in the novel: the hermetic "idyll" of the Cat Mill and the role of Our Lady of Patience, Klaudine Fehleysen. In this connection there is a vast expenditure of the rhetoric of quiescence, renunciation, and withdrawal from the world and society. Even before Klaudine and her refuge are mentioned, the theme is introduced by reference to Goethe, held up as a model by Wassertreter:

> Forty volumes of world fame, eighty-two years of life and only four weeks of untroubled happiness or, better, real comfort [an allusion to a remark of Goethe's to Eckermann, January 27, 1824]—what a consolation for us all is this old boy in his princely crypt in Weimar! Whether one is a great poet and minister of state or a little fool and road-building inspector is a damned indifferent matter—long live all good brave fellows on land and sea, on the level ground and on the golden clouds in the blue ether, the good brave fellows who bear up and don't let themselves be fooled and praise the day in any weather. Do what you like, Leonhard, but in all situations take an example of the old privy councillor and of Cousin Wassertreter; if you die young, you will have enjoyed your lot; if you die old, you can calmly let yourself be called a quietist, lout, or whatever the mob likes: you have saved what belongs to you and can let people talk. (7: 62)

"Quietism" is the operative word here; it is a quality that fills the atmosphere that surrounds Klaudine and dwells in the Cat Mill. She is introduced with cordial praise by the other characters in the alternative community. Wassertreter calls her brave and wise; Nikola addresses her as "Lady Patience"; and Hagebucher at once feels saved and protected in her presence (7: 69, 72). The praise continues unabated on the narrative level, where she is described as of calm and gentle demeanor, a person who alters her environment like a fairy, and the narrator also denominates her Our Lady of Patience (7: 72, 117). Thus the novel, in which practically every purpose turns out to be futile, seems to declare an ideal of flight and passivity, an escapist bourgeois ideology of withdrawal from political and social responsibility.

Modern admirers have naturally not wanted to accept this reading, which is so consistent with the discredited traditional view of Raabe. Sensing the difficulty years ago, Herman Meyer tried to relieve the symbolic locale of the Cat Mill of the odium of quietism: "People have wrongly wanted see in the Cat Mill the realm of 'complete will-less-ness'; rather the realm of the Cat Mill is the center of strength that lends to those who partake of it the strength to endure in the struggle against the world."[4] But this has not been the procedure of other critics, which in general has been to distinguish Raabe's voice from that of the fictional characters and even from the narrative voice. As early as 1940 a scholar of the middle generation argued that Hagebucher does not speak for Raabe and the Cat Mill does not represent a true mastery of life.[5] The more recent procedure has been to call Klaudine's status as wise woman into question. One critic has pointed out that "the actual protection which Frau Klaudine furnishes in the fulfillment of her maternal role seems itself ultimately to be distinctly limited."[6] Another has argued that Klaudine only intensifies Nikola's misfortune, drawing her like a marionette into asocial, sterile stagnation.[7] Some of the most searching questions have been raised by Stephen Gould, who has asserted that the "effusive praise afforded Frau von Fehleysen is . . . not justified by her actions," pointing out that she approves Nikola's ill-fated marriage, suggests Hagebucher's ill-fated lectures, and fails to hold her long-lost son when he does return, committing him to death in America.[8]

We may find some support in the text for these revisionist views if we look hard enough. Klaudine, though she is presented as having a calming and nurturing effect on others, denies that she is clever or wise and is hesitant to give advice (7: 75, 74). Nevertheless, she quite unrealistically promises Hagebucher that, if he reaches the people with his lectures, stones will turn to gold, ill-humor into comfort, and misery into enduring happiness (7: 78). Her patience seems more a discipline than a spiritual achievement, for she is quite impatient with the garrulous Wassertreter, and the patience falls away entirely at the appearance of the returned traveler, from whom she hopes of some news of her son; she becomes so excited that Hagebucher thinks she might be crazy (7: 79-80). To Hagebucher she confesses that her life is quite terrible, as she sits alone, waiting and listening to the water drip in the mill (7: 82). Still, she drew hope from these steady drops, but when her weak, self-tormenting son does reappear, the hopeful drops turn into a stream of dirty water that "poured over the black, broken wheel, made the path swampy, and turned the thicket over a long stretch into an ugly morass. That, too, was like scorn and mockery" (7: 230). At the end the Cat Mill is a picture of total stasis, visited by no one; the two women sit still and silent, and only the drip of the water is heard (7: 382).

Yet Gould has quite rightly stressed that Klaudine and the ideals associated with her are not distanced by irony: "instead of irony one senses only earnestness." He goes on to say that irony "would threaten to turn the entire tale into a burlesque . . . because if Frau Klaudine is not really worthy of Hagebucher's praise, his vision must be as full of illusions as that of the society with which he is conflict." Gould finds in the novel not ironies but antinomies: "The rhetorical support of the von Fehleysen variation conflicts with the support of the Hagebucher episodes and thus contributes negatively to the rhetorical structure of the novel as a whole"; the notorious philistinism passage "completely contradicts the narrator's ironic posture in the first third of the novel and confuses the reader's evaluative participation in the tale."[9] Barker Fairley, who did so much to restore Raabe's reputation in our time, took the hardest line on *Abu Telfan* of just about any friendly modern critic; he found the novel bungled because it does not follow the promise of the three original characters: "the privacy and quietism of the 'Katzenmühle' had taken charge of the book and removed it out of the social-political sphere altogether. . . . Either Raabe never had a central or a leading idea for his social-political novel or he shrank from it and evaded it. This is bad enough, but what makes the case worse is that he does not seem to have realized what was happening, but carries on doggedly to the bitter end."[10]

I agree with Fairley that the initial impetus and promise of the novel do not seem to have been realized, though I am perhaps more sympathetic to the difficulties in which Raabe became entangled. Of all the critics, Gould seems to me to have had the most precise insights into the problem. What we have in the novel is not irony but antinomy, therefore not polyperspectivism but irresolution. We will not be able to force the novel entirely into a critical perspective on Klaudine and the Cat Mill, and therefore on the ideology of quietism and withdrawal; for that its rhetoric is too pervasive. Neither, however, does it sit firmly within such an ideology. Instead it gropes its way along inconsistent vectors, losing its grip on its central character, drifting into formal incongruities, and concluding in a gesture of authorial despair, which is what I take the philistinism passage to imply. What we witness here is the struggle of an author seriously out of harmony with himself. The sharp edge of Raabe's critical instinct is being blunted by a sense of futility. He highly valued the achieved strength and stability of stoic quietism, as the somewhat questionable recourse to Goethe, here and elsewhere, indicates, but it is unreachable for the nervous, high-strung author and therefore does not achieve full plausibility in the novel. Realism struggles here against the utopian dimension of the fiction of the alternative community, and for Raabe, at any rate at this stage of his career, realism meant pessimism; thus the novel ultimately becomes infected with the pessimism that soon will overwhelm *The Rumbledump*. If we understand by interpretation the elucidation of thematic coherence, then *Abu Telfan* is in this sense uninterpretable. It will yield only to an acceptance of its deep incoherence and to an effort to understand the terms of its irresoluteness and the reasons for it.

And yet, and yet. There is something that may still strike us as incomplete in Fairley's impatience with this novel that has so many confusing things to say about patience. We must ask ourselves why competent, sophisticated readers, such as Hans Mayer, continue to admire this flawed work. If the pieces of the novel do not hang comfortably together, many of the pieces themselves are brilliantly executed. The exposure of the community's stolid absence of charity and human interest upon Hagebucher's return, the proletarian bitterness and fierce crusade of Lieutenant Kind, the characterizations of Wassertreter, Täubrich, Nikola, and several minor characters, the wit and ingenuity of much of the dialogue, will animate the thoughtful reader at the same time as he or she may feel structurally ungratified. *Abu Telfan* is perhaps most impressive as an exhibit of Raabe's authorial integrity. The man who so keenly sensed the disingenuousness of much of the literature around him could not fake or pretend. If the constellation of ideas and commitments in his mind and soul did not make sense, then, by heaven, his novel would not make sense either. In the mid-1860s he still had much to do to sort out his mental furniture and make imagination coherent with insight. How very hard this was for him is apparent in *Abu Telfan*; how remarkably he succeeded is apparent in many of the later works.

CHAPTER 16

Fate and Psychology:
At the Sign of the Wild Man
and *Restless Guests*

□

W ITH THE decay of the Christian order, which gave a context to events, purpose to life, and obligations for conduct, questions of the motivation of events and of character became crucial for fiction, particularly the question whether human destiny is motivated externally or internally. One strategy was to replace the potentially scrutable divine will with a more or less inscrutable fate. The range of this strategy could extend from the cheap effects and, sometimes, outright meretriciousness of the Gothic mode to the sublime, as in Schiller's desperate fiction of a Nemesis imposing a justice only all too recognizable as poetic. This form of external determinism has been dislodged in more modern times by materialist social and economic determinisms, and some would argue that "fate" was an ideological, mystifying metonomy for them. Alternatively, one could seek the wellsprings of destiny in the self. Here, too, there are levels, from myths of heroic will and the self-created self to increasingly subtle psychological interrogation. Of course, all kinds of consistent and inconsistent mixtures of these views were possible, and at times it must have seemed imperative to keep both possibilities intact simultaneously. In German fiction, one early and interesting effort to sort these matters out is Eduard Mörike's otherwise little regarded novel *Maler Nolten* (*Painter Nolten*) of 1832, in which there is much inconsistent and, from the point of view of the characters, self-serving talk of "fate," but the catastrophe develops from the interaction of four psychopathic personalities.[1]

Raabe gave these questions no more theoretical articulation than he did any other. But undoubtedly he thought about them, as I imagine that any nineteenth-century realist must have. "The great question with which Raabe wrestles," Perquin observed many years ago, "is whether there is a providence above fate that ultimately holds everything in its hand, or whether fate freely governs the world and is only often subjectively perceived by certain people as providence."[2] Fate, as it appears in Raabe's fiction, exhibits an apparent malignance that is actually indifference. The narrator of *The Rumbledump* expresses this outlook with the bleak resignation characteristic of that novel:

> The demons of the night are not always on the best footing with the demons of the day, and the welfare of a human being, who serves as a shuttlecock and fulfills his poor, empty fate, notoriously and demonstrably troubles the gods very little. Why shouldn't they use their toys? By Styx, ladies and gentlemen, let us put ourselves in their place, and let us be for once—more just than they. (8: 105)

Thus fate figures as more of an absence than a presence, an absence of that sustaining providence to which Romanticism, attempting to square the circle of unbelief, gave the name "Nature." Here Raabe shares a common post-Romantic development, explicit in Heine and Büchner but also evident in less radical writers such as Adalbert Stifter, which can be described poetologically as the ruin of the pathetic fallacy. The metaphoric link between the natural macrocosm and the human microcosm can no longer be plausibly forged; the natural universe has become unbridgeably other, indifferent to human feeling and suffering. In the novella to which we shall turn shortly in this chapter, the protagonist says in connection with his youthful miseries: "it is an error or even a lie when people want to assert that a beautiful countryside and a magnificent, sublime view can conduce to the healing and recovery of a person who is unhappy or beset by trouble and worry. It is simply not true!" (11: 189-90). The concept of fate, therefore, with its genetic connections to Greek nature religion, turns bitter and ironic.

One might trace this employment of the concept through much of Raabe's career. The astronomer Ulex in *The People from the Forest* mourns the passing of astrology: "Today we no longer read people's fate from the stars. They go calmly their eternal way up there; we restlessly wander our short path here below, driven hither and yon like leaves in the wind" (5: 91). Many years later, in *Princess Fish*, the outlook has not changed: "Fate does not differentiate between people and things. It hands them back and forth, and whether there is laughter or tears at these transactions seems a matter of boundless indifference to it" (15: 222). Sometimes Raabe draws on the incalculability of fate to account self-consciously for his insouciant recourse to coincidence in his plotting, thus indirectly paralleling the arbitrariness of fate with that of the manipulating narrator. For example, in *The Hunger Pastor*, the improbable appearance of Lieutenant Götz when Hans Unwirrsch is in deep trouble is presented airily as destiny (*Geschick*) on horseback (6: 178). In *Christoph Pechlin*, where absurd coincidence is a principle of narration, fate appears as the ally of the narrator's humor in frustrating one of Christabel's plots: " '*No!*' replied fate, discourteous and brutal in the highest degree, that is, hiding the gaiety and humor of the affair under the mask of boundless brutality with long-familiar mastery," and the narrator rounds off the flourish with an allusion to Schiller's *Wallenstein*, in full awareness of the extremely ambiguous role fate (read or misread by astrology) plays in that drama (10: 246-47). The orphaned, penniless, and homeless Paul Kohl in *The Lar* wonders what the "ridiculous institute," i.e., fate, has in store for him (17: 252). Fate, as one critic has pointed out, has many synonyms in Raabe, and she goes on to suggest that he employs them to hide his social criticism, thereby blunting it.[3] The tendency to see fate in Raabe as a surrogate for capitalism has understandably gained ground in our time,[4] and indeed there is an element of economic determinism in the concept, as we shall see in due course, but we should refrain from reducing his complex motivation to a single strand and avoid the position that he did not know what he was talking about and signifies something other than what he says.[5] In any case, all this may serve as background to his most remarkable excursion into the narrative equivalent of the genre of fate tragedy.

THE SHOCKER: *At the Sign of the Wild Man*

The opening of *At the Sign of the Wild Man*, first published in 1874 and then included in the *Krähenfeld Stories* in 1879, is exceptionally mannered even by Raabe's standards. As Bulwer-Lytton and Snoopy would say, it is a dark and stormy night. The narrator leads the reader to shelter in the pharmacy At the Sign of the Wild Man, "a quite solid house, judging by appearances [as we obviously ought not to do]" (11: 162), and both of us, narrator and reader, enter, umbrellas in hand, yet we are invisible, observing spirits, umbrellas notwithstanding. As one critic has said: "Entering the house corresponds to entering the realm of fiction."[6] The narrator describes, and shows how he describes, drawing on a reminiscence of the author Raabe to comment on "the terrible bench on which most of us at one time or another have sat and waited [for medication] in feverish anxiety and anguish" (11: 163), and finally taking us into the dwelling of the pharmacist, an aging bachelor named Philipp Kristeller, and his sister Dorette, a hump-backed, grouchy spinster who strikes us at first as a little dim-witted, though we may change our mind about that in the course of the story. Gradually, however, the obtrusive narrator withdraws, remaining generally quiescent through the remainder of the work, much of which is narrated, quite effectively, by two of the characters. Later, some of the events are discussed and commented on by other characters while on their way home from a social gathering, a technique of polyperspective narration of which Fontane was soon to be the master.[7] We are introduced to a modest, comfortable Biedermeier interior, the most striking feature of which is a large collection of prints on the walls; prominent in the midst of the clutter is Dürer's *Melencolia* flanked by two street scenes of the 1848 Revolution. Kristeller himself is a little melancholy on this evening, as it is the thirtieth anniversary of his first sale, and Dorette has solicitously invited two of his friends, the forester and the pastor, to cheer him up. With the arrival of the doctor a little later, we have complete one of Raabe's characteristic circles of petty-bourgeois professionals. In these homely surroundings, among these ordinary people, will occur the most terrifying event in all of his fiction.

Kristeller, quite artfully, begins to tell the curious story of his past. In his youth he was a penniless botanist, engaged to be married but hindered by his lack of means. While botanizing he makes friends with a gloomy, taciturn young man, whom he knows only as August. Kristeller is kind and sympathetic to August, whom he one day finds in a dreadful, nearly hysterical state. August disappears, but in a letter sends Kristeller his whole fortune, 9,500 talers, with which the latter is able to buy his pharmacy. His fiancée, who has urged him to accept the money as a loan, has also suggested that he always keep an empty chair as a sign of his readiness to welcome his benefactor back. But the fiancée dies on their wedding day, and Kristeller is left with the empty chair, faithfully retained for thirty years. Through all that time Kristeller's life has passed nearly without incident. His sole achievement has been the invention of a concoction of bitters, which he advertises and sells, though without conspicuous success. On the strength of this the forester remarks that Kristeller is the only one in the village who has achieved anything, whereupon Dorette warns against praising one's good luck too soon (11: 175-76).

In due course the doctor arrives, bringing with him a foreigner just arrived, a Brazilian colonel named Agostin Agonista. The identity of this personage is not meant to be a secret from the reader, nor is it, for very long, from Kristeller. Promptly this version of the "returnee" assumes the narration. Originally named August Mördling, he came from a family of executioners. His father was not obliged to practice this trade and raised his son in an atmosphere of culture and sensibility. But the son is called upon to perform an execution, and this sets off the emotional crisis witnessed uncomprehendingly by Kristeller. August's transfer of his fortune to Kristeller was not only an act of gratitude, but the shedding of his old identity and the acquisition of a new one as an adventurer in the New World. While Agonista regales his fascinated auditors with tales of his escapades, Raabe foreshortens them considerably; they do not interest him and ought not to interest us. What emerges in the new man is a repression of the acculturated sensibility and its replacement with a cynical ruthlessness. According to his own cheerful account, he has pursued a career of marauding and violence, culminating in a position as a henchman of the Emperor of Brazil. And now the circle of Kristeller's strange fate begins its inexorable closure. Agonista is vivacious, full of bonhommie, and even fuller of plans to take Kristeller into business with him in Brazil. But, as becomes plain, first to Dorette, then to the reader, and finally to Kristeller, he has come, attracted by an advertisement for Kristeller's bitters, to reclaim his loan, with interest, and this despite his ostentatious gesture of burning the old money order he had sent, for he shrewdly senses that Kristeller is not a man to care about legal documents. What then happens is narrated in an extremely low key and somewhat obliquely: Kristeller auctions and mortgages his property, turns over 12,000 talers and the formula for his bitters to Agonista, who vanishes shortly before Christmas, and the pharmacist lives on, reduced to total poverty, which his myopic neighbors ascribe to his own improvidence.

It may seem that many objectively more horrible events occur in Raabe's works, especially in his bloody historical fictions. But it is a matter of record that no other work of his achieved a shock effect comparable to that of *At the Sign of the Wild Man*. So paralyzing is the shock that it even caused the old master, Barker Fairley himself, to stumble: he asserted that "the tale virtually breaks off in the middle" and is an abandoned fragment.[8] There can, of course, be no question of this, and that so attentive and accomplished a critic could perpetrate such a howler testifies to the story's stunning impact. Raabe himself said that none of his novels and novellas had aroused so much turmoil in his public (11: 477); until late in his life he received letters from readers who were outraged by Agonista,[9] an effect doubtless intensified by the circumstance that Raabe, in the teeth of critical reprehension, chose the work for the two-thousandth number of Reclam's Universal Library in 1885.[10] The tough Gottfried Keller, who did not scare easily, was horrified by Agonista (11: 477). Even more horrified was Jensen. His bosom friendship with Raabe notwithstanding, he lashed out at the novella as a betrayal of humanism and idealism, adding somewhat ludicrously that it should be banned by the police because there was nothing edifying in it and it encouraged disgust at the whole human race. He advised Raabe, like the common run of his advisors, to abandon his mannerisms and recommended particularly for the recovery of his humanity Oliver Goldsmith's *Vicar of Wakefield*, a work that was not only 123 years old but is also extremely unsuited to restoring one's faith in the workings of providence (11: 476-77). Some years after the story was first published, Raabe himself wondered whether his friend Sträter had been wise to give it to his boys: "Aren't you afraid of making their young minds acquainted with the beast in man a little too early? In my opinion, one's own life brings everyone soon enough up against Senhor Dom Agostin Agonista."[11]

This raises the question of the source of the shock. Raabe himself, as the quotation above indicates, located it in the combination of invincible vitality and total amoralism in Agonista, and unquestionably many followed him in this, regarding Agonista as an incarnation of radical evil, yet successful in gaining his end, escaping the poetic justice that had been a code in literature for at least a century and that is re-enacted a hundred times a day on modern television. But there is, I believe, more to it than that. The unemphatic conclusion of the novella may delay its most disconcerting effect: the recognition that the life of the kindly, innocent Kristeller has been on loan. This was not a new idea for Raabe; Ulex in *The People from the Forest* reads to a dying man a passage from Epictetus to the effect that everyone is given a role in life that he should play as best he can but that must be given back at the end (5: 204-5). Of course this thought belongs to the oldest wisdom of mankind. But the recognition that "the Lord gave, and the Lord hath taken away" (Job 1:21) must rarely in literature have been enacted in circumstances so pronouncedly arbitrary, so disjoined from the moral qualities of the victim of a cynical fate. These considerations prompt us to look more carefully at Kristeller's character to see if we are reading it correctly.

Kristeller appears to be a modern and therefore somewhat incongruous version of the traditional figure of the Pure Fool. The meaning of his life is focused on gratitude, of which the empty armchair is an icon. He sees the return of his benefactor not as threat but as fulfillment. When his sister reports her insight that the gasconading Agonista is in need of money, Kristeller replies: "But Dorette, that would be wonderful!" (11: 244). He opens his books to Agonista without hesitation and goes about the business of liquidating his modest property with equanimity. It is not surprising, therefore, that Kristeller has been seen as a figure of virtually saintly dimensions, as a man entirely true to himself, internally free, and as a "Raabean person . . . in the grace of Heaven";[12] and Daemmrich has reiterated the view that Kristeller "has remained truly free. In full awareness of the consequences, he has made an existential commitment to the service of others."[13] But perhaps it should trouble us that the "other" who is closest to him, his sister, has nothing but anxiety and misery from this service. Interpretations that stress Kristeller's transcendental freedom ignore Dorette and imply that she is querulous and egotistically short-sighted. While it is true that she is a less attractive figure than her self-effacing brother, and also true that we find her years later, in *Restless Guests*, much in need of healing of her injured spirit, the negative view of her does not seem satisfactory. For she sees where Kristeller does not, and very promptly. What her brother perceives as providence, she perceives as impending doom: "What is falling upon our days now?—So late in life!" (11: 226); unlike the other members of the community she is not entertained by Agonista's ingratiating manner and sees through his fancy projects to his impecuniousness, regarding him as a throatcutter and executioner (11: 238, 246). Agonista evidently spots her as the enemy, for he closets himself with her privately for an hour. We are not told what took place in this interview, but we may guess that he dropped his amiable bearing and took a hard line with her, for she emerges in despair for her brother (11: 240-41). In the end, Kristeller believes that Agonista will send him profits from the manufacture of his bitters; Dorette, of course, does not believe this, and of course she is right. It is difficult to know how we can see Dorette other than as a reproach to Kristeller.

His name, to be sure, suggests some kind of Christ figure. Although, like the great majority of Raabe's characters, he shows no signs of religious commitment, his conduct instinctively resembles an *imitatio Christi*, especially in his indifference to worldly goods, his belief, at what Dorette regards as the catastrophe, that he is lightening the load of property (11: 254). But, as we shall see later in this chapter, one must be very careful and attentive whenever Raabe makes Christian references. One might as easily adduce the Parable of the Ten Talents (Matt. 25:14-30). Kristeller has had a stroke of fortune, and thirty years later he has no more than he was originally given. (In case it is relevant, the interest Agonista extracts works out to less than 0.9% per annum.) This consideration, not unexpectedly, has led to the contemporary view that Kristeller is the victim of an arrested Biedermeier consciousness incompetent in a capitalist age; since Raabe does not quite present him in this light, again the conclusion is urged upon us that Raabe did not understand his own character.[14] This much, in any case, is true: "fate" in this story has much to do with money, the lack of which cripples Kristeller's young life, the bestowal of which establishes him in his modest prosperity, and the loss of which plunges him back into insignificance. It is a cruel irony that, before Agonista's intervention, it is remarked that Kristeller's two predecessors in the pharmacy had gone bankrupt but he had had "luck," as well as "intelligence" in the invention of his bitters (11: 175). Perquin, who as a Jesuit had a clear eye for moral philosophy, denied any victory for Kristeller, since he lacked insight into injustice.[15] It is my view, also, that Raabe did not mean wholly to exculpate Kristeller from any complicity in his fate as a victim, and here, as elsewhere, his perspective on the Christian virtues is an amalgam of admiration and skepticism.

While Kristeller's character presents us with interpretive ambiguities, Agonista is a still more difficult case, because less accessible to realistic codes. He leaves us with a puzzlement that, once again, obliges us to read the work backwards to see if we have been reading it aright. We may first ask whether the image of the wild man in the title and in the apothecary's sign is significant. The wild man is an ancient symbol, well known in the Middle Ages, for the recklessness, aggression, and bestiality barely controlled by the discipline of civilization and the sanctions of morality. Most medieval commentary regarded the wild man as insane, but also as extremely powerful: "No beast, no matter how mighty or savage, is ever secure against the wild man's perpetual aggressiveness."[16] The trouble is, however, that the wild man has become a heraldic device so common that it seems to have lost any iconographic significance it might once have had. It is found in the arms of Raabe's Duchy of Braunschweig as well as those of Prussia and many other principalities; it appeared on the Braunschweig taler coin. A pharmacy At the Sign of the Wild Man need have nothing more to do with savages than a tavern At the Sign of the Red Ox with cattle. However, Raabe was much given to label naming, and we are inclined to suspect that the image is not arbitrary.

The wild man crops up in several places in his fiction. A cannon in *Lorenz Scheibenhart* is designated an "iron wild man" (2: 315, 328). The mad, melancholiac title figure of *Michel Haas* is called a wild man by children (2: 455). The unintegrated returnee Hagebucher in *Abu Telfan* is referred to as a "wild man" (7: 33, 111, 185; also in a draft of Chapter 4, 7: 391). Later, the semi-savage outcast Fuchs in *Restless Guests* is said by the narrator to be a "wild man under the ban of the nature and culture of Europe" (16: 235), and Thedel von Münchhausen in *The Odin Field* relates that he played the wild man to save his poaching friends from the peasants (17: 167). These last two examples are important in the way they associate the wild man not only with savagery or outlawry but also with exceptional vitality and strength of purpose, for a kind of manic energy is characteristic of Agonista's revised self: he repudiates his youthful panic and melancholy as foolishness, and notes to himself that he has remained young while good Kristeller has grown old (11: 214, 229). He also asserts that he has had the devil at his elbow all through his career and that his life has been "shot into the wild" (11: 205-6). We may therefore hold with Daemmrich that Agonista is the " 'wild man' after whom the pharmacy is named,"[17] even though the symbol, as so often, seems to hang in the air somewhat without being fully integrated.

One puzzling problem is the extent to which Agonista's account of himself can be believed. He makes a rather frantic impression, jumping rapidly from a plan to involve Kristeller in a beef-extract industry on a Brazilian hacienda, to another to make a profit on Kristeller's bitters, to a proposal to take the doctor with him to Brazil and make him a millionaire. If this is not all just play-acting, it looks less like the behavior of a coldly calculating villain than high-strung hysteria and perhaps a touch of madness. It is entirely possible, as has been suggested, that his original intentions were not clear,[18] though the claim that he was just a well-meaning person who wanted to make everyone happy is not plausible.[19] More serious is the question of what we are supposed to make of Agonista's tale of having been forced to perform an execution, which derailed him from a conventional course in life.

Traditionally executioners' families were dishonorable and could only marry among themselves; the trade was inherited. (Heine exploited this tradition in his vivid but undoubtedly fictional tale of "Red Sefchen" in his *Memoirs*, but it cannot have influenced Raabe, as the *Memoirs* were not published until 1884.) By Raabe's time this had long since ceased to be the case; executioners had become respectable civil servants. One critic has remarked sensibly that Raabe knew perfectly well that no one in the nineteenth century could be forced to perform an execution.[20] Looking around for other references does not help us much. Raabe knew a man whose grandfather had been an executioner, as he noted in his diary on November 15, 1869. There are, as far as I can recall, only two other executioners in his fiction. One, in the early story, *The Ultimate Justice*, is treated with black humor; he is a vengeful man who plots the ruin of others, but he had not always been an

executioner; he is the son of an Imperial official and became an executioner "with a certain wild irony" (9/1: 50); this occurs in the early
eighteenth century. The other is the nasty foster parent of the orphaned Marten Marten in *The Horn of Wanza*; like many traditional
executioners, he was also a knacker. Both trades were dishonorable,
and so Marten, as he grows up, is also regarded as dishonorable (14:
357-58). This seems to take place around 1809, long before the setting
of *At the Sign of the Wild Man*. Someone, either Agonista or the author
himself, is imposing on us with an implausible anachronism to rather
Gothic effect—an effect reinforced by Agonista's account of having
to carry the headless corpse on his back from the scaffold, leaving
him with a demon that has been riding him until "this very evening"
(11: 216).

This Gothic quality, along with the inconsistencies and opacities in
Agonista's character, makes him more of a mythic force than a realistic
figure, an instrument of an amoral and indifferent fate. Much has been
made of a fairy-tale element in the novella: a treasure found, then lost
by revealing its source.[21] Reference has been made to a fable of Musäus, "The Treasure-Seeker."[22] However, if this connection is to be
taken seriously, it is important to recall that Musäus was an eighteenth-century rationalist who treated his fables in a comic, even
mildly salacious spirit; it will be seen in the next chapter that Raabe
praised these qualities in his essay on Musäus in 1865. "The Treasure-
Seeker" is more like a novella of Boccaccio than a fairy tale of the
Brothers Grimm; the magic substance in it is money, and the drunken
and irresponsible, but also cheerful and generous protagonist is successful. Even in such cases as this we should be careful not to mythify
Raabe too much, for his fundamental disposition was critically rationalistic. This quality appears here in his familiar social themes, particularly in the fatuous fascination of the townspeople with the degenerate Agonista and their complacent blindness to the pathos of
Kristeller, who had always been their friend.

There is, however, one pseudo-rational theme that was on Raabe's
mind here: heredity of character by blood. For the only explanation
available for the transformation of Agonista's character from that
formed in his boyhood to the savagery of his manhood is a genetic
inheritance from his ancestors, the executioners. Even during his first
acquaintance with Kristeller he says that he has inherited "an unfortunate blood" from his forebears and that he must watch out for out-
breaks of fury that he must repress (11: 184). Later he shifts to a
botanical image but with the same implication of genetic affinity: one
must find out to which Linnaean class one belongs and adjust to it

(11: 206). The blood theme is reinforced by another of Raabe's loosely integrated symbols: the granite formation known as the "Blood Throne" (*Blutstuhl*), where human sacrifices may have taken place in the past and where Kristeller's meeting with the despairing August occurs. That his character is family-related is suggested also by his original last name, Mördling, with its strong echo of "murderer." The idea of traits inherited by blood relationship appears occasionally in Raabe's earlier works as well. There is an indication that the character of the *femme fatale* Alida in *One Springtime* is formed by blood inheritance (1: 243), and Klaus Eckenbrecher in *The Holy Spring* cannot be raised to be a scholar or pastor, for his mentor failed to reckon with the musician's blood in his father and the robber's in his mother (3: 33). These are, of course, notions of the nineteenth century, possibly amalgamated in Raabe's mind with popularized Darwinism, that ultimately were to feed into racial theories. He was always interested in such things and picked them out of the air indiscriminately in order to employ them for his fictional purposes. But they really were tentatively and flexibly held notions, experimental in nature as are most things in his imaginative world; they never became obsessive or creedal for him. That this is the case is illustrated by the fact that a decade later he was to return to the scene of *At the Sign of the Wild Man* in a very different narrative spirit.

PSYCHOLOGICAL REALISM: *Restless Guests*

Raabe has sometimes been praised for his psychological insight and subtlety. In general, I think this praise misplaced. His extreme degree of authorial intervention and manipulativeness, with the concomitant emphasis on the fictivity of the narrated, has a tendency to puppetize his characters and thus to work against their psychological autonomy. In *Gutmann's Travels* the narrator comments that no handbook of psychology can explain why the two young lovers-to-be sit silently together (18: 329, 332), the explanation being, no doubt, that the narrator wills it so. Despite the frequent eccentricity of Raabe's characters, his method of characterization is more typological than psychological; that is, his fictional world is more like a Balzacian menagerie than a Proustian web of subliminal subtleties. During Raabe's lifetime one of his most acute critics remarked: "His figures have, for the most part, no very distinct physiognomy; only the narrator has one."[23]

However, as with most generalizations about him, this one has exceptions. There are probes into psychological formation and deformation, particularly as they emerge from childhood experience. The first clear indication of this kind of psychological interest is found in *Three Pens*, especially in regard to the childhood and character development of August Sonntag. One might also think of the effort to capture the mental confusion of the child Eilike, daughter of a mad father, in *Madame Salome*; of the doctor's interpretation, in *Fabian and Sebastian*, of Sebastian's anger and irritability as displaced remorse, an insight that surprises Sebastian and that he immediately suppresses, though the narrator observes that the doctor is "no mean connoisseur of souls" (15: 15); or of the derivation of Scriewer's repellently ambitious character in *Cloister Lugau* from his position as a child struggling for recognition in a large family (19: 44). Most prominently mentioned in this connection has always been Raabe's novel of puberty, *Princess Fish*.[24] However, his masterpiece of psychological fiction seems to me clearly to be *Restless Guests*, and it is of no little significance that in it there is much less overt authorial intervention and a concomitantly greater mass of inner monologue than usual. One scholar has asserted that it is the first of Raabe's larger works that does not once directly address the reader.[25]

Restless Guests: A Novel out of the Saeculum, first published in 1885, returns to the Harz Mountain setting of *At the Sign of the Wild Man*, here plausibly identifiable as Bad Harzburg,[26] an elegant resort then as it is today. Not only was the one work written ten years after the other; the fictional time is also ten years later. But the social setting is different: instead of the solid middle of petty-bourgeois minor officials and professional men, it is shifted more toward the two ends of the social spectrum. In the valley lies the spa, patronized by prosperous, upper-class guests; in the mountains lives a poor peasant community struggling with a meager, infertile environment. *Restless Guests* is in some degree a social novel, a genre rarely executed very successfully in German literature between Goethe's *Die Wahlverwandtschaften* (*Elective Affinities*) of 1809 and Fontane's increasingly masterful examples in the 1880s. It begins with an almost satirical vignette of frivolous tourists gawking at and drawing pictures of the exotic poor. Raabe had touched on this form of class contrast before, for example, very early in *Who Can Change it?*, where the abandoned Heinrich Knispel turns into the best street urchin any lady might want to draw for her album (2: 481), in Windwebel's obsession with drawing Horacker and his mother (see above, p. 142). There are abrasive class and caste conflicts within *Restless Guests*. Still, as has been pointed out, social criticism is not its main burden.[27] Raabe has no intention of opposing modern decadence to a healthy traditional society. The peasant community is deeply riven and its atmosphere is anything but agreeable.

Like most of his true masterpieces, *Restless Guests* tells a relatively simple story. There comes to the resort a young man named Veit von Bielow, an associate professor of political science. Actually he is a Baron von Bielow-Altrippen, but he wants nothing made of this title. Neither, however, does he show any of the signs of an ambitious academic. Clearly of independent means, he is a reasonably intelligent, easygoing, gracious gentleman. He is aware that an old student acquaintance, Prudens Hahnemeyer, is serving as pastor in the peasant community and he goes up to visit him; Prudens, however, is far from delighted to see him. On the way, Veit encounters Prudens's sister Phöbe, a both competent and pious young woman, whom Prudens treats more as a servant than a sister and with whom Veit quickly makes friends. As it happens, the mountain community is in a state of considerable tension. There has been an epidemic of typhoid fever, which has carried off the wife of an angry outcast, a decorated war veteran and semi-criminalized sociopath named Volkmar Fuchs. The local health officer—the same rather shallow doctor we have seen beguiled by Agonista in *At the Sign of the Wild Man*—demands for sanitary reasons that Anna Fuchs be buried in the cemetery, but the hostile, grieving Fuchs insists on burying her in open ground near his isolated hut. Prudens, unwillingly and with justified misgivings, attempts to intervene, but he can make no headway with Fuchs, who regards the pastor as an agent of a social order he profoundly hates. Veit, anxious to be helpful, offers to pay for the burial plot; when this does not quite do the trick, he has an inspiration: he offers to buy plots for himself and Phöbe flanking Anna's, thus, so to speak, protecting her in death from the surrounding community. This singular proposal cuts the knot; it mightily impresses Fuchs, who accepts it as an uncommon act of gentlemanly condescension, though it gives Phöbe quite a jolt.

There now appears on the scene a beautiful and assertive young lady named Valerie, whose existence has only been hinted at thus far but who appears to be Veit's companion and prospective bride. Valerie, far from edified by what she hears, storms into the mountain community, first interrogating Fuchs, then abusing and all but humiliating Phöbe. At this point Veit comes down with the typhoid fever. The spa guests, including Valerie, vanish out of fear of infection, while Phöbe nurses Veit through the illness. Here the reader, attuned to the conventions of nineteenth-century fiction, might expect the poetic justice of true love and a marriage of Veit and Phöbe. But no such thing happens. At the end of the novel Veit, his health thoroughly undermined, is married to Valerie and fleeing death southwards; he writes a long, sorrowful letter to Prudens and Phöbe from St. John's island of Patmos, including a long quote from Sterne's *Tristram Shandy*, Book VII, in which the narrator is fleeing death,[28] and an allusion to Heine's alleged death-bed quip: "Dieu me pardonnera, c'est son métier" (16: 329-330, 333). Valerie sends Phöbe a gift of an early Christian lamp, which Phöbe subtly takes as a sign that Valerie has never forgiven her. Prudens and Phöbe live on as before, while Fuchs, ironically, is reconciled with the community in shared meanspiritedness.

It may be seen from this précis that *Restless Guests* is also something of a shocker, though in a more subdued way. Certainly it was altogether ill-suited to the conventional expectations of the readership of the family magazine, *Die Gartenlaube* (*The Garden Bower*), in which it first appeared, and Raabe had the devil's own time with the editor, who not only demanded the excision of foreign words (like the "saeculum" in the subtitle) and the quotations from Sterne and Heine in Veit's letter, but also attempted to rewrite the ending to make it more sentimental and conciliatory (16: 547). The outraged author resisted the rewriting and restored the other changes in the book version, but the novel had little success until modern times, when it has understandably attracted a great deal of critical attention. This is in large part owing to its leitmotivic density, which invites and challenges interpretation. The "restlessness" of the "guests" upon the earth pervades every character, though in different ways. In a word play irreproducible in English, the restlessness (*Unruhe*) is related to the movement (also *Unruhe*) of a clock, which in turn relates to time, to the temporality of the "saeculum"—worldly life as Vanity Fair. While Valerie in particular is scornfully dismissed by Prudens as "temporality as woman" (16: 270), in fact the "saeculum" infects all of the characters to a greater or lesser degree, for it is the inescapable environment of human life and society, and the polarity of secular worldliness and spiritual value turns out to be a great deal more nuanced and ambiguous that it at first appears to be. Less commonly noticed has been the extent to which the novel recuperates and refines themes and character types adumbrated in earlier works, of which the observations on the tourist and recreational phenomena are but a minor example. The succession of *Restless Guests* to *At the Sign of the Wild Man*, with its similarity of setting and overlapping characters, but quite different tone and form, is but a particularly visible example of the continuity, flux, experimental variation, and progressive artistic refinement in Raabe's career. There would be much to be said about this, but I want to concentrate here on some details of characterization.

Veit von Bielow, for example, may be seen as a descendant of Emil von Schmidt, the narrator of *Master Author*, which also begins with an outing of amiable, educated people of good society. Both are gentlemen of the world, cultivated, articulate, civil, and sensitive to others up to a point. But Veit is more delicately shaped. Schmidt gradually emerges as rather brittle, emotionally impoverished, and lazily self-indulgent; we do not much like him at the end. Veit is kinder, more prepared to give of himself. We might also be reminded of the tepid, ultimately inconsequential Hennig von Lauen in *The Rumbledump*, but Veit is much more of a man and a gentleman; compared to him Hennig is something of a yokel. I do not quite hold with those critics who pass a very harsh judgment on Veit, seeing especially his last letter as weak, lachrymose, and self-centered. It is true that both Prudens and Dorette Kristeller condemn him utterly, the former as a fool and weakling, caught between "frivolity and hypochondria, between vanity and weepiness" (16: 336); the latter as a man without conscience, worse in his own way than Agonista (16: 320). But both of these are observers of limited vision; I do not believe that we are supposed to withhold all sympathy from Veit, especially as in his letter he expresses some awareness of what he has done and contrition for it. But he certainly blunders tragically, out of a lack of self-understanding, out of a certain, perhaps class-determined complacency, out of an unacknowledged conventionality of perception that blinds him to the extraordinary nature of the situation into which he injects himself. Veit has "stepped off the path"—another of the recurring leitmotifs. His fault, however, is not his deviation, but his failure or inability to take full responsibility for its implications. He destabilizes Phöbe's extremely well-formed, integrated, yet strictly bounded self, unintentionally, but carelessly and insensitively nevertheless.

Veit, instinctively and without overt arrogance, invokes his class authority to solve the conundrum of Anna Fuchs's burial. But in grasping for a solution he, as a man of the saeculum, misprizes the organic integrity of the community and the symbolic weight of its rituals of the life cycle. The offer of a common grave site must look to Phöbe like an extraordinary commitment to her personally. That is why she is so shaken by it, evades it for the moment with the, in itself, quite rational consideration that she does not know where "merciful God" will cause her to die (an unconscious expression of her desire to be liberated from this constricted place), and then feels she must turn to the authority of her brother for permission (16: 240).

The "man from temporality" tries to comfort her: "take it merely as a symbol, Phöbe, that we confess one and the same yearning at the bottom of our soul to one and the same realm of undisturbed rest, to eternal peace" (ibid.). This sentiment, perhaps unexceptionable in another context, is out of place here; it appears as liberal-religious blather that is altogether eccentric to Phöbe's universe of discourse. She rather quickly accepts the gesture with happiness and gratitude, while Veit just as quickly comes to regret it in his private thoughts as foolishness. As we think back over the story we can find other evidence of his lack of solidity; for example, he admires the philistine doctor as the only reasonable man in the place (16: 227), and he tells Phöbe that he is without relatives or connections, conveniently neglecting to mention Valerie (16: 232). But his moral being slumbers in his subconscious, and clearly it suffers a wound, for Veit is the only one to come down with the typhoid fever, even though Prudens drinks directly from the bottle in Fuchs's infected house and Valerie eats from Fuchs's pot of stew. Veit is not an evil man, but in a situation of his own making he is weighed and found wanting, and he is to no small extent guilty of the one pervasive dereliction in Raabe's fictional world: the self's unawareness of the other.

Prudens Hahnemeyer also has predecessors. The most obvious of them is Pastor Leutenbacher, the central consciousness of *Elsa of the Fir*. In Leutenbacher's beatification of Elsa (who at the crisis of the story is eighteen years old) as a pure and innocent child there is a subtext of erotic attraction that he is prohibited from acknowledging to himself but that emerges in images and stray thoughts, for example, the image of a rose tree with buds about to open, or the unclear longing that the child causes in his breast (9/1: 171, 176). That the "magic" of nature echoes his loneliness and causes him anxiety attacks (9/1: 174) suggests a lurking, equally unarticulated crisis of faith. One might also think of the monk Festus in *The Holy Spring*, driven mad by unappeasable erotic obsession. But Prudens puts these characters in the shade; he is one of the most memorably delineated figures in all of Raabe's fiction. His harsh, intolerant religiosity is the cracking armor of a soul in virtually terminal torment. He is first of all beset by the bitterness of the educated proletarian who has failed to reach a position in life adequate to his aspirations; this expresses itself in his rude reaction to Veit's ingenuously friendly visit, which arouses resentful memories of the wealthy Veit's guileless charity toward him when he was an impoverished student. He is, however, not unlike Veit in his insensitivity to the other. He seems to have no sense of the beauty and stature of his sister's character and utterly misperceives her achievement in healing Dorette Kristeller's desolated soul; he sneers at Valerie as a pagan Venus and scorns the suffering Veit. An introverted intellectual, he is wholly out of place as pastor of this rough peasant community, with which he stands in a relationship of mutual contempt and hatred. Thus it is an ironic gloss on his situation that the outcast Fuchs, perhaps tactically, treats him as an agent of that community. Prudens, though beset with feelings of anger, perplexity, and futility, confronts Fuchs out of obligation to duty and exhibits courage in drinking from Fuchs's bottle; Fuchs, who is crude but not stupid, fully acknowledges the meaning of this gesture and also recognizes the similarity of his own character to that of the pastor, but he is not to be moved by him all the same.

Prudens's deepest agonies are internal, partly conscious, partly subliminal. He asks Veit to wish him an "immovable heart"—a phrase that, as we shall see, will have quite a future in *The Documents of the Birdsong*—and Veit pities him (16: 205-06). When alone, in one of the most searing passages in all of Raabe, he laughs hysterically, and not for the first time, when his trembling hand falls upon the "hot love songs" of the Canticles, "which *according to the chapter headings* deal with Christ and his church" (16: 207, my emphasis). "Oh Lord my God," he prays, "kill this bitter, wild heart in me, to which no one speaks, before which no one weeps and laughs but that the tone is quenched like a hot iron in a sea of gall" (16: 208). Now, a page earlier the narrator has warned us not to take Prudens at his word in his inner monologue, implying that he is not fully truthful to himself. What this must mean is that Prudens attempts to apply the obsolete and inadequate resources of Pietist self-mortification to a profound crisis of faith and a pathological condition of erotic repression. Prudens is one of Raabe's supremely unlikeable figures, yet he attracts a great deal of the reader's sympathy, even more than Veit, for he is trapped in irredeemable torment, obligated to a religious role for which he is unfit and to a faith that has escaped him, an unwilling skeptic, and thus more a man of the detested saeculum than he is able to acknowledge.

At this point something must be said about the religious dimension of the novel. No other work of Raabe's takes place in so religious an atmosphere. The text is pervaded with so many explicit, implicit, and hidden Biblical allusions from both Testaments that an entire monograph has been devoted to them.[29] Prudens and Phöbe, with their Pietist diction, refer to "the Lord" thirty-four times.[30] Thus there is an understandable temptation to a Christianized interpretation that must nevertheless be resisted.[31] Raabe made a point of this to his editor: "I hardly need to stress that the thing is absolutely not conceived from the standpoint of canting Pietism, but out of its complete opposite!" (16: 547). I have already stated my opinion that Raabe was devoid of traditional religious faith, and it has been rightly said of this novel that "where Raabe probes the religious ground he hits the sand of doubt."[32] Nowhere is this clearer than in Prudens's psychopathology. Clergymen often appear as evil figures in Raabe's fiction. Where they are good, they also exhibit relatively little religious commitment: they show no interest in theology; they do not talk of Christ's redemption or of salvation of the soul (Phöbe does not, either, as has been pointed out);[33] they simply help people as, so to speak, officials of kindness and consolation, though they are not agents of political or social dominance, or repressive moralists, as the pejoratively treated ones may be. This, of course, is the irony of Raabe's dualistic notion of the "saeculum," for the repudiation of worldliness is *also* secular and thus caught up in the saeculum, as are all the characters in the novel.[34] It is important to keep all this in mind when we seek an adequate understanding of Phöbe, the most Christian, the most saintly, the most beautiful soul of all of Raabe's characters.

He originally intended to name her Marie. Fortunately he saw the inappropriateness of this in time and substituted Phöbe, from a passage in Romans 16:1-2: "I commend unto you Phebe our sister, which is a servant of the church which is at Cenchrea: That ye receive her in the Lord, as becometh saints, and that ye assist her in whatsoever business she hath need of you: for she has been a succourer of many, and of myself also" (Veit cites most of the passage verbatim, 16: 190). Thus the naming establishes the traits of discipleship and service in which she finds much of her identity. Her internalized faith suppresses sorrow and has made her calm and steady. We should be careful, however, not to place the Pietist diction and habits of thought that circumscribe her consciousness on Raabe's account. In one place she is said to be "systematic and nun-like" and in another the narrator calls her a "Lutheran nun" (16: 231, 274). We are not to suppose that Raabe regarded nunnishness positively. In *Our Lord God's Chancellory* there is a rather waspish passage concerning a store of meat found in a plundered nunnery proving that "these brides of Christ in temporality did not mortify their earthly bodies all too severely" (4: 327), and the Protestant nuns of *Cloister Lugau*, whose vows are not binding for life, are, for the most part, worldly and cheerful. In one place the narrator makes it clear that Phöbe's Pietist habits of thought and diction are trained reactions: "Thus grace, or, as she was taught to say, the grace of the Lord, has been over her in this evil time" (16: 325).

As in the case of Philipp Kristeller, Raabe exhibits not only the virtues and attractiveness of a person of unalienated faith, but also the limitations and costs. In her Pietist frame of reference Phöbe sees herself as childlike; she is, however, not a child but a woman, clever, observant of others, competent, and harboring an erotic readiness that requires to be nurtured with delicacy and respect.

Veit does not so nurture it; in fact, he does not know what he is doing. No one, neither Veit, nor Prudens, nor Phöbe's friend Spörenwagen senses her erotic awakening because no one, except for the jealous Valerie, perceives her as an erotic being, and, owing to the narrator's beatification of her personality, the reader can miss it too, though as long ago as 1921 one Raabe disciple was amazed by his discovery that Phöbe loves and suffers like other mortals.[35] Raabe once made the characteristically cryptic remark that readers of the future would know why Phöbe "and Little Red Riding Hood from *On the Scrap-Iron* will one day sit on one bench side by side."[36] This suggests that the streetwalker not only shares Phöbe's grace but that Phöbe might potentially share the streetwalker's generous erotic nature, and in any case exhibits the subdued but real liberality, by Victorian standards, in erotic matters in Raabe's fiction. For the careful reader there can be no doubt about the awakening of love in her, nor is it in any way remarkable, for Veit must appear to her as a gracious and thoughtful man compared to the men of her environment, especially her bearish brother. In talking of his studies and his appreciation of the arts Veit is easygoing, moderate, and serious, and even Prudens is softened by his "manly, unaffected cheerfulness of soul" (16: 204). When he speaks of his own experience around the world, in life, science, and art, Phöbe starts to look at him with real interest and begins to smile (16: 187), a sure indication that emancipation would be possible for her. It has been pointed out that, of all the characters, it is Phöbe who speaks most of restlessness.[37]

Like Gretchen in Goethe's *Faust*, Phöbe ignores the polite formula with which Veit offers his arm, but like Gretchen she has begun to pay attention, and Veit notices that she is able to blush and smile (16: 205). (Veit's little liberal-religious sermon may also remind us of Faust's eloquently evasive reply to Gretchen's query of his faith.) Only with Veit does Phöbe feel that she has neglected her garden, an image Veit instinctively and somewhat patronizingly expands into metaphor, calling the world around merely a bigger garden, and she begins to think how imprisoned she is (16: 217, 220). While they walk together her heart beats and she thinks God may have sent him, while the narrator calls up an image of butterflies "like humans in a delicate play of love" (16: 233, 234). She is thus primed for the electric shock of Veit's proposal of the shared grave site, which she takes as expressive of much more profound commitment than it is. Completely candid herself, she does not have the semiotic experience to read the perlocutionary speech acts of worldly society, their widely varying levels of sincerity. It is the sharpest irony of the novel that during their moment of closest physical contact, when they walk hand in hand, Veit is already privately regretting the impulsiveness of his step from the path (16: 241-42). She, however, continues to see his proposal as a bond, which motivates her to nurse him through his illness even though she by then knows their relationship to have been futile. Veit is not a cad or a seducer, as Dorette apparently takes him to be; he is merely inattentive and, despite his seemingly expansive cosmopolitanism, unable to adjust his perceptions to a universe of discourse different from his own or to see in it the potential for change and real response.

The critical record suggests that Phöbe is not an easy character to read. Critics of the older generation often merely sang hymns to her, while more modern interpreters may sometimes go a little far in the other direction. The Marxist, who must see her as a victim of infantile false consciousness and exploitation, and who is able to recognize her suppressed erotic potential, is rather amusingly obliged to take the side of the aristocrat, with his more enlightened and emancipated spirit and his promise of liberation that she is unable to perceive.[38] Another recent critic actually seems to think that Phöbe has harmed Veit; she "has no real understanding of the mental struggles of the adult characters around her"; she is a naive child who damages the world, having "unwittingly precipitated a tragedy she cannot avert."[39] These seem to me examples of constructing what Raabe ought to have meant in place of what he did mean. The observation that Phöbe "retreats behind a wall of faith and personal piety" when her sensual instincts are aroused also seems to me to do her an injustice and to be contrary to the text.[40] It is more important to look at her real potential and its frustration.

Before being forced by her brother into isolation and servitude, she was a teacher in a school for the retarded called Schmerzhausen, and this must strike us as her true vocation, from which her brother deflects her even further with the clear intention of sending her on missionary work. In an inner monologue Phöbe resignedly submits to this purpose in trained obedience: "I will be quite industrious with Prudens in English and Arabic grammar, if it is, perhaps, as he thinks, the Lord's will that He will call me into foreign lands and does not set my last goal here and give me my eternal rest in His grace" (16: 326), a sad twist on her subconscious wish not to be constrained in this place for the rest of her life. In the extraordinary last sentence of the novel, she forlornly imagines herself in the teacher's role again: "In her thoughts she is with her children in Schmerzhausen, and she just smiles and speaks softly: 'Don't any of you disturb the dance, or I must grow angry!' " (16: 337). Fairley felt that the sentence sheds a "chilling, even sinister" light on Phöbe's portrait and contains "a meaning that she was incapable of suspecting."[41] Again I think this judgment does Phöbe an injustice, as Fairley in general makes her out to be less self-aware than I believe she is meant to be; toward the end she realizes that even those who mean well by her do not really understand her (16: 325). But the sentence is tightly packed with psychological ambiguity and conflict: there is the wish to be fulfilling herself somewhere else; there is the contrast between the gentle, nurturing smile and the potential anger; there is the fear of stepping out of line, and the causal link between the step off the path and the resultant anger, all folded back into resignation and willed repression of a sense of loss that the reader must feel all the more acutely.

The other major characters are treated more typologically. The shrewd but shallow, artificially natural, healthy and egotistical Valerie, who at the first moment we see her complains of boredom and family life, with apposite quotes from *Much Ado about Nothing*, might be seen as a descendant of the high-society "witch" Christine von Wittum, whom Emil von Schmidt more or less cheerfully marries in *Master Author*. When Valerie sends Phöbe an ancient lamp with an inscription wishing an early Christian Phoebe eternal peace—an object evidently looted with the energetically required assistance of Valerie's diplomatic connections—it may be a little puzzling to the reader that Phöbe recognizes this gesture as a sign that Valerie has not forgiven her; the unsuspecting Veit, too, is surprised by the gift, as Valerie has always shown signs of anger at any recollection of Veit's "excursion" (16: 335). The only persuasive explanation I have encountered was offered years ago by Pongs: Valerie means to show that Phöbe belongs in an age of primitive Christianity, not in the saeculum, while she, Valerie, is victorious and has won Veit.[42] The lonely, wise carpenter Spörenwagen, who in the past was an unsuccessful suitor of Anna Fuchs and now is Phöbe's good friend, may have an ancestor in the honest carpenter Tellering in *The People from the Forest*. Because of his unselfish, sympathetic nature he is misidentified by others as a gentleman-socialist or even a communist, but in fact his leitmotif, the plane with which he attempts to smooth the knots in his wood and in himself, relates to his inner self and not to society at large; his character and the symbol of the plane attached to him are rather typical for Raabe.

Fuchs is a rather more fully realized character, exhibiting Raabe's penchant to play with names. His name, of course, means "fox," but he is known in the community as the *Räkel*, a word from hunter's language meaning "fox" but also a dialect word meaning "churl"; Raabe had earlier used it in this sense in connection with the uncouth Grünhage in *The Horn of Wanza* (14: 344). Fuch's wife is, correspondingly, called *Feh*, a dialect word meaning a female fox. These animal references imply a pre-civilized character of raw instinct; Fuchs's decoration of his wife's corpse with wildflowers further indicates a pagan quality in the subcivilized underclass that can be seen in the other Harz narratives, *Elsa of the Fir* and *Madame Salome*. He has some reasons in his own experience for his asocial hostility. Yet Raabe detects in the rebel against all authority a slumbering, frustrated authoritarian personality. His astonished change of heart in response to Veit's grand gesture exposes a servile aspect to his nature, and the event leads to his rehabilitation in the community in a way Raabe treats with trenchant sarcasm. The former poacher is now a forester and a table-pounding boor in the tavern, warmly regarded by the congenial villagers, who prefer him to the probably subversive outsider Spörenwagen.

I would suggest that *At the Sign of the Wild Man* and especially *Restless Guests* might be recommended to serious, curious, and competent readers who are invited to determine whether reading Raabe might be worthwhile. They are among the peaks of his artistic achievement, while in them, with the exception of the proem to *At the Sign of the Wild Man*, his more challenging idiosyncrasies are less prominent. These texts require patience and flexibility from the reader, but so does most Victorian fiction. Whoever does not admire these works probably cannot be induced to be one of Raabe's modern readers. Meanwhile, their translation into English would be an interesting and welcome experiment.

CHAPTER 17

Boundaries:
The Pied Piper of Hamelin;
Wunnigel;
Of Old Proteus

◨

ONE OF MY purposes in these essays, already adumbrated several times, is to break up the monolithic image of Raabe that took shape in the first phase of reception. His works were seen as chapter and verse of a great scripture, variegated, to be sure, but organic and integral in their wisdom; works and utterances that did not fit the pattern, however generously the pattern may have been conceived, tended to be shunted to the periphery. There is, to be sure, a great deal of thematic and stylistic continuity. But it should not be stressed at the expense of his variety, his multifaceted openness, his experimental searching within his fictional universe. This chapter calls attention to three examples of what I consider boundary phenomena in his oeuvre: works that are in some degree atypical, situated at outer edges of his possibilities and thus extending his range beyond that perceived by the first generation of his admirers or by most comprehensive literary histories. As it happens, however, all three works involve the relationship of the nineteenth-century writer to the realm of the imagination.

LEGEND INTO FACT: *The Pied Piper of Hamelin*

A thousand guilders! The Mayor looked blue;
So did the Corporation too. . . .
To pay this sum to a wandering fellow
With a gypsy coat of red and yellow! . . .
Besides, our losses have made us thrifty;
A thousand guilders! Come, take fifty!
Robert Browning,
"The Pied Piper of Hamelin"

Prominent among the many literary materials Raabe weaves into his textures are allusions to folk and fairy tales. This fact has been much remarked upon, although as yet there has been no comprehensive study of his use of such sources. The best beginnings have been the studies of Leo Lensing, particularly in regard to *On The Scrap-Iron* and *The Chronicle of Sparrow Alley*.[1] Raabe was much interested in fairy tales and thought at times of writing them himself. In this matter we must be especially careful not to fall victim to stock responses. Lensing points out that, after the failure of 1848, with some writers, like Mörike and Storm, and once very popular authors such as Oskar von Redwitz and Gustav zu Putlitz, "the fairy tale reappeared as an expression of resignation and withdrawal from social and political affairs";[2] Grimm's fairy tales turned from a family book into a children's book, while Andersen's tales, for all their private psychographic coding, were probably children's stories from the outset. Naive harmlessness and escape into a timeless, mythic realm were not Raabe's motives; for that his whole outlook was too rationalistic, skeptical, and just plain obstreperous. Undoubtedly he is the only German writer of his time who would have named a streetwalker "Little Red Riding Hood," though, to be sure, she receives this nickname from "the professors and the gentlemen of the arts . . . as a joke" (16: 444), that is, with the typical insensitivity to other selves of those complacent common spirits outside the alternative community.[3]

Raabe's unusual attitude toward the fairy tale can best be seen in his little essay on Musäus written in 1865 and published in 1867. There was occasion in the last chapter to remark on Musäus's pre-Romantic, Enlightenment attitude toward folk materials, which he subjected to an urbane, rationalistic, and comic perspective. By Raabe's time Musäus had been read out of the canon, supplanted by the Romantic anthropology of the Brothers Grimm and the Romantic poesy of the literary fairy tale. But Raabe rises to the defense of Musäus, his "roguish muse," and his French manners, and in a telling sentence rehabilitates him from Romantic prejudices: "Whoever does not copy the fairy tale in naive beauty and loftiness like Jakob and Wilhelm Grimm, whoever does not sprinkle it with perfumed water like Hans Christian Andersen, for him Orient and Occident will move in the same ironic chiaroscuro as they did for the storyteller of the eighteenth century." To this he adds: "yesterday the irony of the Rococo joked, today the bittersweet present has the floor."[4] Nowhere is it plainer that Raabe felt his own ironic spirit to be related to the irony of the Enlightenment, in repudiation of false poesy and obfuscating ideality.

Thus, at bottom, a "fairy story" meant for him what it often means for us in common usage: a childish fib. Many little asides in his fiction reflect this view. For example, in *Princess Fish*, two characters send a telegram, and the narrator remarks that they could not do that in "fairy-tale books" (15: 359), while in *The Lar* Schnarrwergk and Rosine on their walk in the rain meet an old herb woman who would be pleasantly scary in a fairy tale but in reality does not inspire much confidence (17: 317). However, in *Cloister Lugau*, it is the disagreeable Scriewer who browbeats his fiancée with the observation that they do not live in a fairy-tale world and that the real world is serious (19: 39)—a passage that shows how dangerously close Raabe's skepticism can come to cynicism and how careful he had to be to maintain the horizon of hope and secularized idealism. For he certainly looked at the products of the popular imagination with a disillusioning eye. The narrator of *Old Nests* observes that the childhood world of the fairy tale is amoral: "they all had no conscience in the Brothers Grimm" (14: 34). This may be unjust, but it suggests strongly that morality is a product of civilization and reason. Therefore when a critic argues that for Raabe the fairy tale is a timeless popular ground, more youthful than destructive, loud civilization, and is called on for guidance and aid in the modern world, it seems to me to be a conventionalizing distortion of his actual position.[5] If it is true, as another scholar has argued, that Velten Andres in *The Documents of the Birdsong* hopes to gain from Musäus's tales independence from reality,[6] then it is a misuse of the cheerful rationalist and further evidence of Velten's skewed relationship to the resources of the imagination.

My point is best exemplified by the one occasion, in 1863, when Raabe, instead of drawing on folk and fairy-tale motifs, transformed a popular legend into a complete story. I do not know whether it is still true that nearly all children in the Western world sometime become acquainted with the tale of *The Pied Piper of Hamelin*, but it was doubtless the case in my boyhood. English speakers learn the story in versions descended from Browning's sardonically comic poem of 1842, from which we have the spelling "Hamelin" for the town of Hameln, located on the Weser in Raabe's native landscape. In Browning's now common version, the piper, having magically rid the town of rats, is cheated of his reward, and in revenge leads the children into the Koppelberg, where they disappear, with the exception of one lame boy, who wistfully reports on the utopian vision of a Land of Cockaigne called forth by the piper's music. In Germany, where the story is usually called *Der Rattenfänger von Hameln* (*The Ratcatcher of Hamelin*), the popular tradition runs from a mildly eroticized ballad of Goethe's in 1804, a more folkloric version included by Arnim and Brentano in *Des Knaben Wunderhorn* (*The Boy's Magic Horn*), and a narrative version reported by the Brothers Grimm in the first part of their *Deutsche Sagen* (*German Legends*) in 1816. The story has had a long life and continues to this day to serve a variety of iconographic uses, not least for the tourist trade in Hameln, which elaborately celebrated the seven-hundredth anniversary of the event in 1984.[7]

There are several variants of the tale, and Raabe reconstructs one at the beginning of his story, following in part the Grimms' version. But Raabe is not reproducing legend; he is attempting to retranslate legend into history. To his editor he wrote: "I treat in it the historical fact."[8] It had long been recognized that a historical event must lie behind the story; there continues to be some disagreement about the actual details, though scholars locate it in the late thirteenth century and associate it with the removal of the young people in the town to a German colony in the east, perhaps in Siebenbürgen in Transylvania.[9] However, we need not concern ourselves with the details of this dispute, for Raabe committed himself to a particular, now discredited theory. He found it in an article in the *Holzmindisches Wochenblatt* (*Holzminden Weekly*) of 1786 (9/1: 446), which was quite possibly written by his grandfather, the editor of the paper, and which refers to the theory of a military chaplain named Fein, published in 1749. It associates the legend with an effort by the Abbot of Fulda to sell the thriving town to the Bishop of Minden, with the consequence of a battle that destroyed the town's youth.

This theory was welcome to Raabe because it enabled him to relate the story to his nationalist preoccupations. As the narrator himself stresses, it allowed him to set the story not in 1284, as other theories have it, but in 1259, that is, toward the beginning of the fourteen-year interregnum in the Holy Roman Empire, perceived in German history as a terrible time of anarchy and universal civil war. Thus Raabe is again able to touch upon his pervasive themes of national disunity and the wicked machinations of unpatriotic rulers manipulating the political fate of ordinary people without any regard to their interests. But, as always, the fault in his view lies not only with the lords but also with the people. The "children" of the story are adolescents and young adults, and they are frivolous, selfish, and pleasure-loving despite the peril in which the town finds itself. Here Raabe seems to be reflecting on the popular indifference to the nationalist cause that so exasperated him in Stuttgart.

The youths hold a dance despite a ban on it, and there appears in the community a Wendish piper named Kiza. The young people treat him with rude contempt; for his hunger and thirst they give him a bone and some water in a broken jug. But they oblige him to play, and in hate and anger he turns the affair into a Dionysian orgy, with jealous squabbles and knife fights, until a monk appears, calling the young people to contrition and informing them that the town has been sold to the Bishop of Minden that day. In the ensuing war Kiza is the military piper, for he knows tunes that arouse courage; as a reward he is given a beggar's accommodations. Here the narrator observes: "Kiza, the Wend, might have been quite happy if he had known how to be modest and had been satisfied with the gnawed bone that had fallen as his lot from the table of life. But it is a strange thing about satisfaction; people lose it more easily than any other merits and virtues, and not only by their own fault" (9/1: 142). At a May Day dance celebrating a victory, the sullen Kiza is again forced to play and again creates an orgy, a St. Vitus's dance. When he dances with the belle of the community and kisses her, he is beaten and thrown out; enemy forces find him on the road and Kiza goes over to the other side. He reappears and leads the young men into an ambush, in which both Kiza and his rival are killed. The belle over whom they fought forgets them both and marries a Bremen merchant, and legend, stronger than history, takes over the event.

Apart from his nationalist-historical concerns, Raabe clearly had other things on his mind with this story. Kiza is a version of the outsider as artist, gifted with the ability to move and inspire, as well as to corrupt, but treated with contempt and reduced to beggary. As a Wend he is all the more vulnerable. "Wend" is a general term for the Slavic peoples who were all but exterminated during the German colonization of the east in the twelfth and thirteenth centuries; by Raabe's time they numbered about 150,000 people and were an oppressed minority. His nationalism never extended to xenophobia, and he inserts a passage in the story reviewing the dispossession and suffering of the Wends and the hatred of the Germans for them; of Kiza we are told that he has been driven out of a village occupied by German peasants: "All his relatives and friends had starved and frozen to death, dead and gone; *he* had been saved by his art, though even it provided him only a miserable, outlaw existence subject to every accident" (9/1: 140). Raabe does not sentimentalize the outcast; he is hostile and vengeful, but it is clear that his evil temper stands in a mutual relationship with the intolerance and malevolence in the German community. One of Raabe's early Jewish admirers thought that the mistreated racial outcast might be a parallel case to that of the

253

Jews,[10] and this seems to me probable, if not literally, then typologically.

The story is a relatively minor work in Raabe's oeuvre, but it is of interest because it exhibits his readiness to ground the imagination in reality, to take a legend that has become an amusing children's story and retranslate it into a harsh historical reality, so that the truths about life and history should not be masked by more comfortable mythification. This is more a mid-nineteenth-century than modern approach, far removed from the effort of the contemporary folklorist to uncover, not the historical reality, but the mythic elements in the legend.[11] But Raabe's admirers were not always happy, either; Brandes, for example, found that the historical material overcame the "poesy" in the story[12]—one more succinct example of the urge to drag Raabe back into the conventionality from which he so persistently struggled to be free.

IMAGINATION AS SELF-INDULGENCE: *Wunnigel*

> . . . the narrator himself sails upstream and carries his listeners toward Holzminden on the colorful little magic ship that Lady Imagination, his patron saint, has entrusted to him with many pleasing lessons and charming admonitions. Hoiho, it is a merry little ship, well rigged with flower garlands, gold and silver ornaments and silken sails and pennants. Hoiho, indeed the wind is good, indeed it plays flatteringly with the flowers, pennants, and sails; but the heart of the man at the helm is heavy.
>
> *The Holy Spring* (3: 140-41)

The short novel *Wunnigel* may seem at first to be one more variant on familiar Raabean themes: an outsider whose eccentric vision is measured against the middle way of "normal" people becomes a defeated returnee with no option but to abandon the world and find an alternative harbor outside society. But here there is a shift in the ethics of this constellation that removes the novel from the center of the oeuvre and places it on the boundary as a point of observation. *Wunnigel* is a comic novel with a serious subtext and, despite its tendency rather to undermine the expectations readers have normally brought to Raabe, it has been surprisingly popular.[13]

Wunnigel is a dealer in antiques who obsessively travels around, detaching objects from people who do not know their value. It may be remarked in passing that the antiques dealer is a modern figure, alienating the objects of the past out of their organic settings. On his travels he drags his grown daughter Anselma with him, not knowing what else to do with her. In the central German town in which the story takes place, Anselma becomes ill at an inn and her father, after an unsuccessful attempt to treat her himself, irritably calls in a young doctor named Weyland. As a beginner, Weyland has a small and poor practice, but he clearly is a man of some means, the last of an old family, who lives in a large though somewhat rundown house full, as it happens, of antiques and art objects. *Of course*, as Raabe in his characteristic way makes clear from the outset of the novel, Weyland and Anselma fall in love and marry. Wunnigel, meanwhile, becomes a self-invited house guest of Weyland, but he is delighted at the marriage, since it rids him of his daughter, and he takes the opportunity to disappear. After a few months, plaintive messages start coming from Italy in which Wunnigel complains of having been swindled and robbed. Anselma, who has already warned Weyland not to believe much that her father says, doubts these tales, and when a bedraggled Wunnigel reappears, the true story comes out, though it takes some time to emerge because it is so embarrassing: he has trapped himself in a marriage to an elegant German-Russian virago with the altogether too comic name of Oktavia von Schlimmbesser, a disaster that came about because each erred in estimating the other's financial condition. Wunnigel, having pretended suicide, is now in total flight from his bride, and he hides in the little gatehouse of a ninety-year-old man named Brüggemann, former honorary chief of the citizen's guard, clockmaker, mechanic, tinkerer, and unsuccessful inventor of an automobile (in a novel set around 1872 and first published five years later!). The formidable Oktavia does, naturally, turn up, but the immediate crisis is relieved by the arrival of a Russian diplomat, Paul Petrowitsch Sesamoff, whom Wunnigel lured with the fraudulent prospect of being able to sell him the contents of Weyland's house. This is a different kind of Russian, bluff, big-hearted, and sensible, and in time he takes Oktavia back with him to Russia. But Wunnigel is not restored by this liberation; he refuses all offers to return to Weyland's house, takes himself permanently to bed, and dies in this self-imposed isolation in the following winter.

The story may seem slight, and the narrator goes out of his way to characterize it as comedy. But the reader who has learned that the mature Raabe is not likely to waste his time may feel a little disoriented here. What are we to make of Wunnigel, and how ought we to estimate him by contrast with the "normal" figures, Weyland and Anselma? For all his not inconsiderable faults, Wunnigel is a man of imagination, a lover of beautiful things despite a touch of venality, and an individualist of winsome naivety. When, in Chapter 11, he clumsily smashes a cabinet of porcelain in Weyland's house, he is miserable, not because of the harm to Weyland but because of the loss of the beautiful things, and he demands that Weyland pity *him*, for he, not Weyland, was able to appreciate their aesthetic value. Dr. Weyland, on the other hand, is nobody special. He is a good fellow, pleasant, thoughtful, and reasonable. He may remind us a little of Veit von Bielow in *Restless Guests*, though spared the test that Veit tragically failed. In an odd passage, when he finds himself falling in love, he sees ghosts from trivial novels: "the most conventional literary riff-raff, which here suddenly seemed to be endowed with flesh and blood, bones and muscles, and emerged from the walls" (13: 42)—to be sure, part of the narrator's self-persiflage, very pronounced in this work, as the author of a "love story." And what of Anselma, a nice girl who loves her puzzling father, but who, at Weyland's prompting, admits that she would like to live a normal life like other people, "just for a change" (13: 68-69)? Decade upon decade of the bourgeoisie contending with itself in literature has persuaded us that the "normal" is reprehensible, philistine, bleak, and dull. Thus our sympathy seems to be drawn away from Weyland and Anselma to Wunnigel, who exceeds them in imagination and sensibility, no matter how flawed. This cannot be an improbable reading, since it is the one sponsored by Daemmrich, who sees a nobility ultimately revealed in Wunnigel, "our better self."[14]

The question is whether to take this position is not to fall victim to a different kind of conventionalized reading, to expectations generated by Raabe himself. The fact is that Wunnigel pursues his purposes at the cost of others. He has treated his daughter more as a hindrance than as a person; in the past he has tried to make her sleep in a hammock so that he would have more space for his objects. Clearly he has no wish to be a parent and he is pleased to marry Anselma off, not for the sake of her own happiness—that is just her good luck—but to be free to do as he pleases. According to Anselma's account, his way of life was worrisome and oppressive to his wife as well. He is unreliable and untruthful, perhaps not so much out of calculation, but because his fictional self is more real to him than his real environment. His disingenuousness causes him to trap himself in his disastrous marriage in Italy. He ends utterly introverted, shamed in his own self-regard, unable to accept the genuinely forbearing goodwill of his daughter and son-in-law, and he dies in pathos, isolated except for his comradeship with the ancient Brüggemann. It is important to remember how central sympathy with other selves is to Raabe's ethical outlook; the fact is that Weyland and Anselma, for all their ordinariness, have more of it than Wunnigel. Today we would probably characterize such a personality as narcissistic. In Raabe's fictional universe Wunnigel is a variant of the imaginative type, thus a projection of the author's own self and fate, but in this case, as Fehse pointed out years ago, hyperbolized into the grotesque.[15]

The theme of the imagination in Raabe is a large topic that still awaits a detailed examination. It seems to me to be one point on which a comparison with Gottfried Keller might be undertaken. Keller's imaginative writing exhibits in many places a pronounced suspicion of the imagination. In his most ambitious work, *Green Henry*, a would-be artist achieves nothing but guilt and rueful self-knowledge, and Keller inserted into the novel a chapter entitled in the second version "The Family of Readers," which describes how an entire family goes to hell in a handbasket from reading novels, the daughters becoming unmarriageable sluts surrounded by illegitimate children and the son a gambler, swindler, and convict. Naturally, one must make allowances here for Keller's surreal sense of humor. Nevertheless, in him the imagination was in conflict with common sense, and the artistic vocation with the practical obligations of citizenship; the complex was crucially intensified by his psychological disposition with its large component of self-hatred. One of today's foremost Keller scholars has observed: "For Keller not the bourgeois but the artist is under the pressure of justification, and this justification does not occur in *Green Henry*."[16]

For Raabe the problem was somewhat less existentially acute but also more varied in its aspect. Certainly the imagination was a value for him, and he shows no trace of the sense of guilt about his vocation under which Keller labored. The harmony of reason and imagination was his ideal, but one rarely to be found in reality. In *On Dark Ground* he remarks that people are given two sharp weapons in their fight with life—"understanding and imagination"—but, he goes on to add, how often they are employed for self-destruction (3: 398). One thinks of the series of mad or destroyed artists in his works: the musician Wallinger in *The Children of Finkenrode*, a victim of his otherness from the crude world; the drunken carnival comedian Wolke in *Who Can Change It?* who drowns himself; the erotically maddened monk Festus in *The Holy Spring*, an accomplished painter, and the drunken town musician

Eckenbrecker in the same work; the charlatan alchemist Vinacche in *A Secret*; the brain-damaged Täubrich Pasha in *Abu Telfan*, not exactly an artist but a man who dwells in a utopian fantasy world; the sculptor Querian in *Madame Salome*, driven over the brink by the laughter of his rationalistic "friend" Scholten; the alcoholic, ultimately drowned poet Lippoldes in *Pfister's Mill*; the deranged Paul Ferrari in *German Nobility*, a victim of excessive, rootless imagination, who is told that he would be an original if there had not been millions of his kind before him (13: 229). A comic counterpart is the literal lunatic Löhnefinke in *German Moonshine*, bedevilled by the moon into a poet *malgré lui*.

There are the outsiders who retain their balance at the price of hostility, isolation, or resignation, like the piper Kiza, Master Author, and the "mock-up uncle" Fabian, maker of candy models in *Fabian and Sebastian*, who people think might have been a real artist or sculptor (15: 142). There are the fake artists, such as the breezy, fraudulent actor Schminkert and the cynical, vagabond marionetteer Leppel in *The People from the Forest*, or the pretentious, awful poet Krautworst in *Celtic Bones*, along with the shallow aesthetes, like Brokenkorb in *On the Scrap-Iron*. A further extreme is the willful degeneracy in the person of the corpse photographer and pornographer Blech in *The Lar*, who thinks he might have been a significant artist but could not stand up to the hunger and therefore repudiates resignation:

> I said to myself: poor doll, give it up; this won't do any longer, let other vegetarians in, you have sacrificed yourself enough; the godhead does not want the aesthetic vapor that wafts up from the altar from you to it. And I gave up. In my last highest excitement I kicked not the wall this time, but my own canvas, which the pawnbroker only wanted to take if I were first to dry clean my paint performance from it. (17: 272-73)

The protagonist Kohl in the same novel, for his part, dissolves his aspirations in third-rate journalism.

In numerous places the desirable union of reason and imagination breaks apart: imagination and reality become antinomies instead. The commander of the besieged fortress in *St. Thomas* is a man of "little imagination"; therefore he says straight out that the city is lost, as it is (9/2: 35). Christoph Pechlin, "whose imagination ran away with him more often than his best friends liked," is a self-published, somewhat deluded poet, of whom it is said that he was a true poet at the most foolish moment of his life, his catastrophic engagement with Christabel (10: 295, 383). Of the unworldly Elard Nürrenberg in *Owl's Pen-*

tecost, professor of aesthetics with three paying students and six auditors, the narrator observes that exaltation and confusion are good for
a professor and poet (11: 403). The neighbors say of the lending librarian Achtermann in *German Nobility* that if he were not such a
"Phantastikus" he would not be able to stand his life, but he warns
his young friend Ulrich to take a warning from *Don Quixote* and not
sit around among books, poison his imagination, and make himself
useless for "the real day" (13: 180-81). Often the imagination is seen
as a surrogate for a failed or ungratifying life: the narrator Langreuter
of *Old Nests*, for example, consoles himself with trivial literature and
remarks: "My castle-in-the-air is my house" (14: 148), an aphorism
that Raabeans have often quoted without, perhaps, retaining an
awareness of its context of defeated resignation.

Even when the alternative utopia of the imagination is presented
more positively there is still an undertone of loss and compensation,
as in this meditation on a librarian's catalogue in *German Nobility*:

> and the old magic, the sorcery of the imagination, which from
> the beginning simply and solely holds man firmly in the world,
> the charming, colorful lie, the dear twin sister of truth, once again
> assumed its full reign, *pour corriger la fortune* and to parry bitter
> reality. (13: 283)

Here we have the ancient theme of fiction as lying, deceptive yet
necessary. It is taken up again with particular subtlety in Raabe's
novel of puberty, *Princess Fish*, which the narrator characterizes as "the
great story of the education of a human being through imagination,
dream, and the optical illusion of the young body and the childish
soul of man!" (15: 348). This education of the young Theodor Rodburg consists not in the abandonment of the imagination but in learning to make differentiations by experiencing the pitfalls. Of all his
siblings the only one alive in his imagination is his absent brother
Alexander, who turns out to be a dangerous and evil man; Theodor
gets over his infatuation with the good-looking but slovenly "Princess
Fish," Romana, who is said to have an "unlively," that is, self-indulgent imagination, by looking at her more closely and recognizing her
as an ordinary, aging "earthly madame" (15: 199, 331, 350). It has
been rightly said that the "fundamental tension" in Raabe's whole
oeuvre is "between vision and reality, between the ideal and the practical, the desirable and the possible."[17]

It is in this context that we can see *Wunnigel* as a boundary phenomenon. Wunnigel has imagination, but it is totally introverted, and it
brings grief to himself and others. His imagination, as Weyland rec-

ognizes, seduces him into lying (13: 122). Here is a man, who having gladly married off his daughter in order to pursue his own whims, blames her for having abandoned him when he stumbles into disaster: " 'You alone are to blame, girl! You alone—solely and simply you!' cried Wunnigel from his sofa corner" (13: 124). This is the self-indulgent imagination that reshapes reality to the needs of an immature ego, and it is not far from insanity; but it is not the insanity of the artist driven mad by the recalcitrance of the conventional world. It is misuse of the imagination, and therefore it lies toward one far end of the spectrum of Raabe's persistent meditations on the value and utility of fiction. Its weight, to be sure, is lessened by the comic context of this novel. But the issue was not trivial for Raabe. Wunnigel has an evil predecessor in the invincible *canaille* Dietrich Häussler in *The Rumbledump*, who is credited with imagination, the capacity to dream and idealize reality, and thus sees his own self as the midpoint of the world (8: 37). He will have, as we shall see, a heroically tragic successor in Velten Andres of *The Documents of the Birdsong*.

Constraining Fictions versus Liberating Fantasy: *Of Old Proteus*

> It is a pity; the whole machinery of Romanticism
> is gradually falling apart; we poor devils of story-
> tellers may struggle as much as we like with the
> feather brush and the oil glass: the gears won't
> turn any more, the hooks and levers are broken;
> how long will it be until the thing completely
> stops?
>
> *The People from the Forest* (1862-63, 5: 291)

The comic novella *Of Old Proteus*, first published in 1875-76 and then included as the last of the *Krähenfeld Stories* in 1879, is by a considerable margin the hardest of Raabe's works to interpret satisfactorily. It is even difficult to come to a firm estimate of it in general terms. Is it a weightless, loose-running capriccio, tossed off with the left hand?[18] Or does its apparent arabesque, as critics began to argue long ago, mask serious underlying concerns, perhaps a breach with Schopenhauer and a turning point from pessimism?[19] Our insecurity in regard to this text is owing to the fact that it is different—really different— from anything else Raabe wrote. It is small comfort that he is said to have told his completely baffled editor that he did not know himself what the work meant (E 4: 73). It helps even less that the novella, which maintains, even for Raabe, an exceptionally confrontational posture toward the reader, is in places very hard to read and even to construe; I would not relish the task of translating it into English. I therefore offer what follows in a somewhat tentative spirit, though in the conviction that the novella is a meaningful and potentially interpretable, if perhaps in some ways rather private work.

In order to describe the novella concisely, it will be convenient to approach it out of narrative sequence. At the center of the "plot" we find two frustrated young lovers, improbably named Hilarion Abwarter and Ernesta Piepenschnieder, hindered in their desire to marry by Ernesta's uncle, Baron Philibert von Püterich, who has promised his niece to his friend Magerstedt, an old, lacivious swindler. Püterich has threatened to disinherit Ernesta if she balks him, but this is a ruse, for the profligate Baron is completely ruined and hopelessly in debt to his grasping friend. Here is a situation of the most artless literary conventionality; it might have been drawn directly from the *commedia dell'arte*. Moreover, the young lovers exhibit a banality verging on the moronic. Ernesta chirps away in inflated commonplaces, while the impecunious official Hilarion is a shallow fop who "loved not only his little Ernesta, but also bronze paperweights, crystal inkwells, elegant pens, and fine stationery," on which latter he writes verse "in the prettiest handwriting. If he was not thinking of eternity, of immortality, that was, at least in regard to the poems, a nice touch on his part" (12: 229-30). Like Ernesta, he runs to clichés. When he solemnly quotes *Hamlet*, "There are more things in heaven and earth, Horatio, / Than are dreamt of in your philosophy," the narrator grumps:

> *Nomina sunt odiosa*, but quotations are often much more odious; no god preserves us from having to print anew what the cleverest people constantly present as something fresh! *Crambe bis cocta*, twice-cooked cabbage, can be a delicacy; but when Ernesta, after she has let her beloved finish for the third time, whispers: "Then let the world of spirits hold its protective hand over us!" we believe that we, too, have read that more than twice in a book. . . . (12: 236)

To be sure, the reduction of character and situation to the commonplace is found elsewhere in Raabe; what is not found elsewhere is that the agents of the resolution of the plot to a happy ending are two ghosts and a hermit.

The first ghost is that of Rosa von Krippen, who died of a broken heart when abandoned by Püterich; as a punishment for this foolishness, her shade has been trapped in the wall of Püterich's apartment for thirty years. As a "prudish, pretentious German maiden" (12: 224), it is only just that all these years she has been spread thin between the wall and the wallpaper. But in her outrage at Püterich's plot she struggles free, pushing out a nail holding a portrait of a beautiful actress and dancer, the "sinful" Innocentia. She is the second ghost, but, owing to her wholeness of heart, her purgatory is less onerous; she is confined to the forest as a laughing wood nymph. She, too, died of love, in her case for an officer and gentleman known in the story by the assumed name of Konstantius. He is the hermit, having withdrawn to the forest after having lost the "affected and cranky goose" Rosa (12: 260) to Püterich, while scorning the splendid Innocentia because of her dubious reputation. This tale, too, is nothing but "the *trivialitas trivialitatum*, the ancient, insipid story, that the one loved him, the forest brother, that he loved the other, that this other loved a third, and that this third, namely Baron Püterich, was the only reasonable one of the whole company, since he only loved himself, but took his pleasure how and when he found it!" (12: 259). In this passage there is an audible echo of Heine's poem, *Lyrisches Intermezzo* (*Lyrical Intermezzo*), No. 39 (perhaps best known in Schumann's nimble setting):

> A young man loves a maiden,
> Who chooses another instead,
> This other loves still another
> And these two haply wed.
>
> The maiden out of anger
> Marries, with no regard,
> The first good man she runs into—
> The young lad takes it hard.
>
> It is so old a story,
> Yet somehow always new;
> And he that has just lived it,
> It breaks his heart in two.[20]

At the time of the story, Konstantius is on the edge of a readiness to abandon his life in the forest, where he has been living "with an imperturbability that bordered on stupidity" (12: 202) and where the ghost of Innocentia has been laughing at him for a fool these thirty years. For one thing, he is suffering pain from a piece of acorn caught in a cavity of a tooth and is in pressing need of a dentist. For another, he has discovered that isolation is not possible in the modern world:

But I assure you, dear miss, you have no idea how one is overrun by people here in one's solitude. Fine solitude indeed! If I had set up here a forest tavern with a sign "At the Hermit's," it couldn't be busier in the woods around! If I had announced a marriage bureau in the newspapers, there could not be more perplexed people in need of help wanting to lay claim to my mediation. (12: 257)

Thus Konstantius, fed up with counseling lovers, at first tries to evade Hilarion and Ernesta, but the news that the ghosts of Rosa and Innocentia have appeared to them captures his attention and also galvanizes his return to civilization. In practically no time the disheveled, filthy Konstantius goes to town, has his tooth fixed, gets shaved, finds a tailor to outfit him as a respectable gentleman, visits his banker (he is clearly still a man of means), discomfits Püterich and Magerstedt, and makes Hilarion his heir, enabling him to marry Ernesta and live ever after—whether happily or not, we are not told.

In no other work does Raabe employ elements of fantasy in this way. In a short story written about the same time, *In Retirement*, the ghost of a dead child appears to an elderly couple, but this is to be understood as an enduring presence in memory. The apparitions of the early story *Christmas Spirits* are the products of the punch bowl. In *Owls' Pentecost*, the third item in the *Krähenfeld Stories*, the blessing of the young lovers by the ghost of Prince Alexis XIII (11: 379) is allegorical. The role of the demonic in such works as *Madame Salome* and *The Innerste* is largely a matter of folk psychology, though no less potent for that. But in *Of Old Proteus* we may say, without trying to be paradoxical, that the ghosts are realistically treated. They are really there and are active agents in the story; the question that has been raised as to whether they might be imaginary[21] is easily answered: after Rosa's ghost appears to Hilarion, who has never heard of her before, he verifies her identity in the police archives. Thus Ernesta's wish that the spirit world might protect her and her beloved, scorned by the narrator as a cliché, is literally realized. Marie Jensen observed, with her usual perspicacity: "In this story there is a ghostly realism found nowhere else."[22] Not only are the ghosts real; in contrast to Raabe's customary outlook, there is a kind of transcendental poetic justice operating, if somewhat inscrutably. Both the prudish (or proper) Rosa and the vivacious (or sinful) Innocentia are punished for the absurdity of dying of love, and both become agents of retribution and of the conventional happy ending.

All this takes place in the context of high-strung, convoluted dis-

course on right and wrong readers, on literature and writing. As has
been mentioned in Chapter 12 on narrators, the novella opens with
the question: "How shall we do things in order to appear quite credible to *our* reader?" (12: 199). There follows a set of fragmentary
probes in realism and exotica, but these will not do. For a new beginning the narrator calls up *A Midsummer Night's Dream*, but this atmosphere of romance, too, is at first rejected with the sour remark:
" 'Without Mendelssohn's music the crazy stuff could not be borne
today anymore,' says the public, that is, five-sixths of the public. . . ."
(12: 200). But then the narrator recovers his old hope that there is
an adequate minority readership out there, and decides that this approach will work. The novella is subtitled *A Story of High Summer*,
thus linking its realistic, efficacious ghosts to the ethereal world of
Shakespeare's romance. With this introduction, along with the self-
conscious literariness of the narration and the more or less disrespectful allusions to the reader, it is understandable that one of the best
critics has concluded that "the story is a discussion of literature, with
the emphasis placed . . . on the proper way to write and to read a
story."[23] But what is the best way to write? Surely it cannot be to
write ghost stories, something Raabe never did before or after.

If I understand him correctly here, he is making a distinction, reversed from his implied categories elsewhere, between fiction, understood as the trivialities of conventional literature, and illusion as the
creature of a less fettered imagination. Fiction in this sense puppetizes
consciousness by imposing conventional templates upon it. All the
characters of the novella are victims of preformed fictional plots. Both
Rosa and Innocentia have been constrained to believe that unrequited
love is nobly fatal and are punished for this foolishness by the authority of the narrator's freer imagination. The hermit Konstantius, too,
has fallen into a conventionalized, low-Romantic pattern, one that is
comic by reason of its obsolescence, illustrated by the circumstance
that, after his retirement to the woods, the public payed more attention to an automaton hermit in an amusement park (12: 206). He is a
real hermit, the narrator comments slyly, of the sort that our wives,
aunts, and children *expect* in novels (12: 201). Konstantius comes to
see that "I myself am only the product of an imagination got wholly
out of control" (12: 261). Konstantius is the only living character in
the novel who gains some insight into the enslavement of consciousness by fictional models, helped, no doubt, by the wholesome laughter
of Innocentia's ghost. He begins to question his identity, though without resolution, for, as the narrator says, "Who solves such questions

at all?" (12: 263). He seems to recognize, even as he helps Hilarion and Ernesta to their union, that they, too, are acting out questionable plots that can only descend from imagination to disappointment: "Your wish seems to me foolish: let us retain our illusions as long as possible!" (12: 287).

This brings us to the most famous line in the novella and one of the most often quoted of Raabe's aphorisms: "Give us this day our daily self-delusion!" (12: 239)—added, incidentally, at the last minute in the fair copy of the manuscript (12: 525). But we must look a little at the context, which is another of those knotted, turbid passages that stud this work. It comes at a pause in the story, which the narrator fills up by taking a walk:

> Not fat and stout with the feelings of the philistine who has slaughtered the fattest pig in the community; but not with the feelings of the genius who says: "Today I have experienced again the existence of a hundred individualities in my own, and the *theatrum mundi* can collapse for all I care!"—but slimly and modestly, as the high poet's distant, poor cousin or, rather, half-brother, as the handbooks of aesthetics say, who once again sat around all day and scratched all kinds of smoke pictures of life on his plate. (12: 238)

The reference to the poet's half-brother may be a signal to what this passage is about, for the chief handbook of aesthetics in question is none other than Schiller's essay *Über naive und sentimentalische Dichtung* (*On Naive and Sentimentive Poetry*), with its notorious gibe: "What even the poet, the chaste disciple of the Muse, may permit himself, shall that not be allowed to the novel writer, who is only his half-brother and still so much touches the earth?"[24]—a judgment that made German novelists neurotic throughout much of the nineteenth century. Raabe, though much less intimidated in this matter than most, seems here nevertheless to be ruefully meditating on his vocation.

After speaking of a rare happy man for whom a plate of good food is compensation for "much mental trouble," he goes on:

> The man is right! the man is happy, while the great genius, the aforementioned poet, pictures to himself how Homer forced King Alexander the Great to run around Achilles's tomb—and racks his brains to figure how *he* will manage to move a future hero to get out of breath and break into a sweat on account of his opus. That there is some difficulty with this, he knows, and knows as

well that, for example, Kaiser Wilhelm and Bismarck would not let themselves in for it. With this certainty he can go to the table; but whether the food compensates him, too, for his mental trouble, is another question. Give us this day our daily self-delusion! (12: 238-39).

The passage is opaque and elliptical. Subtly the narrator slips into the role of the great poet from whom he had pretended modestly to distinguish himself by reference to Schiller's tag. At the same time, the required daily self-delusion seems to apply to those authorial ambitions that appeared to be partly intact in the opening meditation on the minority of right readers. Might we then say that the illusionist is engaged in an illusory undertaking? The modern critic, in contrast to those of the past, sees the disillusioning effect in the work as discouraging: "what remains to the characters after their illusions have been destroyed is precious little. . . . If there is more behind the illusions, no one can decipher it."[25]

A soberness about the efficacy of Raabe's kind of fiction is thematic throughout his career. But I do not think things are quite that gloomy here. For we may also cite another odd passage, in which Innocentia's blithe ghost in the treetop trills to Konstantius a line that is said to be from Voltaire, though no one has yet identified it: "C'est le triomphe de la raison, de bien vi, vi, vi, vivre avec les gens, qui n'en ont pas!" (12: 266). For Raabe reason was not, as it was for the Romantics, the antipode of the imagination; for him reason and imagination were allies against petrified, unexamined, conventionally determined habits of mind and conduct. Illusion, even self-delusion, is not pejorative for him *as long as it is conscious*, that is, allied with reason. This is what Konstantius learns in his return to reasonableness, and what the narrator plays out for us when he obliges us to believe in ghosts in a realistic context.

Finally, we must bring up the by no means easy question of the title symbol of Proteus. Raabe employs it in a couple of other places. At the end of *Abu Telfan*, Hagebucher tells the partially demented Täubrich that he is privileged, spared the sense of tragic futility of "all the others, who try to overcome the Egyptian Proteus, life, with cunning or force and must wrestle with it unto death," and he adds: "I tell you, Täubrich, there is among those [reasonable men] not one who can say with certainty whether in his thoughts, wishes, and actions he is truly walking in reality" (7: 380). In a draft of *Princess Fish*, "old Proteus" appears as the image of a man of the moment with a burning imagination, a genius without concentration (15: 611). Hans Butzmann, the editor of *Proteus* in the critical edition, connects the symbol both to the familiar figure of the ever-changing Proteus in the *Odyssey*, with whom Menelaus must wrestle in order to force him to hold one shape and give information, and to the kindly King Proteus in Euripides's *Helen*, with whom Helen finds shelter while her unreal shade is abducted to Troy by Paris (a concept, incidentally, that reappears in the dubious existential status of Helen in Goethe's *Faust*). Thus Butzmann summarizes: "There is the image of the struggle with life, which will not conform to human will; but there is besides the doubt in the security of human perception, a thought that concerns not so much the protagonists as the observer, the author" (12: 523-24).

Butzmann is undoubtedly right about both of these identifications; the question is to what extent the two facets of the tradition cohere. At first there appears to be an identification of Homer's Proteus with Konstantius, who, in trying to evade his visitors, wiggles and writhes so that Hilarion must wrestle with him and hold him fast (12: 255). At the end, however, Konstantius dreams that Innocentia's ghost goes off to join Proteus in the Aegean, "on the bright waters, many-shaped, eternally changing, to help Papa herd the seals" (12: 289). The novel closes with a comment of the narrator on the elusiveness of the imagined world: "the old Proteus escapes once again our grasping arms: he keeps only too gladly all his knowledge of the past, present, and future for himself alone" (ibid.). And as we sit here attempting to fix the Protean image, we are very likely being gulled by the roguish author himself. To his friend Sträter he wrote some years later:

> The old Proteus is indeed good lying-in reading. I am glad that your wife was able to laugh over it. When I was pregnant with the changeling, I also laughed over it frequently—especially when I thought about all the things people would one day say about the pretty child of the Muses.[26]

Perhaps, then, the novella is just a scherzo after all. But it is a scherzo played out on the ground of the imagination, which is insecure to the point of dissolution but absolutely necessary all the same, for it is the only ground on which we can exist with rational integrity. However, we should not take even this interpretation, whether right or wrong, as a generalizing key to Raabe's oeuvre. In the past his admirers transferred the image to its author, calling Raabe himself the old Proteus, and this was more apposite than they themselves perhaps realized. He so referred to himself when selling the *Krähenfeld Stories* to his publisher, calling up at the same time an image of himself as a tightrope walker.[27] Raabe *was* Protean, capable of remarkable changes of shape and form, wriggling often out of our grasp, yet ever again inviting us into quite variously decorated spaces of the rational imagination.

CHAPTER 18

The Mill on the Sewer: *Pfister's Mill* and the Present Relevance of Past Literature

□

> The pride and obstinacy of millers and other in-
> significant people, whom you pass unnoticingly
> on the road every day, have their tragedy too; but
> it is of that unwept, hidden sort that goes on from
> generation to generation, and leaves no rec-
> ord. . . .
>
> George Eliot, *The Mill on the Floss*

I N RECENT years much has been heard about "relevance" in literature, literary criticism, and literary pedagogy. It is an old issue
that has cropped up intermittently in various guises for the last couple
of hundred years, if not longer; we can detect variations of it in the
Renaissance, in ancient Rome, in Rabbinical exegesis, negatively in
Plato. It has been my instinct to react to this concern with a certain
amount of skepticism. My main uneasiness has been that the effect of
a criticism proceeding from a concept of relevance can be to make
ourselves—or our students—more important than the literature, and
thus to conform the literary experience to our own parochial consciousness, rather than expanding ourselves by means of the experience. As I remarked in another context: "I cannot see why . . . to
keep [the text] alive it must be stretched forward to meet us; rather,
the greater benefit to us as readers would seem to me to stretch back
to meet *it*, enriching ourselves, not speciously enriching the text."[1]
There is another danger commonly met with, though more easily detected in the criticism of the past than in our current practice: if we
come to identify our reception of texts with our interests, we may
have to readjust the text to suit them, or, if this proves too difficult,

cast it aside, thus incurring losses in the cultural patrimony. A corollary to this is that texts that become very closely identified with reader interests may slip away from us as these interests change historically, though the texts may never have been precisely perceived in the first place. In general the evaluative principle of present relevance has been a strategy to deal with the demonstrably peripheral importance of literature in our society, and specifically to arouse some modicum of interest in pupils and students with their often exceptionally dim sense of history. Needless to say, such a strategy is necessary and worthwhile, yet it is but a starting point from which to work back into a more comprehensive awareness of the potential significance and enjoyability of texts of the past for us on their own merits. They should not be used as a kind of secular scripture, guiding our thinking and feeling, nor should they be exceptionally praised if they happen to touch chords of interest to us today, for though there is such a thing as historical continuity, detectable in the literary record, there is no such thing as prophecy, except as an accident, nor is there any concrete eschatological shape to real history of the sort that is claimed to justify the "inheritance" principle of official East German cultural doctrine. To be sure, these may be difficult propositions to maintain in these days of the magnification of the reader as the creator of the text (a notion I believe Raabe would have thought preposterous).

Yet, as it happens, in 1884 he himself produced a book that threatens to question the relevance of these very propositions. It is *Pfister's Mill: A Summer Vacation Notebook*, and a quick résumé of its plot will clearly show why. Pfister's mill, which has been in the family for generations, is a working mill to which the local farmers bring their grain to be ground. But, since it is pleasantly located, it has also become a place where the townspeople and students come for outings, to picnic, brew coffee, and drink beer. Pfister is therefore not only a miller but a kind of country tavernkeeper. Like so many of Raabe's positive figures, he is amiable, jovial, and generous, and his relationship with the townspeople of all classes is thoroughly cordial. The tenor of his life is quite cheerful. But as time goes on he is struck down in total innocence by a most pathetic circumstance. In the fall his millstream becomes polluted with a repellent, slimy substance that kills the fish, clogs his wheel, and exudes an unbearable odor. The stink is such that his customers from the town must, with sorrow and regret, abandon him, and his employees finally just quit. This is not much of a mystery; it is apparent that the pollution is caused by the effluent from a sugar-beet factory upstream. Adam Asche, a young chemist, orphaned son of an old friend of Pfister, whom Pfister had made his own son's tutor and otherwise supported, agrees to research the matter and help Pfister bring suit against the factory. The suit is successful, as the factory is ordered to pay the miller an indemnity for every day it pollutes the stream. But this judgment saves neither the stream nor the mill, and the victory cannot console Pfister, who not long afterward dies broken-hearted in the ruin of his honest, gratifying, and generous way of life.

As usual in many of Raabe's most refined works, this story is not told through linear narration, but is mediated in thoughtful reminiscence. The "summer vacation notebook" is a private composition of Pfister's son Ebert, vacationing from his teaching job in Berlin and on his honeymoon, spent in elegiac remembrance in the last four weeks of the mill, which has been sold and is to be torn down to make room for industrial expansion. The architect and the workmen of the new order are scrambling around, a little impatient with the delay. The composition of the memoir continues on the train back to Berlin and in the city, thus indicating the narrator's assimilation into his new, forward-looking way of life. The result is a subtle counterpoint of present and past, with exceptional integration of imaginative resources and imagery, and a slyness of tone on Raabe's part that keeps the reader on the *qui vive. Pfister's Mill* has received little critical attention until relatively recently,[2] though I consider it one of his most finely wrought works. Furthermore, it seems clear that such interest as it has drawn in our time is owing to the apparent relevance of its ecological theme.

According to Raabe, the editor of the first magazine to which he offered *Pfister's Mill* rejected it on the grounds that it stank too much (16: 520-21). The editor's solicitude for the tender sensibilities of the reading public of the 1880s is understandable, for it certainly is the stinkiest German novel I know of in the whole nineteenth century. Whether it is the first German novel to deal significantly with an issue of ecology I am not able to say. Nearly fifty years earlier Karl Immermann's *Die Epigonen (The Epigones,* 1835-36), considered the first German novel to portray an industrial milieu, stressed the oppressive pall of air pollution generated from an industrial enterprise, though the novel is resolved in an evasive and historically futile dismantlement of the industry.[3] In any case, the concern was not new to Raabe. Horst Denkler, in one of the genuinely worthwhile studies of *Pfister's Mill* of recent times,[4] points out that mills associated with polluted streams, as images of obsolescence in changing times, appear elsewhere in Raabe, for example, in *Abu Telfan* (1867), where a mill, put out of business by industry, is a refuge of peace and serenity, but is surrounded by ghostly, dirty water (7: 230), or in *The Innerste* (1876), where there are two mills no longer in existence at the time of the narration (12: 104). The pollution of the Innerste, which makes the stream bloodthirsty and causes it to cry out, goes back to the *eighteenth century*. Other examples might be added to Denkler's. The stream in the town where the candy factory is located in *Fabian and Sebastian* (1882) is polluted (15: 66), and later, in *Stuffcake* (1891), the narrator remarks that the town, which has been spared by history, is free of stink in the atmosphere (18: 156). In the unfinished novel *Altershausen*, a park attendant explains to the protagonist Feyerabend that air pollution is driving out the birds and insects, and Feyerabend predicts to himself that by the end of the twentieth century mankind will have conquered nature and children's nature books will be bibliographical rarities. His desire to learn to take walks again, he muses, is not increased by the Biblical verse (Gen. 1:28): " . . . replenish the earth, and subdue it: and have dominion over the fish of the sea, and over the fowl of the air, and over every living thing that moveth upon the earth" (20: 213-14). This aspect of the advent of the modern world was thus clearly in the front of Raabe's mind for a great many years.

The main thing to notice about *Pfister's Mill* is how difficult he makes it to conform the novel to either of two different sets of pre-formed expectations. The first is the notion, widespread in literary history, that nineteenth-century German fiction was oblivious to modern social and political developments. This is a legend, based on a severely reduced canon, as though Adalbert Stifter were the only mid-century novelist in the German language. It should be laid to rest. In part it is a consequence of measuring German literature of the time against the major novels of France, England, and, to a lesser extent, America. But nineteenth-century German society and politics evolved *differently*, and the German writers, many of whom, like Raabe, were quite cosmopolitan readers, were aware of this. Furthermore, to *resist* modern evolution, to try to salvage values that appear to be threatened, is not to ignore it or to pretend that the changes are not taking place. Such resistance may be conservative—as Raabe to some extent was—or reactionary, which he decidedly was not—but it is one kind of relationship to the modern. If one has a temperamental preference for the progressive over the conservative, as I do, one may regret this, and even feel that it injures the artistic vision. But there are some issues—and ecology is one of them—in which genuine conservative values have been revived in the most progressive minds, coming to war with another sense of the progressive that has come to seem traditional. There are some neat ironies here, which I shall not go into except to say that they require more acuteness of historical sensibility than they regularly receive. An awareness of this irony in our contemplation of *Pfister's Mill* may well make the novel seem unusually "modern" and relevant.

Anyway, as far as alleged indifference to contemporary concerns goes, we can forget about that in the matter of *Pfister's Mill*. It has been known for a long time that the story of the pollution of the millstream, its investigation, and the suit against the factory, is based closely upon an actual event.[5] It was an important case. On the one hand, sugar-beet refining was a significant industry in the economically insecure Duchy of Braunschweig; on the other, the condition of the water was reaching crisis proportions. In the winter after *Pfister's Mill* was published, the drinking water supply of the city of Braunschweig broke down from the pollution.[6] Raabe followed the scientific aspect of the case fairly closely. The "odeur de Pfister" (16: 50) that ruins the mill was, as we know from the historical record and from the novel, the familiar rotten-eggs smell of hydrogen sulfide (16: 76). The excess of slimy algae produced by over-enrichment of the water, so commonplace today, is recognizably described. In other matters Raabe deviated somewhat from the record. One curious detail is that, while in the real case the factory was ordered to pay an indemnity of one thousand marks a day,[7] in the novel the figure is one hundred (16: 165). Whether intentional or not, the effect of this trivialized sum is to deepen the pathos of Pfister's end. Furthermore, as it turned out, the real case was not fully won; two weeks after Raabe finished the manuscript, a higher court reversed part of the judgment in favor of the factory.[8] I do not think Raabe ignored this in the interest of a harmonized conclusion, for the futility of the legal victory is evident enough in his story. There is an avoidance of trivial melodrama as well as a deepened irony in the circumstance that Pfister *wins* the lawsuit, since the victory really makes no difference. The novel deals not with a resolution but with a conflict, as Pfister's lawyer puts it, of "Germany's rivers and trout streams asgainst Germany's sewage and other substances. Germania's green Rhine, blue Danube, blue-green Neckar, yellow Weser against Germania's other effluents" (16: 116). Another point is that the young professor who investigated the case, an acquaintance of Raabe's named Heinrich Beckurts, devoted the rest of his scientific life to campaigning for clean water,[9] while his counterpart in the novel is a very different sort of character, as we shall see.

This brings us to the difficulty with the other preconception that we might bring to the novel as readers. What position should we expect Raabe to take? From start to finish there is a not unremitting but recurrent atmosphere of elegiac melancholy in his writing, which, since it appears to have little ground in the relatively even and placid course of his personal life, must be an environmental and sociological response. The customary view of his consistent thematic concern is well captured in a recent observation on *Altershausen*, in which

> a narrative pattern is easily recognized, which Raabe again and again uses as a ground-plan: the construction of a positive counter-world in contrast to the critically judged reality of the age. The *saeculum*, the reality of the late nineteenth century, presents itself as a stormy civilizing progress that drives out the natural (vegetative and animal) life, then as the world of bourgeois efficiency, of achievement, of rapid careers, of success, of honors and decorations, of public recognition; finally also the thoughtless (not necessarily malign) insensitivity to the suffering of others.[10]

Recently Horst Daemmrich has made a similar point: "In small enclaves, people adhere to spiritual values, gentleness, and love, whereas in the technologically oriented society engineers plan to clear the land for roads, railways, and new housing."[11] In *Pfister's Mill*, Joachim Worthmann has remarked, there is a pervasive opposition of the secluded refuge and the world, of the self-realization of humane individuals versus the mass tendencies of the time, of traditional culture versus technological civilization, of timeless humanity versus temporally bound purpose.[12]

From a novel concerned with industrial water pollution by a writer so described we know what we should expect: a mobilization of conservative resistance, which, in the light of contemporary relevance, has been transformed into progressive resistance. Raabe knew a hundred years ago what we should know now. There is much in *Pfister's Mill* to conform to this expectation. Its very form is elegiac. The lost paradise of childhood is set in parallel with the lost values of the world—one might well think back to Joseph von Eichendorff, whose family estate, retrospectively perceived as a kind of earthy idyll, was lost to the family in the Napoleonic Wars. The mill's function in a world of useful work and communal conviviality has been destroyed, and what is to replace it is unaesthetic, dirty, and crass. Furthermore, the course of events has cost the amiable miller his living and his life. The memoirist is reflective and rather sad, as befits the circumstances.

But that is far from all there is to it. Several strongly stressed features of the novel work across the grain of this reading. It is necessary to observe that significant things have been happening well before the catastrophe sets in. In the first place, a transformation has taken place in the function of the mill, and it is not only that the water-driven mill is becoming obsolete in the industrial age. For, counter to that development, it has become a place of recreation for the townspeople and the students. To be sure, mills had served as entertainment centers well back into history, especially since their smooth floors were suitable for dancing. We find a mention of a mill serving such a function in the scene "Before the Gate" in the first part of Goethe's *Faust* (line 810). Ebert Pfister thinks of his mill as having been a gathering place, especially for student fraternities, far into the past. But we may see the historical depth a little differently; after all, at the time of the story, the fraternities themselves were but two generations old. What he has experienced as a boy is more modern than antiquated: the town is coming to the country and, so to speak, colonizing it. The boundary between the urban and the rural is dissolving; while it looks as though the rural is being made available as a refuge from the urban, in fact it is the urban that is transforming the rural, as we can see in every tourist stop today. This is an aspect of "the transition of the German nation from a peasant people into an industrial state" (16: 114), though that often quoted remark is made in quite another mood, when Pfister grimly takes his traditional miller's ax off the wall to go to law and do battle in the maelstrom of modern times. Ebert puts his own growth into parallel with the development of the German nation: "Like the boy from Pfister's mill, the whole German people had become different; for the years eighteen hundred sixty-six and seventy had happened, and people counted, reckoned, and weighed debit and credit with rather thick, hot heads towards the middle of the seventies" (16: 42; it is reasonable to suspect a satirical allusion here to Gustav Freytag's best-seller, *Debit and Credit*). Even Ebert's childhood memory of the idyllic landscape of his childhood contains here and there "a puffing factory smokestack" (16: 11). Therefore to see in the novel a firm opposition of the traditional and the modern, the timeless and temporal, is inadequate; these boundaries have become porous.

Furthermore, though the Pfisters have been millers for generations, this Pfister has presciently encouraged his son to study so that he might take up a profession. The freedom of sons to deviate from the trades of their fathers and to rise above their horizon is one of the most significant sociological symptoms of the transformation of a traditional into a modern society, one that in nineteenth-century Germany had been bitterly deplored by genuine reactionaries. It is a tribute to Pfister's heart and his wisdom that this has been accomplished by and not against his will. Some inner premonition that the mill would not endure impelled him (16: 20; cf. 47); but it was an educated premonition, for, as he tells his son when he is dying, listening to the conversations of the students and townspeople has taught him why the mill could not survive against the factory (16: 174). While he could not, of course, have foreseen how important this decision would turn out to be, the fact is that he has saved the son from being dragged into the ruin that engulfs the father, and there is a sense in which Ebert's memoir is a loving tribute to his father for having spared him one of the worst of nineteenth-century fates: the technological obsolescence that befell, for example, the weavers in Germany, from the famous proto-revolutionaries of Peterswaldau in 1844, inscribed in literature by Heine and Hauptmann, to Karl May's pauperized father, whose son became a criminal.

Then there is Ebert Pfister's sweet and charming nineteen-year-old wife Emmy. We might call her Thoroughly Modern Emmy. A child of Berlin, she is out of place in the elegiac honeymoon Ebert has inflicted upon her. She loves her husband dearly, and she is not without a certain conventional appreciation for the charm of the deserted mill. She can respect Ebert's feelings about his doomed childhood paradise, but she cannot empathize with them. She sleeps a good deal, and sometimes she can barely keep her eyes open as Ebert reminisces, though she claims to be listening (of course, Raabe is, as usual, quietly provoking the reader here). At one point she regrets that she has not brought her sewing machine with her (16: 77). The reader of today might well be amused at this touch: Emmy quite literally would like to put the machine into the garden. On the whole she finds her husband's feelings about the lost mill somewhat quaint, and she exhibits more interest in the new enterprise that is to replace it. She wonders why the elder Pfister had not covered himself by investing in the sugar-beet factory (16: 118), the sort of thing a more coolly adaptable character, Heinrich Schaumann in *Stuffcake*, was later to do. She is delightfully unburdened by culture. When Ebert quotes an elegiac canzone of Leopardi, she brightly asks: "Did you just write that, little man?" (16: 111-12).

Some critics have quite strangely seen Emmy as a negative figure, as a fluffy, complacent representative of the crass modern.[13] This is wholly impossible; Raabe has given her too many attractive and loving features. Ebert adores her enthusiastically, and he understands perfectly that she was not "in her element" at the mill (16: 163). Fairley observed intelligently that "what [Emmy] shrank from was not so much the ghostly old mill as the side of Ebert's nature that drew him to it,"[14] and Worthmann expanded the point by remarking that in her naivety and gaiety she has the function of preventing Ebert from falling victim to sentimental memories and losing himself in the lost idyll.[15] Ebert himself is wise enough to recognize this: "But Emmy was, thank goodness, not so concerned about it, and I was not, either, nearly so much as by rights I should have been. The child is charming; and we are both healthy and young, and Berlin is a big city, and one can achieve a good deal there if one keeps one's eyes open and also keeps one's other four senses together and is not without grit in one's head" (16: 15). She helps him put his elegiac memories into a perspective that does not burden the present.

However, the real sticking place for a comfortably relevant reading of *Pfister's Mill* is the remarkable character of the young chemist Adam Asche, one of the oddest fellows in Raabe's gallery of often sufficiently eccentric types. Asche is a man of utterly determined practicality, applied not to pure science but to profitable industry. In a wonderfully comic scene, we see him in a shabby laundry, cooking like an alchemist. As an example of Raabe's often hilarious skill at weaving the tag lines of bourgeois culture into inappropriate contexts, the grinning Asche misquotes from Schiller's earnest poem, "The Veiled Statue of Sais": "Heavier, my son than you think, / Is this thin gauze—for your hand / Indeed light, but a hundredweight for my— purse" (16: 59; the replaced word is "conscience"). Asche's very ambience is stink; he has been evicted from every place he has previously lived in because of it. But it can't be helped, he says, "that science in its connection with industry does not have the finest fragrance" (16: 60). (One thinks here involuntarily of the famous and grim quip attributed to Saint-Just that revolutions are not made with musk and rose-water.) Asche has foreseen what has happened to the mill: he points out "that the River Styx flowed right through the land of Arcadia and that everyone in the nineteenth century who has a garden and a mill on the charming water must be prepared for various surprises" (16: 64). Asche's reference to Arcadia is not just a turn of phrase; it reflects his explicit conviction that the idyllic environment of the past is coming to be as irretrievably gone as any of the lost paradises of legend and imagination: "They were very hospitable there, Father Pfister—in Arcadia, namely—and they worshipped the god Pan, and in poesy and imagination it will always remain a paradise—like Pfister's mill for me!—whatever may become of it in the bad real world" (ibid.).

Asche, gratefully loyal to Pfister, is pleased to donate his expertise to make the case against the factory, though he asserts that he himself intends to pollute "a sparkling spring, a crystal stream, a majestic river, in short, some kind of watercourse in the idyllic green German Empire as soon and as infamously as possible" (16: 67). He makes it clear that he is no enemy of the messy water per se, and in one place he cleverly remarks that the millstream stinks "only because mankind can't have its world sweet enough" (16: 87). The reference, of course, is to the sugar produced by the factory, but the point has a larger application: the pollution is a trade-off, a cost, for other values that human beings want. Later Asche is involved in a dry-cleaning establishment, splendidly named Schmurky and Co., whose smell of benzine is worse than the odor of the mill. "Benzine," cries Asche happily. "Grandiose progress, giant achievements, stupefying innovations!" (16: 127). He realizes his ambition to found his own untranslatable "Erdenlappenlumpenundfetzenreinigungsinstitut" (16: 141), and we see this cleaning establishment in the last scene of the novel, polluting the Spree, though the rowboats and sailboats float about as though the mess were "something quite normal and highly indifferent" (16: 177). Asche sits on the veranda reading Homer in the original Greek as an antidote to the pollution.

Fairley remarked: "It may be considered fortunate for Raabe's story or for Vater Pfister that his mill did not stand in Asche's line of progress. Not that he was not a good fellow in his way and highly entertaining in spots."[16] But this characterization does not capture the full peculiarity of the case. In anyone else's novel "the incipient capitalist" (16: 143) would be a horrible example, and the fact is that, generally speaking, the ambitious careerists receive unfriendly treatment in Raabe's fictional universe. As for Asche, he is virtually gross in his allegiance to his own success and material profit come hell or stinking water. He is unburdened by pieties; when Pfister gives him a good silver watch out of gratitude for the care he has taken of Ebert as a boy, he promptly pawns it (16: 39). Pfister, despite his affection for him, says he trusts Asche only as far as he can see him, and he does not put his son into Asche's care as a student (16: 40-41). But the dying Pfister attests him a "sense for the ideal"; if Asche has plunged into this puzzling modern world and joined the side of the factories, "then that is probably the way the dear Lord thinks it best for the coming years and times" (16: 175). Ultimately Pfister transfers to Asche his traditional miller's ax as a symbol of the metamorphosis of one age into another; he does so in return for Asche's promise to see the mill advantageously sold. At one point the impecunious but self-assured young man seems to Ebert to have the character that would qualify him as Bismarck's successor (16: 71). He is a positive personality, even in adversity: Ebert, playing on the circumstance that

Asche's father had been a dyer (*Schönfärber*), says that he never knew anyone "with the same capacity to give the burdens of this world a pleasant coloration" (16: 24). He exhibits that generosity of self that is fundamental to all of Raabe's finest characters. Like them, he expresses himself in the distinctive Raabean idiolect of verbose obliquity and sly allusiveness; he thus clearly belongs to the alternative community, though he is an unusual sort of member of it. His hyperbolic confessions of his own rapacity make him an ironic character, but he is also ironically treated by the author. It seems to me that in Asche's delineation there is a collapse of the fictional and the authorial voice in a larger irony that in its stubborn ambivalence is resistant to interpretive resolution.

Raabe, after all, did not take lightly the offenses to decency and civility spreading in modern society. Instead, the peculiar tone of *Pfister's Mill* suggests that he was visibly and intentionally refusing to take the position that one supposes must have come naturally to him. This refusal generates in the novel an openness, a suspension, that challenges the reader's judgment, as Denkler has acutely argued. Raabe did not want to yield wholly to an elegiac backward-looking sense of the present; he combatted this tendency in himself, which is imaged in the novel by the characters reduced to sterility by their inability to adapt at all to the present: Emmy's father, so alienated from the present that he spends his leisure hours in a cemetery, cheerfully hoping that his grave will stand in the way of progress for thirty years (16: 34); and the alcoholic poet Lippoldes, a cautionary example of the vulnerability of "a too bright, too nervous, too imaginative human being" (16: 83), who drowns in the millstream in a state of inebriation encouraged by the employees of the sugar-beet factory, who have found the old codger amusing. The case is reinforced by reference to the sad end of another failed poet in real life, Ferdinand Alexander Schnezler (16: 133), whose late Romantic poem, "The Abandoned Mill," is threaded through the text. Finally, there is the old servant Christine, who raised Ebert in place of his deceased mother, now so demoralized by the loss of the mill that she would like to be buried on the spot, and she must be shored up by Ebert and Emmy with considerable patience and generosity.

One remarkable feature of the novel is the manner in which the tragic and the pathetic are woven together with the humorous tones and the efforts to maintain good cheer, not harmoniously but dissonantly. An example is the scene of the Christmas dinner to which Asche, who is preparing his chemical analysis, has been invited; the stink of the mill competes with the fragrance of the roast goose. The inebriated Lippoldes, who has been invited to provide a Christmas poem, instead climbs onto the table and recites gloomy verses of impending death and doom, to Pfister's great discomfort (16: 85-86). The imperfectly harmonized layers are also evident in the handling of the time dimensions. Ebert writes his memoir on his summer vacation and thinks of that gloomy Christmas in the past: "How it snows here on these pages despite the summer sunshine! How the north wind blows in cold despite the July heat!" (16: 109). Not only is the sense of a present oppressed by the past palpable; the present itself is dissolving: "The days in the mill seemed to grow ever more beautiful, the more it neared its end. And it neared its end irrevocably, irreparably" (16: 110).

Denkler has usefully assembled evidence that Raabe did not want to stand fast against the present, as much as it worried and sometimes discouraged him, but sought to put some long-term trust in the course of history and to see the present, the *saeculum*, as a temporary epoch from which the endurance of humane individuals would salvage a better future.[17] Denkler rightly says that Raabe's narrative perspective is not wholly identified with any of his characters.[18] For example, one of the effects of Emmy's role in the novella is to make the first-person narrator Ebert responsible for the elegiac Romanticism of its tone, not necessarily the author. But, though Raabe maintains distance from his characters, he is not wholly aloof from them, does not wholly objectify them. They are parts and pieces of his superintending authorial consciousness.

As to the interpretive dilemma the novel poses, Denkler's position, to put it bluntly, is this: Raabe did not understand the issue he was dealing with. His honest bewilderment generates the open form that is a "modern" feature of the work and encourages the modern reader to think the matter through further. In one limited respect I think Denkler is right. Raabe seems primarily to have viewed the matter of pollution *aesthetically*. I say primarily, for the effect upon Pfister is worse than that and indeed fatal. But he does not die from the pollution; he dies in a concatenation of fate deriving from the historical circumstance that, as Asche implies, water-driven mills located downstream from industrial enterprises are doomed. In general, however, the stress is on the assault upon the senses of sight and smell. That the pollution is dangerous to health and life, and, for that matter, ultimately to the overall economic welfare, does not seem to have been in Raabe's mind and I do not think that he knew it. This is not surprising; there are millions of people even today who do not know it. Strictly speaking, there is in this novel no question of ecology, that is, of balance in nature and man's balance with nature. What we have is an offense, but not a threat in the dimensions that enlightened people perceive today.

Otherwise, however, Denkler's argument has a few troubling features. In the first place it takes as a premise that *Pfister's Mill* accepts the economic development of which the pollution is a by-product as historically timely. But this is to evade or to abolish the ironic dilemma the novel poses. The story it tells is *tragic*, though the tragedy appears to be buffered by other considerations. It accepts nothing, it seems to me; it *displays*. In fact, Denkler's argument obliges us to take Pfister's dying peroration, in which he achieves a resigned acceptance of the historical development and even advises Ebert to invest his inheritance, when the mill is sold, in the industry that supersedes it, as the message of the novel, even though Denkler himself has said that the narration does not identify with any of its characters. Pfister's dying speech is eloquent by reason of its humaneness, tolerance, and balance, and it has a summary effect on the reader by reason of its placement very close to the end of the chronologically altered narration. Nevertheless, when seen from the perspective of the novel as a whole, it is but one voice, if a prominent one, among several.

A controlling assumption in Denkler's argument, of conventional Marxist provenance, needless to say, is that the laws of capitalist development were opaque to Raabe. But the problem in *Pfister's Mill* has less to do with capitalism than with industrialization, or, to put it another way, with the élan of the *partial* maximization of human and material resources for *partial* ends.[19] To argue that Raabe saw no solutions to the problem and therefore left the form of the novel open, laying upon the readers the obligation to think the matter through for themselves, is not unreasonable, but to my mind still goes too far toward requiring from the novel a message with a use-value for us, thus perpetuating under different auspices the uses to which his texts were put in the past. What, anyway, is the solution he should have seen? I do not believe it is correct to say that he *accepted* the course of history and the consequences of industrialization presented in the novel, and I am uncomfortable with interpretations based upon an assumption that a writer of his sensibility and acuteness did not understand what he was doing. There is nothing in the text, confidentially written as are all of his works, that suggests he was bewildered or did not see clearly what was happening around him. He did not go out of his way to ascribe positive features to the industrial development. There is no trace of the systematically presented industrial heroism of a novel like Friedrich Spielhagen's *Hammer und Amboß* (*Hammer and Anvil*), a full fifteen years earlier.

One way to approach the question would be to look at *Pfister's Mill* not just in regard to Raabe's view of history, as Denkler does, but in the context of his literary evolution in general. It was absurd that a publisher in rejecting *this* novel complained that his books had come to resemble one another too much (16: 520-21). For it seems to me that this is yet another of his boundary works, in this case an experiment driven across the author's own grain, an effort to integrate into his instinctive and individual outlook aspects of his modern environment that were foreign and troublesome to that outlook. He tests these foreign and hostile aspects to see how far he might go to encompass them with tolerance. His deepest yearning was for peace among men. *Pfister's Mill* might be seen as an exercise on the author's part in the discipline of tolerance for the sake of peaceable relations, *even though he was not of a peaceable nature himself.* The result is not only a stinky, but also a dissonant and in some degree irritating work. The dissonance is not a flaw, nor is it an effect that we are obliged to harmonize with our comprehensive view of Raabe. It is another excursion to an outer boundary, and its experimental nature gives it a special intensity, even nervousness, that certainly was not absent from his disposition.

The relevance of *Pfister's Mill* to our current concerns is an interesting but not necessarily a central feature of the work. We evade the novel more than we approach it if we spend our time worrying whether Raabe did or did not understand the historical, social, and economic determinants of water pollution, whether he did or did not yield to the historical inevitability of industrialism in the German Reich, whether we can or cannot adapt the novel to our contemporary attitudes on these matters. To do so is to fail to attend to its remarkable literary virtues, its stylistic and formal control, its, by Raabe's standards, unusual degree of unforced symbolic integration, its refined irony. It is a good example of the advisability of regarding him, in his alert, self-critical integrity, as a writer very much *dans le vrai* in his own time, bringing his formidable artistic resources to bear on competing values with a flexibility that distinguishes him from the assertive posture of his contemporaries such as Gutzkow, Freytag, Spielhagen, and even, to be frank about it, Keller.

CHAPTER 19

Stuffcake Pro and
Contra

◨

RAABE's expressed opinion that *Stuffcake* (1891) was his best work (18: 426-27) has been seconded, on the whole, by literary criticism. In fact, it is clear that this rich and difficult novel has been one of the main levers for rescuing him from his "friends" and making him available to a more differentiated criticism on modern principles. Romano Guardini's now classic paper on *Stuffcake* of 1932[1] can be seen as the starting point of the modern phase of Raabe criticism. But the history of serious critical attention to this text goes back at least to Ahrbeck's monograph of 1926.[2] In view of the detailed and often subtle care with which the novel has been examined over the years, it may seem presumptuous to offer yet another analytic discussion of it. However, one of the consequences of this finely focused attention has been a slight breakdown in the evaluative consensus. One curious symptom of it emerged in the bosom of the Raabe Society itself: a rather eccentric though not unobservant argument, based on something called "psychobiology," that, since Raabe agreed that all moral life is determined and no one can be held responsible for what he is, the frontal attack on the *canaille* and on Eduard through the figure of Heinrich Schaumann is overwrought.[3] More fiercely, Paul Derks in his psychoanalytic study has denounced one of the troubling features of the dénouement of the story, the apparent abandonment of Störzer's innocent daughter-in-law and grandchildren to the philistine censoriousness of the townspeople, as a further link in the chain of injustice and insensitivity that Schaumann claims to have broken but in fact merely perpetuates.[4] Behind these arguments, acknowledged by both critics, lies a prestigious opinion: that of the French scholar Claude David.[5] For him Schaumann's whole proceeding is a kind of self-deceptive fraud. In purporting to do battle against the philistines, Schaumann in reality recapitulates and reincarnates German philistine postures, especially in his social withdrawal, his extreme self-involvement, and his irresponsibility toward the course of events in which he himself has intervened. *Stuffcake* is a nihilistic humoresque that opens abysses and covers them over immediately. Insofar as the novel is an allegory of Raabe's art, as he claimed, it emerges as sterile, escapist, and conservative. David's reprehension falls upon Raabe himself, for, given Raabe's explicit self-identification with the figure of Schaumann, condemnation of the fictional character tends to reflect upon the author. David's argument is in fact a demurrer against the elevation of Raabe's standing in criticism of recent times.

It is this challenge to which I am attempting to respond. On the one hand, it seems to me that uneasiness about Schaumann's character and consequently about the implications of the story is well justified. But, on the other, it also appears to me that Raabe's moral sensitivity is as much to be trusted as that of any nineteenth-century German writer, though his moral vision was neither simple nor confident. Like much else in him, it was compact of searchings and yearnings. Before devaluating him and a work of such obvious artistic accomplishment, I would be more inclined to ask once again whether we have been reading it aright. Following are some suggestions for reorganizing the insights of modern criticism in pursuit of a consensus on at least some issues and, finally, for relaxing some of the moral and ideological doubts the text has raised.

In the first place, I think it axiomatic that, as some though not all critics have recognized, any comprehensive analysis of *Stuffcake* must begin with the narrator Eduard.[6] To deny this is at the same time to undercut any claim to the novel's excellence. If we assert that this narrator, through whose consciousness the whole story is mediated and who takes up a good deal of our attention, is of no significance, we declare the author incompetent. Indeed, as between Schaumann and Eduard, the latter is the more difficult character to grasp. This is partly because he is located in an area of transition between traditional and modern narration.[7] On the one hand, he is a first-person version of the nineteenth-century omniscient narrator, with a preternatural memory, especially for conversation, and a reliably realistic apprehension of phenomena. This is a convention that as readers we are meant to accept. On the other hand, he is an unreliable narrator, not so much in what he recounts, as in his own response to his experience. He registers what has happened, but he does not seem able fully to comprehend it.[8] This creates a dissonance in the novel that contributes a surprising amount of tension to it, considering its ostentatious absence of plot and its spectacular wordiness. Eduard is, virtually simultaneously, confessional and evasive, and for this reason it is necessary to keep an eye on him at every turn. It might be added parenthetically that Raabe is rather delicate with Eduard. He is not contemptible, nor is he a fool. In fact Raabe identifies Eduard with some of his own views, for example his (narratively totally irrelevant) annoyance at the contemporary German orthographic reform or the passage where Eduard sets his lighted cigar in contrast to the eternal stars (18: 8, 9), which is typical of Raabe's secularly relativized idealism. Hubert Ohl has pointed out that he is not a wholly average type; his imaginative inspiration by Le Vaillant's travel book distinguishes him from his fellow citizens.[9]

It is true that he is a bit of a philistine, as is shown by his assertive claim to culture in the very first sentences, not to speak of his allusion to Platen, of all people, as evidence of it (18: 7), and the juxtaposition of a Spitzweg painting with a lionskin in his South African home (18: 51) is really quite comic. He is smug about his personal acquaintance with the "president" (18: 8; presumably Paul Kruger of the Transvaal). Eduard, of course, tells these things on himself; he is capable of a self-deprecating irony. But his irony floats, as it were, in the liquid of his not very sharply defined self. Some of it is above the surface, self-aware and therefore sovereign, but some is below, more clearly sensed by the reader than by Eduard himself. It has been claimed that Eduard is the only one of Raabe's first-person narrators who lacks a surname,[10] a device that also causes him to float somewhat, as though he lacked an anchor in social existence. Moreover, it would not have taken two explicit allusions (18: 53, 123), to make us think of the "young baron" so named by Goethe in the first sentence of *Die Wahlverwandtschaften* (*Elective Affinities*). Like Goethe's Eduard, he is a not insubstantial person, but a little shallow and a little selfish, and more than a little inadequate to a challenge of serious moral dimensions. Once in a while he expresses highly conventional views, for example, early on when he is thankful that in his boyhood schoolboys were still beaten (18: 26), and near the end when he comments on the refusal of the Royal Post to send a representative to Störzer's funeral after his decades-old crime has been exposed: "and certainly it [the Post] was in this regard not in the wrong; it was wholly right" (18: 203).

It is evident that the Eduard who pens the narration is in flight. (Raabe's often discussed in-joke of naming Eduard's ship "Leonhard Hagebucher" seems to me simply to suggest that he is a mirror image of Hagebucher in *Abu Telfan*, moving in the opposite direction. The Eduard we get to know is not a returnee but a refugee.)[11] His first written words are a sigh of relief: "Back on board!" (18:7). This opening reminds me of the exclamation at the beginning of Thomas Mann's *Tristan*: "Here is 'Einfried,' the sanatorium!" Both are an odd catching of breath, unsettling to the reader and at least retrospectively ominous. In the course of the narration Eduard becomes progressively more stressed, and at times he has to grasp for the self-regard that seemed more or less intact when he began. The prosperous South African colonist and plantation owner has some pride in his accomplishment in life, but before he is halfway through his recollection of his experience he is speaking of his African life as "the most desolate, long-drawn-out, if also most nourishing foreign life" (18: 81), and eventually Schaumann has made him feel his life is simply trivial (18: 109). His increasingly tense obsessiveness as he writes is underlined in his shifts to the narrative present on board ship, an aspect of the text that would itself deserve some detailed critical attention. One occurs after the recollection of his humiliation by Schaumann at their first parting when they were youths; another, following upon his account of his meal with Schaumann and his wife, finds him with a complete loss of appetite, which he ascribes to the tropical climate. To the passengers he seems obsessive and to the captain "ever more eerie," and at length he has the curious thought that the captain might think of him as the ship's Jonah (18: 195). In these shifts there are some objective images set at the authorial level of narration; they all involve potentially impinging powerful forces that are deflected. There seems to be a fire on board, but it is a false alarm; there is a storm, but it turns out to be not serious; the ship lands at St. Helena, but Eduard has too much on his mind with Schaumann to contemplate the ambiguous heroism of Napoleon; and the captain fishes up a shark but, to Eduard's relief, there are no human segments found in it. All this deflection appears to relate more or less symbolically to Eduard's pattern of avoidance.

His fundamental evasiveness lies in his effort to maintain the notion of a cordial friendship between himself and Schaumann, despite the overwhelming evidence against it provided in his own account. As Schaumann forcefully points out to him, Eduard does not think of visiting him during his whole two weeks in his hometown, and the thought occurs only by association with the news of Störzer's death. (In fact he had neglected to look up Störzer, too, despite the man's importance for the shaping of his life, and he regrets this oversight when it is too late. As far as we can see, he has spent the whole two weeks in the tavern gassing with the conventional townspeople.) Both to himself and to Schaumann he constantly tries to deflect the implications of this simple fact. To himself he muses: "Eduard, shall you have saved the best bite of the cake for yourself till the last?" (18: 11), and he thinks of Schaumann as "my other friend of childhood, field, forest, and meadow" (18: 26). That he has never written to this great friend after leaving home he blames on the circumstance that no one writes letters any more in the modern "postcard age" (18: 30), which is patent nonsense. Schaumann, of course, will have none of it; he alternates between contradicting Eduard and devising sarcastic hyperboles about their great friendship. This habit apparently goes back to their youthful relations; at their first parting, when Schaumann has several times told Eduard of the superfluousness of his presence at the scene with Tina, he makes sardonic reference to Damon and Pythias, David and Jonathan (18: 35), and in the course of their conversation he alludes to Pylades (18: 97). Near the end he calls himself Eduard's "most exact friend" (18: 182), an odd locution that in the circumstances has a threatening edge.

We need not go into the textual evidence showing that, while Eduard persistently tries to dissociate himself from the mob of boys that tormented Schaumann (and Tina), Schaumann just as persistently identifies him with them, as this has been noticed by all readers. But despite half-hearted admissions, Eduard never stops twisting and turning. At one point he virtually subverts one of Schaumann's major leitmotifs: "You wanted to talk about the green, living hedges of our youth, old Heinrich, dear old friend!" (18: 83). The hedge is the locus of Schaumann's lonely abandonment, of his forced constitution of himself by himself; Eduard's first-person plural is inappropriate and insensitive. In the train, at the beginning of his precipitate flight, Eduard does his best to trivialize the conflict: "Mankind still had the power to prevail out of fat, calm, tranquillity over against the most sinewy, lean, flighty conquistadorism. Heinrich Schaumann, called Stuffcake, had thoroughly attended to this for me" (18: 204), and he has a last glimpse of Schaumann's fortified retreat, the Red Redoubt, "as a sunlit point in the most beautiful green of home" (18: 206). Dubious and inflated remarks like this have been too often applied as interpretive keys to the text as a whole.

Eduard has another device of evasion that is more subtle and has not been remarked upon by criticism. He makes an intermittent effort to turn his account into a love story, thus sentimentalizing it. To some extent he is tricked into this by Schaumann, who deflects Eduard's attention to Tina. Eduard is clearly much taken with her, even though she is no "Aphrodite" (18: 113) and is in fact a plumpish, graying, near forty-year-old housewife. He is, of course, struck by the contrast with the tigerish girl he remembers from their childhood, a contrast Schaumann wishes to impress on him for his own purposes. But the stress Eduard puts on the affection between Schaumann and Tina is excessive to the point of irrelevance. Raabe told the Jensens: "A love story is just what the thing is not supposed to be,"[12] and we may believe him. Eduard, however, has reasons to wish it were.

This sentimentalizing of Schaumann's domestic existence brings us to a crucial interpretive point. If there is any one concept that permeates both the text of *Stuffcake* and the commentaries on it, it is comfortableness (*Behaglichkeit*) and its cognates. This is important, as it bears on the question whether Raabe, even in one of the latest and most mature of his works, is capitulating to or even advocating the alleged Original Sin of the German bourgeoisie: Biedermeier withdrawal, complacent self-satisfaction, while the rest of the world, with its injustices and social agonies, is left to go hang. Now the reader of *Stuffcake* should note that it is Eduard, starting from his first sight of the renovated Red Redoubt, who reiterates the theme of comfortableness and perceives Schaumann's environment as a *locus amoenus*, a perfected idyll. To be sure, Schaumann systematically encourages him in this impression and, to be sure, it is true as far as it goes: Schaumann has carved out an oasis of gratifying private, even asocial existence. I would argue, however, that this is not the *main point*. If we accept it as the main point, we join Eduard in his evasions. This consideration obliges us to turn from Eduard to Schaumann.

As a personality, Schaumann is marked by two outstanding characteristics: a huge complacency concerning his present self, and an equally huge self-pity concerning his past self. He is also, as Schweckendiek has pointed out, not only addicted to self-praise, but insistently demanding of the praise of others.[13] One must ask if these characteristics do not constitute a kind of psychological antinomy. It is, of course, realistic enough that a childhood filled with humiliation, loneliness, failures to please parents, contemporaries, and governing institutions such as school, along with reiterated assaults on self-worth, is likely to reverberate through a lifetime and remain resistant to cure. But the last thing Schaumann has in mind is to present himself as a neurotic hobbled by his past. He is a victor; he has defeated everyone and realized himself against what he, at any rate, perceives as long odds. Still, there is a vast amount of unresolved tension in him. I must say I find it astonishing that any reader could take Eduard or Schaumann at their word that comfortableness is his governing characteristic.[14] Rather, the almost unbroken and insistent monologue reported by Eduard communicates tension, anger, and aggression.[15] Schaumann is full of ambiguities and antagonisms, which, as Detroy has said, make it difficult for the reader seeking unambiguous virtues to find solid ground.[16] Indeed, Schaumann says himself that the accident of the confrontation with Eduard relieves him of matters that would otherwise churn in his "unnecessarily overstimulated imagination" (18: 166). We are entitled to ask ourselves whether Schaumann is not, in his own way, an unreliable narrator. He is not only ironic and rid-dling, as Ohl has rightly pointed out;[17] he is manipulatively and inten-tionally misleading.

Our first task as readers is to revise the autobiographical account he supplies to Eduard. It may well be that he was fat and slow as a child, and that he felt he had been dropped on the ground like a slice of bread with the buttered side down (18: 66). Given the depth of his self-pity, he is no doubt sincere when he says he would rather have been born "as a jellyfish in the bitter salt flood than as Schaumann's boy, the fat, stupid Heinrich Schaumann" (ibid.). His view that this was all a matter of ineluctable fate—"I can really do nothing about it" (18: 62-63)—or that his mental gift lay in "contemplation" (*Anschauung*: Schau-mann) rather than "concept" (18: 117), I leave to philosophically inclined interpreters. But that the course of his life has been marked by these deficiencies or peculiarities there can be no question; as Ohl has said, his stress on them is a way of "teasing his listener."[18] From the outset he has been independent and strong-minded. This is exhib-ited early in his highly condescending attitude toward his parents.[19] Even in view of the pronounced lack of piety toward parents in Raabe's fictional world, Schaumann's dismissal of "a not only obsti-nate but also weepy Mama and an old man with a downright furious fixation on whatever professional study for his master son was nearest to hand" (18: 34) is striking. He makes up his mind to fail at his university studies "for the sake of my good parents" (18: 38), and ultimately he conquers his father as he does everyone else, extorting acceptance and a certain amount of respect for his course in life. He criticizes Tina for her rather automatic piety toward her dreadful fa-ther, Quakatz (18: 120), and in one passage he speaks of the great height from which he looks down not only on his own father, but on Eduard's, whom he calls "your ghastly old man" (18: 46-47), which is not without significance insofar as Eduard is his father's loyal and unquestioning son, hoping to hand down the parental wisdom to his own children in conservative tradition (18: 12). At an early stage Schaumann fixes his eye on the conquest of the Red Redoubt. The allegedly sluggish boy fights off a whole gang of Tina's tormentors. Although he insists he was unable to learn anything in school, includ-ing Latin, and professes gross embarrassment at Quakatz's request to help him research the *Corpus juris*, his wife contradicts him, saying that he was quite able to do it (18: 108). Tina, who does not play games with people, declares flatly: "he is a much cleverer and more learned person than he pretends to be" (18: 125), as indeed we can easily see. He fails at his university studies not out of incapacity, but out of disgust at the kind of human product such study yields.

Schaumann conquers the Red Redoubt and everyone in it. He faces down the rebellious and threatening servants of the dilapidated farmstead, then makes himself its chief farmhand. He thus must engage in some of the hardest physical labor known to mankind, especially with nineteenth-century tools. Eventually, though, he uses his head to relieve himself of it, leasing part of the land to sugar-beet manufacture and incidentally acquiring capital in the industry. He straightens out Quakatz's confused financial affairs and rescues him from those who tried to take advantage of his inattention and preoccupation with his own trouble. Schaumann has mastered the science of paleontology, in which he is clearly more than a dilettante, though according to him he clambers around the fossil digs only on account of doctor's orders, and when he receives an invitation from a learned society he of course scorns it. Above all he conquers the people. He wins over the ferociously suspicious Quakatz, manipulates him, and eventually manages his life as well as his death, dictating to the pastor the eulogy that not only chastises the townspeople for their prejudgment of Quakatz but also has the consequence of discovering—to Schaumann alone, naturally—Störzer as Kienbaum's killer. It should be observed that this discovery is not an accident, as Schaumann tends to describe it, but a direct result of his cleverness. Moreover, he sculpts the rough, wild girl Tina into the deeply loving, deeply respectful matron we see in Eduard's narration, an accomplishment in which he takes special and reiterated pride.

It would no doubt be anachronistic if today's reader were a little less impressed than Eduard by this accomplishment. Certainly Schaumann's success in civilizing Tina, in driving out her furies, is meant to be seen as a positive accomplishment. Still, one senses a certain loss in the taming of the shrew; a whole dimension of her personality has vanished without a trace. Schaumann is not much more inclined to let Tina talk than he is Eduard; his monologuing rolls over her, cuts her off, insists on thinking for her. One can read that his interruptions are a therapeutic device protecting her from dwelling upon the horrors of her girlhood,[20] but one can only conclude from this that Schaumann is entitled to his self-pity, but Tina is not entitled to hers. Nor is she without limits in her subservience. After he keeps interrupting her about the ideas she has from him, she gets peevish: " 'Naturally! I have everything from you!' cried Madame Valentina, now really somewhat tremulously, excitedly, irritatedly" (18: 112). She retains her religious views in opposition to him. More importantly, she is far from edified by Schaumann's use of his secret concerning the identity of Kienbaum's killer. When she realizes that he has not shared it with her and senses that it is now being used only against Eduard, she is suddenly frightened of him (18: 95), and she is most offended and hurt that Schaumann will not take her into town, where she knows the dénouement—which involves her own life in the profoundest way—will occur; instead she is left behind at home to worry. Here, too, there may be a little less of an idyll than Eduard wishes to perceive. But the main point is that Schaumann's self-presentation is a comedy of misdirection, and perhaps has been since he was a boy; several times he needles Eduard for failing to perceive what was really in him. Inside the fat is not, as the saying goes, a thin man struggling to get out, but a strong, smart, steely, and, one must say, rather dangerous man *in disguise*. As has been observed, his reiterated stress on his weakness of head and foot is in part an ironic appropriation of Eduard's once condescending opinion of him,[21] and his wheezing and groaning during the day with Eduard, his claimed inability barely to perambulate from the garden to the dinner table without assistance, are doubtless part of the same charade.

Most striking is Schaumann's violence and aggressiveness in tone, allusion, and image, unparalleled in Raabe's other writings. It is true that one of his recurrent character types is the gruff curmudgeon, who, before his inevitable goodheartedness is revealed, can be quite drastic, even brutal in manner. But it would be hard to find in Raabe or in any of his contemporaries a match for Schaumann in this regard. Certainly it looks like anything but comfortableness and a great deal like a perpetual, still unresolved pent-up rage. Even as a boy he declares he would be prepared to kill Kienbaum three times over to win the Red Redoubt, and he plays with the idea of strangling his schoolteacher (18: 27). The original impetus to his lust for the Red Redoubt is the story of his hero, Prince Xaver of Saxony, who bombarded the town from it in the Seven Years' War. It is especially gratifying to his imagination that a cannonball from that bombardment is stuck in his father's house. He dreams of shooting not only at the town, but at all humanity (ibid.). Later he and Quakatz happily study the lists of those killed in the bombardment and associate them with their contemporary descendants in the town (18: 99). These feelings are only somewhat sublimated after he has become master of the Red Redoubt; indeed, he would like to haunt the neighborhood after his death (18: 155). His other hero is Frederick the Great, on account of his violent rapacity despite his physical weakness: "The man digested everything!

Vexation, provinces, his own and others' bad luck, and above all his menu personally handwritten every day" (18: 64). We see here as elsewhere that Schaumann's gluttony is more than an amiable vice that he has learned to tolerate in himself. Instead he has turned it into an external correlative of his voracious, hostile emotional constitution. I find odd the insouciance with which his motto, "Gobble it up and gobble your way through!", is regularly treated in the critical literature, as though it were a pleasant and exemplary slogan for the conduct of life. Honest Tina does not much like the phrase (18: 114), and I doubt that it is meant to comfort the reader, either.

The logic of his aggressiveness is grounded in Schaumann's childhood humiliations and the chain of images he appropriates in order to deal with them. This chain begins when Störzer and, later, a schoolteacher, compare Schaumann to a sloth (18: 22, 82). The next link is the fossil mammoth dug up on the farm, which the vengeful Quakatz associates with the Flood; and surely the next is the motto Schaumann attaches to the house and which becomes another leitmotif: "And God spake unto Noah, saying, Go forth of the ark" (Gen. 8:15-16). This cannot mean only, as the critical literature so often seems to suggest: go out and do your own thing as best you can, or, as Helmers has it, an escape from the "culture box."[22] For God spoke these words to Noah after he had destroyed all the rest of mankind, and Schaumann's (and Quakatz's) hostility lives on them through this association.

The last link, concluding Schaumann's evolution from an object of scorn to a figure of competence and accomplishment, is the fossil sloth he himself has found. But this is the prehistoric sloth, a gigantic beast that I daresay one would not care to meet. The image, incidentally, appears earlier in a sardonic passage written by the misanthropic Hahnenberg in *Three Pens*:

> What is man? At any rate not what he imagines himself to be, namely the crown of creation. That would really be worth the trouble, if all these layers of which the scholars speak had all stacked and interpenetrated themselves with all their groups and animal formations in order finally to make possible the existence of this "perfect creature." I will not dispute his right to exist; but it is still to be said that the friendly mammoth, the harmless mastodon, all the comely saurians as well as the delicate megatherium and the comfortable [!] giant sloth also had a right to think themselves something. Every dog and every cat that today peers into the cradle of a young human being must pity him, if they do not hold him in contempt. (9/1: 248)

In carrying over the image to Schaumann, Raabe also carries over some of Hahnenberg's bleak misanthropy, and along with it, some of the distance and even repulsion we must feel toward the figure of Hahnenberg. Detroy has pointed out that the shift of metaphor from the common to the prehistoric sloth occurs at the moment when Schaumann reveals that he knows Kienbaum's killer.[23]

In this connection it is worth remarking that Schaumann not only conquers Quakatz, but also becomes his successor in a more than material sense. Schaumann has no affection for Quakatz; the purpose is to neutralize and pacify him, to turn an obsessive maniac into an ordinary old fool. At one point Schaumann speaks of the "theater of war of Schaumann versus Quakatz" (18: 63). This war could become quite physical; once Schaumann tripped Quakatz and made him fall into the ditch (18: 124), and he calls Quakatz an evil, potentially murderous man whom he was on the verge of killing several times (18: 119). After Quakatz's death his personal possessions are burned in a rite of purification (18: 78-79). But there is clearly also an affinity between Schaumann and Quakatz. As a boy Schaumann identified with him as someone persecuted by the whole world, and he admired Quakatz's fierce dogs (18: 27, 34-35). When Quakatz would like to let all his mice loose on the town, Schaumann offers to be one of the mice (18: 88). Ultimately Schaumann recreates, in more bucolic fashion, Quakatz's barricaded isolation from the world; one of the first things Eduard notices about the Red Redoubt is that the path leading to it is now completely overgrown (18: 50). It may be added that there is also an obvious parallel between Schaumann and the killer Störzer. He, too, has been systematically humiliated and scorned, in his case by the more prosperous and successful, but still loutish Kienbaum, who gives Störzer a mocking nickname similar to Stuffcake's, the untranslatable *Storzhammel* (18: 187), something like "muttonhead." It is no doubt significant for the meaning of the story that the humiliated condition of the weak and rather simpleminded Störzer results, unintentionally, to be sure, in the taking of a life, while the strong and clever Schaumann, despite his bloody-mindedness, has channeled his aggression so that it harms no one and benefits some.

Schaumann differs from the other positive figures of the mature Raabe in his pronounced instinct for power. The posture of Raabe's characters generally is defensive, trying to salvage spaces of humanity and decency against an aggressive and morally crude environment. But Schaumann actively pursues manipulative power over people and events, sometimes quite ruthlessly. He indicates this himself in an expression of hostility toward the town, through which he walks "with the power and actually the highest obligation to bring this idyll this evening into the next volume of the [crime cases] of the *New Pitaval!*" (18: 156). It will be noted that power precedes obligation in this remark. The current object of his power in Eduard's narration is Eduard himself, and it is just this force that Eduard in his narration is attempting to deflect and evade. The primary motive of Schaumann's whole proceeding is to revenge himself on Eduard; he succeeds in this, but only partially.

When Schaumann first catches sight of his visitor, he *springs* at him (18: 53). He cannot be very astonished to see him, for he knows of Eduard's presence in the town from the newspaper. The gesture therefore appears quite threatening, especially in view of Schaumann's normal inertia. Almost his first words to his "friend" are a reproach for visiting him only as an afterthought. Also unsettling in the circumstances is his demonstrative gesture of throat-cutting when he instructs Tina to have a chicken killed for dinner; in any case it sticks in Eduard's memory and he elaborates on it (18: 57-59). Schaumann has been lying in wait for him, as he makes quite clear: "See, Eduard, this is how the superior person, after years of calm waiting, pays back patiently suffered scorn and disregard. For this satisfaction I have waited here in the coolness, while you with your Le Vaillant in hot Africa sweated yourself up on elephant, rhinocerous, and giraffe hunts or in some other useless way" (18: 96). What Schaumann has to say has been all dammed up in him and is released now only on account of Eduard (18: 69).

Schaumann alternates between more or less direct blows and elaborate sarcasm, not all of which Eduard seems prepared to perceive. The hostility appears to go well back into their boyhood relationship. Even then, as Eduard rather oddly recollects, Schaumann identified him with those who gave thanks that they are not Quakatz or Schaumann, and when Eduard protested that he was misunderstood, Schaumann replied: "Not at all, Eduard; it's just that I know you. I know you all, inside and out" (18: 28).[24] All commentators have noticed that, although Schaumann once or twice expresses an interest in hearing something of Eduard's life, he never gives Eduard any opportunity to say anything about it; and indeed, in his several references to Eduard's South African existence, he broadly gives the impression that he already knows as much about it as he needs or cares to. There is similar misdirection in Schaumann's apparent invitation to Eduard to return to the Red Redoubt for dinner after their walk into town. As Eduard eventually senses, there was apparently no intention that he should do so. Schaumann seems to foresee that his revelation will drive Eduard away: "My friend Eduard is travelling home to the Cape of Good Hope, and I am bringing him a little bit on his way" (18: 156). His sarcasm becomes heavy in what I take to be an intentional self-contradiction. He says he is taking Eduard to give him a breath of the fresh air of his hometown (18: 151), but a moment later he remarks on "the disagreeable smell from down there" that will be wafted away at sea (18: 152). In between he has issued another of his misleading invitations to dinner, while remarking in regard to the question of Kienbaum's killer that Eduard "is personally much more deeply involved in it than he so far supposes" (18: 151). All of this is manipulative preparation and trussing up of the victim. The blow of the revelation that Störzer was Kienbaum's killer falls precisely at a moment when Eduard speaks of Störzer as the source of the imaginative inspiration that has shaped the course of his life (18: 162).

The conclusion to be drawn is that the primary purpose of Schaumann's whole procedure has been to strike as heavy a blow as possible to the core of Eduard's self.[25] Certainly Eduard reacts as though this is what has happened. His "world half collapses" and he considers that if he had ever abandoned Schaumann, he has been paid back a thousand times (18: 164, 196). At the same time he feels that he has been abandoned himself to face his distress, while Schaumann can barricade himself again, Quakatz-like (18: 199-200). He flees, first to his hotel, then head over heels from the town, paying a bribe to get his effects moved more quickly and sneaking through back streets. It is a rather disagreeable moment for him that an insouciant citizen remarks in passing: "Without you, Eduard, we might have waited a long time to find out who actually killed Kienbaum" (18: 202). This accidental encounter may be taken as evidence on the authorial level of narration that Eduard has been the catalyst of the revelation. Once on the train, Eduard's memory begins the process of ameliorating the effect that continues, sometimes gropingly, throughout his narration, and it is for this reason that Schaumann's success has been only partial. The view of some critics, for example, Detroy,[26] that Eduard has been chastened and altered for the better by the experience, or that he has been educated into a humorist, I find unconvincing. Schaumann's vengeance has struck a target that is too flaccid for it. Eduard is upset, but in the process of organizing his memories he regains much of his equilibrium. Some of the unease remains, to be sure; yet at the end there is a certain disproportion between Schaumann's means and the end achieved, and a shadow of futility that hangs about his vengeance.

I believe this interpretation can help to explain, if not entirely to resolve, the problem that has been troubling some readers: the circumstance that Schaumann's strategy has the result that Störzer's innocent daughter-in-law and grandchildren become pariahs in the community, stained with Störzer's "crime" by the abstract, philistine moralism of the townspeople. There has been some argument as to whether Schaumann intends to help Frau Störzer in the future. Clearly he twice hints that he will, once with the rather impersonal remark to her: "People manage, and in an emergency others will probably help" (18: 163), and once with a reference to "the vegetable garden, the butter and egg trade of Quakatz Castle" (18: 164). Eduard has it in his own mind at the end that Schaumann promised to help the family (18: 203). But the argument about this is partly off the point for two reasons. On the one hand, Frau Störzer and her children have need not only of vegetables, butter, and eggs, but also of the goodwill of their fellow human beings. A theme of the whole story has been the atrocities that result from the communal withdrawal of such goodwill, and it is by no means clear that Schaumann will be in a position to repair the loss. On the other hand, however, the ostracism of the family is but a side effect of Schaumann's main purpose of crushing Eduard. It is an odd feature of the text that early on Schaumann seems aware of the potential destructive effect of the revelation and shifts the potential blame for it onto Tina and Eduard: there will be gossip "possibly only if you two—you and Eduard—will not be able to keep your mouths shut about it tomorrow" (18: 103).

This suggests that Schaumann's plan is not completely formed in his mind at this point. I believe that his vengeful purpose takes shape and intensifies in the course of his monologue, and in the process he seems to forget the potential consequences: "peoples' yaps will not be able to do any more harm in this matter today" (18: 182). In this Schaumann is clearly wrong, and modern readers have not been mistaken to sense in this whole matter a dissonance in the text.[27] Now I consider it improbable that it might have crept in owing to the author's inattentiveness, and more improbable still that he should have thought the younger Störzers' misfortune of no consequence relative to Schaumann's achievement in shaping his own self. Raabe, after all, wrote for a year and a half on this relatively short novel, and through his thirty-five years of experience his powers of concentration and integration had become all but unparalleled in German letters in his time. From start to finish his moral sense turns on the insensate cruelties in human relations that blight innocent lives, a point on which he so strongly resembles Dickens.

The problem is made more difficult by Raabe's reiterated, unambiguous identification of himself with the title figure. Modern criticism has rightly become skeptical of the binding force of an author's interpretations of his works. But to take the position that an author has no interpretive rights at all violates common sense. In this case, Raabe's customary reticence in offering interpretive aids, especially in autobiographical matters, makes his insistence on his self-identification with Schaumann all the more compelling. I think, by the way, that speculations connecting Schaumann's childhood troubles with Raabe's unsatisfactory school experiences and the like are not convincing. He himself did not do so; he wrote to Sträter that he had been "left lying under the hedge . . . from the fall of 1856 until 1889."[28] These dates are too precise to be ignored. They reach from the appearance of his first novel, *The Chronicle of Sparrow Alley*, in October 1856, to the appearance of the novel preceding *Stuffcake*, *The Lar*. It seems altogether clear that *Stuffcake* is a product of his anger and resentment at his unrealized aspirations as a writer, at the gap between his awareness of his artistic accomplishments, as well as his ambition to be an effectual moral preceptor of the nation, and the recalcitrance of publishers and editors, reflecting in turn the sluggishness of a public to which he was bound in what seemed to him unrequited concern. Schweckendiek is quite right to call *Stuffcake* a case of "abuse of the public" and not altogether wrong in sensing a degree of overkill in it.[29] Thus the curious combination of withdrawal and aggression in Schaumann: like Quakatz; he has shut himself off from his fellow man in resentful and hostile withdrawal, and if, unlike Quakatz, he has applied himself to self-cultivation, the achievement is without echo; but he is not hermetically withdrawn, even if he may think so himself, for he is still obsessed with the urge to set things in human affairs aright. Thus far a moral critique of Schaumann can be made to fall upon Raabe himself.

But by this time in his life, irony, in the modern sense of maintaining incompatibles simultaneously in the mind, had become second nature with him. Gerhart Mayer, in his philosophical study, observed: "As much as Raabe may have regained solid ground under the aegis of a comfortable humor contemptuous of the world, that still did not exclude continuous doubt of the rightness and durability of these solutions."[30] With Raabe things are often not quite what they first appear to be. If Schaumann is a self-projection, he is so less as allegory than as travesty, and not only because of the contrast between the lean, gregarious, paternal author and his fat, anti-social, and childless creation, a contrast of which Beaucamp speaks as "a projection with metamorphosis into an opposite model, in which the polar opposition of his being is evidenced."[31] In the first place, it is clear that Schaumann exhibits a hyperbolic extension of the notorious Raabean narrative garrulity, with its extreme degree of leitmotivic repetitiveness,[32] almost as though it had been a parody by another hand. The "monologist without peer" (18: 62), narrating, as Herman Meyer has put it, like a ruminating cow,[33] may well be a self-critical reflection on Raabe's part; furthermore, the parallel with Schaumann may help to show us why Raabe's customary narration is so relentlessly verbose: he is determined to manage and manipulate a reading audience whose perceptivity and moral sensitivity he mistrusts. When Schaumann says that his ideal from childhood on has not been the Red Redoubt but "Me!" (18:82), it reads like a hyperbolic exaggeration of the Goethean ideal of self-culture. Doubtless Raabe associated himself with the extreme individualization of the Goethean model that can be observed elsewhere is the nineteenth century. At the same time we see some fairly sobering consequences of this extreme posture, and we observe at the end that Schaumann's asocial hostility, born, to be sure, of the same social ideal of justice in common human relations that animates many of Raabe's works, generates further suffering as a careless side effect of strongly focused resentment. Schaumann's failure really to move Eduard in the deep part of his being might well be taken as a resigned if perhaps subliminal recognition of the limits of the Sisyphean task Raabe set himself. The book may be a kind of experiment, in which he for once releases and tests the hostility and malice underlying his kindly public posture and exhibits comfortableness as a defensive facade behind which unresolved tensions continue to vibrate.

Beyond this, I think we can become too solemn about the novel, laying every word and phrase of Schaumann on the jeweler's scale and leafing around in Schopenhauer in search of philosophical authentication. When Raabe wrote in correction of Sträter's perhaps excessively idealistic praise of the novel that it was "one of the most shameless books . . . that have ever been written,"[34] I think he may have been laughing. It would not be unreasonable to take the whole novel as an elaborate joke. As far as Eduard is concerned it is a rather mean joke, but he manages more or less to weasel out of it. In any case, as William T. Webster has argued, we are under no obligation to take Schaumann as a wholly positive figure,[35] and, one might add, thus oblige ourselves to make our estimate of Raabe stand or fall on our estimate of his fictional self-representation. Roy Pascal has said that "the form of [Schaumann's] victory is not exemplary and final, but personal and temporary,"[36] and the same may be said of Raabe. There is a truth about Raabe in the book, as he insisted, but it is a partial truth, hyperbolized, relativized, ironized, dissected, and questioned in that experimental process characteristic of literary realism at its most authentic.

CHAPTER 20

The Split Self:

The Documents of the Birdsong

◨

IN *Stuffcake*, Raabe's fictive persona is turned outward, armored, aggressive, even vengeful. With *The Documents of the Birdsong* of 1896 Raabe turned inward. Of all his major works, this short novel is the most introspective, and it had a long and strenuous genesis. He seems to have begun it in fits and starts, without a clear goal, and it took him twenty-five months to complete; only two other works, *Abu Telfan*, interspersed with other projects, and *Hastenbeck* took longer. He agonized audibly over the process of creation: "I wring and squeeze; it feels like a vice around my brain and like a hot fist at my throat."[1] He ascribed these difficulties to old age, but the real resistance is likely to have lain elsewhere, in the material. When he finished the book he wrote of "years of torment and wringing" and asserted that he could no longer remember what was in it.[2] A few months later he claimed that he had often been on the point of burning it.[3] The intensely personal character of the work has long been recognized. When his friend Hans Hoffmann referred to it as the "*Werther* of the sixty-three-year-old writer" (19: 456), Raabe laughed at him, but the comparison is not so far-fetched, if one could imagine *Werther* narrated by Albert instead of Werther many years after the event. More importantly, Hoffmann saw a double, antithetical self-portrait in the work. This insight has become a commonplace in commentary on the novel, and, unlike many commonplaces in the reception tradition, it is substantially correct. Fehse wrote: "there is no work that gives us so deep an insight into Raabe's experience as this one, not even *Stuffcake*. Indeed, more of his own life flowed into *The Documents of the Birdsong* than he was aware"; it displays an antithesis that "rests upon a split in the author's being such as we see so clearly conveyed in no other of his works."[4] The antithetical quality is immediately evident in the title. The "Birdsong" (*Vogelsang*) is an old neighborhood, at the time of the narration overrun by urban development, but retained in memory as a childhood idyll, a place of trees, hedges, and fields, and modest but comfortable dwellings. The "documents" are the product of the effort of the narrator Karl Krumhardt, a successful, self-disciplined legal official, to bring his memories under rational, orderly control. To capture "birdsong" in "documents" is, needless to say, no easy matter.

As a personality, Krumhardt, whose name suggests both flexibility and hardness, is the most impressive of Raabe's first-person narrators. He is in no way an unreliable narrator; a sober, intelligent, and mature man, he pursues self-knowledge with integrity, without the complacent cynicism of Emil von Schmidt in *Master Author*, the crippled self-regard of Fritz Langreuter in *Old Nests*, or the evasiveness of Eduard in *Stuffcake*. As his record of his memories brings to the surface antithetical traits that he has disciplined out of his existence, his business-like style changes; he visualizes more clearly, and he feels that the most serious things become the most ghostly as the pile of documents threatens to collapse on him (19: 270). He encounters envy in himself, a sense of inadequacy, a touch of alienation from the quality of his life and from his wife and children (19: 295); he learns amazement at himself and the pain of introspection (19: 304); he is becoming a *writer*. Yet in the end he *chooses* his own proper, orderly, bourgeois self, and we respect this choice because it has been earned in self-knowledge, in awareness of the other, and in exploration of limits and alternatives.

The "documents" begin at the end, with a message from a childhood friend, Helene Mungo née Trotzendorff, that another of their friends, Velten Andres, has died in his barely furnished former student room in Berlin, his face turned to the wall. Thus we have once again the familiar cloverleaf of three childhood friends, though this one has been blown apart by incompatibility of temperaments. As we learn at the end of the book, Krumhardt meets Helene at Velten's deathbed, where she urges him to write down their story in sober prose, as a warning to his wife and children. This Krumhardt sets out to do, though as he orders his memories, he finds that sustaining sober prose is a challenging task. The members of the cloverleaf, more explicitly than in any work since *Three Pens*, are conditioned by childhood circumstances and parental influence. Krumhardt's father was a minor official with a special gift for numbers, but he was held back in his career by his lack of a university education. A bitter, rigid man, he raised his son in a highly disciplined way to achieve what the father could not. In this he is successful; the son is orderly, disciplined, and well-adjusted, and he rises to the prestigious official level to which his father had aspired. Krumhardt has internalized many of his father's values and turns to his portrait on the wall for advice; at the same time, his filial relationship was not without stress, for he is more flexible and imaginative. His father quarrels with him about his attraction to the freer games of other children and seemingly disorderly escapades; for the father "understanding remains understanding; sense, sense; nonsense, nonsense; and trash, trash" (19: 244). This combination of attachment to and separation from the father remains a productive force in Krumhardt's personality:

> I look up to the portrait of the old gentleman over my desk with some pangs of conscience and—would truly not wish to be without the leftover feeling of his fierce but sincere fist on my arm, through the whole remainder of my life.

*

> And yet! With what vexation, defiance, and more or less clear resistance did I suffer that good grip in those times when it was more than a memory! And how often did I free myself from it and run off with the two others. . . . (19: 254)

Velten Andres, whose name suggests "otherness," is the son of a deceased, dreamy physician and a kind, nurturing, sunny mother who laughs and smiles without reason and whom Krumhardt's parents find odd and irritating because of her tolerant, unrepressive nature. Velten becomes a self-assured, imaginative, idealistic person without ambition for gain or honors. He is "a master in his realm, which unfortunately was not very much of this world" (19: 261); though more knowledgeable than Krumhardt, he fails in school at first, and he displays his eccentricity on a memorable occasion when he rescues a lumpish boy nicknamed Sloppy from a fall through the ice. Sloppy's father is an important person; Velten is offered his protection and is even introduced to the duke and duchess, but he takes no advantage of this stroke of fortune, to the wonderment and scorn of the community, and especially of Sloppy himself. Krumhardt, as it happens, marries Sloppy's sister, but Sloppy himself is dismissed from this life with a cold twist of phrase that incidentally shows Krumhardt not so distant from Velten's values: "A year ago, he was not torn away from us by a heart attack" (19: 357). The event shows that there is a kind of rigidity in Velten also, which becomes more pronounced as the fate of his life unfolds. He is the "eternally incalculable *odd fellow* of the Birdsong—*who had no harm in him and who had parts if he would use them,* as they said in Cambridge of a similar person, who, according to the opinion of the reasonable people in the world similarly came to little more than a bad end" (19: 266)—this similar person being, as only the reader of an annotated edition is likely to discover, Laurence Sterne.

Helene Trotzendorff, whose name suggests defiance, is the daughter of a fatuously snobbish mother and a German-American fast-buck artist who is absent through much of Helene's childhood, for he has suffered setbacks and has deposited wife and daughter in the, for them, rather déclassé environment of the Birdsong, while he repairs his fortunes in America. He does catch the brass ring on the merry-go-round of American capitalism and returns a triumphant millionaire. Like other figures of more appearance than substance, such as Dietrich Häussler in *The Rumbledump* and Agonista in *At the Sign of the Wild Man*, Charles Trotzendorff is adored by the community for his wealth and success, though both the duke and Krumhardt's father recognize him as an oaf and studiously ignore him. The return to America is quite welcome to Helene, though it tears her away from the cloverleaf. For, in keeping with her parentage, she is ambitious for wealth and social standing. As a child she says:

> But now I am my father's and my mother's child and a free republican and American, and I believe in my father and will also have my salons and servants, black and white, chambermaids and high windows, chandeliers and rugs and riding horses and carriages and my loge in the theater and all the rest! Yes, and now go, Velten, and tell your mother what I said, and that all her goodness and teaching has been thrown away on me; but tell her too that I must cry out so, I don't know what, only because all, all of you, have driven me to it, each in his own way. Oh God, what a poor girl I am and so unhappy in the world! (19: 256-57)

The "servants, black and white," are a nice touch, for the image shows that Helene's instinct is not merely one of shallow avarice but contains a dimension of amoral aestheticism. Her aspirations are as far removed from Krumhardt's bourgeois rectitude as they are from Velten's unworldly idealism; they aim for a different realm of freedom and beauty in secular plenitude, and though her values are definitely not Raabe's as we have learned to know them, there is a certain heroic independence in her invincible determination to realize her own.

Krumhardt's documents purportedly describe the course of Velten's tragic love for Helene and its consequences. Velten firmly believes that Helene does not know her own better self and means to rescue her from herself. She has, he claims, put one of her golden hairs through his nose, but she has "misclimbed" in life (19: 301). This odd verb (*sich verklettern*) first appears in *On the Scrap-Iron*, where it refers to the social-climbing of the aestheticist Brokenkorb's acquaintances, away from the people (16: 347-48).[5] The term had already been literalized in Velten's and Helene's childhood, when she "misclimbs" a tree and Velten cannot get her down, so that others must be called to rescue her. This first "truly lost battle of life" (19: 300) would be recognizable as a bad omen if Velten knew he were a character in a fiction, but as he does not, he follows Helene to America and pursues her, while making his way as a jack-of-all-trades: "scholar, merchant, balloonist, soldier, sailor, journalist—but by bourgeois standards he amounted to nothing" (19: 318). While "balloonist" may seem a particularly apt activity for the unearthly Velten, it is important to note that he does not "amount to nothing" out of incompetence. He is capable of doing anything, it seems, and does, with his left hand, but his only consuming interest is the pursuit of Helene, who, he is persuaded against all evidence, is secretly crying out for him to save her (19: 302), and who, inevitably, marries a multimillionaire named Mungo.

After this, the pace of Velten's life gradually decelerates to stasis. He travels around the world some, then, "very tired," he comes back to live a quiet, "petty-bourgeois" life with his mother, whom he tries to shield from a recognition of his failure in life (19: 350). He takes as his motto an early verse of the "greatest egoist in the history of literature," Goethe:

> Be without feeling!
> An easily moved heart
> Is a miserable possession
> On the wobbling earth. (19: 352)

Now it is well known that this is an occasional poem addressed by Goethe to his friend Behrisch to console him for a discouraging setback, and Raabe somewhat illegitimately generalizes it in support of his persistent view of Goethe as a model of stoic resistance. At the same time it has troubling antecedents. One might be reminded of the misanthropic Hahnenberg in *Three Pens*, who adopts the ancient motto of surgeons: "Be strong, bold, dexterous, and without sympathy" (9/1: 361), or Prudens Hahnemeyer's desire, in *Restless Guests*, that Veit should wish him "an immovable heart" in his dealings with Fuchs (16: 205-6); these are not very positive models. But more important is Velten's eventual recognition that he has not been able to follow the dictum any more than Goethe (19: 370); it is but a mask for a heart too easily moved.

When Velten's mother dies, he burns all her belongings in a strange scene to which we must return shortly, after which he disappears from Krumhardt's sight. Only after Velten's death does Krumhardt learn from Helene that Velten's path had occasionally crossed with hers in various exotic places. At length he returns to the landlady of his student days; though he has plenty of money, he regards himself as propertyless, and he shuts himself up in the room as a hermit, while will and life wind down into death.

It seems to me that the more the reader knows about Raabe, the more uneasy this story is likely to make him. In several prominent characteristics, Velten looks like another of Raabe's metamorphosed alter egos: his struggle for stoicism against a predisposition to labile sensitivity, his individualism, indifferent to the conventional values of the community, his orientation on values more substantial than the materialism and ambition of the dwellers in the saeculum. He seems to understand himself as a lonely knight errant who invests his whole life and sense of self in the effort to draw Helene to himself into his version of the alternative community, though the reader may notice that he dreams of bringing her back to the Birdsong at a time when the neighborhood is disappearing and the Krumhardts are moving out. In the background we sense Raabe's struggle for the preservation of values that are crumbling in the world of the present. Might not Velten's consuming and frustrated effort to win Helene to his universe of values reflect Raabe's effort to impose himself on a stubbornly resistant, conventional public?

It has been pointed out that Raabe died like Velten (and like Wunnigel before him), with his back turned to the world and his face turned to the wall.[6] But the most disconcerting aspect of this identification concerns Velten's mother and his relationship to her.

Frau Andres is recognizable as one of several portraits of Raabe's mother as she lived in his memory and imagination: steadfastly cheerful of disposition and sympathetically tolerant of others but wholly independent of their values. For example, she disapproves of but nevertheless sympathizes with Charles Trotzendorff and his spoiled daughter, and even with Krumhardt's father, who disapproves of her, as a man out of place among "people of imagination" (19: 230-33, 251). Above all, she is lovingly supportive of her son no matter what he does. There is a close bond of intimacy between them; when Velten writes to her from abroad, Krumhardt observes how subtly they understand one another (19: 324). What then are we to make of the extraordinary circumstance that, after his mother's death, Velten begins to burn her (and his father's) effects and eventually stages a mob scene when he invites the community, along with the members of a nearby travelling circus, to plunder the house? Krumhardt seems to understand this—he helps Velten burn his old rocking-horse, even though Krumhardt would have liked to have it for his own boy—and he interprets the action as a great "weariness of possessions" contrasting with and overwhelming his own "joy in property" (19: 372-73).

Possibly, however, this is a place where Krumhardt sees things too much in terms of his own psychological concerns. We are obliged to recall another filial auto-da-fé, the burning of Quakatz's effects after his death in *Stuffcake*. But this is a ritual purification, through which Quakatz's daughter and son-in-law free themselves from the burden of the old maniac's memory. Why should Raabe have repeated the motif here? For Velten is certainly not overtly hostile to his mother; indeed, he exhibits an attachment to her of a perhaps not altogether healthy intensity. On his return from America he thinks his mother knows that he hopes to clutch her skirt and cry "Mama" (19: 347). His return to his Berlin landlady, Frau Feucht, is clearly a return to a surrogate mother. Frau Feucht receives him like a mother, indulging him with sympathy, and he calls her "mother"; in his last days he spends his time reading the books of his childhood in greasy old copies (19: 393, 394). The observation that Velten "returns back into the prespatial, enclosed, cave-like mother-world, which he had really never rightly left" seems obvious enough.[7] After Helene's departure, Velten remarks that he continues to be the object of feminine education: "I remain with the mothers, with the women, and with the girls" (19: 273). In German, the "mothers" must arouse in the reader an unavoidable echo of the mysterious, chthonic realm of the "Mothers" to which Goethe's Faust descends; furthermore, there is a strong implication that Velten's fixation on Helene parallels his fixation on his mother. Later, when he loses Helene, he writes to his mother that "they have taken her from *us*" and that he failed to hold her "for me— *for us*" (19: 325, my emphasis).

But why the burning? It frightens Krumhardt's wife and outrages Velten's old nurse, who cries out that his mother will accuse him on the Day of Judgment and remains unmollified when Velten gives her the house, though she accepts it (19: 369, 379-80). It must seem to us that Velten is not only repudiating property as such, but his mother's property in himself. Now much earlier, in his youth, Velten remarked that it was too bad that he and Helene had been brought up only by their mothers, for even his own fine mother was, after all, only a woman (19: 258). When, after his return, he tries not to destroy his mother's illusion that he has or will heroically overcome the world by force of action (19: 351), he exhibits solicitude for her but perhaps not a great deal of respect. As for Frau Andres, she has moments when she seems to accuse herself of complicity in Velten's failure in life. While contemplating the failings of the Trotzendorff family, she makes a long speech in which she blames herself for not being strict enough and for spoiling her son (19: 251-52). In her readiness to support him, she, too, is willing to believe that Helene is secretly crying out for him (19: 302-3), but later she is assailed by self-doubt: "My God, are we mothers at fault if we give our children our best on their way and thereby make them miserable?" What if we are wrong, he gets his way, and finds that his hopes are nothing but a "fairy-tale yarn, a tauntingly pretty shadow-play on the wall?" (19: 314) When dying, she suffers uncharacteristic uneasiness, and keeps saying that Velten must catch a train, which Velten interprets as the "train to happiness" (19: 363-64).

When we look back in Raabe's career, we notice that it is said of Hans Unwirrsch in *The Hunger Pastor* that it was a good thing he had no tendency to pride, or his head would have been turned by the devotion of his mother and his foster aunt, "the two stupid women" (6: 90), though certainly this remark is meant ironically and affectionately. It has been argued by Karl Hoppe that the relationship of mother and son in *German Nobility* prefigures that in *The Documents of the Birdsong* (13: 436). But this parallel is congruent only if we regard Velten as a victor, one who "passes freely through life." Krumhardt tends to see him this way, asking himself at one point if he is "nothing but the record-keeper in [Velten's] victorious proceeding, against my, against *our* world" and he believes that Velten's wish of conquering the world and dying alone was fulfilled (19: 295, 296). In another place he compares him to Byron and young Goethe, secure of victory, "the conqueror of the world by the grace of frivolity" (19: 308-9). But these are expressions of Krumhardt's envy of the antithetical other.

An acute modern critic, Wilhelm Emrich, is skeptical of the constant praise of Velten's propertylessness as a victory over the world.[8] Velten does not look much like a victor to the reader; he does not survive his obsession into a maturer relationship to life, as, years before, Robert Wolf in *The People from the Forest* survived his hopeless, idealistic love for Eva Dornbluth and his obsession with saving her from her own course. In view of the extent to which, in *The Documents of the Birdsong*, personalities are shaped and prefigured by parents, we might consider what we learn of Velten's deceased father, "a genuine and just suburban doctor, a good-humored person and a good physician," whose real interest was entomology and therefore was "quite often not to be found when he was very needful at a sickbed, an accident, or otherwise in his profession" (19: 220). Here is a form of individualistic unworldliness that is irresponsible because harmful to the community; we see a strand of the narcissistic inwardness that can be detected in Wunnigel.[9] But most explicitly forced upon us is the recognition that the kindly indulgence of Frau Andres is charged with responsibility for Velten's tragic individualism. It is here that we begin to see the significance of Raabe's odd and unexpected late remark: "My blessed mother might have done something more clever seventy years ago than to give me the most foolish part of her dear intellect on my course through life!"[10] Velten's tragedy, his unfitness for life, arises from a total commitment to the imagination, to a fiction obstinately willed in the teeth of a recalcitrant and ultimately invincible reality.

Velten comes into two other sets of personal relationships that are clearly meant to reflect on his personality but that are nevertheless quite difficult to interpret. One is with the des Beaux family in Berlin, especially with the son Leon and the daughter Leonie. They are members of the substantial and historically significant colony of French Huguenots in Berlin from which, incidentally, Theodor Fontane also came. As Raabe presents it, their ambience is the imagination in the form of dreamy aestheticism. Though the des Beaux are the children of a tailor, they live in the memories of past Provençal glories, as Leonie puts it, "in a quiet fairy-tale corner" in Berlin, in what Velten perceives as an atmosphere of troubadour romance (19: 287, 286), and in what one critic has called a dream world more unreal than the Birdsong.[11] They grow up, through their father's fault, in "imagination and dreams" that make them even more unfit for the real world than Velten. Leonie says that Leon has not learned to separate dream and life, so that he is often defeated by the world (19: 289), and the relatively more competent Velten must take charge of the weaker young man, defending him in a duel and later accompanying him on a world tour. Krumhardt, incidentally, is fascinated by the des Beaux; he perceives a light radiating from them, and he is grateful to Velten for this experience, for, with his conventional class instincts, on his own he would have been afraid to be too intimate with a tailor (19: 286). (Actually, Leon is a viscount, though he does not use the title.) It is quite clear from Krumhardt's account that the pretty, gentle Leonie falls silently in love with Velten. For his part, Velten does not so much spurn her love as simply not perceive it in his obsessive fixation on the absent Helene.

Here we see again that insensitivity to the other that is a symptom of an excess of imagination and that has been prefigured in comic form in Wunnigel. Krumhardt, who believes that Leonie would have been right for Velten, laments his blindness to the "miraculous richness belonging to him" and thinks that his fate would have been different if he had had an ear for her sweet voice of love and an eye for her glances. Velten, Krumhardt also notices, did not realize how intimately Leon and Leonie observed him, for he was used to looking through people (19: 309, 319, 294). Krumhardt remarks that Leonie resembles Velten's mother in character (19: 292-93), a subtle point that may give us pause, since Velten so studiously ignores her. As has been pointed out, the des Beaux belong to those characters of Raabe who are imprisoned by the imagination.[12] In time, however, their static aestheticism splits into two directions. Leon turns into a banker and capitalist, while Leonie, propertyless, becomes the deaconess of a religious order, from which she emerges to comfort Velten when he is dying.[13] Thus the bifurcation of the des Beaux reflects, in a more constricted, perhaps slightly more banal dimension, the antithesis of the practical, settled Krumhardt and the unworldly, ultimately isolated Velten.

A more difficult case is the figure of German Fell, the ape-like man who performs as the "missing link" among the circus people invited by Velten to plunder his mother's house, and who has been called one of the most surreal figures in German literature.[14] A good deal of thought has been given to the significance of the names in the novel, but the odd name of German Fell has yet to be decoded satisfactorily. An effort to explain it in connection with unusual English words makes, in my opinion, excessive demands on Raabe's knowledge of that language.[15] We need to find something nearer to hand. "Fell" means "hide" and thus refers to the animal-like quality of the figure. "German" is the Russian form of "Hermann." Might this not suggest that he is both German and exotic, both inside and outside, straddling the realms of reality and imagination like so many of Raabe's figures? This is just a guess, however, and our interpretation is not made any easier by German Fell's claim that he "studied a few semesters in Wittenberg, before I joined the anthropoids" (19: 381). Wittenberg is, of course, where Hamlet studied; is this supposed to give a tragic cast to German Fell, or does his withdrawal to the "anthropoids" in the circus indicate an avoidance of tragedy?

One thing that has not been sufficiently noticed is that when German Fell begins to talk to Velten, his grotesque aspect recedes; he speaks with sense and wit, and in the Raabean idiolect that indicates his membership in the alternative community. He knows something of Velten and implies their relatedness, remarking that both had "misclimbed" in Yggdrasil, the Old Norse tree of life (19: 381). Velten is somewhat stunned by this meeting, and Krumhardt thinks it is a memory from which he will never be free. Velten's landlady reports that at the end of his life he turned himself into an animal, a dog. Thus the relatedness of Velten and German Fell appears certain; Raabe himself remarked on the link through the verb "misclimb" to his friend Hartmann, adding, in his usual cryptic, unhelpful manner: "There is symbolism in it; that was prettily contrived. But who understands all this or even gives himself the trouble of trying?" (19: 452). Well, since then, quite a few have given themselves the trouble. One critic has argued that the confrontation makes Velten see that his rebellion is useless,[16] while one of the finest recent studies of the novel calls German Fell "a distorted reflection of Velten's own position on the fringe of society," and points out that the ape-man "foreshadows the necessary decline of Velten's existence from that day on."[17] But perhaps it ought also to be taken into consideration that German Fell is a survivor. It does not look as though he is headed for the kind of self-dissolution into which Velten drifts. He wears, with irony and exaggeration, the skin with which fate has supplied him. He bends instead of breaking—in this sense he is more like Krumhardt, the "bent-hard," than Velten—and, if he is a defeated outsider, he is not destroyed. Perhaps, therefore, he is meant to be not a grotesque mirror of Velten's fate, but a pointer to a possible road that Velten does not take.

The reason that Velten does not take this road or any other is his single-minded obsession with Helene. This, too, requires a certain amount of interpretive thoughtfulness. Traditional critics have taken a quite harsh view of her, as though she were a successor to the complacently greedy and this-worldly Gertrud Tofote in *Master Author*. Fehse believed that she went to America in flight from Velten's superiority,[18] while in the depths of the Nazi period the ever-astonishing Hermann Pongs amusingly argued that the characterization of Helene was an unwitting prophecy of the modern American woman, "withered in all the forces of her soul, vain, greedy of life, cruel, empty."[19] Even a contemporary critic argues that Velten was wrong about Helene, "a basically shallow, materialistically determined woman" with no strength for depth, a distorted personality who does not allow of subtle interpretation.[20] It strikes me that this makes Velten appear to be rather an idiot. Another of the older critics already found things a little more complicated, remarking upon Helene's strength of will and perseverance, and finding in the text a tension between acknowledgment of her self-assertion and recognition of the emptiness of her values.[21] More recently, Emrich has argued that she is motivated not by greed, but wills her identification with her parents because they are scorned in the Birdsong, because no one respects her dreams and aspirations, and because Velten disregards her human dignity.[22] This last point is the most significant. Helene at the end denies that she was sold, as Velten in his Romantic sentimentality preferred to believe, asserts that she never lied or was cowardly, and insists that what she became arose out of herself; she was the same as a child as she is now (19: 401-2). We are meant to see in her, perhaps, the indestructible Goethean daemon of personality, though not, of course, developed to Goethean ends.

What is certain is that Velten forms of her an imagined self that is not congruent with her real self, which he actually despises. He determines not to let go of Helene her whole life long (19: 291); he seems motivated not so much by love as by a will to power over the other. With this imperialistic imagination he in some degree resembles Stuffcake, but he is unable to manipulate other selves as Stuffcake does, either because the other self in this case is too strong or because he lacks Stuffcake's ruthlessness. Helene tends to the latter view; she sees Velten's strength as imaginary, while she knows him in his weakness: "He was, after all, only a foolish boy, who, with his easily moved heart, at first sought protection from himself in those futile words [i.e., Goethe's verses to Behrisch]" (19: 401). If anyone in this story is a victor, it is Helene in her own self-estimation; she revels in her own strength and scorns Leonie as a weak person who could never have understood Velten (19: 402). But her own capacity for feeling does not seem to run very deep; she displays a rather theatrical sentimentality herself at the end when she quotes *Richard II*: "Let us sit upon the ground and tell sad stories of the death of kings" (19: 400), perhaps bearing in mind King Richard's abject weakness and self-pity when he recites these lines. From her own account it appears that she regarded Velten's devotion to her as a possession, one that she has enjoyed in their occasional meetings around the world. Nor does grief over the loss of Velten paralyze her social life. She declines Krumhardt's invitation to accompany her to the Birdsong, for that evening she has an engagement at the home of the American minister, where the famous English actor Henry Irving is to perform. She asks Krumhardt to come along, but he, naturally, declines her invitation in turn. Perhaps we might say that Helene is reality incarnate, so that the unworldly Velten, oriented outside reality in the realm of the imagination, was bound to fail in his quest of her.

311

However, some pages back I indicated that the documents are only purportedly about the love story of Velten and Helene. We have learned by now that the mature Raabe almost never put love stories at the center of his narrative interest, and it was observed long ago that, while Krumhardt may believe he is writing the story of Velten and Helene, he is actually writing about the burden of Velten's riddle for himself, in the course of which his effort for sobriety and neutrality fails, as does his official style.[23] The narrative style is marked by an increasing degree of nervousness; it has been computed that Krumhardt shifts between the frame of the narrative present and the narrated past no fewer than sixty times.[24] His sense of security and identity becomes increasingly fragile. What he documents is the "self-reflection, the self-confrontation, the self-division" of the writer, a crisis of consciousness that ends with the acceptance of the necessary life-lie.[25] His vision begins to develop the polyperspectivism so characteristic of Raabe himself; one critic has observed that he looks at Velten with bourgeois eyes, but at the bourgeois world with Velten's eyes.[26] At one point Krumhardt is reminded of Lessing, who claimed that he published the fragments of the freethinker Reimarus because "he did not want to live with him alone under the same roof any more." Krumhardt intensifies the thought: "since he is gone forever, he wants to maintain his right as a guest more firmly than ever: but I *cannot live alone with him under one roof any longer.* So I keep writing" (19: 358). Velten at one point is clever enough to foresee that Krumhardt has taken much from him that will lie heavily on him and his children in the future; whenever Krumhardt thinks of that remark, his secure four walls seem to close in on him, the floor seems insecure, he feels uncomfortable in his house and his life, he gets fearful and asthmatic—as Raabe himself was asthmatic (19: 366).

Krumhardt's wife functions in the background as a worried, warning chorus. She grows increasingly distressed about Krumhardt's labor on the documents, for she senses the hold that Velten's potentially anarchistic imagination maintains on her husband's spirit. She becomes a little nervous as soon as Helene's letter reporting Velten's death has come; she is especially protective of the Krumhardt children and takes the position that she is to maintain throughout: "Heaven protect them from too much imagination and preserve for them a clear head and a calm heart." To which Krumhardt sighs: "Quite my opinion, dear Anna" (19: 216). But if Frau Krumhardt had acute hearing, she might have been made all the more uneasy when he tries to calm her at the first news: "Why are you so startled? It concerns you and your children only quite indirectly" (19: 215). *Her* children? Here is the seed of what she fears most: that the spirit of Velten will alienate Krumhardt from his allegiance to the family and to the order in which it resides. She has always seen Velten as dangerous; she liked him well enough, but did not want him as a godfather to her child (19: 359).

When Velten begins to burn his mother's property, she gets genuinely frightened because she fears that Krumhardt might become like him; she has a dream that Krumhardt burns a photograph of her and their child (19: 371). But Krumhardt keeps going right on back to Velten, and she feels Velten is changing him under her hands (19: 373-74). The burning makes her angry with her husband and she cries out: "I hold fast to my property in the world!" (19: 383). Thus the security of possessions is central for her as it is for Helene, but for a different reason. For Helene property is aesthetic and an objective correlative of her self-realization; Frau Krumhardt cares first and foremost about the family. At the end she envies Helene's riches—but for the sake of the children (19: 408). Her worry is made all the more intense by the fact that she, too, is impressed by Velten and even attracted to him. When she first meets him, she finds him to be quite different from her expectations, pronounces Helene a goose for having let him get away, and asserts quite surprisingly that *she* would have waited "for this awful person" and not given up her right to him, adding that, if she were a man in this society, she could be envious of such an awful man (19: 348-49). It is very important that Raabe included this moment, for it prevents us from thinking of her as a mere stolid, unimaginative bourgeoise, grimly hanging on to property and conventionality. She senses with empathic instinct the salient point in Krumhardt's feelings about Velten, which is envy, and is able to feel the force of the alternative she fears.

Krumhardt registers his wife's anxiety, but he is not much deflected by it in his effort to work the problem out for himself. He does share the anxiety, however; in one place he writes: "What would happen if I could not call upon my dear wife, my dear children, to help against this 'lost,' this—propertyless man?" (19: 295) One recent critic has given a Jungian interpretation to Krumhardt's struggle for integrity of the self, regarding Velten as his "shadow," a second soul to be overcome and integrated.[27] But we do not need the Jungian terminology to see that Velten incarnates an unused but also unappeased potential in Krumhardt's self, one whose unworldly, willfully unanchored values are incompatible with his way of life, with his commitments to the paternal superego and to his role in society. But he can hang on by accepting the recognition that his life is a role that he plays—and that he can *choose*. Well before the end of the documents, when he still has much psychic work to do, Velten's ghost appears to him and mockingly asks: "Well, old fellow, not yet sick of the game?" Krumhardt, despite all disappointment, boredom, and disgust, firmly replies: "*No!*" and adds to himself: "I have and hold my children's inheritance. The playthings of man on earth, which after all will one day drop from my hands, they may pick up, and I—I still feel myself responsible to them for it!" (19: 345) The awareness that life is a matter of playing out one's assigned role is something Krumhardt may have learned from Velten, who has told him that "everyone's role is grown onto his body" (19: 333). Velten pursues this theater metaphor for two full pages, observing that in his own case "it is a heavy ticket price that has to be paid for the tragicomedy of existence" (19: 334).

This resolution is fine for Krumhardt. It restores his soul; without losing his disciplined equilibrium, he can retain the Veltenesque component of his self as an enrichment of his inner, private culture. But for Raabe it is not so fine; it leaves him in the quandary with which he began. For as a writer and artist he cannot do without the imagination with all its dubious, stressful implications. In the narrative consciousness of the novel, as opposed to Krumhardt's, there is still a gap, even an abyss, between the Krumhardtian and the Veltenesque. In that dilemma of inside-outside that German Fell may symbolize, Velten is too far *out*, not even clearly in focus, while Krumhardt is too far *in*, obliged to renounce in his life's role the plenitude of the author's imagination. Clearly there was a side of Raabe that was drawn to the Krumhardtian normality. It is evident in the quality of his external life, modest, ordinary, domestic, familial, patriarchal. It must have occurred to him that his way of life might not have been much different if he had been a hard-working, middle-level official rather than the major novelist of his generation, and possibly a good deal more gratifying and less agitating. Beyond this, I believe that, even as a writer, he may have longed for greater normality, for a more effective capacity to communicate with, let us say, the Helenes of this world. But the otherness of the Velten Andres in him was not to be exorcised or subordinated, for it *was* the imagination, and as such the prerequisite of his vocation. This vocation he plainly saw as tragic, as condemning him to isolation from the larger community, to the appearance of eccentricity no matter how conventionally he might conduct himself, to propertylessness in a both literal and metaphorical sense. In *The Documents of the Birdsong* he does not unify the components of his self but drives a wedge into them. For him, Velten in all his attractiveness is a warning example as he is for Krumhardt and his family, but for him, Krumhardt is impossible. It is little wonder that Raabe found the novel so hard to write, or that he could not remember what was in it when he had finished. Three or four years later, he would begin one last effort to unify and harmonize his sense of self. It failed, as we shall see in the next chapter.

In my opinion, *The Documents of the Birdsong* is the finest work of a great career, an outstanding late nineteenth-century novel of European stature. Even Kientz, so ready to devalue Raabe, managed to praise it as a "beau livre" and allowed that it may be his masterpiece, adding: "Toute l'opposition, chère à Thomas Mann, entre Bürger et Künstler est préfigurée dans ce roman."[28] It is not surprising that critics have repeatedly thought of Thomas Mann, especially of the biography of the demonically possessed composer Adrian Leverkühn as recounted by the intelligent but normal Serenus Zeitblom in *Doctor Faustus*.[29] Recently Preisendanz has warned that this comparison is superficial,[30] and perhaps it should not be pressed too far, as the structure of the contrast between bourgeois and artist is quite different. But there is a comparable narrative acumen, and the self-awareness of the modern bourgeois artist as alienated from himself, one of Mann's enduring themes, is no less intensely explored in Raabe's novel. Like Mann, and unlike Balzac or Flaubert and their innumerable progeny, Raabe does not pour scorn on the bourgeoisie from the aristocratic height of artistic sensibility, but honestly recognizes the irreducible bourgeois component of his own consciousness. But Raabe does not, like Stifter and Keller, repel the energy of imagination as a threat to only partially analyzed bourgeois allegiances, for that would be the death of art, as, in my opinion, it turned out to be in Stifter and recurrently threatened to be in Keller. Instead, in *The Documents of the Birdsong* he sacrificed himself in Velten Andres while continuing to plug along as Karl Krumhardt, a trick of having it both ways that, as Raabe doubtless profoundly knew, can only be executed in fiction.

CHAPTER 21

The Unclosed Circle:
The Fragment
Altershausen

□

RAABE completed his last historical novel, *Hastenbeck*, in August
of 1898. Six months later he wrote to Jensen: "Mentally, that
is, literarily, I have been cleaned out since *Hastenbeck* as never before
and never before have I felt so much like an empty sack."[1] Nevertheless, eleven days earlier, on February 2, 1899, he had already noted
in his diary the beginning of a new novel, *Altershausen*. Nothing more
is heard of it until the fall; he completed the first chapter on November
4, the second on November 21, the third on December 6, the fourth
on December 27, the fifth on January 18, 1900, the sixth on January
23. This may seem more rapid than it was; the chapters are short, and
this much comes only to some thirty-five pages in modern print; still,
it was a good pace at this time of his life. After this comes a pause of
several months, but then the record picks up again: Chapter 7 was
finished in May 1900, 8 in June, 9 in August, 10 in September, 11 in
October, 12 in November. This regularity is in itself rather striking;
it is hard to know whether it is a symptom of steady creativity or of
dutifulness. But it continues to be a good pace, as the diary shows
that Raabe was very busy at this time, especially with the preparation
and proofreading of new editions of his previous works.

Now, however, comes a long pause of more than a year. A diary
entry of February 4, 1902, indicates that he consulted with his friend
Brandes about the work. In June Raabe re-read the twelve chapters
and wrote a thirteenth, then a fourteenth in July and a fifteenth in
August. He began Chapter 16 in that month, but it breaks off in the
middle of a conversation. The manuscript shows several lines crossed
out at the end (deciphered 20: 507). With those deletions he put an
end to his career as a writer of fiction. Friends and publishers generally knew about *Altershausen*, for they encouraged him to get on with
it, but he always fended them off with such remarks as: "Whatever

else I have written in this place [Braunschweig] in the course of a generation, I leave on my retirement tract of Altershausen, as writer (ret.), to the assessment of posterity."[2] To his publisher Grote, who kept pressing him about it, he wrote very near the end of his life: "Reattaching the broken threads in *Altershausen* to one another for your purposes is something that cannot be done; it is a bitter thing that I began to spin in 1899 and 1900 *at bottom for myself alone*" (Raabe's emphasis).[3] After his death it was edited and published by his son-in-law, Paul Wasserfall. Since then it has been an object of much curiosity, as Raabe quite likely foresaw.

Fragmentary texts present literary criticism with a particular set of problems. For despite all the now anti-Romantic, now meta-Romantic revolutions in modern theory, a certain organicist presupposition continues to lurk in our attitude toward texts. We expect them as crafted objects to be fully framed with a beginning and end, bounded from the unstructured universe of discourse outside the work. The point has been made succinctly by Robert Scholes: "A story is a narration that attains a certain degree of completeness, and even a fragment of a story or an unfinished story will imply that completeness as an aspect of its informing principle—the intentionality that governs its construction."[4] A fragment tends to balk interpretation while at the same time seeming to invite speculative completion; well known are the examples of literary fragments that have been completed by other hands. Of course, there are different kinds of fragments. Size makes a big difference for interpretation—whether it is merely a scrap, as is the case with many texts of antiquity, or a 1,600-page torso like Robert Musil's *Mann ohne Eigenschaften* (*Man Without Qualities*). Things turn out to be much easier if we have the end, as with Büchner's *Lenz*, than if we are unsure about the end, as with Büchner's *Woyzeck*.

Beyond this, I should like to suggest, merely heuristically for present purposes, that there are five types of fragments: intentional, sufficient, frustrated, abandoned, and inhibited. We associate the intentional fragment with Romanticism, particularly with the theories of Friedrich Schlegel. The Romantic fragment enacts in its form the recognition that the finite text can never capture the infinite totality that the Romantic imagination strives for but necessarily fails to comprehend. Jean Paul, in his "excuse" to the public for the unfinished state of *Die unsichtbare Loge* (*The Invisible Lodge*), translated this view into terms that might well have appealed to Raabe:

If one asks why a work has not been completed, it is just as well that one does not ask why it was begun. What life do we see in the world that is not interrupted? And if we complain that an incomplete novel does not inform us what came of Kunz's second love affair and Elsa's despair over it, and how Hans saved himself from the claws of the country magistrate and Faust from the claws of Mephistopheles—then let us be consoled by the fact that man sees round about him in his present nothing but knots,—and the solutions lie only on the other side of the grave;—and all world history is an incomplete novel for him.[5]

The sufficient fragment is similar, if we disregard the question of intentionality; despite its apparent or explicit fragmentariness, it seems to us as complete as it can be or needs to be. Heine designated several of his texts, such as *The Harz Journey* and the long poem "Jehuda ben Halevy" as fragments, though they are certainly interpretable as wholes; in his case the practice seems to have had less to do with Romantic theory than with the habitual dissatisfaction with his accomplishment that set in when his works were about to be published. A frustrated fragment is a work that would almost certainly have been completed if it had not been for some external hindrance. The most obvious such hindrance is the death of the author; among many examples one might think of Schiller's *Demetrius* or Dickens's *Edwin Drood*. But a work might also be frustrated by failing powers and encroaching age, such as Keller's last novel *Martin Salander*, which he originally projected as a work of two volumes, but lacked the strength to complete. As for abandoned fragments, they are so common in the history of literature that to give examples would be otiose. The author outgrows his project, or loses interest in it, or foresees that it will not satisfy him, or becomes otherwise preoccupied, or postpones its completion to never-never day. Finally, an inhibited fragment is one that develops its fatal frustrations internally: in the working out of the fiction, contradictions and antinomies emerge that the author cannot resolve; the author comes to be so much at odds with himself that the project seizes up and resists recasting. Years ago I tried to show that Ludwig Tieck's unfinished novel *Franz Sternbalds Wanderungen* (*Franz Sternbald's Wanderings*) is a case of this kind.[6] Heine's three fragmentary novels, in my opinion, also belong in this category.[7]

To be sure, making such assignments in practice may sometimes be far from easy. What, for instance, shall we do with Kafka's novels? It is also not obvious into which rubric Raabe's *Altershausen* falls, and different answers to the question have been given at different times. While Raabe's claim that it was a private work written only for himself suggests that it might be classified as abandoned, he was usually at pains to present it as a frustrated fragment. Most of his comments ascribe the failure to complete the novel to failing energy and mental powers. Possibly there is something to this; he was a man of seventy whose work pace had clearly been slowing down. The draft and first chapter of *Gutmann's Travels* in 1890-91 required eleven months, and he regarded *Stuffcake* as the end point of his career.[8] In 1903, when he had laid down his pen for good, he wrote that Jensen's "literature mill is still merrily running; on mine the wheel is stopped, as in my Cat Mill;—the coagulation doesn't yield the lousiest drop any more."[9] Several years later he mused: "in my seventy-eighth year I prefer that people should say: 'Too bad that he stopped' rather than 'he really ought to stop at last.' "[10]

But several things make it difficult to be satisfied with these explanations. For one thing, Raabe had been complaining grievously about old age for years and years, at least since he was fifty, when much of his finest work was ahead of him. For another, as an old man he certainly did not make an impression of diminished vigor upon those who knew him, who regularly commented on his liveliness, his walking pace that left ordinary pedestrians breathless, and the wit of his conversation. Only with his broken collarbone in 1909 does he seem clearly to go into a decline. Thirdly, it is difficult to detect failing powers in the text, which exhibits some of the roughness of a first draft but no signs of senility in the undiminished brilliance of style, which is here very careful and delicate, a little like Proust in its detailed recovery of memory, if less elaborate. One critic saw in it an early example of modern stream-of-consciousness narration.[11] Furthermore, it certainly seems to be a sign of sustained mental vigor that Raabe introduced yet another variant of narrative perspective that he had not yet tried: the narrator begins in the third person, then identifies himself as "*I*, now the writer of these pages" (20: 204), continues for a few pages of introduction in the first person, then narrates the rest in the third person, a device enacting the distanced observation of the self by the self, and suggesting besides that others of Raabe's third-person narrations are also distanced fictions of the authorial self.[12]

Some observers, especially in the oldest generation of his admirers, have regarded *Altershausen* as a sufficient fragment. Jensen, in a public "letter" to his deceased friend, asserted that the work needed no conclusion, for it said what it wanted to say.[13] Among modern critics, Daemmrich has regarded it as complete enough, though for reasons less comforting than Jensen's: "If one regards *Altershausen* as Raabe's last attempt to portray an individual and his secret sharer as well as his final expression of an unresolved doubt whether a single individual can ever hope to achieve complete harmony with the world, the novel appears complete."[14] Martini, too, has found the work complete enough, since, like life, it could not have closure, but he adds the speculation that if Raabe did intend a closure to the novel, it would not have been harmonious or unambiguous.[15]

But this recognition of unresolved doubt in the text has led most modern critics to treat it, in one way or another, as an inhibited fragment. Meinerts, one of the earliest of Raabe's perceptive critics, recognized that it takes up again some of the problems of *The Documents of the Birdsong* and observed that Raabe himself realized there was no solution to them and that it was not his way to make peace with life or to find a permanent solution of stasis in dream and death.[16] Years earlier, Perquin had found the theme of the novel in the question of what happens to one in death, and added: "in view of the philosophical character of the work, where a cheerful last evening of life as a final apotheosis would have been downright childish, one can rightly assume that the pantheistic solution did not satisfy Raabe and that his life work ended with a question mark after all."[17] Lukács, from his quite different perspective, argued, apparently with *Altershausen* in mind, that if Raabe had logically carried through his premises, "he would have, *sans phrase*, without any reservation, opted for childhood against the world of the 'adults'; no space would be found here for the complicated dialectical for-and-against of such life feelings and attitudes toward life; thus the aging Raabe would sink into sentimental entertainment literature or become a subjectivist décadent," adding characteristically: "In his weak works, in the weak sections of the good writings of his late period, he came close to both."[18] A more recent critic gives more credit to Raabe's perception and integrity, arguing that in the fragment repetition becomes the principle of time and narration; while the narrator keeps gesturing for a consoling alternative to the cyclical emptiness, Raabe could see no way out.[19] My own understanding has benefited greatly from these and other critical initiatives. My emphasis, however, is a little different. I believe *Alterhausen* is a true example of an inhibited fragment, that it failed internally and could not be continued. I shall try to show that Raabe made some errors of judgment that are intimately connected with his enduringly irreconcilable contradictions, and I submit that in recognition of the fact that he ultimately could not in honesty say what he might have liked to say if he could have believed it, he called a halt to his novel and his career.

Altershausen begins with the word "Survived!" (20: 203). What has been survived is the seventieth-birthday celebration of Fritz Feyerabend, a prominent physician and medical scientist, now contemplating retirement and the evening of his life. He is a well-preserved but somewhat isolated man whose child and wife have died; he lives with his sister, whose management and mothering he likes well enough. He also does not dislike the honors that have come upon him, but it occurs to him that afterwards people will no longer think about him very much. Clearly, an inchoate unease and dissatisfaction lurks in this prosperous, successful man, who exhorts himself: "Physician, heal thyself!" (20: 208), and who in the face of increasing age is obliged to buck himself up with aphorisms such as "Stay in your boots, man!" (20: 216). He is evidently addicted to the doubtfully efficacious stoic exercises often encountered in Raabe's fiction. The physician's first publication, we are told, dealt with habituation to medicines; "now, however, it is a matter of how, with greater or lesser success, he has made himself immune to the toxic and infectious agents of earthly existence, even after having concluded his seventieth year" (20: 208), a formulation that may well remind us of Velten Andres's futile effort to be "without feeling" in *The Documents of the Birdsong*. He wonders himself if it is a sign of senility that he is beset by a longing to return to his home town, Altershausen. Here, incidentally, we see more examples of Raabe's perhaps excessively explicit label naming: "Feyerabend" means "quitting time," while "Altershausen" means something like "old home"; since the man and the place would have had these names when the man was still young and the place not yet his old home, the device drifts from symbolism toward allegory.

Feyerabend is well aware that his sister would think him crazy if she knew of his plan to return to his old home, though she would have accepted his claim to have business in "Paris, London, Rome . . . Madrid, Rio Janeiro [sic], or New York" (20: 226), so he slips away without revealing his destination. Here we see already the narrator's alienation even from those closest to him. His most clearly articulated desire is to see again his childhood friend Ludchen Bock, whom he left behind as a bright, vigorous ten-year-old. But when he returns, to his initial shock he finds Ludchen as a whining, infantile old man, capable only of performing the simplest tasks for drinking money, and a figure of fun in the community. For it turns out that Ludchen at age twelve had a fall from a tree that caused brain damage and arrested his development. He is now in the care of an elderly woman, Minchen Ahrens, who was a childhood friend of Ludchen and Feyerabend; thus Raabe's familiar childhood cloverleaf is here restored in old age, and Feyerabend seems immensely comforted in Minchen's calm, timeless presence. However, it is in the middle of a conversation with her that the novel breaks off.

The deeply personal dimension of the fragment must immediately strike any informed reader. In fact, Fehse thought that Raabe's main motive was to arm himself against the stresses of his own impending seventieth-birthday celebrations.[20] It has been argued that the depiction of Altershausen corresponds in detail to Raabe's childhood home of Stadtoldendorf, a resemblance that also seemed plausible to me when I visited there.[21] Minchen Ahrens, it turns out, was the name of a servant in the Stadtoldendorf household to whom Raabe retained a fond attachment for many years (20: 505). Even more important is the search for a sense of closure, for meaning in the life cycle as a career ends and the end of life approaches. It seems all but certain that *Altershausen* was conceived as a last work, a final summation and stocktaking. At the same time, one must be cautious about autobiographical identification. Raabe's habit was always to project images of his own self so metamorphosed that they exaggerate partial features of his personality and develop alternative, contrasting aspects of a possible, imagined self, from the perspective of which the author pursues self-analysis and often self-criticism.

Feyerabend differs from Raabe in significant respects. In the first place, he is a successful man of worldly affairs, such as Raabe did not believe himself to be, and a type of figure often regarded with suspicion in his fiction. Since Feyerabend is admired and honored, while the retarded Ludchen is an object of teasing and mild ill will, we may be inclined to think that Raabe has again split his imagined self into two contrasting extremes, as in *The Documents of the Birdsong*. Feyerabend is, on the surface at any rate, much more of the complacent, well-adjusted Wilhelminian bourgeois than Raabe was ever able to be. It is here that we must be especially careful about our interpretive responses to several aspects of Feyerabend's mentality that may be irritating to the modern reader. The most troubling of these is his remark on Altershausen's well, from which the stork brings up children "in sufficient numbers against intruding and obtruding Semitism, Frenchiness [*Welschentum*], and Slavism" (20: 268).[22] In our time Horst Denkler has been very troubled by this passage, which he sees as a reflex of anxiety about Germany's encirclement and to which he applies a psychosocial interpretation.[23] But this rude xenophobia does not really sound much like Raabe, and some of our own anxiety about it might be relieved if we open a space between the author and his fictional persona. Not that he was incapable of such thoughts, but they flicker in a broader and more generous cast of mind; Feyerabend at the outset is a somewhat stuffier, more tightly corseted personality than his author, and it is possible that Raabe meant to bring him, through his experiences in Altershausen, into a more relaxed and humanized condition. Certainly he appears drawn to his hometown by a hope for some as yet undefined redemption.

The encounter with the retarded Ludchen Bock was evidently meant to be one instrument of this redemption. Ludchen would be an excellent candidate in a contest for the most perversely misinterpreted of Raabe's characters. One critic has spoken of him as a figure of true instinct, superior to Feyerabend, "in possession of the true reality of life," a figure of childish simplicity against disharmonious reason, close to the roots of being.[24] Another has claimed that Ludchen remains mentally twelve years old, and, with reference to a passage in Schopenhauer's *The World as Will and Representation*, emphatically marked in Raabe's copy, to the effect that brain damage or madness cannot affect the heart, the seat of individuality, concludes that Ludchen is "an existence fully harmonious in itself," the consequence of a "childlikeness joyful in life."[25] In a more recent study, Ludchen's mind is again described as having remained the same, a figure "who can live in the other world without having to compromise or break apart like Leonhard [Hagebucher] or Velten [Andres]."[26] Yet another contemporary study argues that the teased, mistreated Ludchen "incarnates symbolically the contempt and scorn for the ideals of the past in the present."[27] These are all examples of willful misreading of what is before us on the page. Ludchen has not remained the same; he bears no resemblance to a twelve-year-old boy and certainly none to the merry, energetic scamp Feyerabend retains in his memory. His only link to his boyhood self is a retained affinity for nature. Otherwise he is a whiny, greedy old idiot, childish rather than childlike. What ideals of the past can this sorry wreck of a man incarnate? Other critics, to be sure, have seen more clearly: Roy Pascal has pointed out that Ludchen is not childlike, that he is disturbing and causes anxiety, that he never gives the answer Feyerabend wants, and that therefore he is not what Feyerabend is seeking.[28] Martini has said rightly that Ludchen exhibits childhood in the form of caricature, though he then takes an odd tack by arguing that Feyerabend begins to show signs of Ludchen's idiocy and that he is associated with Raabe's theme of the necessity of illusion and dream over the abyss.[29] More recently, critics have seen that Ludchen is an insecure and miserable figure who suffers "countless repetitions of the unrelieved anguish of the wounded child,"[30] and that Raabe actually gives "a striking illustration of the undesirability of the childhood idyll's continuation into adult life."[31]

323

This interpretive confusion, however, is the fault not only of the interpreters but also of the author. In my admittedly speculative opinion, Raabe blundered with the figure of Ludchen Bock. I suspect that he really intended to imagine a figure representing temporal stasis, but his purpose was sabotaged by his realistic common sense. The observation that Ludchen's condition is not medically and psychologically realistic is not of great importance.[32] But a twelve-year-old boy is not an idiot, at least, in my paternal experience, not all the time. While he may retain childish characteristics, he is likely to resemble an adult more than Ludchen does. After his accident Ludchen avoids boys and plays only with girls (20: 285), very likely a sign, as with Velten Andres's obsession with girls and women, of a drift into a dysfunctional fantasy world; he is unable to learn and forgets much of what he already knew. Ludchen is *not* an arrested twelve-year-old, whatever that might look like, and therefore cannot serve the purposes several critics have ascribed to him. Raabe must have seen this in the process of creation, and the recognition that the figure was misconceived may well have contributed to the abandonment of the novel.

Even so, we may still have not grasped Ludchen's intended function. For there are symptoms in the text of a subliminal hostility between Ludchen and Feyerabend. In what turns out to be a blind motif owing to the fragmentary character of the work, Feyerabend, at one of the most dignified moments of his birthday celebration, suddenly remembers Ludchen denouncing him to their school rector as "unclean"; that is, he had a louse (20: 220). This may be a hint that the memory of Ludchen was to serve as a lever to bring to the surface something that is not altogether in order in Feyerabend's adult self. Later, when Feyerabend and Ludchen play nine men's morris, a children's game popular in Germany under the name of "Mühle," Feyerabend accuses Ludchen of cheating, "smiling out of all his superiority, yet with the most complete seriousness," whereupon Ludchen offers to beat him up as he had sixty years before (20: 303-4). Earlier, however, Ludchen seems to be fighting down a fear of Feyerabend, who remarks retrospectively: "Who could know what perhaps was rising up in the darkened soul out of far, past, bright days?" (20: 288). Might these "bright days" have turned out to be a self-delusive memory of the sort in which Eduard in *Stuffcake* repeatedly indulges? Perhaps Feyerabend's desire to find out what Ludchen had to say about life might not have turned out comfortably for him, though one critic has argued that he must have found something positive, since the narrative is written after his return from his journey.[33] Nevertheless, with respect to Ludchen, several kinds of tensions and contradictions are building in the text. We cannot tell if they are running counter to Raabe's original intention, but the project of discovering the meaning of life or unravelling the "terrible secret of self-awareness" (20: 240) by means of Ludchen seems doomed.

As regards the third member of the reconstituted cloverleaf, Minchen Ahrens, I am afraid I again find that much in the critical tradition is unsatisfactory. Repeatedly the calm, nurturing Minchen has been compared with Phöbe in *Restless Guests*.[34] Even a contemporary critic has claimed that Minchen "surpasses" Phöbe, adding that "the connection to the world-secret occurs in the quiet self-surrender of sacrifice, near to life and outlasting time."[35] Apart from the question of how Phöbe might be "surpassed," Minchen is by contrast a positively diminished figure, colorless, placid, and passive; when she fails to recognize Feyerabend at their first encounter, she is instinctively deferential to him as an upper-class person (20: 269). Phöbe is polite and respectful, but never deferential for so artificial a reason as class distinction. It is true that we hear briefly of a futile love affair in Minchen's past (20: 309), but this is merely a sad loss in no way comparable to Phöbe's jarring encounter with Veit von Bielow. Raabe seems in real danger here of regressing to the stasis of Klaudine and the Cat Mill that generated so much thematic discordance in *Abu Telfan*. Feyerabend, at any rate, appears to be mesmerized by Minchen and comes to be nearly ecstatic in her presence (20: 300). He says that she belongs in a book entitled *Mother Germany and her People* (20: 277). His conversation with her gives him sustenance that no dream can: "the great open world secret lay in its whole beauty before him in the light of this present day and—he was glad that he was *along in the world* and belonged to the miracle" (20: 299). I regret to say that passages like this, often admired in the past, strike me as twaddle, not least because they are totally unearned in the figuration of Minchen. Thus it is not surprising that the most thoughtful critics have suspected that Minchen might have been the fatal problem in the fragment or that Raabe must have seen that the distance between Feyerabend and Minchen was unbridgeable.[36] It does seem ominous that the fragment breaks off in the middle of one of Feyerabend's allegedly so redeeming conversations with her.

However, a significant symptom of the antinomies that threaten to sabotage the novel appears somewhat earlier, in a remarkable dream scene. Feyerabend has two dreams in the fragment. The first is a rather forced allegory of the political experiences of his lifetime. As the bells of Altershausen ring the hours, the critical years of German history pass in review, beginning with 1848; as a matter of fact, this vision is the first and only representation of the revolution of 1848 in Raabe's works. The dates continue through the Crimean War, the war between Austria and France of 1859, the Prussian wars against Denmark of 1864 and against Austria of 1866, which last wakes him up, and finally the Franco-Prussian War, which makes him irritable, so that he turns over and "sleeps through the number seventy from the Altershausen church tower" (20: 259). This dream has been interpreted to mean that Bismarck's wars against Denmark and Austria were the high point of modern German development for Raabe, while the consequences of the Franco-Prussian War, the actual constitution of the Reich, were but a disappointment for him.[37] It also possible, however, that it is another device for separating Feyerabend from the author; Raabe, though certainly disappointed by many things in the German Reich, did not "sleep through" 1870-71, but followed events with enthusiastic attention.

The second dream is a different matter altogether. It is the most deftly devised, the most realistically dream-like of all his fictional dreams. It appears in Chapter 14, one of the latest segments of the fragment, completed in July 1902, that is, several months after Raabe's own seventieth-birthday celebrations. The scene is the last Christmas in Feyerabend's childhood home in Altershausen. Feyerabend, to the surprise of no one in the household, has been metamorphosed into a nutcracker. Actually he is the worn-out nutcracker of the previous Christmas, about to be discarded: "Let's see someone crack earth-nuts until his seventieth birthday and keep his previous so brilliantly 'dazzling blue' eyes and not let his once so gleamingly black mustache hang greyly, thinly, raggedly over his 'old and tired lips'!" (20: 292). A toy whip appears as an "old, hideous, unfruitful Megaera" (20: 294) urging Feyerabend to let out all the poison and gall that he has accumulated in his life, but she is rejected. The successor nutcracker appears, and Feyerabend gives him a nut, urging him to crack on and not to despair. Now the old nutcracker is re-metamorphosed into Feyerabend, but just at that moment his nurse arrives to use him, "the old horror" (20: 298) for tinder on the fire.

At the beginning of this dream there is a literary allusion to the empty-headed Baroness Emerentia von Schnuck-Puckelig-Erbsenscheucher in Karl Immermann's *Münchhausen*, who falls in love with a nutcracker that is thrown in the trash. Raabe, as we have seen, justly admired *Münchhausen* as a satirical novel, but the allusion may mask another one to a more familiar example of the nutcracker motif: E.T.A. Hoffmann's tale of 1816, *Nußknacker und Mäusekönig* (Nut-

cracker and Mouse-King), with its subtle and somewhat grim subtext, full of conflict and vengeance, probing not only the isolation of the realm of poesy from the common run of hostile realists, but also the artist's internal threat of artificiality. Like Raabe, Hoffmann anatomizes an imagined self, in his case dramatizing the conflict between his dexterous imagination and his frustrated, unattractive persona in the form of the hyperbolically ugly storyteller and ingenious clockwork artist Drosselmeier, and then in an even more grotesque third self in the form of the beleaguered but brave nutcracker. It cannot be proved that Raabe knew Hoffmann's *Nutcracker*; it is not among the three volumes of Hoffmann found in his preserved library.[38] But it certainly is the sort of thing he might have read; Fehse thought it a source for the early story *Christmas Spirits*, at the beginning of which the narrator, with an allusion to Hoffmann, buys a doll at a street auction; the story develops into an elaborate dream scene in which the Christmas presents come to life (2: 281).[39] Raabe might have been reminded of the motif by the news of Tchaikovsky's ballet in 1892.

Feyerabend cannot decide whether he owes the dream to the weakness of age, to the renewed puberty that Goethe ascribed to the genius, or to his "*maternal* inheritance" (20: 289; Raabe's emphasis); once again the ambivalent quality of fantasy is traced to the mother's side. The most realistic aspect of the dream is the dreamer's shifting, dissolving identity among present self as honored old man, past self as ten-year-old child, and nutcracker, once shiny and new, now worn and dilapidated. But its most significant feature is the nervously oscillating dialectic between a cyclical, therefore tragic-stoic, and a progressive, therefore hopeful, future-oriented outlook. Feyerabend as the old nutcracker professes to wish his successor well and gives him a nut to crack, at which he succeeds, for both came "from the same famous factory," but, the dreamer continues somewhat cryptically, "even if the world as it was did not perish, it was not made very different by the new substitute." He then gives his successor some advice:

> Keep on cracking, there is always something better, and—when you have chewed and cracked yourself tired and [stand] soberly before the pile of shells, then do as I do: don't fret and fume! Besides one's annoyance and disgust one still has once in a while some fun and pleasure, and besides one's disgrace also one's honors. Look [around] the table: a year ago, when I was young here, it was the same company around me. (20: 297; the brackets indicate editorial emendations to the manuscript)

At this the successor nutcracker echoes Feyerabend's encouragement but begins to weep tears of resin. The room takes on a magical aura with sweet odors and shining lights: "The wax candles on the tree that had been blown out by Father Feyerabend [flamed] up again for a supplementary celebration of his seventieth birthday, but with a magic light *sub specie aeternitatis*" (ibid.). All the toys cry out joyfully that the cracking will go on, except for the prettiest doll, who weeps bitterly. Now the old nutcracker is re-metamorphosed back into the "Acting Privy Councillor Professor Doctor Feyerabend" who wonders what he should say to the doll in consolation: "That her daughters will become as beautiful as she?" (20: 298) And he watches in his own person as his metaphorical self is taken as tinder for the fire, since his childhood self now has a new nutcracker.

The waking Feyerabend attempts to repress the implications of this dream: "It no longer snowed into the Christmas night of two generations ago, but everything still lay in the most beautiful late-summer afternoon sunshine in the current year, in which he was *present* in Altershausen, where he was invited to drink coffee with Minchen Ahrens and his friend Ludchen Bock!" (20: 299) As we have seen, Feyerabend believes himself to be *dans le vrai* with Minchen, enjoying a sustenance that no dream can give. But the remarkable dream is not to be erased from the reader's memory by these means and, if the text is to make sense at all, it must represent some true level of Feyerabend's consciousness. It generates a rhetoric of consolation that fails to come into equilibrium. The recognition that life goes on, that the task of nutcracking must be passed on to the successor generation, does not neutralize the sorrow of loss and impending death; the intended atmosphere of celebratory joy is punctuated by bitter tears, reflecting the ambivalence of the birthday celebration. In Raabe's own psychic constitution, the awareness of the pleasures and honors enjoyed in life could not balance deeply rooted feelings of anger and resentment, as we can easily see in his moods during his decade of retirement. The aggressive satire incarnated by the whip is rejected by the dream-Feyerabend, but Raabe's art and spirit could not do without satire; to reject the whip would have required a self-repudiation of which I do not think he was capable. In the most general sense, *Altershausen* is an effort to shore up the narrating self against death. Raabe was intensely aware of the inevitability of death but could not assent to it. The ethos of the novel tries to freeze reality in the stasis of an eternal present, but both the dream, with its antinomy of recurrence and progression, of preservation and loss, and the illogical figuration of Ludchen Bock as a self stopped in time show the futility of the effort. In the fragment Raabe was whistling in the dark, and he knew that he was.

The word "home" (*Heimat*) in German has an emotional charge not easily reproduced in English. It connotes a kind of eschatology of the self, a paradise of psychic wholeness and belonging toward which the alienated self, battered by adulthood and reality, yearns. It is a metaphorical place to which the self longs to return. In the early story *The Way to Laughter* Raabe gave the concept conventionally sentimental expression: "An infinite wistfulness overcame him, a feeling that can only be designated by the term—homesickness. . . . Man's home is in—happiness. If the child of the earth yearns for a higher, more blessed happiness, his farther—unknown home, then he calls his yearning—*faith*; if it longs for a lost earthly happiness, then he calls his yearning—*homesickness!*" (2: 237) But Raabe soon emancipated himself from these stammering, low-Romantic vapors. Instead, the recognition becomes thematic in his oeuvre that one cannot go home again, neither to an unaltered place, nor with an unaltered self. Chapter 27 of *The People from the Forest* begins with the heading: "Robert Wolf proves that one can return to the old place without looking at the world from there in the old way" (5: 313). *Old Nests* demonstrates the impossibility of going home again; the flow of time and change is recognized and accepted. Castle Werden cannot be restored as Ewald dreamt, and its stones are, with typically explicit symbolism, employed for a bridge. Ewald had imagined in Ireland "that she [Irene] and it [the castle] and we would have remained what we were" (14: 213), but he must learn otherwise.[40] Theodor Rodburg in *Princess Fish* has to learn that he cannot go home again, that he is homeless at home, and that his childhood and youth are a corpse (15, 368, 382). When he goes off to the university, his elderly mentor Tieffenbacher prophesies that Theodor will have a comfortable old age with his friends in his hometown, such as he himself believes he has found, but the prophecy is false and occurs just before Tieffenbacher's own life is destroyed by the elopement of his wife with Theodor's brother Alexander (15: 352). Theodor is struck with terror when he returns to his hometown, which has undergone changes in time, and he turns his back on it (15: 384-85). The departure from home, like the separation from the family, repeatedly appears as part of the process of maturation and individuation.

In *Altershausen*, Raabe seems to be trying to reverse this process. Of course, we cannot be certain that Feyerabend himself was not to undergo a reversal, an acceptance of the impossibility of his quest. A few details in the text seem to hold this option open. Feyerabend initially wonders whether his access of homesickness is a symptom of senility (20: 217). When he arrives in Altershausen, he at first finds the place strange and changed, and he feels like Odysseus on his return home (20: 232-33). "It is easier," he thinks to himself, "to orient oneself in a strange world than to make oneself at home again in a world become strange!" (20: 238). But he soon acclimates himself and the feeling of strangeness wears away, to be replaced by a sense of recognition and even of stasis. When he gets away from the redeveloped center of town, he finds that all is as it was two generations ago, like the town of Vineta sunken underwater (20:240)—a recurrent motif, incidentally, of German poetry. As far as the fragment goes, it can appear that a "return to childhood [is] . . . a timorous and ultimately self-defeating exercise based on an illusory conception of the timelessness of existence."[41]

If this rather hard judgment is fair, then we must also recognize that the fragmentariness of the novel represents an act of integrity. With *Altershausen*, I infer, Raabe endeavored to close the circle of his life. But the circle would not close. The stoic equanimity, the benign acceptance for which he and his characters repeatedly strove, could not be truthfully achieved. Death and loss are death and loss and not some other thing. The self cannot return to the lost paradise of its origins, if indeed there ever was any such paradise. Anger and bitterness, the memory of discouragement and disappointment, ought to be dissoluble in an old age full of honors and recognition, but are not. Raabe may have wished that certain things were so, but wishing never made them so for him. His characters might draw sustenance from necessary and inevitable illusion, but in the last analysis illusion and reality remained for him separate realms. He was the most honest of fictionalists; he could not close the circle by force of pretense. Thus *Altershausen* is a fragment inhibited by the author's own candor with himself. It remained open and unresolved, as the entire oeuvre has been found by modern criticism to be open and unresolved, transcending by the unforced release of the rational imagination even the author's own ideological commitments, his would-be convictions, his preceptorial allegiances, into polyperspective and often ironic complexity.

IN LIEU OF A CONCLUSION

> Literature not only sustains a historical experience
> and continues a tradition. It also—through moral
> risk and formal experimentation and verbal hu-
> mor—transforms the conservative horizon of the
> readers and helps liberate us all from the deter-
> minisms of prejudice, doctrinal rigidity and bar-
> ren repetition.
>   The narrative voice contributes to our presence
> as the active subjects rather than the passive ob-
> jects of history. The novel is a question that can-
> not be contained by a single answer, because it is
> social and society is plural. The novel is an an-
> swer that always says: "the world is unfinished
> and cannot be contained by a single question."
>   Carlos Fuentes[1]

IN SOME quarters an uncomfortable feeling has been developing that
many of the canonical texts of our literary tradition are showing signs
of interpretive exhaustion. The practice of academic criticism operates
necessarily on a theorem that great texts are in their essence inexhaustible. There is always room for yet another discourse on a poem of
Wordsworth or Hölderlin. Given the probability that literary criticism, history, and theory constitute, in sheer numbers of practition-
ers, the vastest intellectual enterprise in the Western world, this ever-
expanding discourse must mean that the texts are literally without
definable limits, are infinite in their generative possibilities. An outsider might well wonder if this is logical. An imperfectly articulated
suspicion that it might not be has, in my view, infected the contemporary practice of literary study.

It is not only that criticism and theory, in their professional specialization and quantitative ramification, have become so abstruse, refined well beyond the comprehension or possibly the patience of the
majority of educated and cultured readers. More subtly, there has
been a proliferation of theories that privilege the reader as the creator
of the text, which therefore becomes an artifact of doubtful ontological
status and little more than an occasion for the creativity and ingenuity
of the interpreter. The author fades into the oversoul of language it-

self, while the interpreter becomes the artist. There are now really no limits in the name of interpretive validity, and it sometimes seems that anyone may say anything about anything and offer it as discourse on literature. I am fully aware of the epistemological considerations from which these theories and practices derive. But a sociologist of knowledge might conclude that the adherence to this particular set of epistemological positions rather than another is motivated by an interest in preserving the institutional structure of literary scholarship by making its exhaustion impossible, in thus preserving the status or, perhaps these days, merely the employment of literary scholars.

It is in this context that the topic of Wilhelm Raabe seems so welcome and refreshing. It is very far from exhaustion, and the coming years will doubtless bring much vigorous discussion in the international critical community, refining details as well as our overview of his place in literary, social, and political history. On innumerable occasions in the preceding pages I have felt how much more could be said, either by myself or, more likely, by a more acute observer. I realize that, by attempting to juggle the whole oeuvre, I may have blurred important distinctions and perspectives, despite my pursuit of nuances. Even my efforts at more detailed interpretation, it seems to me, keep the texts rather in the middle distance. In my own estimation, this book belongs to the pioneering phase of our modern understanding of Raabe, the fuller maturation of which still lies in the future.

At the same time, however, the topic does not have to be worked up from a primitive state. There has been a long tradition of empirical research, and most of the basic philological work has been done. A substantial body of valuable modern criticism already exists, although a good deal of it is unpublished. All of this, as I have tried in the preceding pages to acknowledge, is of value to the inquirer. Still, the philological base is not yet so complete as to make primary research unnecessary. Several of the texts in the critical edition have had to be re-edited, either in new printings of volumes of the edition or in other formats. Some of the annotation has become antiquated. Raabe's nonfiction works and other paralipomena have still not appeared in the critical edition at this writing. The most disappointing volumes of the critical edition are those containing his letters. Except for the correspondence with the Jensens, only a selection has been included, leaving out, for example, most of Raabe's correspondence with his publishers, so that the thorough student must still have recourse to Fehse's differently selected volume of 1940. The annotation in the critical edition is cursory. Fortunately, a complete edition of the correspondence is being prepared by Hans-Werner Peter and William T. Webster. Furthermore, although at the outset of this enterprise I shared the general view that Raabe's diary would not bear publication, I have had recourse to it so often that I welcome the recent news that such a project is under consideration. No one, of course, would want to *read* it qua diary, but for internal purposes of Raabe scholarship it would be valuable to have it, and perhaps also his notebooks, edited and, above all, indexed. This would be a daunting research task, however, that would probably require a team of scholars.

There continues to be plenty of room for interpretive dialogue on both matters of detail and more comprehensive issues. One task remaining before us is to complement the highly sophisticated studies of Raabe's narrative technique with an equally intense examination of his style. He developed the most idiosyncratic style of any German writer of his time, of a sort that irritated his general public and more conventional critics but whose originality the most perceptive of critics were able to recognize even then. In 1881 Eduard Engel wrote in a review of the *The Horn of Wanza*: "Raabe has a *style* and it is his own. Whereas I, who have a reputation of attending more to form than content, find it absolutely impossible, from a page of Hans Hopfen or Spielhagen or even Wilbrandt to guess the author without a glance at the title page, I would undertake—without boasting—among ten other works, from ten lines of a story of Wilhelm Raabe unknown to me, to pick out this rare man with his original, particular style."[2] Naturally this salient feature of his writing has attracted comment from the critics. Christa Hebbel, in a relatively early study, devoted some attention to style, pointing out that Raabe avoids the straightforward declarative sentence whenever he can and that he exhibits two levels: "an idealizing manner of speaking, elevating the object in various ways out of the subjective perspective, and a humoristic-ironic posture tending in the opposite direction, relativizing the object in its significance."[3] But actually things are more complicated than this, for the idealizing and ironizing rhetorics interpenetrate to the point where they are the same, internally antithetical posture, and Raabe can lurch from one rhetorical level to another, sometimes within the same sentence or clause, with disconcerting abruptness. Hermann Helmers has contributed two good essays, one stressing Raabe's sometimes esoteric rhetorical habits that insistently challenge the reader, the other his alienation of style from common habits of diction: his shifts of levels, grotesquely mixed metaphors, rhetorical devices, intentionally irrelevant allusions, and subversion of clichés.[4] But more can be done to build on these beginnings with more closely focused methods such as detailed analysis of characteristic passages or even a taxonomy of the kinds of sentences he wrote.

His historical placement remains another continuing challenge, which is beset by several difficulties. For one thing, the need to free him from the ideological vise of his disciples has given much of the discussion an apologetic cast, which I am quite aware is not absent from my own approach to him and perhaps still tends to burden discourse about him. If one writes a book about, say, George Eliot, one does not have to devote space to an argument that she is an important and excellent writer. For another, he often seems to us oddly out of his time, even though literary sociology has rightly warned against supposing that even the most original and idiosyncratic writers can somehow be magically liberated from the consciousness-forming determinants of time, place, and society. The problem is made no easier by the circumstance that Raabe had strongly articulated, explicitly class-oriented ideological commitments that nevertheless develop manifold and to some degree contradictory facets in the polyperspectivism imposed by the fictional imagination.

Since he was, as I have argued, an eminently literary kind of writer, it would seem appropriate to attempt to situate him historically by situating him in literary history, and this will oblige us to raise the question of realism. To take this tack, however, is unlikely to make the task any easier or more comfortable, the definition of realism being as recalcitrant as we all know it to be. Often in the preceding pages I have consciously employed the terms "realism" and "realistic" in the most commonplace way, innocent of any particular theoretical burden, for there seemed to be no convenient way to broach the theoretical issues while attempting to get on with the business at hand. One must first decide whether realism is to be measured according to retrospectively applied norms à la Lukács or according to the principles extant in Raabe's own time. These principles, which began to be explicitly articulated around mid-century, were aggressively ideological and bourgeois; the function of realism was to assure the middle class of the rightness of its collective view of things and buoy up its confidence. The influential theorist Julian Schmidt declared that the novel should "seek the German people where they are to be found in their competence [*Tüchtigkeit*], namely in their work,"[5] an admonition Gustav Freytag promptly set as the motto to his anti-aristocratic, anti-revolutionary, anti-Semitic, and, above all, anti-Polish best-seller of 1855, *Debit and Credit*. Hartmut Steinecke, commenting on the way in which Freytag's novel realized Schmidt's program, observed that "order, discipline, moderation are set as values for the realistic novel. The writing of novels thus becomes a trade, 'work' that is worth the effort of the burgher." Thus "work acquires a high value of acculturation, it transmits the bourgeois virtues and habits of behavior: industriousness and order, regularity and sense of duty." It is not, however, work itself that is the central value—one might add here that the Jew Itzig in *Debit and Credit* is repugnant partly because he works too hard—but realism's revelation of the positive aspect of reality: "For realism means from the beginning: *health* and *optimism*. It demands the discovery in reality of the positive and the healthy, the beautiful, pleasant, comfortable; everything unhealthy, sickly, negative, pessimistic should be repelled."[6]

It is completely clear that Raabe wanted nothing to do with this program, as was repeatedly marked up against him by his reviewers, one of whom, the prominent Young Hegelian Robert Prutz, hoped as early as 1863 that he was finding his way "out of his blurry manner to a firm, true-to-life plasticity" (5: 448). Thus he appears to reside on a boundary of Friedrich Sengle's vastly complex category of Biedermeier, though as one of the youngest authors who can be so denominated. But Sengle points out that, by Biedermeier standards, Raabe is a much more orderly and conscious narrator and disposes his rhetorical devices in a more disciplined fashion.[7] A closer examination would show that the apparently untheoretical Raabe must have given a great deal of thought to the problems of realism, for reflections on them can be found in many places in the fiction. But I do not think that such an examination would be able to extract a coherent position. Instead, we find him turning the familiar conundrums of realism this way and that, and apparently coming to different tentative conclusions in different places.

Raabe's main commitment was to truthfulness of representation. His remark of 1866, "There is much lying in our literature, and for my poor part I will do what I can with all my strength to expose it, although I know quite well that the comfort of my life will not benefit from it,"[8] has often been cited as a crucial utterance, and rightly so, especially as it can be applied against the alleged truthfulness of the programmatic realism. But, like others before and after him, he found that truthfulness of representation is not always identical with mimetic representation. To begin with, he inherited and never entirely abandoned an idealism that distinguished mean, shallow reality from higher, more spiritual truths. Thus, in *Three Pens*, one might hear an echo of Schiller, for whom "realism" was a deeply pejorative term, in August Sonntag's account of the way in which his amoral mentor Pinnemann attempted to seduce him into a corrosive cynicism:

335

All enthusiasm, all inspiration, every beautiful illusion this companion and guide had to tear out of my soul; he was a Mephisto, a negating spirit, and in addition, despite all his cunning, a crude, uncultured, foolish one. His wit was flat, false, and common; but I was too immature to be able to defend myself against it. I was dragged by this Pinnemann through the theaters, the concerts, the exhibitions of art works, and even today I grind my teeth in anger when I recall how he tried to stifle every enthusiastic surge of feeling. This half-educated maliciousness, this impotent foaming of nullity against the true and beautiful, against every hope and joy of sacrifice are the most terrible thing that civilization begets in its womb. In it mankind strikes itself in the face, and the thought that basically people like my guide have the most influence on the masses and everywhere have the first and last word is enough to embitter the most loyal and honorable person and drive him into the deepest disgust. (9/1: 304)

Sonntag goes on to remark that Pinnemann drove out the true and eternal with the triviality of detail (9/1: 305). Later the shallowly common-sensical Mathilde Sonntag asserts with her characteristic conceit that she is the only rational person of the bunch, while the rest are floating into the blue sky each with his "air balloon full of high-mindedness and philosophy" (9/1: 398). In other places Raabe can sound a little like Stifter, who argued that it was the calm, regular, small things of life that were real, not violent upheavals in nature or great passions in mankind.

But this secularized idealism by no means defines every facet of his position. In some places he or his characters express an almost cynical disillusionment with idealism as delusion or prettification; in others realistic mimesis is rejected as naturalism. Elsewhere it will appear that realism is not mimetic enough, compared, say, to a photograph (see *Christoph Pechlin*, 10: 286), or that reality is less realistic than fiction, in those cases—e.g., *Gedelöcke*, *The Geese of Bützow*—where he draws absurd or bizarre tales from real-life sources. Yet again in other cases, such as *In the Victory Wreath* and *Pfister's Mill*, real-life sources can afford realistic narration in the more commonplace sense of the term. Just as Gottfried Keller was inspired to write his most famous novella, *Romeo and Juliet in the Village*, by an item in the newspaper, so Raabe drew the initial situation of *On the Scrap-Iron* from a set of newspaper clippings (reproduced 16: 573-77), which he followed quite closely in details. Perhaps for this very reason he began the novel with a reminder that reality, unlike fiction, lacks a beginning and an end, and that his novel is fiction, not reality (see above, p. 178).

It is here that we can see him struggling on two fronts at once. On the one hand, he often found reality discouraging and associated a realistic outlook with heartlessness. Thus there is a certain pressure toward flight into the realm of the ideal. But, on the other hand, he continuously resisted this pressure, seeking instead a space of play and freedom between reality and fantasy, in touch with both. He did not, however, find this space easy to define. He objected to what he was pleased to regard as the aesthetic attitude because he found it reductive. Yet he was an artist; he knew very well that art organizes, selects, abstracts reality. He tried to maintain an awareness of the multiplicity of reality within an awareness of the fictionality of fiction, and thus he developed a realism of narration rather than of the narrated. As Eduard Beaucamp has said, his realism "consists not in a reproduction of reality, but in a contention with it."[9] It is in the hopeful fiction of the alternative community that one can see this contentiousness most clearly.

He was not simply a "realist," nor did he adhere, like some of his contemporaries, to a definitive theory of realism. Instead, he was *inside* the notorious aporias of realism, and knew himself to be there. The paradox that the real must be represented in the fictive was constantly before his eyes. He kept his eyes open, loosened the fiction to accommodate as much of the multiplicity of reality as possible, and accommodated at the same time the imaginative alternatives to reality that burgeon in fiction, skeptically acknowledging their necessity along with their seductive dangers. When this realism about realism comes to be more clearly defined, more exactly related to the details of his strategies and struggles, I believe that his significance among the writers of the international Victorian age will become manifest.

NOTES

All text references, unless otherwise indicated, are taken from Wilhelm Raabe, *Sämtliche Werke*, ed. Karl Hoppe et al. (Göttingen: Vandenhoeck & Ruprecht, 1960-), identified by volume and page number; supplementary volumes are designated by E (Ergänzungsband). The following abbreviations are used throughout:

Mitt.: *Mitteilungen für die Gesellschaft der Freunde Wilhelm Raabes* (1911-43); *Der Raabefreund* (1944); *Mitteilungen der Raabe-Gesellschaft* (1948-). Volumes numbered consecutively.

RJ: *Jahrbuch der Raabe-Gesellschaft* (1960 ff.). Since there have been other Raabe Yearbooks in the past, the periodical lacks volume numbers, and only the year is given.

Otherwise full references are given for the first occurrence within the notes for each chapter and short titles thereafter.

INTRODUCTION

1. There have been few translations of his works into English and even fewer are extant. Until recently, the most easily accessible have been an abridged and not very graceful version of *The Hunger Pastor* in *The German Classics*, Vol. 11 (New York: The German Publication Society, 1914), and a parallel text edition of *Elsa of the Fir* (here titled *Elsa of the Forest*) by James C. O'Flaherty and Janet K. King (University, Alabama: University of Alabama Press, 1972). A new beginning has been made with the publication of Wilhelm Raabe, *Novels*, ed. Volkmar Sander, The German Library, Vol. 45 (New York: Continuum, 1983). It contains *Horacker* and *Stuffcake*, the latter unfortunately titled *Tubby Schaumann*.

2. Norbert Fuerst, *The Victorian Age of German Literature: Eight Essays* (University Park and London: Pennsylvania State University Press, 1966).

3. Some may wish to nominate Jeremias Gotthelf here. Although there is no doubt that he was a capable realist and a vigorous, earthy stylist, his stony conservatism and homiletic fundamentalism seem to me to disqualify him from the first rank of novelists. At bottom I hold to the perhaps old-fashioned notion that excellence in literary art has something to do with the progress, refinement, enlightenment, and deepened sensitivities of the human race, values to which Gotthelf's contribution was minimal.

4. See my article, "The Mystery of the Missing *Bildungsroman*, or: What Happened to Wilhelm Meister's Legacy?" *Genre* 14 (1981): 229-46.

5. Wilhelm Emrich, "Personalität und Zivilisation in Wilhelm Raabes 'Die Akten des Vogelsangs,'" *RJ* 1982, pp. 7-25.

6. Eberhard W. Meyer, "Raabe—mit Vergnügen," *Diskussion Deutsch* 12 (1981): 3-5.

PART I: IN SEARCH OF RAABE
CHAPTER 1: WOLFENBÜTTEL

1. To Paul Heyse, July 16, 1874, E 2: 175-76.
2. To Sigmund Schott, July 18, 1891, E 2: 303-4.
3. To Thaddäus Lau, May 23, 1861, E 2: 66-68.
4. To the Jensens, Feb. 13, 1870, E 3: 92.
5. Diary, Sept. 11, 1865.
6. Hermann Anders Krüger, "Erster Besuch auf dem Weghause," *Wilhelm Raabe und sein Lebenskreis: Festschrift zum 100. Geburtstag des Dichters*, ed. Heinrich Spiero (Berlin-Grunewald: Klemm, 1931), pp. 132-34. Krüger's book appeared as *Der junge Raabe: Jugendjahre und Erstlingswerke nebst einer Bibliographie der Werke Raabes und der Raabeliteratur* (Leipzig: Xenion-Verlag, 1911).
7. Hans Martin Schultz, "Der alte Herr," *Raabe-Gedenkbuch: Im Auftrage der Gesellschaft der Freunde Wilhelm Raabes*, ed. Constantin Bauer and Hans Martin Schultz (Berlin-Grunewald: Klemm, 1921), p. 144.
8. To Edmund Sträter, Mar. 24, 1890, E 2: 278.
9. To Hans von Wolzogen, Aug. 28, 1883, E 2: 242.
10. Geoffrey Patrick Guyton Butler, "England and America in the Writings of Wilhelm Raabe: A Critical Study of his Knowledge and Appreciation of Language, Literature and People" (Diss. [University of London], 1961), p. 452.
11. To Karl Leiste, Sept. 9, 1863; to Margarethe Raabe, Oct. 27, 1886, E 2: 100-1, 254.
12. Joachim Müller, "Erzählstruktur und Symbolgefüge in Wilhelm Raabes 'Unruhigen Gästen,' " *RJ* 1962, p. 127.
13. Klara Behrens-Raabe, "Erinnerung aus meinem Vaterhause," *Wilhelm Raabe und sein Lebenskreis*, pp. 17-18.
14. Ernst-August Roloff [Sen.], "Legenden um Raabe," *Mitt.* 41 (1954): 50.
15. A list of his works along with other materials from the family tradition will be found in Paul Wasserfall, "Vom Hause Raabe," *Raabe-Gedenkbuch*, ed. Bauer and Schultz, pp. 3-22.
16. His father exhibited some skills of observation and writing; see Karl Hoppe, "Eine Brockenwanderung von Raabes Vater anno 1821," *Mitt.* 46 (1959): 1-7, and Gustav Raabe, "Als Student zu Fuss nach Göttingen," *RJ* 1964, pp. 122-25.
17. To the Jensens, Nov. 18, 1874, E 3: 232.
18. To Emilie Raabe, Nov. 15, 1874, E 2: 178.
19. Sigmund Freud, "Eine Kindheitserinnerung aus *Dichtung und Wahrheit*," *Studienausgabe*, Vol. 10 (Frankfurt am Main: S. Fischer, 1969), p. 266. The thought was originally developed in the *Interpretation of Dreams*.
20. To Hans von Wolzogen, Aug. 5, 1901, *"In alls gedultig": Briefe Wilhelm Raabes (1842-1910)*, ed. Wilhelm Fehse (Berlin: Grote, 1940), p. 352.
21. To Justus Jeep, Dec. 22, 1869, E 2: 147.
22. Wilhelm Brandes, "Ein Aufsatzheft des jungen Raabe," *Raabe-Gedenkbuch*, ed. Bauer and Schultz, pp. 33-39.

23. Wilhelm Brandes, *Wilhelm Raabe: Sieben Kapitel zum Verständnis und zur Würdigung des Dichters*, 2nd ed. (Wolfenbüttel and Berlin: Julius Zwissler, Otto Janke, 1906), p. 4.

24. For details, see Karl Hoppe, *Wilhelm Raabe: Beiträge zum Verständnis seiner Person und seines Werkes* (Göttingen: Vandenhoeck & Ruprecht, 1967), pp. 11-26.

25. To Philipp Spandow, May 13, 1900, E 2: 412.

26. Hans Oppermann, "Wilhelm Raabe der Dichter," *RJ* 1961, p. 24.

27. See to Louis Tappe, January 28, 1874, E 2: 174.

28. To Adolf Glaser, Oct. 10, 1863, E 2: 101-2.

29. These items have not yet appeared in the modern critical edition of Raabe's works. They will be found in Wilhelm Raabe, *Sämtliche Werke* (Berlin-Grunewald, Klemm [1913-1916]), Series III, 6: 519-47.

30. Collections of the drawings may be found in Karl Hoppe, *Wilhelm Raabe als Zeichner* (Göttingen: Vandenhoeck & Ruprecht, 1960), and in Hans-Werner Peter, *Wilhelm Raabe: Der Dichter in seinen Federzeichnungen und Skizzen* (Rosenheim: Rosenheimer Verlagshaus, 1983).

31. Leo A. Lensing, "Fairy Tales in the Novel: Generic Tension in Wilhelm Raabe's *Die Chronik der Sperlingsgasse*," *Wilhelm Raabe: Studien zu seinem Leben und Werk*, ed. Leo A. Lensing and Hans-Werner Peter (Braunschweig: pp-Verlag, 1981), p. 15.

32. Horst S. Daemmrich, *Wilhelm Raabe* (Boston: Twayne, 1981), p. 35; Joachim Worthmann, *Probleme des Zeitromans: Studien zur Geschichte des deutschen Romans im 19. Jahrhundert* (Heidelberg: Carl Winter, 1974), p. 132.

33. See Stephen A. Gould, "Ontology and Ethics: The Rhetorical Role of the Narrator in Wilhelm Raabe's Early Novels" (Diss. University of Nebraska, 1976), pp. 62-64.

34. For a detailed comparison of the two versions, see Julius Kühn, "Ein Blick in Raabes dichterische Werkstatt: Im besonderen eine Betrachtung von Raabes 'Ein Frühling,' " *Mitt.* 45 (1958): 3-14.

35. See, for example, her letter to a friend of May 6, 1867, excerpted E 4: 64.

CHAPTER 2: STUTTGART

1. See Raabe to Eduard Hallberger, Dec. 19, 1861, E 2: 76.

2. To Auguste Raabe, Sept. 2, 1863, E 2: 99.

3. *The Rumbledump* is my effort to reproduce at least the sound of Raabe's untranslatable title, *Der Schüdderump*, an old colloquial term for a crude cart used to collect and dump the corpses of plague victims, which serves as a leitmotif on the level of narrative commentary in the novel.

4. To Adolf Glaser, Feb. [16], 1866, E 2: 112 (the letter is exactly dated in the commentary to *Gedelöcke*, 9/2: 456-57).

5. See 9/1: 457-64 and Hans Oppermann, "Wilhelm Raabe der Dichter," *RJ* 1961, pp. 28-29.

6. To Auguste Raabe, May 7, 1868, E 2: 129.

7. A good account of Raabe's life and personal associations in Stuttgart will be found in Jochen Meyer, *Wilhelm Raabe: Unter Demokraten, Hoflieferanten und Philistern. Eine Chronik seiner Stuttgarter Jahre* (Stuttgart: Fleischhauer & Spohn, 1981).

8. To the literary historian Harry Maync, Nov. 21, 1900, E 2: 419.

9. To Auguste Raabe and family, Sept. 11, 1866, E 2: 116. Raabe also remarked on this in his diary, Aug. 7, 1866. Given the style of mid-nineteenth-century government in the German states, his suspicion was entirely plausible.

10. Fritz Hartmann, *Wilhelm Raabe: Wie er war und wie er dachte*, 2nd ed. (Hanover: Sponholtz, 1927), p. 63.

11. Sigmund Freud, "Der Wahn und die Träume in W. Jensens *Gradiva*," *Studienausgabe*, Vol. 10 (Frankfurt am Main: S. Fischer, 1969), pp. 9-85.

12. "Drei unveröffentlichte Briefe von Wilhelm Jensen († 1911). Zur Geschichte von Freuds Gradiva-Analyse," *Die psychoanalytische Bewegung* 1 (1929): 207-11.

13. Reproduced E 4: 85. It is now in the Deutsches Literaturarchiv, Marbach.

14. In general I have been satisfied by the treatment of the relationship given by Else Hoppe, "Wilhelm Raabe und Marie Jensen, Mythos einer Freundschaft," *RJ* 1966, pp. 25-57. But Horst Denkler, "Wohltäter Maienborn: Ängste und ihre Bewältigung im Werk Wilhelm Raabes," *RJ* 1984, p. 21, takes a different view, intuiting a suppressed erotic attraction. Denkler's biographical note, "Marie Jensen: Angaben zur Person einer schönen Unbekannten," *Mitt.* 73 (1986): 5-8, appeared just in the nick of time to allow me to make corrections of traditional errors concerning Marie's origins.

15. Marie Jensen to Raabe, Mar. 13, 1892, E 3: 464.

16. To the Jensens, June 17, 1876, E 3: 258.

17. E.g., Marie Jensen to Raabe, Apr. 17, 1889, Jan. 1, 1908, E 3: 431-33, 575-76.

18. Marie Jensen to Raabe, Jan. 27, 1869, E 3: 38-39.

19. To the Jensens, [Feb. 9], 1869, E 3: 46-47.

20. Marie Jensen to Raabe, Feb. 19, 1869; Wilhelm Jensen to Raabe, Mar. 1869, Sept. 18, 1869, E 3: 47, 48-49, 69.

21. Marie Jensen to Raabe, [June 6], 1876, E 3: 255.

22. To Jensen, Nov. 10, 1871, Apr. 30, 1872, E 3: 152, 173. Christian II of Denmark appears in *Karin of Sweden* as a homicidal maniac.

23. See Marie Jensen to the Raabes, Dec. 20, 1883, E 3: 358-59, and Wilhelm Fehse, *Raabe und Jensen: Denkmal einer Lebensfreundschaft* (Berlin: Grote, 1940), pp. 122-25.

24. Marie Jensen to Raabe, Aug. 29, 1870, E 3: 114.

25. To Marie Jensen, Apr. 21, 1889, E 3: 434.

26. Wilhelm Jensen to Raabe, Sept. 9, 1896, E 3: 508.

27. Jensen's political involvements at this time are not entirely clear. In Stuttgart he was publicly accused of being a "press whore" in Prussian pay

(Fehse, *Raabe und Jensen*, p. 15). Louis Kientz, *Wilhelm Raabe: L'homme, la pensée, l'oeuvre* (Paris: Didier, 1939), pp. 53-54, elaborates from this circumstance an argument that Jensen was a propaganda agent of Bismarck and owed his prosperity to Bismarck's secret support, although the only evidence he offers is the claim that the newspaper Jensen joined in Flensburg, the *Norddeutsche Allgemeine Zeitung*, was subsidized by Bismarck. The mid-1860s are a little early for Bismarck's practice of suborning journalists and newspapers; see Irene Fischer-Frauendienst, *Bismarcks Pressepolitik* (Münster: Fahle, 1963), where it appears (p. 54) that Bismarck did control the *Norddeutsche Allgemeine Zeitung*, but Jensen was not its chief editor. As for Jensen's Stuttgart paper, the *Schwäbische Volkszeitung*, there was a belief in Bismarck's circles that it *might* be won over (p. 56), but Fischer-Frauendienst indicates no evidence of a subsidy.

28. Berthe Raabe to the Jensens, June 6, 1870, E 3: 106.

CHAPTER 3: BRAUNSCHWEIG

1. To Karl Leiste, Mar. 15, 1870, E 2: 148.

2. E.g., Karl Hoppe, "Die Übersiedlung Raabes nach Braunschweig: Eine Richtigstellung," *Wilhelm Raabe: Beiträge zum Verständnis seiner Person und seines Werkes* (Göttingen: Vandenhoeck & Ruprecht, 1967), pp. 26-38.

3. To Wilhelm Jensen, Feb. 13, 1877, E 3: 273.

4. To Josef Bass, Mar. 8, 1910, E 2: 499-500.

5. See Heinrich Spiero, "Wilhelm Raabes literatur- und zeitgeschichtliche Stellung," *Raabe-Gedenkbuch: Im Auftrage der Gesellschaft der Freunde Wilhelm Raabes*, ed. Constantin Bauer and Hans Martin Schultz (Berlin-Grunewald: Klemm, 1921), p. 48; cf. Eduard Beaucamp, *Literatur als Selbstdarstellung: Wilhelm Raabe und die Möglichkeiten eines deutschen Realismus* (Bonn: Bouvier, 1968), p. 188. For a rather unsympathetic view of Raabe's treatment of the city, restricted to the earliest works, *The Chronicle of Sparrow Alley* and *The People from the Forest*, see Marilyn Sibley Fries, *The Changing Consciousness of Reality: The Image of Berlin in Selected German Novels from Raabe to Döblin* (Bonn: Bouvier, 1980), pp. 8-42.

6. On Dulk, see Jochen Meyer, *Wilhelm Raabe: Unter Demokraten, Hoflieferanten und Philistern. Eine Chronik seiner Stuttgarter Jahre* (Stuttgart: Fleischhauer & Spohn, 1981), passim.

7. Cf. S. Radcliffe, "Wilhelm Raabe and the Railway," *New German Studies* 2 (1974): 131-44. Radcliffe sees Raabe's view as more conservative and closed to the modern than I do.

8. Anna-Margarete Ehninger, geb. Behrens-Raabe, "Erinnerungen an Wilhelm Raabe, seine Familie und sein Heim," *Wilhelm Raabe: Studien zu seinem Leben und Werk*, ed. Leo A. Lensing and Hans-Werner Peter (Braunschweig: pp-Verlag, 1981), p. 489.

9. Fritz Hartmann, "Gespräche mit Raabe," *Raabe-Gedenkbuch*, ed. Bauer and Schultz, p. 131.

10. For a discussion of "Raabe's Contacts with the English and the Ameri-

cans," see Geoffrey Patrick Guyton Butler, "England and America in the Writings of Wilhelm Raabe: A Critical Study of his Knowledge and Appreciation of Language, Literature and People" (Diss. [University of London], 1961), pp. 452-67.

11. Hollon A. Farr, whose name Raabe misspelled as "Pfarr" (diary, Aug. 18, 1908); there was also some further correspondence with him in 1909 and 1910. See my note, "Professor Pfarr aus Yale: Ein Rätsel in Raabes Tagebuch," *Mitt.* 71 (1984): 17-18.

12. Paul Wasserfall, "Vom Hause Raabe," *Raabe-Gedenkbuch*, ed. Bauer and Schultz, p. 16.

13. To the Jensens, Sept. 7, 1904, E 3: 558.

14. To Karl Schönhardt, Dec. 29, 1892, E 2: 339.

15. To Heinrich Falkenberg, Feb. 9, 1910, E 2: 499.

CHAPTER 4: RAABE AND HIS PUBLIC

1. Karl Heim, "Wilhelm Raabe und das Publikum" (Diss. University of Tübingen, 1953), p. 189. This unpublished dissertation is the best source for this topic and for this chapter I have drawn copiously on it, hereinafter cited as Heim with page number. Heim summarized his results in "Wilhelm Raabe und das Publikum," *Mitt.* 42 (1955): 1-12.

2. To Ernst Schotte, Mar. 2, 1859, E 2: 27.

3. To the editorial staff of the *Allgemeine Kunst-Chronik*, May 7, 1894, E 2: 353.

4. To Glaser, Oct. 13, 1869; to George Westermann, same date; to Glaser, Oct. 17, 1869; to Karl Leiste, Oct. 26, Nov. 3, 1869, E 2: 135-45. This controversy was particularly unnecessary, since *The Rumbledump* and *Abu Telfan* are almost exactly the same length, differing by only two pages in modern print.

5. To G. Grote, Verlag, Sept. 15, 1891, *"In alls gedultig": Briefe Wilhelm Raabes (1842-1910) im Auftrage der Familie Raabe herausgegeben*, ed. Wilhelm Fehse (Berlin: Grote, 1940), p. 266.

6. Karl Hoppe, "Aphorismen Raabes: Chronologisch geordnet," *Wilhelm Raabe: Beiträge zum Verständnis seiner Person und seines Werkes* (Göttingen: Vandenhoeck & Ruprecht, 1967), p. 117. With "California," Raabe probably meant the very popular German novels about America, perhaps especially those of Friedrich Gerstäcker; "Norway" doubtless refers to Ibsen, and "Russia" probably to Turgenev and perhaps also Tolstoy.

7. To the Jensens, 1 July 1867, E 3: 8.

8. To Schotte, Oct. 2, 1861; to Glaser, July 24, 1863, E 2: 73, 97.

9. Heim, p. 95.

10. To G. Grote, Verlag, July 13, 1910, E 2: 503-4.

11. In *Gutmanns Reisen*, Raabe referred to the chauvinistic language purifiers, in a virtually untranslatable phrase, as authors of "teutschtuende Entrüstungsartikel" ("teutonizing outrage articles") whom the devil should take (18: 244).

12. See Heim, p. 106.

344

13. To Siegmund Schott, July 18, 1891, E 2: 304; see also 14: 460.

14. Ernst August Roloff [Sen.], "Wilhelm Raabe in zeitgenössischer Kritik," *Mitt.* 40, No. 2 (1953): 15-16.

15. Heinrich von Kleist to Marie von Kleist, late fall 1807, *Sämtliche Werke und Briefe*, ed. Helmut Sembdner (Munich: Hanser, 1965), 2: 796.

16. Heinrich and Julius Hart, *Kritische Waffengänge* (Leipzig: Wigand, 1882), No. 2, p. 54, quoted Leo A. Lensing, *Narrative Structure and the Reader in Wilhelm Raabe's "Im alten Eisen"* (Bern, Frankfurt am Main, and Las Vegas: Peter Lang, 1977), p. 87.

17. See my discussion of this in *Heinrich Heine: The Elusive Poet* (New Haven and London: Yale University Press, 1969), pp. 123-24.

18. Stephen A. Gould, "Ontology and Ethics: The Rhetorical Role of the Narrator in Wilhelm Raabe's Early Novels" (Diss. University of Nebraska, 1976), p. 218. Gould titles his chapter on *The Rumbledump* "Narrator versus Reader."

19. See to Jensen, Dec. 18, 1869, E 3: 78.

20. To C. Müller-Grote, Sept. 22, 1884, E 2: 243.

21. Hoppe, "Aphorismen Raabes," p. 89. Also quoted 7: 388.

22. To Paul Heyse, Jan. 6, 1886, E 2: 250. Raabe had written unusually frank and revealing letters to Heyse on Feb. 26 and Mar. 2, 1875, E 2: 179-80, 182-83.

23. To Marie Jensen, Dec. 23, 1882; to the Jensens, July 18, 1883, E 3: 350, 355.

24. To the Jensens, Feb. 15, 1874, E 3: 214.

25. To J. L. Kober, Sept. 17, 1859, E 2: 44.

26. To the Jensens, Oct. 3, 1873, E 3: 206.

27. To J. L. Kober, Sept. 17, 1859, E 2: 45.

28. See, for example, Ernst-August Roloff [Sen.], "Legenden um Raabe," *Mitt.* 41 (1954): 39-51.

29. Raabe prefixed to his diary a list of his works with honoraria; it is reproduced in E 4: 382-87.

30. To Auguste Raabe, Jan. 21, 1864, E 2: 104.

31. To Carl Freund, Mar. 10, 1896, E 2: 376-77; cf. to Dr. Julius Stinde of the same date, E 2: 377-78. This figure, to be sure, conflicts with his diary entry on his income tax at the end of 1894. The difference is probably his grant from the Schiller Foundation, discussed immediately below.

32. To Karl Schönhardt, Dec. 30, 1902, E 2: 444.

33. To Paul Heyse, Aug. 9, 1879, E 2: 202.

34. Heim, p. 184.

35. To Glaser, Oct. 10, 1863, after the completion of *The Hunger Pastor* (E 2: 102).

36. To Edmund Sträter, Sept. 21, 1889, E 2: 267-68.

37. To Auerbach, Apr. 22, 1884, E 2: 222. The dating of the letter is corrected in E 4: 345-46.

38. "Wilhelm Raabe," *The Bookman* 14 (1901/2): 220-22 (with photograph of Raabe).

39. Ulrike Koller, "Vom 'Lesepöbel' zur Leser-'Gemeinde.' Raabes Beziehung zum zeitgenössischen Publikum im Spiegel der Leserbehandlung," *RJ* 1979, p. 124, n. 111.

40. Friedrich Sack, "Raabe unter den 'Besten zwölf Büchern,'" *Mitt.* 17 (1927): 153-56. Ahead of him came Keller, Freytag, Bismarck, and Nietzsche. *The Hunger Pastor* was the Raabe text most often mentioned; the author of the report found its dominance regrettable (ibid., p. 154).

41. *Mitt.* 19 (1929): 109-10.

42. To Dr. S., Dec. 19, 1892, E 2: 336-37.

43. To Siegmund Schott, Dec. 17, 1899, E 2: 408.

44. Heim, pp. 284-88.

CHAPTER 5: PESSIMISM

1. Gerhart Mayer, *Die geistige Entwicklung Wilhelm Raabes: Dargestellt unter besonderer Berücksichtigung seines Verhältnisses zur Philosophie* (Göttingen: Vandenhoeck & Ruprecht, 1960), p. 46.

2. Nicolaas Cornelis Adrianus Perquin, S.J., *Wilhelm Raabes Motive als Ausdruck seiner Weltanschauung* (Amsterdam: H. J. Paris, 1927), pp. 124-25. This study, curiously enough by a Dutch Jesuit, though naturally dated, is exceptionally intelligent for its time and contains many thoughtful perceptions. It has unjustly slipped into obscurity in the history of Raabe criticism.

3. To Karl Emil Franzos, Jan. 28, 1893, *"In alls gedultig": Briefe Wilhelm Raabes (1842-1910) im Auftrage der Familie Raabe herausgegeben,* ed. Wilhelm Fehse (Berlin: Grote, 1940), p. 294.

4. Anton Bettelheim, *Berthold Auerbach: Der Mann—Sein Werk—Sein Nachlaß* (Stuttgart and Berlin: Cotta, 1907), p. 359.

5. Clifford Albrecht Bernd, *German Poetic Realism* (Boston: Twayne, 1981), p. 105. A more thorough treatment of the historical and political context will be found in Helmut Richter, "Die Chronik der Sperlingsgasse," *Raabe in neuer Sicht,* ed. Hermann Helmers (Stuttgart: Kohlhammer, 1968), pp. 312-16.

6. Georg Lukács, "Wilhelm Raabe," *Deutsche Realisten des 19. Jahrhunderts* (Berlin: Aufbau-Verlag, 1952), p. 239. This in some respects unfriendly essay dates from 1939, thus from Lukács's most Stalinist phase.

7. Hermann Helmers, *Die bildenden Mächte in den Romanen Wilhelm Raabes* (Weinheim: Beltz, 1960), pp. 15-16.

8. Karl Hoppe, "Aphorismen Raabes: Chronologisch geordnet," *Wilhelm Raabe: Beiträge zum Verständnis seiner Person und seines Werkes* (Göttingen: Vandenhoeck & Ruprecht, 1967), p. 112.

9. No one has been able to find the source for this in the Koran. It is possible that Raabe had it from a novella of his now little-remembered contemporary, M. Solitaire (Woldemar Nürnberger). See 7: 414.

10. Monika Weber Clyde, "Der Bildungsgedanke bei Wilhelm Raabe" (Diss. University of California, Berkeley, 1968), p. 67.

11. To Leonhard Korth, July 19, 1894, E 2: 357-58.

12. Stephen A. Gould, "Ontology and Ethics: The Rhetorical Role of the Narrator in Wilhelm Raabe's Early Novels" (Diss. University of Nebraska, 1976), pp. 118-20.

13. To Karl Geiger, Jan. 16, 1910, E 2: 498.

14. To Ferdinand Avenarius, Sept. 21, 1907, E 2: 475.

15. See especially Th. C. van Stockum, "Schopenhauer und Raabe, Pessimismus und Humor," *Neophilologus* 6 (1921): 169-84; Reinhold Weinhardt, "Schopenhauer in Wilhelm Raabes Werken," *Jahrbuch der Schopenhauer-Gesellschaft* 25 (1938): 308-28; Gerhart Mayer, *Die geistige Entwicklung Wilhelm Raabes*, esp. pp. 42-46, 78-98. Even efforts to deny Schopenhauer's influence or to show that Raabe's thinking did not correspond to Schopenhauer's philosophy are, to my mind, useful but not strictly necessary. See for example Friedrich Neumann, "Wilhelm Raabes Schüdderump," *Zeitschrift für Deutsche Philologie* 71 (1951-53): 325; and E.A. Roloff [Sen.], "Triumph und Überwindung der Kanaille. Raabes Pessimismus im Spiegel der Novelle 'Zum wilden Mann,' " *Raabe-Jahrbuch 1949*, ed. E.A. Roloff [Sen.] (Braunschweig: Appelhans, 1949), pp. 32-33.

16. To Karl Schönhardt, Dec. 30, 1907, E 2: 476. As an afterthought Raabe mentions Kant also.

17. To Wilhelm Röseler, Sept. 20, 1873, E 2: 172.

18. To the Jensens, Nov. 18, 1874, E 3: 233.

19. See Theodore Ziolkowski, *Dimensions of the Modern Novel: German Texts and European Contexts* (Princeton: Princeton University Press, 1969), pp. 215-57.

20. To Karl Schönhardt, Dec. 31, 1890, E 2: 289.

21. To P. J. Meier, Oct. 19, 1910, E 2: 508.

22. Needless to say, this hint has been taken up: Thea Heinrich, "Der Tod in der Dichtung Wilhelm Raabes" (Diss. University of Munich, 1949); Christel Schmitz, "Das Todesproblem im Werk Wilhelm Raabes" (Diss. University of Bonn, 1950). Neither study seems to me at all adequate to the problem. Schmitz, p. 93, makes the astounding claim that there are only two cases of suicide in Raabe's works. Suicides and suicidal moods abound in his fiction, especially in the earlier works.

23. See Heinrich Anz, " 'Leichenbegängnisse.' Zum Verfahren der geschichtlichen Erzählung in Raabes 'Gedelöcke,' " *RJ* 1982, p. 123.

24. Fritz Martini, "Das Problem des Realismus im 19. Jahrhundert und die Dichtung Wilhelm Raabes," *Dichtung und Volkstum* 36 (1935): 299-300.

25. Wilhelm Fehse, *Wilhelm Raabe: Sein Leben und seine Werke* (Braunschweig: Vieweg, 1937), p. 44.

26. This, to my mind quite eccentric, even obscurantist view was propagated in the 1920s by one Helene Dose in more than a dozen publications, the most elaborated of which are *Aus Wilhelm Raabes mystischer Werkstatt* (Hamburg: Hanseatische Verlags-Anstalt, 1925), and *Die Magie bei Wilhelm Raabe* (Berlin-Grunewald: Klemm, 1928).

27. Raabe has slyly conflated two verses here, Eccles. 11:9 and 12:1. Among the excisions is the beginning phrase of 12:1: "Remember now thy Creator in the days of thy youth. . . ."

CHAPTER 6: THE CASE AGAINST RAABE

1. Georg Lukács, "Wilhelm Raabe," *Deutsche Realisten des 19. Jahrhunderts* (Berlin: Aufbau-Verlag, 1952), p. 261.

2. Ernst Bloch, "Demokratie als Ausnahme," *Politische Messungen, Pestzeit, Vormärz* (Frankfurt am Main: Suhrkamp, 1970), pp. 160-61. The essay dates from 1938.

3. *Deutsche Philologie im Aufriß*, ed. Wolfgang Stammler et al., 2nd ed. (Berlin: Erich Schmidt Verlag, 1955-62) Vol. 2: cols. 1511-12.

4. Gerhard Nebel, *Unter Partisanen und Kreuzfahrern* (Stuttgart, 1950), quoted *Mitt.* 54 (1967): 27.

5. E.V.K. Brill, "Raabe's Reception in England," *German Life and Letters* N.S. 8 (1954/55): 305-6.

6. See Volkmar Sander, "Corviniana non leguntur. Gedanken zur Raabe-Rezeption in Amerika und England," *RJ* 1981, pp. 118-27; Jean Royer, "Bericht über die Raabeforschung in Frankreich," *Wilhelm Raabe: Studien zu seinem Leben und Werk*, ed. Leo A. Lensing and Hans-Werner Peter (Braunschweig: pp-Verlag, 1981), pp. 574-75.

7. Louis Kientz, *Wilhelm Raabe: L'homme, la pensée et l'oeuvre* (Paris: Didier, 1939), p. 119. It is interesting, however, that one of the most committed but also most broad-minded of Raabe's traditional admirers, Constantin Bauer, defended Kientz against the total rejection of the Raabe community, saying that the book contains, along with much that is false, "an abundance of pertinent observations and ingenious remarks": Bauer, "Raabe im Ausland," *Mitt.* 43 (1956): 8.

8. Barker Fairley, "The Modernity of Wilhelm Raabe," *German Studies Presented to Leonard Ashley Willoughby by his Pupils, Colleagues and Friends on his Retirement*, [ed. J. Boyd] (Oxford: Blackwell, 1952), p. 74.

9. Gerhard Kaiser, *Gottfried Keller: Das gedichtete Leben* (Frankfurt am Main: Insel, 1981), p. 315.

10. See the now classical study by Herman Meyer, *Der Sonderling in der deutschen Dichtung* (Munich: Hanser, 1963), esp. the chapter "Neue Synthese der Gestaltung im Werke Wilhelm Raabes," pp. 229-89. The monograph of Stanley Radcliffe, *Der Sonderling im Werk Wilhelm Raabes* (Braunschweig: pp-Verlag, 1984), came into my hands too late to be integrated into this study. Radcliffe, who treats Raabe's eccentrics more as incarnations of ideas than as literary characters, differentiates them perceptively but stresses their relative withdrawal from or accommodation to conventional society rather than their movement into an alternative community as I do.

11. Wilhelm Raabe, *Werke in Auswahl*, ed. Hans-Werner Peter (Braunschweig: pp-Verlag, 1981), 3, p. 216. The review concerns *The Horn of Wanza*. I will return to this matter in the concluding chapter.

12. To Eduard Engel, July 4, 1881, E 2: 230-31.

13. To Dike Captain Müller, Nov. 19, 1900, E 2: 417. The quotation is from *The Vicar of Wakefield.*

14. What is probably the most thoroughly hostile treatment of Raabe in contemporary scholarship is directed against his symbolism, in this case his weather imagery: F. C. Delius, *Der Held und sein Wetter: Ein Kunstmittel und sein ideologischer Gebrauch im Roman des bürgerlichen Realismus* (Munich: Hanser, 1971), pp. 38-61. This unrelievedly disagreeable study is of interest primarily as an example of the mode of employing intellectual work as a form of guerrilla warfare.

15. *Mitt.* 11 (1921): 51.

16. *Mitt.* 14 (1924): 26.

17. Wilhelm Brandes, *Wilhelm Raabe: Sieben Kapitel zum Verständnis und zur Würdigung des Dichters*, 2nd ed. (Wolfenbüttel and Berlin: Julius Zwissler, Otto Janke, 1906), p. 34.

18. *Mitt.* 29 (1939): 33-35; 30 (1940): 1. It is my guess that Hitler cared as much for the devotions of the Raabe Society as he did for the man in the moon. For the calligraphic novella he returned a two-line telegram of thanks that has every appearance of having been composed by a member of his staff. *Mitt.* 29 (1939), No. 2 proudly printed it.

19. Hahne, "Eine ketzerische Betrachtung über W. Raabe," *Mitt.* 29 (1939): 68-75.

20. *Mitt.* 23 (1933): 73; 29 (1939): 1-3.

21. Hahne, "Raabe und die nationale Revolution"; Fehse, "Die Alten und die Jungen"; Johannes Iltz, "Raabe und Hitler," *Mitt.* 23 (1933): 67-69; 24 (1934): 1-8, 8-17.

22. *Mitt.* 26 (1936): 134.

23. Fehse, "Goethe, Raabe und die deutsche Zukunft," *Mitt.* 12 (1922): 14.

24. Wilhelm Stapel, "Raabes Deutschheit," *Raabe-Gedenkbuch: Im Auftrage der Gesellschaft der Freunde Wilhelm Raabes*, ed. Constantin Bauer and Hans Martin Schultz (Berlin-Grunewald: Klemm, 1921), pp. 94-102.

25. Fehse, "Raabes Erzählung 'Frau Salome.' Ihre Entstehung und ihre Deutungen," *Mitt.* 14 (1924): 41-58.

26. Heinrich Mohr, "Wilhelm Raabe und die nordische Rasse"; Hahne, "Raabe vom Rassenstandpunkt betrachtet," *Mitt.* 17 (1927): 18-39; 24 (1934): 114-22.

27. Heinz Hertel, "Wie stellt sich die heutige Jugend zu Raabe?" *Mitt.* 21 (1931): 60.

28. It has been argued, for example, that Raabe, like Nietzsche, reflected the threat of the proletarization of the petty-bourgeoisie by capitalism, so it is understandable that both became heroes of fascism: Uwe Heldt, *Isolation und Identität: Die Bedeutung des Idyllischen in der Epik Wilhelm Raabes* (Frankfurt am Main, Bern, and Cirencester: Peter D. Lang, 1980), pp. 137-38.

29. An analysis of the social class distribution of the membership will be

found in Eugen Rüter, *Die Gesellschaft der Freunde Wilhelm Raabes: Rezeptions-steuerung als Programm* (Darmstadt: Thesen Verlag, 1977).

30. Brandes, *Sieben Kapitel*, pp. 77, 70-71. One contemporary observer has denominated Brandes a proto-fascist: Günther Matschke, *Die Isolation als Mittel der Gesellschaftskritik bei Wilhelm Raabe* (Bonn: Bouvier, 1975), p. 11. I think this is extreme, unless one takes the position that bourgeois ideology necessarily evolves into fascism.

31. *Mitt.* 35 (1948): 37; E. A. Roloff [Jun.], "Aus der Chronik der Raabe-Gesellschaft," *Mitt.* 38, No. 2 (1951): 8-14. This account goes so far as to suggest a resistance legend.

32. Adolf Suchel, "Literarische Einflüsse auf Raabes Novelle 'Frau Salome,' " *Mitt.* 35 (1948): 7-19.

33. Walter Buchholz, "Ein Nachwort zu Wilhelm Raabes 'Stopfkuchen,' " *Mitt.* 38, No. 1 (1951): 6-11.

34. Bauer, "Raabe im Ausland," *Mitt.* 43 (1956): 1-10. Of Bauer's comparatively decent conduct during the Nazi period there will be something more to say in the next chapter.

35. M. Töteberg and J. Zander, "Die Rezeption Raabes durch die 'Gesellschaft der Freunde Wilhelm Raabes' 1911 bis 1945," *RJ* 1973, pp. 178-93. One of the old guard, the bibliographer Fritz Meyen, attempted to repel this critique: *RJ* 1974, pp. 105-11, but the editors of the journal defended Töteberg and Zander against the protests from the membership (ibid., p. 111). This was but one of the many generational skirmishes in and around the Raabe Society, which have begun to calm down but still have not entirely come to rest. The study by Rüter cited above (n. 29) is more thorough, but it is one-sided and sometimes unreliable in regard to facts. See the detailed review by Hans-Jürgen Schrader, *RJ* 1977, pp. 166-83.

PART II: THEMES
CHAPTER 7: RAABE AND THE JEWS: THE CASE OF
The Hunger Pastor

1. Gordon A. Craig, *The Germans* (New York: Putnam, 1982), p. 139. This view of Raabe has been of long duration. Ernest K. Bramsted, in his useful book, *Aristocracy and the Middle-Classes in Germany: Social Types in German Literature 1830-1900*, rev. ed. (Chicago: University of Chicago Press, 1964), p. 148, n. 1, calls arguments against viewing *The Hunger Pastor* as an anti-Semitic book "whitewashing." A more balanced view is achieved by Pierre Angel, *Le personnage juif dans le roman allemand (1855-1915): La racine littéraire de l'antisémitisme Outre-Rhin* (Montreal, Paris, and Brussels: Didier, 1973), pp. 23-34, 182-87.

2. The first detailed argument of the case appeared in a Jewish periodical: Josef Bass, "Die Juden bei Wilhelm Raabe," *Monatsschrift für Geschichte und Wissenschaft der Juden* 54 (1910): 641-88. See also Bass, "Die jüdischen Gestalten bei Raabe," *Raabe-Gedächtnisschrift*, new rev. ed., ed. Heinrich Goebel (Hildesheim and Leipzig: August Lax, 1931), pp. 62-90.

3. A beginning has been made by Dieter Arendt, " 'Nun auf die Juden!' Figurationen des Judentums im Werk Wilhelm Raabes," *Tribüne* 19, No. 74 (1980): 108-40.

4. Josef Kunz, "Wilhelm Raabe, 'Die Holunderblüte.' Versuch einer Interpretation," *RJ* 1973, pp. 88-108.

5. Raabe made this connection in *The Chronicle of Sparrow Alley* (1: 167), where he quoted Psalms 137:5: "If I forget thee, O Jerusalem, let my right hand forget her cunning," remarking that this sentiment kept the pieces of a people together through the millenia, and adding: "If I forget thee, Germany, great fatherland, let my right hand forget her cunning." He saw the Jews, like the Germans, as a perpetually harassed people; Leah in *Höxter and Corvey* observes bitterly: "my fathers have never had peace since Emperor Titus" (11: 339).

6. Robert Anthony Graves, "The Integral Personality: The Relationship Between the Female Characters and the World in Selected Works of Theodor Fontane and Wilhelm Raabe" (Diss. University of Bristol, 1978), pp. 154-55. The traditional anti-Semitic observer can see the matter in a different light, and point out that Salome is a disgusted outsider in the Jewish community: Wilhelm Fehse, "Raabes Erzählung 'Frau Salome.' Ihre Entstehung und ihre Deutungen," *Mitt.* 14 (1924): 55. Nor is Raabe to be pinned down in such matters. The spoiled, emancipated Kleophea Götz in *The Hunger Pastor*, who elopes with the evil Jew, praises the naked Greeks and announces that she belongs to them (6: 257).

7. See Adolf Suchel, "Literarische Einflüsse auf Raabes Novelle 'Frau Salome,' " *Mitt.* 35 (1948): 7-19 and, more persuasively, Katherine Starr Kaiser, "Structure and Narrative Technique in Wilhelm Raabe's *Krähenfelder Geschichten*" (Diss. Brown University, 1974), p. 60. Many years later, Velten Andres in *The Documents of the Birdsong* would refer admiringly to Heine as "the Jew or Semitic Hellene" (19: 368), thus again linking Jew and Greek.

8. A parallel between Haeseler's early life and that of Heine has been suggested by Gerald Opie, "Raabe and the Classical Tradition: Some Reflections on *Der Dräumling*," *Wilhelm Raabe: Studien zu seinem Leben und Werk*, ed. Leo A. Lensing and Hans-Werner Peter (Braunschweig: pp-Verlag, 1981), p. 137.

9. To Heinrich Laube, Apr. 19, 1869, *"In alls gedultig": Briefe Wilhelm Raabes (1842-1910) im Auftrage der Familie Raabe herausgegeben*, ed. Wilhelm Fehse (Berlin: Grote, 1940), p. 77.

10. To Erich Liesegang, Nov. 20, 1900; to Robert Lange, Jan. 3, 1901, E 2: 418, 420. Meyer's middle name was Moritz.

11. E.g., *The Children of Finkenrode* (2: 69); *The Holy Spring*, Chapter 21 and especially 3: 320-23; *The Rumbledump* (8: 84).

12. Wilhelm Jensen to Raabe, Jan. 4, 1910, E 3: 587.

13. His name was Crohn or Krohn: diary, Sept. 7, 1906, Apr. 9, Sept. 27, 1908.

14. Julius Heinrich Dessauer, *Geschichte der Israeliten mit besonderer Berücksichtigung der Kulturgeschichte derselben; von Alexander dem Grossen bis auf gegen-*

wärtige Zeit; nach den besten vorhandenen Quellen (Erlangen: Palm, 1846). See Wilhelm Fehse, *Wilhelm Raabe: Sein Leben und seine Werke* (Braunschweig: Vieweg, 1937), pp. 218-21.

15. Raabe to Auerbach, Apr. 22, 1884, E 2: 221-22. The letter is misdated 1881 in this place; see the correction, E 4: 345-46.

16. Among them was Bass (see n. 2 above). In a monograph of the Nazi period, Günther Vogelsang, *Das Ich als Schicksal und Aufgabe in den Dichtungen Raabes* (Braunschweig: Appelhans, 1942), pp. 207, 209, Bass is identified as a Jew. A Viennese, Bass appears to have been totally assimilated, judging from his contributions, e.g., "Welsche und deutsche Liebe bei Raabe," *Mitt.* 19 (1929): 19-36, and "Wie ich zu Wilhelm Raabe kam," *Wilhelm Raabe-Kalender 1913,* ed. Otto Elster and Hanns Martin Elster (Berlin: Grote, 1912), pp. 129-35. In the latter reminiscence it appears that it was just *The Hunger Pastor* that first aroused Bass's enthusiasm for Raabe.

17. In 1918, when Freytag's reputation was still high, Heinrich Spiero had no difficulty comparing them: "Wilhelm Raabe und Gustav Freytag," *Raabe-studien: Im Auftrag der "Gesellschaft der Freunde Wilhelm Raabes,"* ed. Constantin Bauer (Wolfenbüttel: Heckner, 1925), pp. 138-43. More cautious is Walter Silz, "Freytag's *Soll und Haben* and Raabe's *Der Hungerpastor,*" *Modern Language Notes* 39 (1924): 10-18. Originally, Hermann Pongs in *Wilhelm Raabe: Leben und Werk* (Heidelberg: Quelle & Meyer, 1958), p. 215, tried to weaken the connection, but he seems to have come to accept it when editing the critical edition (6: 469). It is stressed by Friedrich Sengle, "*Der Hungerpastor* (1863/64): Zum Problem der frühen Biedermeiertradition," *Wilhelm Raabe,* ed. Lensing and Peter, pp. 84-87. Louis Kientz, *Wilhelm Raabe: L'homme, la pensée et l'oeuvre* (Paris: Didier, 1939), pp. 80-81, takes it for granted. Surprisingly, in view of Kientz's tendency to denigrate Raabe on every possible ground, here he defends him against anti-Semitism, though he then (p. 83) charges him with a kind of intellectual anti-Semitism derived from the circle around Wolfgang Menzel and directed against Heine. Raabe's alleged discipleship to Menzel is one of Kientz's many inventions.

18. As part of his pattern of resentment in these matters, Raabe claimed that Freytag had excluded any mention of him from his influential journal *Die Grenzboten;* see to Karl Geiger, June 29, 1909, E 2: 490. The somewhat fluffy Käthchen Nebelung in *Owls' Pentecost* reads only contemporary literature, such as Gutzkow's *Ritter vom Geiste* (*Knights of the Spirit*), Auerbach's *Schwarzwälder Dorfgeschichten* (*Black Forest Village Tales*), and Freytag's *Debit and Credit* (11: 384). In a notebook entry Raabe remarked that some books one reads with the heart, like Goethe's *Dichtung und Wahrheit* (*Poetry and Truth*), others lying on the sofa, like *Debit and Credit* (11: 517).

19. Sharp contrasts are drawn by Gerhart Meyer, "Wilhelm Raabe und die Tradition des Bildungsromans," *RJ* 1980, p. 105.

20. See my discussion of these matters in "The Evaluation of Freytag's 'Soll und Haben,' " *German Life and Letters* N.S. 22 (1968/69): 315-24.

21. This was first suggested by Bass, "Die Juden bei Wilhelm Raabe," pp. 658-59.

22. Marketa Goetz-Stankiewicz, "Die böse Maske Moses Freudensteins. Gedanken zum Hungerpastor," *RJ* 1969, pp. 7-32. It has also been argued that Moses is a Mephistopheles figure having nothing to do with anti-Semitism: Rudolf Mohr, " 'Der Hungerpastor'—Ein Pfarrerroman?" *RJ* 1977, p. 62. Cf. also Sengle, *"Der Hungerpastor,"* p. 87, who follows Goetz-Stankiewicz.

23. Gerhart Mayer, *Die geistige Entwicklung Wilhelm Raabes: Dargestellt unter besonderer Berücksichtigung seines Verhältnisses zur Philosophie* (Göttingen: Vandenhoeck & Ruprecht, 1960), p. 34.

24. It is a curious detail that Joachim Müller, more recently the tolerated bourgeois literary scholar in East Germany, was, under earlier political auspices, able to speak of Moses as "this Jewish creature, which Raabe grasped with unheard-of racist clear-sightedness": "Das Weltbild Wilhelm Raabes," *Deutsche Vierteljahrsschrift* 21 (1943): 203.

25. This scene is implausible for two reasons. For one thing, it seems unlikely that the modestly enthusiastic theology student Hans (who was tutored in Hebrew by Moses) could have learned enough Hebrew to converse in the language; for another, Orthodox Eastern Jews of the time would have regarded Hebrew as a holy tongue restricted to liturgical purposes and would have conversed only in Yiddish. There is a regrettable coda to the scene: on Hans's return train journey on Christmas Eve, he encounters no unpleasant Jews, who, the narrator suggests, do not seem to travel in the cold (6: 418).

26. Mark Howard Gelber, "Aspects of Literary Anti-Semitism: Charles Dickens' *Oliver Twist* and Gustav Freytag's *Soll und Haben*" (Diss. Yale University, 1980), p. 19. Sengle, *"Der Hungerpastor,"* p. 86, also speaks of "literary anti-Semitism."

27. I have used here the translation by Elizabeth Wyckoff, *The Complete Greek Tragedies*, ed. David Grene and Richmond Lattimore (Chicago: University of Chicago Press, 1959), 2: 176. Unfortunately it is not as pithy as the German: "Nicht mitzuhassen, mitzulieben bin ich da." In 1881, Ignaz Döllinger, the once reactionary, later rebellious Catholic theologian, also quoted the line in a plea for tolerance of the Jews, whereupon Auerbach, in the last publication of his life, gratefully acknowledged Döllinger's employment of the quotation. See M. I. Zwick, *Berthold Auerbachs sozialpolitischer und ethischer Liberalismus: Nach seinen Schriften dargestellt* (Stuttgart: Kohlhammer, 1933; originally a Columbia University dissertation), p. 112.

28. Raabe, to be sure, nowhere admits to a dependence on *Debit and Credit*. But in the text of *The Hunger Pastor* there is an obscure joke: one of the odd fellows in a reserved table group distinguishes himself by buttoning his coat on the left one day and on the right the other, which habit he refers to as his "Debet" and "Kredit" (6: 208). I strongly suspect a buried allusion here. In *Pfister's Mill* there is a more direct one: "the whole German people had become different; for the years eighteen hundred sixty-six and seventy had taken place

and people counted, reckoned, and weighed debit and credit with rather thick, hot heads into the middle of the seventies" (16: 42). An occurrence of the phrase in *On the Scrap-Iron* (16: 395-96) may be only casual without a specific allusion.

29. Philippine Ullmann's letter was first published by G. Rülf, "Ein Nach-trag zu 'Wilhelm Raabe und die Juden,'" *Monatsschrift für Geschichte und Wissenschaft der Juden* 55 (1911): 247-51. This is a supplement to Bass's essay, n. 2 above.

30. Eliza Davis to Charles Dickens, June 22, 1863, *Anglo-Jewish Letters, (1158-1917)* ed. Cecil Roth (London: Soncino, 1938), pp. 304-5.

31. Roland Freymond, *Der Einfluß von Charles Dickens auf Gustav Freytag* (Prague: Bellmann, 1912). Raabe's original intention of having Moses drown in a shipwreck was obviously motivated by the fate of Steerforth in *David Copperfield*.

32. Dickens to Eliza Davis, July 10, 1863, *Anglo-Jewish Letters*, p. 306-07.

33. Gelber, "Aspects of Literary Anti-Semitism," pp. 78-79, is not per-suaded that the revisions did much to relieve the anti-Semitic impact of *Oliver Twist*.

34. Raabe to Philippine Ullmann, Feb. 4, 1903, E 2: 445. Like Fontane, Raabe must have known perfectly well that educated Jews were an important segment of his public. According to his diary, he received on Feb. 26, 1903, the congratulations of the graduates of a Jewish Business Academy in Prague, to whom he returned thanks on Mar. 24.

35. Raabe to S. Bachenheimer, Feb. 24, 1902, E 2: 437-38. Here Raabe refers to the Jews as "your tribal and our guest comrades," which suggests that even then he was far from accepting the idea of "German citizens of the Jewish faith."

36. Raabe to M. Schulze, Nov. 21, 1883, E 2: 242-43. In his diary, Aug. 28, 1884, he notes the receipt of a brochure from Vienna on the Jewish ques-tion, which he acknowledged Nov. 18; on Dec. 3, 1887, he records the receipt of another anti-Semitic periodical.

37. Franz Hahne, "Raabes Stellung im Dritten Reich," *Mitt.* 23 (1933): 102-3. Hahne clearly believed that an ethically admirable position *must* be anti-Semitic.

38. Heinrich Spiero, *Raabe: Leben—Werk—Wirkung* (Darmstadt: Hofmann, 1924); *Raabe-Lexikon* (Berlin-Grunewald: Klemm, [1927]); *Wilhelm Raabe und sein Lebenskreis* (Berlin-Grunewald: Klemm, 1931).

39. Spiero, *Raabe: Leben*, p. 53.

40. Heinrich Spiero, *Schicksal und Anteil: Ein Lebensweg in deutscher Wendezeit* (Berlin: Volksverband der Bücherfreunde, 1929). The assimilation obviously hid nothing; although this book has practically nothing to do with Jews, the copy in the Yale University Library bears the stamp of the "Library for Re-search into the Jewish Question, Frankfurt / M," a Nazi institution. Spiero's Christianity was militant and bombastic. See his book, *Die Heilandsgestalt in*

der deutschen Dichtung (Berlin: Eckart, 1926), which attempts to Christianize Raabe (pp. 249-52).

41. Spiero, *Raabe: Leben*, p. 2.

42. *Mitt.* 23 (1933): 120; cf. 24 (1934): 61.

43. Wilhelm Fehse, "Dasein und Leben," *Mitt.* 27 (1937): 2. Fehse is the only one of Raabe's "friends" of that epoch to have suffered for his conduct; he died in a Russian internment camp in 1946 (*Mitt.* 42 [1955]: 21). I have heard that he starved to death. A eulogy of Fehse by a member of the successor generation, Hans Oppermann, not mentioning such things as his sonnet to Hitler, appeared in *Mitt.* 44 (1957): 66-72.

44. *Mitt.* 23 (1933): 66. Among the retrospective obituaries in the post-war *Mitt.* 35 (1948): 36, there is one of Spiero, who died in Berlin in 1947; it remarks that he was working on a new edition of his biography to the end, but wastes no words on an ejection that must have been traumatic for him. The Raabe community tacitly readmitted him by including his article, "Wilhelm Raabe und Berlin," in *Wilhelm Raabe-Kalender 1947*, ed. E. A. Roloff [Sen.] (Goslar: Deutsche Volksbücherei, 1946), pp. 47-50. His name is given incorrectly as "Wilhelm" in the list of contributors (p. 151).

45. E 2: 445. The phrase is an abridgment of Matthew 5:45; Raabe employs variants of it in several other places.

46. Hahne prided himself on being one of those who introduced the ideas of Gobineau into Germany; see *Mitt.* 31 (1941): 31. Ludwig Schemann, translator, biographer, and explicator of Gobineau, was one of Raabe's correspondents (diary, July 11, July 12, 1902; Mar. 11, 1905; Mar. 7, 1907). When he sent Raabe some of his studies, Raabe replied cordially, remarking that his attention had first been drawn to Gobineau by Schopenhauer (Raabe to Schemann, July 31, 1902, E 2: 440). Schemann, in *Gobineau: eine Biographie* (Strassburg: Trübner, 1913-16), 1: 495, praises his "friend" Hahne for his translations of Gobineau's travel novellas, and in *Gobineaus Rassenwerk: Aktenstücke und Betrachtungen zur Geschichte und Kritik des Essai sur l'inégalité des races humaines* (Stuttgart: Fromann, 1910), p. 174, Schemann cites Hahne as one of the schoolteachers who found Gobineau's race theories pedagogically valuable.

47. Dieter Arendt, "Die Heine-Rezeption im Werk Wilhelm Raabes," *Heine-Jahrbuch* 1980, pp. 188-221. Spiero went out of his way to praise the anti-Semitic literary historian, both in *Raabe: Leben*, p. 252-53, and in "Wilhelm Raabes literatur- und zeitgeschichtliche Stellung," *Raabe-Gedenkbuch: Im Auftrage der Gesellschaft der Freunde Wilhelm Raabes*, ed. Constantin Bauer and Hans Martin Schultz (Berlin-Grunewald: Klemm, 1921), p. 42. This is an especially sad example of the blindness of which the assimilated, nationalistic German Jews have often been accused. The subsequent post-war president of the Raabe Society, Ernst-August Roloff [Sen.], also found occasion during the Nazi years to praise Bartels on his eightieth birthday: *Mitt.* 33 (1943): 31-33.

48. See, apart from Raabe's correspondence with Frenssen, Raabe to Siegmund Schott, July 22, 1902, E 2: 439. Raabe was by no means uncritical of the rather bizarre Frenssen; see E 4: 238.

49. Gustav Frenssen, *Lebensbericht* (Berlin: Grote, 1941). For a penetrating, if in places debatable, sociological analysis of the success of *Jörn Uhl*, see Uwe-K. Ketelsen, "Literatur in der Industrialisierungskrise der Jahrhundertwende: Eine historische Analyse der Erzählkonzeption von Gustav Frenssens Roman 'Jörn Uhl,' " *RJ* 1984, pp. 173-97. I shall return briefly to the question of Frenssen in my chapter on Raabe's relationship to literature.

50. Wilhelm Brandes, *Wilhelm Raabe: Sieben Kapitel zum Verständnis und zur Würdigung des Dichters*, 2nd ed. (Wolfenbüttel and Berlin: Julius Zwissler, Otto Janke, 1906), p. 89. Note that this book, first published in 1901, appeared during Raabe's lifetime and, so to speak, under his eyes.

51. See my article, "Wilhelm Raabe as Successor to Young Germany," *Monatshefte* 77 (1985): 449-59.

CHAPTER 8: POLITICS

1. These early political activities are reviewed by Heinrich Leonard, "Wilhelm Raabe und der Deutsche Nationalverein," *Wilhelm Raabe und sein Lebenskreis: Festschrift zum 100. Geburtstag des Dichters namens der Gesellschaft der Freunde Wilhelm Raabes*, ed. Heinrich Spiero (Berlin: Grunewald: Klemm, 1931), pp. 43-49.

2. To Karl Leiste, Dec. 19, 1863, E 2: 102-3.

3. Fritz Hartmann, "Gutmanns Reisen. Raabes politischer Roman," *Mitt.* 29 (1931): 158-59.

4. Fritz Hartmann, "Gespräche mit Raabe," *Raabe-Gedenkbuch: Im Auftrage der Gesellschaft der Freunde Wilhelm Raabes*, ed. Constantin Bauer and Hans Martin Schultz (Berlin-Grunewald: Klemm, 1921), p. 133.

5. Paul Wasserfall, "Vom Hause Raabe," *Raabe-Gedenkbuch*, ed. Bauer and Schultz, p. 19.

6. Hartmann, "Gespräche mit Raabe," *Raabe-Gedenkbuch*, ed. Bauer and Schultz, p. 126.

7. To Edmund Sträter, Sept. 13, 1897, E 2: 396.

8. To the *Berliner Tageblatt*, Feb. 1, 1905, E 2: 461.

9. To Edmund Sträter, Apr. 2, 1909, E 2: 486.

10. To Klara [sic] Zetkin, Mar. 10, 1908, E 2: 477-78; for Zetkin's letter, see Karl Hoppe, *Wilhelm Raabe: Beiträge zum Verständnis seiner Person und seines Werkes* (Göttingen: Vandenhoeck & Ruprecht, 1967), pp. 57-58.

11. Horst Daemmrich, *Wilhelm Raabe* (Boston: Twayne, 1981), p. 41, has commented on "Raabe's technique of criticizing social phenomena by concentrating on their deforming effects on individuals."

12. Hermann Helmers, *Wilhelm Raabe* (Stuttgart: Metzler, 1968), p. 13, echoed by Günther Matschke, *Die Isolation als Mittel der Gesellschaftskritik bei Wilhelm Raabe* (Bonn: Bouvier, 1975), p. 10. Karl Hotz, *Bedeutung und Funktion des Raumes im Werk Wilhelm Raabes* (Göppingen: Kümmerle, 1970), p. 126, has rightly warned: "By stressing Raabe's social criticism, which is unquestiona-

bly present, one is just to only *one* Raabe, the Raabe one *wants*, but not to his highly differentiated and polyphonic narrative art."

13. See Dieter Kafitz, *Figurenkonstellation als Mittel der Wirklichkeitserfassung: Dargestellt an Romanen der zweiten Hälfte des 19. Jahrhunderts (Freytag, Spielhagen, Fontane, Raabe)* (Kronberg: Athenäum, 1978), p. 167. Kafitz calls particular attention to John Stuart Mill's *On Liberty*, which Raabe acquired in German translation in 1860 (p. 191).

14. To Eduard Engel, Nov. 28, 1899, E 2: 407.

15. To Wildenbruch's widow, Jan. 17, 1909; to the "Neue Kunstvereinigung," Berlin, Feb. 8, 1909, E 2: 482-83, 483-84.

16. To Edmund Sträter, Apr. 4, 1895, E 2: 369.

17. To Auguste Raabe, May 7, 1868, July 17, 1870, E 2: 130, 151.

18. To Karl Leiste, Mar. 13, 1868, E 2: 128.

19. To Wilhelm Kosch, Nov. 16, 1908, E 2: 481.

20. Herman Meyer, *Der Sonderling in der deutschen Dichtung* (Munich: Hanser, 1963), p. 261.

21. To Dr. Paul Zimmermann, Oct. 19, 1896, E 2: 383-84.

22. Georg Lukács, "Wilhelm Raabe," *Deutsche Realisten des 19. Jahrhunderts* (Berlin: Aufbau-Verlag, 1952), p. 235.

23. Jochen Meyer, *Wilhelm Raabe: Unter Demokraten, Hoflieferanten und Philistern. Eine Chronik seiner Stuttgarter Jahre* (Stuttgart: Fleischhauer & Spohn, 1981), p. 9.

24. Hoppe, "Raabes Stellung in der Geschichte des deutschen Geistes," *Wilhelm Raabe*, p. 147.

25. Meyer, *Wilhelm Raabe: Unter Demokraten*, p. 17.

26. See on this Friedrich Röttger, *Volk und Vaterland bei Wilhelm Raabe* (Graz: Stiasny, 1930), esp. pp. 14-15. While the spirit of this study will be found today to be obsolete (the author, incidentally, was Dutch, not German), it is not without insight into the national-liberal positions that Raabe held in common with many of his generation.

27. Hermann Pongs, *Wilhelm Raabe: Leben und Werk* (Heidelberg: Quelle & Meyer, 1958), p. 206.

28. To Marie Jensen, Nov. 22, 1895, E 3: 498.

29. To Jensen, Dec. 31, 1884, E 3: 375.

30. To Heyse, Mar. 2, 1875, E 2: 183.

31. To Eduard [sic] de Morsier, Oct. 25, 1890, E 2: 285-86.

32. To Eduard Hallberger, Apr. 10, 1867, E 2: 120-21.

33. To Siegmund Schott, July 18, 1891, E 2: 303.

34. Even in the Nazi period the novella was taken to be a warning against colonialism twenty years before Bismarck's policy. See Friedrich Bamler, "St. Thomas," *Mitt.* 29 (1939): 107-12.

35. To Gustav Frenssen, May 25, 1900, E 2: 413.

36. To Paul Gerber, Jan. 4, 1900, E 2: 411.

37. Hans Martin Schultz, *Raabe-Schriften: Eine systematische Darstellung* (Wolfenbüttel: Heckner, 1931), p. 88.

38. Fritz Hartmann, *Wilhelm Raabe: Wie er war und wie er dachte*, 2nd ed. (Hanover: Sponholtz, 1927), p. 67.

39. Wilhelm Fehse, *Wilhelm Raabe: Sein Leben und seine Werke* (Braunschweig: Vieweg, 1937), p. 263. The caution should always be kept in mind that one can never be sure whether the entries in Raabe's notebooks represent his own thoughts or are notes for one of his fictional voices.

40. Karl Heim, "Wilhelm Raabe und das Publikum" (Diss. University of Tübingen, 1953), pp. 18-19.

41. Among the few who have spoken well of the novel on political grounds are Röttger, *Volk und Vaterland bei Wilhelm Raabe*, pp. 78-96, and Fehse, *Wilhelm Raabe*, pp. 162-67. A fair modern assessment will be found in Laurel Ellen Eason, "Beginning and Conclusion: Structure and Theme in the Early Novels of Wilhelm Raabe" (Diss. Vanderbilt University, 1979), pp. 164-97.

42. In 1923 this passage was inserted into the left-wing periodical, *Die Weltbühne* 19, pt. 1 (1923): 434, as a critique of the Weimar Republic, probably by Tucholsky. See Leo A. Lensing, "Reading Raabe: The Example of Kurt Tucholsky," *Seminar* 19 (1983): 130-31.

43. To Jensen, Dec. 22, 1891; to Edmund Sträter, Jan. 4, 1892, E 3: 461; E 2: 319.

44. To Sträter, Jan. 4, 1892, E 2: 319.

45. The rather simpleminded poem has been subjected to an intensive ideological and psychosocial analysis by Rainer Noltenius, *Dichterfeiern in Deutschland: Rezeptionsgeschichte als Sozialgeschichte am Beispiel der Schiller- und Freiligrath-Feiern* (Munich: Fink, 1984), pp. 113-43. While Noltenius is ready with sometimes dubious psychonanalytic speculations, he barely mentions *The Dräumling Swamp*. More apposite is Anneliese Klingenberg's East German edition, *Der Dräumling: Mit Dokumenten zur Schillerfeier 1859.* (Berlin and Weimar: Aufbau-Verlag, 1984). Among the documents is the program of the Wolfenbüttel celebration. Klingenberg gives a generally fair if somewhat superficial account of Raabe's political development.

46. I am not the only one to have been struck by this similarity. See Ernst-Stephan Bauer, "Heilsames Lachen in heillosem Fremdsein. Zur Aufnahme Raabescher Motive in Hesses 'Steppenwolf,' " *RJ* (1984), pp. 198-207. *The Dräumling Swamp* was one of Hesse's favorite works. See his account of his visit to Raabe in 1909, Hermann Hesse, *Gesammelte Werke* (Frankfurt am Main: Suhrkamp, 1970) 10: 163-73.

47. To Heinrich Raabe, Apr. 20, 1871, *"In alls gedultig": Briefe Wilhelm Raabes (1842-1910)*, ed. Wilhelm Fehse (Berlin: Grote, 1940), p. 109. Also cited 10: 454.

48. Cf. Irene Stocksieker Di Maio, *The Multiple Perspective: Wilhelm Raabe's Third-Person Narratives of the Braunschweig Period* (Amsterdam: John Benjamins, 1981), pp. 78-79.

49. Nicolaas Cornelis Adrianus Perquin, S.J., *Wilhelm Raabes Motive als Ausdruck seiner Weltanschauung* (Amsterdam: H. J. Paris, 1927), p. 166.

CHAPTER 9: HISTORY

1. Berthold Auerbach, *Gesammelte Schriften* (Stuttgart and Augsburg, Cotta: 1857), I: viii.

2. To the Creutzsche Buchhandlung, Feb. 3, 1889, E 2: 262-63.

3. Raabe's antithetical relationship to the objective claims of historiography in his time is pursued in detail by Philip James Brewster, "Wilhelm Raabes historische Fiktion im Kontext: Beitrag zur Rekonstruktion der Gattungsproblematik zwischen Geschichtsschreibung und Poesie im 19. Jahrhundert" (Diss. Cornell University, 1983).

4. Contemporary critics who have found it more worthy of critical attention than I have been able to do are Josef Kunz, "Wilhelm Raabes Novelle 'Des Reiches Krone.' Versuch einer Interpretation," *RJ* 1966, pp. 7-24, and Karl-Friedrich Hahn, "Wilhelm Raabes 'Des Reiches Krone.' Geschichte als erzählerisches Mittel," *RJ* 1982, pp. 125-41. In the light of my understanding of Raabe I found the latter interpretation too religious.

5. Brewster, "Wilhelm Raabes historische Fiktion," also argues for a less dismissive view of the early fiction and (pp. 147, 152) singles out *The Holy Spring*.

6. To Edmund Sträter, June 13, 1891, E 2: 302.

7. Horst S. Daemmrich, *Wilhelm Raabe* (Boston: Twayne, 1981), pp. 76-77. Brewster, "Wilhelm Raabes historische Fiktion," pp. 180-92, finds traces of Hegel here and there, as others have, but he argues persuasively that Raabe grew totally skeptical of teleological schemes, and such philosophy of history as he had was an anti-philosophy, denying the intelligibility of history from the perspective of its victims or any transcendental plan. Thus, as Brewster remarks, his philosophy of history is coded in his narrative technique (p. 191).

8. Uwe Heldt, *Isolation und Identität: Die Bedeutung des Idyllischen in der Epik Wilhelm Raabes* (Frankfurt am Main, Bern, and Cirencester: Peter D. Lang, 1980), p. 136.

9. Brewster, "Wilhelm Raabes historische Fiktion," several times (e.g., p. 351) also points out that the repetitive recurrence of the bad in human affairs is coupled with the hope that the cycle might be brought to an end.

10. See Daemmrich, *Wilhelm Raabe*, pp. 52-55, for a treatment from a somewhat different perspective of *St. Thomas* as one solution to the problematics of historical fiction.

11. *Goethes Werke* (Hamburger Ausgabe), ed. Erich Trunz (Hamburg: Wegner, 1949-60), 10: 252-53.

12. To Auguste Raabe, May 7, 1868, July 17, 1870, E 2: 130, 151.

13. See on this and the historical placement of the novella generally the essay of Hans-Jürgen Schrader in his edition of *Höxter und Corvey* (Stuttgart: Reclam, 1981), esp. p. 202.

14. Katherine Starr Kaiser, "Structure and Narrative Technique in Wilhelm Raabe's *Krähenfelder Geschichten*" (Diss. Brown University, 1974), p. 111.

15. Hans Oppermann, "Raabes Erzählung 'Höxter und Corvey,' " *Mitt.* 42

(1955): 46-55. This is a good example of the inappropriateness of measuring Raabe against "classical" canons of form.

16. Fritz Martini, "Wilhelm Raabes 'Höxter und Corvey,' " *Der Deutschunterricht* 5, No. 1 (1953): 76-92.

17. For a fine, detailed explication and defense of the structure, see Kaiser, "Structure and Narrative Technique," pp. 97-132.

18. See especially Benno von Wiese, "Wilhelm Raabe: Die Innerste," *Die deutsche Novelle von Goethe bis Kafka: Interpretationen* (Düsseldorf: Bagel, 1964-65) 2: 198-215; Siegfried Hajek, "Wilhelm Raabes Erzählung 'Die Innerste,' " *RJ* 1977, pp. 30-47; and Kaiser, "Structure and Narrative Technique," pp. 67-96.

19. Jeffrey L. Sammons, "Raabe's Ravens," *Michigan Germanic Studies* 11 (1985): 1-15. Brewster, "Wilhelm Raabes historische Fiktion," pp. 331-76, offers a detailed and engrossing interpretation of the raven battle in his exemplary discussion of *The Odin Field* as a historical novel. He does not, however, relate the image to Raabe's self-representation as I do.

20. To Robert Lange, September 19, 1898, E 2: 400.

21. See John Hibberd, *Salomon Gessner: His Creative Achievement and Influence* (Cambridge: Cambridge University Press, 1976), p. 100.

22. Friedrich von Blanckenburg, *Versuch über den Roman* (Leipzig and Liegnitz: David Siegerts Wittwe, 1774).

CHAPTER 10: HUMOR

1. Karl Hoppe, "Aphorismen Raabes: Chronologisch geordnet," *Wilhelm Raabe: Beiträge zum Verständnis seiner Person und seines Werkes* (Göttingen: Vandenhoeck & Ruprecht, 1967), p. 91.

2. *Princeton Encyclopedia of Poetry and Poetics*, ed. Alex Preminger et al. (Princeton: Princeton University Press, 1965), pp. 143-47, 271-72, 738-40, 897-98. There is, to be sure, an entry under "Comedy of Humors" (p. 147), but that is a special technical term.

3. Gero von Wilpert, *Sachwörterbuch der Literatur*, 4th ed. (Stuttgart: Kröner, 1964), p. 285.

4. Jean Paul, *Vorschule der Ästhetik*, Werke, ed. Norbert Miller (Munich: Hanser, 1960/65), 5: 125. I have cited the English translation of Margaret R. Hale, *Horn of Oberon: Jean Paul Richter's School for Aesthetics* (Detroit: Wayne State University Press, 1973), pp. 88-89. This passage is directly applied to Raabe by Herman Meyer, "Raum und Zeit in Wilhelm Raabes Erzählkunst," *Deutsche Vierteljahrsschrift* 27 (1953): 256-57.

5. Keller to Hermann Hettner, May 29, 1850, Emil Ermatinger, *Gottfried Kellers Leben, Briefe und Tagebücher* (Stuttgart and Berlin: Cotta, 1924/25), 2: 234.

6. Friederich Theodor Vischer, *Ästhetik oder die Wissenschaft des Schönen* (Stuttgart: Carl Mäcken, 1846/57), pt. 1, sect. 2, B, c, p. 448.

7. Hermann Hesse, *Gesammelte Werke in zwölf Bänden* (Frankfurt am Main: Suhrkamp, 1970), 7: 156. The connection is discussed by Ernst-Stephan

Bauer, "Heilsames Lachen in heillosem Fremdsein: Zur Aufnahme Raabe-scher Motive in Hesses 'Steppenwolf,' " *RJ* 1984, p. 199.

8. To J. L. Kober, Mar. 21, 1859, E 2: 28.

9. Ernst Bode, "Über Wilhelm Raabes Verhältnis zur Philosophie," *Wilhelm Raabe-Kalender 1913*, ed. Otto Elster and Hanns Martin Elster (Berlin: Grote, 1912), p. 82.

10. G. A. O. Collischonn, "Horacker," *Raabestudien*, ed. Constantin Bauer (Wolfenbüttel: Heckner, 1925), pp. 262-63 (originally *Mitt.* 5 [1915]).

11. Adolf Suchel, "Über die Formen des Komischen bei Wilhelm Raabe," *Mitt.* 29 (1939): 45-56. One consequence of such arbitrary distinctions is that *Horacker* appears here not as a humorous but as a tragicomic work (p. 46).

12. Georg Lukács, "Wilhelm Raabe," *Deutsche Realisten des 19. Jahrhunderts* (Berlin: Aufbau-Verlag, 1952), p. 256.

13. Horst S. Daemmrich, *Wilhelm Raabe* (Boston: Twayne, 1981), p. 123.

14. Dieter Arendt, "Auf der Bühne des Welttheaters," *RJ* 1983, p. 29. There are many interesting insights into Raabe in Wolfgang Preisendanz's stimulating book *Humor als dichterische Einbildungskraft: Studien zur Erzählkunst des poetischen Realismus*, 2nd ed. (Munich: Fink, 1976). However, I have so many difficulties with Preisendanz's tendency to identify humor with the poetic imagination in general and with narrative irony in particular that I believe I should leave it aside with this respectful notice.

15. To Ernst Eckstein, Aug. 10, 1877, E 2: 193.

16. To W. Spemann and Julius Stettenheim, Aug. 10, 1885, E 2: 244-45.

17. Friedrich Sengle, in his elaborate literary history of the period, devoted well over a hundred pages to the verse epic: *Biedermeierzeit*, Vol. 2, *Die Formenwelt* (Stuttgart: Metzler, 1972), pp. 626-742.

18. I have taken over here the translation of John E. Woods in Wilhelm Raabe, *Novels* (New York: Continuum, 1983), p. 103, because I cannot do any better, though I am not sure it quite captures the send-up of rigidity and energetic conformism in the original:

Stramm, stramm, stramm;
Alles über einen Kamm.

19. To G. Grote Verlag, Jan. 10, 1876, E 2: 185.

20. To Edmund Sträter, Feb. 5, 1890, E 2: 275.

21. Fritz Martini, "Parodie und Regeneration der Idylle. Zu Wilhelm Raabes 'Horacker,' " *Literatur und Geistesgeschichte: Festgabe für Heinz Otto Burger*, ed. Reinhold Grimm and Conrad Wiedemann (Berlin: Erich Schmidt Verlag, 1968), pp. 249, 256.

22. Volkmar Sander, "Illusionszerstörung und Wirklichkeitserfassung im Roman Raabes," *Deutsche Romantheorien: Beiträge zu einer historischen Poetik des Romans in Deutschland*, ed. Reinhold Grimm (Frankfurt am Main and Bonn: Athenäum, 1968), p. 222.

23. A. Weber, "Lehrerfiguren in Raabes *Horacker*," *Formen realistischer Erzählkunst: Festschrift for Charlotte Jolles in Honour of her 70th Birthday*, ed. Jörg Thunecke with Eda Sagarra (Nottingham: Sherwood Press, 1979), p. 230.

24. Martini, "Parodie und Regeneration der Idylle," p. 237.

25. Wilhelm Fehse, *Wilhelm Raabe: Sein Leben und seine Werke* (Braunschweig: Vieweg, 1937), p. 234, argued that *Celtic Bones* was the only work of Raabe's to show a clear influence from Jean Paul, namely from *Dr. Katzenbergers Badereise* (*Dr. Katzenberger's Spa Journey*, 1809), the cynical protagonist of which steals bones from cemeteries and caves, collecting them along with freaks of nature, and traps and threatens a spa doctor who wrote bad reviews of his works. This opinion has been repeated frequently since then, though I can find no merit in it. It is an example of the habit of older literary scholars of grasping at an unusual motif—in this case the theft of old bones—and deducing influence from it.

26. To unknown, Jan. 9, 1896, E 2: 372-73. Raabe added that if the author were to turn it into a comedy for a "dignified stage" as opposed to a "Tivoli theater," he would have nothing against it.

27. Daemmrich, *Wilhelm Raabe*, p. 125.

28. Kathryn Louise Albaugh, "The Influence of William Makepeace Thackeray on Wilhelm Raabe" (Diss. Stanford University, 1941), p. 181. Albaugh continues: she has "peculiarities which his German women do not seem to have, but which Thackeray constantly stressed in connection with his maidens" (p. 182).

29. See Robert Anthony Graves, "The Integral Personality: The Relationship between the Female Characters and the World in Selected Works of Theodor Fontane and Wilhelm Raabe" (Diss. University of Bristol, 1978); Margrit Bröhan, *Die Darstellung der Frau bei Wilhelm Raabe und ein Vergleich mit liberalen Positionen zur Emanzipation der Frau im 19. Jahrhundert* (Frankfurt am Main and Bern: Peter D. Lang, 1981); and Irene Stocksieker Di Maio, "The 'Frauenfrage' and the Reception of Wilhelm Raabe's Female Characters," *Wilhelm Raabe: Studien zu seinem Leben und Werk*, ed. Leo A. Lensing and Hans-Werner Peter (Braunschweig: pp-Verlag, 1981), pp. 406-13.

30. Anna-Margarete Ehninger, "Erinnerungen an Wilhelm Raabe, seine Familie und sein Heim," *Wilhelm Raabe*, ed. Lensing and Peter, p. 479.

31. To the Jensens, Sept. 6, 1910, E 3: 592. It is not clear to me whether Margarethe ever had any success as a painter. She does not seem to have made out too well. By the 1930s all of Raabe's descendants, including Margarethe, were in financial difficulties and required charitable assistance from the Schiller Foundation. See Helmut Richter, ed., *Die Akte Wilhelm Raabe* (Weimar: Archiv der Deutschen Schillerstiftung, [1963]).

32. Josef Bass, "Die 'verlorenen Mädchen' bei Wilhelm Raabe," *Wilhelm Raabe-Kalender 1914*, ed. Otto Elster and Hanns Martin Elster (Berlin: Grote, 1913), pp. 74-96. It is perhaps even more surprising to see him defending homosexuality with remarkable liberality in 1905 (E 4: 186).

33. The contemporary Swabian author Hermann Lenz has commented on Raabe's "astonishingly incorrect Swabian": "Raabe: 'Des Südens warmer Gruss,'" *Schwäbische Curiosa*, ed. Georg Kleemann, 2nd ed. (Tübingen: Rainer

Wunderlich Verlag Hermann Leins, 1974), p. 211. I am grateful to Leo Lensing for the reference. See also 10: 489.

34. Jörg Thunecke, "Wilhelm Raabes angelsächsische Sprachhaltung in 'Christoph Pechlin,'" *Akten des VI. Internationalen Germanistenkongresses Basel 1980 (Jahrbuch für Internationale Germanistik*, Series A, Vol. 8, 2), pp. 263-66.

35. James Robert Reece, "Narrator and Narrative Levels in Wilhelm Raabe's Stuttgart Novels" (Diss. University of Oregon, 1975), p. 196.

36. Peter Michelsen, "Der Rektor und die Revolution: Eine Interpretation der 'Gänse von Bützow,'" *RJ* 1967, pp. 58-59.

37. It has been so treated by Philip James Brewster, "Wilhelm Raabes historische Fiktion im Kontext: Beitrag zur Rekonstruktion der Gattungsproblematik zwischen Geschichtsschreibung und Poesie im 19. Jahrhundert" (Diss. Cornell University, 1983), pp. 162-75.

38. Michelsen, "Der Rektor und die Revolution," pp. 70-71. For a similar conclusion see Eberhard Kirchhoff, "Einige Anmerkungen zu den philosophischen Einflüssen bei Wilhelm Raabe," *Diskussion Deutsch* 12 (1981): 304-7.

39. Daemmrich, *Wilhelm Raabe*, p. 59.

Chapter 11: Literature

1. Wilhelm Fehse, *Wilhelm Raabe: Sein Leben und seine Werke* (Braunschweig: Vieweg, 1937), p. 48.

2. Marie Jensen to Bertha Raabe, November 1, 1870, E 3: 121.

3. Herman Meyer, *The Poetics of Quotation in the European Novel*, tr. Theodore and Yetta Ziolkowski (Princeton: Princeton University Press, 1968), p. 204. Fritz Jensch, *Wilhelm Raabes Zitatenschatz* (Wolfenbüttel: Heckner, 1925), attempted to catalogue the quotations, but he himself knew that his 2,100 items were far from exhaustive.

4. Dieter Arendt, "Lessing-Rezeption bei Wilhelm Raabe: Ein Beitrag zur Geschichte des Bildungsbürgertums," *RJ* 1984, pp. 156, 153-54.

5. Arendt, "Lessing-Rezeption," pp. 142-43 and passim.

6. Ernst-August Roloff [Jun.], "Wilhelm Raabes Entwicklungsroman 'Prinzessin Fisch' und seine Bedeutung für das Gesamtwerk" (Diss. University of Göttingen, 1951); see also Roloff [Jun.], " 'Prinzessin Fisch' als entwicklungspsychologisches Problem," *Raabe-Jahrbuch 1950*, ed. E. A. Roloff [Sen.] (Braunschweig: Appelhans, 1950), pp. 87-108.

7. Meyer, *The Poetics of Quotation*, p. 213, n. 12.

8. Dorothea Bänsch, "Die Bibliothek Wilhelm Raabes nach Sachgebieten geordnet," *RJ* 1970, p. 93.

9. Jeffrey L. Sammons, "Wilhelm Raabe as Successor to Young Germany" *Monatshefte* 77 (1985): 449-59. Of the older Raabe scholars, I believe that Karl Hoppe was the only one to see that Raabe's relationship to Young Germany required clarification. See "Raabes Universitätsstudium" (originally 1956), *Wilhelm Raabe: Beiträge zum Verständnis seiner Person und seines Werkes* (Göttingen: Vandenhoeck & Ruprecht, 1967), p. 20.

10. Diary, Apr. 24, May 3, 8, 1859; see also to Auguste Raabe, May 5, 1859, E 2: 36.

11. To the Jensens, Dec. 25, 1878, E 3: 301.

12. See my effort to do this in *Six Essays on the Young German Novel* (Chapel Hill: University of North Carolina Press, 1972), pp. 124-50.

13. To Heyse, Feb. 26, 1875, E 2: 180.

14. To Edmund Sträter, May 22, 1892, E 2: 329.

15. To Eduard Engel, June 22, July 4, 1881, E 2: 229-30, 231.

16. To Fontane, Dec. 30, 1889; to Max Wolff, May 6, 1910, E 2: 272, 501. For Fontane's judgment on Raabe, see Kurt Schreinert, "Theodor Fontane über Wilhelm Raabe," *RJ* 1962, pp. 182-90.

17. The relationship with Heyse is discussed by Karl Heim, "Wilhelm Raabe und das Publikum" (Diss. University of Tübingen, 1953), p. 168, and Karl Hoppe, "Aus Raabes Briefwechsel," *Wilhelm Raabe*, pp. 39-55.

18. Marie Jensen to Raabe, Sept. 4, 1877, E 3: 280.

19. To Jensen, Feb. 13, 1890, E 3: 449: to Edmund Sträter, Mar. 24, 1890, E 2: 278. These were reactions to the publication of Storm's correspondence with Emil Kuh; Raabe felt the same way about the Storm-Keller correspondence; see to Jensen, Feb. 13, 1904, E 3: 553.

20. To Paul Heyse, Mar. 2, 1875, E 2: 183.

21. Leo A. Lensing believes that Raabe constructed *On the Scrap-Iron* in conscious parodistic opposition to Marlitt's type of women's magazine novel: "The Caricatured Reader in *Im alten Eisen*: Raabe, Marlitt and the 'Familienblattroman,' " *German Life and Letters* N.S. 31 (1977/78): 318-27. See also Lensing, *Narrative Structure and the Reader in Wilhelm Raabe's "Im alten Eisen"* (Bern, Frankfurt am Main, and Las Vegas: Peter Lang, 1977), pp. 87-93.

22. To Georg Scherer, Aug. 10, 1870, E 2: 154.

23. To the Leipziger Verlag, Feb. 8, 1909, E 2: 483. By the standards of our time this does not seem very liberal; but note that it is not sexuality but "sadism," hurting others, that offends him. In 1881 Raabe evaded an invitation to contribute to a journal edited by Sacher-Masoch, *Auf der Höhe*, because its internationalist policy did not appeal to him (to Sacher-Masoch, Sept. 20, 1881, E 2: 232: see also Hartmann's account of the event, E 4: 84-86). Nationalists and anti-Semites vigorously opposed Sacher-Masoch's internationalist and pro-Jewish enterprise. See David Biale, "Masochism and Philosemitism: The Strange Case of Leopold von Sacher-Masoch," *Journal of Contemporary History* 17 (1982): 307.

24. Hesse's report on the visit was written much later and not published until 1933. It can also be found in Hesse, *Gesammelte Werke in zwölf Bänden* (Frankfurt am Main: Suhrkamp, 1970), 10: 163-73. On Hesse's reponse to Raabe, see Hoppe, *Wilhelm Raabe*, pp. 63-65.

25. See to Frenssen, May 25, 1900; Nov. 26, 1901; and, somewhat less enthusiastically, to Siegmund Schott, July 22, 1902, E 2: 412-13; 434; 439. See also Raabe's frank admission to Sträter, Oct. 27, 1902, that his positive view of Frenssen was owing to the latter's discipleship (E 2: 442).

26. Philip J. Brewster, "Onkel Ketschwayo in Neuteutoburg: Zeitge-schichtliche Anspielungen in Raabes 'Stopfkuchen,' " *RJ* 1983, p. 117, n. 42.

27. Eugen Rüter, *Die Gesellschaft der Freunde Wilhelm Raabes: Rezeptionssteu-erung als Programm* (Darmstadt: Thesen Verlag, 1977), p. 83.

28. To Frenssen, May 25, 1900, E 2: 413.

29. To the Freie Bühne, May 18, 1894, E 2: 354-55.

30. To Siegmund Schott, Apr. 3, 1892, E 2: 325.

31. To Siegmund Schott, July 18, 1891, E 2: 303.

32. The only discussion of Raabe's Greek I know is Josef Bass, "Grie-chisches bei Raabe," *Mitt.* 20 (1930): 36-42.

33. Bänsch, "Die Bibliothek Wilhelm Raabes," p. 127.

34. A diary entry of Jan. 31, 1865, makes it probable that Raabe met Tur-genev in Stuttgart in the company of his friend and translator Moritz Hart-mann. In that year Raabe contributed a little poem to an album for Turgenev's companion, the singer Pauline Viardot-Garcia (20: 408; see also the correction to the dating by Karl Hoppe, "Miszellen," *RJ* 1968, pp. 137-39). The album was a project of Raabe's Stuttgart club in honor of the singer; a diary entry of Jan. 17, 1865, suggests that Hartmann urged Raabe to contribute. The Austrian liberal Hartmann was at first a friend of Raabe's, but they became estranged politically, possibly a motive for Raabe's irritable view of Hart-mann's protégé Turgenev. I have all this from unpublished researches of Leo A. Lensing, which he graciously turned over to me and which I hope he will pursue and publish.

35. To Edmund Sträter, Sept. 21, 1892, E 2: 332.

36. To Jensen, Oct. 16, 1877, E 3: 284.

37. To Richard Wrede, Apr. 15, 1897, E 2: 392.

38. To Wilhelm Kosch, Feb. 27, 1909, E 2: 484.

39. To Jensen, Feb. 14, 1910, E 3: 588. An unpersuasive effort to explain Raabe's fascination is Wolfgang Giegerich, "Dumas' 'Le Comte de Monte-Christo [sic]' und Wilhelm Raabe," *RJ* 1971, pp. 49-71.

40. Geoffrey Patrick Guyton Butler, "England and America in the Writings of Wilhelm Raabe: A Critical Study of his Knowledge and Appreciation of Language, Literature and People" (Diss. [University of London], 1961), pp. 159-63. This unfortunately unpublished dissertation is the most thorough study of Raabe's knowledge of English language and literature. The subject, however, is far from exhausted and will bear further examination.

41. See Butler, "England and America," pp. 135-58, who takes a rather schoolmasterly view of the matter. However, if Raabe was actually able to read Thackeray's *Memoirs of Mr. C. J. Yellowplush*, as indicated in his diary in 1865 (see p. 165), his grasp of English must have been pretty sound, for this work is written in orthographic representation of the footman's lower-class dialect, with many verbal jokes and puns of which the narrator is unconscious.

42. See Hoppe, *Wilhelm Raabe*, p. 24.

43. See Butler, "England and America," p. 274.

44. To Jensen, Feb. 14, 1879, E 3: 302.

45. Wilhelm and Marie Jensen to Raabe, May 4, 1872, E 3: 173. American literature generally was less important to Raabe than English. However, we find him citing a ballad of Longfellow in English in *After the Great War* (4: 41), and in his diary on Apr. 21, 1910, he noted the death of Mark Twain. He also read Captain Marryat's *Diary in America* (diary, Nov. 21, 1866).

46. To Edmund Sträter, Apr. 27, 1892, E 2: 327.

47. Louis Kientz, *Wilhelm Raabe: L'homme, la pensée et l'oeuvre* (Paris: Didier, 1939), devotes a substantial section, pp. 95-119, to demonstrating Raabe's slavish imitations of Dickens.

48. The one monographic study of the relationship, Emil Doernenburg and Wilhelm Fehse, *Raabe und Dickens: Ein Beitrag zur Erkenntnis der geistigen Gestalt Wilhelm Raabes* (Magdeburg: Creutz'sche Verlagsbuchhandlung, 1921), is hopelessly out of date. It began as a 1908 University of Pennsylvania master's thesis by a German-American academic who despised the United States as inferior to German culture; afterwards it was revised by Fehse.

49. E.g., Laurel Ellen Eason, "Beginning and Conclusion: Structure and Theme in the Early Novels of Wilhelm Raabe" (Diss. Vanderbilt University, 1979), p. 210.

50. H. R. Klieneberger, "Charles Dickens and Wilhelm Raabe," *Oxford German Studies* 4 (1969): 90-117, reprinted in Klieneberger, *The Novel in England and Germany: A Comparative Study* (London: Oswald Wolff, 1981), pp. 108-44. Klieneberger deals with Raabe in the received clichés of the case against him and is a worthy modern successor to Kientz.

51. The most thorough study is an unpublished dissertation, Kathryn Louise Albaugh, "The Influence of William Makepeace Thackeray on Wilhelm Raabe" (Diss. Stanford University, 1941). In the chronology of Raabe studies this was a long time ago; Albaugh evidently worked with Fehse and thus absorbed a view of Raabe that is no longer our own.

52. Albaugh, "Influence," p. 37.

53. To Wilhelm Kosch, Feb. 27, 1909, E 2: 484.

54. Bänsch, "Die Bibliothek Wilhelm Raabes," p. 137.

55. Dieter Arendt, "Auf der Bühne des Welttheaters," *RJ* 1983, pp. 14-15.

56. Albaugh, "Influence," pp. 17-18, 27-28, 32-35, 39. Albaugh points out, p. 23, that another influential tastemaker of the time, Julius Rodenberg, who knew Thackeray personally, had more insight into the reasons for his mode of narration and defended him.

CHAPTER 12: NARRATORS

1. Karl Hoppe, "Aphorismen Raabes: Chronologisch geordnet," *Wilhelm Raabe: Beiträge zum Verständnis seiner Person und seines Werkes* (Göttingen: Vandenhoeck & Ruprecht, 1967), p. 97.

2. James Robert Reece, "Narrator and Narrative Levels in Wilhelm Raabe's Stuttgart Novels" (Diss. University of Oregon, 1975), p. 321.

3. Karl Hotz, *Bedeutung und Funktion des Raumes im Werk Wilhelm Raabes* (Göppingen: Kümmerle, 1970), p. 55. I believe Hotz's figure of twenty-one

frame stories is too high, for he includes among them all first-person narrations of reminiscence. The claim that all but one of the narrators is isolated in a garret (ibid.) is simply not true and a reflex of old prejudices about Raabe.

4. See Charlotte C. Prather, "C. M. Wieland's Narrators, Heroes and Readers," *Germanic Review* 55 (1980): 64-73.

5. See Dieter Kafitz, *Figurenkonstellation als Mittel der Wirklichkeitserfassung. Dargestellt an Romanen der zweiten Hälfte des 19. Jahrhunderts (Freytag, Spielhagen, Fontane, Raabe)* (Kronberg: Athenäum, 1978), pp. 19-20.

6. Wayne C. Booth, *The Rhetoric of Fiction* (Chicago: University of Chicago Press, 1961), p. 122.

7. Barker Fairley, "The Modernity of Wilhelm Raabe," *German Studies Presented to Leonard Ashley Willoughby by Pupils, Colleagues and Friends on his Retirement*, [ed. J. Boyd] (Oxford: Blackwell, 1952), p. 74.

8. Michael Boyd, *The Reflexive Novel: Fiction as Critique* (Lewisburg: Bucknell University Press, 1983), pp. 24, 35.

9. Boyd, *The Reflexive Novel*, p. 33. Boyd's position is not the only possible one in contemporary criticism. Not until my own work was completed did I come across George Levine's absorbing study of the varieties of Victorian narrative resources, *The Romantic Imagination: English Fiction from Frankenstein to Lady Chatterley* (Chicago and London: University of Chicago Press, 1981). Levine demonstrates persuasively that the "great novels of the nineteenth century were never so naive about narrative conventions or the problems of representation as later realists or modern critics have suggested" (p. 7) and that "there was no such thing as naive realism—simple faith in the correspondence between word and thing—among serious Victorian novelists" (p. 12). This study would be a valuable guide in a project to situate Raabe precisely in the Victorian context; so much of what Levine has to say about Thackeray fits Raabe so exactly that I feel vindicated in the conclusions about their affinity to which I had come.

10. Christa Hebbel, "Die Funktion der Erzähler- und Figurenperspektiven in Wilhelm Raabes Ich-Erzählungen" (Diss. University of Heidelberg, 1960), pp. 127, 139.

11. Hoppe, "Aphorismen Raabes," p. 111.

12. To Klara [sic] Zetkin, Mar. 10, 1908, E 2: 477.

13. Wolfgang Preisendanz, "Die Erzählstruktur als Bedeutungskomplex der 'Akten des Vogelsangs,'" *RJ* 1981, p. 210; Wolfgang Jehmüller, *Die Gestalt des Biographen bei Wilhelm Raabe* (Munich: Fink, 1975), p. 11.

14. To the Verein zur Förderung der Kunst, Mar. 4, 1901, E 2: 421.

15. Wilhelm Raabe, *Werke in Auswahl: Studienausgabe*, Vol. 5: *Unruhige Gäste: Ein Roman aus dem Säkulum*, ed. Hans-Werner Peter (Braunschweig: pp-Verlag, 1981), p. 166. The novel was, to be sure, published in the renowned *Gartenlaube*, but it was not suited for that magazine, as was recognized by the editor, who plagued Raabe with demands for significant changes, and it failed with the readership.

16. Reece, "Narrator and Narrative Levels," p. 282.

17. Stephen A. Gould, "Ontology and Ethics: The Rhetorical Role of the Narrator in Wilhelm Raabe's Early Novels" (Diss. University of Nebraska, 1976), pp. 72-78.

18. Gould, "Ontology and Ethics," p. 218.

19. Reece, "Narrator and Narrative Levels," p. 33-35.

20. Laurel Ellen Eason, "Beginning and Conclusion: Structure and Theme in the Early Novels of Wilhelm Raabe" (Diss. Vanderbilt University, 1979), p. 227.

21. Cf. Heine in *Die Bäder von Lucca* (*The Baths of Lucca*), Chapter 9: ". . . I cannot promise you much entertainment in the next chapters. If you are bored by the tedious stuff that will appear in them, console yourself with me, who even had to write all this stuff. I advise you to skip a few pages occasionally, then you will finish the book more quickly—ah, I wish I could do the same!" Heinrich Heine, *Sämtliche Schriften*, ed. Klaus Briegleb et al. (Munich: Hanser, 1967-76), 2: 426.

22. For more extensive critical comment on these devices, see Irene Stocksieder Di Maio, *The Multiple Perspective: Wilhelm Raabe's Third-Person Narratives of the Braunschweig Period* (Amsterdam: John Benjamins, 1981), p. 76, and Leo A. Lensing, *Narrative Structure and the Reader in Wilhelm Raabe's "Im alten Eisen"* (Bern, Frankfurt am Main, and Las Vegas: Peter Lang, 1977), esp. Chapter 1.

23. Hoppe, "Aphorismen Raabes," p. 89.

24. Katherine Starr Kaiser, "Structure and Narrative Technique in Wilhelm Raabe's *Krähenfelder Geschichten*" (Diss. Brown University, 1974), p. 152.

25. Reece, "Narrator and Narrative Levels," p. 193.

26. Horst S. Daemmrich, *Wilhelm Raabe* (Boston: Twayne, 1981), pp. 32, 34.

27. For an attempt at a typology of Raabe's first-person narrators, see Jehmüller, *Die Gestalt des Biographen*, p. 19.

28. Daemmrich, *Wilhelm Raabe*, p. 93. As a predecessor in multiple narration Daemmrich mentions Wilkie Collins's *The Woman in White* (1860). I know of no evidence that Raabe knew Collins, but the temporal coincidence is striking. The comparison with Collins was first made by Arno Schmidt. See Horst Denkler, "Der untrügliche Spürsinn des Genius für seinesgleichen: Arno Schmidts Verhältnis zu Wilhelm Raabe," *RJ* 1985, p. 147.

29. The best study of *Three Pens* is Joachim Bark, "Raabes 'Drei Federn' (1865): Versuche fiktiver Biographik. Zugleich ein Beitrag zum deutschen Erziehungsroman," *RJ* 1981, pp. 128-48.

30. See Frederick J. Beharriell, "The Hidden Meaning of Goethe's 'Bekenntnisse einer schönen Seele,' " *Lebendige Form: Interpretationen zur deutschen Literatur. Festschrift für Heinrich E. K. Henel*, ed. Jeffrey L. Sammons and Ernst Schürer (Munich: Fink, 1970), pp. 37-62. More recently, the subtle unreliability of the narrator in *Werther* has been seen more clearly: Erika Nolan, "Goethes 'Die Leiden des jungen Werther': Absicht und Methode," *Jahrbuch der Deutschen Schillergesellschaft* 28 (1984): 191-222.

31. Gould, "Ontology and Ethics," p. 97.

32. Gould, "Ontology and Ethics," pp. 102, 106.

33. Valuable insights may be found in Daemmrich, *Wilhelm Raabe*, pp. 115-22; Siegfried Hajek, " 'Meister Autor'—Sprachschichten und Motive," *RJ* 1981, pp. 149-68; and Fritz Martini, "Wilhelm Raabes Verzicht auf 'Versöhnung.' Bemerkungen zu 'Meister Autor,' " *RJ* 1981, pp. 169-93.

34. Hajek, " 'Meister Autor,' " p. 153.

35. Martini, "Wilhelm Raabes Verzicht," pp. 182-84.

36. Hajek, " 'Meister Autor,' " p. 152.

37. Siegfried Hajek and Fritz Martini, "Diskussionshorizonte: 'Meister Autor' im Kontext realistischen Erzählens," *RJ* 1982, p. 101.

38. Jost Schillemeit, "Ruminationen. Zur Entstehungsweise Raabescher Erzählungen," *RJ* 1981, p. 46.

39. Daemmrich, *Wilhelm Raabe*, p. 32.

40. Booth, *The Rhetoric of Fiction*, p. 123.

CHAPTER 13: THE DEFECTIVE FAMILY

1. Fritz Martini, *Die Stadt in der Dichtung Wilhelm Raabes* (Greifswald: Hans Adler, E. Parzig, 1934), p. 38.

2. Erich Weniger, "Wilhelm Raabe und das bürgerliche Leben," *Raabe in neuer Sicht*, ed. Hermann Helmers (Stuttgart: Kohlhammer, 1968), p. 78.

3. Siegfried Hajek, "Wilhelm Raabe im Deutschunterricht. 'Die Akten des Vogelsangs,' " *Diskussion Deutsch* 12 (1981): 8.

4. W. H. Riehl, *Die Familie*, 11th ed. (Stuttgart: Cotta, 1897), p. 75.

5. Riehl, *Die Familie*, p. vi.

6. Riehl, *Die Familie*, p. 102. Cf. Volume 1 of the *Naturgeschichte des Volkes als Grundlage einer deutschen Sozial-Politik, Land und Leute*, 9th ed. (Stuttgart: Cotta, 1894), p. vi: "I . . . found the natural class divisions on my way without looking for them."

7. Riehl, *Die Familie*, pp. xiii, 121, 147.

8. Riehl, *Die Familie*, p. 209.

9. Riehl, *Die Familie*, pp. 248-49.

10. A. Tilo Alt, *Theodor Storm* (New York: Twayne, 1973), p. 20.

11. Adalbert Stifter, *Der Nachsommer, Gesammelte Werke in sechs Bänden*, ed. Michael Benedikt and Herbert Hornstein (Gütersloh: Bertelsmann, 1956/57), 4: 736-37.

12. Friedrich Theodor Vischer, *Ästhetik oder die Wissenschaft des Schönen* (Stuttgart: Carl Mäcken, 1846/57), pt. 3, sect. 2, b, pp. 1313-14.

13. Lists of these characters will be found in the German version of this essay, Jeffrey L. Sammons, "Die defekte Familie bei Wilhelm Raabe und die Fiktion der alternativen Gesellschaft: Ein Versuch," *RJ* 1985, pp. 27-43. I cannot swear to the completeness or exactness of the figures, for there are many minor characters whose family relations are not quite clear. Also there are cases where the family relations of a character change in the course of the story. Similar, less complete tables will be found in William T. Webster,

Wirklichkeit und Illusion in den Romanen Wilhelm Raabes (Braunschweig: pp-Verlag, 1982), pp. 359-63. Webster does not systematically integrate these observations into his interpretation but remarks on one occasion: "fewer than a third of the families described in his works can . . . be considered as complete" (p. 261).

14. Karl Hotz, *Bedeutung und Funktion des Raumes im Werk Wilhelm Raabes* (Göppingen: Kümmerle, 1970), p. 133.

15. Riehl, *Die Familie*, p. 217: "We have gained in 'prudery' because the family spirit is growing stronger again. . . . We may therefore congratulate ourselves that our theater public begins to become so prudish again."

16. Katherine Starr Kaiser, "Structure and Narrative Technique in Wilhelm Raabe's *Krähenfelder Geschichten*" (Diss. Brown University, 1974), p. 76.

17. Riehl, *Die Familie*, p. viii.

18. Wilhelm Fehse, "In Raabes Werkstatt," *Raabe-Gedenkbuch*, ed. Constantin Bauer and Hans Martin Schultz (Berlin-Grunewald: Klemm, 1921), p. 84.

19. Gerald Opie, "Childhood and the Childlike in the Fiction of Wilhelm Raabe" (Diss. University of Exeter, 1971), p. i.

20. Opie, "Childhood and the Childlike," p. 59.

21. Raabe to the Jensens, Oct. 2, 1874, E 3: 230.

22. To be sure, Raabe's fatherly feelings were not without limits and doubts. To Edmund Sträter he wrote on May 7, 1890, that it was consoling to ask oneself whether one is really responsible for the fate of one's children (E 2: 280). When his daughter Klara and her family moved into the apartment above his, it seems not to have delighted him very much; see to Jensen, Feb. 14, 1908, E 3: 577.

23. In conversation with his son-in-law Paul Wasserfall, E 4: 18. In a perhaps more authentic place it is the city of Magdeburg that prevented him from becoming "a mediocre lawyer, schoolmaster, physician, or even pastor" (to Müller-Brauel, Aug. 9, 1906, E 2: 467).

24. Margrit Bröhan, *Die Darstellung der Frau bei Wilhelm Raabe und ein Vergleich mit liberalen Positionen zur Emanzipation der Frau im 19. Jahrhundert* (Frankfurt am Main: Peter D. Lang, 1981), p. 206: the "omnipotence of the father becomes a destructive force in the middle-period works. . . . Fathers have become the founders of unhappiness."

25. Leo A. Lensing, *Narrative Structure and the Reader in Wilhelm Raabe's "Im alten Eisen"* (Bern, Frankfurt am Main, and Las Vegas: Peter Lang, 1977), pp. 88, 90.

26. Wolfgang Jehmüller, *Die Gestalt des Biographen bei Wilhelm Raabe* (Munich: Fink, 1975), p. 51.

27. Fritz Martini, "Wilhelm Raabe und das literarische Biedermeier," *Mitt.* 23 (1933): 43.

28. Uwe Heldt, *Isolation und Identität: Die Bedeutung des Idyllischen in der Epik Wilhelm Raabes* (Frankfurt am Main, Bern, and Cirencester: Peter Lang, 1980), p. 216.

29. Dieter Kafitz, *Figurenkonstellation als Mittel der Wirklichkeitserfassung. Dargestellt an Romanen der zweiten Hälfte des 19. Jahrhunderts (Freytag, Spielhagen, Fontane, Raabe)* (Kronberg: Athenäum, 1978), p. 178.

30. Michael Limlei, "Die Romanschlüsse in Wilhelm Raabes Romanen *Stopfkuchen* und *Die Akten des Vogelsangs*," *Wilhelm Raabe: Studien zu seinem Leben und Werk*, ed. Leo A. Lensing and Hans-Werner Peter (Braunschweig: pp-Verlag, 1981), p. 351. Limlei gives no examples and I think they would be hard to find, leaving aside the relationship of a son to his widowed mother. The childhood *environment* is often agreeably and nostalgically remembered, but that is not identical with the family.

CHAPTER 14: THE FICTION OF THE ALTERNATIVE COMMUNITY

1. Kenneth Burke, "The Rhetoric of Hitler's 'Battle,' " *Terms for Order*, ed. Stanley Edgar Hyman and Barbara Karmiller (Bloomington: Indiana University Press, 1964), pp. 107, 117. The essay dates from 1939.

2. My own translation from "Manifest der Kommunistischen Partei," Karl Marx and Friedrich Engels, *Ausgewählte Schriften in zwei Bänden* (Berlin: Dietz Verlag, 1960), 1: 26.

3. Herman Meyer, *Der Sonderling in der deutschen Dichtung* (Munich: Hanser, 1963), p. 289.

4. Volkmar Sander, "Illusionszerstörung und Wirklichkeitserfassung im Roman Raabes," *Deutsche Romantheorien: Beiträge zu einer historischen Poetik des Romans in Deutschland*, ed. Reinhold Grimm (Frankfurt am Main and Bonn: Athenäum, 1968), p. 223.

5. Renate Möhrmann, *Der vereinsamte Mensch. Studien zum Wandel des Einsamkeitsmotivs im Roman von Raabe bis Musil* (Bonn: Bouvier, 1974), p. 33.

6. Stephen A. Gould, "Ontology and Ethics: The Rhetorical Role of the Narrator in Wilhelm Raabe's Early Novels" (Diss. University of Nebraska, 1976), p. 125.

7. Joachim Bark, "Raabes 'Drei Federn' (1865): Versuche fiktiver Biographik. Zugleich ein Beitrag zum deutschen Erziehungsroman," *RJ* 1981, p. 144.

8. Horst S. Daemmrich, *Wilhelm Raabe* (Boston: Twayne, 1981), p. 116.

9. I have always wondered whether this is an echo of the well-known leitmotivic advice given by another mentor, the misanthropic uncle in Stifter's *Der Hagestolz (The Bachelor)*: "Everyone is there for his own sake" (Adalbert Stifter, *Studien* [Stuttgart: Insel, 1958], 2: 376). There is no way to know this, though we do know that Raabe admired Stifter.

10. Katherine Starr Kaiser, "Structure and Narrative Technique in Wilhelm Raabe's *Krähenfelder Geschichten*" (Diss. Brown University, 1974), pp. 51-52.

11. Hermann Böschenstein, *Deutsche Gefühlskultur: Studien zu ihrer dichterischen Gestaltung* (Bern: Paul Haupt, 1954), p. 241.

Part III: Interpretations
Chapter 15: Irresolute Form: *Abu Telfan*

1. Mayer's essay, which appeared in *Die Zeit* on July 18, 1980, p. 39, was slightly expanded for *ZEIT-Bibliothek der 100 Bücher*, ed. Fritz J. Raddatz (Frankfurt am Main: Suhrkamp, 1980), pp. 278-82, and in this form was reprinted in *Wilhelm Raabe: Studien zu seinem Leben und Werk*, ed. Leo A. Lensing and Hans-Werner Peter (Braunschweig: pp-Verlag, 1981), pp. 128-32.

2. James Robert Reece, "Narrator and Narrative Levels in Wilhelm Raabe's Stuttgart Novels" (Diss. University of Oregon, 1975), p. 209. Reece goes on to observe, however, that "the potentially most exciting portions occur as the oral reconstructions of several of the work's characters" (ibid.).

3. Louis Kientz, *Wilhelm Raabe: L'homme, la pensée et l'oeuvre* (Paris: Didier, 1939), pp. 145-46.

4. Herman Meyer, *Der Sonderling in der deutschen Dichtung*, 2nd ed. (Munich: Hanser, 1963), p. 253. The objection is directed against Perquin.

5. Hans Jürgen Meinerts, *"Die Akten des Vogelsangs": Raabestudien auf Grund einer Sprachuntersuchung* (Berlin: Junker und Dünnhaupt, 1940), p. 196, n. 14.

6. Robert Anthony Graves, "The Integral Personality: The Relationship between the Female Characters and the World in Selected Works of Theodor Fontane and Wilhelm Raabe" (Diss. University of Bristol, 1978), p. 149.

7. Margrit Bröhan, *Die Darstellung der Frau bei Wilhelm Raabe und ein Vergleich mit liberalen Positionen zur Emanzipation der Frau im 19. Jahrhundert* (Frankfurt am Main and Bern: Peter D. Lang, 1981), pp. 147-48.

8. Stephen A. Gould, "Ontology and Ethics: The Rhetorical Role of the Narrator in Wilhelm Raabe's Early Novels" (Diss. University of Nebraska, 1976), p. 185. Gould titles his chapter on *Abu Telfan* "Confusion of Distance."

9. Gould, "Ontology and Ethics," pp. 185-86, 182, 187.

10. Barker Fairley, *Wilhelm Raabe: An Introduction to his Novels* (Oxford: Clarendon Press, 1961), pp. 166-68. Cf. Wilhelm Fehse, *Wilhelm Raabe: Sein Leben und seine Werke* (Braunschweig: Vieweg, 1937), p. 289, who had already seen the disunity of the novel; he argues that the theme of Hagebucher is finished with the lecture, and that the tale of Lieutenant Kind and the Serena episode are add-ons. This is a judgment, however, that does not engage the problematics of the text as a whole.

Chapter 16: Fate and Psychology:
*At the Sign of
the Wild Man* and *Restless Guests*

1. See my discussion in "Fate and Psychology: Another Look at Mörike's *Maler Nolten*," *Lebendige Form: Interpretationen zur deutschen Literatur. Festschrift für Heinrich E. K. Henel*, ed. Jeffrey L. Sammons and Ernst Schürer (Munich: Fink, 1970), pp. 211-27.

2. Nicolaas Cornelis Adrianus Perquin, S.J., *Wilhelm Raabes Motive als Ausdruck seiner Weltanschauung* (Amsterdam: H. J. Paris, 1927), p. 244.

3. Elisabeth Rockenbach Trafton, "Resignation in Wilhelm Raabes Stuttgarter Trilogie" (Diss. University of California, Los Angeles, 1978), pp. 85-86, 97, and passim.

4. Uwe Heldt, *Isolation und Identität: Die Bedeutung des Idyllischen in der Epik Wilhelm Raabes* (Frankfurt am Main, Bern, and Cirencester: Peter D. Lang, 1980), p. 223.

5. A timely warning against seeing *At the Sign of the Wild Man* as an allegory of capitalism is given by Eberhard Völker, "Raabes Harzburger Erzählungen," *RJ* 1984, p. 28.

6. Katherine Starr Kaiser, "Structure and Narrative Technique in Wilhelm Raabe's *Krähenfelder Geschichten*" (Diss. Brown University, 1974), p. 25.

7. See Peter Demetz, *Formen des Realismus: Theodor Fontane. Kritische Untersuchungen* (Munich: Hanser, 1964), pp. 137-45.

8. Barker Fairley, *Wilhelm Raabe: An Introduction to his Novels* (Oxford: Clarendon Press, 1961), p. 247.

9. Karl Heim, "Wilhelm Raabe und das Publikum" (Diss. University of Tübingen, 1953), p. 94.

10. On the importance of the Reclam publication for the work's popularity, see Ulrike Koller, "Vom 'Lesepöbel' zur Leser-'Gemeinde.' Raabes Beziehung zum zeitgenössischen Publikum im Spiegel der Leserbehandlung," *RJ* 1979, p. 125.

11. To Edmund Sträter, Nov. 8, 1894, E 2: 361.

12. Paul Spruth, "Zur Psychologie des Apothekers Philipp Kristeller und des Obersten Don Agostin Agonista in Raabes Novelle 'Zum wilden Mann,' " *Mitt.* 42 (1955): 101-3; Adolf Suchel, "Wilhelm Raabes Stellung zum Problem der Willensfreiheit," *Mitt.* 46 (1959): 21.

13. Horst S. Daemmrich, *Wilhelm Raabe* (Boston: Twayne, 1981), p. 100.

14. Wilfried Thürmer, "Entfremdetes Behagen. Wilhelm Raabes Erzählung 'Zum wilden Mann' als Konkretion gründerzeitlichen Bewußtseins," *RJ* 1976, pp. 155, 161.

15. Perquin, *Wilhelm Raabes Motive*, pp. 182-84.

16. Richard Bernheimer, *Wild Men in the Middle Ages: A Study in Art, Sentiment, and Demonology* (Cambridge, Mass.: Harvard University Press, 1952), p. 11. Bernheimer goes on to say (p. 12): "To the present day, in certain country districts of Bavaria, a mentally deranged person is actually called a wild man."

17. Daemmrich, *Wilhelm Raabe*, p. 99. The connection was also made by Kaiser, "Structure and Narrative Technique," p. 26, who has a note on the iconography, pp. 218-19, n. 8.

18. Kaiser, "Structure and Narrative Technique," p. 35.

19. E. A. Roloff [Sen.], "Triumph und Überwindung der Kanaille. Raabes Pessimismus im Spiegel der Novelle 'Zum wilden Mann,' " *Raabe-Jahrbuch 1949*, ed. E. A. Roloff [Sen.] (Braunschweig: Appelhans, 1949), p. 47.

20. Roloff, "Triumph und Überwindung der Kanaille," p. 52.

21. See Daemmrich, *Wilhelm Raabe*, p. 98.

22. Hans Butzmann, "Musäus' Schatzgräber und Raabes Erzählung 'Zum wilden Mann,' " *Mitt.* 36 (1949): 81-83. The fable may be conveniently found in Johann Karl August Musäus, *Märchen und Sagen*, ed. Hans Marquardt (Munich: Kösel Verlag, 1972), 2: 395-452.

23. Leo Berg, "Wilhelm Raabe als Erzähler," *Neue Essays* (Oldenburg and Leipzig: Schulze, 1901), p. 279. The essay was first published in 1897, as a review of the fourth volume of Raabe's collected stories.

24. See especially Ernst-August Roloff [Jun.], "Wilhelm Raabes Entwicklungsroman 'Prinzessin Fisch' und seine Bedeutung für das Gesamtwerk" (Diss. University of Göttingen, 1951). Roloff's psychology, however, is idealistic and makes no reference to Freud. Wilhelm Fehse, *Wilhelm Raabe: Sein Leben und seine Werke* (Braunschweig: Vieweg, 1937), p. 476, asserted with some exaggeration that *Princess Fish* is the only work that puts a psychological problem at the center. The one allegedly psychiatric study of Raabe's figures is of little help, as it merely puts labels on conditions: Maria Vogel, "Darstellung der von Wilhelm Raabe geschilderten seelischen Abnormitäten und Versuch einer psychiatrischen Deutung" (M.D. Diss. University of Frankfurt am Main, 1949). Vogel (p. 12) claimed to have identified seventy psychotics in Raabe's works, to all of whom the author is sympathetic. Rather more thoughtful is the study of William T. Webster, "Psychiatrische Betrachtungen oder Gesellschaftskritik? Zur Darstellung geistiger Abnormitäten im Werk Wilhelm Raabes," *Wilhelm Raabe: Studien zu seinem Leben und Werk*, ed. Leo A. Lensing and Hans-Werner Peter (Braunschweig: pp-Verlag, 1981), pp. 324-41.

25. Heim, "Wilhelm Raabe und das Publikum," p. 258. The argument is repeated in Heim's more accessible essay, "Wilhelm Raabe und das Publikum," *Mitt.* 42 (1955): 8. The view expressed by the editor Günter Heumann of the edition of *Restless Guests* in Wilhelm Raabe, *Werke in Auswahl*, ed. Hans-Werner Peter (Braunschweig: pp-Verlag, 1981), 5: 166, that the more conventional narrative style was a concession to the reader of the popular *Gartenlaube*, in which the work first appeared, is, I believe, wholly unacceptable. For one thing, *Restless Guests* was not written for *Die Gartenlaube* but was sent in by request, and it was not a success either with the magazine's editor, who attempted to force crippling revisions, or with its readership. Heumann may have this idea from Hermann Pongs, *Wilhelm Raabe: Leben und Werk* (Heidelberg: Quelle & Meyer, 1958), p. 500.

26. Völker, "Raabes Harzburger Erzählungen," pp. 41-42.

27. W. T. Webster, "Social Change and Personal Insecurity in the Late Novels of Wilhelm Raabe," *Formen realistischer Erzählkunst: Festschrift for Charlotte Jolles in Honour of her 70th Birthday*, ed. Jörg Thunecke with Eda Sagarra (Nottingham: Sherwood Press, 1979), p. 234.

28. This is the longest uninterrupted literary quote in Raabe's works. Geoffrey Patrick Guyton Butler, "England and America in the Writings of Wilhelm Raabe: A Critical Study of his Knowledge and Appreciation of Language, Literature and People" (Diss. [University of London], 1961), p. 274,

argues that no interpretation of the novel is valid without taking it into account.

29. Gertrud Höhler, *Unruhige Gäste: Das Bibelzitat in Wilhelm Raabes Roman* (Bonn: Bouvier, 1969).

30. Höhler, *Unruhige Gäste*, p. 76.

31. For an example of what I regard as an excessively Christianized interpretation, see Rainer Gruenter, "Ein *Schritt vom Wege*. Geistliche Lokalsymbolik in Wilhelm Raabes *Unruhige Gäste*," *Euphorion* 60 (1966): 209-21. The view of Rolf-Dieter Koll, *Raumgestaltung bei Wilhelm Raabe* (Bonn: Bouvier, 1977), p. 147, that the novel exhibits an atypical "resignation into the religious" I consider also untenable.

32. Joachim Müller, "Erzählstruktur und Symbolgefüge in Wilhelm Raabes 'Unruhigen Gästen,' " *RJ* 1963, p. 102.

33. Höhler, *Unruhige Gäste*, p. 140.

34. The idea of the saeculum appears elsewhere, for example, in *Abu Telfan*, where it is said of the isolated Klaudine that "nothing more out of the saeculum will so easily come over the old woman in the mill" (7: 120); and in more comic form in *The Dräumling Swamp*, where Fischarth, locked up in Haeseler's studio with cigars, good food, and brandy, has no further care for the saeculum outside (10: 144). Siegfried Hajek, " 'Meister Autor'—Sprachschichten und Motive," *RJ* 1981, p. 151, sees the ultimate definition of the saeculum in *Master Author*. The editor of *Die Gartenlaube*, allergic to foreign words as always, changed "saeculum" in the subtitle to "society" (Fehse, *Wilhelm Raabe*, p. 489).

35. Karl Lorenz, "Der Liebesroman Phöbes und Veits in den 'Unruhigen Gästen,' " *Mitt.* 11 (1921): 132-39.

36. To Edmund Sträter, Sept. 21, 1889, E 2: 268.

37. Höhler, *Unruhige Gäste*, p. 125.

38. Walter Schedlinsky, *Rolle und industriegesellschaftliche Entwicklung: Die literarische Vergegenständlichung eines sozialgeschichtlichen Phänomens im Werk Wilhelm Raabes* (Frankfurt am Main: R. G. Fischer, 1980), pp. 351-74.

39. Gerald Opie, "Childhood and the Childlike in the Fiction of Wilhelm Raabe" (Diss. University of Exeter, 1971), pp. 169, 176-79.

40. Webster, "Social Change and Personal Insecurity," pp. 234-35.

41. Fairley, *Wilhelm Raabe*, p. 156.

42. Pongs, *Wilhelm Raabe*, p. 510.

CHAPTER 17: BOUNDARIES
The Pied Piper of
Hamelin; Wunnigel; Of Old Proteus

1. Leo A. Lensing, *Narrative Structure and the Reader in Wilhelm Raabe's "Im Alten Eisen"* (Berne, Frankfurt am Main, and Las Vegas: Peter Lang, 1977), Chapter 3, and "Fairy Tales in the Novel: Generic Tension in Wilhelm Raabe's *Die Chronik der Sperlingsgasse*," *Wilhelm Raabe: Studien zu seinem Leben*

und Werk, ed. Leo A. Lensing and Hans-Werner Peter (Braunschweig: pp-Verlag, 1981), pp. 14-43.

2. Lensing, "Fairy Tales in the Novel," pp. 16-17.

3. The interpretation of the figure of Little Red Riding Hood touched off a lively debate at a symposium in 1981, during which several prestigious critics took widely differing positions. See "Zur Vorlage: Charlotte Jolles: 'Im alten Eisen.' Wirklichkeit im Märchenton," *RJ* 1982, pp. 85-87.

4. "Der alte Musäus," Wilhelm Raabe, *Sämtliche Werke* (Berlin-Grunewald: Klemm, [1913/16]), Series III, Vol. 6: 539-40.

5. Eduard Beaucamp, *Literatur als Selbstdarstellung: Wilhelm Raabe und die Möglichkeiten eines deutschen Realismus* (Bonn: Bouvier, 1968), pp. 97-99.

6. Rolf-Dieter Koll, *Raumgestaltung bei Wilhelm Raabe* (Bonn: Bouvier, 1977), p. 71.

7. See Wolfgang Mieder, "Der Rattenfänger von Hameln in der modernen Literatur, Karikatur und Werbung," *Muttersprache* 95 (1984/85): 127-50 (with amusing illustrations).

8. To Julius Niedner, Mar. 27, 1863, E 2: 92-93.

9. One of the modern students of the problem, Heinrich Spanuth, has discussed Raabe's relationship to it in "Raabe und die Hämelschen Kinder," *Mitt.* 45 (1958): 14-23. Browning, incidentally, knew of the Transylvanian theory, to which he adverts in his poem.

10. Josef Bass, "Die Juden bei Wilhelm Raabe," *Monatsschrift für Geschichte und Wissenschaft der Juden* 54 (1910): 658-59.

11. See Gerhard Goebel, "Apoll in Hameln. Ein Nachtrag zu den 'Göttern im Exil,' " *Germanisch-romanische Monatsschrift* N.S. 32 (1982): 286-99; Goebel, linking his interpretation to Heine's theory of the Christian demonization of the pagan gods, views the piper as a demonized Apollo.

12. Wilhelm Brandes, *Wilhelm Raabe: Sieben Kapitel zum Verständnis und zur Würdigung des Dichters*, 2nd ed. (Wolfenbüttel and Berlin: Julius Zwissler, Otto Janke, 1906), p. 41.

13. One index of its popularity is that it ran in installments in the fall of 1878, that is, immediately upon publication, in the *New Yorker Musikzeitung*, edited by Leopold Damrosch, even though the paper was otherwise entirely devoted to musical matters, with which *Wunnigel* has nothing to do. Raabe noted the fact in his diary on Oct. 22, 1878. See my note in *Mitt.* 71 (1984): 12.

14. Horst S. Daemmrich, *Wilhelm Raabe* (Boston: Twayne, 1981), pp. 136-37.

15. Wilhelm Fehse, *Wilhelm Raabe: Sein Leben und seine Werke* (Braunschweig: Vieweg, 1937), pp. 429-30.

16. Gerhard Kaiser, *Gottfried Keller: Das gedichtete Leben* (Frankfurt am Main: Insel, 1981), p. 214.

17. William T. Webster, *Wirklichkeit und Illusion in den Romanen Wilhelm Raabes* (Braunschweig: pp-Verlag, 1982), p. 71.

18. For example, Heinrich Spiero, *Raabe: Leben—Werk—Wirkung*, 2nd ed.

(Wittenberg: Ziemsen, [1925]), pp. 196-97: "The search for symbols and the belief that something must always be hidden behind things belabor this droll prose in vain."

19. See, for example, Otto Berth, "Vom alten Proteus," *Mitt.* 16 (1926): 1-11; Fehse, *Wilhelm Raabe*, pp. 415-16; Beaucamp, *Literatur als Selbstdarstellung*, pp. 44-51; Karl Hoppe, "Wilhelm Raabe einst und heute," *RJ* 1961, p. 15. A thoughtful and valuable effort at interpretation will be found in Katherine Starr Kaiser, "Structure and Narrative Technique in Wilhelm Raabe's *Krähenfelder Geschichten*" (Diss. Brown University, 1974), pp. 162-212.

20. *The Complete Poems of Heinrich Heine: A Modern English Version by Hal Draper* (Boston: Suhrkamp/Insel, 1982), p. 65.

21. Kaiser, "Structure and Narrative Technique," p. 176.

22. Wilhelm and Marie Jensen to Raabe, Dec. 21, 1877, E 3: 288. Wilhelm Jensen, perhaps predictably, did not care for the novella and preferred *Wunnigel* (ibid.).

23. Kaiser, "Structure and Narrative Technique," pp. 185-86.

24. Friedrich Schiller, *Sämtliche Werke*, ed. Gerhard Fricke et al. (Munich: Hanser, 1958-62), 5: 741.

25. Kaiser, "Structure and Narrative Technique," p. 178. When she argues, however, that the passage on self-delusion is part of a satire on philistines and "geniusses" (p. 190), I do not agree with her; I read it as implicating the narrator himself.

26. To Edmund Sträter, Feb. 18, 1892, E 2: 323.

27. To G. Grote, Verlag, Feb. 15, 1877, *"In alls gedultig": Briefe Wilhelm Raabes (1842-1910)*, ed. Wilhelm Fehse (Berlin: Grote, 1940), p. 154.

CHAPTER 18: THE MILL ON THE SEWER: *Pfister's Mill* AND THE PRESENT RELEVANCE OF PAST LITERATURE

1. Jeffrey L. Sammons, *Literary Sociology and Practical Criticism: An Inquiry* (Bloomington: Indiana University Press, 1977), p. xi.

2. Barker Fairley, with his reliable sense of quality, is an exception; he devoted a chapter (pp. 37-53) to *Pfister's Mill* in *Wilhelm Raabe: An Introduction to his Novels* (Oxford: Clarendon Press, 1961). He also published an annotated edition of the text (London: Duckworth, 1956), which I have not seen.

3. See Jeffrey L. Sammons, *Six Essays on the Young German Novel* (Chapel Hill: University of North Carolina Press, 1972), pp. 132, 138-39.

4. Horst Denkler, "Wilhelm Raabe: Pfisters Mühle (1884). Zur Aktualität eines alten Themas und vom Nutzen offener Strukturen," *Romane und Erzählungen des Bürgerlichen Realismus*, ed. Denkler (Stuttgart: Reclam, 1980), esp. pp. 302-3. The article is identical to the afterword of Denkler's edition of *Pfisters Mühle* (Stuttgart: Reclam, 1980), pp. 225-51.

5. The case history is set out by Ludwig Popp, " 'Pfisters Mühle': Schlüsselroman zu einem Abwasserprozess," *Städtehygiene* 10 (1959): 21-25. Special printing for the Raabe Society, 1979.

6. See Denkler, "Wilhelm Raabe: Pfisters Mühle," p. 297.

7. Popp, " 'Pfisters Mühle,' " p. 23.

8. Popp, " 'Pfisters Mühle,' " p. 25; see also Denkler, "Wilhelm Raabe: Pfisters Mühle," p. 297.

9. Popp, " 'Pfisters Mühle,' " p. 24.

10. Siegfried Hajek, "Die Freiheit des Gebundenen. Bemerkungen zu Raabes 'Altershausen,' " *RJ* 1974, p. 28. I am far from certain, incidentally, that this passage accurately infers the tendency of the *Altershausen* fragment, but that is another matter that cannot be pursued in this place.

11. Horst S. Daemmrich, *Wilhelm Raabe* (Boston: Twayne, 1981), p. 116; the comment refers to *Master Author*.

12. Joachim Worthmann, "Die 'erinnerte' Zeit—Wilhelm Raabes 'Pfisters Mühle,' " in Worthmann, *Probleme des Zeitromans: Studien zur Geschichte des deutschen Romans im 19. Jahrhundert* (Heidelberg: Carl Winter, 1974), p. 132.

13. For example, Denkler, "Wilhelm Raabe: Pfisters Mühle," p. 303, dismisses her in phrases that I find barely comprehensible. Keith Bullivant, "Wilhelm Raabe and the European Novel," *Orbis Litterarum* 31 (1976): 274, working from theoretical premises not unlike Denkler's, observes by contrast that Emmy's "presence and all that she represents for Ebert bring to the narration another perspective, emphasizing all the time how times have changed, so that the book is continually shot through with a mood of optimism and happiness that eventually outweighs the sense of regret at the passing of the world embodied in Pfisters Mühle."

14. Fairley, *Wilhelm Raabe*, p. 46.

15. Worthmann, "Die 'erinnerte' Zeit," p. 139.

16. Fairley, *Wilhelm Raabe*, p. 43.

17. Denkler, "Wilhelm Raabe: Pfisters Mühle," pp. 298-99. Cf. Bullivant, "Wilhelm Raabe and the European Novel," p. 274: "The very structure of his novel, the oscillation between the past and the narrative present, brings out Raabe's profound sense of living between two opposed worlds."

18. Denkler, "Wilhelm Raabe: Pfisters Mühle," p. 303.

19. Denkler here seems to have fallen a little into the widespread contemporary habit of calling everything one dislikes about the modern world "capitalist" or "bourgeois." Surely he is aware that the so-called socialist countries are developing ecological problems quite as bad as those in the "capitalist" West and are doing much less about them. He might consider Budapest, where I experienced a fragrance of coal smoke and a patina of soot on every surface that vividly recalled my boyhood in Cleveland. That, at least, is now gone from American cities. There is every reason to believe that democratic society has a better chance of solving ecological problems, or at least of keeping them on the public agenda.

CHAPTER 19: *Stuffcake* PRO AND CONTRA

1. Romano Guardini, "Über Wilhelm Raabes 'Stopfkuchen,' " reprinted in *Raabe in neuer Sicht*, ed. Hermann Helmers (Stuttgart: Kohlhammer, 1968), pp. 12-43.

2. Hans Ahrbeck, *Wilhelm Raabes Stopfkuchen: Studien zu Gehalt und Form von Raabes Erzählungen* (Borna-Leipzig: Noske, [1926]), a Göttingen dissertation. Ahrbeck is doubtless to be seen as still in the original community of disciples, as he was the son-in-law of Raabe's confidant Edmund Sträter, but his dissertation was, for its time, not without insight.

3. Adolf Schweckendiek, "Wilhelm Raabes 'Stopfkuchen': Eine ketzerische Betrachtung," *RJ* 1974, pp. 75-97.

4. Paul Derks, *Raabe-Studien. Beiträge zur Anwendung psychoanalytischer Interpretationsmodelle: Stopfkuchen und Das Odfeld* (Bonn: Bouvier, 1976), pp. 9-23. Even Ahrbeck, after talking around this matter for some pages, remained baffled by it (*Wilhelm Raabes Stopfkuchen*, pp. 18-24). Several critics, including some excellent contemporary ones, evade all or part of the difficulty.

5. Claude David, "Über Wilhelm Raabes *Stopfkuchen*," *Lebendige Form: Interpretationen zur deutschen Literatur. Festschrift für Heinrich E. K. Henel*, ed. Jeffrey L. Sammons and Ernst Schürer (Munich: Fink, 1970), pp. 259-75. Perhaps there is something particularly French in David's outlook, for a similar set of doubts was expressed around the same time by Pierre Bange, "Stopfkuchen de W. Raabe. Le solipsisme de l'original et l'humour," *Etudes Germaniques* 24 (1969): 4: "Au fond, l'humour ne peut sans doute jouer son rôle que dans une certaine mauvaise conscience ou avec une inappréciable part de naïveté et d'auto-illusion." As Roy Pascal's considerable appreciation of Raabe seems to be qualified by his experience of English realism, so Bange observes a lack of materialistic determinism, the "milieu balzacien" (ibid.).

6. Prominent among those who have thought Eduard insignificant are Roy Pascal, "The Reminiscence-Technique in Raabe," *Modern Language Review* 49 (1954): 343, and David, "Über Wilhelm Raabes *Stopfkuchen*," p. 263. Those who have acknowledged his importance include Christa Hebbel, "Die Funktion der Erzähler- und Figurenperspektiven in Wilhelm Raabes Ich-Erzählungen" (Diss. University of Heidelberg, 1960), pp. 86, 190-93; Peter Detroy, *Wilhelm Raabe: Der Humor als Gestaltungsprinzip im "Stopfkuchen"* (Bonn: Bouvier, 1970), p. 54 and passim; and especially Hubert Ohl, "Eduards Heimkehr oder Le Vaillant und das Riesenfaultier. Zu Wilhelm Raabes 'Stopfkuchen,' " *Raabe in neuer Sicht*, ed. Helmers, pp. 247-78. As will be seen, I am in substantial agreement with Ohl.

7. See Hubert Ohl, *Bild und Wirklichkeit: Studien zur Romankunst Raabes und Fontanes* (Heidelberg: Stiehm, 1968), p. 104, and Detroy, *Wilhelm Raabe*, p. 24.

8. Cf. William T. Webster, "Idealisierung oder Ironie? Verstehen und Mißverstehen in Wilhelm Raabes 'Stopfkuchen,' " *RJ* 1978, p. 156.

9. Ohl, "Eduards Heimkehr," p. 270.

10. Cf. Paul Derks, "Eduard als Kunstfigur. Zu Wilhelm Raabes *Stopfkuchen*," *RJ* 1976, p. 62, and Hermann Helmers, *Die bildenden Mächte in den Romanen Wilhelm Raabes* (Weinheim: Beltz, 1960), p. 93.

11. Cf. Ohl, "Eduards Heimkehr," p. 269.

12. To the Jensens, Dec. 30, 1890, E 3: 454.

13. Schweckendiek, "Wilhelm Raabes 'Stopfkuchen,' " pp. 78-81.

14. Even Karl Hoppe, *Wilhelm Raabe: Beiträge zum Verständnis seiner Person und seines Werkes* (Göttingen: Vandenhoeck & Ruprecht, 1967), p. 219, found that "in the figure of Stuffcake this imperturbability has been escalated to a weird degree." I should think so. Cf. Schweckendiek, "Wilhelm Raabes 'Stopfkuchen,' " p. 91: "I cannot befriend myself with the expression 'comfortable contempt of the world,' with which Schaumann 'looks down' on the people in the town." This discomfort can be relieved if we emancipate ourselves from the need to see Schaumann and his resolutions as exemplary. Detroy, *Wilhelm Raabe*, p. 40, is closer to the point when he characterizes the idyll as "a deceptive calm."

15. Ohl speaks of Schaumann "in his exceptional state of tension" ("Eduards Heimkehr," p. 256).

16. Detroy, *Wilhelm Raabe*, pp. 67-70. It is from this perspective that we can confront Claude David, who accepts the unambiguous exemplary reading and puts a negative judgment upon it.

17. Ohl, "Eduards Heimkehr," p. 249.

18. Ohl, "Eduards Heimkehr," pp. 252-53.

19. See Helmers, *Die bildenden Mächte*, pp. 72-73.

20. Christine Wrangel, "Verknüpfungsformen in Wilhelm Raabes späten Romanen *Pfisters Mühle, Stopfkuchen* und *Altershausen*" (Diss. New York University, 1970), pp. 154-56.

21. Hebbel, "Die Funktion der Erzähler- und Figurenperspektiven," p. 193.

22. Helmers, *Die bildenden Mächte*, p. 85.

23. Detroy, *Wilhelm Raabe*, p. 74. The remainder of Detroy's interesting discussion of the sloth image differs considerably from my own view.

24. It has, of course, not escaped the commentators that this phrase becomes the leitmotif of "Aunt Knowthemall" in *Cloister Lugau*, who sees through everybody. But this echo simply points up how idiosyncratic *Stuffcake* is among Raabe's works. *Cloister Lugau* is, if anything, one of the more softly tempered of his mature novels. Aunt Knowthemall is one of his typical elderly heroines, who helps lead a victory of several decent human beings over an unappetizing villain; though she has moments of total exasperation, the war of one against all characteristic of Schaumann is not evident in her.

25. Cf. Ohl, "Eduards Heimkehr," p. 258: "Schaumann's whole narration is aimed at Eduard."

26. Detroy, *Wilhelm Raabe*, pp. 49-54, 123.

27. Detroy, *Wilhelm Raabe*, pp. 40-41, sees it as a pessimistic commentary on the inability of society to learn compassion, but does not deal with Schaumann's responsibility.

28. To Edmund Sträter, Jan. 3, 1891, E 2: 290.

29. Schweckendiek, "Wilhelm Raabes 'Stopfkuchen,' " p. 94. Schweckendiek is alluding to Peter Handke's then-contemporary, obstreperous assault on the theater audience, *Publikumsbeschimpfung*.

30. Gerhart Mayer, *Die geistige Entwicklung Wilhelm Raabes: Dargestellt unter*

besonderer Berücksichtigung seines Verhältnisses zur Philosophie (Göttingen: Vanden-hoeck & Ruprecht, 1960), p. 84.

31. Eduard Beaucamp, *Literatur als Selbstdarstellung: Wilhelm Raabe und die Möglichkeiten eines deutschen Realismus* (Bonn: Bouvier, 1968), p. 27.

32. Hebbel, "Die Funktion der Erzähler- und Figurenperspektiven," p. 115, counted the repetitions.

33. Herman Meyer, "Raum und Zeit und Wilhelm Raabes Erzählkunst," *Raabe in neuer Sicht*, ed. Helmers, p. 109.

34. To Sträter, June 13, 1891, E 2: 301.

35. Webster, "Idealisierung oder Ironie?" pp. 157-66.

36. Roy Pascal, *The German Novel: Studies* (Toronto: University of Toronto Press, 1968), p. 160.

CHAPTER 20: THE SPLIT SELF:
The Documents of the Birdsong

1. To Edmund Sträter, Nov. 8, 1894, E 2: 360.

2. To Paul Gerber, Sept. 16,. 1895; to Sträter, same date, E 2: 370, 371.

3. To Sträter, Jan. 13, 1896, E 2: 374.

4. Wilhelm Fehse, *Wilhelm Raabe: Sein Leben und seine Werke* (Braunschweig: Vieweg, 1937), pp. 567-68.

5. The concept appeared earlier in *Villa Schönow* as *Verkletterung*. See Hans Jürgen Meinerts, *"Die Akten des Vogelsangs": Raabestudien auf Grund einer Sprach-untersuchung* (Berlin: Junker und Dünnhaupt, 1940), pp. 91-92.

6. Meinerts, *"Die Akten des Vogelsangs,"* pp. 172-73. See also the commentary in 19: 450.

7. Rolf-Dieter Koll, *Raumgestaltung bei Wilhelm Raabe* (Bonn: Bouvier, 1977), p. 76.

8. Wilhelm Emrich, "Persönlichkeit und Zivilisation in Wilhelm Raabes 'Die Akten des Vogelsangs,' " *RJ* 1982, p. 12.

9. The first critic, I believe, to have called attention to the importance of this apparently passing remark is Regina Schmid-Stotz, *Von Finkenrode nach Altershausen: Das Motiv der Heimkehr im Werk Wilhelm Raabes als Ausdruck einer sich wandelnden Lebenseinstellung, dargestellt an fünf Romanen aus fünf Lebensab-schnitten* (Bern, Frankfurt am Main, and New York: Peter Lang, 1984), p. 130.

10. To Hans von Wolzogen, Aug. 5, 1901, E 2: 429.

11. Meinerts, *"Die Akten des Vogelsangs,"* p. 86.

12. Eduard Beaucamp, *Literatur als Selbstdarstellung: Wilhelm Raabe und die Möglichkeiten eines deutschen Realismus* (Bonn: Bouvier, 1968), pp. 114-15.

13. This turn of affairs has caused some critics to associate Leonie with Phöbe in *Restless Guests*, e.g., Siegfried Hajek, "Wilhelm Raabe im Deutschun-terricht. 'Die Akten des Vogelsangs,' " *Diskussion Deutsch* 12 (1981): 14, n. 10, and Karl Hotz, *Bedeutung und Funktion des Raumes im Werk Wilhelm Raabes* (Göppingen: Kümmerle, 1970), p. 158. In my view, this similarity should not

be insisted upon; if the timid, unassertive Leonie resembles Phöbe, it is in quite diminished form. I regard Phöbe as a unique character in Raabe's works.

14. Emrich, "Persönlichkeit und Zivilisation," pp. 21-22.

15. One of the editors of the text in the critical edition—it is not clear which—takes "German" as "bodily (related)," as in "cousin-german," and "Fell" in the sense of "gloom, irritation" (19: 479). I think there has been some misunderstanding of the dictionary here; "german" does not mean "bodily" in the literal sense, but, from Latin *germanus*, having the same parents, and for a substantive "fell" the *OED* gives only an obsolete rare usage, "gall, bitterness."

16. William T. Webster, *Wirklichkeit und Illusion in den Romanen Wilhelm Raabes* (Braunschweig: pp-Verlag, 1982), p. 189.

17. Nancy A. Kaiser, "Reading Raabe's Realism: *Die Akten des Vogelsangs*," *Germanic Review* 59 (1984): 7.

18. Wilhelm Fehse, "Die literarischen Symbole in den 'Akten des Vogelsangs.' Ein Nachruf auf Dr. Margarete Bönneken," *Mitt.* 11 (1921): 53.

19. Hermann Pongs, "Frauenehre bei Raabe," *Mitt.* 34, No. 2 (1944): 14-15.

20. Webster, *Wirklichkeit und Illusion*, pp. 180-82.

21. Meinerts, *"Die Akten des Vogelsangs,"* p. 74.

22. Emrich, "Persönlichkeit und Zivilisation," pp. 17-18.

23. Meinerts, *"Die Akten des Vogelsangs,"* pp. 11, 15-17. Meinerts also made the valuable suggestion that Krumhardt is a latent possibility of Velten's being, as Velten is of Krumhardt's, and that there is a "far-reaching identity" between them (pp. 8-9).

24. Walther L. Hahn, "Zum Erzählvorgang in Raabes 'Akten des Vogelsangs,' " *RJ* 1972, p. 64.

25. Wolfgang Preisendanz, "Die Erzählstruktur als Bedeutungskomplex der 'Akten des Vogelsangs,' " *RJ* 1981, pp. 214, 220, 223. Given Raabe's deep thought about the "life-lie," it is a pity he was not more sympathetic to Ibsen, who so acutely codified the concept in *The Wild Duck*.

26. Christa Hebbel, "Die Funktion der Erzähler- und Figurenperspektiven in Wilhelm Raabes Ich-Erzählungen" (Diss. University of Heidelberg, 1960), p. 221.

27. Frank Zwilgmeyer, "Archetypische Bewusstseinsstufen in Raabes Werken, insbesondere in den 'Akten des Vogelsangs,' " *RJ* 1984, pp. 99-120, esp. p. 120.

28. Louis Kientz, *Wilhelm Raabe: L'homme, la pensée et l'oeuvre* (Paris: Didier, 1939), pp. 271, 298.

29. E.g., Roy Pascal, "The Reminiscence-Technique in Raabe," *Modern Language Review* 49 (1954): 345; Wolfgang Jehmüller, *Die Gestalt des Biographen bei Wilhelm Raabe* (Munich: Fink, 1975), pp. 143-46.

30. Preisendanz, "Die Erzählstruktur als Bedeutungskomplex," p. 220.

Chapter 21: The Unclosed Circle:
The Fragment *Altershausen*

1. To Jensen, Feb. 13, 1899, E 3: 521.

2. To Müller-Brauel, Aug. 9, 1906, E 2: 468.

3. To G. Grote, July 13, 1910, *"In alls gedultig": Briefe Wilhelm Raabes (1842-1910)*, ed. Wilhelm Fehse (Berlin: Grote, 1940), p. 415.

4. Robert Scholes, *Semiotics and Interpretation* (New Haven and London: Yale University Press, 1982), p. 60.

5. Jean Paul, *Werke*, ed. Norbert Miller (Munich: Hanser, 1959-66), 1: 13. Philip James Brewster, "Wilhelm Raabes historische Fiktion im Kontext: Beitrag zur Rekonstruktion der Gattungsproblematik zwischen Geschichtsschreibung und Poesie im 19. Jahrhundert" (Diss. Cornell University, 1983), pp. 188-92, calls particular attention to the importance of this passage.

6. Jeffrey L. Sammons, "Tieck's *Franz Sternbald*: The Loss of Thematic Control," *Studies in Romanticism* 5 (1965-66): 30-43.

7. See my argument in the chapter entitled "The Elusive Novel: *Der Rabbi von Bacherach, Schnabelewopski,* and *Florentinische Nächte*" in *Heinrich Heine, the Elusive Poet* (New Haven and London: Yale University Press, 1969), pp. 301-34.

8. To the Jensens, Dec. 30, 1890; to Siegmund Schott, Feb. 21, 1891, E 3: 454; E 2: 292.

9. To the Jensens, Dec. 30, 1903, E 3: 550.

10. To Hans von Wolzogen, May 2, 1909, *"In alls gedultig,"* ed. Fehse, p. 398.

11. Frank C. Maatje, "Ein früher Ansatz zur 'Stream of Consciousness'-Dichtung: Wilhelm Raabes 'Altershausen,' " *Neophilologus* 45 (1961): 305-22.

12. On this, see James Robert Reece, "Narrator and Narrative Levels in Wilhelm Raabe's Stuttgart Novels" (Diss. University of Oregon, 1975), esp. pp. 64-67.

13. Wilhelm Fehse, *Raabe und Jensen: Denkmal einer Lebensfreundschaft* (Berlin: Grote, 1940), p. 180.

14. Horst S. Daemmrich, *Wilhelm Raabe* (Boston: Twayne, 1981), p. 151.

15. Fritz Martini, "Wilhelm Raabes 'Altershausen,' " *RJ* 1964, pp. 82, 104, 88.

16. Hans Jürgen Meinerts, *"Die Akten des Vogelsangs": Raabestudien auf Grund einer Sprachuntersuchung* (Berlin: Junker und Dünnhaupt, 1940), pp. 167-68.

17. Nicolaas Cornelis Adrianus Perquin, S.J., *Wilhelm Raabes Motive als Ausdruck seiner Weltanschauung* (Amsterdam: H. J. Paris, 1927), p. 236.

18. Georg Lukács, "Wilhelm Raabe," *Deutsche Realisten des 19. Jahrhunderts* (Berlin: Aufbau-Verlag, 1952), p. 249.

19. Eckart Oehlenschläger, "Erzählverfahren und Zeiterfahrung. Überlegungen zu Wilhelm Raabes *Altershausen*," *Wilhelm Raabe: Studien zu seinem Leben und Werk*, ed. Leo A. Lensing and Hans-Werner Peter (Braunschweig: pp-Verlag, 1981), pp. 381-405.

20. Wilhelm Fehse, *Wilhelm Raabe: Sein Leben und seine Werke* (Braunschweig: Vieweg, 1937), pp. 594-95.

21. Wolfgang Schlegel, "Wilhelm Raabes Weserheimat in seinen Werken— eine Geschichtslandschaft," *RJ* 1981, p. 98. "Altershausen" and the Low German "-oldendorf," doubtless originally "-oldendorp," are etymologically similar.

22. I find it quite difficult to capture the tone of this phrase in English: "gegen ein- und andringendes Semiten-, Welschen- und Slawentum."

23. Horst Denkler, "Wohltäter Maienborn: Ängste und ihre Bewältigung im Werk Wilhelm Raabes," *RJ* 1984, pp. 7-25. This article suffers a little throughout, I think, from a failure to distinguish fictive, narrative, and authorial voices precisely enough from one another.

24. Siegfried Hajek, *Der Mensch und die Welt im Werk Wilhelm Raabes* (Warendorf: Schnell, 1950), pp. 91-93.

25. Gerhart Mayer, "Raabes Romanfragment 'Altershausen': Grundzüge einer Interpretation I. Teil," *RJ* 1962, pp. 160-62.

26. Regina Schmid-Stotz, *Von Finkenrode nach Altershausen: Das Motiv der Heimkehr im Werk Wilhelm Raabes als Ausdruck einer sich wandelnden Lebenseinstellung, dargestellt an fünf Romanen aus fünf Lebensabschnitten* (Bern, Frankfurt am Main, and New York: Peter Lang, 1984), pp. 112-13.

27. Dieter Kafitz, *Figurenkonstellation als Mittel der Wirklichkeitserfassung. Dargestellt an Romanen der zweiten Hälfte des 19. Jahrhunderts (Freytag, Spielhagen, Fontane, Raabe)* (Kronberg: Athenäum, 1978), p. 225.

28. Roy Pascal, "Warum ist 'Altershausen' Fragment geblieben?" *RJ* 1962, pp. 150-51. I owe a number of insights to this excellent essay.

29. Martini, "Wilhelm Raabes 'Altershausen,' " pp. 100, 102-3.

30. W. T. Webster, "Hesitation and Decision: Wilhelm Raabe's Road to Reality," *Forum for Modern Language Studies* 15 (1979): 80.

31. Gerald Opie, "Childhood and the Childlike in the Fiction of Wilhelm Raabe" (Diss. University of Exeter, 1971), p. 222.

32. Maria Vogel, "Darstellung der von Wilhelm Raabe geschilderten seelischen Abnormitäten und Versuch einer psychiatrischen Deutung" (M.D. Diss. University of Frankfurt am Main, 1949), p. 13.

33. Mayer, "Raabes Romanfragment 'Altershausen,' . . . I. Teil," p. 159. If, however, we compare the case of Eduard in *Stuffcake*, this argument is not wholly compelling.

34. Mayer, "Raabes Romanfragment 'Altershausen': Grundzüge einer Interpretation II. Teil," *RJ* 1963, p. 66; Hans Schomerus, "Zeugnis des Selbstbewußtseins: Raabe und Montherlant," *RJ* 1965, p. 56.

35. Karl Hotz, *Bedeutung und Funktion des Raumes im Werk Wilhelm Raabes* (Göppingen: Kümmerle, 1970), p. 183.

36. See Maatje, "Ein früher Ansatz," pp. 317-19; Mayer, "Raabes Romanfragment 'Altershausen' . . . II. Teil," pp. 73-74.

37. Brewster, "Wilhelm Raabes historische Fiktion," pp. 228-29.

38. Dorothea Bänsch, "Die Bibliothek Wilhelm Raabes nach Sachgebieten

geordnet," *RJ* 1970, pp. 91-92. These in any case look like late acquisitions. Two of them are undated Reclam editions and the third, which may not have belonged to Raabe, is an edition of *Die Elixiere des Teufels (The Elixirs of the Devil)* published in 1908.

39. Fehse, *Wilhelm Raabe*, p. 105. The identification is taken over without acknowledgment by the editor Hans Oppermann in the critical edition, 2: 568.

40. On the illusory nature of the return to the land of youth in *Old Nests*, see Hotz, *Bedeutung und Funktion des Raumes*, p. 117.

41. Webster, "Hesitation and Decision," p. 80.

In Lieu of a Conclusion

1. Carlos Fuentes, "The Novel Always Says: The World Is Unfinished," *New York Times Book Review*, Mar. 31, 1985, p. 25.

2. *Das Magazin für die Literatur des In- und Auslandes* 50: (June 11, 1881): 350, quoted in Wilhelm Raabe, *Werke in Auswahl: Studienausgabe*, ed. Hans-Werner Peter, Vol. 3, *Das Horn von Wanza*, ed. Joachim Müller and Hans-Werner Peter (Braunschweig: pp-Verlag, 1981), p. 216.

3. Christa Hebbel, "Die Funktion der Erzähler- und Figurenperspektiven in Wilhelm Raabes Ich-Erzählungen" (Diss. University of Heidelberg, 1960), pp. 159-63.

4. Hermann Helmers, "Über Wilhelm Raabes Sprache," *RJ* 1962, pp. 9-21; "Die Verfremdung als epische Grundtendenz im Werk Raabes," *RJ* 1963, pp. 7-30.

5. Julian Schmidt, "Aus: Geschichte der Deutschen Litertur im neunzehnten Jahrhundert," *Romantheorie: Dokumentation ihrer Geschichte in Deutschland 1620-1880*, ed. Eberhard Lämmert et al. (Cologne and Berlin: Kiepenheuer & Witsch, 1971), p. 327.

6. H. Steinecke, "Gustav Freytags *Soll und Haben*—ein 'realistischer' Roman?" *Formen realistischer Erzählkunst: Festschrift for Charlotte Jolles in Honour of her 70th Birthday*, ed. Jörg Thunecke with Eda Sagarra (Nottingham: Sherwood Press, 1979), pp. 110, 112. Steinecke makes essentially the same point in "Gustav Freytag: *Soll und Haben* (1855): Weltbild und Wirkung eines deutschen Bestsellers," *Romane und Erzählungen des Bürgerlichen Realismus: Neue Interpretationen*, ed. Horst Denkler (Stuttgart: Reclam, 1980), pp. 143-44.

7. Friedrich Sengle, "*Der Hungerpastor* (1863/64): Zum Problem der frühen Biedermeiertradition," *Wilhelm Raabe: Studien zu seinem Leben und Werk*, ed. Leo A. Lensing and Hans-Werner Peter (Braunschweig: pp-Verlag, 1981), p. 82.

8. To Adolf Glaser, Feb. [16], 1866, E 2: 112.

9. Eduard Beaucamp, *Literatur als Selbstdarstellung: Wilhelm Raabe und die Möglichkeiten eines deutschen Realismus* (Bonn: Bouvier, 1968), p. 176.

BIBLIOGRAPHY

THIS IS a selected bibliography; essentially it is a record of my own research experience, restricted to materials directly pertinent to Raabe. No evaluation or recommendation is implied by the inclusion of any item. Nor is any discrimination implied against the many editions of individual texts currently in print by the listing below of several that have been of particular use to me. Volumes of collected essays are listed once, by editor. The following abbreviations are used throughout: *Mitt.: Mitteilungen für die Gesellschaft der Freunde Wilhelm Raabes* (1911-43); *Der Raabefreund* (1944); *Mitteilungen der Raabe-Gesellschaft* (1948-). The essential items from the first nine years of the *Mitteilungen* are reprinted in Bauer, ed., *Raabestudien* (see below), and therefore are not listed separately in this bibliography. *RJ: Jahrbuch der Raabe-Gesellschaft* (1960-).

PRIMARY LITERATURE

EDITIONS

Sämtliche Werke. Berlin-Grunewald: Klemm, [1913/16]. 18 vols. in 3 series.
Sämtliche Werke. Berlin-Grunewald: Klemm, [1934]. 15 vols. in 3 series.
Sämtliche Werke, ed. Karl Hoppe et al. Göttingen: Vandenhoeck & Ruprecht, 1960-. 20 vols. in 21 plus 4 supplementary vols. A fifth supplementary vol. is planned.
Werke in vier Bänden, ed. Karl Hoppe. Munich: Winkler, 1961/63. 4 thin-paper vols.
Werke in Auswahl: Studienausgabe, ed. Hans-Werner Peter et al. Braunschweig: pp-Verlag, 1981. 9 vols. in paperback.
Die Akten des Vogelsangs, ed. Karl Hoppe and Hans-Werner Peter. Munich: Deutscher Taschenbuch Verlag, 1981.
Der Dräumling: Mit Dokumenten zur Schillerfeier 1859, ed. Anneliese Klingenberg. Berlin and Weimar: Aufbau-Verlag, 1984.
Höxter und Corvey, ed. Hans-Jürgen Schrader. Universal-Bibliothek, No. 7729[3]. Stuttgart: Reclam, 1981.
Pfisters Mühle: Ein Sommerferienheft, ed. Horst Denkler. Universal-Bibliothek, No. 9988[3]. Stuttgart: Reclam, 1980.

IN ENGLISH

Novels, tr. John E. Woods and Barker Fairley, ed. Volkmar Sander; foreword by Joel Agee. The German Library, 45. New York: Continuum, 1983. *Horacker* and *Tubby Schaumann* (i.e., *Stopfkuchen*).

Else von der Tanne [*Elsa of the Forest*], tr. and ed. James C. O'Flaherty and Janet K. King. University, Alabama: University of Alabama Press, 1972. German and English in parallel text.

LETTERS

"In alls gedultig": Briefe Wilhelm Raabes (1842-1910). Im Auftrage der Familie Raabe herausgegeben von Wilhelm Fehse. Berlin: Grote, 1940.

DRAWINGS

Hoppe, Karl. *Wilhelm Raabe als Zeichner.* Göttingen: Vandenhoeck & Ruprecht. 1960.

Peter, Hans-Werner. *Wilhelm Raabe: Der Dichter in seinen Federzeichnungen und Skizzen.* Rosenheim: Rosenheimer Verlagshaus, 1983.

ARCHIVAL LOCATIONS

Raabe-Verzeichnis: Bestände in Braunschweig, Marbach/Neckar und Wolfenbüttel, ed. Manfred R. W. Garzmann and Wolf-Dieter Schuegraf, with an essay by Horst Denkler. Braunschweig: Stadtarchiv und Städtische Bibliothek, 1985.

SECONDARY LITERATURE

Abert, Paul. "Vom Schauplatz der 'Frau Salome.' " *Mitt.* 15 (1925): 21-26.

Ahrbeck, Hans. *Wilhelm Raabes Stopfkuchen: Studien zu Gehalt und Form von Raabes Erzählungen.* Borna-Leipzig: Noske, [1926].

Albaugh, Kathryn Louise. "The Influence of William Makepeace Thackeray on Wilhelm Raabe." Diss. Stanford University, 1941.

Angel, Pierre. *Le personnage juif dans le roman allemand (1855-1915): La racine littéraire de l'antisémitisme Outre-Rhin.* Montreal, Paris, and Brussels: Didier, 1973.

Anon., "Wilhelm Raabe." *The Bookman* 14 (1901-2): 220-22.

Anz, Heinrich. " 'Leichenbegängnisse.' Zum Verfahren der geschichtlichen Erzählung in Raabes 'Gedelöcke.' " *RJ* 1982, pp. 110-24.

Arendt, Dieter. "Auf der Bühne des Welttheaters." *RJ* 1983, pp. 7-32.

———. "Die Heine-Rezeption im Werk Wilhelm Raabes." *Heine-Jahrbuch 1980*, pp. 188-221.

———. "Lehrer-Figurationen im Werk Wilhelm Raabes oder Die unglückliche Liebe des Sekundaners zur Bildung." *Diskussion Deutsch,* 12 (1981): 35-56.

———. "Lessing-Rezeption bei Wilhelm Raabe. Ein Beitrag zur Geschichte des Bildungsbürgertums." *RJ* 1984, pp. 121-56.

———. " 'Nun auf die Juden!' Figurationen des Judentums im Werk Wilhelm Raabes." *Tribüne* 19, No. 74 (1980): 108-40.

————. "Wilhelm Raabe und der 'romantische Schlachtruf: Krieg den Philistern!' " *RJ* 1981, pp. 55-83.

————. "Wilhelm Raabes Dramaturgie der Erzählkunst." *RJ* 1980, pp. 7-42.

Bachmann, Doris. "Die 'Dritte Welt' der Literatur. Eine ethnologische Methodenkritik literaturwissenschaftlichen Interpretierens, am Beispiel von Raabes Roman 'Abu Telfan oder Die Heimkehr vom Mondgebirge.' " *RJ* 1979, pp. 27-71.

Bachmann, Wilhelm. "Der Lar und Drei Federn." *Mitt.* 11 (1921): 20-28.

Bänsch, Dorothea. "Die Bibliothek Wilhelm Raabes nach Sachgebieten geordnet." *RJ* 1970, pp. 87-165.

————. "Zur Sprache und Sprachentwicklung bei Wilhelm Raabe." *RJ* 1960, pp. 140-88.

Bärend, Irmhild. "Das Bibelzitat als Strukturelement im Werk Wilhelm Raabes." *RJ* 1969, pp. 33-52.

Bamler, Friedrich. "St. Thomas." *Mitt.* 29 (1939): 107-12.

Bange, Pierre. "*Stopfkuchen* de W. Raabe. Le solipsisme de l'original et l'humour." *Etudes Germaniques* 24 (1969): 1-15.

Bark, Joachim. "Raabes 'Drei Federn' (1865): Versuche fiktiver Biographik. Zugleich ein Beitrag zum deutschen Erziehungsroman." *RJ* 1981, pp. 128-48.

Bass, Josef. "Griechisches bei Raabe." *Mitt.* 20 (1930): 36-42.

————. "Die Juden bei Wilhelm Raabe." *Monatsschrift für Geschichte und Wissenschaft der Juden* 54 (1910): 641-88.

————. "Welsche und deutsche Liebe bei Raabe." *Mitt.* 19 (1929): 19-36.

Bauer, Constantin. "Die Anfänge der Raabe-Gesellschaft." *Mitt.* 38, No. 2 (1951): 2-8.

————. "Raabe im Ausland." *Mitt.* 43 (1956): 1-10.

————, ed. *Raabestudien: Im Auftrag der "Gesellschaft der Freunde Wilhelm Raabes."* Wolfenbüttel: Heckner, 1925.

Bauer, Constantin, and Hans Martin Schultz, eds. *Raabe-Gedenkbuch: Im Auftrage der Gesellschaft der Freunde Wilhelm Raabes.* Berlin-Grunewald: Klemm, 1921.

Bauer, Ernst-Stephan. "Heilsames Lachen in heillosem Fremdsein. Zur Aufnahme Raabescher Motive in Hesses 'Steppenwolf.' " *RJ* 1984, pp. 198-207.

Beaucamp, Eduard. *Literatur als Selbstdarstellung: Wilhelm Raabe und die Möglichkeiten eines deutschen Realismus.* Bonn: Bouvier, 1968.

Beitter, Ursula E. "Mythologische Symbolik in Raabes 'Else von der Tanne.' " *RJ* 1980, pp. 43-51.

Berg, Leo. "Wilhelm Raabe als Erzähler (1897)"; "Hastenbeck." Pp. 269-83, 426-33 in Berg, *Neue Essays.* Oldenburg and Leipzig: Schulze, 1901.

Bernd, Clifford Albrecht. *German Poetic Realism.* Twayne's World Author Series, 605. Boston: Twayne, 1981.

Berns, Jörg Jochen. "Der Pegnitzschäfer Raabe. Kommentar zu sieben vergessenen Briefen." *RJ* 1975, pp. 16-32.

Berth, Otto. "Noch einmal Velten Andres." *Mitt.* 14 (1924): 58-64.

———. "Vom alten Proteus." *Mitt.* 16 (1926): 1-11.

Bönneken, Margarete. *Wilhelm Raabes Roman "Die Akten des Vogelsangs."* 2nd ed., Marburg: Elwert, 1926.

Bothe, Käthe. "Günther Wallinger und Friedemann Bach." *Mitt.* 10 (1920): 51-54.

Brand, Jürgen. "Strukturelle Symmetrien in Raabes 'Die Chronik der Sperlingsgasse.' " *RJ* 1983, pp. 49-58.

Brandes, Wilhelm. " 'Die Königin von Saba,' ein epischer Entwurf Wilhelm Raabes." *Mitt.* 11 (1921): 1-7.

———. "Raabe und Washington Irving." *Mitt.* 13 (1923): 75-79.

———. *Wilhelm Raabe: Sieben Kapitel zum Verständnis und zur Würdigung des Dichters.* 2nd ed., Wolfenbüttel and Berlin: Julius Zwissler, Otto Janke, 1906.

Brate, Gertrud. "Form und Inhalt in Wilhelm Raabes 'Else von der Tanne oder Das Glück Domini Friedemann Leutenbachers, armen Dieners am Wort Gottes zu Wallrode im Elend.' " *RJ* 1973, pp. 54-70.

Brewster, Philip J[ames]. "Onkel Ketschwayo in Neuteutoburg. Zeitgeschichtliche Anspielungen in Raabes 'Stopfkuchen.' " *RJ* 1983, pp. 96-118.

———. "Wilhelm Raabes historische Fiktion im Kontext: Beitrag zur Rekonstruktion der Gattungsproblematik zwischen Geschichtsschreibung und Poesie im 19. Jahrhundert." Diss. Cornell University, 1983.

Brill, E.V.K. "Raabes Englisch-Übersetzer." *Mitt.* 45 (1958): 24-29.

———. "Raabe's Reception in England." *German Life and Letters* N.S. 8 (1954/55): 304-12.

Bröhan, Margrit. *Die Darstellung der Frau bei Wilhelm Raabe und ein Vergleich mit liberalen Positionen zur Emanzipation der Frau im 19. Jahrhundert.* Frankfurt am Main and Bern: Peter D. Lang, 1981.

Brües, Otto. "Raabe und die junge Generation." *Mitt.* 21 (1931): 47-55.

Buchholz, Walter. "Ein Nachwort zu Wilhelm Raabes 'Stopfkuchen.' " *Mitt.* 38, No. 1 (1951): 6-11.

Bullivant, Keith. "Wilhelm Raabe and the European Novel." *Orbis Litterarum* 31 (1976): 263-81.

———. "Realismus und Romanästhetik: Überlegungen zu einem problematischen Aspekt der deutschen Literatur." *Orbis Litterarum* 39 (1984): 1-13.

Burchardt, Hannelore. "Wilhelm Raabes 'Eulenpfingsten.' " *RJ* 1968, pp. 106-35.

Burggraf, Gudrun. "Wie stellt sich die heutige Jugend zu W. R.?" *Mitt.* 21 (1931): 55-58.

Butler, Geoffrey Patrick Guyton. "England and America in the Writings of Wilhelm Raabe: A Critical Study of his Knowledge and Appreciation of Language, Literature and People." Diss. [University of London], 1961.

Butzmann, Hans. "Musäus' Schatzgräber und Raabes Erzählung 'Zum wilden Mann.' " *Mitt.* 36 (1949): 81-83.

————. [See also under Dittrich, Wolfgang, below.]

Clyde, Monica Weber. "Der Bildungsgedanke bei Wilhelm Raabe." Diss. University of California, Berkeley, 1968.

————, Monica D. "Stopfkuchen: Raabe's Idyllic Sloth." *Pacific Coast Philology* 9 (1974): 25-30.

Coenen, F. E. "Wilhelm Raabe's Treatment of the Emigrant." *Studies in Philology* 34 (1937): 612-26.

Daemmrich, H[orst S.]. "Situationsanpassung als Daseinsgestaltung bei Raabe und Fontane." Pp. 244-51 in *Formen realistischer Erzählkunst: Festschrift for Charlotte Jolles in Honour of her 70th Birthday*, ed. Jörg Thunecke with Eda Sagarra. Nottingham: Sherwood Press, 1979.

————. *Wilhelm Raabe*. Twayne's World Authors Series, 594. Boston: Twayne, 1981.

David, Claude. "Über Wilhelm Raabes *Stopfkuchen*." Pp. 259-75 in *Lebendige Form: Interpretationen zur deutschen Literatur. Festschrift für Heinrich E. K. Henel*, ed. Jeffrey L. Sammons and Ernst Schürer. Munich: Fink, 1970.

Delius, F. C. *Der Held und sein Wetter: Ein Kunstmittel und sein ideologischer Gebrauch im Roman des bürgerlichen Realismus*. Munich: Hanser, 1971.

Denkler, Horst. "Marie Jensen: Angaben zur Person einer schönen Unbekannten." *Mitt.* 73 (1986): 5-8.

————. "Wilhelm Raabe: Pfisters Mühle (1884). Zur Aktualität eines alten Themas und vom Nutzen offener Strukturen." Pp. 293-309 in *Romane und Erzählungen des Bürgerlichen Realismus: Neue Interpretationen*, ed. Denkler. Stuttgart: Reclam, 1980.

————. "Der untrügliche Spürsinn des Genius für seinesgleichen: Arno Schmidts Verhältnis zu Wilhelm Raabe." *RJ* 1985, pp. 138-53.

————. "Wohltäter Maienborn. Ängste und ihre Bewältigung im Werk Wilhelm Raabes." *RJ* 1984, pp. 7-25.

Derks, Paul. "Eduard als Kunstfigur. Zu Wilhelm Raabes *Stopfkuchen*." *RJ* 1976, pp. 60-68.

————. "Raabe und die Droste." *RJ* 1975, pp. 33-41.

————. *Raabe-Studien: Beiträge zur Anwendung psychoanalytischer Interpretationsmodelle. Stopfkuchen und Das Odfeld*. Bonn: Bouvier, 1976.

Detering, Heinrich. "Apokalyptische Bedeutungsstrukturen in Raabes 'Das Odfeld.' " *RJ* 1984, pp. 87-98.

Detroy, Peter. *Wilhelm Raabe: Der Humor als Gestaltungsprinzip im "Stopfkuchen."* Bonn: Bouvier, 1970.

Dierkes, Hans. "Der 'Zauber des Gegensatzes.' Schopenhauer und Wilhelm Raabes 'Stopfkuchen.' " *Schopenhauer-Jahrbuch* 54 (1973): 93-107.

Dietze, Walter. "Zeitstimmung und Zeitkritik in Wilhelm Raabes 'Chronik der Sperlingsgasse.' " *Monatshefte* 61 (1969): 337-46.

Di Maio, Irene Stocksieker. *The Multiple Perspective: Wilhelm Raabe's Third-Person Narratives of the Braunschweig Period*. Amsterdam: John Benjamins, 1981.

Dittrich, Wolfgang. "Hans Butzmann und sein Beitrag zur Raabe-Philologie.

Mit einer unpublizierten Studie (1957) zu editorischen Fragen der 'Braun-schweiger Ausgabe.' " *RJ* 1984, pp. 51-67.

Doernenburg, Emil. "Lawrence [sic] Sterne und Wilhelm Raabe." *Germanic Review* 6 (1931): 154-82. Tr. as "Wilhelm Raabe und Laurence Sterne." *Mitt.* 29 (1939): 10-18, 56-68.

———. *Wilhelm Raabe und die deutsche Romantik*. Philadelphia: Americana Germanica Press, 1919.

Doernenburg, Emil, and Wilhelm Fehse. *Raabe und Dickens: Ein Beitrag zur Erkenntnis der geistigen Gestalt Wilhelm Raabes*. Magdeburg: Creutz'sche Verlagsbuchhandlung, 1921.

Dose, Helene. *Die Magie bei Wilhelm Raabe*. Berlin-Grunewald: Klemm, 1928.

———. *Aus Wilhelm Raabes mystischer Werkstatt*. Hamburg: Hanseatische Verlags-Anstalt, 1925.

Eason, Laurel Ellen. "Beginning and Conclusion: Structure and Theme in the Early Novels of Wilhelm Raabe." Diss. Vanderbilt University, 1979.

Eckhardt, Juliane. "Die Werke Wilhelm Raabes im Literaturunterricht." *Diskussion Deutsch* 12 (1981): 16-33.

Ehninger, Annemargret. "Zum Schicksal des Raabehauses." *Mitt.* 34, No. 2 (1944): 43-45.

Eisele, Ulf. *Der Dichter und sein Detektiv: Raabes 'Stopfkuchen' und die Frage des Realismus*. Tübingen: Niemeyer, 1979.

Elster, Otto, and Hanns Martin Elster. *Wilhelm Raabe-Kalender 1912*. Berlin: Grote, 1911.

———. *Wilhelm Raabe-Kalender 1913*. Berlin: Grote, 1912.

———. *Wilhelm Raabe-Kalender 1914*. Berlin: Grote, 1913.

Emrich, Wilhelm. "Personalität und Zivilisation in Wilhelm Raabes 'Die Akten des Vogelsangs.' " *RJ* 1982, pp. 7-25.

Esser, Aloise. "Zeitgestaltung und Struktur in den historischen Novellen Wilhelm Raabes." Diss. University of Bonn, 1953.

Fairley, Barker. "A Misinterpretation of Raabe's 'Hastenbeck.' " *Modern Language Review* 57 (1962): 575-78.

———. "The Modernity of Wilhelm Raabe." Pp. 66-81 in *German Studies Presented to Leonard Ashley Willoughby by Pupils, Colleagues and Friends on his Retirement*, [ed. J. Boyd]. Oxford: Blackwell, 1952. Reprinted pp. 253-71 in Fairley, *Selected Essays on German Literature*, ed. Rodney Symington. New York, Berne, Frankfort am Main, and Nancy: Peter Lang, 1984. Tr. as "Das Moderne an Wilhelm Raabes Erzähltechnik." *Mitt.* 42 (1955): 74-89.

———. "Raabe and Mark Twain: A Point of Contact." *RJ* 1963, pp. 76-77.

———. "Two Coincidences." *RJ* 1962, pp. 74-77.

———. *Wilhelm Raabe: An Introduction to his Novels*. Oxford: Clarendon Press, 1961.

———. "Wilhelm Raabes 'Stopfkuchen.' " Pp. 203-17 in *Interpretationen*, Vol. 3, *Deutsche Romane von Grimmelshausen bis Musil*, ed. Jost Schillemeit.

Fischer-Bücherei, No. 716. Frankfurt am Main and Hamburg: Fischer, 1966.

Fechter, Paul. "Ein Urteil über Raabe." *Mitt.* 23 (1933): 110-13.

Fehse, Wilhelm. "Die Alten und die Jungen." *Mitt.* 24 (1934): 1-8.

———. "Dämon und Tyche." *Mitt.* 24 (1934): 101-14.

———. "Dasein und Leben." *Mitt.* 27 (1937): 1-16.

———. "Goethe, Raabe und die deutsche Zukunft." *Mitt.* 12 (1922): 11-25.

———. *Im Spiegel des alten Proteus: Wilhelm Raabe als Seher unserer Zeit.* Berlin: Verlag Deutsche Rundschau, 1931.

———. "Die literarischen Symbole in den 'Akten des Vogelsangs.' Ein Nachruf auf Dr. Margarete Bönneken." *Mitt.* 11 (1921): 8-20, 33-57.

———. *Raabe und Jensen: Denkmal einer Lebensfreundschaft.* Berlin: Grote, 1940.

———. "Raabes Erzählung 'Frau Salome.' Ihre Entstehung und ihre Deutungen." *Mitt.* 14 (1924): 41-58.

———. "Von Aurora entführt." *Mitt.* 30 (1940): 25-27.

———. "Wilhelm Raabe als Briefschreiber." *Mitt.* 30 (1940): 45-58.

———. *Wilhelm Raabe: Sein Leben und seine Werke.* Braunschweig: Vieweg, 1937.

———. *Wilhelm Raabes Leben.* Berlin-Grunewald: Klemm, 1928.

———. "Zwei Briefe Theodor Fontanes an Wilhelm Raabe." *Mitt.* 28 (1938): 85-88.

Fink, August. "Ein Brief über Raabe." *RJ* 1962, pp. 191-93.

Folkers, Gernot. *Besitz und Sicherheit: Über Entstehung und Zerfall einer bürgerlichen Illusion am Beispiel Goethes und Raabes.* Kronberg: Scriptor, 1976.

Fries, Marilyn Sibley. *The Changing Consciousness of Reality: The Image of Berlin in Selected German Novels from Raabe to Döblin.* Bonn: Bouvier, 1980.

Friese, Hans. "Durch Aurora entführt." *Mitt.* 28 (1938): 54-56.

———. "Erwin Guido Kolbenheyer." *Mitt.* 34, No. 2 (1944): 33-41.

———. "Wilhelm Raabe und die Antike." *Mitt.* 32 (1942): 104-15.

Fröhlich, Walter. "Das Verhältnis der Wackerhahnschen zum Bienchen von Boffzen." *Mitt.* 44 (1957): 22-24.

Fuchtel, Paul. "Raabe und Wolfenbüttel." *Mitt.* 25 (1935): 34-47.

Gerber, Paul. *Wilhelm Raabe: Eine Würdigung seiner Dichtungen.* Leipzig: Wilhelm Friedrich, [1897].

Gerloff, Ludwig. "Wilhelm Raabe—der Philosoph?" *RJ* 1977, pp. 26-29.

Giegerich, Wolfgang. "Dumas' 'Le Comte de Monte-Christo [sic]' und Wilhelm Raabe." *RJ* 1971, pp. 49-71.

Glockner, Hermann. "Griffelkünstler Proteus." *RJ* 1962, pp. 66-73.

Gloy, Hans. "Die Innerste: Die Kritik eines Kommentars." *Mitt.* 32 (1942): 98-104.

Goebel, Heinrich, ed. *Raabe-Gedächtnisschrift.* New rev. ed., Hildesheim and Leipzig: August Lax, 1931.

Goedsche, Charlotte L. "Wilhelm Raabe's 'Die Chronik der Sperlingsgasse': An Analysis of its Structure." Diss. Northwestern University, 1980.

Göhmann, Herbert W., and Matthias Göhmann. *Wilhelm Raabe und das We-*

serbergland: Ein Führer zu den Orten und Werken seiner Weserheimat. Holzminden: Hüpke & Sohn, Weserland-Verlag, 1979.

Goetz-Stankiewicz, Marketa. "Die böse Maske Moses Freudensteins. Gedanken zum Hungerpastor." *RJ* 1969, pp. 7-32.

―――. "Des Dichters 'Pflicht.' Gedanken zu Raabes Einstellung zum Kunstwerk." *RJ* 1971, p. 21-48.

―――. "The Short Stories: A Possible Clue to Wilhelm Raabe." *Germanic Review* 37 (1962): 55-67.

―――. "The Tailor and the Sweeper: A New Look at Wilhelm Raabe." Pp. 152-76 in *Essays on German Literature in Honour of G. Joyce Hallamore*, ed. Michael S. Batts and Marketa Goetz Stankiewicz. Toronto: University of Toronto Press, 1968. Tr. as "Der Schneider und der Feger. Zwei Grundgestalten bei Wilhelm Raabe." *RJ* 1972, pp. 31-60.

Golz, Bruno. "Rabelais und Raabe." *Mitt.* 10 (1920): 46-51.

Gould, Stephen A. "Ontology and Ethics: The Rhetorical Role of the Narrator in Wilhelm Raabe's Early Novels." Diss. University of Nebraska, 1976.

Graumann, Hans. "Schlüssel zum Verständnis von Raabes Stopfkuchen." *Mitt.* 46 (1959): 49-57.

Graves, Robert Anthony. "The Integral Personality: The Relationship between the Female Characters and the World in Selected Works of Theodor Fontane and Wilhelm Raabe." Diss. University of Bristol, 1978.

Gruenter, Rainer. "Ein *Schritt vom Wege.* Geistliche Lokalsymbolik in Wilhelm Raabes *Unruhige Gäste.*" *Euphorion* 60 (1966): 209-21.

Hahn, Karl-Friedrich. "Wilhelm Raabes 'Des Reiches Krone.' Geschichte als erzählerisches Mittel." *RJ* 1982, pp. 125-41.

Hahn, Walter L. "Zum Erzählvorgang in Raabes 'Akten des Vogelsangs.' " *RJ* 1972, pp. 61-71.

Hahne, Franz. "Die andre Welt: eine raabische Betrachtung." *Mitt.* 34, No. 1 (1944): 1-15.

―――. "August Raabe"; "August Raabe als Historiker." *Mitt.* 26 (1936): 71-82; 103-15.

―――. "Erinnerungen an Wilhelm Raabe." *Mitt.* 31 (1941): 29-33.

―――. "Jeremias Gotthelf und Raabe." *Mitt.* 28 (1938): 34-51.

―――. "Ein Nachfolger Raabes als politischer Dichter." *Mitt.* 31 (1941): 93-97.

―――. "Eine ketzerische Betrachtung über Wilhelm Raabe." *Mitt.* 29 (1939): 68-75.

―――. "Raabe und die nationale Revolution." *Mitt.* 23 (1933): 67-69.

―――. "Raabe vom Rassenstandpunkt betrachtet." *Mitt.* 24 (1934): 114-22.

―――. "Raabes Sehnen und des Führers Erfüllung." *Mitt.* 29 (1939): 33-35.

―――. "Raabes Stellung im Dritten Reich." *Mitt.* 23 (1933): 97-110.

―――. "Raabes Stellung zum Theater." *Mitt.* 30 (1940): 27-30.

―――. "Was will Wilhelm Raabe mit seinem Roman 'Im alten Eisen'?" *Mitt.* 18 (1928): 149-61.

―――. "Zu Raabes 'Prinzessin Fisch.' " *Mitt.* 36 (1949): 72-77.

Hajek, Siegfried. "Die Freiheit der Gebundenen. Bemerkungen zu Raabes 'Altershausen.' " *RJ* 1974, pp. 24-40.

———. " 'Meister Autor'—Sprachschichten und Motive." *RJ* 1981, pp. 149-68.

———. *Der Mensch und die Welt im Werk Wilhelm Raabes.* Warendorf: Schnell, 1950.

———. "Wilhelm Raabe im Deutschunterricht: 'Die Akten des Vogelsangs.' " *Diskussion Deutsch* 12 (1981): 6-15.

———. "Wilhelm Raabe und die Jugend unserer Zeit." *RJ* 1960, pp. 9-20.

———. "Wilhelm Raabes Erzählung 'Die Innerste.' " *RJ* 1977, pp. 30-47.

Hajek, Siegfried, and Fritz Martini. "Diskussionshorizonte: 'Meister Autor' im Kontext realistischen Erzählens." *RJ* 1982, pp. 99-109.

Hampe, Edgar. "Die Symbolik in Raabes 'Lar.' " *Mitt.* 27 (1937): 77-86.

Hanson, William P. "Raabes erste Chronik." *RJ* 1983, pp. 33-48.

———. "Raabe's Poems." *Modern Language Review* 80 (1985): 858-70.

———. "Some Basic Themes in Raabe." *German Life and Letters* N.S. 21 (1967/68): 122-30.

Hartmann, Fritz. "Gutmanns Reisen. Raabes politischer Roman." *Mitt.* 21 (1931): 156-71.

———. "Im Silberkranz. Unser erstes Vierteljahrhundert." *Mitt.* 26 (1936): 123-34.

———. *Wilhelm Raabe: Wie er war und wie er dachte.* 2nd ed., Hanover: Sponholtz, 1927.

Hebbel, Christa. "Die Funktion der Erzähler- und Figurenperspektiven in Wilhelm Raabes Ich-Erzählungen." Diss. University of Heidelberg, 1960.

Heim, Karl. "Wilhelm Raabe und das Publikum." Diss. University of Tübingen, 1953.

———. "Wilhelm Raabe und das Publikum." *Mitt.* 42 (1955): 1-12.

Heinrich, Thea. "Der Tod in der Dichtung Wilhelm Raabes." Diss. University of Munich, 1949.

Heiseler, Ingrid von. "Die geschichtlichen Quellen und ihre Verwendung in Raabes Erzählung 'Hastenbeck.' " *RJ* 1967, pp. 80-104.

Heldt, Uwe. *Isolation und Identität: Die Bedeutung des Idyllischen in der Epik Wilhelm Raabes.* Frankfurt am Main, Bern, and Cirencester: Peter D. Lang, 1980.

Helmers, Hermann. *Die bildenden Mächte in den Romanen Wilhelm Raabes.* Weinheim: Beltz, 1960.

———. "Die Figur des Erzählers bei Raabe." *RJ* 1965, pp. 9-33.

———. "Über Wilhelm Raabes Sprache." *RJ* 1962, pp. 9-21.

———. "Die Verfremdung als epische Grundtendenz im Werk Raabes." *RJ* 1963, pp. 7-30.

———. *Wilhelm Raabe.* Sammlung Metzler, M71. Stuttgart: Metzler, 1968.

———. "Wilhelm Raabe und Heinrich Böll." *RJ* 1981, pp. 105-17.

———, ed. *Raabe in neuer Sicht.* Sprache und Literatur, 48. Stuttgart, Berlin, Cologne, and Mainz: Kohlhammer, 1968.

395

Hertel, Heinz. "Wie stellt sich die heutige Jugend zu Raabe?" *Mitt.* 21 (1931): 59-61.

Hirata, Tatsuji. " 'Zum wilden Mann.' Ein Interpretationsversuch." *RJ* 1983, pp. 59-70.

Hirschstein, Hans. "Der wirtschaftliche Hintergrund in Raabes Zeitromanen." *Mitt.* 15 (1925): 99-111.

Höfer, Conrad. *Wilhelm Raabe zum Gedächtnis.* Eisenach: [Kühner], 1932.

Höhler, Gertrud. *Unruhige Gäste. Das Bibelzitat in Wilhelm Raabes Roman.* Bonn: Bouvier, 1969.

Höse, Karl. "Juristische Bemerkungen zu Raabes 'Stopfkuchen.' " *RJ* 1962, pp. 136-46.

Hoffmeister, Kurt. *Wilhelm Raabe und seine Braunschweiger Freunde.* Braunschweig: privately printed, 1979.

Hoppe, Else. "Raabes eigener Weg zum Lachen." *RJ* 1962, pp. 47-65.

———. "Vom tödlichen Lachen im Werk Wilhelm Raabes." *RJ* 1960, pp. 21-59.

———. "Wilhelm Raabe und Marie Jensen, Mythos einer Freundschaft." *RJ* 1966, pp. 25-57.

Hoppe, Karl. "Aphorismen Raabes chronologisch geordnet." *RJ* 1960, pp. 94-139.

———. "Aus Raabes Briefwechsel." *RJ* 1963, pp. 31-63.

———. "Eine Brockenwanderung von Raabes Vater anno 1821"; Gustav Raabe, "Als Student zu Fuss nach Göttingen." *Mitt.* 46 (1959), 1-7; *RJ* 1964, pp. 122-25.

———. "Entstehung und Veröffentlichung von 'Altershausen.' " *RJ* 1967, pp. 72-79.

———. "Micheline. Ein Fragment." *RJ* 1969, pp. 80-84.

———. "Miszellen: 1. Börries von Münchhausen und Raabe. 2. Zwei Briefe von Ernst Barlach." *RJ* 1967, pp. 105-9.

———. "Miszellen: 1. Der Stand der Raabe-Ausgabe; 2. Das Stuttgart Albumblatt Raabes; 3. Gelegenheitsverse." *RJ* 1968, pp. 136-39.

———. "Miszellen: 1. 60 Jahre Raabe-Gesellschaft; 2. Chronologisches Verzeichnis von Raabes Werken." *RJ* 1971, pp. 118-25.

———. "Niedersächsische Wesenszüge im Werk Wilhelm Raabes." *Mitt.* 29 (1939): 35-44.

———. "Die Übersiedlung Raabes nach Braunschweig. Eine Richtigstellung." *RJ* 1965, pp. 112-24.

———. "Die weltanschaulichen Grundzüge in Raabes Stopfkuchen." *Mitt.* 41 (1954): 77-89.

———. *Wilhelm Raabe: Beiträge zum Verständnis seiner Person und seines Werkes.* Göttingen: Vandenhoeck & Ruprecht, 1967.

———. "Wilhelm Raabe einst und heute." *RJ* 1961, pp. 7-20.

Hotz, Karl. *Bedeutung und Funktion des Raumes im Werk Wilhelm Raabes.* Göppingen: Kümmerle, 1970.

————. "Raumgestaltung und Raumsymbolik in Wilhelm Raabes Erzählung 'Else von der Tanne.' " *RJ* 1968, pp. 83-90.

Huth, Otto. "Raabe und das Neue Testament." *RJ* 1965, pp. 103-11.

Iltz, Johannes. "Die Kinder bei Wilhelm Raabe." *Mitt.* 15 (1925): 14-21, 55-73.

————. "Raabe und Hitler." *Mitt.* 24 (1934): 8-17.

Jehmüller, Wolfgang. *Die Gestalt des Biographen bei Wilhelm Raabe.* Munich: Fink, 1975.

Jensch, Fritz. "Der Schmied von Jüterborg." *Mitt.* 14 (1924): 12-21.

————. "Unaufgeklärte Zitate bei Raabe." *Mitt.* 14 (1924): 140-47; "Nachträge," 16 (1926): 204-7; 18 (1928): 39-41; 19 (1929): 87-92; 21 (1931): 71-75.

————. "Von Einem, der auszog, das Fürchten zu lernen." *Mitt.* 12 (1922): 49-62.

————. *Wilhelm Raabes Zitatenschatz.* Wolfenbüttel: Heckner, 1925.

Johanson, Klara. "Der Gaukler von Braunschweig. Ein Nachruf aus dem Jahre 1910." *RJ* 1969, pp. 53-56.

Jolles, Charlotte. " 'Im alten Eisen.' Wirklichkeit im Märchenton." *RJ* 1981, pp. 194-209.

Joost, Ulrich. "Das 'Buch der Schöpfung' im 'Zusammenhang der Wissenschaften.' Zum motivgeschichtlichen Hintersinn des gelehrten Buchbinders Baumann-Bruseberger in Wilhelm Raabes 'Prinzessin Fisch.' " *RJ* 1980, pp. 69-90.

Junge, Hermann. *Wilhelm Raabe: Studien über Form und Inhalt seiner Werke.* Dortmund: Ruhfus, 1910.

————. "Wilhelm Raabes Religiosität." *Mitt.* 28 (1938): 20-21.

Kafitz, Dieter. *Figurenkonstellation als Mittel der Wirklichkeitserfassung. Dargestellt an Romanen der zweiten Hälfte des 19. Jahrhunderts: Freytag, Spielhagen, Fontane, Raabe.* Kronberg: Athenäum, 1978.

Kahn, Ludwig. "Fortschrittsglaube und Kulturkritik im bürgerlichen Roman: Gustav Freytag und Wilhelm Raabe." Pp. 252-67 in *Corona*, ed. Arno Schirokauer and Wolfgang Paulsen. Durham: Duke University Press, 1941.

Kaiser, Katherine Starr. "Structure and Narrative Technique in Wilhelm Raabe's *Krähenfelder Geschichten.*" Diss. Brown University, 1974.

Kaiser, Nancy A. "Reading Raabe's Realism: *Die Akten des Vogelsangs.*" *Germanic Review* 59 (1984): 2-9.

Kientz, Louis. "Raabe und Frankreich." *Mitt.* 21 (1931): 130-36.

————. *Wilhelm Raabe: L'homme, la pensée et l'oeuvre.* Paris: Didier, 1939.

Killy, Walther. "Geschichte gegen die Geschichte. Raabe: Das Odfeld." Pp. 146-65 in Killy, *Romane des 19. Jahrhunderts: Wirklichkeit und Kunstcharakter.* Göttingen: Vandenhoeck & Ruprecht, 1967.

————. "Das Odfeld." Pp. 128-45 in *Der deutsche Roman*, Vol. 2, ed. Benno von Wiese. Düsseldorf: Bagel, 1965.

King, Janet K. "Raabe's *Else von der Tanne*." *German Quarterly* 40 (1967): 653-63.

Kirchhoff, Eberhard. "Einige Anmerkungen zu den philosophischen Einflüssen bei Wilhelm Raabe." *Diskussion Deutsch* 12 (1981): 304-7.

Klein, Arpad. *Versuch einer Interpretation von Raabes Werk.* Raabe-Forschungen, ed. Hans-Werner Peter, 3. Braunschweig: pp-Verlag, 1983.

Klein, Johannes. "Raabes 'Schüdderump.' " *RJ* 1968, pp. 7-22.

———. "Raabes 'Schüdderump' in seiner und unserer Zeit." *RJ* 1965, pp. 65-82.

———. "Vorwegnahme moderner Formen in Raabes 'Gänsen von Bützow.' " *RJ* 1962, pp. 99-107.

———. "Wilhelm Raabe als Formkünstler in seinen Novellen." *Mitt.* 26 (1936): 48-54, 82-93.

Klieneberger, H. R. "Charles Dickens and Wilhelm Raabe." *Oxford German Studies* 4 (1969): 90-117. Reprinted pp. 108-44 in Klieneberger, *The Novel in England and Germany: A Comparative Study.* London: Oswald Wolff, 1981.

Klopfenstein, Eduard. *Erzähler und Leser bei Wilhelm Raabe: Untersuchungen zu einem Formelement der Prosaerzählung.* Bern: Paul Haupt, 1969.

Klotz, Volker. "Stadtflucht nach innen: Raabes *Die Chronik der Sperlingsgasse*." Pp. 167-93 in Klotz, *Die erzählte Stadt: Ein Sujet als Herausforderung des Romans von Lesage bis Döblin.* Munich: Hanser, 1969.

Köttgen, Gerhard. "Raabe und Spielhagen." *Mitt.* 33 (1943): 20-27.

———. *Wilhelm Raabes Ringen um die Aufgabe des Erziehungsromans.* Berlin: Ebering, 1939.

Kolbe, Hans. *Wilhelm Raabe: Vom Entwicklungs- zum Desillusionierungsroman.* Berlin: Akademie-Verlag, 1981.

Koll, Rolf-Dieter. *Raumgestaltung bei Wilhelm Raabe.* Bonn: Bouvier, 1977.

Koller, Ulrike. "Vom 'Lesepöbel' zur Leser-'Gemeinde.' Raabes Beziehung zum zeitgenössisschen Publikum im Spiegel der Leserbehandlung." *RJ* 1979, pp. 94-127.

Krebs, Reinhard. "Raabe-Renaissance auch in der Schule?" *Diskussion Deutsch* 12 (1981): 199-200.

Krüger, Herm[ann] Anders. *Der junge Raabe: Jugendjahre und Erstlingswerke nebst einer Bibliographie der Werke Raabes und der Raabeliteratur.* Leipzig: Xenien-Verlag, 1911.

Kühn, Julius. "Ein Blick in Raabes dichterische Werkstatt: Im besonderen eine Betrachtung von Raabes 'Ein Frühling.' " *Mitt.* 45 (1958): 3-14.

Kunz, Josef. "Die Novellenkunst Raabes dargestellt an seiner Novelle 'Im Siegeskranze.' " *RJ* 1964, pp. 106-21.

———. "Raabe und die Geschichte. Noch ein Wort zu dem Roman 'Das Odfeld.' " Pp. 476-93 in *Kritische Bewahrung: Beiträge zur deutschen Philologie. Festschrift für Werner Schröder zum 60. Geburtstag,* ed. Ernst-Joachim Schmidt. Berlin: Erich Schmidt Verlag, 1974.

———. "Wilhelm Raabe 'Die Holunderblüte.' Versuch einer Interpretation." *RJ* 1973, pp. 88-108.

———. "Wilhelm Raabes Novelle 'Des Reiches Krone.' Versuch einer Interpretation." *RJ* 1966, pp. 7-24.

Lamprecht, Helmut. *Studien zur epischen Zeitgestaltung in Wilhelm Raabes Roman "Das Odfeld."* Diss. University of Frankfurt am Main, 1958.

Lensing, Leo A. " 'Auch das Wort "Roman" ist überflüssig.' Zwei unveröffentlichte Briefe zur Publikation von Wilhelm Raabes 'Der Schüdderump.' " *RJ* 1980, pp. 91-96.

———. "The Caricatured Reader in *Im alten Eisen*: Raabe, Marlitt and the 'Familienblattroman.' " *German Life and Letters* N.S. 31 (1977/78): 318-27.

———. *Narrative Structure and the Reader in Wilhelm Raabe's "Im alten Eisen."* Berne, Frankfurt am Main, and Las Vegas: Peter Lang, 1977.

———. "Raabe und K. E. Franzos' 'Deutsche Dichtung.' Zwei unbekannte Briefe." *RJ* 1979, pp. 128-31.

———. "Reading Raabe: The Example of Kurt Tucholsky." *Seminar* 19 (1983): 122-35.

Lensing, Leo A., and Hans-Werner Peter, eds. *Wilhelm Raabe: Studien zu seinem Leben und Werk. Aus Anlaß des 150. Geburtstages (1831-1981)*. Braunschweig, pp-Verlag: 1981.

Lenz, Hermann. "Dankesrede zur Raabe-Preisverleihung 1981." *RJ* 1982, pp. 56-60.

———. "Raabe: 'Des Südens warmer Gruss.' " Pp. 201-12 in *Schwäbische Curiosa*, ed. Georg Kleemann. 2nd ed., Tübingen: Rainer Wunderlich Verlag Hermann Leins, 1974.

Lorenz, Albert. "Eros in Raabes Werk." *RJ* 1965, pp. 125-47.

———. "Raabe und Berlin." *RJ* 1961, pp. 40-52.

Lorenz, Karl. "Der Liebesroman Phöbes und Veits in den 'Unruhigen Gästen.' " *Mitt.* 11 (1921): 132-39.

Lozinskaja, L., and E. Fradkina. "Wilhelm Raabe." Tr. from the Russian by Helene Fiedler. *RJ* 1978, pp. 107-45.

Luginbühl, Emil. "Poetische Grenzüberschreitungen: Jeremias Gotthelf und Wilhelm Raabe." *Schweizer Monatshefte* 63 (1983): 923-37. Reprinted *RJ* 1984, pp. 157-72.

———. *Wilhelm Raabe und die deutsche Geschichte*. St. Gallen: Kommisionsverlag der Fehr'schen Buchhandlung, 1952.

Lukács, Georg. "Wilhelm Raabe." Pp. 231-61 in Lukács, *Deutsche Realisten des 19. Jahrhunderts*. Berlin: Aufbau-Verlag, 1952.

Maatje, Frank C[hristiaan]. *Der Doppelroman: Eine literatursystematische Studie über duplikative Erzählstrukturen*. Groningen: Wolters, 1964.

———. "Ein früher Ansatz zur 'Stream of Consciousness'-Dichtung: Wilhelm Raabes 'Altershausen.' " *Neophilologus* 45 (1961): 305-22.

Manthey, Jürgen. "Wilhelm Raabe und das Scheitern des deutschen Liberalismus." *RJ* 1976, pp. 69-106.

Margotton, Jean-Charles. "*Stopfkuchen* de W. Raabe: A propos de la structure narrative du roman." *Etudes Germaniques* 36 (1981): 291-305.

Martini, Fritz. "Auswanderer, Rückkehrer, Heimkehrer. Amerikaspiegelungen im Erzählwerk von Keller, Raabe und Fontane." Pp. 178-204 in *Amerika in der deutschen Literatur: Neue Welt—Nordamerika—USA*, ed. Sigrid Bauschinger et al. Stuttgart: Reclam, 1975.

———. "Der Bauer in der Dichtung Wilhelm Raabes." *Mitt.* 24 (1934): 69-77.

———. "Ironischer Realismus: Keller, Raabe und Fontane." Pp. 113-41 in *Ironie und Dichtung*, ed. Albert Schaefer. Munich: C. H. Beck, 1970.

———. "Parodie und Regeneration der Idylle. Zu Wilhelm Raabes 'Horacker.' " Pp. 232-66 in *Literatur und Geistesgeschichte: Festgabe für Heinz Otto Burger*, ed. Reinhold Grimm and Conrad Wiedemann. Berlin: Erich Schmidt Verlag, 1968.

———. "Das Problem des Realismus im 19. Jahrhundert und die Dichtung Wilhelm Raabes." *Dichtung und Volkstum* 36 (1935): 271-302.

———. *Die Stadt in der Dichtung Wilhelm Raabes.* Greifswald: Hans Adler, E. Parzig, 1934.

———. "Wilhelm Raabe." Pp. 528-56 in *Deutsche Dichter des 19. Jahrhunderts*, ed. Benno von Wiese. Berlin: Erich Schmidt Verlag, 1969.

———. "Wilhelm Raabe und das literarische Biedermeier." *Mitt.* 23 (1933): 33-45.

———. "Wilhelm Raabe und das XIX. Jahrhundert." *Zeitschrift für deutsche Philologie* 58 (1933): 326-43.

———. "Wilhelm Raabes 'Altershausen.' " *RJ* 1964, pp. 78-105.

———. "Wilhelm Raabes 'Höxter und Corvey.' " *Der Deutschunterricht* 5, No. 1 (January, 1953): 76-92.

———. "Wilhelm Raabes Verzicht auf 'Versöhnung.' Bemerkungen zu 'Meister Autor' " *RJ* 1981, pp. 169-93.

Matschke, Günther. *Die Isolation als Mittel der Gesellschaftskritik bei Wilhelm Raabe.* Bonn: Bouvier, 1975.

Mattenklott, Gundel. "Exkurs über Wilhelm Raabes 'Akten des Vogelsangs.' " Pp. 28-32 in Mattenklott, *Sprache der Sentimentalität: Zum Werk Adalbert Stifters.* Frankfurt am Main: Akademische Verlagsgesellschaft, 1973.

Mayer, Gerhart. *Die geistige Entwicklung Wilhelm Raabes: Dargestellt unter besonderer Berücksichtigung seines Verhältnisses zur Philosophie.* Göttingen: Vandenhoeck & Ruprecht, 1960.

———. "Raabes Romanfragment 'Altershausen': Grundzüge einer Interpretation." *RJ* 1962, pp. 155-65; 1963, pp. 64-75.

———. "Wilhelm Raabe und die Tradition des Bildungsromans." *RJ* 1980, pp. 97-124.

———. "Zum Wesen von Raabes humoristischer Sprachform." *RJ* 1960, pp. 77-93.

Mayer, Hans. *Aussenseiter*. Frankfurt am Main: Suhrkamp, 1975.

Mehring, Franz. "Wilhelm Raabe. Dezember 1910." Pp. 97-99 in Mehring, *Aufsätze zur deutschen Literatur von Hebbel bis Schweichel. Gesammelte Schriften*, ed. Thomas Höhle et al. Vol. 11, Berlin: Dietz, 1961.

Meinerts, Hans Jürgen. *"Die Akten des Vogelsangs": Raabestudien auf Grund einer Sprachuntersuchung*. Berlin: Junker und Dünnhaupt, 1940.

Meyen, Fritz. "Berichtigungen und Ergänzungen zur Raabe-Bibliographie von 1955." *RJ* 1961, pp. 53-71.

———. "Einige Bemerkungen zu Töteberg / Zander: Die Rezeption Raabes durch die 'Gesellschaft der Freunde Wilhelm Raabes' 1911 bis 1945 im 'Jahrbuch der Raabe-Gesellschaft' 1973, Seite 178-193." *RJ* 1974, pp. 105-11.

———. "Zur Neuauflage der Wilhelm-Raabe-Bibliographie." *RJ* 1973, pp. 109-16.

Meyer, Eberhard W. "Raabe—mit Vergnügen." *Diskussion Deutsch* 12 (1981): 3-5.

Meyer, Herman. "Raum und Zeit in Wilhelm Raabes Erzählkunst." *Deutsche Vierteljahrsschrift* 27 (1953): 236-67. Reprinted pp. 239-79 in *Zur Poetik des Romans*, ed. Volker Klotz. Darmstadt: Wissenschaftliche Buchgesellschaft, 1965; pp. 253-93 in *Die Werkinterpretation*, ed. Horst Enders. Darmstadt: Wissenschaftliche Buchgesellschaft, 1967.

———. *Der Sonderling in der deutschen Dichtung*. 2nd ed., Munich: Hanser, 1963.

———. "Wilhelm Raabe 'Hastenbeck.' " Pp. 186-206 in Meyer, *Das Zitat in der Erzählkunst*. 2nd ed., Stuttgart: Metzler, 1967. Pp. 204-29 in Meyer, *The Poetics of Quotation in the European Novel*, tr. Theodore and Yetta Ziolkowski. Princeton: Princeton University Press, 1968.

Meyer, Jochen. *Wilhelm Raabe: Unter Demokraten, Hoflieferanten und Philistern. Eine Chronik seiner Stuttgarter Jahre*. Stuttgart: Fleischhauer & Spohn, 1981.

Meyer-Krentler, Eckhardt. *"Unterm Strich": Literarischer Markt, Trivialität und Romankunst in Raabes "Der Lar."* Paderborn: Schöningh, 1986.

Michelsen, Peter. "Der Rektor und die Revolution. Eine Interpretation der 'Gänse von Bützow.' " *RJ* 1967, pp. 51-71.

Misslack, Johannes. "Der Lar." *Mitt.* 10 (1920): 73-81.

Möhrmann, Renate. *Der vereinsamte Mensch: Studien zum Wandel des Einsamkeitsmotivs im Roman von Raabe bis Musil*. Bonn: Bouvier, 1974.

Mohr, Heinrich. "Wilhelm Raabe und die nordische Rasse." *Mitt.* 17 (1927): 18-39.

Mohr, Rudolf. " 'Der Hungerpastor'—ein Pfarrerroman?" *RJ* 1977, pp. 48-85.

Morold, Max. "Wilhelm Raabe und Oesterreich." *Mitt.* 21 (1931): 123-30.

Morsier, Edouard de. "Wilhelm Raabe." Pp. 313-401 in Morsier, *Romanciers allemands contemporains*. Paris: Perrin, 1890.

Müller, Joachim. "Erzählstruktur und Symbolgefüge in Wilhelm Raabes 'Frau Salome.' " *RJ* 1970, pp. 37-62.

———. "Erzählstruktur und Symbolgefüge in Wilhelm Raabes 'Unruhigen Gästen.' " *RJ* 1962, pp. 121-35; 1963, pp. 89-102.

———. "Interpretation von Raabes Erzählung 'Frau Salome.' " *RJ* 1970, pp. 37-62.

———. "Das Weltbild Wilhelm Raabes." *Deutsche Vierteljahrsschrift* 21 (1943): 196-227.

———. "Das Zitat im epischen Gefüge. Die Goethe-Verse in Raabes Erzählung 'Die Akten des Vogelsangs.' " *RJ* 1964, pp. 7-23.

Müller, Theodor. "Der zeitgeschichtliche Hintergrund der Raabeschen Erzählung 'Zum wilden Mann.' " *Mitt.* 28 (1938): 76-81.

Nauck, Gerhart. "Das Gesellschaftsproblem bei Raabe." *Mitt.* 13 (1923): 31-36.

Naumann, Hans. "Braunschweiger Festrede über Wilh. Raabe." *Mitt.* 22 (1932): 1-13.

Neubauer, Konrad. "Das Sterben bei Wilhelm Raabe." *Mitt.* 22 (1932): 38-40.

Neumann, Friedrich. "Erlebte Geschichte in Raabes Erzählung 'Im Siegeskranze.' " *RJ* 1962, pp. 108-20.

———. "Wilhelm Raabes Erzählung 'Zum wilden Mann.' Eine Interpretation." *RJ* 1960, pp. 60-76.

———. "Wilhelm Raabes Schüdderump." *Zeitschrift für deutsche Philologie* 71 (1951/53): 291-329.

Neumann, Peter Horst. "Generalstreiklektüre. Über Wilhelm Raabes literarischen Rang und Nachruhm." *RJ* 1982, pp. 40-55.

Noltenius, Rainer. "Der Schriftsteller Wilhelm Raabe—Städtische Feier in Wolfenbüttel." Pp. 113-43 in Noltenius, *Dichterfeiern in Deutschland: Rezeptionsgeschichte als Sozialgeschichte am Beispiel der Schiller- und Freiligrath-Feiern.* Munich: Fink, 1984.

Oberdieck, Wilhelm. "Gestalt und Gestaltung von Weisheit im Werk Wilhelm Raabes." *RJ* 1980, pp. 125-38.

———. "Wilhelm Raabes Begegnung mit dem Absurden." *RJ* 1968, pp. 91-105.

———. "Vom Glück der Entsagenden. Goethes 'Wilhelm Meister' und Raabes 'Horn von Wanza.' " *RJ* 1973, pp. 117-35.

Ohl, Hubert. *Bild und Wirklichkeit: Studien zur Romankunst Raabes und Fontanes.* Heidelberg: Stiehm, 1968.

———. "Der Bürger und das Unbedingte bei Wilhelm Raabe." *RJ* 1979, pp. 7-26.

Opie, Gerald. "Childhood and the Childlike in the Fiction of Wilhelm Raabe." Diss. University of Exeter, 1971.

Oppermann, Hans. "Das Bild der Antike bei Wilhelm Raabe." *RJ* 1967, pp. 58-79.

————. "Existentialismus und Humor. (Raabe und Camus)." *Mitt.* 41 (1954): 90-101.

————. "Glockenklang. Ein Heimatgedicht Wilhelm Raabes." *RJ* 1962, pp. 78-85.

————. "Literatur zu Wilhelm Raabe aus dem Jahr 1959 (mit Nachträgen)." *RJ* 1960, pp. 189-97.

————. "Mythische Elemente in Raabes Dichtung." *RJ* 1968, pp. 48-82.

————. "Neue Literatur zu Raabe." *RJ* 1962, pp. 194-201.

————. "Neue Literatur zu Wilhelm Raabe." *RJ* 1961, pp. 72-94; 1963, pp. 112-25; 1966, pp. 146-60; 1967, pp. 110-21; 1968, pp. 140-55; 1969, pp. 88-96; 1970, pp. 166-70.

————. "Der passive Held. Raabe, 'Das Odfeld.' " *RJ* 1967, pp. 31-50.

————. "Pastor Nodt. Zu 'Gutmanns Reisen.' " *RJ* 1969, pp. 84-87.

————. *Raabe.* rororo Bildmonographie, 165. Reinbek bei Hamburg: Rowohlt, 1970.

————. "Raabe und Fontane." *Mitt.* 36 (1949): 59-64.

————. "Raabes Erzählung 'Höxter und Corvey.' " *Mitt.* 42 (1955): 46-55.

————. "Wilhelm Fehse." *Mitt.* 44 (1957): 66-72

————. "Wilhelm Raabe der Dichter." *RJ* 1961, pp. 21-39.

————. "Zum Problem der Zeit bei Wilhelm Raabe." *RJ* 1964, pp. 57-77.

Pascal, Roy. "The Reminiscence-Technique in Raabe." *Modern Language Review* 49 (1954): 339-48.

————. "Warum ist 'Altershausen' Fragment geblieben?" *RJ* 1962, pp. 147-54.

————. "Wilhelm Raabe (1831-1910)." Pp. 143-77 in Pascal, *The German Novel.* Toronto: University of Toronto Press, 1968.

Perquin, Nicolaas Cornelis Adrianus, S.J. *Wilhelm Raabes Motive als Ausdruck seiner Weltanschauung.* Amsterdam: H. J. Paris, 1927.

Peschken, Bernd, and Claus-Dieter Krohn, eds. *Der liberale Roman und der preußische Verfassungskonflikt: Analyseskizzen und Materialien.* Stuttgart: Metzler, 1976.

Peter, Hans-Werner. "Der unbekannte Briefwechsel: Hans Hoffmann / Wilhelm Raabe." *RJ* 1977, pp. 86-102.

————. "Wilhelm Raabe: Ein sozialistischer Ethiker? Ein Versuch zur Bestimmung seiner sozialen Grundhaltung." *RJ* 1974, pp. 65-74.

Pfeiler, Wm. K. "41 Jahre mit Raabe in USA." *Mitt.* 54 (1967): 27-28.

Pongs, Hermann. "Frauenehre bei Raabe." *Mitt.* 34, No. 2 (1944): 3-18.

————. "Raabe und das Reich." *Mitt.* 23 (1933): 1-13.

————. *Wilhelm Raabe: Leben und Werk.* Heidelberg: Quelle & Meyer, 1958.

Popp, Ludwig. "Fritz Limmer, der Photograph Wilhelm Raabes.—Zum Titelbild der Festschrift." *RJ* 1981, pp. 7-9.

————. " 'Pfisters Mühle': Schlüsselroman zu einem Abwasserprozess." *Städtehygiene* 10 (1959): 21-25. Special printing for the Raabe Society, 1979.

Preisendanz, Wolfgang. "Die Erzählstruktur als Bedeutungskomplex der 'Akten des Vogelsangs.' " *RJ* 1981, pp. 210-24.

Preisendanz, Wolfgang. *Humor als dichterische Einbildungskraft: Studien zur Er-zählkunst des poetischen Realismus.* 2nd ed., Munich: Fink, 1976.

———. "Provokativer Humor—Wilhelm Raabes 'Horacker.' " *RJ* 1977, pp. 9-25.

Puschnig, Otto. "Bekenntnis eines Österreichers zu Wilhelm Raabe." *Mitt.* 22 (1932): 40-42.

Radcliffe, S[tanley]. "The Diary of a Somebody? Wilhelm Raabe's Record of his Life." *New German Studies* 10 (1982): 107-22.

———. "Historical Realities in Raabe's *Im Siegeskranz.*" Pp. 209-15 in *Formen realistischer Erzählkunst: Festschrift for Charlotte Jolles in Honour of her 70th Birthday*, ed. Jörg Thunecke with Eda Sagarra. Nottingham: Sherwood Press, 1979.

———. "Raabe, Jensens 'Altes Wort' and 'The Quarterly Review.' " *RJ* 1982, pp. 142-47.

———. *Der Sonderling im Werk Wilhelm Raabes.* Braunschweig: pp-Verlag, 1984.

———. "Wilhelm Raabe und der Dreierklub zu Braunschweig." *RJ* 1978, pp. 11-16.

———. "Wilhelm Raabe, der Dreißigjährige Krieg und die Novelle." *RJ* 1969, pp. 57-70.

———. "Wilhelm Raabe and the Railway." *New German Studies* 2 (1974): 131-44.

Reece, James Robert. "Narrator and Narrative Levels in Wilhelm Raabe's Stuttgart Novels." Diss. University of Oregon, 1975.

Reid, James H. "Wilhelm Raabe." Pp. 251-71 in *German Men of Letters*, Vol. 5, ed. Alex Natan. London: Oswald Wolff, 1969.

Reuter, Hans-Heinrich. "Fünf ungedruckte Briefe Wilhelm Raabes." *RJ* 1962, pp. 173-81.

Richter, Helmut, ed. *Die Akte Wilhelm Raabe.* Weimar: Archiv der Deutschen Schillerstiftung, [1963].

Rieder, Heinz. *Liberalismus als Lebensform in der deutschen Prosaepik des neunzehn-ten Jahrhunderts.* Germanische Studien, 122. Berlin: Ebering, 1939.

Ringel, Karl Jürgen. "Raabes metaphysischer Agnostizismus—ein Kapitel aus einer 'Hastenbeck'-Interpretation." *RJ* 1970, pp. 63-71.

———. *Wilhelm Raabes Roman "Hastenbeck." Ein Beitrag zum Verständnis des Al-terswerkes.* Bern: Herbert Lang, 1970.

———. "Die zitierte Idylle. Arkadische Sehnsucht und soziale Kritik in 'Has-tenbeck.' " *RJ* 1981, pp. 225-42.

Ritter, Alexander. "Vorbild und Einfluß: Crébillons d. J. Roman 'L'Écumoire' und Raabes 'Abu Telfan.' " *RJ* 1973, pp. 135-55.

Ritterson, Michael Lee. "Narrators and Narration in Six Later Novels of Wilhelm Raabe." Diss. Harvard University, 1973.

———. "Rückwendung, Vorausdeutung und Erzählablauf in Wilhelm Raabes 'Das Odfeld' und 'Hastenbeck.' " *RJ* 1976, pp. 107-32.

Rölleke, Heinz. "Brentano-Zitate bei Wilhelm Raabe." *Jahrbuch des Freien Deutschen Hochstifts* 1981, pp. 365-69.

Röttger, Friedrich. *Volk und Vaterland bei Wilhelm Raabe.* Graz: Stiasny, 1930.

Rohse, Eberhard. "Raabe und der junge Brecht. Zur Rezeption früher historischer Erzählungen Wilhelm Raabes in Bertolt Brechts Gymnasiasten-Drama 'Die Bibel.' " *RJ* 1978, pp. 17-62.

Roloff, Ernst-August [Sen.]. "Elfhundert Jahre Ringen um Nation und Reich. Eine nationalgeschichtliche Betrachtung zum elfhundertsten Jahrestage des Vertrages von Verdun, 11. August 1943, aus der Sicht Wilhelm Raabes." *Mitt.* 33 (1943): 100-7.

————. "Erreichtes und Erstrebtes. Bericht über die Arbeit und das Planen der 'Gesellschaft der Freunde Wilhelm Raabes e. V.' " *Mitt.* 35 (1948): 1-6.

————. "Geschichte und Dichtung im Werk Wilhelm Raabes." *Mitt.* 32 (1942): 81-98.

————. "Legenden um Raabe." *Mitt.* 41 (1954): 39-51.

————. "Ein vereitelter Versuch zur Reichseinheit im 12. Jahrhundert." *Mitt.* 31 (1941): 113-21.

————. "Wilhelm Raabe in zeitgenössischer Kritik." *Mitt.* 40, No. 2 (1953): 12-20.

————, ed. *Raabe-Jahrbuch 1949.* Braunschweig, Appelhans, 1949.

————, ed. *Raabe-Jahrbuch 1950.* Braunschweig: Appelhans, 1950.

————, ed. *Wilhelm Raabe-Kalender 1947.* Goslar: Deutsche Volksbücherei, 1946.

————, ed. *Wilhelm Raabe-Kalender 1948.* Goslar: Deutsche Volksbücherei, 1948.

Roloff, E[rnst-]A[ugust] [Jun.]. "Aus der Chronik der Raabe-Gesellschaft." *Mitt.* 38, No. 2 (1951): 8-14.

————. "Wilhelm Raabes Entwicklungsroman 'Prinzessin Fisch' und seine Bedeutung für das Gesamtwerk." Diss. University of Göttingen, 1951.

Rülf, G. "Ein Nachtrag zu 'Wilhelm Raabe und die Juden.' " *Monatsschrift für Geschichte und Wissenschaft der Juden* 55 (1911): 247-51.

Rüter, Eugen. *Die Gesellschaft der Freunde Wilhelm Raabes: Rezeptionssteuerung als Programm.* Darmstadt: Thesen Verlag, 1977.

Ruhl-Anglade, Gabriele. "Angst und Trost. Zur Motivik in Raabes 'Hastenbeck.' " *RJ* 1983, pp. 119-33.

Ruprecht, Erich. "Raabes Erzählung 'Holunderblüte.' Wende zum Tragischen." *RJ* 1970, pp. 72-86.

Sack, Friedrich. "Raabe unter den 'Besten zwölf Büchern.' " *Mitt.* 17 (1927): 153-56.

Sammons, Jeffrey L. "Die defekte Familie bei Wilhelm Raabe und die Fiktion der alternativen Gemeinschaft: Ein Versuch." *RJ* 1985, pp. 27-43.

————. "The Mill on the Sewer: Wilhelm Raabe's *Pfister's Mill* and the Present Relevance of Past Literature." *Orbis Litterarum* 40 (1985): 16-32.

Sammons, Jeffrey L. "Professor Pfarr aus Yale: Ein Rätsel in Raabes Tage-buch." *Mitt.* 71 (1984): 17-18.

————. "Raabe's Ravens." *Michigan Germanic Studies* 9 (1985): 1-15.

————. "Wilhelm Raabe and his Reputation among Jews and Anti-Semites." Pp. 169-91 in *Identity and Ethos: A Festschrift for Sol Liptzin on the Occasion of his 85th Birthday*, ed. Mark Gelber. New York, Berne, and Frankfurt am Main: Peter Lang, 1986.

————. "Wilhelm Raabe as Successor to Young Germany." *Monatshefte* 77 (1985): 449-59.

————. " '*Wunnigel*' in der '*New Yorker Musikzeitung*' " *Mitt.* 71 (1984): 12.

Sander, Volkmar. "Corviniana non leguntur. Gedanken zur Raabe-Rezeption in Amerika und England." *RJ* 1981, pp. 118-27.

————. "Illusionszerstörung und Wirklichkeitserfassung im Roman Raabes." Pp. 218-32 in *Deutsche Romantheorien: Beiträge zu einer historischen Poetik des Romans in Deutschland*, ed. Reinhold Grimm. Frankfurt am Main and Bonn: Athenäum, 1968.

Schaukal, Richard von. "Raabe." *Mitt.* 21 (1931): 87-92.

Schedlinsky, Walter. *Rolle und industriegesellschaftliche Entwicklung: Die litera-rische Vergegenständlichung eines sozialgeschichtlichen Phänomens im Werk Wil-helm Raabes.* Frankfurt am Main: R. G. Fischer, 1980.

Schillemeit, Jost. "Ruminationen. Zur Entstehungsweise Raabescher Erzäh-lungen." *RJ* 1981, pp. 35-54.

Schiller, Herbert. *Die innere Form W. Raabes.* Borna-Leipzig: Noske, 1917.

Schlegel, Wolfgang. "Über Wilhelm Raabes Geschichtsbild." *RJ* 1962, pp. 22-31.

————. "Wilhelm Raabes Weserheimat in seinen Werken—eine Geschichts-landschaft." *RJ* 1981, pp. 84-104.

Schmid-Stotz, Regina. *Von Finkenrode nach Altershausen: Das Motiv der Heimkehr im Werk Wilhelm Raabes als Ausdruck einer sich wandelnden Lebenseinstellung, dargestellt an fünf Romanen aus fünf Lebensabschnitten.* Bern, Frankfurt am Main, and New York: Peter Lang, 1984.

Schmidt, Wilh[elm]. "Raabe und die Naturwissenschaften." *Mitt.* 26 (1936): 83-91.

————. "Wahrheit, Sage und Dichtung in Raabes 'Des Reiches Krone.' " *Mitt.* 36 (1949): 9-15.

Schmiedeke, Udo. "Der Harz in Raabes Werken." *Mitt.* 68 (1981): 49-69.

Schmitz, Christel. "Das Todesproblem im Werk Wilhelm Raabes." Diss. University of Bonn, 1950.

Schneider, Hilde. *Wilhelm Raabes Mittel der epischen Darstellung.* Berlin: Ebe-ring, 1936.

Schomerus, Hans. "Salas y Gomez und die Rote Schanze. Von der Ein-samkeit des Menschen." *RJ* 1968, pp. 41-48.

————. "Über die Gestalt des Bösen in den Werken Wilhelm Raabes." *RJ* 1962, pp. 32-46.

————. "Zeugnis des Selbstbewußtseins. Raabe und Montherlant." *RJ* 1965, pp. 49-57.

Schrader, Hans-Jürgen. "Joseph Goebbels als Raabe-Redner." *RJ* 1974, pp. 112-15.

————. "Zur Vergegenwärtigung und Interpretation der Geschichte bei Raabe." *RJ* 1973, pp. 12-53.

Schrader, Hans-Jürgen, Kenneth Bruce Beaton, Eberhard Rohse, and Ulrike Koller. "Protokoll vom Internationalen Symposion zur Raabe-Forschung 14.-16. September 1981 im Zeughaus der Herzog August Bibliothek, Wolfenbüttel." *RJ* 1982, pp. 61-98.

Schreinert, Kurt. "Theodor Fontane über Wilhelm Raabe." *RJ* 1962, pp. 182-90.

Schüddekopf, Jürgen. "Raabe in Rußland." *Mitt.* 33 (1943): 41-44.

Schultz, Hans Martin. *Raabe-Schriften: Eine systematische Darstellung.* Wolfenbüttel: Heckner, 1931.

Schultz, Hartwig. "Werk- und Autorintention in Raabes 'Alten Nester' und 'Akten des Vogelsangs.' " *RJ* 1979, pp. 132-54.

Schultz, Werner. "Barock, Rokoko und Goethezeit in 'Hastenbeck.' " *RJ* 1966, pp. 80-91.

————. "Einwirkungen des 'Romantikers' E.T.A. Hoffmann auf den 'Realisten' Wilhelm Raabe." *RJ* 1976, pp. 133-50.

————. "Die Lehrjahre Wilhelm Raabes 1856 bis 1862." *RJ* 1972, pp. 7-30.

————. "Neue Literatur zu Wilhelm Raabe." *RJ* 1972, pp. 75-84.

————. "Schicksal und Zufall im Werk und Weltbild Wilhelm Raabes." *RJ* 1975, pp. 91-123.

————. "Wilhelm Raabes Briefwechsel mit Freunden und Verwandten." *RJ* 1973, pp. 156-77.

Schweckendiek, Adolf. "Der harmonische Mensch." *RJ* 1969, pp. 71-79.

————. "Wilhelm Raabes 'Stopfkuchen': Eine ketzerische Betrachtung." *RJ* 1974, pp. 75-97.

Schweikert, Rudi. " 'Vom Hunger will ich handeln.' Überlegungen zur 'Hunger'-Metapher und zum Licht-Dunkel-Gegensatz in Wilhelm Raabes Roman 'Der Hungerpastor.' " *RJ* 1978, pp. 78-106.

Senk, Herbert. "Bemerkungen zu Raabes Federzeichnungen." *Mitt.* 41 (1954): 110-30.

Silz, Walter. "Freytag's *Soll und Haben* and Raabe's *Der Hungerpastor.*" *Modern Language Notes* 39 (1924): 10-18.

————. "Pessimism in Raabe's Stuttgart Trilogy." *PMLA* 39 (1924): 687-704.

Škreb, Zdenko. "Die Gestalt des jungen Mannes in Raabes Erzählwerk." *RJ* 1975, pp. 124-45.

————. "Zum Raabe-Ton. Die künstlerische Wirkung erzählender Prosa." *RJ* 1981, pp. 10-34.

Spanuth, Heinrich. "Raabe und die Hämelschen Kinder." *Mitt.* 45 (1958): 14-23.

Speyer, Marie. *Raabes "Hollunderblüte."* Regensburg: Habbel, 1908.

Spiero, Heinrich. *Raabe: Leben—Werk—Wirkung*. 2nd ed., Wittenberg: Ziemsen, [1925].

———. *Raabe-Lexikon*. Berlin-Grunewald: Klemm, [1927].

———. *Schicksal und Anteil: Ein Lebensweg in deutscher Wendezeit*. Berlin: Volksverband der Bücherfreunde, 1929.

———, ed. *Wilhelm Raabe und sein Lebenskreis: Festschrift zum 100. Geburtstag des Dichters namens der Gesellschaft der Freunde Wilhelm Raabes und der Verlagsanstalt Hermann Klemm A. G*. Berlin-Grunewald: Klemm, 1931.

Sporn, Thomas. "Wilhelm Raabe: Ökologisch?" *Diskussion Deutsch* 12 (1981): 56-63.

Sprengel, Peter. "Interieur und Eigentum. Zur Soziologie bürgerlicher Subjektivität bei Wilhelm Raabe." *Jahrbuch der Jean-Paul-Gesellschaft* 9 (1974): 127-76.

Spruth, Paul. "Eilike. Eine Mädchengestalt bei Wilhelm Raabe." *RJ* 1971, pp. 93-102.

———. " 'Stopfkuchen'—Raabes bestes Buch?" *Mitt.* 45 (1958): 29-35.

———. "Zur Psychologie des Apothekers Philipp Kristeller und des Obersten Don Agostin Agonista in Raabes Novelle 'Zum wilden Mann.' " *Mitt.* 42 (1955): 101-3.

Stammler, Heinrich A. "Ironie und Pathos in Raabes Novelle 'Sankt Thomas.' " *RJ* 1962, pp. 86-98.

Stern, J. P. "Wilhelm Raabe: Home and Abroad." Pp. 139-62 in Stern, *Idylls & Realities: Studies in Nineteenth-Century German Literature*. London: Methuen, 1971.

Stockum, Th. C. van. "Schopenhauer und Raabe, Pessimismus und Humor." *Neophilologus* 6 (1921): 169-84.

Suchel, Adolf. "Literarische Einflüsse auf Raabes Novelle 'Frau Salome.' " *Mitt.* 35 (1948): 7-19.

———. "Über die Formen des Komischen bei Wilhelm Raabe." *Mitt.* 29 (1939): 45-56.

———. *Wilhelm Raabe aus Anlaß der 100. Wiederkehr seines Geburtstages der deutschen Jugend dargestellt*. Berlin-Grunewald: Klemm, [1931].

———. "Wilhelm Raabes Stellung zum Problem der Willensfreiheit." *Mitt.* 45 (1958): 53-66; 46 (1959): 17-29.

Tebbe, Walter. "Das geistliche Dreigestirn Jerusalem, Holtnicker und Störenfreden. Bemerkungen eines Theologen zu 'Hastenbeck.' " *RJ* 1971, pp. 72-92.

Thürmer, Wilfried. "Entfremdetes Behagen. Wilhelm Raabes Erzählung 'Zum wilden Mann' als Konkretion gründerzeitlichen Bewußtseins." *RJ* 1976, pp. 151-61.

———. "Die Schönheit des Vergehens. Zur Produktivität des Negativen in Wilhelm Raabes Erzählung 'Pfisters Mühle' 1884." *RJ* 1984, pp. 68-86.

Thunecke, Jörg. "Verhinderte Dichter. Wilhelm Buschs Balduin Bählamm und Wilhelm Raabes Dr. Neubauer. Ein Beitrag zur Sozialkritik der Gründerzeit." *RJ* 1983, pp. 71-95.

BIBLIOGRAPHY

————. "Wilhelm Raabes angelsächsische Sprachhaltung im 'Christoph Pechlin.' " Pp. 263-66 in *Akten des VI. Internationalen Germanistenkongresses Basel 1980* (*Jahrbuch für Internationale Germanistik*, Series A, Vol. 8,2), ed. Heinz Rupp and Hans-Gert Roloff. Bern, Frankfurt am Main, and Las Vegas: Peter Lang, 1980.

Töteberg, M., and J. Zander. "Die Rezeption Raabes durch die 'Gesellschaft der Freunde Wilhelm Raabes' 1911-1945." *RJ* 1973, pp. 178-93.

Trafton, Elisabeth Rockenbach. "Resignation in Wilhelm Raabes Stuttgarter Trilogie." Diss. University of California, Los Angeles, 1978.

Ueda, Noboyuki. "Bericht über die Raabe-Forschung in Japan." *RJ* 1977, pp. 149-55.

Völker, Eberhard. "Raabes Harzburger Erzählungen." *RJ* 1984, pp. 26-50.

Vogel, Maria. "Darstellung der von Wilhelm Raabe geschilderten seelischen Abnormitäten und Versuch einer psychiatrischen Deutung." M.D. Diss. University of Frankfurt am Main, 1949.

Vogelsang, Günther. *Das Ich als Schicksal und Aufgabe in den Dichtungen Raabes*. Braunschweig: Appelhans, 1942.

Walther, Theodor. "Meine Begegnung mit Wilhelm Raabe." *Mitt.* 15 (1925): 29-32.

Warnke, Gisela. "Das 'Sünder'-Motiv in Wilhelm Raabes *Stopfkuchen*." *Deutsche Vierteljahrsschrift* 50 (1976): 465-76.

Wassermann, Felix M. "Die *Akten des Vogelsangs* und das Problem der bürgerlichen Existenz im neuen Reich." *German Quarterly* 36 (1963): 421-33.

Weber, A. "Lehrerfiguren in Raabes *Horacker*." Pp. 216-32 in *Formen realistischer Erzählkunst: Festschrift for Charlotte Jolles in Honour of her 70th Birthday*, ed. Jörg Thunecke with Eda Sagarra. Nottingham: Sherwood Press, 1979.

Webster, W[illiam] T. "Hesitation and Decision: Wilhelm Raabe's Road to Reality." *Forum for Modern Language Studies* 15 (1979): 69-85.

————. "Der 'Hinhocker' und der 'Weltwanderer': Zur Bedeutung der Reise bei Wilhelm Raabe." *RJ* 1982, pp. 26-39.

————. "Idealisierung oder Ironie? Verstehen und Mißverstehen in Wilhelm Raabes 'Stopfkuchen,' " *RJ* 1978, pp. 146-70.

————. "Social Change and Personal Insecurity in the Late Novels of Wilhelm Raabe." Pp. 233-43 in *Formen realistischer Erzählkunst: Festschrift for Charlotte Jolles in Honour of her 70th Birthday*, ed. Jörg Thunecke and Eda Sagarra. Nottingham: Sherwood Press, 1979.

————. "Thomas Mann, Wilhelm Raabe und die realistische Tradition in Deutschland." *Zeitschrift für deutsche Philologie* 99 (1980): 254-76.

————. *Wirklichkeit und Illusion in den Romanen Wilhelm Raabes*. Raabe-Forschungen 1, ed. Hans-Werner Peter. Braunschweig: pp-Verlag, 1982.

Weidenhaun, Karl. "Wilhelm Raabe als Dichter des Nachmärz." *Mitt.* 20 (1930): 133-45.

Weinhardt, Reinhold. "Schopenhauer in Wilhelm Raabes Werken." *Jahrbuch der Schopenhauer-Gesellschaft* 25 (1938): 306-28.

Weniger, Erich. " 'Erlebnis' und 'Dichtung' im Werk Wilhelm Raabes." *Die Sammlung* 13 (1958): 613-23.

————. "Die Quellen zu Wilhelm Raabes 'Odfeld.' " *RJ* 1966, pp. 96-124.

Westerburg, Hans. "Wilhelm Raabe als Ethiker." *Mitt.* 21 (1931): 146-56.

Wiese, Benno von. "Wilhelm Raabe, Die Innerste." Pp. 198-215 in von Wiese, *Die deutsche Novelle von Goethe bis Kafka: Interpretationen*, Vol. 2. Düsseldorf: Bagel, 1965.

Wischniewski, Horst. "Die Akten des Vogelsangs. Freiheit in Wilhelm Raabes Roman." *RJ* 1974, pp. 98-101.

Witschel, Günter. *Raabe-Integrationen: "Die Innerste," "Das Odfeld," "Stopf-kuchen."* Bonn: Bouvier, 1969.

Wittkowski, Wolfgang. "Handeln, Reden und Erkennen im Zusammenhang der Dinge: Raabes *Horn von Wanza* und Fontanes *Irrungen Wirrungen*—ethisch betrachtet." Pp. 346-76 in *Wege der Worte: Festschrift für Wolfgang Fleischhauer*, ed. Donald C. Riechel. Cologne and Vienna: Böhlau, 1978.

Worthmann, Joachim. "Die 'erinnerte Zeit'—Wilhelm Raabes 'Pfisters Mühle.' " Pp. 130-43 in Worthmann, *Probleme des Zeitromans: Studien zur Geschichte des deutschen Romans im 19. Jahrhundert.* Heidelberg: Carl Winter, 1974.

Wrangel, Christine. "Verknüpfungsformen in Wilhelm Raabes späten Romanen *Pfisters Mühle, Stopfkuchen* und *Altershausen*." Diss. New York University, 1970.

Zornemann, Erich B. "Herbert Schillers Angriff auf Raabes Künstlertum. Ein Versuch zur Klärung." *Mitt.* 17 (1927): 129-38.

Zwilgmeyer, Franz. "Archetypische Bewußtseinsstufen in Raabes Werken, insbesondere in den 'Akten des Vogelsangs.' " *RJ* 1984, pp. 99-120.

INDEX OF
RAABE'S WORKS

Places where works are discussed in detail are indicated with italic type.

TITLES IN ENGLISH

TITLES IN GERMAN

LIBRARY OF CONGRESS CATALOGING-IN-PUBLICATION DATA

Sammons, Jeffrey L.
Wilhelm Raabe: the fiction of the alternative community.

Bibliography: p.
Includes indexes.
1. Raabe, Wilhelm Karl, 1831-1910—Criticism
and interpretation. I. Title.
PT2451.Z5S2 1987   833'.8   86-30267
ISBN 0-691-06709-0 (alk. paper)